D1785248

**Fodor's** upCLOSE

# LOS ANGELES

*the complete guide, thoroughly up-to-date*

**SAVVY TRAVELING: WHERE TO SPEND, HOW TO SAVE**

*packed with details that will make your trip*

**CULTURAL TIPS: ESSENTIAL LOCAL DO'S AND TABOOS**

*must-see sights, on and off the beaten path*

**INSIDER SECRETS: WHAT'S HIP AND WHAT TO SKIP**

*the buzz on restaurants, the lowdown on lodgings*

**FIND YOUR WAY WITH CLEAR AND EASY-TO-USE MAPS**

FODOR'S TRAVEL PUBLICATIONS
NEW YORK • TORONTO • LONDON • SYDNEY • AUCKLAND
*www.fodors.com*

**COPYRIGHT © 2000 BY FODOR'S TRAVEL PUBLICATIONS**

Fodor's is a registered trademark of Random House, Inc.

Fodor's upCLOSE is a trademark of Random House, Inc.

All rights reserved under International and Pan-American Copyright Conventions. Published in the United States by Fodor's Travel Publications, a division of Random House, Inc., New York, and simultaneously in Canada by Random House of Canada, Limited, Toronto. Distributed by Random House, Inc., New York.

*No maps, illustrations, or other portions of this book may be reproduced in any form without written permission from the publisher.*

Second Edition

ISBN 0–679–00390-8

ISSN 1098–7541

**FODOR'S UPCLOSE LOS ANGELES**

**EDITOR:** Jennifer Paull

**Editorial Contributors:** Sasha Abramsky, Sue Alexander, Jennifer L. Kasoff, Lina Lecaro, Lisa Oppenheimer, Nancy Rones, Bill Stern, Bobbi Zane

**Editorial Production:** Tom Holton

**Maps:** David Lindroth Inc., Eureka Cartography, *cartographers*; Robert Blake, *map editor*

**Design:** Fabrizio La Rocca, *creative director*; Allison Saltzman, *cover and text design*; Jolie Novak, *photo editor*

**Production/Manufacturing:** Mike Costa

**Cover Art:** Bob Torrez/Tony Stone Images

**SPECIAL SALES**

Fodor's upCLOSE Guides and all Fodor's Travel Publications are available at special discounts for bulk purchases for sales promotions or premiums. Special editions, including personalized covers, excerpts of existing guides, and corporate imprints, can be created in large quantities for special needs. For more information, contact your local bookseller or write to Special Markets, Fodor's Travel Publications, 201 East 50th Street, New York, NY 10022. Inquiries from Canada should be directed to your local Canadian bookseller or sent to Random House of Canada, Ltd., Marketing Department, 2775 Matheson Blvd East, Mississauga, Ontario L4W 4P7. Inquiries from the United Kingdom should be sent to Fodor's Travel Publications, 20 Vauxhall Bridge Road, London SW1V 2SA, England.

**IMPORTANT TIP**

Although all prices, opening times, and other details in this book are based on information supplied to us at press time, changes occur all the time in the travel world, and Fodor's cannot accept responsibility for facts that become outdated or for inadvertent errors or omissions. So **always confirm information when it matters,** especially if you're making a detour to visit a specific place.

PRINTED IN THE UNITED STATES OF AMERICA

10 9 8 7 6 5 4 3 2 1

# CONTENTS

# 3. FOOD 85

# 4. WHERE TO SLEEP 120

# 5. AFTER DARK 139

# 6. OUTDOOR ACTIVITIES AND SPORTS 160

# 7. SHOPPING 182

# 8. NEAR LOS ANGELES 196

# INDEX 229

# TRAVELING
# UPCLOSE

S troll up the Venice Boardwalk. Swoop along the freeways. Bask on the beach. Culture-vulture your way along the Miracle Mile and take in the Getty. Shop for a picnic at a farmers' market. Catch a flick at a restored movie palace. In other words, if you want to experience the heart and soul of Los Angeles, whatever you do, don't spend too much money.

The deep and rich experience of Los Angeles that every true traveler yearns for is one of the things in life that money can't buy. In fact, if you have it, don't use it. By traveling lavishly you risk turning into a sideline traveler. Restaurants with white-glove service are great—sometimes—but they're usually not the best place to find the perfect enchilada. Doormen at plush hotels have their place, but not when your lookalike room could be anywhere from Düsseldorf to Detroit. Better to stay in a more intimate place that truly gives you the atmosphere you traveled so far to experience. Don't just stand and watch—jump into the spirit of what's around you.

If you want to see Los Angeles up close and savor the essence of the city and its people in all their stylish and sometimes outlandish glory, this book is for you. We'll show you the local culture, the offbeat sights, the bars and cafés where tourists rarely tread, and the B&Bs and other hostelries where you'll meet fellow travelers—places where the locals would send their friends. And because you'll probably want to see the famous places if you haven't already been there, we give you tips on losing the crowds, plus the quirky and lively facts you want as well as the basics everyone needs.

## OUR GANG

Who are we? We're artists and poets, slackers and straight arrows, and travel writers and journalists who in our less hedonistic moments report on local news and spin out an occasional opinion piece. What we share is a certain footloose spirit and a passion for Los Angeles, which we celebrate in this guidebook. We've revealed all of our favorite places and our deepest, darkest travel secrets, all so that you can experience the best part of Los Angeles to the fullest.

Native Londoner **Sasha Abramsky** lives in New York but spends as much time as possible in L.A., visiting his much-loved grandmother in Studio City. He can't afford to own a classic sports car, so he satisfies his craving by visiting the Petersen Automotive Museum and gawking inanely. His other favorite thing to do in L.A. is to walk along Santa Monica beach at sunset. He writes travel articles and feature stories for British and American magazines.

A transplant from the Big Apple, **Sue Alexander** updated both our Basics and Outdoor Activities and Sports chapters. She's covered many an L.A. freeway mile interviewing Angelenos in her job as a freelance magazine writer and editor, but still hasn't completed her ultimate West Coast quest: to find a quality bagel in a city with more doughnut shops per capita than any other city in the nation.

Trekking through Los Angeles' often glamorous, sometimes gritty nightlife scene, **Lina Lecaro** has been writing about clubs, bars, bands, and everything else the city has to offer after dark for nearly eight years. A longtime regular contributor to *L.A. Weekly*, she is also the clubs editor for *Glue*, not to mention a writer for *BAM* and *Venice* magazines and Internet sites like the *Los Angeles Times'* Calendar Live and Music Now's Woodstock.com. The native Angeleno's secret for getting into the hottest spots in town? Look fine, act friendly, and be fierce.

**Lisa Oppenheimer**, our Near Los Angeles updater, has spent her career penning features on Southern California for books and magazines. A lifelong and firmly rooted Northeasterner, she nevertheless enjoys writing about year-round sunshine and balmy temperatures, topics that would constitute fiction in her home town in Massachusetts. Lisa has contributed to several Fodor's guides; her work has also appeared in *Sesame Street Parents, Disney Magazine,* and *Robb Report* magazines.

As a recent New York transplant, **Nancy Rones** was in the midst of discovering L.A.'s shopping scene— so it was natural for her to undertake this guide's shopping chapter. The perk she found about living in L.A.? "You only need a one-season wardrobe, give or take a jacket, so you never have to rationalize how long you'll get to wear a purchase before the serious heat or cold hits." For her full-time gig, she plugs away as a senior editor at *Teen* magazine.

Before settling in Los Angeles, **Bill Stern**, a native New Yorker, ate his way from Peoria to Paris and from Umbria to Uzbekistan. Since then he has reviewed restaurants for several publications, including the *Los Angeles Times, L.A. Weekly, Buzz Weekly,* and the *L.A. Reader*. He created the symposium "Breaking Bread: A Series of Forums on Food and Community in California, 1775–1995," which was held at the Los Angeles Central Library in 1995.

**Bobbi Zane** has watched Los Angeles grow from the small city of her childhood to the megametropolis of today. She has a lifelong collection of the city's hidden treasures, including some of the "wonderful one-stars" she reviewed for our lodging chapter. She has contributed to several other Fodor's guides, including *California's Best Bed & Breakfasts, California,* and *San Diego*. Her byline also appears in regional magazines and newspapers, including *Westways* and the *Los Angeles Times*.

Editor **Jennifer Paull** grew up behind the Orange curtain; thanks to her fab family, she knows plenty of colorful chinks in Orange County's bland facade. She's also had countless high- and low-brow adventures in L.A. proper. Now a New York City resident, one of her favorite homecoming sights is the giant "Nude Nudes" sign near LAX. She couldn't resist sprinkling oddball factoids throughout this edition, the better to paint the city's glorious goofiness.

## A SEND-OFF

Always call ahead. We knock ourselves out to check all the facts, but everything changes all the time, in ways that none of us can ever fully anticipate. Whenever you're making a special trip to a special place, as opposed to merely wandering, always call ahead. Trust us on this.

And then, if something doesn't go quite right, as inevitably happens with even the best-laid plans, stay cool. Missed your train? Stuck in the airport? Use the time to study the people. Strike up a conversation with a stranger. Study the newsstands or flip through the local press. Take a walk. Find the silver lining in the clouds, whatever it is. And do send us a postcard to tell us what went wrong and what went right. You can E-mail us at: editors@fodors.com (specify the name of the book on the subject line) or write the Los Angeles editor at Fodor's upCLOSE, 201 East 50th Street, New York, NY 10022. We'll put your ideas to good use and let other travelers benefit from your experiences. In the meantime, bon voyage!

LOS ANGELES

SAN FERNANDO
Foothill Fwy.
NORTHRIDGE
SAN FERNANDO VALLEY
CANOGA PARK
RESEDA
BURBANK
GLENDA
Ventura Fwy.
VAN NUYS
NORTH HOLLYWOOD
STUDIO CITY
UNIVERSAL CITY
Griffith Park
Mulholland Dr.
SHERMAN OAKS
SANTA MONICA MTS.
WEST HOLLYWOOD
HOLLYWOOD
LOS FELIZ
SILVE LAK
BEL AIR
BEVERLY HILLS
Topanga State Park
UCLA
BRENTWOOD
WESTWOOD
Wilshire Blvd.
DOWNTOWN
PACIFIC PALISADES
Sunset Blvd.
Santa Monica Blvd.
J. Paul Getty Museum
MALIBU
Santa Monica Fwy.
USC
SANTA MONICA
CULVER CITY
SOUTH CENTRAL
San Diego Fwy.
Slauson Ave.
VENICE
MARINA DEL REY
INGLEWOOD
Lincoln Blvd.
Santa Monica Bay
Los Angeles International Airport
Imperial Hwy.
WA
EL SEGUNDO
Sepulveda
Hawthorne
Crenshaw Blvd
Western Ave.
Harbor
Central Ave.
MANHATTAN BEACH
HERMOSA BEACH
GARDENA
TORRANCE
San Diego
CA
REDONDO BEACH
Pacific Coast Hwy.
Avalon Blvd.
PACIFIC OCEAN
PALOS VERDES ESTATES
RANCHO PALOS VERDES
Palos Verdes Dr. S.
SAN PEDRO

N

0    5 miles
0    5 km

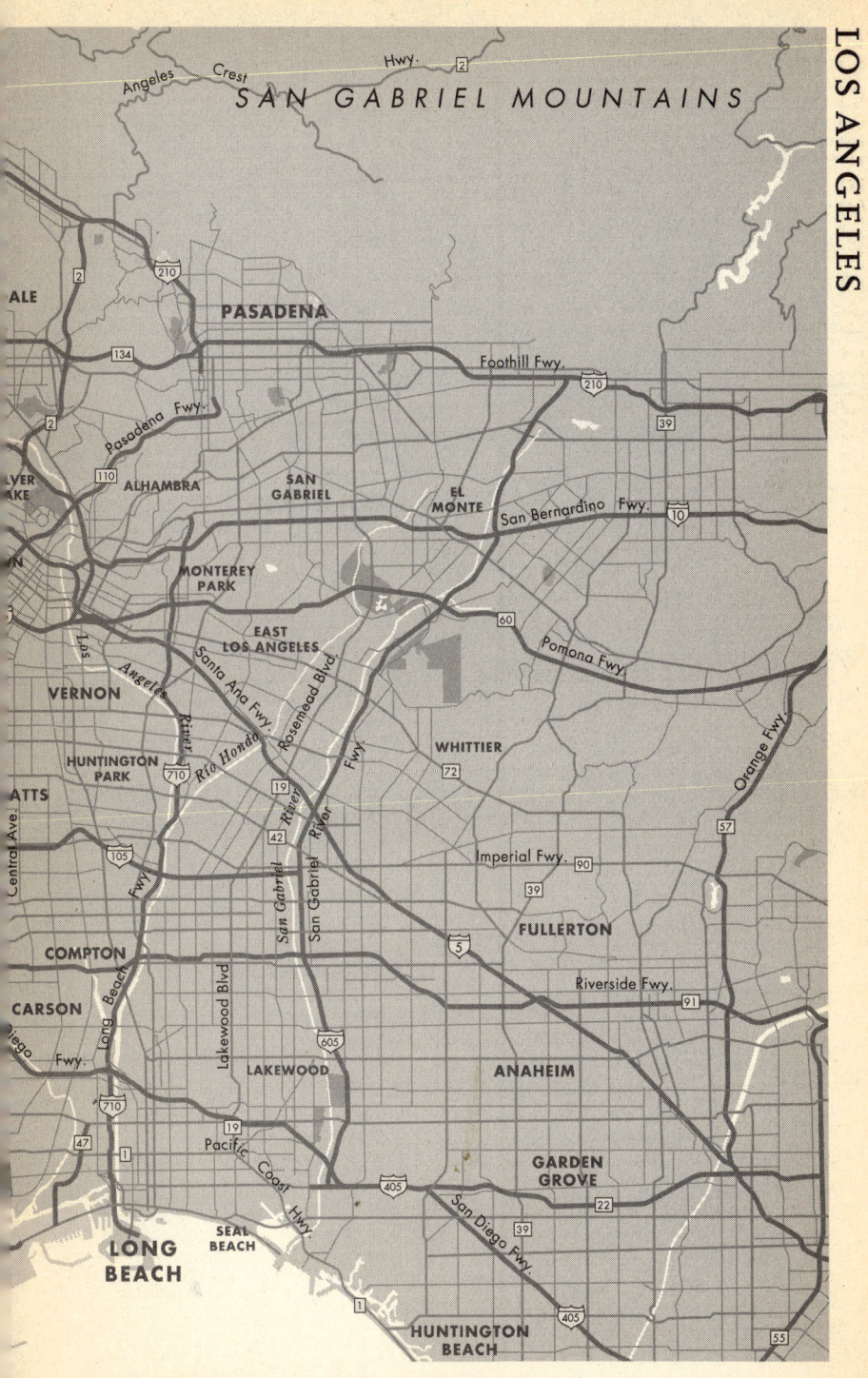

SAN GABRIEL MOUNTAINS

Angeles Crest Hwy. 2

2

210

PASADENA

134

Foothill Fwy. 210

ALE

2

Pasadena Fwy.

39

110

ALHAMBRA

SAN GABRIEL

EL MONTE

San Bernardino Fwy. 10

LVER AKE

MONTEREY PARK

60

EAST LOS ANGELES

Pomona Fwy.

VERNON

Santa Ana Fwy.

Rosemead Blvd.

Angeles River

Rio Hondo

WHITTIER

72

Orange Fwy.

HUNTINGTON PARK

710

19

Fwy.

57

ATTS

105

42

San Gabriel River

San Gabriel River

Imperial Fwy. 90

Central Ave.

39

Fwy.

FULLERTON

COMPTON

Lakewood Blvd.

5

CARSON

Long Beach

605

Riverside Fwy.

91

Diego Fwy.

LAKEWOOD

ANAHEIM

710

47

19

Pacific Coast Hwy.

405

GARDEN GROVE

22

1

SEAL BEACH

San Diego Fwy.

39

LONG BEACH

1

405

55

HUNTINGTON BEACH

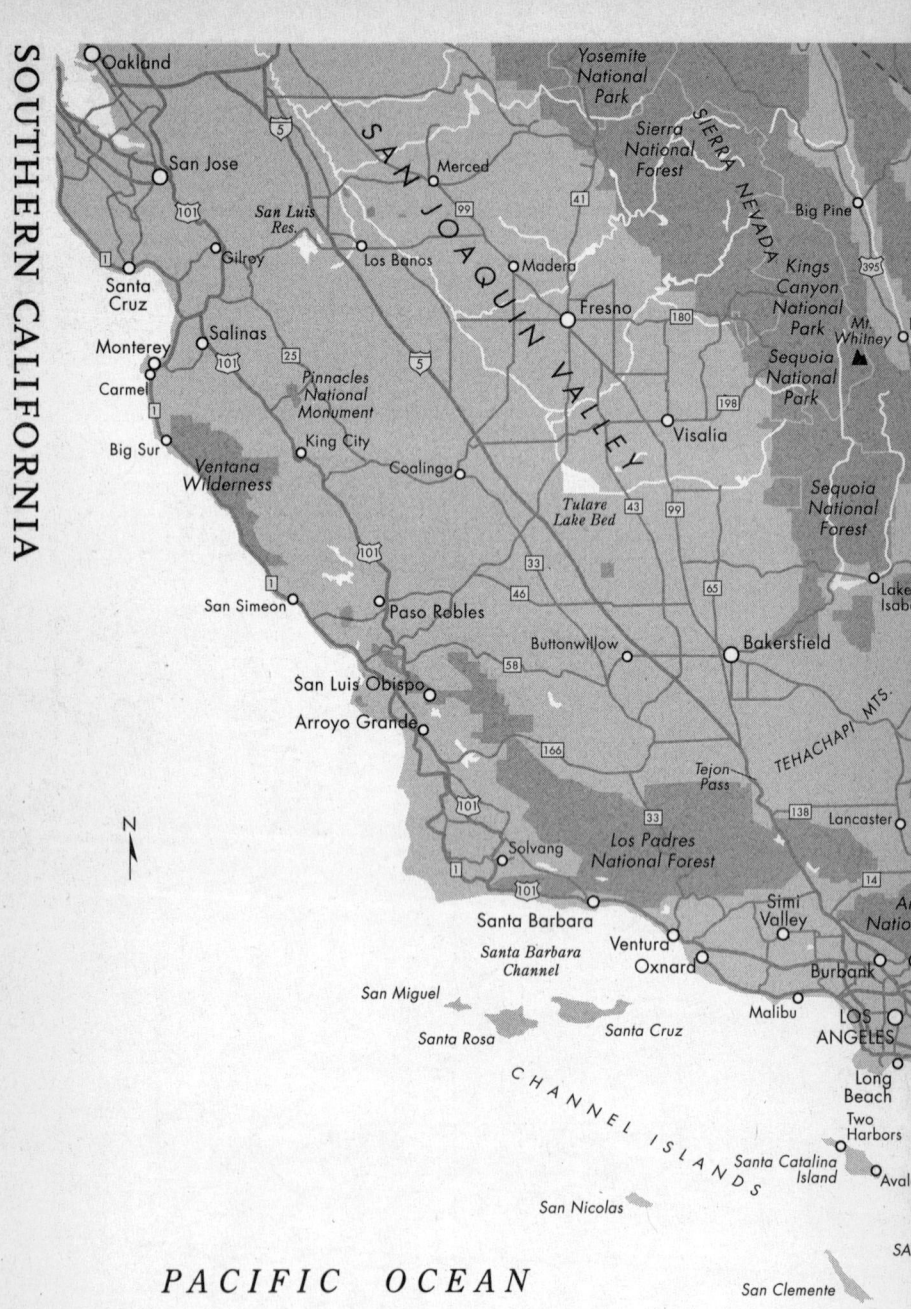

SOUTHERN CALIFORNIA

Oakland
San Jose
101
5
San Luis Res.
Gilroy
Los Banos
Santa Cruz
Salinas
Monterey
101
25
Carmel
Pinnacles National Monument
Big Sur
1
Ventana Wilderness
King City
Coalinga
San Simeon
1
Paso Robles
San Luis Obispo
Arroyo Grande
101
N
Solvang
1
101
Santa Barbara
Santa Barbara Channel
Ventura
Oxnard
San Miguel
Malibu
Santa Rosa
Santa Cruz
CHANNEL ISLANDS
San Nicolas

SAN JOAQUIN VALLEY
Yosemite National Park
Merced
41
99
Madera
Fresno
180
Visalia
198
43
99
Tulare Lake Bed
33
46
65
Buttonwillow
58
166
Tejon Pass
33
Los Padres National Forest

Sierra National Forest
SIERRA NEVADA
Big Pine
395
Kings Canyon National Park
Mt. Whitney
Sequoia National Park
Sequoia National Forest
Lake Isabe
Bakersfield
TEHACHAPI MTS.
138
Lancaster
14
Simi Valley
An Natio
Burbank
LOS ANGELES
Long Beach
Two Harbors
Santa Catalina Island
Aval
San Clemente
SA

PACIFIC OCEAN

0        50 miles
0        75 km

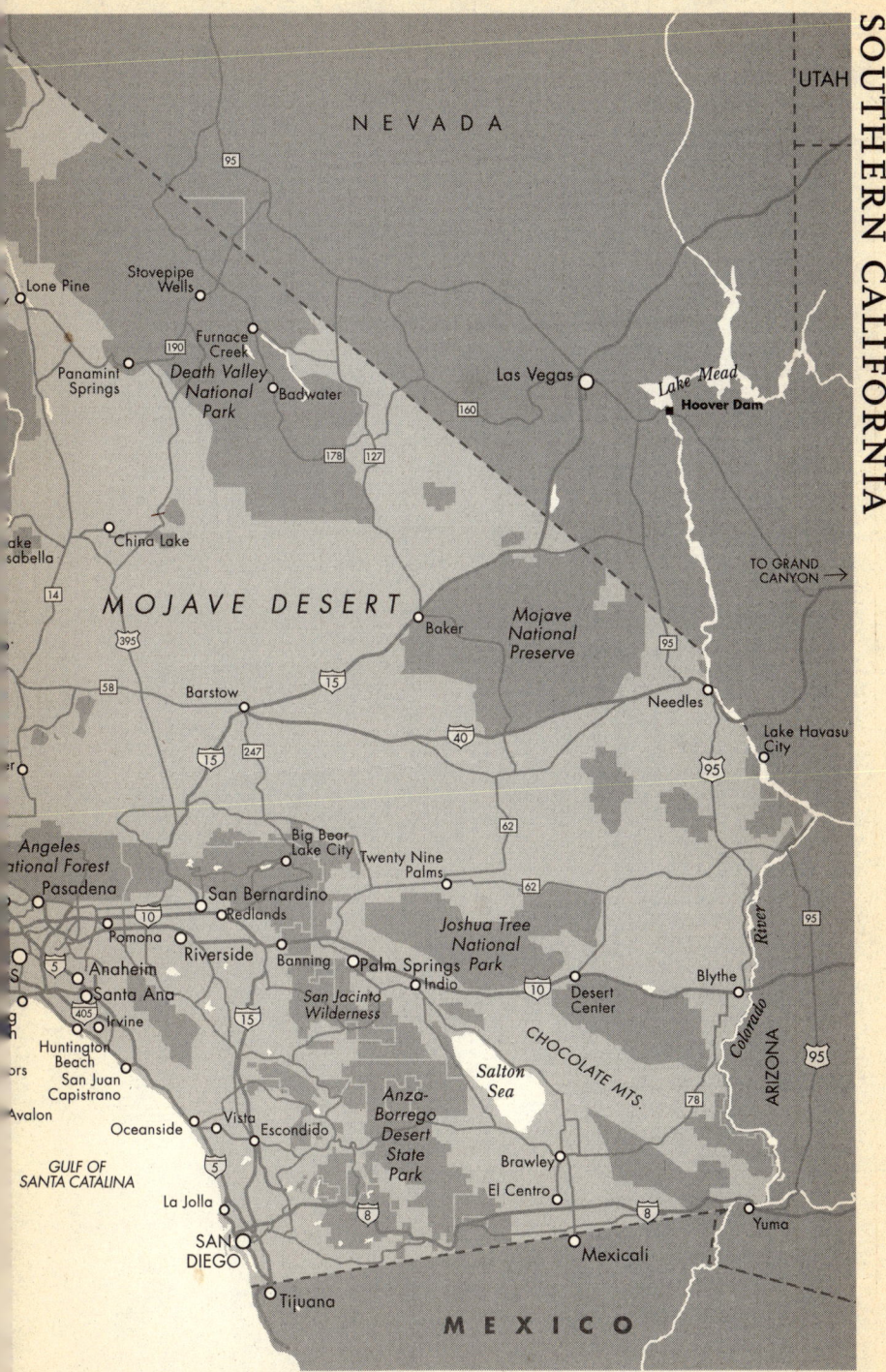

UTAH

NEVADA

95

Lone Pine

Stovepipe
Wells

Furnace
Creek

190

Panamint
Springs

*Death Valley
National
Park*

Badwater

Las Vegas

*Lake Mead*

■ Hoover Dam

178 127

ake
sabella

China Lake

M O J A V E   D E S E R T

14

395

Baker

*Mojave
National
Preserve*

TO GRAND
CANYON →

95

58

Barstow

15

Needles

Lake Havasu
City

15 247

40

US 95

Big Bear
Lake City

62

Twenty Nine
Palms

*Angeles
National Forest*

Pasadena

San Bernardino

Redlands

62

*Joshua Tree
National
Park*

95

Pomona

Riverside

Banning

Palm Springs

10

Desert
Center

Blythe

5

Anaheim

Santa Ana

405

Irvine

15

Indio

*San Jacinto
Wilderness*

*Colorado River*

95

Huntington
Beach

San Juan
Capistrano

C H O C O L A T E   M T S.

ARIZONA

Avalon

Oceanside

Vista

Escondido

*Anza-
Borrego
Desert
State
Park*

*Salton
Sea*

*GULF OF
SANTA CATALINA*

Brawley

La Jolla

El Centro

78

Yuma

8

8

SAN
DIEGO

Mexicali

Tijuana

M E X I C O

160

# BASICS

*Basic Information on Traveling in Los Angeles,*
*Savvy Tips to Make Your Trip a Breeze, and Companies*
*and Organizations to Contact*

I

f you've ever traveled with anyone, you know that there are two types of people in the world—the planners and the nonplanners. Travel brings out the worst in both groups. Left to their own devices, the planners will have you goose-stepping from attraction to attraction on a cultural forced march, while the nonplanners will invariably miss the flight, the bus, and maybe even the point. This chapter offers you a middle ground; we hope it provides enough information to help you plan your trip to Los Angeles without nailing you down. Stay flexible and remember that the most hair-pulling situations will turn into the best travel stories back home.

## AIR TRAVEL

### BOOKING YOUR FLIGHT

When you book **look for nonstop flights** and **remember that "direct" flights stop at least once.** Try to avoid connecting flights, which require a change of plane.

### CARRIERS

**MAJOR AIRLINES** • **Air Canada** (tel. 800/776–3000). **America West** (tel. 800/235–9292). **American** (tel. 800/433– 7300; 0345/789–789 in the U.K.). **British Airways** (tel. 800/247–9297; 0345/222–111 in the U.K.). **Continental** (tel. 800/231–0856). **Delta** (tel. 800/241–4141; 0800/414–767 in the U.K.). **Japan Air Lines** (tel. 800/525–3663). **Northwest** (tel. 800/225–2525). **TWA** (tel. 800/892–4141). **United** (tel. 800/241–6522; 0800/888–555 in the U.K.). **US Airways** (tel. 800/428–4322). **Virgin Atlantic** (tel. 01293/747–747 in the U.K.).

**SMALLER AIRLINES** • **Alaska Airlines** (tel. 800/426–0333). **Carnival Air Lines** (tel. 800/824–7386). **Midwest Express** (tel. 800/452–2022). **Reno Air** (tel. 800/736–6247). **Southwest** (tel. 800/435–9792).

### CHECK-IN & BOARDING

Assuming that not everyone with a ticket will show up, airlines routinely overbook planes. When that happens, airlines ask for volunteers to give up their seats. In return these volunteers usually get a certificate for a free flight and are rebooked on the next flight out. If there are not enough volunteers, the airline must choose who will be denied boarding. The first to get bumped are passengers who checked in late and those flying on discounted tickets, so **get to the gate and check in as early as possible,** especially during peak periods.

Always **bring a government-issued photo I.D. to the airport.** You will be asked to show it at the check-in counter.

Curbside check-in can save you standing in a long line at the indoor airline counters. Uniformed baggage handlers will check your ticket and I.D., ask a few security questions, tag and send off your luggage, and give you your gate number. Be sure to tip them at least a dollar per bag.

## CUTTING COSTS

The least-expensive airfares to Los Angeles must usually be purchased in advance and are nonrefundable. It's smart to **call a number of airlines, and when you are quoted a good price, book it on the spot**—the same fare may not be available the next day. Always **check different routings** and look into using different airports. Travel agents, especially low-fare specialists (*see* Discounts & Deals, *below*), are helpful.

Consolidators are another good source. They buy tickets for scheduled international flights at reduced rates from the airlines, then sell them at prices that beat the best fare available directly from the airlines, usually without restrictions. Sometimes you can even get your money back if you need to return the ticket. Carefully read the fine print detailing penalties for changes and cancellations, and **confirm your consolidator reservation with the airline.**

When you **fly as a courier** you trade your checked-luggage space for a ticket deeply subsidized by a courier service. These flights are only international, jetting between L.A. and business hubs like London and Sydney. There are several catches to the deal; you may have to fly on just a few days' notice, and there may be restrictions on how long you can stay.

**CONSOLIDATORS • Cheap Tickets** (tel. 800/377–1000). **Up & Away Travel** (tel. 212/889–2345). **Discount Airline Ticket Service** (tel. 800/576–1600). **Unitravel** (tel. 800/325– 2222). **World Travel Network** (tel. 800/409–6753).

**COURIERS • International Bonded Couriers** (tel. 310/665– 1760). **Jupiter Air** (tel. 310/670–1197).

## ENJOYING THE FLIGHT

For more legroom **request an emergency-aisle seat.** Don't sit in the row in front of the emergency aisle or in front of a bulkhead, where seats may not recline. If you have dietary concerns, **ask for special meals when booking.** These can be vegetarian, low-cholesterol, or kosher, for example. On long flights, try to maintain a normal routine, to help fight jetlag. At night **get some sleep.** By day **eat light meals, drink water** (not alcohol), and **move around the cabin** to stretch your legs.

## FLYING TIMES

Nonstop flights from New York to L.A. take about six hours; a nonstop from Chicago takes roughly four hours. A nonstop from London will last a leg-cramping 10 hours.

## HOW TO COMPLAIN

If your baggage goes astray or your flight goes awry, complain right away. Most carriers require that you **file a claim immediately.**

**AIRLINE COMPLAINTS • U.S. Department of Transportation Aviation Consumer Protection Division** (C-75, Room 4107, Washington, DC 20590, tel. 202/366–2220). **Federal Aviation Administration Consumer Hotline** (tel. 800/322–7873).

## AIRPORTS & TRANSFERS

The major airports are **Los Angeles International (LAX), Burbank- Glendale-Pasadena Airport, Ontario International Airport,** and **John Wayne Orange County Airport.**

**Los Angeles International Airport,** 17 mi southwest of downtown L.A. off I–405, is a snarl of traffic and tourists. It's the fourth-largest airport in the world in terms of passenger traffic, and every airline you can think of flies here. The international terminal (Bradley Terminal) has a currency exchange office and information booths open daily 7 AM–11 PM. In addition to dispensing the usual tourist pamphlets, the staff here can help you find accommodations. There is free shuttle service between all the terminals and the Metro Green Line. The shuttle runs daily from 4:30 AM to 12:15 AM, making stops on the lower level at each terminal. Most shuttles are wheelchair accessible. Travelers with disabilities can arrange personalized van service around LAX. Electronic lockers are available in all terminals behind the security checkpoint. You can pay for lockers with cash, ATM cards, and credit cards. Supervised luggage storage (tel. 310/646–0222) is available in the Bradley International Terminal on the departure level next to Malaysia Airlines. The service is open from 6 AM to 12:30 AM.

The smaller, gentler **Burbank-Glendale-Pasadena Airport** (2627 N. Hollywood Way, at Thornton Ave., Burbank) is close to Hollywood and only 1 mi south of I–5. For journeys up and down the West Coast (to San Francisco, say, or Seattle), flights into and out of Burbank are often cheaper than LAX flights. There's no luggage storage area or lockers.

**Ontario International Airport,** about 35 mi east of L.A., is preferred by many over LAX because it is small and easily managed. The airport is on Airport Drive and Vineyard Avenue, 2 mi east of downtown Ontario, just off the San Bernardino Freeway (I–10). There are information booths on the east and west sides of the main terminal. There's a currency exchange booth in Terminal 2, and luggage storage lockers in both terminals.

**Long Beach Airport** (off the I-405 south at Lakewood Blvd. N, 4100 Donald Douglas Dr.) is another option if you're looking for a smaller airport. You will be limited in your pick of carriers, though, as its terminal is served only by American Airlines and America West Airlines.

Glossy **John Wayne Orange County Airport** (off MacArthur Blvd. at I–405, Santa Ana) is most convenient for stays in Anaheim and the Orange County coast. It's a very manageable airport as there's just one terminal (with a 9-ft. bronze John Wayne statue to boot). If your takeoff seems steeper than usual, don't worry; some planes make a relatively sharp ascent or landing to comply with the airport's noise-level standards.

**AIRPORT INFORMATION • Los Angeles International Airport** (tel. 310/646–5252). **Burbank-Glendale-Pasadena Airport** (tel. 818/840–8847). **Ontario International Airport** (tel. 909/937–2700). **Long Beach Airport** (tel. 562/570–2600). **John Wayne Orange County Airport** (tel. 949/252–5006).

## TRANSFERS

Outside the baggage claim area in each of **LAX**'s terminals is a Quick-Aid computer, which provides ground transportation information, including public bus routes from the airport. More costly transportation options include shuttle buses and taxis, which are convenient but expensive.

**BUSES • The MTA** (tel. 213/626–4455) also offers limited airport service to all areas of greater L.A. from LAX; bus lines depart from bus docks directly across the street from Parking Lot C. Prices vary from $1.35 to $3.10; some routes require transfers. The best line to take downtown is Number 42 ($1.35) or the express line Number 439 ($1.85). Both take about 70 minutes.

To reach downtown from the Burbank Airport, take Bus 94; for Hollywood take Bus 163. There are no direct public bus routes from Ontario, Long Beach, or John Wayne airports into L.A.

**COMMUTER TRAINS •** If you're not too pressed for time and don't have too many bags to lug, you can get to both LAX and the Long Beach Airport via the **Metro Rail** trains. For LAX, take the Green Line to the Aviation/I-105 stop, then hop the "G" shuttle to the airport. To get to Long Beach Airport, you'll need to take the Blue Line train to 1st Street Station, walk over to shelter C at the adjacent transit mall, and transfer to Long Beach bus #111 to the airport.

**SHUTTLES •** If you'd like a shuttle to take you to the airport, you'll need to call the company for an advance reservation. To be on the safe side, call at least a day in advance. Companies generally have agents stationed outside the airports' baggage claim areas to arrange for shuttles into town.

**SuperShuttle** (tel. 310/782–6600 or 800/554–3146) offers direct service 24 hours a day between LAX and downtown hotels for about $12 one-way in seven-passenger vans. **Apollo Xpress Shuttle** (tel. 818/247–1515) offers door-to-door service anywhere in the greater L.A. area 24 hours every day. Fares run $10–$30 one-way depending on pickup and drop-off location. **Prime Time Shuttle** (tel. 661/295–0134) also has 24 hour service to the greater L.A. area; a one-way ticket should be in the $10–$25 range. They go into Orange County as well. **Airport Bus** (tel. 800/772–5299) provides regular service between LAX and the Pasadena and Anaheim areas. They pick up and drop off at certain hotels in each area; a one-way ticket is $12 to Pasadena and $14 to Buena Park. The buses run roughly from 8 AM to 9 PM. They also make runs to John Wayne Airport every half-hour from 7:30 AM to 6:30 PM. **Van Nuys Flyaway Service** (7610 Woodley Ave., at Saticoy St., tel. 818/994–5554) shuttles between LAX and its base station round the clock for $3.50 one-way. Unlike most shuttles, you don't need to make a prior reservation.

From Ontario International, ground transportation possibilities include **SuperShuttle** (tel. 909/428–6600), **Metropolitan Express** (tel. 310/417–5050), and **Inland Express** (tel. 909/626–6599). All of these offer 24-hour, door-to-door service; Inland Express and Metropolitan Express add an extra fee for late-night runs. Expect to pay more than $50 to reach downtown L.A.

From John Wayne airport, you can catch an **Airport Bus** (tel. 800/772–5299) to one of their scheduled hotels in the Anaheim area. Their booth is near the baggage claim exits on the lower level of Terminal B; the fare is $10, and the service operates roughly from 8 AM to 10:30 PM. **SuperShuttle** (tel. 714/517–6600) vans provide 24-hour door-to-door service. Fees vary depending on your pickup or drop-off point; they range from around $12 for a hotel in the Disneyland area to $30–$40 for hotels in L.A.

**TAXIS** • A taxi ride to downtown from LAX can take as little as 30 minutes, but substantially longer in traffic. Request the flat fee ($24) to downtown. A ride to Hollywood will cost about $32, from LAX to North Hollywood about $37, and from LAX to Malibu about $50. Keep in mind that a group of more than two splitting a cab from the airport will cost you about the same as a shuttle (*see above*). There are specific taxi points at all terminals.

# BUS TRAVEL TO AND FROM LOS ANGELES

## GREEN TORTOISE ADVENTURE TRAVEL

It's not just a bus ride; it's often the most memorable part of your vacation. It's also *the* cheap alternative to humdrum public transportation. Green Tortoise's "Alternative Commuter" buses crawl their way from Los Angeles up the West Coast to San Francisco ($35 one-way) and Seattle ($79 plus $3 for food, one-way) and back down again. They're equipped with sleeping pads and stereos (but not, unfortunately, toilets). Tortoise also offers various package trips, including a summer trek to Alaska and winter tours to Mexico and Baja, along with summer season treks from Los Angeles to Boston via Chicago ($349 plus $111 for food) and spring and fall trips from L.A. to Beantown via New Orleans ($389 plus $121 for food). Reservations are required. The buses often stop for a cookout, sauna, or swim. You'll need to reserve a seat from five to seven days in advance and pay the driver in cash.

Green Tortoise stops once weekly in Hollywood (behind McDonald's on Vine St., between Santa Monica and Sunset Blvds.), in Santa Monica (at AYH, 1434 2nd St.), in downtown Los Angeles (at the TV Cafe, 1777 Olympic Blvd., at Alameda Ave.), at LAX (at Backpacker's Paradise, 4200 W. Century Blvd., Inglewood), in Long Beach (at Wardlow Station, Pacific Pl. near Long Beach Blvd.), and in Huntington Beach (at Max's Foods, 15300 Goldenwest, at Georgetown St.) before continuing up to Seattle or across America.

## BY GREYHOUND

Incontestably the cheapest—and potentially the most entertaining—way of getting to Los Angeles is by Greyhound, which offers daily service to L.A.'s downtown station (1716 E. 7th St., at Alameda St., tel. 213/629–8400) from many U.S. and Canadian cities, including San Francisco (8–12 hours, $69 round-trip) and San Diego (3½ hours, $22 round-trip). The station is in a blighted neighborhood, so try to arrive during daylight hours. The Greyhound station in Hollywood (1409 N. Vine St., between Sunset Blvd. and De Longpre Ave., tel. 213/466–6384) offers roughly equivalent fares. All fares fluctuate according to the date of travel.

Greyhound's Ameripass, valid on all U.S. routes, can be purchased in advance in cities throughout the United States; spontaneous types can also buy one up to 45 minutes before the bus leaves from the terminal. The pass allows purchasers unlimited travel within a limited time period: seven days ($199), 15 days ($299), 30 days ($409), or 60 days ($599). Foreign visitors can get slightly lower rates. Call ahead for the discount offers; you could net a bargain by buying your ticket at least a week in advance, for instance. Discounts are also available by joining the student or senior citizen savings clubs.

### FARES & SCHEDULES •

**Green Tortoise** (tel. 800/867–8647; in 415 and 510 area codes, tel. 415/956–7500). **Greyhound** (tel. 800/231–2222).

## BUS TRAVEL WITHIN LOS ANGELES

The **Metropolitan Transit Authority (MTA)** provides buses to get around town, but not many people use them. Those who do complain that half their lives are spent in transit on said buses. Still, you gotta give the folks at the MTA credit: They *are* trying to get people out of their cars and onto mass transit to help cut down on pollution and general stress. Also, they're slowly building up a larger fleet of buses (with clean fuel instead of diesel), so service will become more frequent and reliable over the next few years.

However, they do *not* publish a comprehensive map of the bus system, a mysterious fact you can ponder while spending endless hours calling to get a schedule or searching for individual route guides at Union Station. The best way to plan your bus ride is to call the information line (*see below*); the operators will give you directions.

Not surprisingly, a bus trip in Los Angeles sometimes requires freeway travel. MTA buses have five Freeway Express Zones that are priced according to where and how far you're going.

The orange-and-white and newer yellow-and-white MTA buses provide thorough but slow-as-molasses transportation through L.A. Generally, MTA buses numbered 1–99 serve downtown L.A., Buses 100–199 run east–west, and Buses 200–299 run north–south. During rush hours (5 AM–8 AM and 3 PM–6 PM), commuter express buses run to and from downtown; these buses are in the 400–499 range. Bus stops are well marked with orange-and-black signs, and buses arrive every 10–30 minutes, depending on routes and days. Late-night service is skimpy (infrequent and with limited stops), so swing by a visitor center (*see* Visitor Information, *below*) for a schedule. Most MTA buses have wheelchair access.

The Department of Transportation (DOT) runs another system, called **DASH (Downtown Area Short Hop).** These short-distance minibus shuttles hit 19 communities: Downtown, El Sereno/City Terrace, Fairfax, Highland Park/Eagle Rock, Hollywood, Leimert/Slauson, Lincoln Heights/Chinatown, Midtown/Chinatown, Panorama City/Van Nuys, Park La Brea, Pico Union/Echo Park, Sherman Oaks, Southeast, Van Nuys/Studio City, Warner Center, Watts, Watts/North, Wilmington, and Wilshire Center/Koreatown. While each DASH line has a different timetable, buses generally run every 10 to 20 minutes, weekdays about 7–7; some run on weekends, some don't.

Though some MTA buses loop through the city of Santa Monica, more thorough service is provided by Santa Monica's **Big Blue Bus,** which also takes passengers from the beach to LAX, Westwood, downtown L.A., and as far north as the Getty Center. Signs reading "Big Blue Bus" mark the bus stops. Additionally, a city-operated shuttle called the **Tide** connects several downtown Santa Monica attractions, including Main Street, the Promenade, the pier, and some motels. The shuttle operates Sunday–Thursday noon–10, Friday and Saturday noon–midnight, with departures every 15 minutes.

**FARES & SCHEDULES** • MTA bus fare is a flat $1.35 (two-hour transfers 25¢ plus 50¢ per zone when traveling the freeway). The DASH is 25¢. The Big Blue Bus fare is 50¢ ($1.25 to downtown), with one free transfer (depending on destination). Transfers to MTA bus lines are available for 25¢. The Tide shuttle fare is 25¢. Carry exact fare (dollar bills are okay) because drivers cannot make change.

To save money, you can buy bus token packs and passes. Discount tokens are sold in bags of 10 for $9. Weekly passes cost $11, semimonthly passes cost $21, and monthly passes cost $42. You can also get Freeway Express Stamps for $15 per zone, up to a maximum of 5 zones.

Getting an MTA schedule can be quite a challenge. You can call for route schedules (expect to be on hold for a while) or look for individual route guides at Union Station. Big Blue Bus and Tide route maps and schedule info can be picked up at their office (1660 7th St., at Olympic Blvd., Santa Monica). The L.A. Department of Transportation can mail you DASH maps in advance, or you can get them at Union Station.

**MTA** (tel. 213/626–4455). **DASH** (tel. 808–2273 from any local area code). **Big Blue Bus** (tel. 310/451–5444). **The Tide** (tel. 310/398–3289).

# CAMERAS & PHOTOGRAPHY

L.A.'s sunsets can be spectacular—a side effect of all that smog—so now's your chance to capture a gorgeously red-orange sky. If you bring your camera to the beach, keep it in a plastic bag or wrapping to protect it from sand and salt water.

**PHOTO HELP** • **Kodak Information Center** (tel. 800/242– 2424). *Kodak Guide to Shooting Great Travel Pictures,* available in bookstores or from Fodor's Travel Publications (tel. 800/533–6478; $16.50 plus $4 shipping).

## EQUIPMENT PRECAUTIONS

Always **keep your film and tape out of the sun.** Carry an extra supply of batteries, and **be prepared to turn on your camera or camcorder** to prove to security personnel that the device is real. Always **ask for hand inspection of film,** which becomes clouded after successive exposures to airport X-ray machines, and **keep videotapes away from metal detectors.**

# CAR RENTAL

In Los Angeles it's not a question of whether wheels are a hindrance or a convenience: They're virtually a necessity. More than 35 major companies and dozens of local rental companies serve a steady demand for cars at Los Angeles International Airport and various city locations.

Rates in L.A. begin at $29 a day and $125 a week for an economy car with air-conditioning, automatic transmission, and unlimited mileage. This does not include tax, which is 8.25%.

**MAJOR AGENCIES** • **Alamo** (tel. 800/327–9633; 0181/759– 6200 in the U.K.). **Avis** (tel. 800/331–1212; 800/879–2847 in Canada; 02/9353–9000 in Australia; 09/525–1982 in New Zealand). **Budget** (tel. 800/527–0700; 0144/227–6266 in the U.K.). **Dollar** (tel. 800/800–4000; 0181/897–0811 in the U.K., where it is known as Eurodollar; 02/9223–1444 in Australia). **Hertz** (tel. 800/654–3131; 800/263–0600 in Canada; 0990/90–60–90 in the U.K.; 02/9669–2444 in Australia; 03/358–6777 in New Zealand). **National InterRent** (tel. 800/227–7368; 0345/222525 in the U.K., where it is known as Europcar InterRent).

## CUTTING COSTS

To get the best deal **book through a travel agent who will shop around.** Also **price local car-rental companies,** although the service and maintenance may not be as good as those of a major player. Remember to ask about required deposits, cancellation penalties, and drop-off charges if you're planning to pick up the car in one city and leave it in another. If you're traveling during a holiday period, also make sure that a confirmed reservation guarantees you a car.

Do **look into wholesalers,** companies that do not own fleets but rent in bulk from those that do and often offer better rates than traditional car-rental operations. Payment must be made before you leave home.

**LOCAL AGENCIES** • **Avon** (1100 S. Beverly Dr., between Pico and Olympic Blvds., Beverly Hills, tel. 310/277–4455); no airport shuttle. **Bob Leech's** (4490 W. Century Blvd., LAX, tel. 310/673– 2727 or 800/635–1240 for reservations and free airport pickup). **Lucky** (8620 Airport Blvd., LAX, tel. 310/641–2323 or 800/400– 4736 for reservations and free airport pickup). **Fox** (10211 S. La Cienega Blvd., LAX, tel. 310/641–3838 or for free pickup, call from courtesy phone in baggage claim area). **Rent-a-Wreck** (10860 Burbank Blvd., at Vineland Ave., Burbank, tel. 818/623–0804); free shuttle service to and from Burbank Airport and local hotels.

**WHOLESALERS** • **Auto Europe** (tel. 207/842–2000 or 800/223–5555).

## INSURANCE

When driving a rented car you are generally responsible for any damage to or loss of the vehicle as well as for any property damage or personal injury that you may cause. Before you rent see what coverage your personal auto-insurance policy and credit cards already provide.

For about $15 to $20 per day, rental companies sell protection, known as a collision- or loss-damage waiver (CDW or LDW), that eliminates your liability for damage to the car. Some states, including California, have capped the price of the CDW and LDW. In most states you don't need a CDW if you have personal auto insurance or other liability insurance. However, **make sure you have enough coverage to pay for the car.** If you do not have auto insurance or an umbrella policy that covers damage to third parties, purchasing liability insurance and a CDW or LDW is highly recommended.

## REQUIREMENTS & RESTRICTIONS

In California you must be 21 to rent a car, and rates may be higher if you're under 25. There is no top age limit. You'll pay extra for child seats (about $3 per day), which are compulsory for children under five, and for additional drivers (about $2 per day). Non-U.S. residents will need a reservation voucher, a passport, a driver's license, and a travel policy that covers each driver, in order to pick up a car.

## SURCHARGES

Before you pick up a car in one city and leave it in another **ask about drop-off charges or one-way service fees,** which can be substantial. Note, too, that some rental agencies charge extra if you return the car before the time specified in your contract. To avoid a hefty refueling fee **fill the tank just before you turn in the car,** but be aware that gas stations near the rental outlet may overcharge.

# CAR TRAVEL

Traffic in L.A. is less apocalyptic than it's often portrayed in movies and on TV—though not by much. And although the popularity of drive-by shootings has waned, carjacking incidents are on the rise. The *Thomas Guide Los Angeles County Street Guide and Directory* ($16.95) is almost heavy enough to fill any self-defense needs, but its primary purpose is to help you figure out where the hell you are and how to get where you're going. Worshiped throughout the Southland, this comprehensive book of maps and indexes is available in area bookstores and gas stations, and it should be the first thing a visiting driver buys.

Traffic is hell into downtown in the morning from 7 to 10 and out of downtown from 4 to 8 on all free-ways. Sometimes if you cleverly utilize your Thomas Guide, it's easier and faster to take city streets instead of the freeways. You will probably end up driving a greater distance, but at least you will be moving. Remember, you are almost always guaranteed a consistent ETA on surface streets, whereas driving from point A to point B on the freeway could take you 20 minutes or two hours, depending on traffic.

## EMERGENCIES

**Call 911** for emergency police, fire, and ambulance services. If your car breaks down, try to pull over to the shoulder or side of the road and either wait for a state trooper to arrive or, if you have another pas-senger that can safely wait in the car, walk to the nearest roadside emergency phone. (These are sta-tioned along all major freeways.) Being a member of the American Automobile Association can really pay off if you have car trouble. Membership covers emergency road service as well as several basic ser-vices like jumping your car.

**AUTO ASSISTANCE • American Automobile Association** (tel. 800/564–6222).

## FREEWAY DRIVING

Spending time on the freeway will be an unavoidable part of your trip here. And it seems that Angelenos interpret signs reading 65 MPH as the minimum speed allowed on the freeway, not the maximum. Visit-ing speed demons will feel right at home, as everyone, including old ladies in Cadillacs, zooms by. Part of the speed mania also seems to be the implicit understanding between drivers that no one will slow down for you as you merge onto the freeway. Another related rule of thumb: Don't hit the freeway unless you already know exactly how to get where you're going. Exits occur frequently, on both sides of the free-way, and you should be prepared to bolt into the appropriate lane. During commuting hours, however, traffic is not just slow but almost at a standstill. Avoid traveling on any freeway that goes into downtown from 7 to 10 AM and any freeway heading out of downtown from 4 to 8 PM. If a car breaks down or there is a minor accident, traffic becomes paralyzed, and there's an instant jam. You should try to steer clear of drivers busy talking on their cell phones; their extra distraction could put you on the receiving end of a fender bender.

Freeways generally have a car pool lane on the far left side; these are marked by diamonds painted on the tarmac. These lanes are strictly for vehicles with two or more passengers, and they normally move more quickly than the standard lanes. They can be very tempting if you're stuck in a traffic jam, but don't risk it if you're driving solo—if you get caught, a ticket can run you over $300.

People refer to freeways both by name and by number. The rundown is as follows: **I–5** (the Golden State Freeway) runs through downtown, continuing north to the California–Oregon border and south to San Diego. **I–10** (the Santa Monica Freeway, called the San Bernadino Freeway farther east) runs east from Santa Monica, continuing through L.A.'s boring 'burbs to Palm Springs and San Bernadino. **I–405** (the San Diego Freeway) runs parallel to but west of I–5; take this to reach the L.A. International Airport, the coast, and points south. **Highway 1,** also known as the **Pacific Coast Highway (PCH),** meanders along the coastline, passing through L.A.'s beach communities on its way north to San Francisco and south toward San Diego. **U.S. 101** runs north–south (east of I–405) and is called the Hollywood Freeway within L.A.; farther north it is referred to as the Ventura Freeway. It runs into Ventura County and through downtown and is used as an alternate to I–5 when coming into Los Angeles. **I–110** runs north–south from Pasadena to San Pedro and is called the Pasadena Freeway north of downtown L.A. and the Har-bor Freeway south of downtown.

## GASOLINE

Gas prices can fluctuate quite a bit, dipping to around a dollar and rising to $1.75 or more. In general, a gallon should hover around $1.25–$1.35.

# DRIVING LIKE AN ANGELENO

*In Los Angeles driving is as much a part of the daily routine as, say, breathing—and neither is easy. You and your car will feel right at home if you follow these simple steps. First, get hip to L.A.'s driving lingo: Interstate 5 is "the Five" and U.S. 101 is "the One-oh-One." Next, rent a cellular phone so you can conduct animated conversations while weaving recklessly. As you cruise, never concede space to merging traffic. If you're pulled over, free yourself from the tedium of a ticket by casually mentioning that you're employed by Hollywood agencies ICM or CAA (and expect a cop-movie screenplay in the mail two weeks later). And, finally, always have your auto "detailed"; never have it "washed."*

## PARKING

The first rule of on-street parking in the land of the automobile is to read signs carefully. Take a stroll up and down the street if necessary, because although parking signs are minuscule and infrequent, parking tickets are neither. For some sample parking ticket fines (to think about while you're considering blocking that fire hydrant), *see* Rules of the Road, *below*. Most stores and restaurants have parking lots or parking garage validation (discounts) for patrons. Street parking is ample at metered spaces (carry quarters in your glove box), except in downtown on weekdays, when you will almost certainly have to pay for a garage. Most garages have an early-bird special (before 9) of $3–$10 for the whole day. The best way to find a good parking deal is to play shark and circle the streets for a while until you find a nice price. If you are heading downtown, it's easier and cheaper to park your car at one of the Metro stations in the outlying areas and take the Metro in (*see* Subways & Commuter Trains, *below*). A fancy way to rid yourself of the old clunker is by using the valet services that abound on Melrose Avenue and Sunset Boulevard and other nighttime hot spots. The cost of valets can range from free to $25 and sometimes more. Don't surrender your car to a valet or a parking garage without finding out how much it is going to cost you for a specified amount of time. Remember that all the nasty, sneaky fees and "$5 every 10 minutes" are always written in covert peewee print.

## RULES OF THE ROAD

Drivers and all passengers must wear seat belts in California. Tickets for not wearing a seat belt are about $25 per person—and cops can and will pull you over just to fine you for this violation. Motorcycle helmets are required by law. Tickets for not wearing a helmet start at $68 and quickly escalate as penalty assessments mount. Speed limits on freeways vary from 55 to 70 mph. Most of the time most cars exceed the speed limit, which is not to say you should. Tickets for speeding start with a violation ticket of $35; the rest of the fine is assessed in court depending on exactly how fast you were going and how many prior moving violation tickets you have had. For example, someone with no prior violations who had been driving 20 mi over the speed limit might be fined $225 in court. Most parking tickets range from $20 to $60, depending on the city and the type of violation (e.g., meter out of money, parking in a residential permit area). But wait, we're just getting started. Keep in mind that parking in a zone designated for drivers with disabilities will land a $330 ticket on your windshield. Parking in a red zone is verboten and is just asking for your car to be towed or at least plastered with an expensive ticket. The moral of the story? Always, always read the signs around you to make sure you aren't poised for a ticket. And don't forget that the more tickets you get, the higher the fines for your next ticket.

## TRAFFIC REPORTS

Traffic reports are broadcast every 10 minutes on most radio stations during rush hours. Try KFWB at 980, KNX at 1070, or KPCC-FM at 89.3 for news and traffic. Announcers generally refer to the freeways by their given names, although they sometimes refer to the freeway numbers (*see* Freeway Driving, *above*).

# CHILDREN IN LOS ANGELES

Keep an eye out for the helpful (and free) publication *L.A. Parent*; you can find issues in newsboxes on street corners and sometimes in bookstores or coffee shops. For information on children's events, check *Los Angeles* magazine's "Kid Stuff" column in its listings section. The *Los Angeles Times* also has plenty of children's activities listings, plus a kids-oriented page in "Section Gee!"

If you are renting a car don't forget to **arrange for a car seat** when you reserve.

### FLYING

If your children are two or older **ask about children's airfares.** As a general rule, infants under two not occupying a seat fly at greatly reduced fares or even for free.

Experts agree that it's a good idea to use safety seats aloft for children weighing less than 40 pounds. Airlines set their own policies: U.S. carriers usually require that the child be ticketed, even if he or she is young enough to ride free, since the seats must be strapped into regular seats. Do **check your airline's policy about using safety seats during takeoff and landing.** And since safety seats are not allowed just everywhere in the plane, get your seat assignments early.

*If you get momentarily discombobulated, remember that freeways running east and west are even-numbered; freeways running north and south are odd-numbered.*

When reserving, **request children's meals or a freestanding bassinet** if you need them. But note that bulkhead seats, where you must sit to use the bassinet, may lack an overhead bin or storage space on the floor.

### LODGING

Most hotels in Los Angeles allow children under a certain age to stay in their parents' room at no extra charge, but others charge for them as extra adults; be sure to **find out the cutoff age for children's discounts.**

# CONSUMER PROTECTION

Whenever shopping or buying travel services in Los Angeles, **pay with a major credit card** so you can cancel payment or get reimbursed if there's a problem. If you're doing business with a particular company for the first time, **contact your local Better Business Bureau and the attorney general's offices** in your state and the company's home state, as well. Have any complaints been filed? Finally, if you're buying a package or tour, always **consider travel insurance** that includes default coverage (*see* Insurance, *below*).

**LOCAL BBBS • Council of Better Business Bureaus** (4200 Wilson Blvd., Suite 800, Arlington, VA 22203, tel. 703/276–0100, fax 703/525–8277).

# CUSTOMS & DUTIES

When shopping, **keep receipts** for all purchases. Upon reentering the country, **be ready to show customs officials what you've bought.** If you feel a duty is incorrect or object to the way your clearance was handled, note the inspector's badge number and ask to see a supervisor. If the problem isn't resolved, write to the appropriate authorities, beginning with the port director at your point of entry.

### IN AUSTRALIA

Australia residents who are 18 or older may bring home $A400 worth of souvenirs and gifts (including jewelry), 250 cigarettes or 250 grams of tobacco, and 1,125 ml of alcohol (including wine, beer, and spirits). Residents under 18 may bring back $A200 worth of goods. Prohibited items include meat products. Seeds, plants, and fruits need to be declared upon arrival.

**INFORMATION • Australian Customs Service** (Regional Director, Box 8, Sydney, NSW 2001, tel. 02/ 9213–2000, fax 02/9213–4000).

## IN CANADA

Canadian residents who have been out of Canada for at least 7 days may bring home C$500 worth of goods duty-free. If you've been away less than 7 days but more than 48 hours, the duty-free allowance drops to C$200; if your trip lasts 24–48 hours, the allowance is C$50. You may not pool allowances with family members. Goods claimed under the C$500 exemption may follow you by mail; those claimed under the lesser exemptions must accompany you. Alcohol and tobacco products may be included in the 7-day and 48-hour exemptions but not in the 24-hour exemption. If you meet the age requirements of the province or territory through which you reenter Canada, you may bring in, duty-free, 1.14 liters (40 imperial ounces) of wine or liquor *or* 24 12-ounce cans or bottles of beer or ale. If you are 16 or older, you may bring in, duty-free, 200 cigarettes and 50 cigars. Check ahead of time with Revenue Canada or the Department of Agriculture for policies regarding meat products, seeds, plants, and fruits.

You may send an unlimited number of gifts worth up to C$60 each duty-free to Canada. Label the package UNSOLICITED GIFT—VALUE UNDER $60. Alcohol and tobacco are excluded.

**INFORMATION • Revenue Canada** (2265 St. Laurent Blvd. S, Ottawa, Ontario K1G 4K3, tel. 613/993–0534; 800/461–9999 in Canada).

## IN NEW ZEALAND

Homeward-bound residents 17 or older may bring back $700 worth of souvenirs and gifts. Your duty-free allowance also includes 4.5 liters of wine or beer; one 1,125-ml bottle of spirits; and either 200 cigarettes, 250 grams of tobacco, 50 cigars, or a combination of the three up to 250 grams. Prohibited items include meat products, seeds, plants, and fruits.

**INFORMATION • New Zealand Customs** (Custom House, 50 Anzac Ave., Box 29, Auckland, New Zealand, tel. 09/359–6655, fax 09/359–6732).

## IN THE U.K.

From countries outside the EU, including the U.S., you may bring home, duty-free, 200 cigarettes or 50 cigars; 1 liter of spirits or 2 liters of fortified or sparkling wine or liqueurs; 2 liters of still table wine; 60 ml of perfume; 250 ml of toilet water; plus £136 worth of other goods, including gifts and souvenirs. If returning from outside the EU, prohibited items include meat products, seeds, plants, and fruits.

**INFORMATION • HM Customs and Excise** (Dorset House, Stamford St., Bromley Kent BR1 1XX, tel. 0171/202–4227).

## IN THE U.S.

Non-U.S. residents ages 21 and older may import into the United States 200 cigarettes or 50 cigars or 2 kilograms of tobacco, 1 liter of alcohol, and gifts worth $100. Meat products, seeds, plants, and fruits are prohibited.

**INFORMATION • U.S. Customs Service** (inquiries, 1300 Pennsylvania Ave. NW, Washington, DC 20229, tel. 202/927–6724; complaints, Office of Regulations and Rulings, 1300 Pennsylvania Ave. NW, Washington, DC 20229; registration of equipment, Registration Information, 1300 Pennsylvania Ave. NW, Washington, DC 20229, tel. 202/927–0540).

# DISABILITIES & ACCESSIBILITY

California is a national leader in making attractions and facilities accessible to travelers with disabilities. Since 1982 the state building code has required all construction for public use to include access for people with disabilities. But although awareness of the needs of travelers with disabilities increases every year, budget allocations to implement these needs are harder to find. Always ask if discounts are available, either for you or for a companion. In addition, plan your trip and make reservations far in advance, since companies that provide services for people with disabilities go in and out of business regularly.

There is good news, however: Many of Los Angeles's hotels, restaurants, and attractions are accessible to travelers with disabilities. State laws provide special privileges as well, such as license plates allowing special parking spaces, unlimited parking in time-limited spaces, and free parking in metered spaces. ID from states other than California is honored.

**LOCAL RESOURCES • Los Angeles City Department on Disability** (700 E. Temple St., Room 380, tel. 213/485– 6334).

## COMPLAINTS

**Disability Rights Section** (U.S. Department of Justice, Civil Rights Division, Box 66738, Washington, DC 20035-6738, tel. 202/514–0301; 800/514–0301; 202/514–0301 TTY; 800/514–0301 TTY, fax 202/307–1198) for general complaints. **Aviation Consumer Protection Division** (*see* Air Travel, *above*) for airline-related problems. **Civil Rights Office** (U.S. Department of Transportation, Departmental Office of Civil Rights, S-30, 400 7th St. SW, Room 10215, Washington, DC 20590, tel. 202/366–4648, fax 202/366–9371) for problems with surface transportation.

## LODGING

When discussing accessibility with an operator or reservations agent **ask hard questions.** Are there any stairs, inside *or* out? Are there grab bars next to the toilet *and* in the shower/tub? How wide is the doorway to the room? To the bathroom? For the most extensive facilities meeting the latest legal specifications **opt for newer accommodations.**

## TRANSPORTATION

Most Metropolitan Transit Authority buses have wheelchair lifts and lock-downs, and the Metro is fully accessible.
**LOCAL RESOURCES • MTA services** (tel. 213/626–4455, 800/266– 6883 [800/COMMUTE], or 800/252–9040 for TDD/TTY).

## TRAVEL AGENCIES

In the United States, although the Americans with Disabilities Act requires that travel firms serve the needs of all travelers, some agencies specialize in working with people with disabilities.
**TRAVELERS WITH MOBILITY PROBLEMS • Access Adventures** (206 Chestnut Ridge Rd., Rochester, NY 14624, tel. 716/889–9096). **Accessible Journeys** (35 W. Sellers Ave. Ridley Park, PA 19078, tel. 610/521–0339 or 800/846–4537, fax 610/521–6959). **Accessible Vans of Southern California** (3393 E. 19th St., Long Beach, CA 90804, tel. 800/242–4111). **CareVacations** (5-5110 50th Ave., Leduc, Alberta T9E 6V4, tel. 780/986–6404 or 877/478–7827, fax 780/986–8332). **Flying Wheels Travel** (143 W. Bridge St., Box 382, Owatonna, MN 55060, tel. 507/451–5005 or 800/535–6790, fax 507/451–1685). **Hinsdale Travel Service** (201 E. Ogden Ave., Suite 100, Hinsdale, IL 60521, tel. 630/325–1335, fax 630/325–1342).
**TRAVELERS WITH DEVELOPMENTAL DISABILITIES • New Directions** (5276 Hollister Ave., Suite 207, Santa Barbara, CA 93111, tel. 805/967–2841 or 888/967–2841, fax 805/964–7344).

# DISCOUNTS & DEALS

Student, senior, and children's discounts are often available for admission fees for sights, attractions, and public transportation in L.A. If you're a student, be sure you have an acceptable student ID card (*see* Students, *below*); if you're a senior, you may need to show your driver's license or other proof of age.

While your travel plans are still in the fantasy stage, study the travel sections of major Sunday newspapers and flip through a few travel magazines. You can often find tempting ads and helpful contacts for discount travel packages and cheap flights. Surfing the Internet can also reap a deal, whether it's package and flight info, or a promotional bargain for a specific establishment. Travel agents are another obvious resource; agencies on or near university campuses can be especially helpful since they're used to dealing with budget travelers. *See also* Tours & Packages *and* Travel Agents, *below.*

Be a smart shopper and **compare all your options** before making decisions. A plane ticket bought with a promotional coupon from travel clubs, coupon books, and direct-mail offers may not be cheaper than the least expensive fare from a discount ticket agency. And always keep in mind that what you get is just as important as what you save.

## DISCOUNT RESERVATIONS

To save money **look into discount-reservations services** with toll-free numbers, which use their buying power to get a better price on hotels, airline tickets, even car rentals. When booking a room, always **call the hotel's local toll-free number** (if one is available) rather than the central reservations number— you'll often get a better price. Always ask about special packages or corporate rates.

**AIRLINE TICKETS** • tel. **800/FLY–4–LESS.** tel. **800/FLY– ASAP.**

**HOTEL ROOMS** • **Accommodations Express** (tel. 800/444– 7666). **Central Reservation Service (CRS)** (tel. 800/548– 3311). **Hotel Reservations Network** (tel. 800/964–6835). **Quickbook** (tel. 800/789–9887). **Room Finders USA** (tel. 800/473–7829). **RMC Travel** (tel. 800/245–5738). **Steigenberger Reservation Service** (tel. 800/223–5652).

## DIVERS' ALERT

**Do not fly within 24 hours of scuba diving.**

## ELECTRICITY

Overseas visitors will need to bring adapters to convert their personal appliances to the U.S. standard: AC, 110 volts/60 cycles, with a plug of two flat pins set parallel to one another.

## EMERGENCIES

**DENTISTS** • **UCLA Dental Center** (2337 Le Conte Ave., at Tiverton Ave., tel. 310/825–2337). **USC School of Dentistry** (925 W. 34th St., tel. 213/740–2800).

**EMERGENCY SERVICES** • Dial 911 for **police, ambulance,** and **fire.**

**LOW-COST HOSPITALS AND CLINICS** • **Hollywood-Sunset Free Clinic** (3324 Sunset Blvd., at Silverlake Blvd., tel. 323/660–2400). **Los Angeles County Hospital at USC Medical Center** (1200 N. State St., at Marengo, tel. 323/226–2622). **Los Angeles Free Clinic** (8405 Beverly Blvd., at Orlando, tel. 323/653–1990). **South Bay Free Clinic** (1807 Manhattan Beach Blvd., 1 block west of Aviation Blvd., Manhattan Beach, tel. 310/376–0791).

**24-HOUR PHARMACIES** • **Kaiser Bellflower Pharmacy** (9400 E. Rosecrans Ave., Bellflower, tel. 562/461–4213).

## GAY & LESBIAN TRAVEL

Gay men and lesbians enjoy a certain amount of freedom in larger cities. Despite these supportive environments, gay bashing continues to occur, so always be aware of your surroundings if you're with your same-sex lover. There are heaps of excellent resources and organizations for gay folks in Los Angeles. Publications by and for gays can be found in gay community bookstores and cafés in West Hollywood, Santa Monica, and elsewhere. In Orange County, Laguna Beach is one of the most welcoming environments.

**GAY- AND LESBIAN-FRIENDLY TRAVEL AGENCIES** • **Different Roads Travel** (8383 Wilshire Blvd., Suite 902, Beverly Hills, CA 90211, tel. 323/651–5557 or 800/429–8747, fax 323/651–3678). **Kennedy Travel** (314 Jericho Turnpike, Floral Park, NY 11001, tel. 516/352–4888 or 800/237–7433, fax 516/354–8849). **Now Voyager** (4406 18th St., San Francisco, CA 94114, tel. 415/626–1169 or 800/255–6951, fax 415/626–8626). **Skylink Travel and Tour** (1006 Mendocino Ave., Santa Rosa, CA 95401, tel. 707/546–9888 or 800/225–5759, fax 707/546–9891), serving lesbian travelers.

**LOCAL RESOURCES** • **BiNet LA** (tel. 323/882–4402). **South Bay Lesbian/Gay/Bi Community Center** (2009 Artesia Blvd., Suite A, Redondo Beach, tel. 310/379–2850). **Gay and Lesbian Community Yellow Pages** (tel. 323/469–4454). **L.A. Shanti** (1616 N. La Brea Ave., between Hollywood and Sunset Blvds., tel. 323/962–8197). **L.A. Gay and Lesbian Center** (1625 N. Schrader Blvd., 4 blocks west of Vine St., Hollywood, tel. 323/993–7400).

## HOLIDAYS

Major national holidays include New Year's Day (Jan. 1); Martin Luther King, Jr., Day (3rd Mon. in Jan.); President's Day (3rd Mon. in Feb.); Memorial Day (last Mon. in May); Independence Day (July 4); Labor Day (1st Mon. in Sept.); Thanksgiving Day (4th Thurs. in Nov.); Christmas Eve and Christmas Day (Dec. 24 and 25); and New Year's Eve (Dec. 31).

# INSURANCE

The most useful travel insurance plan is a comprehensive policy that includes coverage for trip cancellation and interruption, default, trip delay, and medical expenses (with a waiver for preexisting conditions).

Without insurance you will lose all or most of your money if you cancel your trip, regardless of the reason. Default insurance covers you if your tour operator, airline, or cruise line goes out of business. Trip-delay covers expenses that arise because of bad weather or mechanical delays. Study the fine print when comparing policies.

British and Australian citizens need extra medical coverage when traveling overseas.

Always **buy travel policies directly from the insurance company**; if you buy it from a cruise line, airline, or tour operator that goes out of business you probably will not be covered for the agency or operator's default, a major risk. Before you make any purchase **review your existing health and home-owner's policies** to find what they cover away from home.

**TRAVEL INSURERS** • In the U.S. **Access America** (6600 W. Broad St., Richmond, VA 23230, tel. 804/285–3300 or 800/284–8300), **Travel Guard International** (1145 Clark St., Stevens Point, WI 54481, tel. 715/345–0505 or 800/826–1300). In Canada **Voyager Insurance** (44 Peel Center Dr., Brampton, Ontario L6T 4M8, tel. 905/791–8700; 800/668–4342 in Canada).

**INSURANCE INFORMATION** • In the U.K. the **Association of British Insurers** (51–55 Gresham St., London EC2V 7HQ, tel. 0171/600–3333, fax 0171/696–8999). In Australia the **Insurance Council of Australia** (tel. 03/9614–1077, fax 03/9614–7924).

# LODGING

For information and listings for hotels, motels, and hostels *see* Chapter 4.

## APARTMENT RENTALS

If you want a home base that's roomy enough for a family and comes with cooking facilities **consider a furnished rental.** These can save you money, especially if you're traveling with a group. Home-exchange directories sometimes list rentals as well as exchanges.

**INTERNATIONAL AGENTS** • **Hometours International** (Box 11503, Knoxville, TN 37939, tel. 423/690–8484 or 800/367– 4668). **Vacation Home Rentals Worldwide** (235 Kensington Ave., Norwood, NJ 07648, tel. 201/767–9393 or 800/633–3284, fax 201/767–5510). **Hideaways International** (767 Islington St., Portsmouth, NH 03801, tel. 603/430–4433 or 800/843–4433, fax 603/430–4444; membership $99).

## HOME EXCHANGES

If you would like to exchange your home for someone else's, **join a home-exchange organization,** which will send you its updated listings of available exchanges for a year and will include your own listing in at least one of them. It's up to you to make specific arrangements.

**EXCHANGE CLUBS** • **HomeLink International** (Box 650, Key West, FL 33041, tel. 305/294–7766 or 800/638–3841, fax 305/294–1448; $93 per year). **Intervac U.S.** (Box 590504, San Francisco, CA 94159, tel. 800/756–4663, fax 415/435–7440; $83 for catalogues.

## HOSTELS

No matter what your age you can **save on lodging costs by staying at hostels.** In some 5,000 locations in more than 70 countries around the world, Hostelling International (HI), the umbrella group for a number of national youth-hostel associations, offers single-sex, dorm-style beds and, at many hostels, couples rooms and family accommodations. Membership in any HI national hostel association, open to travelers of all ages, allows you to stay in HI-affiliated hostels at member rates (one-year membership is about $25 for adults; hostels run about $10–$25 per night). Members also have priority if the hostel is full; they're eligible for discounts around the world, even on rail and bus travel in some countries.

**ORGANIZATIONS** • **Australian Youth Hostel Association** (10 Mallett St., Camperdown, NSW 2050, tel. 02/9565–1699, fax 02/9565–1325). **Hostelling International—American Youth Hostels** (733 15th St. NW, Suite 840, Washington, DC 20005, tel. 202/783–6161, fax 202/783–6171). **Hostelling International—Canada** (400–205 Catherine St., Ottawa, Ontario K2P 1C3, tel. 613/237–7884, fax 613/237–7868). **Youth Hostel Association of England and Wales** (Trevelyan House, 8 St. Stephen's Hill, St.

Albans, Hertfordshire AL1 2DY, tel. 01727/855215 or 01727/845047, fax 01727/844126). **Youth Hostels Association of New Zealand** (Box 436, Christchurch, New Zealand, tel. 03/379–9970, fax 03/365–4476). Membership in the U.S. $25, in Canada C$26.75, in the U.K. £9.30, in Australia $44, in New Zealand $24.

# MAIL

The standard domestic letter rate is 33¢; a postcard costs 20¢ to mail. Sending letters overseas costs 60¢ for ½ ounce, $1 for an ounce; a postcard costs 55¢.

If you need to have mail sent to you in L.A., but don't have a specific address, it could be sent to you care of General Delivery to the downtown post office branch (760 N. Main St., 90086). If you're an American Express cardmember, you could also have mail held for you at one of the local AmEx offices. The sender should write "client mail" on the envelope. Remember to bring a piece of official identification when picking up your mail.

## POST OFFICES

The central post office in L.A. is the Worldway Postal Center Station (5800 W. Century Blvd., at LAX, 90009, 800/275–8777). It's open 24 hours for midnight stamp or mail runs. Check a local phone book for the address of the branch nearest you, but note that all L.A. post offices now use the central 800 number.

# MEDIA

## NEWSPAPERS & MAGAZINES

The *Los Angeles Times* (25¢, Sunday $1.50), widely considered the West Coast's best newspaper, is especially valuable on Sundays: The "Calendar" section contains a trove of entertainment information. There's also a great weekend planning section that's included in the Thursday paper. For slightly hipper up-to-the-minute entertainment listings, pick up a copy of *L.A. Weekly* or the *New Times,* two free weeklies available at cafés, supermarkets, and bookstores; new issues hit the stands every Thursday. *L.A. Weekly* is the more comprehensive, often seeming to weigh more than a small child.

*Los Angeles* magazine ($2.95) is for the most part a fluffy monthly, but they do publish "The Guide: Los Angeles at Your Fingertips" in the back of each issue, with listings for music, restaurants, cafés, and things going on around town. In July they publish a "Best of L.A." issue, which is invaluable. *Glue* ($2.50), a slim, alternative, bimonthly magazine, is packed with funky style, gossip, and scenester tips. There are also two hysterical columns: one, by Mink Stole (check your John Waters credits), dishes advice while the other, by Vaginal Davis, dishes attitude.

*La Opinion* is the major Spanish-language newspaper in L.A. Pick it up at any newsstand for info and news about and for Latinos. The Chicano Studies Research Library (B307 Murphy Hall, tel. 310/825–2363) is a noncirculating library that has books and newspapers on and for the Latino community.

## RADIO & TELEVISION

Check the *Los Angeles Times* Sunday edition for Radio Highlights, which lists interesting upcoming radio programs. **KLON** (88.1) of Long Beach State plays jazz and blues. **KCRW** (89.9) is the local National Public Radio station. **KKBT** (92.3) plays hip-hop and rhythm and blues music while **KIKF** (94.3) plays country. Check out Mark and Brian in the morning on **KLOS** (95.5), an alternative and rock station. Howard Stern contaminates the airwaves on **KLSX** (97.1) weekday mornings; it's an all-talk station. **KLAX** (97.9) tosses ranchero music on the airwaves. **KYSR** (98.7) plays Top 40 and retro '80s tunes and wakes up L.A. every weekday morning with Jamie, Frosty, and Frank. **KRTH** (101.1) plays the oldies but goodies. For a dose of Mariah Carey and her ilk, turn the dial to **KIIS** (102.7), home of Rick Dees. **KROQ** (106.7), one of the best-known stations in the Southland, plays alternative rock and constantly gives out tickets to shows. Weekday morning DJs Kevin and Bean have a passionate following. **Y107** (107.1) has a modern rock format.

**CBS** is on Channel 2, **NBC** on Channel 4, **ABC** on Channel 7. The **Warner Bros. Network** can be found on KTLA, Channel 5. **Fox** is on KTTV, Channel 11. **PBS** is on KCET, Channel 28; **KOCE** on Channel 50; **KLCS** on Channel 41. The independent stations are Channels 9, 18, 43, 51, 56, 62, and 68.

# MONEY MATTERS

Prices throughout this guide are given for adults. Substantially reduced fees are almost always available for children, students, and senior citizens.

## ATMS

**ATM LOCATIONS • Cirrus** (tel. 800/424–7787). **Plus** (tel. 800/843–7587).

## CREDIT CARDS

Major credit cards are widely accepted in L.A.'s restaurants, hotels, and other establishments. You'll need a credit card in order to rent a car or to make purchases (such as event tickets) over the phone. And they provide some consumer protection and recourse in case there's a problem with the product or service. Diner's Club and Discover are accepted somewhat less frequently than American Express, Visa, and MasterCard.

**REPORTING LOST CARDS •** To report lost or stolen credit cards, call the following toll-free numbers: American Express (tel. 800/327–2177); Discover Card (tel. 800/347–2683); Diners Club (tel. 800/234–6377); MasterCard (tel. 800/307–7309); Visa (tel. 800/847–2911).

## EXCHANGING MONEY

For the most favorable rates, **change money through banks.** Although fees charged for ATM transactions will be higher than at home, Cirrus and Plus rates are excellent, because they are based on wholesale rates offered only by the major banks. You won't do as well at exchange booths in airports or train or bus stations. To save yourself a frantic cash search on arrival, remember to **get some local currency before you leave home.**

## TRAVELER'S CHECKS

Using traveler's checks tends to be easier in L.A. rather than in the smaller, nearby towns. They're generally treated as the equivalent of cash in most hotels and restaurants, with one exception: you'll need a photo I.D. to use them. Lost or stolen checks can usually be replaced within 24 hours. To ensure a speedy refund, buy your own traveler's checks—don't let someone else pay for them, since irregularities like this can cause replacement delays. The person who bought the checks should make the call to request a refund. Also, remember to keep a tally of the checks as you spend them.

**REPORTING LOST CHECKS •** American Express (tel. 800/221–7282).

# PACKING

One important thing to keep in mind while packing is that you should **be prepared for temperature changes.** If you plan to head up to the mountains or spend time on the ocean, there can a marked temperature drop; the city cools off considerably at night. Bring clothes you can layer—cotton Ts, a sweater or two, a pair of long pants. And while L.A. is known for seemingly eternal sunshine, it doesn't hurt to bring a slicker or collapsible umbrella. Style-wise, think casual but not sloppy. Black clothes are a safe bet. Comfortable shoes are a must, even if you're humming "nobody walks in L.A." while you pack—you'll need them for sightseeing. Finally, don't forget your sunglasses, bathing suit, and sunblock.

You've heard it before and you'll hear it again: **Pack light.** The heaviness of your luggage is always directly proportional to how many days you've been lugging it around. In your carry-on luggage **bring an extra pair of eyeglasses or contact lenses** and **enough of any medication you take** to last the entire trip. You may also want your doctor to write a spare prescription using the drug's generic name, since brand names may vary from country to country. In luggage to be checked, **never pack prescription drugs or valuables.** To avoid customs delays, carry medications in their original packaging. When packing containers of gooey liquids like shampoo, use containers that seal tightly (tape the top down if necessary) and pack them in a separate waterproof bag. The pressure on airplanes can cause lids to pop off and create instant goo-slicks inside your luggage. If you'll be hitting hostels, find out whether you'll need a sleep sheet. And don't forget to copy down and carry addresses of offices that handle refunds of lost traveler's checks.

Other stuff you might not think to take but will be damn glad to have: a miniature flashlight; a pocketknife; a water bottle; several large zip-top plastic bags; a travel alarm clock; a palm-sized sewing kit; extra batteries; a good book; and a day pack.

## CHECKING LUGGAGE

How many carry-on bags you can bring with you is up to the airline. Most allow two, but not always, so make sure that everything you carry aboard will fit under your seat, and get to the gate early. Note that if you have a seat at the back of the plane, you'll probably board first, while the overhead bins are still empty.

If you are flying internationally, note that baggage allowances may be determined not by piece but by weight—generally 88 pounds (40 kilograms) in first class, 66 pounds (30 kilograms) in business class, and 44 pounds (20 kilograms) in economy.

Airline liability for baggage is limited to $1,250 per person on flights within the United States. On international flights it amounts to $9.07 per pound or $20 per kilogram for checked baggage (roughly $640 per 70-pound bag) and $400 per passenger for unchecked baggage. You can buy additional coverage at check-in for about $10 per $1,000 of coverage, but it excludes a rather extensive list of items, shown on your airline ticket.

Before departure **itemize your bags' contents** and their worth, and label the bags with your name, address, and phone number. (If you use your home address, cover it so that potential thieves can't see it readily.) Inside each bag **pack a copy of your itinerary**. At check-in **make sure that each bag is correctly tagged** with the destination airport's three-letter code. If your bags arrive damaged or fail to arrive. at all, file a written report with the airline before leaving the airport.

## PASSPORTS & VISAS

**U.K. CITIZENS • U.S. Embassy Visa Information Line** (tel. 01891/200–290; calls cost 49p per minute, 39p per minute cheap rate) for U.S. visa information. **U.S. Embassy Visa Branch** (5 Upper Grosvenor Sq., London W1A 1AE) for U.S. visa information; send a self-addressed, stamped envelope. Write the **U.S. Consulate General** (Queen's House, Queen St., Belfast BTI 6EO) if you live in Northern Ireland. Write the **Office of Australia Affairs** (59th fl., MLC Centre, 19-29 Martin Pl., Sydney NSW 2000) if you live in Australia. Write the **Office of New Zealand Affairs** (29 Fitzherbert Terr., Thorndon, Wellington) if you live in New Zealand.

### PASSPORT OFFICES

The best time to apply for a passport or to renew is during the fall and winter. Before any trip, check your passport's expiration date, and, if necessary, renew it as soon as possible.

**AUSTRALIAN CITIZENS • Australian Passport Office** (tel. 131–232).

**NEW ZEALAND CITIZENS • New Zealand Passport Office** (tel. 04/494–0700 for information on how to apply; 04/474–8000 or 0800/225–050 in New Zealand for information on applications already submitted).

**U.K. CITIZENS • London Passport Office** (tel. 0990/210– 410) for fees and documentation requirements and to request an emergency passport.

## SAFETY

Los Angeles is as safe as any other large American city. What's different about L.A. is that the vast majority of the populace spends most of their time in cars; the opportunities for assaults, rapes, and holdups just aren't there. Drivers should keep their doors locked; pedestrians should exercise the usual precautions.

Determining the safety of Los Angeles neighborhoods is tricky. Bad, scary areas are peppered throughout basically safe areas. MacArthur Park and South-Central tend to the more dangerous side, especially at night. Generally, you should exercise caution at night in any neighborhood, especially if you are alone; avoid deserted or dark streets. Walk at a brisk, confident pace. Carjacking happens to the poor, the rich, the famous, and the unknown in every neighborhood in L.A; keep your car doors locked and remember that you can buy another car but not another life. As in all big cities, stay aware of your surroundings. Don't leave valuables in your car—better yet, don't bring anything you really cherish with you on vacation. Obviously, if you are somewhere that makes you feel uncomfortable or in danger, leave.

Money belts may be dorky and bulky, but it's better to be embarrassed than broke and/or stranded. You'd be wise to carry all cash, traveler's checks, credit cards, passport, and other essentials there or in some other inaccessible place, like a neck pouch. If you carry a bag or backpack, keep it attached to you; never leave it unguarded, even for a minute. If you're sitting somewhere, like a restaurant, keep your bag in your lap or between your feet, not slung on the back of a chair or on a seat next to you, where it could be easily swiped.

## ALCOHOL

California's legal drinking age is a strictly enforced 21. It's essential to carry picture identification (passport or driver's license), or you may not be allowed into places that serve alcohol. (For all you night owls, bear in mind that alcohol can't be purchased, served, or consumed in public establishments between the hours of 2 AM and 6 AM.) Do not—repeat, *do not*—drink and drive. If the alcohol content in your blood exceeds the legal .08% limit, you'll be arrested, your license will be suspended, and you'll face fines starting at about $400 (not to mention the costly court fees and mandatory rehab sessions).

# SENIOR-CITIZEN TRAVEL

To qualify for age-related discounts **mention your senior-citizen status up front** when booking hotel reservations (not when checking out) and before you're seated in restaurants (not when paying the bill). When renting a car ask about promotional car-rental discounts, which can be cheaper than senior-citizen rates.

**EDUCATIONAL PROGRAMS** • **Elderhostel** (75 Federal St., 3rd fl., Boston, MA 02110, tel. 877/426–8056, fax 877/426– 2166).

# SMOKING

California's rep as an anti-smoking bastion is well founded; in Los Angeles, you're not allowed to smoke in most public buildings, including restaurants and bars. If you're a nic fiend, L.A.'s good weather will be on your side since it shouldn't be too painful to go outside to smoke. Many bars and restaurants have outdoor seating areas, but you should check their smoking policy before lighting up.

# STUDENTS

There are enough student discounts in L.A. to make things easier for those on a tuition-cramped budget. Most of the city's museums have student rates, as do most movie theaters. Students can also qualify for monthly discounts on public transportation. The amount is based strictly on where you're coming from and going to, so call the MTA information line (*see* Bus Travel Within Los Angeles, *above*) for full details.

To save money, **look into deals available through student-oriented travel agencies** and the various other organizations involved in helping out student and budget travelers. Typically, you'll find discounted airfares, rail passes, tours, lodgings, and other travel arrangements, and you don't necessarily have to be a student to qualify.

The big names in the field are STA Travel, with some 100 offices worldwide and a useful Web site (http://www.sta-travel.com), and the Council on International Educational Exchange (CIEE or just Council for short; http://www.ciee.org), a private, nonprofit organization that administers work, volunteer, academic, and professional programs worldwide and sells travel arrangements through its own specialized travel agency, Council Travel. Travel CUTS, strictly a travel agency, sells discounted airline tickets to Canadian students from offices on or near college campuses. The Educational Travel Center (ETC) books low-cost flights to destinations within the continental United States and around the world. And Student Flights, Inc., specializes in student and faculty airfares.

Most of these organizations also issue student identity cards, which entitle their bearers to special fares on local transportation and discounts at museums, theaters, sports events, and other attractions, as well as a handful of other benefits, which are listed in the handbook that most provide to their cardholders. Major cards include the International Student Identity Card (ISIC) and Go 25: International Youth Travel Card (GO25), available to nonstudents as well as students age 25 and under; the ISIC, when purchased in the United States, comes with $3,000 in emergency medical coverage and a few related benefits. Both the ISIC and GO25 are issued by Council Travel or STA in the United States, Travel CUTS in Canada, at student unions and student-travel companies in the United Kingdom, and by STA in Australia. The International Student Exchange Card (ISE), issued by Student Flights, Inc., is available to faculty members as well as students, and the International Teacher Identity Card (ITIC), issued by Travel

CUTS, provides similar benefits to teachers in all grade levels, from kindergarten through graduate school. All student ID cards cost between $10 and $20.

**STUDENT IDS & SERVICES • Council on International Educational Exchange** (CIEE, 205 E. 42nd St., 14th fl., New York, NY 10017, tel. 212/822–2600 or 888/268–6245, fax 212/822–2699) for mail orders only, in the U.S. **Council Travel in Southern California** (Los Angeles, tel. 310/208– 3551; Long Beach, tel. 562/621–6603; San Diego, tel. 619/270–6401). **Educational Travel Center** (tel. 608/256– 5551 or 800/747–5551). **STA in Southern California** (Los Angeles, tel. 323/934–8722; Santa Monica, tel. 310/394–5126; Westwood, tel. 310/824–1574). **Student Flights** (tel. 480/951–1177 or 800/255– 8000). **Travel Cuts** (187 College St., Toronto, Ontario M5T 1P7, tel. 416/979–2406 or 800/667–2887) in Canada.

# SUBWAYS & COMMUTER TRAINS

L.A.'s entrée into subway and commuter rail travel is quite recent; trains started running in the early 1990s. The MTA's MetroRail system has three lines: the Red Line subway and the Blue and Green Line above-ground commuter trains. The Blue and Green lines are called MetroLink.

True to its word, the MTA keeps the L.A. subway system chugging along. As of press time, the Red Line route had expanded to thirteen stations, stretching as far west as Hollywood and Vine from its eastern starting point in downtown's Union Station. The expansion into Hollywood has certainly made it easier to hop from downtown sights like Olvera Street, Chinatown, and Little Tokyo to the glitter of Mann's Chinese Theater and the Walk of Fame. In a city as vast and sprawling as L.A., though, the Red Line's current usefulness is limited. Happily, the subway system is scheduled to expand into the San Fernando Valley by mid-2000, with stops at Hollywood Boulevard and Highland Avenue, Universal City, and North Hollywood. Optimists say that by 2001 the Red Line will run 300 mi throughout the greater Los Angeles area. We'll see.

Quite a bit of planning (and money) went into the stations' design, and each has its own distinct look. Some of the best include the Vermont/Beverly station, with its imposing, glass-clad columns juxtaposed with rock formations, and the Hollywood/Vine station, which has recycled film reels on the ceiling, original Paramount Pictures film projectors from the 1930s, and floor paving that looks like the yellow brick road from *The Wizard of Oz.*

If you need to travel a bit farther afield, the MTA's Blue and Green Line commuter trains might do the trick. The Blue Line runs north to south from downtown's 7th Street/Metro Center stop (where it meets the Red Line subway) to 1st Street Station in Long Beach. The Green Line runs east to west from Norwalk to Redondo Beach and includes a stop near LAX. It intersects the Blue Line at the Rose Parks (Imperial/Wilmington) station.

## FARES & SCHEDULES

The fare for a one-way ride on the Red, Green, or Blue Line subway is $1.35; a transfer for another train line or an MTA bus costs 25¢. The same discount token packs and passes used for the MTA bus system (*see above*) are used for the subways and commuter trains.

Trains for all lines run every 5–10 minutes during weekday rush hours, otherwise every 7–20 minutes. Service runs from 5 AM to 11 PM.

**SUBWAY INFORMATION • MTA** (tel. 213/626–4455 or 800/COMMUTE).

# TAXIS

Usually you can't hail a taxi on the street; instead you phone for one. All taxi companies in Los Angeles County charge the same rate: an initial $1.90 plus $1.60 per mile. Taxis are a good idea if you're out at a club in a bad area, or if you and your companions have been drinking. Cabs are expensive—and no doubt you'll have a long way to go—but your safety is worth it. Within the downtown area a taxi ride will cost about $4. For information on taking a taxi from LAX into the city, *see* Airports & Transfers, *above*. Most taxi companies operate 24 hours daily.

**TAXI COMPANIES • L.A. Taxi** (tel. 213/627–7000). **United Independent Taxi** (tel. 323/653–5050). **Yellow Cab Co.** (tel. 800/200–1085).

# TELEPHONES

For local directory assistance, dial 411. For long-distance help, dial the area code plus 555–1212.

## AREA CODES

Area codes are changing all over the country, and southern California is certainly no exception. In some (but not all) cases, the telephone companies provide a grace period that allows callers to dial the old area code for a few months. The following are some recent area code changes:

Areas surrounding downtown Los Angeles (including most of Hollywood) now use 323 instead of 213. At press time, there was a dust-up over the addition of a new area code to west L.A. (currently the 310 area code). Consumer protest has so far kept a new area code at bay.

San Gabriel Valley switched to 626 from 818. The southern portion of Orange County now uses 949 rather than 714.

## CALLING LONG DISTANCE

AT&T, MCI, and Sprint long-distance services make calling home relatively convenient and let you avoid hotel surcharges. In the United States you typically dial an 800 number to access these carriers.

**TO OBTAIN ACCESS CODES • AT&T** USADirect (tel. 800/874–4000). **MCI** Call USA (tel. 800/444–4444). **Sprint** Express (tel. 800/793– 1153).

## INTERNATIONAL CALLS

Calls between the United States and Canada are not considered international calls and can be dialed as regular long-distance numbers. To call any other country, dial 011, the country code, the city code (dropping the initial zero if there is one), then the actual number. If you get stuck, dial 00 for a long-distance operator, who can help you. The country code for Great Britain is 44, New Zealand 64, and Australia 61.

*Even if you're not planning to take the Red Line subway, duck into the Civic Center Station, at 1st and Hill streets, to check out the mannequins suspended from the ceiling.*

## PUBLIC PHONES

Instructions for pay telephones should be posted on the phone, but generally you insert your coins— 35¢ for most local calls—in a slot and wait for the steady hum of the dial tone before dialing the number. If you dial a long-distance number, the operator will come on the line and tell you how much more money you must insert for your call to go through.

# TIME

Los Angeles is in the Pacific Standard Time zone. It is three hours behind New York, two hours behind Chicago, eight hours behind London, and 17 hours behind Sydney.

# TIPPING

Gratuities are normally not included on restaurant bills, although some places do include it for large parties, usually six or more. The basic tip is 15 percent, 20 percent for excellent service. Give at least a dollar per bag to luggage handlers.

# TOURS & PACKAGES

On a prepackaged tour or independent vacation everything is prearranged so you'll spend less time planning—and often get it all at a good price.

## BOOKING WITH AN AGENT

Travel agents are excellent resources. But it's a good idea to collect brochures from several agencies because some agents' suggestions may be influenced by relationships with tour and package firms that reward them for volume sales. If you have a special interest **find an agent with expertise in that area**; ASTA (*see* Travel Agencies, *below*) has a database of specialists worldwide.

Make sure your travel agent knows the accommodations and other services of the place they're recommending. Ask about the hotel's location, room size, beds, and whether it has a pool, room service, or programs for children, if you care about these. Has your agent been there in person or sent others whom you can contact?

Do some homework on your own, too: Local tourism boards can provide information about lesser-known and small-niche operators, some of which may sell only direct.

## BUYER BEWARE

Each year consumers are stranded or lose their money when tour operators—even large ones with excellent reputations—go out of business. So **check out the operator.** Ask several travel agents about its reputation, and try to **book with a company that has a consumer-protection program.** (Look for information in the company's brochure.) In the United States, members of the National Tour Association and United States Tour Operators Association are required to set aside funds to cover your payments and travel arrangements in case the company defaults. It's also a good idea to choose a company that participates in the American Society of Travel Agent's Tour Operator Program (TOP); ASTA will act as mediator in any disputes between you and your tour operator.

Remember that the more your package or tour includes the better you can predict the ultimate cost of your vacation. Make sure you know exactly what is covered, and **beware of hidden costs.** Are taxes, tips, and transfers included? Entertainment and excursions? These can add up.

**TOUR-OPERATOR RECOMMENDATIONS • American Society of Travel Agents** (*see* Travel Agencies, *below*). **National Tour Association** (NTA, 546 E. Main St., Lexington, KY 40508, tel. 606/226–4444 or 800/682–8886). **United States Tour Operators Association** (USTOA, 342 Madison Ave., Suite 1522, New York, NY 10173, tel. 212/599–6599 or 800/468–7862, fax 212/599–6744).

## PACKAGES

The companies listed below offer vacation packages in a broad price range.

**AIR/HOTEL/CAR • American Airlines Fly AAway Vacations** (tel. 800/321–2121). **Continental Vacations** (tel. 800/634–5555). **Delta Dream Vacations** (tel. 800/872–7786). **United Vacations** (tel. 800/328–6877). **US Airways Vacations** (tel. 800/455–0123).

**HOTEL ONLY • SuperCities** (139 Main St., Cambridge, MA 02142, tel. 800/333–1234).

**CUSTOM PACKAGES • Amtrak's Great American Vacations** (tel. 800/321–8684). **Budget World-Class Drive** (tel. 800/527–0700, 0800/181181 in the U.K.) for self-drive itineraries.

**FROM THE U.K. • British Airways Holidays** (Astral Towers, Betts Way, London Rd., Crawley, West Sussex RH10 2XA, tel. 01293/723–121). **Jetsave** (Sussex House, London Rd., East Grinstead, West Sussex RH19 1LD, tel. 01342/312–033). **Key to America** (1–3 Station Rd., Ashford, Middlesex TW15 2UW, tel. 01784/248–777). **Kuoni Travel Ltd.** (Kuoni House, Dorking, Surrey RH5 4AZ, tel. 01306/742–222). **Premier Holidays** (Premier Travel Center, Westbrook, Milton Rd., Cambridge CB4 1YG, tel. 01223/516–688). **Trailfinders** (42– 50 Earls Court Rd., London W8 6FT, tel. 0171/937–5400; 58 Deansgate, Manchester M3 2FF, tel. 0161/839–6969).

# TRAIN TRAVEL

**Amtrak** is the only passenger rail service in the United States. In Los Angeles Amtrak stops at the historic Union Station, in a semisleazy neighborhood downtown. The *Coast Starlight* arrives here from Seattle via Portland and Oakland, while the *Sunset Limited* travels to Los Angeles from Orlando via New Orleans. The *Texas Eagle* arrives from San Antonio, while the *Southwest Chief* arrives from Chicago. All of these arrive daily. The best way to get fares and schedules is to call Amtrak (*see below*). From Los Angeles's **Union Station** you can hop on the Metro Red Line, MetroLink long-distance commuter trains, or MTA buses to points within L.A. and to outlying areas (*see* Bus Travel *and* Subway & Commuter Trains, *above*). Luggage storage is available from 6:30 AM to 10:00 PM and costs $1.50 per item. Union Station itself is open 24 hours.

**TRAIN INFORMATION • Amtrak** (tel. 800/872–7245). **Union Station** (800 N. Alameda St., at César Chávez Ave., tel. 213/683–6729).

## RAIL PASSES

Amtrak's **All-Aboard Pass** is good for people who plan their itinerary in advance. The pass, which is actually a booklet of tickets, allows Amtrak riders special fares for three stops made in 45 days of travel within a region. Ticket agents need to know your dates of travel and intended destinations for ticketing, so call Amtrak in advance. Amtrak also provides free but limited shuttle services for pass holders whose routes don't connect.

Amtrak's **USARail Pass** works to the advantage of the foreign budget traveler (it's not available to U.S. or Canadian citizens) because it requires no formal itinerary, works on any of Amtrak's U.S. routes, and allows for spontaneous planning (within a specified time period). A 15-day pass costs $355 ($245 off-season), a 30-day pass $440 ($350 off-season). Buy them at an international travel agency before entering the United States or from an Amtrak office (passport and visa required for purchase).

## RESERVATIONS

Reservations are necessary for long-distance travel; you can make them by calling Amtrak's general number (*see* Train Information, *above*) or by hitting the website (http://www.amtrak.com). If you call early, you can save money, since the fares go up as seats fill.

# TRANSPORTATION AROUND LOS ANGELES

Moving around L.A. is difficult at best. First, L.A. is just plain big. Second, the bus system is slow and tedious, and the subway system isn't terribly thorough. Third, if you drive on the freeways, you will get lost and confused unless you spend hours consulting maps (FYI: Spend those hours—it's worth it in the end). Most Angelenos choose cars over mass transit because cars allow you to go where you want, when you want; driving is a local pastime; and sitting in traffic can be educational provided you're tuned into NPR. So to be noble and suffer on mass transit or to be selfish and suffer in traffic and aggravation?— that is the question. *See* Bus Travel, Subways & Commuter Trains, *and* Driving *above* for more insight. For information on how to get to your destination in Los Angeles from one of the area airports, *see* Airports & Transfers, *above*.

# TRAVEL AGENCIES

A good travel agent puts your needs first. Look for an agency that has been in business at least five years, emphasizes customer service, and has someone on staff who specializes in your destination. In addition **make sure the agency belongs to a professional trade organization.** The American Society of Travel Agents (ASTA), with 27,000 agents in some 170 countries, is the largest and most influential in the field. Operating under the motto "Integrity in Travel," it maintains and enforces a strict code of ethics and will step in to help mediate any agent-client disputes if necessary. ASTA also maintains a Web site that includes a directory of agents. (Note that if a travel agency is also acting as your tour operator, *see* Buyer Beware *in* Tours & Packages, *above*.)

**LOCAL AGENT REFERRALS • American Society of Travel Agents** (ASTA, tel. 800/965–2782 24-hr hot line, fax 703/684–8319, www.astanet.com). **Association of British Travel Agents** (68–271 Newman St., London W1P 4AH, tel. 0171/637– 2444, fax 0171/637–0713). **Association of Canadian Travel Agents** (1729 Bank St., Suite 201, Ottawa, Ontario K1V 7Z5, tel. 613/521–0474, fax 613/521–0805). **Australian Federation of Travel Agents** (Level 3, 309 Pitt St., Sydney 2000, tel. 02/9264–3299, fax 02/9264–1085). **Travel Agents' Association of New Zealand** (Box 1888, Wellington 10033, tel. 04/499–0104, fax 04/499–0786).

# VISITOR INFORMATION

**TOURIST INFORMATION •** For general information about Los Angeles and its environs, contact these tourism bureaus before you go. When you arrive, stop by the visitor information centers in downtown Los Angeles or Hollywood.

**CITY • Los Angeles Convention and Visitors Bureau** (633 W. 5th St., Suite 6000, 90071, tel. 213/624–7300 or 800/228–2452) offers the free "Destination Los Angeles," an annually updated information book with suggestions for entertainment, lodging, dining, and a list of special events. Los Angeles also maintains a 24-hour toll-free multilingual line with visitor information and the scoop on upcoming events (tel. 213/689–8822). There are two visitor information centers: **Downtown Los Angeles** (685 S. Figueroa St., tel. 213/689–8822); **Hollywood** (6541 Hollywood Blvd., tel. 213/689–8822).

**METRO AREA • Beverly Hills** (239 S. Beverly Dr., 90212, tel. 310/248–1000 or 800/345–2210). **Channel Islands** (2731 S. Victoria Ave., Oxnard, 93035, tel. 800/994–4852). **Hollywood** (7018 Hollywood Blvd., 90028, tel. 323/469–8311). **Long Beach Area Convention and Visitors Bureau** (1 World Trade Center, Suite 300, 90831, tel. 562/436–3645). **Malibu Chamber of Commerce** (23805 Stuart Ranch Rd., #100, 90265, tel. 310/456–9025). **Marina del Rey Visitor & Convention Bureau** (9800 S. Sepulveda Blvd., Suite 214, Westchester, 90045, tel. 310/821–0555). **Pasadena** (171 S. Los Robles Ave., 91101, tel. 626/795–9311). **Santa Monica Visitors Center** (1400 Ocean Ave., 90401, tel. 310/393–7593). **Venice** (P.O. Box 202, 90294, tel. 310/396–7016). **West Hollywood** (8687 Melrose Ave., Suite M26, 90069, tel. 310/289–2525).

**STATE • California Office of Tourism** (801 K St., Suite 1600, Sacramento, CA 95814, tel. 916/322–2882 or 800/862–2543) has a free visitor's guide.

**IN THE U.K. • California Tourist Office** (ABC California, Box 35, Abingdon, Oxfordshire OX14 4TB, tel. 0891/200–278). Calls cost 50p per minute peak rate or 45p per minute cheap rate. Brochures can be obtained by sending a check for £3 made out to ABC California to the above address.

## WEB SITES

**Check out the World Wide Web** when you're planning your trip. You'll find everything from up-to-date weather forecasts to virtual tours. Fodor's Web site, www.fodors.com, is a great place to start your online travels.

We could point you to 2,000 L.A.-related Web sites, but, hell, if you know how to connect to the Web, you probably know how to use search engines. Glance at these sites to get started; most have links that will connect you with related L.A. ephemera.

**Calendar Live!.** The arts and entertainment branch of the *Los Angeles Times*'s Web site (*see below*) isn't just a rehash of what you can read in hard copy. Its own staff of writers and editors pumps out news and reviews about everything fun and interesting in L.A. It's great for upcoming events—everything from a blues festival on Catalina to a celebrity book-signing in Hollywood. *http://www.calendarlive.com.*

**Glue.** Use this bimonthly magazine's page to get a gossip fix; the gossip and music scene riffs are updated every week or two. *http://www.gluemag.com.*

**L.A. Weekly.** Read L.A.'s hip weekly paper (without being subjected to endless liposuction ads) before you even get here. *http://www.laweekly.com.*

**Los Angeles Convention & Visitors Bureau.** Check out the neighborhood synopses and sample itineraries here; they've also got a monthly calendar, visitor resources, and more. *http://www.lacvb.com.*

**Los Angeles County Metropolitan Transportation Authority.** L.A.'s public transportation is notoriously confusing, but this site makes things a little clearer. There's plenty of general info (fares, schedules, and the like), updates on the subway and commuter rail construction projects, and a trip planner. *http://www.mta.net.*

**Los Angeles Magazine.** Bypass the celeb-profile cover stories and get right to the useful stuff: restaurant reviews and the monthly events listing guide. *http://www.lamag.com.*

**Los Angeles Times.** The site for the city's major paper will get you up to speed on local events. *http://www.latimes.com.*

**The Official City of L.A. Site.** This site is useful for its calendar listings and links to better sites. *http://www.ci.la.ca.us.*

**Time Out.** While *Time Out* doesn't publish a magazine in L.A., their local scouts put up monthly events selections, arts reviews, and the like on the general Web page. *http://www.timeout.com.*

## WHEN TO GO

Generally, Los Angeles's weather embodies the "sunny California" stereotype. From November through March, however, L.A. experiences a misty season—somewhat welcome because it cleans up the air. Unfortunately, it does necessitate the beautiful people garaging their convertibles and closing their sunroofs, which is such a bother. In June things start to heat up, although the coastal areas get a fair amount of morning fog, locally known as "June Gloom." In summer smog infiltrates every district, and clever folks head to the beach, where it's always a little cooler and breezier. At night it almost always cools down (remember, you're in a desert disguised as a city), so do as Mama said and bring a sweater.

# CLIMATE

**FORECASTS** • **Los Angeles County weather number** (tel. 213/554– 1212). **Weather Channel Connection** (tel. 900/932–8437), 95¢ per minute from a Touch-Tone phone.

**RESOURCES** • Check the weather and the smog situation in the *Los Angeles Times* or try the **Surf and Beach Report** (tel. 310/578–0478) and the **South Coast's Air Quality Management District** (tel. 800/288–7664).

The following chart shows the average highs and lows in Los Angeles.

| | | | | | | | | |
|---|---|---|---|---|---|---|---|---|
| *Jan.* | 64°F | 18°C | *May* | 69°F | 21°C | *Sept.* | 75°F | 24°C |
| | 46 | 8 | | 53 | 12 | | 60 | 16 |
| *Feb.* | 64°F | 18°C | *June* | 71°F | 22°C | *Oct.* | 73°F | 23°C |
| | 44 | 7 | | 57 | 14 | | 55 | 13 |
| *Mar.* | 66°F | 19°C | *July* | 75°F | 24°C | *Nov.* | 56°F | 13°C |
| | 48 | 9 | | 60 | 16 | | 48 | 9 |
| *Apr.* | 66°F | 19°C | *Aug.* | 75°F | 24°C | *Dec.* | 66°F | 19°C |
| | 51 | 11 | | 62 | 17 | | 46 | 8 |

# FESTIVALS

The Los Angeles **Cultural Affairs Department** (tel. 213/485–2433) publishes an annual "Festivals of Los Angeles" booklet, available at visitor centers (*see* Visitor Information, *above*). It should be especially appealing to lovers of jazz and film, for which monthly festivals abound.

**JANUARY** • The New Year's Day **Tournament of Roses Parade** (tel. 626/449–4100) attracts thousands; people sleep overnight on the streets of Pasadena in order to claim a prime slab of concrete. Their efforts hardly seem heroic compared to those of the glue wielders who affix more than 25 million flowers to the mammoth floats. For a chiller experience, hit the **Annual New Year's Day Swim** (tel. 310/833–1377) on Cabrillo Beach with the Cabrillo Beach Polar Bears club; join in or stay warm and watch from shore. In Little Tokyo the **Oshogatsu Festival** (tel. 213/625– 0414) ushers in the Japanese New Year.

**FEBRUARY** • The Golden Dragon Parade—which falls on a different day in February each year—is the pinnacle of the monthlong **Chinese New Year Festivities** (tel. 213/617–0396) in Chinatown.

**MARCH** • The 26-mi **Los Angeles Marathon** (tel. 310/444–5544), held the first Sunday of the month, attracts international competitors and hordes of spectators. At the **St. Patrick's Day Parade** in Century City, expect green beer—and the sort of people green beer is likely to attract. In the week surrounding St. Joseph's Day (Mar. 19), the Mission San Juan Capistrano hosts the *Fiesta de las Golindrinas* (**Festival of the Swallows**), celebrating the springtime return of the swallows from Argentina. There isn't a snowball's chance in hell you'll get invited to the **Academy Awards** (tel. 310/247–3000), held on the last Sunday of the month, but you could try to catch a glimpse of the stars as they stalk or sashay up the red carpet. Beginning in 2001, the ceremony is scheduled to be held at the new venue at Hollywood and Highland. The **Grunion Run,** from March through July, is a nighttime fish-breeding orgy that allows voyeurs to observe wiggling, ecstatic grunions. Not all southern Californian beaches run with grunions, the only fish species that comes ashore to mate, so check with the Cabrillo Marine Aquarium (tel. 310/548–7563), which sponsors a grunion-peeping program. Further inland in Santa Clarita you can line-dance your way to the **Cowboy Poetry and Music Festival** (tel. 805/286–4078); this annual event is hosted at Gene Autry's Melody Ranch (film location for *High Noon*), where cowboy poets, storytellers, and musicians celebrate the romance of life on the range. Tickets range from $7 to $90 per performance.

**APRIL** • During the **Blessing of the Animals** (tel. 213/628– 1274), held the Saturday before Easter, a cow leads a procession of animals down Olvera Street to a cardinal, who then blesses the pets, from puppies to parakeets. The southern California **Renaissance Pleasure Faire** (Glen Helen Regional Park, tel. 800/523–2473) is packed with lads and lassies trying to re-create jolly olde 16th-century England every Saturday and Sunday from late April through June. Down in San Juan Capistrano, locals pitch in to help renovate the facades of their historic mission buildings at the annual **Mud Slinging Festival** (tel. 949/248– 2049); all are welcome to join in the muck tossing, food, and entertainment.

**MAY** • A 36-block section of downtown is jammed with Latino music and carnival rides during **Cinco de Mayo** (tel. 213/624– 3660), the May 5 commemoration of the defeat of the French at an important battle in Puebla. At the end of the month UCLA holds the free two-day **Jazz and Reggae Festival** (tel. 310/825–9912). On the first weekend in May, the **UCLA Pow Wow** (tel. 310/206– 7513) gathers

# PARADING IN PASADENA

*The creators of Pasadena's Doo Dah Parade (tel. 626/440–7379) freely admit that this Rose Parade spoof was conceived over a few beers with crestfallen friends who weren't allowed to participate in the respected flower fest. Doo Dah has grown to alarmingly oddball proportions, with Dread Zeppelin, Torment of Roses, the Hibachi Barbecue Drill Team, Lounge Lizards, and hundreds of other spoofsters leading the insanity. It's held the Saturday after Thanksgiving on the Old Pasadena stretch of Colorado Blvd.*

together representatives from different Native American tribes to share their traditional music, dance, and food.

**JUNE** • Summer brings out all the neighborhood celebrations, including the **NoHo Theater and Arts Fair** (tel. 818/508–5155) in North Hollywood and the **Santa Monica Street Fair** at the Third Street Promenade (tel. 310/319–6263). Check the *L.A. Weekly* for a full listing of festival dates and offerings. Most feature live music, food, and crafts—just a big ol' block party. The **Mariachi USA Festival** (tel. 213/848–7717) at the Hollywood Bowl is not to be missed if you like mariachi music, ballet *folklórico*, or fireworks. The **Los Angeles Gay & Lesbian Pride Celebration** (tel. 323/969–8302), in West Hollywood, commemorates the 1969 Stonewall riots in New York City and honors gay people past and present. Five hundred thousand people regularly show up for the four-hour parade on a Sunday in late June and the moms and dads in the Parents, Friends, and Family of Lesbians and Gays (PFLAG) contingent usually get the loudest cheers. On the same weekend, the **Los Angeles Dyke March** (tel. 323/692–1029) starts on Santa Monica Boulevard (at Doheny Drive) and ends with a block party with dancing, laughing, and fun.

**JULY** • Watch the **Fourth of July Fireworks** from coastal communities such as Marina del Rey; most take place around sunset. The **Lotus Festival** (tel. 213/485–1310) celebrates Pacific Rim cultures with crafts, music, and dragon boat races in Echo Park, near the largest lotus bed outside of China. It's usually held the first weekend after the Fourth of July. From July through August both amateurs and pros at the **International Surf Festival** (tel. 310/305–9546) shred on raspy waves along Los Angeles's South Bay beaches. Landlubbers can hang out at the sand castle design contest. **Absolut Chalk** (tel. 626/440–7379) is the world's largest chalk mural festival with more than 400 artists participating; it happens at Pasadena City Hall in late June or early July, and there's a $7 admission. Laguna Beach has a couple of cool festivals that run through July and August. The most impressive is the **Pageant of the Masters** (tel. 949/494–1145; for tickets call 800/487–3378). Every night, in an outdoor amphitheater, actors re-create some of the world's most famous artworks as "living pictures." Paired with the Pageant of the Masters is the **Festival of the Arts,** a fine art and craft show and sale held on the grounds in front of the amphitheater. Across the road is the **Sawdust Festival** (tel. 949/494–3030), a much more laid-back arts fair.

**AUGUST** • The **Nisei Week Japanese Festival** (tel. 213/687–7193) takes place the first full weekend in August and features a parade, a carnival, and a 5K run in Little Tokyo. On the same weekend, you could hear world-class musicians at the **Long Beach Jazz Festival** (tel. 562/436–7794), held in Rainbow Lagoon Park overlooking the *Queen Mary*. Speakers, music, dance, and an African marketplace are pulled together in mid-August to commemorate Marcus Garvey at the **Marcus Garvey Day Parade and Festival** (tel. 323/735–9642). Pull out your accent on a mid-August weekend and gorge yourself at Santa Monica's **Festa Italia** (tel. 310/364–1964). Of course, there'll be some cultural stuff, too, like opera singers and Venetian mask makers.

**SEPTEMBER** • On the fifth of the month **Los Angeles's Birthday** (tel. 213/628–1274) is celebrated on Olvera Street in El Pueblo de Los Angeles Historic Park with a civic ceremony and festivities honoring the 44 black, mestizo, and Spanish city founders with birthday cake. If you're in Catalina at the beginning of the month, test your athletic skill at the **Invitational Buffalo Chip Toss** (tel. 310/510–0303) in Two Harbors—yes, you'll be handling the real thing. Mid-September marks the celebration of **Mexi-**

can **Independence** (tel. 213/624– 3660) on Olvera Street. At the end of the month South-Central's free one-day **Watts Towers Jazz Festival** (tel. 213/485–1795) attracts top performers from all over the world. For more than 20 years the annual **Koreatown Festival** (tel. 213/480–1115), also celebrated at the end of the month, hosts a lavish parade, traditional dancing, and martial arts demonstrations.

**OCTOBER** • The three-day **Santa Monica Oktoberfair** (tel. 310/393–9287, ext. 326), which takes place at the beginning of the month, is an epic street fair, with German oompah bands, carnival rides— and maybe just a little beer. **The Los Angeles International Film Festival** (tel. 323/856–7707) runs for a week at the end of the month, screening the best and brightest in American and international cinema. It now uses the recently renovated American Cinematheque's Egyptian Theatre as its main venue. General admission tickets are $8.50. For lobster lovers, the annual **Redondo Beach Lobster Festival** (tel. 310/374–2171) is a must; it's $7 admission to crack claws and enjoy other seafood specialties. It's usually held in early or mid-October.

**NOVEMBER** • **Día de los Muertos** (tel. 213/628–1274), or Day of the Dead, is celebrated at the beginning of the month on Olvera Street with activities both silly and somber, from dancing humans dressed as skeletons to a candlelight procession at dusk.

**DECEMBER** • If you're looking for traditional holiday fare, catch the **Hollywood Christmas Parade** (tel. 323/469–2337) which goes down Hollywood Boulevard the Sunday after Thanksgiving. Besides seeing the high school bands, floats, and Santa Claus, you could sight a celeb (like David Hasselhoff) doing the grand-marshal honors. There's also the annual African-American **Kwanzaa Festival and Parade** (tel. 323/789–5654), held during the last week of the year in Leimert Park. **Las Posadas** (tel. 213/968– 8492), a candlelight procession depicting Mary and Joseph's journey for shelter, illuminates the night at El Pueblo de Los Angeles Historic Monument every evening during the week before Christmas. And it wouldn't be the holidays without a drive through the somewhat hokey but still impressive **Griffith Park Light Festival** (tel. 323/913–4688), which starts roughly two weeks before Christmas.

*If you had any doubt about how seriously Angelenos take their wheels, head to the Blessing of the Cars (tel. 323/663–1265) in Glendale where a priest blesses pre-1968 cars, from hot rods to touring cars. It's held on the last Saturday in July.*

# 2 EXPLORING LOS ANGELES

BY ANDREW DEAN NYSTROM AND ELIZA ENGELBERG

UPDATED BY SASHA ABRAMSKY

I n Los Angeles reality is a slippery subject. From the Venice Beach canals (which simulate their Italian namesakes) to the hills of Malibu (easily recognizable as the Korean landscape of *M\*A\*S\*H*), sights in the City of Angels are not always what they seem. Any sight worth its salt—especially in Hollywood, West Hollywood, and Beverly Hills—comes with an attendant catalog of the celebrities who lived or died or made love there. The truly superior sight also will have appeared in a movie or television show (never mind the architecture of the Bradbury Building, let's discuss its appearances in *Blade Runner*). Budding postmodernist-theory nerds will enjoy the blurring of traditional history with motion picture history. Is the former home of Beach Boy Brian Wilson at 10452 Bellagio Road in Beverly Hills a legitimate sight? How about the house down the street at 10431, used as the evil boss's mansion in the movie *9 to 5*? In the long run you'll be better off if you skip the cultural analysis and let yourself enjoy the exoticism of celebrity homes along with the eerie familiarity of buildings you've visited before at the movies.

Shocking as it may seem, however, there are whole sections of the city whose value and charm owe virtually nothing to the entertainment world. If you belong to that unusual breed of tourist whose interest in Los Angeles extends beyond the TV set or movie screen, head to the often-overlooked downtown area, where you can find traces of history that predate the movie business, and indeed, Spanish California's entry into the Union. It's actually not too hard to discover whole neighborhoods of people whose involvement with the film world begins and ends with an occasional trip to the video store. East L.A., across the Los Angeles River from downtown, is the heart of the city's Latino community, who now make up more than a quarter of the L.A. population; a visit there will give you a taste of the Latino-majority California-to-be. The museums of the Miracle Mile, in the Wilshire District (west of downtown), and the stunning Getty Center demonstrate that Angeleno culture extends beyond celluloid and sound bites. Going all the way west brings you to the ocean and Santa Monica and Venice, where universal beach culture coexists with some of southern California's quirkiest charms. And you can always rollerblade down the coast to the South Bay settlements of Manhattan, Hermosa, and Redondo beaches.

Although parts of the city are served by a relatively new subway system (better a century late than never), most Angelenos don't seem to realize this. Cars are basically a prerequisite for living here, and exploring the city from behind a steering wheel is still the best, most convenient method. But even with a car you will do well to plan your itinerary by neighborhood, as trips across town can last hours when commuter traffic kicks in. The city has infamously inadequate public transportation, especially given the size of its sprawl. Catching a public bus, not to mention figuring out the routes, is a chancy affair. Hoofing it is generally not an option unless you're a marathon walker. However you choose to handle your exploration, get a good map, use common sense about safety, and by all means, keep your eyes peeled for celebrities.

# DOWNTOWN

The idea of a downtown runs counter to L.A.'s image of the endless suburb, but on a smogless day you can indeed see the cluster of skyscrapers that mark the city's center. The elegant, shining towers may be filled with some of L.A.'s business elite by day and a handful of well-heeled hotel guests and loft-dwellers by night, but the majority of downtown is surrendered to the have-nots when the lifeblood of the city's power structure retreats westward at the end of business hours. Evidence remains amid the urban decay that this was once the stronghold of L.A.'s elite: crumbling but beautiful Beaux Arts buildings, fantastical movie theaters that now house flea markets. Most tourists come here for the museums (perhaps the **Museum of Contemporary Art** or the **Geffen Contemporary**) or historic attractions (**El Pueblo**) and scramble away to safer environs at dusk. But if you limit your exploration of downtown to the sanitized fortress of museums, office buildings, and hotels or see the area as a relic of a bygone era, you will be missing a vital part of the downtown experience: the people, communities, and commerce that form the backbone of the new L.A.

Downtown proper lies right in the center of the freeway jumble where the Hollywood, Pasadena, Santa Ana, and Harbor freeways cross. West of Hill Street loom the skyscrapers and formal cultural institutions of **Bunker Hill**. North past U.S. 101 are the original centers of the city, **Union Station** and **Chinatown**. Go south to see where **Broadway** and the surrounding few blocks form a bustling strip of discount stores and eateries, the center of downtown's less elegant commerce. Continuing east past Main Street, the buildings thin out, and the terrain turns to vacant lots, wholesalers, and single-room-occupancy hotels, with **Little Tokyo** a prosperous anomaly at the north end of San Pedro Street. Parking prices follow the economic landscape. Avoid the meters for long stays and head to the bargain lots east of Main Street. Or be an L.A. iconoclast and take public transportation. Scads of MTA buses run throughout downtown. DASH bus routes A, B, C, D, E, and F cover the area on weekdays; on weekends, only the E, F, and DD routes operate. (The DD is a weekend-only route which combines parts of the regular A and B routes to include Chinatown, Little Tokyo, and other tourist attractions.) There's also the subway—the Red Line starts at Union Station and heads west, with one branch going over to Wilshire, the other to Hollywood. The Blue Line commuter trains run through downtown, heading south from the 7th Street Metro Center. For more general information on public transportation, *see* Chapter 1.

*See the Downtown Los Angeles map.*

## BUNKER HILL

This *Blade Runner* landscape of multicolor glass-and-metal buildings is the primary stomping ground of business folk, wealthy tourists, and museum goers. The architecture is awesome or ominous (depending on your political and aesthetic leanings), but either way, there's plenty of art and culture to absorb within the futuristic cityscape, from the Museum of Contemporary Art (MOCA) to the Los Angeles Public Library. In keeping with L.A.'s pro-automobile sentiment, pedestrian access can be tricky in this area, and many a cultural critic has lambasted the privatization of public space, now turned into office plazas and tucked-away terraces. If you drive, park in a lot south or east of the elegance for the best prices; otherwise, take DASH Routes A, B and D. The closest subway stations are the Red Line's Pershing Square and Civic Center/Tom Bradley stops.

### CITY HALL

Although the 1928 Los Angeles city hall is now dwarfed by surrounding skyscrapers, as an icon it stands larger than life. TV addicts have seen the building in many guises—it served a stint as the *Daily Planet* office in the *Superman* TV series and stood in for the Vatican in the TV movie *The Thorn Birds*. At press time, the building was closed for seismic renovation; it should reopen in 2001. The area around this grand pillar of justice tends to be iffy after dark. *200 N. Spring St., between Temple and W. 1st Sts. Free tours weekdays at 10 and 11.*

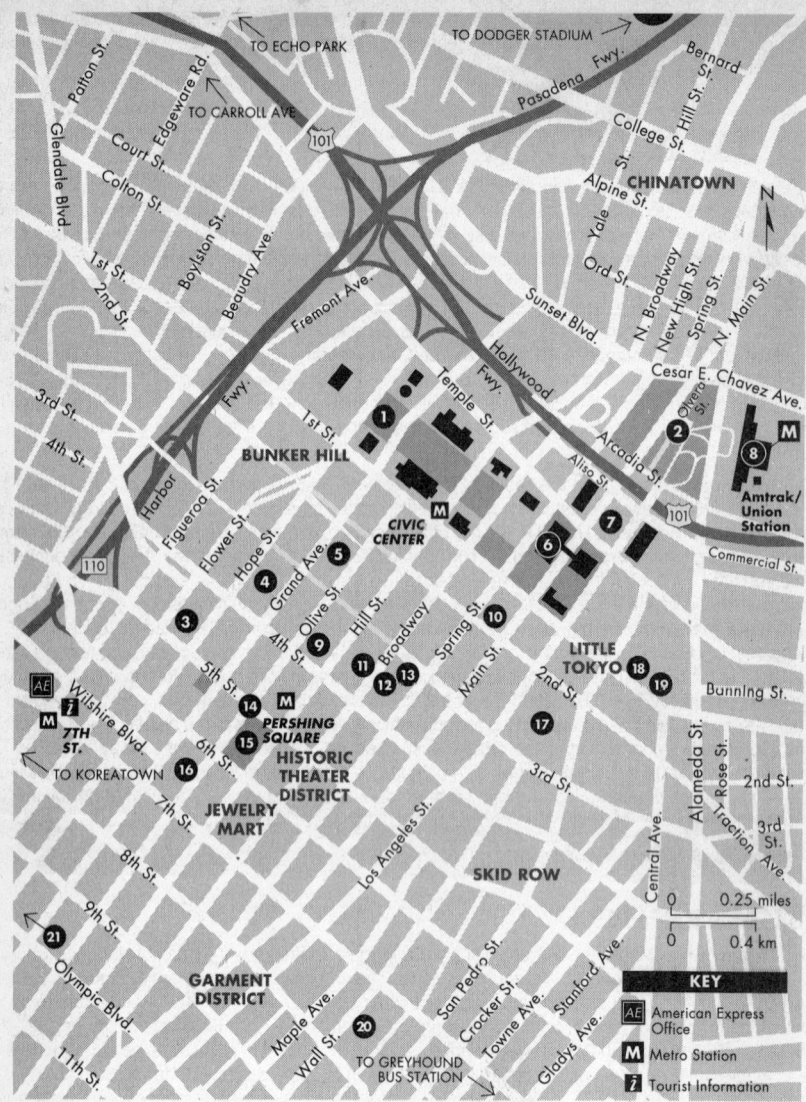

TO ECHO PARK

TO DODGER STADIUM

TO CARROLL AVE.

101

Bernard St.

Pasadena Fwy.

College St.

Hill St.

Alpine St.

**CHINATOWN**

N

Glendale Blvd.

Patton St.

Court St.

Edgeware Rd.

Colton St.

Boylston St.

Beaudry Ave.

1st St.

2nd St.

Fremont Ave.

Sunset Blvd.

Ord St.

Yale St.

N. Broadway

New High St.

Spring St.

N. Main St.

Cesar E. Chavez Ave.

3rd St.

4th St.

Harbor Fwy.

Figueroa St.

Flower St.

Fwy.

1st St.

**BUNKER HILL**

Temple St.

Hollywood Fwy.

Arcadia St.

Aliso St.

① 

Opera St.

② 

M

⑧ 

**Amtrak/ Union Station**

101

Commercial St.

110

Hope St.

Grand Ave.

Olive St.

⑤ 

④ 

**CIVIC CENTER**

M

⑥ 

⑦ 

**LITTLE TOKYO**

Banning St.

4th St.

Hill St.

Broadway

Spring St.

Main St.

2nd St.

⑨ 

⑩ 

⑪ 

⑫ ⑬ 

⑱ 

⑲ 

⑰ 

AE

i

M

**7TH ST.**

Wilshire Blvd.

5th St.

6th St.

⑭ 

M

**PERSHING SQUARE**

⑮ 

⑯ 

TO KOREATOWN

7th St.

**HISTORIC THEATER DISTRICT**

3rd St.

Los Angeles St.

2nd St.

3rd St.

Central Ave.

Alameda St.

Rose St.

Traction Ave.

**JEWELRY MART**

8th St.

9th St.

**SKID ROW**

0    0.25 miles

0    0.4 km

⑳ 

**GARMENT DISTRICT**

Maple Ave.

Wall St.

San Pedro St.

Crocker St.

Towne Ave.

Stanford Ave.

Gladys Ave.

**KEY**

AE  American Express Office

M  Metro Station

i  Tourist Information

Olympic Blvd.

11th St.

TO GREYHOUND BUS STATION

# TELEPHONES

For local directory assistance, dial 411. For long-distance help, dial the area code plus 555–1212.

## AREA CODES

Area codes are changing all over the country, and southern California is certainly no exception. In some (but not all) cases, the telephone companies provide a grace period that allows callers to dial the old area code for a few months. The following are some recent area code changes:

Areas surrounding downtown Los Angeles (including most of Hollywood) now use 323 instead of 213. At press time, there was a dust-up over the addition of a new area code to west L.A. (currently the 310 area code). Consumer protest has so far kept a new area code at bay.

San Gabriel Valley switched to 626 from 818. The southern portion of Orange County now uses 949 rather than 714.

## CALLING LONG DISTANCE

AT&T, MCI, and Sprint long-distance services make calling home relatively convenient and let you avoid hotel surcharges. In the United States you typically dial an 800 number to access these carriers.

**TO OBTAIN ACCESS CODES • AT&T** USADirect (tel. 800/ 874–4000). **MCI** Call USA (tel. 800/444–4444). **Sprint** Express (tel. 800/793– 1153).

*Even if you're not planning to take the Red Line subway, duck into the Civic Center Station, at 1st and Hill streets, to check out the mannequins suspended from the ceiling.*

## INTERNATIONAL CALLS

Calls between the United States and Canada are not considered international calls and can be dialed as regular long-distance numbers. To call any other country, dial 011, the country code, the city code (dropping the initial zero if there is one), then the actual number. If you get stuck, dial 00 for a long-distance operator, who can help you. The country code for Great Britain is 44, New Zealand 64, and Australia 61.

## PUBLIC PHONES

Instructions for pay telephones should be posted on the phone, but generally you insert your coins— 35¢ for most local calls—in a slot and wait for the steady hum of the dial tone before dialing the number. If you dial a long-distance number, the operator will come on the line and tell you how much more money you must insert for your call to go through.

# TIME

Los Angeles is in the Pacific Standard Time zone. It is three hours behind New York, two hours behind Chicago, eight hours behind London, and 17 hours behind Sydney.

# TIPPING

Gratuities are normally not included on restaurant bills, although some places do include it for large parties, usually six or more. The basic tip is 15 percent, 20 percent for excellent service. Give at least a dollar per bag to luggage handlers.

# TOURS & PACKAGES

On a prepackaged tour or independent vacation everything is prearranged so you'll spend less time planning—and often get it all at a good price.

## BOOKING WITH AN AGENT

Travel agents are excellent resources. But it's a good idea to collect brochures from several agencies because some agents' suggestions may be influenced by relationships with tour and package firms that reward them for volume sales. If you have a special interest **find an agent with expertise in that area**; ASTA (*see* Travel Agencies, *below*) has a database of specialists worldwide.

Make sure your travel agent knows the accommodations and other services of the place they're recommending. Ask about the hotel's location, room size, beds, and whether it has a pool, room service, or programs for children, if you care about these. Has your agent been there in person or sent others whom you can contact?

Do some homework on your own, too: Local tourism boards can provide information about lesser-known and small-niche operators, some of which may sell only direct.

## BUYER BEWARE

Each year consumers are stranded or lose their money when tour operators—even large ones with excellent reputations—go out of business. So **check out the operator.** Ask several travel agents about its reputation, and try to **book with a company that has a consumer-protection program.** (Look for information in the company's brochure.) In the United States, members of the National Tour Association and United States Tour Operators Association are required to set aside funds to cover your payments and travel arrangements in case the company defaults. It's also a good idea to choose a company that participates in the American Society of Travel Agent's Tour Operator Program (TOP); ASTA will act as mediator in any disputes between you and your tour operator.

Remember that the more your package or tour includes the better you can predict the ultimate cost of your vacation. Make sure you know exactly what is covered, and **beware of hidden costs.** Are taxes, tips, and transfers included? Entertainment and excursions? These can add up.

**TOUR-OPERATOR RECOMMENDATIONS • American Society of Travel Agents** (see Travel Agencies, below). **National Tour Association** (NTA, 546 E. Main St., Lexington, KY 40508, tel. 606/226–4444 or 800/682–8886). **United States Tour Operators Association** (USTOA, 342 Madison Ave., Suite 1522, New York, NY 10173, tel. 212/599–6599 or 800/468–7862, fax 212/599–6744).

## PACKAGES

The companies listed below offer vacation packages in a broad price range.

**AIR/HOTEL/CAR • American Airlines Fly AAway Vacations** (tel. 800/321–2121). **Continental Vacations** (tel. 800/634–5555). **Delta Dream Vacations** (tel. 800/872–7786). **United Vacations** (tel. 800/328–6877). **US Airways Vacations** (tel. 800/455–0123).

**HOTEL ONLY • SuperCities** (139 Main St., Cambridge, MA 02142, tel. 800/333–1234).

**CUSTOM PACKAGES • Amtrak's Great American Vacations** (tel. 800/321–8684). **Budget World-Class Drive** (tel. 800/527–0700, 0800/181181 in the U.K.) for self-drive itineraries.

**FROM THE U.K. • British Airways Holidays** (Astral Towers, Betts Way, London Rd., Crawley, West Sussex RH10 2XA, tel. 01293/723–121). **Jetsave** (Sussex House, London Rd., East Grinstead, West Sussex RH19 1LD, tel. 01342/312–033). **Key to America** (1–3 Station Rd., Ashford, Middlesex TW15 2UW, tel. 01784/248–777). **Kuoni Travel Ltd.** (Kuoni House, Dorking, Surrey RH5 4AZ, tel. 01306/742–222). **Premier Holidays** (Premier Travel Center, Westbrook, Milton Rd., Cambridge CB4 1YG, tel. 01223/516–688). **Trailfinders** (42– 50 Earls Court Rd., London W8 6FT, tel. 0171/937–5400; 58 Deansgate, Manchester M3 2FF, tel. 0161/839–6969).

# TRAIN TRAVEL

**Amtrak** is the only passenger rail service in the United States. In Los Angeles Amtrak stops at the historic Union Station, in a semisleazy neighborhood downtown. The *Coast Starlight* arrives here from Seattle via Portland and Oakland, while the *Sunset Limited* travels to Los Angeles from Orlando via New Orleans. The *Texas Eagle* arrives from San Antonio, while the *Southwest Chief* arrives from Chicago. All of these arrive daily. The best way to get fares and schedules is to call Amtrak (see below). From Los Angeles's **Union Station** you can hop on the Metro Red Line, MetroLink long-distance commuter trains, or MTA buses to points within L.A. and to outlying areas (see Bus Travel *and* Subway & Commuter Trains, *above*). Luggage storage is available from 6:30 AM to 10:00 PM and costs $1.50 per item. Union Station itself is open 24 hours.

**TRAIN INFORMATION • Amtrak** (tel. 800/872–7245). **Union Station** (800 N. Alameda St., at César Chávez Ave., tel. 213/683–6729).

## RAIL PASSES

Amtrak's **All-Aboard Pass** is good for people who plan their itinerary in advance. The pass, which is actually a booklet of tickets, allows Amtrak riders special fares for three stops made in 45 days of travel but is officially named Nuestra Señora La Reina de Los Angeles. Completed in 1822, this was the pueblo's first religious establishment, and today hosts the largest Latino congregation in California. Although the main church is a 1960s addition (complete with a mosaic of Jesus beside a saguaro cactus), the adjoining chapel is an original building reasonably true to its decorative roots. Both areas are very much in use, so tread lightly among the congregants. *535 N. Main St., across from Main Plaza, tel. 213/629–3101. Open daily 5:30 AM–8 PM.*

**OLVERA STREET** • The oldest thoroughfare in the city, Olvera Street is now a mishmash of souvenir stalls and mariachis who animate (or, depending on your point of view, undermine) this living history lesson. Walking from the Avila Adobe to the Old Plaza Church, you'll pass by tons of stalls hawking *churros*, crafts, and the inevitable El Pueblo T-shirts, and you'll probably hear the energetic chords of a mariachi band. The street is also jammed with restaurants, but frankly, there are better deals on Mexican food in many other parts of the city. If you need to rest your dogs, head to the Plaza, where there are plenty of benches. The Plaza is also where priests hold the springtime Blessing of the Animals. *Between Cesar E. Chavez Ave. and Arcadia St.*

## UNION STATION

The old Union Station and the Union Pacific Railroad connected Los Angeles to San Francisco in 1876 and helped transform L.A. from an underpopulated farming community to a bustling metropolis. An eclectic mix of Spanish colonial, Southwestern, and art deco styles, the station is also the best example of 1930s L.A. architecture—a rare combination of marble floors, wrought-iron gas lamps, wood paneling, and engraved ceilings. It's now an Amtrak depot, linked with regional and local mass-transit lines. *800 N. Alameda St., just north of U.S. 101, tel. 213/683–6729.*

*There are many ways to ascend to the heavens in the City of Angels. One of the coolest is a hike up the First Interstate Steps (also called Bunker Hill Steps), which wind past fountains and sculptures from 5th Street up to Hope.*

# AROUND BROADWAY

Decades ago, Broadway was downtown's dose of glittery shopping and entertainment. A stroll around this area now will take you past art deco and art nouveau buildings in varying degrees of neglect, including the elaborate Oviatt Building and the serene Bradbury Building. At the center of it all is the Grand Central Market, a vortex of bargain trade. The nearby movie houses of the historic Theater District are noteworthy, not only for the splendor they once were but also for the reflection of downtown they now are: Cheap clothing and appliance stores and a few fundamentalist Christian congregations have moved into these splendid movie theaters where the rich once gathered. Check out the bargain wedding chapels and Mexican pharmacies along a strip that's a little bit pre-renovation Times Square, a little bit Tijuana. The Red Line subway runs through here; the closest stops are Pershing Square and Civic Center/Tom Bradley. DASH buses A, B, and D also cross the area.

## ANGELS FLIGHT RAILWAY

The "world's shortest railway," Angels Flight is a restored wooden cable car that starts behind the Grand Central Market, on Hill Street (between 3rd and 4th streets), and ascends to a plaza behind Grand Street. For 25¢ a ride (five rides for $1) you can enjoy this creaky old funicular, which claims to have carried more passengers per mile since its construction in 1901 than any railway in the world. The name has a slightly sinister connotation in modern L.A.: The car rises from the gritty Broadway area to a celestial land of money and power in one short block. *Tel. 213/626–1901. Open daily 6:30 AM–10 PM.*

## BIDDY MASON PARK

This plaza is tucked away somewhat surreptitiously among office buildings. That's too bad, because Biddy Mason, a slave who walked all the way to Gold Rush California with her master, was a major downtown landowner and power broker who deserves more than the plain bas-relief honoring her here. After she was freed in 1856, Mason saved her money and bought up the land where the relief now stands and in the area of Spring Street between 4th and 7th streets. *Between Broadway and Spring, and 3rd and 4th Sts. Most easily accessed across from Ronald Reagan State Bldg., on Spring.*

## BRADBURY BUILDING

Constructed in 1893, the Bradbury Building was designed by an obscure draftsman named George Wyman to be a textile factory for mining millionaire Lewis Bradbury. Although the outside is unassuming, the interior is literally breathtaking. Elaborate wrought-iron staircases and elevator cages rise through the wood-paneled inner courtyard towards a massive skylight five stories above. The sweatshops are long gone; now the building is lined with offices. The effect is so peaceful you'd never know you were two feet from the crazed Broadway strip. It's one of the city's most unexpected pleasures—and if it looks familiar, you most likely saw it in *Blade Runner*. *304 S. Broadway, between 3rd and 4th Sts., tel. 213/626–1893. Open weekdays 9–5 (doors usually open Sat.).*

## GRAND CENTRAL MARKET

This colorful maze of produce and fishmonger stalls, butcher shops and bakeries is both the largest and the oldest market in Los Angeles—it's been up and running since 1917. The taco stands and chop suey counters offer the best lunch deals downtown. Check the grocery area for some remarkable bargains (five pounds of tomatoes for 99¢), eavesdrop on the frenetic buying and selling, or just feast your eyes on the vast heaps of produce. A *tortillería* close to the Broadway entrance offers what are arguably the freshest tortillas for miles—poured, baked, and bagged before your eyes. This is about as close to a genuine Mexican market experience as L.A. offers. *317 Broadway, between 3rd and 4th Sts., tel. 213/624–2378. Open daily 9–6.*

## HISTORIC THEATER DISTRICT

From 1918 to 1932 roughly a dozen lavish movie theaters were built on and around Broadway between 3rd and 11th streets. Sadly, in the heart of the motion picture capital of the world, almost all have closed their doors, been converted into evangelical churches and storefronts, or fallen into disrepair. Even in their dilapidated and transformed states, however, the theaters merit a walk down Broadway—to see the once grand exteriors and to occasionally peek into the ornate lobbies.

Start with the **Million Dollar Theater** (307 Broadway, at 3rd St., tel. 213/617–7799), built in 1918 and now the Universal Church. Beneath the archway carved with harp-strumming cherubs, the marquee now reads JESUS CHRIST IS LORD in Spanish. If there is a service going on, you can walk in and see the theater, still splendidly baroque, but with a giant photograph of the Holy Land and congregants speaking in tongues where the screen used to be. (Next door, at 301 Broadway, is the **Botanica Million Dollar,** now a pharmacy where you can buy a candle in the shape of the devil, oil to make your spouse stay at home, and a Sacred Heart of Jesus air freshener.)

Continuing south on Broadway past 5th, three theaters in a row—the **Roxie,** the **Cameo,** and the **Arcade**—have all become clothing or electronics stores. All have fabulous old neon signs, and the Roxie, built in 1932, has the remains of a grand facade. Past 6th Street at 615 South Broadway, the **Los Angeles** (1931) has towering columns and a carved archway over the marquee. The interior is decorated beyond belief with frescoes, fountains, and crystal chandeliers. Ironically, the theater is now mainly a shooting location for period movies. You can call 213/629–2939 to request to see the interior, but you may have to pretend you're scouting for the next Spielberg film.

Across the street, the **Palace** survives as a first-run theater (630 South Broadway, between 6th and 7th Sts., tel. 213/239–0959), although its tiny crowds are mainly homeless people looking for a brief escape from the streets. You can sneak a peek inside if there's a nice person working the ticket booth, but most of the ornamentation is gone. Continue past the ghosts of the **State** (703 S. Broadway) and the **Globe** (744 S. Broadway) to the also defunct **Tower** (802 S. Broadway, at 8th St.). In addition to the clock tower from which it derives its name, the theater has beautiful arches, columns, urns, and stained glass along its 8th Street side.

After the rainbow neon sign of the **Rialto** (810 S. Broadway), now a series of shops, lies the district's other functioning theater, the **Orpheum** (842 S. Broadway, between 8th and 9th Sts., tel. 213/239–0939). Go to a $3 Tuesday movie and catch a first-run flick or just wheedle your way in past the ticket taker to see the scalloped velvet sofas in the lobby, the heavenly steps to the now off-limits balcony, the stained-glass exit signs, and the naked bronze ladies who serve as lighting fixtures.

Although there are no more movies at the **United Artists** theater (933 Broadway, between 9th St. and Olympic Blvd.), the marquee beneath the faux-Egyptian statuettes announces that televangelist Dr. Gene Scott gives sermons there every Sunday at 11. Walk on if you don't need saving. Take a right on Olympic and a left onto Hill for the last and wackiest theater in the district. The **Mayan** (1038 S. Hill St., between Olympic and 11th Sts.) rejected the usual Greco-Roman-Egyptian decor in favor of a New World theme. Pre-Columbian gods and glyphs painted in primary colors surround the doorway and the marquee, and a simulated ruin occupies a display case near the ticket booth. Since the 1980s the theater has been a nightclub (*see also* Chapter 5).

## JEWELRY MART

Centered on Hill St., mainly between 5th and 7th streets, this cluster of shops—L.A.'s answer to New York's Diamond District—is a must for anyone with a passion for wholesale and discounted jewelry (and credit enough to indulge). In addition to marked-down Cartier baubles and Rolex watches, this urban gold mine has a brilliant selection of loose gemstones, and attracts an increasing number of top-quality jewelers. But be aware: Merchants take quick offense when you ask if the jewels are real.

## L.A. TIMES BUILDING

See the cutting edge of journalism for absolutely free—and get a reporter's notebook and pencil to boot. This laid-back tour takes you the length of the city-block-long building where the *L.A. Times* comes to life each day. Your guide will show you the oddly sedate newsroom, the ergonomically crafted furniture and big-screen computers of the new design and graphics departments, and even the kitchen where the food writers prepare and photograph their culinary creations. Children under 10 are not admitted on the tour. If you're into the mechanics of it all, you can also take a separate tour of the Olympic printing plant. *145 S. Spring St., on Times–Mirror Square between 1st and 2nd Sts., tel. 213/237–5000. Admission free. Tours weekdays at 11:15.*

## OVIATT BUILDING

Haberdasher James Oviatt's splendid art deco taste is preserved beautifully in this building, which housed his store on the ground floor and his apartment at the top. An expensive restaurant has replaced the hat shop, but the penthouse has been restored to resemble Oviatt's original digs and is now rented out for movie shoots and weddings. If you call in advance, you can ride in L.A.'s last remaining manually operated elevator and walk around what was no doubt one of L.A.'s swankiest homes in the 1920s. The sunken terra-cotta bathtub and the accompanying olive-green tiled massage room are the apartment's most seductive features. More recently the building has been used in a Billy Idol music video and in the movies *Pretty Woman* and *Indecent Exposure.* If you can't fit in a tour, the building's outside, with its Lalique glass awning, arched, carved, stone window frames, and elaborate wrought-iron gates, is worth at least a walk-by. *617 Olive St., between 6th and 7th Sts., tel. 213/622–6096. Admission for tours free with appointment. Open weekdays 9–4.*

## PERSHING SQUARE

Established as a park in 1866, Pershing Square was renamed for General John J. Pershing after the First World War. Now dotted with palm trees, pink pillars, salmon spheres, and statues of overachievers like Beethoven, the square surrounds a large purple aqueduct that spills water into an amorphous puddle below. Although it's not exactly an oasis of soothing nature, the park has benches and a nice lawn where you can rest your feet and enjoy great views of the skyscrapers. Since the opening of its subway station in 1998, the park also feels safer. *Between S. Olive, S. Hill, W. 5th, and W. 6th Sts. Open daily 5–10.*

## REGAL BILTMORE HOTEL

If you face Olive Street from within Pershing Square, you'll notice the Biltmore as a charming example of 1920s architecture in a sea of futuristic skyscrapers. The outside of this expensive grand dame is understated brick with sculpted balconies, but the rooms within explode in rococo excess. Enter through the tearoom (don't forget to look up at the ornate Byzantine ceiling) and proceed through the gilded archway of cherubs and grapes to the lobby. Wherever you wander through the hotel, it's worth your while to check the ceilings; not one inch of plain white plaster peeks through the gaudiness. *506 S. Grand Ave., at W. 5th St., tel. 213/624–1011.*

# EASTSIDE

Down where the wholesale district meets Skid Row, you can buy just about anything from pink-plastic tricycles to Chia Pets to fashions and flowers—not to mention not-so-legal wares. If you walk south to the Flower or Fashion markets, you will pass through one of Los Angeles's most impoverished, down-at-heels neighborhoods. Take the necessary precautions and be aware that wandering tourists might not be a welcome sight to the people on the streets. Do *not* walk in this area after dark. Walking north, the area gentrifies rather suddenly at Little Tokyo, whose shops and museums provide less gritty sightseeing. Parking is cheap and reliable in the lots on Los Angeles Street or near the Geffen Contemporary in Little Tokyo. The Red Line's Pershing Square station is the closest subway stop; DASH buses D and E shuttle through the neighborhood.

# SPOUSE NOT INCLUDED

*Short on dough but desperate to make a lifelong legally binding commitment to your loved one? No need to rush to Las Vegas—for $140, the Guadalupe Wedding Chapel (237 S. Broadway, between 2nd and 3rd Sts., tel. 213/628–0551) will give you all the necessaries for your nuptials, including a honeymoon. The only thing you won't get for the $140 is a spouse, so come prepared. The storefront of the chapel advertises in Spanish the many services available within: legal marriages (including marriage to minors), divorces (should things go awry), restraining orders (should things go greatly awry), and a hodgepodge of other services ranging from immigration to income tax. But the specialty of the house is weddings. After filling out the requisite forms, you can choose one of the five chapels (depending on the color scheme you prefer). Do you envision taking the leap beneath a sky-blue ceiling, or would you prefer red roses and hearts? In any event, you can fit 50 guests in the chapel, and you can even get married by an actual minister or priest. Your $140 also rents a bridal gown and buys you two rings, the license, and a 36-hour honeymoon tour of Las Vegas. Although the Guadalupe Chapel is the oldest in town, there is a veritable wedding industry along the Broadway strip in between the doughnut shops and the bargain clothing stores. If you've got the mate and you've got the notion, the only question remaining is: Why pay more?*

## FLOWER MARKET

Each day before dawn florists make a pilgrimage to this block-long series of fragrant shops and stalls crowded into several large buildings on Wall Street (between 7th and 8th streets). On Monday, Wednesday, Friday, and Sunday from 8 on and on Tuesday, Thursday, and Saturday from 6 on, early risers jostle with wholesalers and florists to pick out enormous bouquets of every imaginable flower at wholesale prices. Most stalls close down by about 11, although they're technically open until noon. *Tel. 213/627–2482.*

## GARMENT DISTRICT

A slew of cut-rate clothing stores is wedged into the blocks between Santee Street, Maple Avenue, 12th Street, and Pico Boulevard. The four-floor **Cooper Building** (860 S. Los Angeles St., at 9th St., tel. 213/622–1139), open Monday–Saturday 9:30–5:30 and Sunday 11–5, is filled with aesthetically challenged department store leftovers, including garb by Calvin Klein and DKNY, but the prices don't promote impulse buying. But at the smaller shops, like **Fashion Mart** (930 S. Santee St., No. 219, between 9th St. and Olympic Blvd., tel. 213/689–8700) and **Comedy Club** (930 S. Santee St., No. 7, tel. 213/891–9311), you'll find cheap and decent stuff. Most stores are closed on Sunday.

## GEFFEN CONTEMPORARY

Anyone who hasn't quite figured out the meaning of *postmodern* should take an educational field trip to the (David) Geffen Contemporary (formerly the catchily named Temporary Contemporary). The building has strong ties to its past life as a warehouse—the interior looks more like a site for a rave than a museum—but it lends itself to extremely hip displays. Temporary exhibits are spread out among the scaffolding and high ceilings of the main part of the building. Although the museum does not consider itself MOCA's avant-garde arm, its flexible space allows for wacky installations and large multimedia projects such as the complete group of Richard Serra's mammoth steel *Torqued Ellipses*. Shows scheduled for 2000 include an exhibition on the past 100 years of architectural achievements and a retrospective of Adrian Piper's audio and video installations. Also, the first large-scale exhibit ever devoted to minimal art will be mounted in 2001. The $6 admission will get you into the MOCA as well, and both museums are serviced by DASH Route A. *152 N. Central Ave., at 1st St., Little Tokyo, tel. 213/621–2766. Admission $6, free with MOCA admission and Thurs. after 5. Open Tues.–Wed. and weekends 11–5, Thurs. 11–8.*

## JAPANESE VILLAGE PLAZA

The Village Plaza and the Japanese-American Cultural and Community Center Plaza across the street are the two shopping centers that form the heart of Little Tokyo. The Village Plaza is purely commercial, with some interesting shops and restaurants spanning a broad range of prices. Within the Cultural and Community Center Plaza there is a gallery showcasing contemporary Japanese and Japanese-American artists and a theater that puts on such traditional Japanese performances as *noh* and Kabuki. In the middle of the plaza stands a massive granite sculpture by Isamu Noguchi dedicated to the *issei,* the Japanese who were denied American citizenship until 1952. *E. 2nd St., between San Pedro and Central Aves.*

## JAPANESE-AMERICAN NATIONAL MUSEUM

*Mexico City and Guadalajara are the only two cities in the world with Latino populations larger than Los Angeles County's 3.3 million.*

These two museum buildings are quite a contrast—the original brick building faces the glass-and-steel curves of a new pavilion across a courtyard. The 1925 building still has a ceremonial entrance on the side; at press time it was used for temporary shows and activities. In the new pavilion, you can check out displays on the *issei* (first Japanese immigrants, who arrived in the 19th century) and their descendents. There are plenty of remnants from daily life, like a basket of essentials for a "picture bride," dolls and portable Buddhist shrines from the WWII incarceration camps, even a salvaged portion of a camp barrack. There are also computers with which Japanese-American visitors can look up genealogical information and locate war veterans. *369 E. 1st St., at Central Ave., tel. 213/625–0414. Admission $6, free Thurs. 5–8 and all day on 3rd Thurs. of month. Open Tues., Wed., Fri.–Sun. 10–5; Thurs. 10–8.*

## LITTLE TOKYO

More like a mall than a neighborhood, Little Tokyo (bordered by Temple, Los Angeles, 3rd, and Alameda streets and served by DASH Route A) nonetheless offers many bits of interest amid lots of touristy schlock. As you stroll through, ignore the overpriced gift shops and focus on the Japanese bookstores, pharmacies, and grocery stores. A row of restored old buildings on East 1st Street (between Central and San Pedro streets) lets you envision the Japanese-American community before its forced relocation into internment camps during World War II. On the other side of East 1st Street, slightly removed from the street, the Koyosan Buddhist Temple (342 E. 1st St., at Central Ave., tel. 213/624–1267) occupies a beautiful building and offers an English-language service open to the public every Sunday at 10 AM.

## MUSEUM OF NEON ART

The glowing rainbow arch at the entrance to the MONA marks the beginning of a subterranean world lighted only by the art itself. Installments range from traditional signs to elaborate seascapes. The sculptures move, hiss, and flash, bringing the entire room to life. After seeing the work and watching the 15-minute video on the artists, you may be convinced, as the MONA would like you to be, that neon has its place in the pantheon of the fine arts. Most of the museum's collection of old neon now graces the Universal CityWalk (*see* Studios, *below*), but you can still see the Van de Kamp's windmill in one of the outside windows and an old RCA sign inside. If you want to learn more about the alchemy of creating neon, museum founder Lili Lakich offers workshops, and first-time works of her students grace the walls of the entryway. It's a bit out of the way, but there are plenty of DASH stops nearby. *501 W. Olympic Blvd., at S. Hope St., tel. 213/489– 9918. Admission $5, free 2nd Thurs. of month. Open Wed.–Sat. 11–5, Sun. noon–5.*

## SKID ROW

The area near 5th and San Pedro is thick with poverty. People without permanent homes line the streets, sleeping, hanging out, and conducting business. Outside the missions and the transient hotels,

# THERAPY AT 70 MPH

*The following drives offer the best of Los Angeles from the comfort of your car—convertibles optional. Joan Didion and others have been inspired by the private moments provided by these amazing concrete public spaces.*

*By Day:*

*PCH from the South Bay north to Point Magu or vice versa for breezy beachfront views.*

*Circumnavigate the Palos Verdes Peninsula on Palos Verdes Drive for breathtaking views of Catalina Island and the Pacific Ocean.*

*Sunset Boulevard west toward the ocean at dusk.*

*Glendale Freeway (State Highway 2) south from the I–210 interchange for great views of downtown.*

*By Night:*

*I–405 south from the San Fernando Valley into L.A. Basin for a look at the glittering computer-chip-esque monstrosity that is L.A. by night.*

*Mulholland Drive from U.S. 101 (Hollywood Freeway) to the L.A./Ventura county line for a winding, rustic look at an unknown side of the city.*

*I–105 (Century Freeway) in the east carpool lane to I–110 (Harbor Freeway) north for an unequaled elevated glimpse of the L.A. Basin.*

*Tunnels on 2nd and 3rd streets in downtown for déjà vu movie and television flashbacks.*

*State highway 110 (Pasadena Freeway) north through downtown to Pasadena for a roller-coaster ride on one of the city's oldest freeways.*

*Laurel Canyon or Beverly Glen Blvds. between the San Fernando Valley and L.A.—the night views of the Valley from the latter are especially spectacular.*

rectangles are painted on the sidewalk. Above them, signs explain that the rectangles mark SLEEPING ZONES, and warn that SLEEPING ONLY WILL BE ALLOWED INSIDE THE RED PAINTED AREA BETWEEN THE HOURS OF 7:30 PM AND 6 AM. It is unlikely that the people populating skid row wish to become a tourist attraction, and crime here is a real presence, but if you want to see the ultimate antithesis of Bunker Hill opulence, you can walk along San Pedro north toward Little Tokyo or south toward the Flower Market. Every Sunday the streets are particularly crowded as a variety of church groups passes through to hand out meals and the priest known as Dollar Man makes his weekly appearance. Wearing his collar and a white baseball cap, Dollar Man stands at the corner of 5th and Towne streets handing out $1 each to the hundreds of people who stand in line waiting. Rumor has it he gives out $3,000 every Sunday.

# NEAR DOWNTOWN

An interesting assortment of neighborhoods lines the perimeter of downtown. Westward on Olympic (roughly between Normandie and Wilton) lies Koreatown, a living, breathing community that lacks the theme-park trappings of other "ethnic" neighborhoods. Leaving downtown west on Cesar E. Chavez (which soon becomes Sunset) brings you into the heart of L.A.'s up-and-coming home of hipsters, Echo Park. So far the neighborhood's growing appeal among the white boho crowd has not edged out the dominant group of Central American immigrants. Tucked away east of Echo Park Lake on Carroll Avenue are some of L.A.'s surviving Victorian homes. Heading west on Wilshire brings you to MacArthur Park, made famous by the eponymous song by Richard Harris (not to mention Donna Summers's version). It is a beautiful public space where a rather tough crowd hangs out, though your visit won't shed much light on the mysterious lyrics: "Someone left the cake out in the rain." The Red Line subway has a MacArthur Park station; a branch also goes farther west along Wilshire to Koreatown.

## ANGELINO HEIGHTS/CARROLL AVENUE

During the real-estate boom of the 1880s, Angelino Heights was a swank place to live. Like much of downtown, it has suffered economic decline since its heyday, but Carroll Avenue, with the highest concentration of Victorian houses in Los Angeles, seems to be en route to becoming fancy again. For the one-block tour of birthday-cake homes, start at Douglas Avenue and walk east along Carroll. The houses range from fully restored and freshly painted to dilapidated and likely to be haunted, with many in the process of being renovated. Most spectacular is **Sessions House** (1330 Carroll Ave.). Built in 1888, it is covered in fish-scale shingles, with rounded turrets and circular openings to the upper and lower porches. It's also worth strolling the blocks around Carroll Avenue to look for the occasional mansion.

*Art historians compare the Watts Towers (encrusted with colorful glass shards) to Gaudi's Barcelona cathedrals, whereas prominent bass man and folk-art historian Charles Mingus, who grew up nearby, compares them to upside-down ice-cream cones.*

## ECHO PARK

The once and future home of L.A.'s bohemian set, Echo Park is a diverse neighborhood, both ethnically and economically. Home to a large community of Central American immigrants, the area is now attracting artistic types, along with lawyers and bankers who like a funky ambience. Cruising Sunset west of downtown (roughly between Elysian Park and East Hollywood), you can see cafés and art galleries popping up among the nail salons and small-appliance shops. Of particular note is **Echo Park** itself, at the corner of Bellevue and Echo Park streets, with its palm trees and walking trail surrounding a lake filled with water lotuses. Although it's a pleasant place by day, it gets a little rough after dark. Continuing past the park on Glendale, you pass a monument of L.A. religious history: the **Angelus Temple** (1100 Glendale Blvd., at Park Ave., tel. 213/484–1100), home to Aimee Semple McPherson's Foursquare Gospel Church. (Something to ponder: Why is the Foursquare temple round?) McPherson is a heroine of the Christian fundamentalist movement she helped pioneer in the 1920s. Her stunts, showy revival meetings, and "healing powers" were nationally famous. In 1926 she mysteriously disappeared while swimming, but turned up roughly a month later, claiming to have been kidnapped. The authorities, however, accused her of skipping town with a married man, and the ensuing sensational court hearings seriously smirched her reputation. The church has services Sunday at 10:45 and 6; you may also call to schedule a weekday tour.

## KOREATOWN

Caution to pedestrians: The Korean section of L.A. covers a large area, and it's not clear exactly where it begins and ends. Just west of downtown, the boundaries are loosely defined by Wilshire Boulevard to the north and Pico Boulevard to the south, but the only real clue that you've arrived are the Korean-language signs above the myriad strip malls. Mostly residential and commercial, Koreatown does not cater much to tourists. In fact, the **Korean Cultural Center** (5505 Wilshire Blvd., at Dunsmuir Ave., tel. 323/936– 7141), which has an art gallery and a library, sits outside the neighborhood. It's a good place to start your tour if you want a more formal introduction to Korean culture, and if you are lucky enough to find a human being working within, you may get tips on where to explore within Koreatown proper. Eating is always an option, but Korean restaurants tend to be fancy and expensive. For truly cheap eats, poke around the many shopping centers for more accessible Korean barbecue.

## MACARTHUR PARK

Although MacArthur Park is beautiful from a passing car, it is more a center of urban squalor than an idyllic Olmsteadian retreat. The lake in the middle sports an island with palm trees and a dramatic fountain, and the entire park is filled with lovely greenery. But there are a lot of young men loitering on the benches and lawns, so it's not a very inviting spot for unaccompanied women, and the park should be avoided by all after dark. There's a MacArthur Park Red Line subway station, so at least it's easy to reach without a car. The surrounding area is filled with bustling swap meets, most notably one at the former **Westlake Theater,** at the corner of 7th and Alvarado streets. Walk past the laser art and communion dresses and look up at the dramatic ceiling fresco and engravings that remain.

# SOUTH-CENTRAL

There are two distinct perspectives from which the neighborhoods south and west of downtown are perceived. To outsiders, that is, the majority of Angelenos and visitors, the words *South-Central* bring to mind the mysteriously dangerous, gang-riddled area south of the Santa Monica Freeway (I–10) that lies between the San Diego (I–405) and Long Beach (I–710) freeways—or those run-down places they glimpse from the elevated carpool lane on the Harbor Freeway (I–110). The racially diverse mix of long-time African-American residents and recent Mexican, Central-American, and Asian and Pacific Islander arrivals sees a different reality: a sprawl of traditional communities in flux, recently torn apart by racial tensions, an influx of drugs and attendant gang turf wars, and crippling poverty brought on by years of political and economic neglect. As it stands, South-Central has become the most publicized and politicized ghetto of L.A. It is evolving into a crucible that Angelenos, and Californians in general, can study closely as the gap between rich and poor grows and the ethnic makeup of the state shifts away from a white majority.

Some of the best times to visit South-Central are during several free annual music festivals that help to break down some of the physical (freeways) and psychological (race) barriers that segregate Angelenos from one another. The **Central Avenue Jazz Festival** (Dunbar Hotel, 4225 S. Central Ave., tel. 213/485–0709), held at the end of July, revives the spirit of the '40s and '50s, when the Central Avenue strip was considered the place to be seen by people of all colors. In mid-September the vibrant **Leimert Park Jazz Festival** (tel. 323/960–1625) brings together local musicians, eateries, and craftspeople to preserve the legacy of jazz. At the end of September the free **Watts Towers Day of the Drum Festival** (Watts Towers Arts Center, 1727 E. 107th St., tel. 213/485–1795 or 213/847–4646) attracts an astounding international array of percussionists from around the world. The following day the free **Simon Rodia Festival** features smokin' jazz, gospel, and rhythm and blues on the same stage.

The best way to get here is to drive; remember that many areas are not safe after dark, and plan your time here accordingly. The closest commuter rail stops are the Blue Line's 103rd Street station and the Rosa Parks (Imperial/Wilmington) station, where the Blue and Green commuter rail lines intersect.

*See the South-Central map.*

## DUNBAR HOTEL

The Dunbar was built in 1928 by Dr. John Alexander Somerville as the most posh hotel in town catering to blacks. Take a quick turn through the lobby to see the impressive cultural display of black Los Angeles, including a history of black vaudeville performers like Bill "Bojangles" Robinson, who migrated to the City of Angels to seek his fortune in Hollywood. The building now contains private apartments. *4225 S. Central Ave.*

## EXPOSITION PARK

Originally developed in 1880 as an open-air farmers' market, this 160-acre public space hosted Olympic festivities in 1932 and 1984 in conjunction with the adjacent **Memorial Coliseum** and **Sports Arena** (*see* Spectator Sports *in* Chapter 6). Today the park is beginning to show signs of exhaustion and neglect, but it remains home to a fascinating collection of museums. The pool in the **Olympic Swimming Stadium,** next to the Coliseum, is open to the public during the summer. Between museum visits, take a picnic lunch and, in season, stroll through the spectacular 7-acre **Rose Garden** (open daily 8–sunset), just east of the Natural History Museum of Los Angeles County (*see below*). It is possible to comfortably visit all the attractions in a long day and still experience a larger-than-life movie at the **IMAX Theater** (*see* Movie Houses *in* Chapter 5). Economical four-hour metered parking is available along

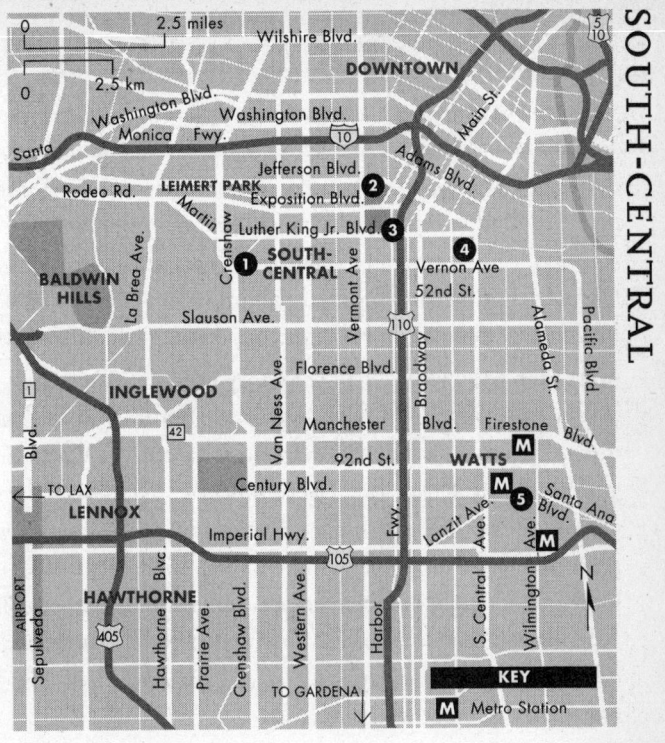

Dunbar Hotel, **4**
Exposition Park, **3**
Leimert Park, **1**
University of
Southern
California, **2**
Watts Towers, **5**

Exposition Boulevard on the northern edge of the park, across the street from USC; otherwise pay $3 to park in a secure lot near the IMAX, off State Drive.

**CALIFORNIA SCIENCE CENTER** • The kind of place that children serve as an excuse for grown-ups to visit, this complex links several corporate-sponsored museums. There's the **Kinsey Hall of Health** (don't miss the demonstration of how drugs—licit and illicit— damage your body), **Technology Hall** (with the Earthquake Experience simulator), the **South Science** building (with mostly temporary exhibits, plus a virtual-reality space walk), and the **3D IMAX Theater** (tel. 213/744–2014, $7.50). Although most of the educational exhibits and interactive displays are designed to pique children's interest, post-puberty audiences will still be able to find awe-inspiring moments, especially in the **Aerospace Hall.** Hands-on displays chronicle the history of propulsion, liftoff, and aerial navigation. An authentic used space capsule, fighter planes, robots, and an ominous looming LAPD helicopter round out the lineup. The old IMAX theater and snack bar are just outside, near the grounded United plane. *700 State Dr., tel. 213/744–7400. From I– 110, exit at Exposition Blvd., proceed west and follow signs. Admission free. Open daily 10–5.*

**CALIFORNIA AFRICAN AMERICAN MUSEUM** • This museum explores the history, art, and cultural legacy of black people in the United States. Three galleries stage rotating exhibitions of African folk art and contemporary multimedia installations. Paintings and sculptures capture African-American experiences over the past few centuries. *600 State Dr., tel. 213/744–7432. Admission free. Open Tues.– Sun. 10–5.*

**NATURAL HISTORY MUSEUM OF LOS ANGELES COUNTY** • Born as the Los Angeles County Museum of History, Science, and Art in 1913, this Spanish Renaissance structure has been expanding and evolving ever since its inception. The most recent addition to the 35-gallery building is the Hall of Native American Cultures, delving into the troubled history of the original settlers of the Southland. Exhibits of gems and minerals, American history, fossils and dinosaurs, and pre-Columbian artifacts cover the first floor. Kids flock to the second floor for the interactive bird, mammal, and marine life exhibits, presented in credibly replicated habitats. The bottom floor deals exclusively with California history and houses a research library and a cafeteria. On the free admission day the place tends to be

# THE FIRE THIS TIME

*Government-sanctioned segregation ended in 1964 with the passage of the Civil Rights Act, but issues of race, ethnicity, and economics have lent the city of Los Angeles a segregated geography. Los Angeles's neighborhoods are fiercely stratified, and many residents of various communities only cross paths on the freeways. This segregation exploded in the faces of Angelenos in April 1992, when devastating riots followed the acquittal of four white officers charged in the beating, recorded on videotape, of a black man, Rodney King.*

*More than seven years later the Rodney King riots have taken their place in the history books next to the riots that shook Watts in 1965. But although empty federal promises were able to extinguish the fires in Watts, South-Central has grown disillusioned with government "solutions." Instead, grassroots organizations are initiating their own revitalization programs. GED preparation courses, employment training, small-business loans, job placement programs, and alliances with other economically depressed ethnic communities have recently been implemented in an attempt to strengthen the economy from the ground up. Several well-publicized gang truces have also been forged since the worst days of territorial violence.*

mobbed with school groups. Free one-hour tours are given daily at 1. *900 Exposition Blvd., at Menlo Ave., tel. 213/763–3466. Admission $8; free 1st Tues. of month. Open weekdays 9:30–5, weekends 10–5.*

## GARDENA

Welcome to "Vegas in L.A.," with the most sinners per capita this side of Hollywood. Snuggled in the crook of I–110 and Highway 91, just north of I–405, this city has a convenient ordinance that legalizes certain forms of gambling. Vermont and Western avenues are the major strips for dens of cocktail sin, although the recent construction of a large casino in Inglewood (*see below*) forced several older clubs to fold their hands. This is also the only part of town (other than the **South Bay**'s beach huts; *see* Chapter 3) where you'll find Hawaiian-style restaurants. Gardena is also home to the largest concentration of Japanese in the United States.

The swinging **Normandie Casino and Showroom** (1045 W. Rosecrans Ave., at S. Vermont Ave., tel. 310/352–3400 or 800/540–8006) is a good place to start a tour of Gardena excitement. The Normandie has been catering to middle-class Asian-Americans in the ritzy Red Dragon Room since 1948. Phyllis Diller, Juice Newton, and a host of quality Filipino crooners have appeared in the showroom. It's open 24 hours to those over 21 and doles out surprisingly good food and drinks at decent prices ($6 lunch buffet 11–2). You can also get free instruction in tantalizing games like Texas Hold 'Em, Omaha, and EO Eleven. To find the action from the I–110, exit at Rosecrans Avenue and head west until you hit Vermont.

For a dose of Gardena's prevalent Asian culture, stop by the **Japanese Cultural Institute** (16215 S. Gramercy Pl., between Western and Van Ness Aves., tel. 310/324–6611). It's open weekdays 9–5. Parlay your winnings into a savory sushi picnic at the **Pacific Supermarket** (1620 W. Redondo Beach Blvd., between Western and Normandie Aves., tel. 310/323–7696).

## INGLEWOOD

This town is billed by its boosters as the City of Champions, but the only winners you're likely to find here today are hustlers who haunt the Hollywood Park Racetrack and Casino (*see below*). Two miles east of the Los Angeles International Airport, the gaming complex sits just south of the **Great Western Forum,** once the Lakers' turf and now home of the WNBA Sparks (*see* Spectator Sports *in* Chapter 6). The casino, racetrack, and Forum are all grand places in which to observe humanity at its extremes.

The horses at **Hollywood Park Racetrack** (Century Blvd. and Prairie Ave., tel. 310/419- -1500) gallop Wednesday–Sunday at 1 PM from mid-April through mid-July and again from mid-November until December 24. Fridays are $1 nights, with a 7 PM post time and only a buck each for admission, a beer, and a hot dog. Call for tips on other special events, simulcast racing, and giveaways. General admission costs $6 and includes free parking; walk-ins and bus riders receive a $1 discount, except on Friday.

The plush, 24-hour **Hollywood Park Casino** (3883 W. Century Blvd., at Prairie Ave., tel. 310/330–2800 or 800/888–4972) boasts free gaming instruction, both live and on video, so-called fine dining, parimutuel wagering in a huge sports lounge, a karaoke bar, a health club, and a certifiably shady clientele. You can find some action on several poker variations and on unique California casino games like Pai Gow and pan. The house dealers supervise all play but hold no interest in the house winnings—this means you are obliged to fork over hourly seat-rental as well as small per-hand fees. Seated players are frequently offered 99¢ deals on breakfast, margaritas, and pancakes—and men are occasionally propositioned.

To get to Inglewood from I–405, exit east on Century Boulevard and follow signs down the backstretch. From I–105, exit north on Prairie Avenue and follow signs around the final curve. From I–110, merge west to I–105, exit north on Prairie Avenue, and follow the signs.

*You gotta love the tongue-in-cheek Pig Murals that grace the walls of the Farmer John meatpacking building (3049 E. Vernon St., near Soto St., in Vernon). Artist Leslie Grimes died in a fall from shaky scaffolding while working on his trompe l'oeil folk masterpiece.*

## LEIMERT PARK

In the middle of the Crenshaw Boulevard strip, you could easily overlook this tiny triangle of shops and greenery, about a mile north of Slauson Avenue and a few miles east of I–405. Make the effort to find it. The middle-class community of Leimert Park (with the park of the same name on the corner of Crenshaw Boulevard and Vernon Avenue as its locus) has emerged as an oasis of African-American culture amid the postuprising blight of South-Central. The shops on 43rd Place and Degnan Boulevard sell African clothing, art, jewelry, food, and music. Swing by **Fifth Street Dick's Coffee Company** (3347½ W. 43rd Pl., tel. 323/296–3970) for a robust cup of Ethiopian coffee and some of the best jazz in Los Angeles. Most jams take place after midnight (*see* Live Music *in* Chapter 5). Look to the **Great Negus Wordsmith & Roots Empire** (3335 W. 43rd Pl., no phone) gallery and performance space, owned by the same couple, for more spoken-word, drama, and open-mike freestyle rap events. The free **Museum in Black** (4331 Degnan Blvd., between 43rd St. and 43rd Pl., tel. 323/292–9528) presents a jam-packed selection of African textiles, slavery-era documents, and religious figurines. It's open Tuesday–Saturday 10–6. You'll find plenty of friendly elder statesmen playing dominoes and shooting the breeze in the park, the site of the annual **Kwanzaa Festival** (*see* Festivals *in* Chapter 1) during the last week of the year. To reach the park, take Crenshaw Boulevard south from I–10 or Slauson Avenue east from I–405, heading left (north) on Crenshaw to the Vernon intersection.

## UNIVERSITY OF SOUTHERN CALIFORNIA

Founded in 1880, USC (dubbed the "university of spoiled children" by crosstown rival UCLA) is the oldest major private school on the West Coast. Tree-shaded Spanish-style and contemporary brick buildings provide the backdrop for this enclave of wealth and privilege—a secure village that's home to some 24,000 students—in a sea of relative poverty. The film school has graduated the likes of George Lucas, Ron Howard, and John Singleton, and the football team, the Trojans, once starred a young Orenthal James Simpson. A stroll across campus can be rewarding for movie buffs: Snippets of *The Graduate, The Hunchback of Notre Dame,* and *Forrest Gump* were all shot here. Interesting stops include the beautiful main lobby and reading room of the **Doheny Memorial Library,** the tiny clapboard **Widney Hall** (Alumni House), constructed in the early 1880s, and the oddly shaped **Los Angeles Shrine Auditorium** (665 W. Jefferson Blvd., tel. 213/749–5123), just north of campus, which has been one of the major venues for the Academy Awards. (The red carpet was last rolled out in spring 2000.) Students congregate in the quad, under the watchful eye of their mascot, Tommy Trojan. Maps of the campus are available at all eight entrance gates, and free one-hour walking tours are given weekdays 10–3; for reservations call the Alumni House (tel. 213/740–2300). *Bounded by Figueroa St., Jefferson Blvd.,*

Exposition Blvd., and Vermont Ave. and adjacent to Exposition Park, tel. 213/740–2311 for campus info. From I–110, exit at Exposition and proceed west. Enter campus at Gate 1 on Exposition or turn right on Figueroa and enter at Gate 2.

Just north of the USC campus, across Jefferson Boulevard on Hoover Street, you'll run into the **University Village** shopping center; its **International Food Court,** open daily 8- -8, houses a conglomeration of the best cheap, quick, and eclectic eats in the area. The lunch hour is crowded with students, but lickety-split service does the trick. The nostalgic **Headlines!** (621 W. Jefferson Blvd., tel. 213/746–1284) welcomes the USC crowd for cheap diner meals.

## WATTS TOWERS

The riots of 1965 devastated the neighborhood around these improbable monuments. And the Rodney King uprisings set the area aflame again in 1992. But Watts and surrounding neighborhoods have greater notoriety than perhaps they deserve, though they remain the most downtrodden and poverty-stricken sections of Los Angeles. The Watts Towers, a masterpiece of Los Angeles urban art, are wire spires constructed willy-nilly by itinerant tile setter and Italian immigrant Simon Rodia entirely of discarded objects he collected between 1921 and 1954. The tallest of the three main bricolage structures rises almost 100 ft. Despite several private and city-led efforts to raze them, the towers still stand, now the centerpiece of a state historic park and cultural center. Due to long-term renovation efforts, tours have been suspended until summer 2001; in the meantime, you can peek through the scaffolding. Do not linger here after dark. *1765 E. 107th St., next to Watts Towers Arts Center. Take I–110 to I–105 east; exit north at S. Central Ave., turn right onto 108th St., left onto Graham Ave. Admission free. Open daily 10–5.*

## WATTS TOWERS ARTS CENTER

Besides hosting workshops and other events, this center mounts rotating art exhibits (often of Southern Californian artists) and a permanent folk instrument display. February is consumed by special celebrations and exhibits for Black History Month, and a music festival is held every July. *1727 E. 107th St., at Graham Ave., tel. 213/847–4646. Open Tues.–Sat. 10–4, Sun. noon–4.*

# EAST L.A.

Drive east on Cesar E. Chavez Avenue from downtown into the neighborhoods of East L.A., and you'll suddenly be reminded that people of color outnumber Anglos in the L.A. area: In East L.A. English is the seldom-heard second language. Boyle Heights, City Terrace, and the adjoining neighborhoods of East L.A. are interesting places to visit, though there are few formal sights-to-see. Keep in mind that the area is economically depressed and plagued by gang activity; both locals and visitors risk being in the wrong place at the wrong time. It's best to drive here rather than depending on public transportation. Exercise caution by exploring during daylight hours and sticking to major streets, but don't let fear deter you from investigating one of the most vibrant communities in Los Angeles.

## CESAR E. CHAVEZ AVENUE

It's the main drag in Boyle Heights. And it is hard to recognize Cesar E. Chavez Avenue as the same piece of concrete that turns into Sunset Boulevard west of downtown and hits the ocean in Malibu. The street's name change from Brooklyn Avenue to Cesar E. Chavez was a symbolic final act in the neighborhood's transition from primarily Jewish (note the remains of an old synagogue at 247 Breed Street) to primarily Latino. Spanish-language bookshops, discount clothing stores, *taquerías,* and produce markets line this lively street, making for an interesting drive or stroll. Keep an eye out for the many murals that decorate commercial establishments and for the occasional *mariachi* (musician) playing tunes on the avenue in hopes of being hired.

## MURALS OF EAST L.A.

In the midst of all its corporate art and well-marketed mass culture, Los Angeles has nearly 2,000 murals by and for the people. The history and background of these murals are as multicultural as the city itself, originating with the now-vanished efforts of a Scandinavian immigrant in 1912, with later bursts of activity aided by New Deal projects of the 1930s and community empowerment movements of the 1960s and '70s. If you visit the murals of East L.A., look for the myriad representations of the Virgin of Guadalupe, an icon who embodies both the Catholic Virgin Mary and the Aztec earth goddess Tonantzin. Cesar Chavez also makes numerous appearances on the street that now bears his name. The greatest concentration of public paintings is in the Latino community of Boyle Heights, where the Mexican mural tradition has taken on its own *norteño* look. Indeed, there are few commercial blocks in Boyle Heights without murals, so don't limit yourself to our designated sights. If you want a more complete tour, look in museum and independent bookstores for *Street Gallery: Guide to 1000 Los Angeles Murals,* by Robin Dunitz (RJD Enterprises; $24.95).

If you drive down Olympic Boulevard past Los Angeles's largest fleet of taco trucks, you will pass the Estrada Courts Housing Projects (between Grande Vista and Lorena Sts.). There are several murals on the walls of the projects, ranging from '70s fantasy scenes to reinterpretations of van Gogh. The most notable section of the artwork is a fierce portrait of Che Guevara pointing at the onlooker, with "We are not a minority" emblazoned below his militant stare.

Head to the mural *One Stop Immigration,* at the corner of Whittier and Esperanza, to check out a sly play on commercialism: The Coca-Cola logo is transformed into the empowerment message "Tome conciencia" (Drink consciousness). The vivid colors of Superman and the Statue of Liberty (crying tears of blood) are styled after the socialist muralists Diego Rivera and David Siqueiros. A lower caption reads, in Spanish: "The present is about struggle, the future is ours."

Continue to the corner of 1st Street and Lorena Avenue and look behind El Mercado de Los Angeles to see a uniquely L.A. juxtaposition of Hollywood hype and community art: a portrait of actor-director Edward James Olmos. The mural was commissioned in 1988 by *Time* magazine for their cover on this East Los Angeles activist and star.

One of the better murals depicting the Spanish invasion of Mexico can be found on the side of the Moctezuma Café, on Cesar E. Chavez Avenue, near Bernal Avenue. The Aztec-styled battle scene also serves to advertise the air-conditioned restaurant within, where you can enjoy a hearty meal underneath another wall of murals continuing the scene of struggle.

Continue on Chavez to Indiana Street to see the mural *Barrios United Is Peace and Power,* which depicts important political events in Latino history, from the signing of the Treaty of Guadalupe Hidalgo to the passage of Proposition 187. This mural has a unique 3-D twist: a metal sculpture of a man in chains hanging from the wall.

*Director Cecil B. DeMille, who lit the proverbial fire under Hollywood, nearly set up shop in Flagstaff, Arizona. But he was dissatisfied with what he saw from the train station—it wasn't "western enough"—so he continued west, and the rest is history.*

The Treaty of Guadalupe Hidalgo makes another appearance in the *Story of Our Struggle* mural at the corner of 1st Street and Townsend Avenue. Biblical figures join United Farm Workers members beneath the archways of the First Street Store. This mural is actually a mosaic; the tiles were baked and painted in Mexico before being assembled here.

*Homeboy,* a portrayal of modern East L.A. youth culture, is worth a detour to 4th Street between Pecan and Gless avenues. Mexican revolutionary Emiliano Zapata, an Aztec warrior, and the Virgin Mary accompany homeboys decked out in Ben Davis clothing and gang tattoos.

## PLAZA DE LOS MARIACHIS

The main concentration of traditional traveling musicians for hire can be found at the Plaza de los Mariachis. The mariachis here play weddings, *quincianeras* (the equivalent of a sweet 16 for a 15-year-old Latina girl), and the occasional hip Westside gathering. Rates are negotiable, but you can generally plan on spending $100 an hour to get two or three musicians to play your event. Mariachi music centers on the guitar, both the large Mexican version and the more compact Americanized form. Larger combos can include violin and horns, and the sentimental songs are sung in beautiful harmony. If you don't have the dough to bring a mariachi band back to your hostel, consider eating at a nice sit-down restaurant like **La Parilla** (*see* East L.A. *in* Chapter 3), where you can eavesdrop on other diners' serenades or get a personal performance for about $5 a song. Most songs are popular folk ballads familiar to the people who grew up with them, but it's okay if you can't sing along. *Corner of 1st St. and Boyle Ave.*

## LINCOLN PARK

If you need a spot of green in the midst of your inner-city tour, swing by Lincoln Park in Boyle Heights. In addition to the usual lake, fountain, and palm trees that garnish most Los Angeles city parks, there are faux Aztec pyramids for children to scale. The park is pleasant and family oriented by day, but like most urban parks, should be avoided after dark. At one corner of the park is the **Plaza de la Raza,** a small courtyard with a fountain, a crafts store, and frequent community events, from children's craft classes to musical performances on the plaza's stage. *Corner of Valley Blvd. and Mission Rd.*

## EL MERCADO DE LOS ANGELES

Also known as *el mercadito* (the little market), this large, busy indoor market in Boyle Heights is an East L.A. institution. On the bottom floor you can buy anything from fresh produce, meats, and fish to clothing, jewelry, herbs, and allegedly magical potions. There are also inexpensive taquerías if you want a quick bite to eat. Upstairs are a few sit-down restaurants (*see* East L.A. *in* Chapter 3) where you can get a more leisurely and slightly more expensive meal. If you go in the evening, there's a chance of live musical entertainment, as likely to be *norteño* as mariachi. *Corner of 1st and Lorena Sts.*

# HOLLYWOOD

Like the rags-to-riches star Norma Jean Mortenson, better known as Marilyn Monroe, modern Tinseltown came from inauspicious beginnings. Quiet, farmland Hollywood was forced to consolidate with Los Angeles in order to tap into the city's water supply in 1910. A year later, the first studio was established; in 1913, the city took off when Cecil B. DeMille produced the hit western *The Squaw Man* in a German immigrant's barn at the corner of Sunset Boulevard and Gower Street.

In Hollywood's seminal years directors flocked from the East Coast, fleeing bad weather and patent laws for the land of eternal sunshine and boundless natural beauty. The cheap rent in Hollywood attracted studios that had originally settled downtown, and the industry quickly spawned an attendant playground for the rich and infamous. The big Studios-with-a-capital-S blossomed here: MGM, Paramount, Columbia, and more. It was film's Olympus—the Barrymores, Errol Flynn, Greta Garbo, Marlene Dietrich, Humphrey Bogart, Bette Davis, you name 'em, they were there. Those days are long gone: Paramount is the only original major studio still physically located in Hollywood (*see* Studios, *below*). The others have fled over the hills, attracted by cheaper real estate in Burbank. All the same, this now-tattered area is full of hidden treasures. The eternal pimp-versus-cop struggle seems finally to have been won by the latter, and streets once dominated by boarded-up buildings are benefiting from large doses of urban renewal, all ostensibly aimed at recapturing Hollywood's glory days. The refurbished El Capitan and Egyptian movie palaces gave the boulevard a new fix of neon glam. The geodesic Cinerama Dome Theater at Sunset Boulevard is being renovated, and another new theater-and-restaurant center will be bumping up against Mann's Chinese Theater. But the biggest player will be the Hollywood and Highland development, under construction at press time. This massive complex, at the corner of the streets it's named after, will include a theater for the Academy Awards; they're due to host the Oscars beginning in 2001. Hopefully, the area won't be overrun by megamalls—on the quieter side, small, hip restaurants like Les Deux Cafés are sneaking into the area.

The majority of the sites listed below are within a rectangle formed by Highland (west), Franklin (north), and North Vermont (east) avenues and Sunset Boulevard (south), and you can easily walk the strip in an afternoon. The bronze stars embedded in the pavement along the boulevard will be the first clue that you've reached the much-ballyhooed Hollywood Walk of Fame (*see below*)—if the fleets of tour buses and gaggles of jovial pensioners haven't already tipped you off. Forming an ominous Bermuda Triangle where all good taste mysteriously disappears, the **Hollywood Wax Museum** (6767 Hollywood Blvd., at Highland Ave., tel. 323/462–5991), the **Guinness Book of World Records Museum** (6764 Hollywood Blvd., at Highland Ave., tel. 323/463–6433), and **Ripley's Believe It or Not!** (6780 Hollywood Blvd., at Highland Ave., tel. 323/466–6335) feature lots of Marilyn Monroe displays and other trivialities for just under a tenner. Save your money for a movie.

To make a sweep through the obligatory tourist traps, hop on MTA Bus 1 along Hollywood Boulevard or park in one of the residential areas near the intersection of Hollywood Boulevard and Highland Avenue. Check signs to make sure it's legal; some areas restrict parking to residents only. You could also use the Red Line subway, which runs through the bowels of Hollywood Boulevard. There's a stop at Hollywood and Vine, and another at Hollywood and Highland Avenue is due to open in mid-2000.

*See the Hollywood map.*

## BARNSDALL ART PARK AND HOLLYHOCK HOUSE

This hilltop art community was founded by oil heiress Aline Barnsdall in 1915, when the surrounding lowlands were still being farmed. As she was a friend of architect Frank Lloyd Wright, she commissioned him to design the complex (only three buildings were completed). Hollyhock House, built between 1919

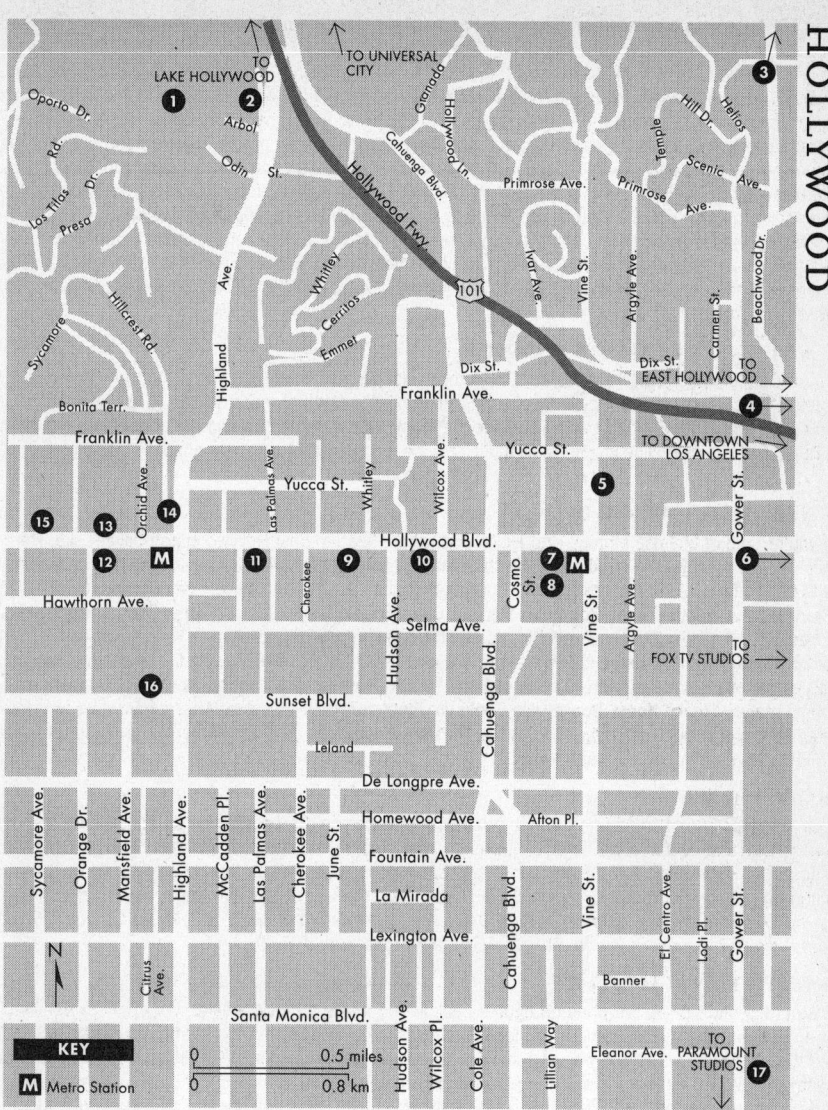

Oporto Dr.
Rd.
Los Tilas Dr.
Presa
Arbot
Odin St.
Hillcrest Rd.
Sycamore
Bonita Terr.
Franklin Ave.
Orchid Ave.
Hawthorn Ave.
Highland
Whitley
Cerritos
Emmet
Franklin Ave.
Yucca St.
Hollywood Blvd.
Cherokee
Selma Ave.
Hudson Ave.
Sunset Blvd.
Leland
De Longpre Ave.
Homewood Ave.
Fountain Ave.
La Mirada
Lexington Ave.
Las Palmas Ave.
Whitley
Wilcox Ave.
Granada
Hollywood In.
Cahuenga Blvd.
Hollywood Fwy.
Primrose Ave.
Ivar Ave.
Vine St.
Argyle Ave.
Carmen St.
Dix St.
Franklin Ave.
Yucca St.
Cosmo St.
Vine St.
Argyle Ave.
Cahuenga Blvd.
Temple
Scenic Ave.
Primrose Ave.
Hill Dr.
Helios
Beachwood Dr.
Dix St.
TO EAST HOLLYWOOD
TO DOWNTOWN LOS ANGELES
Gower St.
TO FOX TV STUDIOS

Sycamore Ave.
Orange Dr.
Mansfield Ave.
Highland Ave.
McCadden Pl.
Las Palmas Ave.
Cherokee Ave.
June St.
Citrus Ave.
Cahuenga Blvd.
Vine St.
Afton Pl.
El Centro Ave.
Ladl Pl.
Gower St.
Banner
Santa Monica Blvd.
Hudson Ave.
Wilcox Pl.
Cole Ave.
Lillian Way
Eleanor Ave.
TO PARAMOUNT STUDIOS

N

**KEY**

M  Metro Station

0        0.5 miles
0        0.8 km

Barnsdall Art Park
and Hollyhock
House, **6**

Capitol Records
Tower, **5**

Eco-Home, **4**

Egyptian
Theatre, **11**

Frederick's of
Hollywood, **9**

Hollywood Bowl, **1**

Hollywood
Entertainment
Museum, **15**

Hollywood Farmers'
Market, **8**

Hollywood Heritage
Museum, **2**

Hollywood High
School, **16**

Hollywood History
Museum, **14**

Hollywood Memorial
Park Cemetery, **17**

The Hollywood
Sign, **3**

Hollywood Walk
of Fame, **7**

Los Angeles
Contemporary
Exhibitions, **10**

Mann's Chinese
Theater, **13**

Motion Picture
Coordination
Office, **12**

and 1921, was his first—and probably most unusual—project in Los Angeles. The design is a marked departure from the horizontal lines of Wright's Prairie style. Stylized versions of Mrs. Barnsdall's favorite hollyhock flowers are used inside and out; the structure's massiveness hints at Mayan architecture. Pueblo Indian and Asian influences are also evident in the "organic" architectural scheme, which aims to blend the structure into the surroundings. And there are experimental touches, like a water-filled moat surrounding the living room fireplace and inward-sloping walls on the second floor. A few of the doorways measure only 5 feet, 7 inches—the "perfect" height for an entryway according to the short-of-stature Wright. The furniture is original Wright as well—as was his perfectionist wont, he designed the interiors to match. The Art Park is also home to the **Los Angeles Municipal Art Gallery** (tel. 213/485–4581), known for its excellent contemporary art exhibitions. The June 9 annual blockbuster Frank Lloyd Wright birthday celebration includes free tours of the Hollyhock House and hands-on architecture workshops for children. *4800 Hollywood Blvd., at N. Vermont Ave., tel. 323/913–4157. Hollyhock tours ($2) Wed.–Sun. noon, 1, 2, and 3.*

## CAPITOL RECORDS TOWER

When Capitol needed new offices in 1956, singer Nat King Cole and songwriter Johnny Mercer suggested the company build a cylindrical tower resembling a stack of records. And voilà, it was done. If you peek through the windows, you can see the lobby, where numerous awards for gold and platinum albums line the walls. The crowning bit of kitsch: The red beacon atop the tower spells out "Hollywood" nonstop in Morse code. *1750 N. Vine St., at Hollywood Blvd.*

## EAST HOLLYWOOD

If you're tired of Melrose attitude and Hollywood grime, head to East Hollywood and Silver Lake. Here, near the intersection of Franklin and North Vermont avenues, you'll find a newish café and club scene that has so far avoided the pretense and posing that accompany almost every emerging L.A. trend. On Franklin have a coffee at the **Bourgeois Pig** (*see* Cafés and Coffeehouses *in* Chapter 3) or dine at **Prizzi's Piazza** (*see* Chapter 3). If you're itching to reach deeper into your pocket, pick up a smart-ass T- shirt or an A-line dress at **X-Large** (1768 N. Vermont Ave., tel. 323/666–3483)—one in the chain of hip-hop stores partially owned by Kim Gordon of Sonic Youth. Researchers hunting for surreal tabloid cover-photo material make **Koma Books** (*see* Books *in* Chapter 7) their first stop. After a hard day's window-shopping and people-watching, stop by the **Dresden Room** (*see* Bars *in* Chapter 5) for liquid refueling to the accompaniment of Sinatra tunes.

## ECO-HOME

Los Angeles, land of smog and excess, is hardly the place you'd expect to find an ecologically friendly household that features all sorts of low-cost, earth-friendly features, from solar energy panels to Xeriscapes (low-water, low-maintenance landscaping). In order to see the house, you must take an informative two-hour tour, during which you'll get tips on how you, too, can make your house an eco-home. Reservations are essential. *4344 Russell Ave., near Vermont Ave., Los Feliz, tel. 323/662–5207. Admission $7. Tours Oct.–June, Sun. 2–4:30; July–Sept., Sun. 4–6:30.*

## EGYPTIAN THEATRE

It's not too often that giant pharaoh figures beckon you inside a movie theater. Entrepeneur Sid Grauman, the man behind the famous Chinese Theater (*see below*), created this theme movie palace in the 1920s. By the early 1990s it was a wreck, and the severe earthquake in 1994 almost finished it off. But with an amazing run of luck and the perseverance of the American Cinematheque film association, it was stunningly restored and reopened in 1998. Now you can see a film under a crimson-and-gold sunburst and hear the mighty Wurlitzer—just as though it were Hollywood's first golden age. *See also* Movie Houses *in* Chapter 5. *6712 Hollywood Blvd., at Las Palmas Ave., tel. 323/466– 3456.*

## FREDERICK'S OF HOLLYWOOD

This legendary palace of licentious lingerie is a great place to pick up a pair of crotchless satin panties for the folks back home. Their well-endowed **Bra Museum** (admission free) in the back of the store features several titillating exhibitions, including the "History of the Bra" and the "Celebrity Lingerie Hall of Fame," featuring undergarb worn by Mae West, panties from Zsa Zsa Gabor, a Madonna bustier, and even a bra that belonged to Milton Berle. Though the museum was looted during the 1992 uprisings (what better way to vent your rage than to go on a panty raid?), most heisted items were later returned—one repentant man turned in his booty (pun very much intended) to a bemused priest. *See also* Chapter 7. *6608 Hollywood Blvd., at Whitley Ave., tel. 323/466–8506. Open weekdays 10–9, Sat. 10–7, Sun. 11–6.*

## HOLLYWOOD AND VINE

Once considered the heart of Hollywood, today this intersection is frequented by hustlers and gawking tourists, not stars of the silver screen. Ostensibly, out-of-towners come here to get their bearings and activate their nostalgia receptors, but they are more likely to be taken for all they are worth. If you must gawk, look for the **Taft Building** on the southeast corner of the intersection, once home to many agents and therefore a magnet for wanna-be starlets. The **Equitable Building,** on the northeast corner, also housed the agents of such luminaries as Clark Gable and Greta Garbo. You'll also find the stars of the Apollo astronauts here. Perhaps that's the reason for the spaced-out looks on the faces of disillusioned visitors. Gone are the days when this area was known as Little Paris, when it was the locus of the burgeoning radio and movie industries. Gone also is the famous Brown Derby restaurant, which used to stand on the southeast corner—so many famous faces ate there that it was called the commissary of Hollywood.

## HOLLYWOOD BOWL

The Hollywood Bowl, a striking white band shell nestled in the Hollywood foothills, is the summer home of the **Los Angeles Philharmonic** and the **Hollywood Bowl Orchestra** (see Classical Music, Dance, and Opera in Chapter 5). On clear summer nights thousands of picnic-toting Angelenos head here for performances of classical, jazz, and contemporary music. Thirteen outdoor dining areas surround the Bowl, and they get crowded; arrive an hour or two before kickoff to claim a spot. You can pick up any supplies you forgot at the Bowl's concession stands: hot dogs, beer, pesto chicken, wine, whatever—though you'll pay for the convenience. Seat prices vary by type of performance and proximity, usually ranging from about $10 (student and senior rush tickets) to about $35. You can catch rehearsals for free Tuesday–Friday 9:30–noon. Call ahead to make sure a rehearsal is scheduled. *2301 N. Highland Ave., ¾ mi north of Hollywood Blvd., tel. 323/850–2000 for performance and BowlExpress info. BowlExpress Park & Ride service ($5 round-trip) from 15 locations in L.A. County; or MTA Bus 163 or 420. Performances June–Sept., Tues.–Sun.*

*The nonprofit Hollywood Heritage Society sponsors walking tours that highlight the often invisible glamour of old Hollywood. Their Boulevard Walk departs from the Capitol Records building. Call 323/874–4005 for more information and reservations.*

## HOLLYWOOD ENTERTAINMENT MUSEUM

A large space for a rather small museum is set aside in Hollywood's Galaxy complex. Interactive exhibits allow you to hear the voices of luminaries such as Katherine Hepburn and Orson Welles. The most interesting display is a timeline chronicling celluloid history from the first commercial screening in 1896 through the present day. *7021 Hollywood Blvd., at Sycamore St., tel. 323/465–7900. Admission $7.50. Open Thurs.–Tues. 11–6.*

## HOLLYWOOD FARMERS' MARKET

Every Sunday a couple of blocks of Ivar Street (between Hollywood Boulevard and Selma Avenue) metamorphose into a festive street fair. Huge crowds flock to the pedestrians-only area to sample ethnic foods and listen to lively musical entertainment as they peruse stalls packed chockablock with farm-fresh produce and crafts. During the market, the Ivar Theater sponsors an outdoor coffee shop where celebs often appear. *Tel. 323/463–3171.*

## HOLLYWOOD HERITAGE MUSEUM

The Hollywood Heritage Society salvaged this old barn where Cecil B. DeMille shot his first full-length film, *The Squaw Man,* in 1913. A screening room shows reels of vintage Hollywood footage, and old movie props are on display. *2100 N. Highland Ave., at Odin St., tel. 323/874–2276. Admission $4. Open by appointment on weekdays, weekends 11–4.*

## HOLLYWOOD HIGH SCHOOL

The diverse students here speak 40 languages, quite a contrast to the days when stars such as Carol Burnett, Linda Evans (*Dynasty*), James Garner (*Rockford Files*), and Lana Turner attended. *1521 N. Highland Ave., at Sunset Blvd.*

## HOLLYWOOD HISTORY MUSEUM

Slated to open in summer 2000, in the old art deco Max Factor building, this will be a paean to Hollywood. Permanent and temporary exhibits of costumes, props, posters, and equipment will examine

# WALK OF FAME TOUR

GEORGE & IRA GERSHWIN: 7083 Hollywood Blvd. ALFRED HITCHCOCK: 7013 Hollywood Blvd. W. C. FIELDS: 7004 Hollywood Blvd. MICHAEL JACKSON: 6927 Hollywood Blvd. GRETA GARBO: 6901 Hollywood Blvd. GROUCHO MARX: 6821 Hollywood Blvd. ELVIS PRESLEY: 6777 Hollywood Blvd. MARILYN MONROE: 6776 Hollywood Blvd. CHARLIE CHAPLIN: 6751 Hollywood Blvd. SYLVESTER STALLONE: 6712 Hollywood Blvd. LUCILLE BALL: 6436 Hollywood Blvd. BETTE DAVIS: 6225 Hollywood Blvd. CLARK GABLE: 1608 Vine St. MARLON BRANDO: 1765 Vine St. JOHN LENNON: 1750 Vine St.

moviemaking from its beginning to its recent innovations. The museum will also host guest speakers and lectures on a regular basis. *1660 N. Highland Ave., tel. 323/464–7776.*

## HOLLYWOOD MEMORIAL PARK CEMETERY

Fame *is* immortal. Just ask the groundskeepers here, who have seen countless tourists drive up in rented convertibles, stand on the gravesites of their favorite stars, and take snapshots of the hallowed tombstones with disposable cameras. Mel Blanc, Douglas Fairbanks, Sr., Marion Davies, and other notables are buried here, denied privacy even in death by a tour-of-the-dead-stars map available free in the cemetery office. Walk from the entrance on the lake area, and you'll find the crypt of filmmaker Cecil B. DeMille. Fans, the press, and the famous Lady in Black used to turn up at the Cathedral Mausoleum every August 23 to honor Rudolph Valentino on the anniversary of his death. If you'd like to visit the permanent homes of additional stars, *see* Cemeteries *in* Stars, Sets, and Death Sites, *below. 6000 Santa Monica Blvd., between Gower St. and Van Ness Ave., tel. 323/469–1181. Open weekdays 8–5, weekends 10–3.*

## THE HOLLYWOOD SIGN

Erected on top of 1,640-ft Mt. Lee in 1923 to publicize *Los Angeles Times* publisher Harry Chandler's Hollywoodland housing development, the sign lost its LAND and was deeded to the Hollywood Chamber of Commerce in 1945. This highly visible civic symbol has proven a favorite subject of pranksters, who have successfully modified it to read OLLYWOOD, in honor of Oliver North during the Iran-Contra hearings, and HOLLYWEED, in support of a medicinal marijuana ballot initiative. Though years have passed since the last failed starlet took a swan dive from one of the sign's 50-ft-tall Os, questions about this famous landmark are routinely intercepted by Griffith Park rangers with a curt "It's off-limits." Local opinions are mixed, from "You can't hike up there" to "Hell, yeah, you can hike up there, but you'll be slapped with a $103 fine." One look at the expressway-size trails blazing up the hillside from the ends of Deronda and Innsdale drives, and you know that—-despite the apparent illegality—people *do* climb up there. But to stick to the straight and narrow, use the public Mt. Lee Trail, which goes right by the sign (*see* Hiking *in* Chapter 6). The letters were rebuilt in 1978 with money (nearly $28,000 a pop) donated by concerned industry celebs like Alice Cooper.

## HOLLYWOOD WALK OF FAME

Terrazzo and brass stars were first embedded at the corner of Highland Avenue and Hollywood Boulevard in 1960. In the four decades since, more than 2,000 other famous and not-so-famous names have been added between La Brea Avenue and Argyle Avenue, as well as along Vine Street. This kind of immortality doesn't come cheap: The personality in question (or more likely his or her studio or record company) must pay $7,500 for the honor. The celebrities' stars are classified by one of five logos: a motion picture camera, a radio microphone, a television set, a record, or a theatrical mask. Don't bump into other starstruck gawkers as you walk. Call the Hollywood Chamber of Commerce (tel. 323/469–8311) voice-mail info center for a current schedule of special events, like Walk of Fame induction ceremonies.

## LAKE HOLLYWOOD

Built in 1917 by William Mulholland as part of his ambitious water-stealing plan, the lavishly landscaped Lake Hollywood (also known as the **Hollywood Reservoir**) is the most secluded body of water in the city. When you've had enough of the smog, head into the Hollywood Hills: If you have a map, good orienteering skills, and some patience, you may stumble across a sliver of park northeast of the reservoir that offers a fantastic view of the legendary HOLLYWOOD sign. Stressed-out industry execs often pound the pavement on the trail around the lake. Many scenes from *Chinatown* and *Earthquake* were shot around the reservoir in 1974. Along the way you'll also be able to see some of L.A.'s architectural jewels, including homes designed by Frank Lloyd Wright, R. M. Schindler, and Richard Neutra. Call the Department of Water and Power at 818/909–3000 for a reservoir status report; the path is occasionally closed for mysterious reasons. *See also* Chapter 6. *Take U.S. 101 north to Barham Blvd. exit; head north ¼ mi to Lake Hollywood Dr., turn right and descend to lakeshore. Follow Tahoe Dr. around lake to Canyon Lake Dr. and turn right; park is on left. Open daily 6–sunset. Reservoir path open weekdays 6:30–10 and 2– 7:30, weekends 6:30 AM–7:30 PM.*

## LOS ANGELES CONTEMPORARY EXHIBITIONS (LACE)

Since 1977 this small collective has provided a welcoming venue for all manner of exhibitions, ranging from well-known touring installations to emerging local artists. Be sure to check out the bookstore, which stocks an exhaustive selection of periodicals. Validated parking is $2, and there's a suggested donation of $3. *6522 Hollywood Blvd., at Wilcox St., Hollywood, tel. 323/957–1777. Open Wed.–Sat. noon–6.*

*Legend had it that Lana Turner was discovered at Schwab's drugstore (8024 Sunset Blvd., now gone). This may not have been quite true, but Schwab's was a big Hollywood hangout. F. Scott Fitzgerald had a heart attack here while on a cigarette run.*

## MANN'S CHINESE THEATER

Commissioned by impresario Sid Grauman in 1927, this outlandish approximation of a Chinese pagoda was yet another addition to his family of exotic-themed movie palaces, including the Egyptian Theatre (*see above*) and the Mayan Theater (now a nightclub, 1038 S. Hill St.) downtown. During the rip-roaring '30s, opening nights drew enormous crowds anxious to glimpse arriving stars in person. Today, though first-run movies are still shown in the opulent Chinese Theater, the main attraction is a collection of some 160 cement imprints of celebs' digits, feet, even a nose (Jimmy Durante), outside the lobby. The famous courtyard started off as an accident: In 1927, actress Norma Talmadge stepped in wet cement on her way into a premiere. Stars have been following her lead ever since—from golden-era leads like Humphrey Bogart and Joan Crawford to more recent names (John Travolta). If you see a movie here, be sure it's playing in the main theater and not in one of two unremarkable adjoining halls added in 1980. *6925 Hollywood Blvd., between Orange Dr. and Orchid Ave., tel. 323/464–8111.*

## MOTION PICTURE COORDINATION OFFICE

This is an invaluable resource if you're determined to see at least one celebrity (though you may have to settle for the cast and crew of a low-budget HBO thriller). Pick up the office's free shoot sheet, which describes what's being filmed around town each day: It lists the kind of shoot (film, TV, music video, still photography), who's involved, and when and where it's happening. Once you find the set, you may be allowed a closer inspection—perhaps even an autograph—if you remain polite and free of hysterics. *7083 Hollywood Blvd., 5th fl., tel. 323/957–1000. Open weekdays 8–6.*

## MULHOLLAND DRIVE

This famous thoroughfare, named after former L.A. water chief William Mulholland—whose engineering feats brought water to the dry-as-a-bone L.A. basin—winds its way from the base of the Hollywood Hills, just west of the Hollywood Freeway (U.S. 101), traversing the spine of the Santa Monica Mountains, crossing the San Diego Freeway (I–405), and continuing westward as Mulholland Highway. It passes through several rural communities before diving into the Pacific Ocean some 100 mi later. Driving (or cycling) any portion of its length is slow going, but you'll be rewarded with sensational views of the city, the San Fernando Valley, and the expensive homes along the way. *Take U.S. 101 north from downtown to Barham Blvd. exit; turn left and head west uphill.*

# WEST HOLLYWOOD AND MELROSE AVENUE

West Hollywood has long since replaced Hollywood proper as a center of wealth and celebrity. As Hollywood grew more seedy and affordable, West Hollywood, which roughly covers Beverly Boulevard north through the hills above Sunset from La Brea to Doheny, became increasingly posh and precious. Representing all that outsiders love to hate about Los Angeles, West Hollywood's only sights have a simulated quality to them, tracing their importance in one way or another to the entertainment world. Drink at the bar that Johnny Depp owns, gawk at the hotel where John Belushi died, eat at the table where Marilyn Monroe and Joe DiMaggio had their blind date. Leave your conscience at home and come prepared to enjoy decadent consumption, or at least voyeurism, and save your brain cells for another part of your trip.

The apex of the West Hollywood scene can be found along the Sunset Strip between Doheny and Fairfax. From its trendy cafés, nightclubs, and restaurants to its signature show business billboards, the famously named boulevard reeks of glamour. Since celebrities come to this area to eat, party, and in several noteworthy cases, die, there's always a sense that a star is just around the corner. A few blocks south, the Santa Monica strip serves as the center of the L.A. gay, lesbian, and bisexual community. Some of the city's best cafés and dance clubs are here, and like Sunset, it is a prime spot to spy on the beautiful people.

Still farther south, Melrose Avenue is the shopping locus for the platforms-and-polyester crowd, and its ever-changing clothing boutiques outfit L.A.'s lower-budget trendsetters and trend followers. Just west of the strip on Melrose is the Pacific Design Center and surrounding Avenues of Design, which will enable you to make your home as fashionable and ostentatious as your person. *See* West Hollywood and Melrose Avenue *in* Chapter 7 for more thorough reviews of places to make your credit cards scream for mercy.

Sunset Strip is serviced by MTA Lines 2, 3, 302, and 409; take MTA Lines 4 and 304 to poke along Santa Monica Boulevard's La Cienega–to–Doheny segment. To hit the main section of Melrose Avenue, between Fairfax and La Brea avenues, take MTA Lines 10 and 11. The subway doesn't serve this part of town. Parking shouldn't be too much of a hassle if you troll the sidestreets.

*See the West Hollywood, Beverly Hills, and the Westside map.*

## MELROSE AVENUE

A straighter crowd frequents the Melrose strip (between Fairfax and La Brea avenues) in search of the excitement and, of course, the latest fashions. The serious shopper will make a quick stop farther west of the main drag at **Fred Segal** (8118 Melrose Ave., at Crescent Heights Blvd.) to view the haute version of the Melrose strip knockoffs. Once back among the fluorescent-lit shotgun stores and scruffy kids east of Fairfax, head to the vintage and oddball boutiques for the best finds. Keep in mind that you come to Melrose to look, feel, and act trendy, so put your inner cultural critic to rest, unless you stop at **Melrose News** (647 N. Martel Ave., at Melrose Ave., tel. 323/655–2866) or at the **Cosmopolitan Book Shop** (7017 Melrose Ave., tel. 323/938–7119), oases of intellectual stimulation in the fashion desert. At **Off the Wall Antiques** (7325 Melrose Ave., tel. 323/930–1185) you can shell out the big bucks for a larger-than-life statue of Bob's Big Boy or a neon naked lady with light-up parts. **Condomania** (7306 Melrose Ave., tel. 323/933–7865) sells both practical and playful prophylactics. Hit **Wasteland** (7428 Melrose Ave., at Vista St., Melrose, tel. 323/653-4028) for vintage frocks or bell bottoms. Eat off your shopping anxiety at **Pink's Famous Chili Dogs** (709 N. La Brea Ave., tel. 323/931–4223), offering satisfyingly bad hot dogs popular among grungy young stars. Perhaps the strip's most unique store is **Necromance** (7220 Melrose, tel. 323/934–8684), specializing in skulls, insect exoskeletons, and all things dead to decorate your home or body. For more on both fabulous bargains and obscenely priced fashion errors, *see* West Hollywood and Melrose Avenue *in* Chapter 7. If you must.

## PACIFIC DESIGN CENTER/DESIGN DISTRICT

So, enough about me, let's talk about my furniture. Once you have finished perfecting your body, hair, and wardrobe, it's time to bring your home up to par. Well, at least you can daydream about it at the Pacific Design Center (PDC), a monstrous-looking building aptly nicknamed the Blue Whale (8687 Melrose Ave., at San Vicente Blvd., tel. 310/657–0800). The building is open to the public to look (weekdays 9–5), but you'll need an interior decorator's license to buy. The stores within offer everything from rococo antique mirrors to ultramodern slablike sofas; you can find furnishings for your home, office, and garden. If you are not sufficiently impressed to blow your life savings on a new bedroom set, move on to the surrounding blocks: Melrose Avenue and Robertson, San Vicente, La Brea, and Beverly boulevards, known collectively as the **Avenues of Design** and offering a more offbeat selection of wares. **Circa 1910 Antiques** (7206 Melrose Ave., at Formosa Ave., tel. 323/965–1910) sells furnishings, glassware, and pottery somewhere between art nouveau and art deco, while **Frewil** (605 N. La Brea Ave., tel. 323/934–8474) has a more contemporary, avant-garde collection.

## SANTA MONICA BOULEVARD

Although Ellen DeGeneres, her lip-lock Anne Heche, and a few other high-profile performers are openly gay, many Hollywood stars remain frustratingly ensconced in their well-stocked walk-in closets. Still, L.A. has plenty of gay pride, colorfully visible on the Santa Monica strip, between La Cienega and Doheny. The locale of L.A.'s annual Gay and Lesbian Pride Parade, the strip is lively day and night, with lots of restaurants, cafés, and dance clubs. If you have been in L.A. too long without a bona fide celebrity sighting, consider settling for a look at some still-undiscovered beautiful people. As the proliferation of gyms suggests, body culture is alive and well on the Santa Monica strip, and there is a constant parade of toned bodies in various stages of undress. If you want a traditional café (read: heavily caffeinated beverages), the boulevard has plenty to offer. The **Abbey** (692 N. Robertson Blvd., at Santa Monica Blvd., tel. 310/289–8410; see Cafés and Coffeehouses in Chapter 3) is popular at all hours, with lovely outdoor seating and a sophisticated. Euro ambience. Get your café reading material or add to your gay library at **A Different Light Bookstore** (8853 Santa Monica Blvd., at San Vicente Blvd., tel. 310/854–6601; see Books in Chapter 7), open late and well stocked with gay fiction and nonfiction.

*A perfect example of "famous for being famous": Angelyne, L.A.'s landmark pneumatic babe. Her busty-blonde billboards are sprinkled over the city, but don't try to pin her down to a profession. In her own words, "I don't do—I AM!"*

## SUNSET BOULEVARD

This strip of outsized and elaborate movie billboards and celebrity overdoses also has some of L.A.'s most famous nightspots. Catch a known or unknown act at the hard-rocking **Whisky** (8901 Sunset Blvd., at Hilldale Ave.), the reputed birthplace of go-go dancing and the locale of more than one Doors concert. The nearby **Roxy** (9009 Sunset Blvd., between Hilldale Ave. and Doheny Dr.) also hosts big names in loud music, and the sidewalk outside both places fills with a tastefully rough-looking crowd just around show time. If you don't feel sufficiently rock and roll for the evening, make your way to **Sunset Strip Tattoo** (8418 Sunset Blvd., at La Cienega Blvd.), where Cher and other stars have had their flesh enhanced. The **Viper Room** (8852 Sunset Blvd., at Larrabee Ave.), famous as actor River Phoenix's last stop before dying of a drug overdose just outside, has established its live music creds. Other famous Sunset area drug deaths include those of Lenny Bruce, in an apartment in the hills above **Sunset Plaza** (Sunset Blvd. and Sunset Plaza Dr.), and John Belushi, in the palatial **Chateau Marmont** (8221 Sunset Blvd., at Sweetzer). Belushi's OD blew the hotel's cover as a place where celebrities could go when they wanted to be alone, and inquiring minds can read all about the stars who soiled the sheets there in former owner Raymond L. Sarlot's book, *Life at the Marmont*. If you prefer a more elegant celebrity aura, swing by the **Rainbow Bar and Grill** (9015 Sunset Blvd., at Doheny Dr.) to see where Joe DiMaggio first made the acquaintance of Marilyn Monroe and where Vincente Minnelli proposed to Judy Garland. The beautiful art deco tower of the **Argyle Hotel** (8358 Sunset Blvd., at Olive Dr.) sets the scene in both written and visual noir: It was a filming location for *Murder, My Sweet* and was also frequented by Raymond Chandler's literary private eye, Philip Marlowe.

# GRIFFITH PARK

Northeast of Hollywood in the Santa Monica Mountains, Griffith Park's 4,213 acres constitute the largest municipal park in the United States. Most of the original acreage was bequeathed to the city in 1896 by mining tycoon Colonel Griffith J. Griffith, who gifted the land with the understanding that some would be reserved for the rich and famous to ultimately retire in style. Today the park includes three golf courses, endless trails, pony rides, a miniature railway, a beautiful antique carousel, and recreation facilities; a famous cemetery (**Forest Lawn**, see Cemeteries in Stars, Sets, and Death Sites, below), the **Greek Theater** (see Chapter 5), and such tourist attractions as the **L.A. Zoo** (see below), the **Autry Museum of**

**Western Heritage,** and the HOLLYWOOD sign, which rests atop Mt. Lee. Though portions of the park have been developed for human pursuits, the bulk remains in a relatively pristine state. Hiking, cycling, and horseback riding are all options (*see* Chapter 6); for safety's sake, if you're alone, stay on maintained, populated trails and make your exit before dark.

## COMING, GOING, AND GETTING AROUND

The park is bordered on the west by the Hollywood Freeway (U.S. 101), on the east by the Golden State Freeway (I–5), on the north by the Ventura Freeway (U.S. 134), and on the south by Los Feliz Boulevard. There are four main entrances. **Western Canyon Road** branches north off Los Feliz Boulevard at the south end of the park and passes through the Fern Dell, a half mile of lush, shaded paths and waterways, and continues climbing to the Griffith Observatory (*see below*). The **Vermont Canyon Road** entrance, on the south end, provides access to the Greek Theater and the Roosevelt golf course. On the northeast side of the park, over the hills in the San Fernando Valley off Riverside Drive, take **Crystal Springs Drive** to the ranger station and Wilson and Harding golf courses. Finally, at the north end of the park, off the Ventura Freeway (Highway 134), you can reach Travel Town and Forest Lawn Memorial Park by exiting at Victory Boulevard south to **Zoo Drive.** When approaching from the north or south, the Golden State Freeway (I–5) is your best bet; when coming from the east or west, take the Ventura Freeway (Highway 134).

**VISITOR CENTER** • Orient yourself here by picking up road and trail maps, attraction brochures, and information about free guided hikes. The park's gates are open daily 5 AM–10 PM, but most mountain roads and trails are off-limits after dusk. *Ranger headquarters: 4730 Crystal Springs Dr., at Griffith Park Dr., tel. 323/665–5188. West of I–5, between Hwy. 134 and Los Feliz Blvd. From I–5, exit at Los Feliz Blvd., Griffith Park, or Zoo Dr. and follow signs. From Hwy. 134, exit at Forest Lawn Dr.*

## AUTRY MUSEUM OF WESTERN HERITAGE

If ever there were a politically correct cowboy museum, this is it. The huge, sophisticated collection of artifacts (and props and videos of TV westerns) presents a fond look at the Old West without perpetuating myths and stereotypes about the era. The collection includes Annie Oakley's gold-plated Smith and Wessons and Buffalo Bill Cody's saddle. It's across the parking lot and just east of the L.A. Zoo (*see below*). *4700 Western Heritage Way, Griffith Park–Hollywood, tel. 323/667–2000. Enter at Griffith Park Dr. and follow signs. MTA Bus 96. Admission $7.50. Open Tues.–Sun. 10–5.*

## BRONSON CAVES

Hidden in the hills in the southwest corner of Griffith Park, these caves were the hero's hideaway in the bif-pow-whamo television version of *Batman*, the site of many gunfights in *Gunsmoke* and *Bonanza*, and the stand-ins for the moonscapes in science fiction flicks like *Invasion of the Body Snatchers* and television shows like *Star Trek*. The trailhead you'll want (Brush Canyon) is on the right (east) side of the road near the red wall. Head through the white pipe gate past trail sign number 49; it's a quarter mile to the caves. Prepare yourself for some serious déjà vu. *From U.S. 101, exit north on Van Ness, turn left on Franklin Ave., right on Canyon Dr. or Bronson Ave., and head uphill 1 mi into Griffith Park until road ends. Open daily 6–sunset.*

## GRIFFITH OBSERVATORY AND PLANETARIUM

This copper-domed observatory houses a science museum, a planetarium, a laserium, and a 12-inch telescope. Film crews love this place, as viewers of *Rebel Without a Cause* and *The Terminator* can attest. If you're wondering how much you'd weigh on Mars, head to the **Hall of Science** (free), which has interactive computers and exhibits designed for both kids and adults. In the main hall you can buy tickets for the hour-long **Planetarium** presentation ($4) or for the **Laserium** ($7), a laser-beam show set to the tunes of bands like Led Zeppelin, U2, and Pink Floyd. (Beware the hordes of red-eyed youths who flock here on Friday and Saturday nights; it's the unofficial meeting place of the just-say-yes crowd.) On clear evenings (7–9:45) peer through the telescope (free) at Jupiter or the Orion nebula. Call the Observatory Sky Report (tel. 323/663–8171) to hear what's new in the heavens above Los Angeles. *2800 E. Observatory Rd., tel. 323/664–1191 or 818/997- -3624 for Laserium show times. Enter Griffith Park from Los Feliz Blvd. and follow signs. Observatory open summer, daily 12:30–10; winter, Tues.–Fri. 2–10, weekends 12:30–10.*

## L.A. ZOO

If you need a break from the urban jungle, head to the zoo. Considerable effort (and a constant stream of corporate money) has been expended to give the 1,200 animals here some semblance of a natural habitat, making this an example of comparatively humane captivity. The newest exhibit is the Chimpanzees of

Mahale Mountains habitat, part of a larger plan for a **Great Ape Forest.** At press time, construction had started on the Red Ape Rain Forest section. The vast complex is well worth an afternoon's exploration, so wear comfortable shoes. *5333 W. Zoo Dr., tel. 323/644–4200. Enter Griffith Park at Los Feliz Blvd. or Zoo Dr. and follow signs. Admission $8.25. Open Sept.–June, daily 10–5, July–Aug., daily 10–6.*

# WILSHIRE DISTRICT

Wilshire Boulevard, named for real estate speculator and Marxist H. Gaylord Wilshire, begins in downtown Los Angeles and runs all the way west to the Pacific. The most interesting parts of the boulevard are the section west of MacArthur Park up through the Miracle Mile of museums; the former center of the Jewish community, the Fairfax District; and tony Hancock Park. A center of commerce since the 1920s, Wilshire Boulevard is still the home of some of L.A.'s finer art deco stores and office buildings.

Museums have replaced stores as the premier attraction of the Miracle Mile, and many old buildings are used only for filming period movies, but a drive down Wilshire still gives a sense of the area's history. The Los Angeles County Museum of Art is worthy of an entire day's visit; clustered nearby are more eclectic collections, from miniatures to cars. For more street life and good kosher eats, head north from Wilshire onto Fairfax Avenue. For a unique visit with a deliberate community of artists, head to St. Elmo Village, reached by taking La Brea south from Wilshire and going east on St. Elmo's Drive.

Parking can be expensive for the Miracle Mile museums; go on Sunday when meters are free and spaces plentiful or be prepared to pay a minimum of $4 in one of the many lots. To follow Wilshire by bus, use MTA Lines 20, 21, and 22; to go from Wilshire onto Fairfax, take Line 217. The subway's Red Line has a few stops along Wilshire: Western Avenue; Normandie Avenue; and Vermont Avenue.

*See the Wilshire District map.*

## AMBASSADOR HOTEL
East of the Miracle Mile sits the fenced-off shell of the Ambassador Hotel and its once-hip dining room, the Coconut Grove, where the Academy Awards ceremony took place several times before the birth of the Chandler Pavilion. Although the hotel and restaurant were a see-and-be-seen locale for the 1920s movie crowd, its fame has been replaced by notoriety as the site where Robert Kennedy was assassinated in 1968. Now the exterior stucco is chipping, and the palm trees stand lonely in the desolate front lawn. *3400 Wilshire Blvd., at Wilshire Pl.*

## BULLOCKS WILSHIRE BUILDING
This gorgeously imposing, art deco department store closed in 1992, but after years of neglect the building was resuscitated by the Southwestern Law School. It now serves a less consumerist purpose; the school installed its library here. The terra-cotta exterior, copper detailing, and stern tower can seem daunting, but the interior is a blast—it was decorated by some of L.A.'s top artists of the 1920s. At press time, they planned to schedule regular free tours beginning in 2000. *3050 Wilshire Blvd., at Alexandria Ave., tel. 213/738–6814.*

## CAROL AND BARRY KAYE MUSEUM OF MINIATURES
If Las Vegas can have the Eiffel Tower, it should surprise no one that L.A. has its own versions of the Venetian Doges' Palace, Fontainebleau, and Hampton Court Palace—all in miniature. This museum is a combination of the ultrakitsch—twee miniature chalets— and the amazing. Fortunately, it leans more toward the latter. The buildings are perfectly re-created, one side reproducing the exterior, the other cut away to reveal room interiors. Peer at the incredible detailing, from gargoyles to tiny chandeliers lit with minute electric bulbs. *5900 Wilshire Blvd., between Curson Ave. and Ogden Dr., tel. 323/937–6464. Admission $7.50. Open Tues.–Sat. 10–5, Sun. 11–5.*

## CRAFT AND FOLK ART MUSEUM
Crafts from around the world—both contemporary and folk—are displayed here on a rotating basis. Six to eight major exhibitions, covering everything from sunglasses and jewelry to architecture, are arranged each year. *5814 Wilshire Blvd., at Curson Ave., tel. 323/937–4230. Admission $3.50. Open Tues.–Sun. 11–5.*

## FAIRFAX DISTRICT
Drive or take MTA Bus 217 north from Wilshire along Fairfax Avenue to reach one of L.A.'s original Jewish settlements, the Fairfax District, which is concentrated mainly between Melrose and Beverly

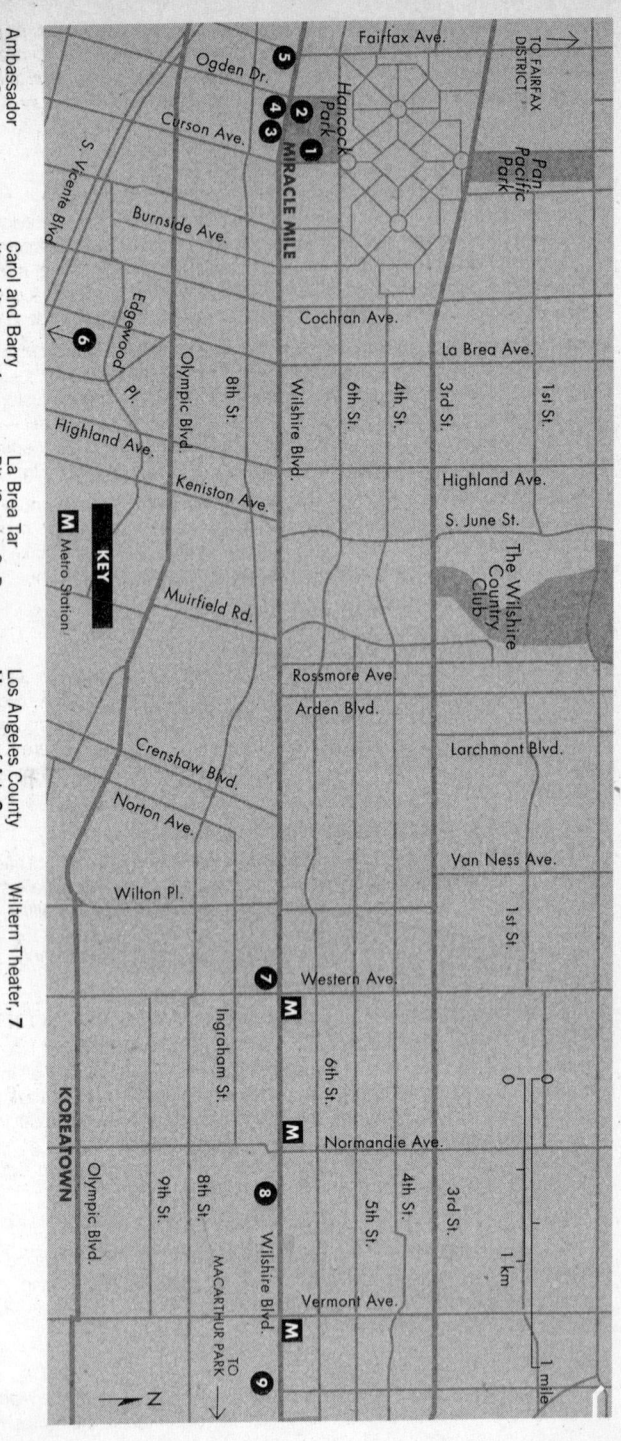

# WILSHIRE DISTRICT

Ambassador
Hotel, **9**

Bullocks Wilshire
building, **8**

Carol and Barry
Kaye Museum of
Miniatures, **4**

Craft and Folk Art
Museum, **3**

La Brea Tar
Pits/George C. Page
Museum of La Brea
Discoveries, **1**

Los Angeles County
Museum of Art, **2**

Petersen Automotive
Museum, **5**

St. Elmo Village, **6**

Wiltern Theater, **7**

avenues. Although the Jewish founders of the Hollywood motion picture industry kept their ethnicity under wraps, the Orthodox Jews of the Fairfax District have no problem showing their colors. Many Jews have now left the area in favor of the San Fernando Valley, but the remaining numbers maintain their visibility through the kosher restaurants, religious shops, and Jewish community organizations that line the avenue. Remember that places generally close for the Jewish Sabbath on Saturday, and often close early on Friday. **Canter's** deli (419 N. Fairfax Ave., between Melrose Ave. and Beverly Blvd., tel. 323/651–2030; see Hollywood in Chapter 3), a longtime Fairfax institution, hosts a substantial and diverse crowd, serving up their famous matzo ball soup 24 hours a day. After dark the restaurant's adjoining bar, the Kibitz Room, fills with neighborhood regulars along with club hoppers in high-fashion attire. Although there aren't many formal sights in the neighborhood (with the exception of the historical mural of Jewish L.A. alongside Canter's), a walk down the Fairfax strip feels like a sojourn into another world, or at least another era. Check out **Hatikvah Music** (436 N. Fairfax Ave., between Oakwood and Rosewood Aves., tel. 323/655–7083; see Music in Chapter 7) to examine the broad range of Jewish recordings: Mel Brooks and Carl Reiner's *2000 Year Old Man* beside Cantor Josef Rosenblatt's *Masterpieces of the Synagogue*. They also stock the best selection of Israeli pop music in all L.A. Next door, **Atara's Books and Gifts** (452 N. Fairfax Ave., between Oakwood and Rosewood Aves., tel. 323/655–3050) carries Jewish paraphernalia of all kinds, from cookie cutters in the shape of the Star of David to a child's musical windup toy that plays Torah tunes. When you get hungry, you can't miss with Canter's or the numerous kosher restaurants, which range from traditional Ashkenazi (Eastern European) style at **La Glatt** (446 N. Fairfax Ave., between Oakwood and Rosewood Aves., tel. 323/658–7730) to unusual Chinese dishes, some kosher, at **Genghis Cohen** (740 N. Fairfax Ave., near Melrose Ave., tel. 323/653–0640).

*If you approach anyone holding a clipboard at Mann's Chinese Theater, you'll likely walk away with a slew of free movie tickets.*

**FARMERS' MARKET** • Just south of the Fairfax strip on 3rd Street stands one of L.A.'s landmark institutions, the Fairfax Farmers Market, built to showcase the prowess of California's produce. Better fruits and vegetables can be found at the Hollywood Farmers' Market or downtown at the Grand Central Market (see Farmers' Markets in Chapter 3), but this market has a pleasantly historical feel and some decent places to eat. **DuPar's** (tel. 323/933–8446) is a classic L.A. coffee shop worth experiencing, and the **Gumbo Pot** (tel. 323/933–0358) serves up good New Orleans cooking. *6333 W. 3rd St., at Fairfax Ave., tel. 323/933–9211. Open June–mid-Sept., Mon.–Sat. 9–7, Sun. 10–6; mid-Sept.–May, Mon.–Sat. 9:30–6:30, Sun. 10–5.*

## LA BREA TAR PITS/GEORGE C. PAGE MUSEUM OF LA BREA DISCOVERIES

Forty thousand years ago animals wandered into this pungent primordial watering hole and unwittingly sacrificed themselves to archaeological discovery. You can stand on Wilshire Boulevard (for free) and gaze at the bubbling tar pits and a reenactment of a woolly mammoth mother getting stuck in the muck while her baby cries at the shore. There are actually dozens of tar pits spitting bubbles here in **Hancock Park,** but if you are interested in seeing examples of the thousands of Ice Age bones excavated from the tar, pay $6 to go into the Page museum, where they have reconstructed the skeletons of the mammals that once roamed Los Angeles. A mangy-looking animatronics model of a saber-toothed tiger swings its fangs repeatedly at the neck of a giant sloth in a display that is part *Jurassic Park*, part puppet show. Rather than risk your life in the pits themselves, you can enjoy the simulated experience of trying to pull your legs out of the interactive tar mechanism. The museum's spookiest part is the hologram of the inside and outside of La Brea Woman, a prehistoric homicide victim found in the tar pits. *5801 Wilshire Blvd., at Curson Ave., tel. 323/857–6311 or 323/934–7243. Admission $6, free 1st Tues. of month. Open June–Aug., weekdays 9:30–5, weekends 10–5; Sept.–May, Tues.–Fri. 9.30–5, weekends 10–5.*

## LOS ANGELES COUNTY MUSEUM OF ART (LACMA)

This massive concrete-and-glass structure at the west end of the Miracle Mile on Wilshire houses more art than the armchair aesthete can fit comfortably into one day. If the $7 admission discourages you from making multiple trips, brace yourself for a full day of culture or choose your wings and exhibits selectively. You can always relax between wings in the wonderful **Gerald B. Cantor Sculpture Garden,** which is studded with statues, including several Rodins. The museum consists of the **Frances and Armand Hammer Building,** a showcase for a wide range of modern Western works; the **Pavilion for Japanese Art**; the enormous **Ahmanson Building,** which spans international art across time; the **Robert O. Anderson Building,** the museum's site for 20th-century art; the **Leo S. Bing Center,** where you can

# MUSEUMS ON THE CHEAP

*Visitors planning a museum blitz should get their hands on the Art-Cee-LA card, which entitles holders to free admission at 16 local museums, including MOCA, the Southwest Museum, the L.A. County Natural History Museum, and the UCLA/Armand Hammer Museum. Membership also entitles holders to purchase half-price tickets to sports events and dance, music, and theater performances, subject to availability. The standard annual fee is $40, but cards are available to students and tourists for $25. Box 789, La Cañada-Flintridge 91012-0789, tel. 818/957–9400.*

snack and catch a flick; and the **Times-Mirror Central Court,** which hosts jazz every Friday afternoon and big-band and chamber music every Sunday afternoon. A stone's throw away on Wilshire is the **LACMA West** building, once a department store. Now it's mainly used for high-profile traveling exhibitions; there's also a branch of the Southwest Museum inside. Ask at the ticket booth for a brochure laying out the specific exhibits and consult the brief guide below. Exhibits scheduled for 2000 include "Pharaohs of the Sun: Akhenaten, Nefertiti, and Tutankhamen," a contemporary ceramics show, and a retrospective on Charles and Ray Eames. Some special exhibits have a separate admission fee, and tickets need to be booked in advance. *5905 Wilshire Blvd., at Ogden Dr., tel. 323/857–6000. Admission $7, free 2nd Tues. of the month. Open Mon., Tues., and Thurs. noon–8, Fri. noon–9, weekends 11–8; call for hrs of individual galleries.*

**THE AHMANSON GALLERY** • The museum equivalent of Humanities 101, the Ahmanson Gallery is the biggest and most culturally inclusive wing of LACMA, emphasizing non-Western and pre-20th-century art.

To your left as you enter on the ground floor are several rooms full of ancient Mexican ceramics, from animal-shaped vessels to warrior figures. To the right of the entrance is a small display of West African crafts, such as ceremonial masks and carved ivory; this leads abruptly to American paintings and decorative arts from the 18th to the early 20th centuries. Wander through these rooms and you'll see examples of Colonial portraiture and Hudson River School landscapes, a smooth Georgia O'Keeffe painting and the clean lines of Stickley or Greene & Greene Arts and Crafts furniture, a genteel Sargent portrait and Remington's snapping bronze, *The Bronco Buster.*

Going down one floor brings you to collections of Chinese and Korean art, with many pieces dating back thousands of years. There are sturdy bronze cauldrons and Buddhist statues, jade ceremonial objects, delicate porcelain, lacquerware, and painted scrolls.

Take the elevator up to the vast second floor, where you could easily lose yourself for several hours. While the collections of each period aren't especially deep, this floor covers a lot of ground, and in every room you should spot something cool. If you tackle the rooms in roughly chronological order, start with Egyptian tomb art, the walls of Assyrian reliefs from Iraq, circa 870 BC, and the collection of Iranian bronze ware that dates to 1350 BC. There are rooms full of the requisite Greek and Roman marble statuary and Greek red- and black-figure ceramics, followed by medieval European art (lots of altarpieces) and early Renaissance work, like della Robbia's terra cotta sculpture. Racing into the 17th and 18th centuries, you can spot Rembrandt portraits and softly melancholy paintings by Watteau. In a gallery devoted entirely to Rodin's sculpture, there's an interesting display on the process of creating a bronzed nude. You'll wind up in the late 19th century galleries, hung with Cézanne still lives and a few Impressionist works. Throughout the second floor, fine art is interspersed with decorative arts, such as glassware, ceramics, and enamels.

But save some energy for the beautiful collection of Islamic art on the third (and final) floor. Exhibits range from Koranic calligraphy to a beautiful stained-glass mosque lamp. Nearby is an equally impressive collection of South Asian art where you can surround yourself with statues of Hindu deities and examine intensely colored and detailed folios.

**PAVILION FOR JAPANESE ART** • Start your tour with the elevator, which takes you to the top floor while a voice-over explains that the gallery's lighting is designed to mimic the paper windows of a traditional Japanese home. The pavilion winds you gracefully down curving ramps, past arts and crafts that date from as early as the middle Jomon period (3000 BC) up to the early 20th century. The top floor is filled with drawings and paintings from the 19th century as well as Samurai armor, ceramics, bronze ware, and lacquer boxes from throughout Japanese history. Continuing down, you pass painted scrolls and screens that portray battle scenes and Zen vistas of paradise, *ukiyo-e* scenes of pleasure and careful nature studies. (These images should be "read" from right to left.) A fountain that runs the length of the bottom floor fills the building with the sound of falling water. At ground level is the Netsuke Gallery, which holds a collection of miniature figurines (called *netsuke*) used to clasp lacquer boxes, in lieu of pockets, to the sash of a kimono. These intricate sculptures, about the size of a baby's fist, range in material from wood to ivory and depict animals, humans, and dragons.

**THE FRANCES AND ARMAND HAMMER BUILDING** • Much of this wing contains rotating exhibits of modern art, crafts, and photography. The small permanent exhibit includes Impressionist and post-Impressionist works by big guys like Monet and Gauguin, the photography of W. Eugene Smith, works of German Expressionism, and late-19th-century European art. The temporary installations cover a lot of interesting ground, with recent examples including a show of Mexican artist Diego Rivera and an exclusive exhibit on Pompeii.

*If you've got a flexible schedule, keep an eye out for flyers begging for movie extras. You could spend a day or two on a film set as part of a background crowd, experience the often snail-like pace of filmmaking, and even make a little extra pocket money.*

**ROBERT O. ANDERSON BUILDING** • Although the bottom floor hosts changing contemporary exhibits, the top two floors have a permanent collection of 20th-century art. Take the elevator, the size of a modest artist's studio apartment, to the third floor to check out modern art from 1900 to 1970. You will see much-reproduced pieces by Pablo Picasso, Diego Rivera, Jackson Pollock, and L.A.'s own David Hockney. Of particular Hollywood note is the Steve Martin Gallery, devoted to the work of intrawar Europe, including Max Ernst and Rene Magritte. On the second floor, the post-1970 exhibit is as outlandish as you could hope, with a wall of flashing video screens by Nam June Paik, a Rachel Lachowicz sculpture of urinals made from lipstick, and Ed Kienholz's tableau, *The Back Seat Dodge '38*. Rooms are organized into themes like "Politics and Identity" and "The Performative"; there are plenty of art-world darlings like Cindy Sherman photos. When you get to Michael McMillen's re-creation of an old garage, go right in.

**THE LEO S. BING CENTER** • If all that art makes you hungry, you can get the usual overpriced museum food here. More important, you'll find the Bing Theater, one of L.A.'s best repertory movie houses (*see* Movie Houses *in* Chapter 5). Films screen here several nights a week, costing around $6, although prices vary. Call the museum for shows, times, and prices. The movies are grouped by theme; subjects of past festivals have included a Blake Edwards retrospective and new British films.

## THE MIRACLE MILE

Once a field of oil derricks, the strip of Wilshire Boulevard running from La Brea to Fairfax was developed in the 1920s as the world's first automobile-oriented shopping district. The towering buildings had large ground-floor windows whose displays were designed to seduce passing motorists, and all the stores provided parking. Although museums and office buildings have replaced most shops, a few relics of car-inspired architecture remain. A notable example is the former **May Company** department store, at the intersection of Wilshire and Fairfax, distinguished by the large gold silo on its corner. It's now known as LACMA West (*see* LACMA, *above*), and its windows showcase exhibits rather than gussied-up mannequins. Across Fairfax, **Johnie's** coffee shop holds true to its original function as well as form. Originally called Romeo's Times Square, Johnie's exemplifies the drive-up (as opposed to drive-in) diner, pioneered in Los Angeles, with its easy parking and large windows meant to convince cruisers to come in for a bite. Farther east, the **El Rey** theater (5515 Wilshire Blvd., between Fairfax and La Brea Aves., tel. 323/769–5500), now a nightclub, still stands as an example of the art deco style that once dominated the block. Save your shopping for Melrose or Rodeo Drive, but the Miracle Mile is still good for a joy ride en route to the museums.

# SCIENCE FICTION IN THE KITCHEN

*Sci-fi buffs will want to tour Forrest J. Ackerman's fab 300,000-piece collection of movie stills, costumes, props, and other unique artifacts, including the models for the Martian ships in "War of the Worlds," all housed in his Frank Lloyd Wright home in Los Feliz. Call 323/666–6326 for directions and dates of his free Saturday open houses. To reach his home, follow North Vermont Avenue into the hills to 2495 Glendower Avenue.*

## PETERSEN AUTOMOTIVE MUSEUM

Learn more about the Miracle Mile and nearly every other side effect of the car you can imagine at the Petersen—including the fact that since 1922 an average of over 30,000 Americans a year have lost their lives to road accidents. The first two floors are set up like a car show, with gleaming examples of motorized opulence, oddity, and celebrity. The top floor has educational exhibits on how cars work. Stroll from Clark Gable's Mercedes and Greta Garbo's 1925 Lincoln to the functioning car from the movie *The Flintstones*. If hot-rodding does it for you, peruse the sumptuously painted low riders, chop tops, and classic roadsters. The second floor has a roomful of Harleys that would make a Hell's Angel swoon. Even if cars are not your particular fetish, the ground floor of the museum is worthwhile for its artful display of the intertwined history of Los Angeles and the automobile. Had the streetcar not lost out to the automobile in a 1920s power struggle (see the movie *Who Framed Roger Rabbit?*), L.A. may not have evolved into the city of suburbs, billboards, and drive-in everything it is today. The museum gives careful attention to all kinds of automobile aftershocks, from TV shows and movies devoted to cars to youth culture's many four-wheeled mating rituals. *6060 Wilshire Blvd., at Fairfax Ave., tel. 323/930–2277. Admission $7. Open Tues.–Sun. 10–6.*

## ST. ELMO VILLAGE

South of Wilshire Boulevard off La Brea Avenue lies a Los Angeles anomaly: a village of artists who keep their doors open to the public in an attempt to create a sense of community within the concrete jungle. Founding village member Roderick Sykes encourages visitors to knock on his door at 4830 St. Elmo Drive at any time; he'll tell you if he's indisposed, and if he's not, he'll take the time to give you a tour of his utopian settlement and explain the principles behind the establishment of St. Elmo Village. Wander through the art-filled courtyard surrounded by 10 tiny brown-shingled houses, seven of which are home to the artist-teachers of the village. Every Saturday (10–1), the residents offer workshops in photography, painting, metal sculpture, and acting, primarily aimed at children but open to all interested parties. On Wednesday from 6 to 9 there's an additional artistic workshop geared for adults. Every Sunday is an open house, and on Memorial Day weekend they put on a festival celebrating art and community. Since the village's founding in 1969, its members have devoted themselves to transforming urban detritus into art and to encouraging the surrounding neighborhood to partake in the experience. Sykes expresses remorse that the world views his settlement as an "oasis" rather than the norm, but he notes that the village has increased the sense of community in a poor area where neighbors once avoided and feared one another. Come by to get creative on a Saturday or another time when the anonymity of Los Angeles and the corporate-sponsored art of the Miracle Mile and downtown threaten to sour you toward humanity. *4830 St. Elmo Dr., between Rimpau and La Brea Blvds., tel. 323/931–3409.*

## WILTERN THEATER

This towering turquoise building still functions as a theater, so if you want a look at its splendid art deco interior, you'll have to buy tickets to one of its frequent concerts or plays (*see* Chapter 5). If not, it's worth a drive-by or a walk-by to see the exterior's elaborate teal tiles, the massive carved-wood doors with ornate silver borders, and the distinctive neon sign. Outside the ticket booth you can look at the black-and-white photographs of the interior and decide if it's worth an evening of cultural inundation to see the goods firsthand. *3790 Wilshire Blvd., at Western Ave., tel. 213/380–5005.*

# BEVERLY HILLS

Set like an opulent gem in the surrounding encrusted ring—historic Hollywood, flamboyant West Hollywood, futuristic Century City—the wealthy reality of Beverly Hills is a dream to most and enjoyed by a fairly invisible but well-known few. This is one of the few remaining locales where flaunting your riches isn't considered gauche. Most tourists come here to shop; for comprehensive coverage of spots to blow your summer savings, *see* Shopping by Neighborhood *in* Chapter 7. Walking the sterile sidewalks outside the Golden Triangle (Wilshire Boulevard, Little Santa Monica Boulevard, and Cañon Drive; *see below*) has been known to attract the attention of Beverly Hills's finest; the area is often referred to as "the best-policed six square miles on earth." This is also prime Star Map territory, but before you shell out $5–$10 to a roadside vendor, realize that most maps are outdated, and famous estates are usually hidden behind imposing walls. Just across Sunset Boulevard from the Beverly Hills Hotel, you'll find the city's other golden triangle, tranquil Will Rogers Memorial Park, filled with fountains and fishponds.

Architectural landmarks include the renovated Spanish baroque city hall and the more contemporary Spanish Deco Civic Center (both on the corner of Rexford Dr. and Santa Monica Blvd.), the cantilevered Union 76 Gas Station (Rexford Dr. at Little Santa Monica Blvd.), and the noble 1933 Italian Renaissance U.S. Post Office building (9300 Santa Monica Blvd., between Crescent and Cañon Drs.), whose interior walls are covered by Depression-era WPA murals. And for something a little more unusual, check out the "witch's house" at Walden Drive and Carmelita Avenue; the steep-roofed house looks like something from a *Hansel and Gretel* set. The Beverly Hills Visitors Bureau (239 S. Beverly Dr., between Charleville Blvd. and Gregory Way, tel. 310/248–1015) hands out free maps; ask them where to catch the free Beverly Hills Trolley for a tour of downtown.

*A fabulous photo op: Tail o' the Pup (329 N. San Vicente Blvd., at Beverly Blvd., tel. 310/652–4517), a restaurant shaped like a hot dog, complete with mustard. Sit down and have a frank.*

Although the subway doesn't reach into Beverly Hills, you can take Bus 20 along Wilshire Boulevard. It's as close to Beverly Hills as you'll get without a car. Parking in this incorporated city is fairly easy; many streets have meters.

*See the West Hollywood, Beverly Hills, and the Westside map.*

## ACADEMY OF MOTION PICTURE ARTS AND SCIENCES

The exhibitions of movie accoutrements here—from animation cells to props and costumes—will teach you more about the industry than many of Burbank's whiz-bang studio tours. Recent exhibitions have included an anniversary show of Alfred Hitchcock materials: production designs, scripts, advertisements, costumes, and correspondence. *8949 Wilshire Blvd., Beverly Hills, tel. 310/247–3600. Admission free. Open Tues.–Fri. 10–5, weekends noon–6.*

## BEIT HASHOAH MUSEUM OF TOLERANCE

The Museum of Tolerance takes on the unenviable task of trying to make the MTV generation think about the Holocaust. To this end, they engage hundreds of flickering television monitors flashing with jump-cut videos, along with life-size dioramas, voice-overs, and interactive exhibits, in place of traditional artifacts and placards. One half of the museum addresses contemporary examples of intolerance, ranging from the L.A. riots to the war in Bosnia, while the other half focuses exclusively on the Holocaust.

The contemporary section is self-guided and interactive: You can choose which parts of the events leading up to the 1992 riots to watch on video, pausing after each segment to answer questions about race, class, and prejudice, and then compare your answers to those of previous museum visitors. Or you can walk through a dark hallway while a disembodied voice hisses derogatory epithets at you ("Fag! Nigger! Chink!") and signs urge you to "think. . . think twice. . . now don't say it." There are short films on contemporary ethnic violence throughout the world and on the civil rights movement of the 1950s and '60s. At every turn the contemporary exhibits draw parallels between intolerance in modern America and the mentality that allowed the Nazis to exterminate 6 million Jews. It's preachy, but it gets the message across.

The second half of the museum is a fully automated, guided tour through exhibits on the Holocaust. You walk past dioramas depicting between-the-wars Germany, displays of anti-Semitic propaganda, and finally through the doors of a simulated concentration camp chamber. Throughout the 65-minute tour

# WEST HOLLYWOOD, BEVERLY HILLS, AND THE WESTSIDE

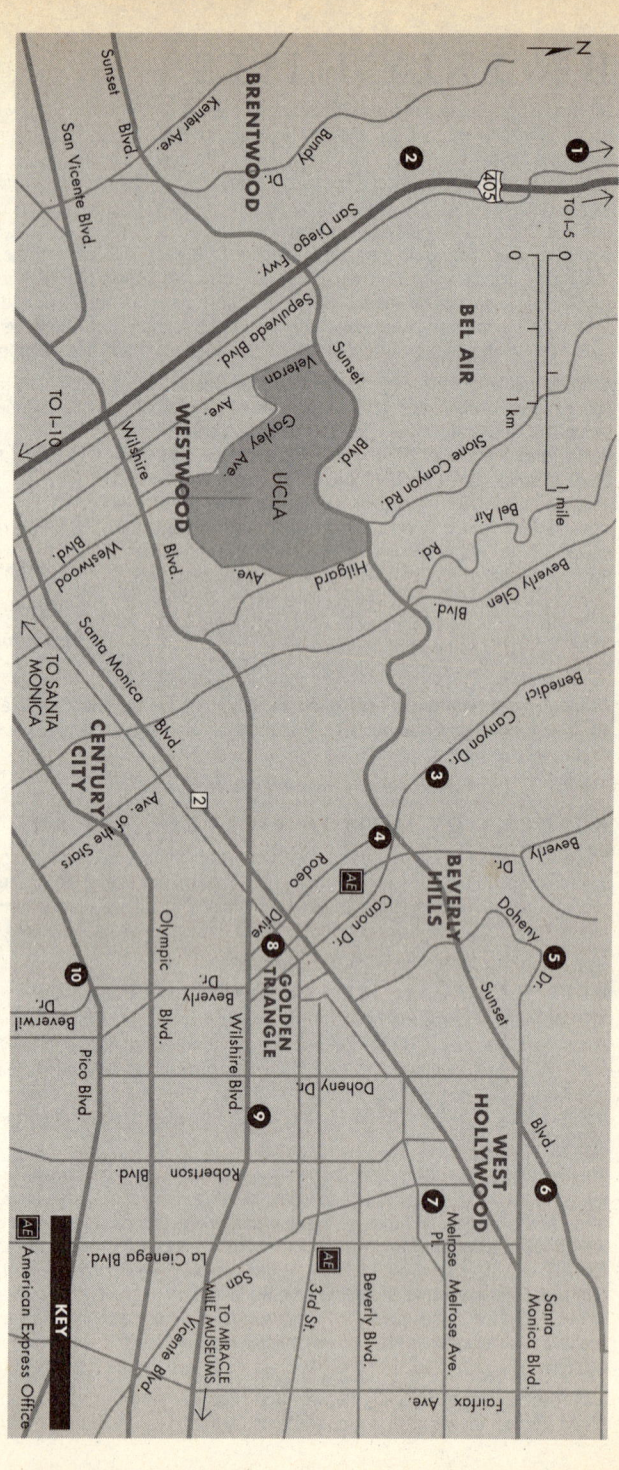

60

voice-overs expound on the history of the years preceding the Holocaust. To further illustrate the events, you're given a child's photo "passport"; while going through the exhibit you learn more about the child's fate. The museum's second floor uses multimedia workstations for on-the-spot education sessions on the war, the Holocaust, German politics, and much more; and the third floor has the only examples of traditional museum artifacts, ranging from Jewish religious objects confiscated by the Nazis to concentration camp uniforms. If you already know a lot about the Holocaust, you may find the museum superficial and its exhibits both flashy and pedantic. Nonetheless, by aligning the Holocaust with more familiar examples of hatred, the museum makes a good stab at promoting tolerance, especially among the young and the easily bored. Reservations are a good idea; also note that the museum closes on Jewish holidays. *9786 W. Pico Blvd., at Roxbury Dr., near Beverly Hills, tel. 310/553– 8403. Admission $8.50. Open Mon.–Thurs. 10–4, Fri. 10–3, Sun. 10:30–6.30.*

## BEVERLY HILLS HOTEL

Known as the Pink Palace, this landmark hotel has come to symbolize good service and the city's hedonistic lifestyle. This fine example of Spanish Colonial Revival architecture is considered the city's first citizen—it opened in 1912, two years prior to incorporation. It has the requisite celebrity status; the reclusive Garbo once lived here, and its Polo Lounge still buzzes with deal-cutting. You can furtively explore the lush acres of tropical gardens under the pretense of eating breakfast in the all-pink coffee shop. *9641 Sunset Blvd., between Beverly and Rodeo Drs., tel. 310/276–2251 or 800/283–8885.*

## CENTURY CITY

If this is the prototypical city of the future, then prepare yourself for a sterile, dehumanizing 21st century. Century City is strictly business. Once the fabled back lot of Twentieth Century Fox, the only remaining attraction of any note is the **ABC Entertainment Center,** on the Avenue of the Stars, home to the **Shubert Theatre** (tel. 310/201–1558) and the **Cineplex Odeon Century Plaza Cinemas** (tel. 310/ 553–4291). The Cineplex's 600-seat Theater Two is one of the best places in the city to take in a first-run movie. The theaters validate tickets for reduced parking lot fees, but rates are still exorbitant during the business day. If you come for a matinee, think about ditching your car in the **Century City Shopping Center** lots (10250 Little Santa Monica Blvd., at Century Park W, tel. 310/277–3898), which allow three free hours, and then walking to the theater. Century City's one nod to culture and history is the Beit Hashoah Museum of Tolerance (*see above*).

## GOLDEN TRIANGLE AND RODEO DRIVE

Beverly Hills's famous retail area—bounded by **Wilshire Boulevard, Cañon Drive,** and **Little Santa Monica Boulevard**—is affectionately known as the Golden Triangle by the sort of people who shower affection on expensive clothes. The showpiece **Rodeo Drive** (pronounced ro-*day*-oh) is frequently and mistakenly compared to other famous shopping strips—Madison Avenue in New York, for example, or Rue de Faubourg St.-Honoré. Paris it is not; on Rodeo the tacky, banal architecture does disservice to the famous designers' opulent window displays. Shopping in the Rodeo's by-appointment-only boutiques is best left to the high-muck-a-mucks and Saudi sheiks, but the people-watching from outdoor patios of several restaurants is top drawer (*see* Beverly Hills and Century City *in* Chapter 3). Haute couture designers and jewelers like Armani, Bijan, Cartier, and Yves St. Laurent attract plenty of filthy-rich stars with their limo drivers in tow, but the best way to soak up the cheeky atmosphere is on foot.

## GREYSTONE MANSION

Beverly Hills's Doheny Drive is named for oilman Edward Doheny, the original owner of this 55-room Tudor-style manor, which was built in 1927. Films like Jack Nicholson's *The Witches of Eastwick* and *Indecent Proposal* were filmed on the expansive grounds. The gardens are open for self-guided tours, some areas are designated for picnicking, and free concerts are held sporadically in the mansion's courtyard on summer afternoons. *905 Loma Vista Dr., tel. 310/550–4796. Admission free. Open Apr.–Oct., daily 10–6; Nov.–Mar., daily 10–5.*

## MUSEUM OF TELEVISION AND RADIO

This handsome museum perfectly illustrates the primary paradox of television: It makes the world smaller while isolating its inhabitants from one another. The museum is divided into a library and several screening rooms; a small exhibit area at the front displays costumes from *Star Trek: The Next Generation* and the like. If you feel like a communal experience, check out one of the several screenings of historic TV episodes, advertisements, and news broadcasts available that day. In the library (really a room filled with computers next to a room filled with TV monitors), you can enjoy the eerie experience of sitting in a room with dozens of other headphone-wearing people, each watching his or her own TV.

You can use the computers to search the index of the museum's collection of 75,000 TV shows, radio programs, and advertisements, select three at a time, and then ask the librarian to call them up on the video monitors next door and enjoy up to two hours of solitary nostalgia. Make sure you specify that you want to use the library when you buy your ticket: A library ticket will allow you access to the screening rooms, but a regular ticket for the same price mysteriously will not admit you to the library. *465 N. Beverly Dr., at Little Santa Monica Blvd., Beverly Hills, tel. 310/786–1000. Suggested donation: $6. Open Wed. and Fri.–Sun. noon–5, Thurs. noon–9.*

## PICKFAIR MANSION

Benedict Canyon Drive is hallowed ground for star-tour aficionados, not the least for Pickfair (1143 Summit Drive), the legendary haunt established by Mary Pickford and Douglas Fairbanks, Sr., in 1919. The major players of the movie industry followed on Pickford's and Fairbanks's coattails, and Benedict Canyon—once just lima bean fields—quickly became the fashionable neighborhood of Hollywood's biggest stars. The famous Tudor mansion itself is hardly visible from the street, but you can glimpse the impressive surrounding grounds through the gates. If you continue farther up the canyon, you'll pass the Manson murder site, whose address has been changed from 10050 Cielo Drive to 10048 in an attempt to confuse gawkers. For more locales of famous fatalities, *see* Stars, Sets, and Death Sites, *below.*

# THE WESTSIDE

In the districts west of La Cienega, including Westwood, Brentwood, and Bel Air, a platinum card seems like the common denominator. But luckily there's more to absorb here than gossip from personal trainers—there are also excellent art collections, with the fantastic Getty Center as the King of the Hill.

The pedestrian-friendly (!) streets of Westwood Village teem with well-scrubbed kids from the University of California at Los Angeles (UCLA) out spending their parents' money. The area is also the center of a large expatriate Iranian community. Tidy Brentwood has a dark streak in its polish: The Simpson/Goldman double murder occurred here in 1995, as did Marilyn Monroe's drug overdose in 1962 (*see* Stars, Sets, and Death Sites, *below*).

It can be hard to find parking here during the week; there are several validated parking lots in Westwood Village, but you'll have to look for something streetside in Brentwood. Though the subway doesn't reach this far, you can take bus 20, or the express bus 320, down Wilshire Boulevard from downtown. From Santa Monica, take the Big Blue Bus number 14. To get to the Getty Center, take bus 561.

*See the West Hollywood, Beverly Hills, and the Westside map.*

## GETTY CENTER

If any museum could make nonchalant Angelenos lose their cool and sputter a few exclamations, this is it. The Getty Center is the new home of much of the art collection of the late oil billionaire J. Paul Getty, as well as a center for art scholarship, education, and conservation. The gleaming museum roosts above the city, surrounded by gorgeous grounds and drinking in stunning views. Unfortunately, the depth of the collections often lags. It's no Metropolitan, but the total experience of the architecture, gardens, educational resources, and vistas should take up the slack.

Getty began collecting art in the 1930s, concentrating on three distinct areas: Greek and Roman antiquities, Baroque and Renaissance paintings, and 18th-century decorative arts. Until 1997, the entire collection was kept in the J. Paul Getty Villa in Malibu (*see below*), which is now being renovated to house only the antiquities.

The dramatic, new Richard Meier–designed museum is organized as a series of pavilions around an outdoor courtyard. The buildings' geometric exteriors are textured with rough-cut travertine; at dusk, the sunset light seems to saturate the stone. Channels and reflecting pools mark the courtyard; from here you can scrutinize the city and ocean views before heading down into the central garden.

Exhibits draw from both the permanent collection and traveling shows. The museum has added collections of drawings, photography, manuscripts, and European sculpture to Getty's own foci. If you can resist the distractions of the views, explore highlights like the Italian Renaissance and French Impressionist paintings (Fra Bartolommeo's *The Holy Family*, van Gogh's *Irises*), American photography, or the pair of reconstructed, 18th-century, French salons. The complex also includes an auditorium, a conservation institute with scientific labs and training facilities, and a research institute with library and archives.

The catch, however, is getting in. If you plan to drive, you must make a reservation for a parking space well in advance (we're talking weeks, not days). If you take a bus or a cab, you may have to wait in line and, worst-case scenario, there's the possibility of being turned away. Once you're admitted, a tram shuttles you up the hill to the complex. *1200 Getty Center Dr., Brentwood, tel. 310/440–7300. Admission free; $5 parking fee. Open Tues.–Wed. 11–7, Thurs.–Fri. 11–9, weekends 10–6.*

## SKIRBALL CULTURAL CENTER AND MUSEUM

The permanent exhibit at the lavish Skirball Cultural Center (just above Bel Air) showcases artifacts from throughout Jewish history, starting with the old temple in Jerusalem, and tracing the Diaspora (dispersion) of the Jewish people to Spain, North Africa, China, Eastern Europe, and eventually the United States. You can see a beer jug from ancient Israel, costumes of the Tunisian Jews, and a reconstruction of the New Synagogue in Berlin (destroyed during the Nazi pogrom *Kristallnacht* [Night of the Broken Glass] in 1938). Most objects are from immigrants to the United States between the 17th century and the 1880s. There is a model of the gateway to New York's Ellis Island (through which most East Coast immigrants passed), a diorama of an immigrant's kitchen from the turn of the century, and video clips of Jews describing what it means to be Jewish in 20th-century America. The cultural center offers classroom and conference space to interested parties and a simulated ancient archaeological dig for schoolchildren. *2701 N. Sepulveda Blvd., at Mulholland Dr., Bel Air, tel. 310/440–4500. Admission $8. Open Tues.–Sat. noon–5, Sun. 11–5.*

## WESTWOOD VILLAGE/UCLA CAMPUS

*UCLA served as a poor stand-in for the U.C. Berkeley campus during the filming of The Graduate.*

The sprawling campus is defined by Gayley and Veteran avenues to the west, Sunset Boulevard to the north, Hilgard Avenue to the east, and Le Conte Avenue and Westwood Village to the south. Most extracurricular action takes place on **Broxton Avenue,** which is lined with shops and eateries catering to students on the lam, as well as 10—count 'em, 10—deluxe movie houses, including a few palaces dating from the golden age of theater design. Built in 1931 and now part of the Mann chain, the vintage **Village** (961 Broxton Ave., tel. 310/208–5576) retains its original flourishes and boasts a 70-ft-wide screen, a dynamic sound system, and a romantic balcony. Erected in 1970, the **National** (10925 Linbrook Ave., at Westwood Blvd., tel. 310/208–4366) is the youngest large single-screen theater in the city. Weekend lines for exclusive engagements have been known to give rise to small-scale riots, but Westwood remains one of the few places in L.A. where you can still experience the thrill of an opening-night premiere. Before checking out the campus, stop by **Diddy Riese** (926 Broxton Ave., at Le Conte Ave., tel. 310/208–0448) for a 25¢ cookie.

Worthwhile on-campus stops include the **Ackerman Student Union,** which has a well-stocked bookstore and a ride-share board; the **Tree House** (main level), a popular place to pick up a snack; and the **Morgan Center** sporting Hall of Fame, where athletic memorabilia and trophies are on display. Architecturally notable are the original Romanesque **Royce Hall** and **Powell Library** structures, which have survived many a trembler. Throughout the school year the Department of Film and Television sponsors screenings from its extensive archives, in **Melnitz Hall** (tel. 310/206–3456). The **University Research Library**'s fascinating film-oriented collection is also open to the public. The **Fowler Museum of Cultural History** (tel. 310/825–4361) hosts well-curated rotating exhibits of non-Western art. Admission is $5 (free Thursday), and it's open Wednesday and Friday–Sunday noon–5, Thursday noon–8. Free 90-minute campus walking tours are conducted weekdays at 10:30 and 1:30. There is some free street parking near campus along Wilshire, Hilgard, Weyburn, and Gayley avenues. You can get a free campus map from the drive-by kiosk, just past the main entrance on Westwood Plaza Drive. Free off-site parking and shuttles are available on busy summer evenings at the Federal Building (Wilshire Blvd. and Veteran Ave.) when streets in Westwood Village are closed to car traffic. *Exit I–405 east at Wilshire Blvd. and follow signs to Westwood Blvd. Turn left into Westwood Village and cross Le Conte Ave. to campus parking lots ($5). Tel. 310/825–4321 for UCLA switchboard, 310/206–0616 for visitor center.*

**FRANKLIN D. MURPHY SCULPTURE GARDEN** • Don't miss the opportunity to stroll among the more than 50 modern works, including pieces by Jacques Lipchitz, Gaston Lachaise, Matisse, and Rodin, in this outdoor garden in the heart of the north campus. Free guided walking tours of the garden are available weekdays by making a reservation through the campus Art Council (tel. 310/825–3264), or you can pick up a free self-guided walking brochure at a campus information booth.

**WIGHT ART GALLERY** • Behind the sculpture garden, this museum mounts exhibits of work by UCLA students; you could find paintings, sculpture, or multimedia pieces. *Tel. 310/825–9287. Admission free. Open Tues.–Fri. 11–5, weekends 1–5.*

**ARMAND HAMMER MUSEUM OF ART AND CULTURAL CENTER** • The permanent collection at this richly endowed museum, just south of campus, includes oils by van Gogh, Cassatt, Rubens, Monet, and Rembrandt, as well as some original manuscripts penned by Leonardo da Vinci; and an extensive collection of satirical works by 19th-century French lithographer and sculptor Honoré Daumier. More intriguing are the exhibitions curated from the critically acclaimed Grunwald Center for the Graphic Arts collection, which includes works by Albrecht Dürer, Cézanne, and Jasper Johns. The Hammer also sponsors free outdoor summer cultural events, including a potpourri of jazz and world-beat musicians, special children's workshops, and symposia. Validated parking in the museum garage is $2.75. *10899 Wilshire Blvd., at Westwood Blvd., tel. 310/443– 7000. Admission $4.50, free Thurs. after 6. Open Tues.–Wed. and Fri.–Sat. 11–7, Thurs. 11–9, Sun. 11–5. Free docent tour daily at 1.*

**MILDRED MATHIAS BOTANICAL GARDEN** • Nestled in the southeast section of campus, off Tiverton Avenue at the corner of Hilgard and Le Conte avenues, this garden is home to a diverse group of unusual and well-labeled botanicals, which are conveniently divided by region. Unlike the other campus sights, it's closed during university holidays. *Tel. 310/825–1260. Admission free. Open weekdays 8–5, weekends 8–4.*

# MALIBU

Most people associate Malibu with wealth and fame, but recently, its image has been tarnished by natural disasters. It suffered badly from the 1994 Northridge earthquake, then from fire, then mud slides in the heavy rains of 1995; three years later, El Niño battered its coastline. Angelenos, however, know the area is still filled with natural splendors. Some of the finest beaches and most dramatic hills in the L.A. area are found amid Malibu's 27 MILES OF SCENIC BEAUTY (as promised when you cross the border on Pacific Coast Highway—PCH). Although many of its residential neighborhoods are exclusive and gated, anyone who makes the trip north will have access to the beaches and to many of the spectacular inland roads.

Founded by Spanish rancheros, Malibu was taken over by land baron Frederick Rindge, whose widow started the area's members-only tradition by building a private railroad in hopes of preventing a public one from accessing her home. In 1929, however, PCH made it possible for all kinds of riffraff to enjoy Malibu, as they continue to do today. Although stars and the anonymous wealthy still seclude themselves in such protected enclaves as the famous Malibu Colony (it's off Malibu Road east of Webb Way, in case you secure yourself an invite), the beaches and strip malls are filled with all kinds of normal folk, including a disproportionate number of hippies and surfers. Indeed, if Malibu were not known for its famous residents or its scenery, it would still be noted for some of the best surfing in the United States. Even the earliest inhabitants, the Chumash Indians, enjoyed a surfing of sorts in their large wooden canoes, and today Malibu is second only to Orange County (some would say it's first) as the preferred surfing locale in southern California. So even if none of the historical sights, such as the Paramount Ranch or Adamson's House, appeals to you, come to Malibu to enjoy the beaches and watch an awesome display of surf culture.

Malibu is most easily reached by heading north from Santa Monica on PCH. You can also take a nice drive on Sunset Boulevard due west till you hit PCH right on the Santa Monica–Pacific Palisades border. Head right (north) to reach Malibu. Most of the town's commercial life centers around PCH; look for coastal access signs as you drive. Some interior roads are private, but others are open to all and make for beautiful drives through the rolling coastal hills. Parking is somewhat scarce; try the lot on the corner of PCH and Sunset Boulevard, next to Gladstone's restaurant. To get to Malibu by bus, take the 20 or 320 down Wilshire Boulevard and transfer to the 434 heading north up Ocean Avenue.

## ADAMSON HOUSE

Owned by the neighborhood's first Anglos, the Rindge family (whose daughter married an Adamson and lived here), the Adamson House is an early example of the enviable lifestyle of the Malibu elite. Its beautifully landscaped lawns and gardens lead right up to the **Malibu Lagoon** and **Malibu Surfrider Beach** (*see* Chapter 6). The Rindges were famous as the owners of the Malibu Potteries, and you can see vividly colored tiles in the Spanish Moorish–revival style inside and outside the home. You can arrange for a tour or poke around the house and the grounds on your own. Inside you'll find a short exhibit on the history of Malibu. Crowded with photos and tiny captions, it's not the most thoughtfully designed display, but it does contain important tidbits from Malibu's colorful history, including information on the area's protosurfers, the Chumash Indians, and a who's who of the movie business. Try to find parking on PCH, or you will have to pay a $6 fee at the lot. *23200 PCH, at Malibu Lagoon State Park, tel. 310/456–8432. Admission $2. Open Wed.–Sat. 11–3.*

## BEACHES

All right, let's skip the culture and cut to the chase: You've come to Malibu to laze about at the beach. Although you can't go wrong hitting any of the coastal access spots off PCH, different beaches have different strong points. **Malibu Surfrider Beach,** as the name suggests, is the best place to watch a free surf show. Make sure your skills are up to snuff if you decide to hit the swells (*see* Surfing *in* Chapter 6). You can also enjoy the birds and wetlands of **Malibu Lagoon State Beach** (23200 PCH, tel. 818/880–0350), and there are nice walks both up and down the coast. Park along PCH if at all possible; otherwise you'll have to spend $6 at the pay lots. If you head to the **Malibu Seafood Patio Cafe** (*see* Pacific Palisades and Malibu *in* Chapter 3), you will find yourself across the street from **Coral Beach,** a narrow strip of sand that is one of the more low-key sunning spots in Malibu. Perhaps the most popular beach is **Zuma,** about 6 mi north of Malibu's commercial center. The remarkably wide beach stretches literally for miles, so even if it's crowded, you can strike out to find yourself some space. Again, try parking on PCH or on one of the nearby side streets (you can enter the pay lot and exit onto Westward Beach Road, which sometimes has spots) to avoid a $6 fee. The northern tip of Zuma, known as **El Matador,** tends to have some nude bathers, weather permitting. Just south of Zuma is **Point Dume,** a beautiful state park, usually among the least crowded Malibu beaches. You'll have to pay a $5-per-vehicle fee; leave your car behind and hike to the park.

## THE GETTY VILLA

You can only gaze from afar at the imitation Roman villa that houses part of J. Paul Getty's massive collection of classical art because the facility will be closed for remodeling until the year 2002. Go instead to the Getty Center, off I–405 (*see* The Westside, *above*), to see all the post-Greek and post-Roman work and a smattering of his ancient sculptures, pottery and jewelry collection. Still, the exterior of this Malibu museum is worth a glance as you drive by on PCH. *17985 PCH, between Sunset and Topanga Canyon Blvds.*

## PARAMOUNT RANCH

If you don't want to spend your money on a studio tour, you can see a Wild West facade for free at the hot and dusty Paramount Ranch. Originally the locale for shoots of Paramount westerns, the site was also used for the filming of the hit TV series *Dr. Quinn: Medicine Woman*; fans of the show will recognize the church and the graveyard. Other than that, there's not a lot happening here. There are a few walking trails around the ranch that might make the trip worthwhile; ask at the ranger station for more information. (Then again, it might be worth paying for the Paramount tour in Hollywood, where you'll get a cute guide with two hours' worth of anecdotes.) *Tel. 805/370–2300. Take U.S. 101 to Agoura Hills, exit at Kanan Rd., go south to Cornell, and turn left; ranch is 2½ mi on right. Admission free. Open daily sunrise–sunset.*

## PEPPERDINE UNIVERSITY

Also known as Surfer U., Pepperdine does not have the most sterling reputation among Angelenos, who see the school as a place where celebrity spawn can buy a diploma. The university had a close brush with Whitewater independent counsel Kenneth Starr in 1998; Starr accepted, postponed, and then reneged on the deanship of its law and public policy schools. Starr was not only embroiled with his investigation at the time, but facing down accusations of a conflict of interest, since the school is heavily funded by a conservative, anti-Clinton muckraker. Pepperdine wouldn't be a bad place to spend your college years, however—set as it is on beautiful rolling hills above the Pacific. It's a Christian university, and as such has rules against what many college students see as rites of passage: inappropriate clothing, drinking, and staying out all night; dancing wasn't allowed on campus until 1989. Technically, the school is not open to the public, but if you tell the security guard you just want to take a look, he or she will probably oblige you. The modern buildings aren't much to look at, but the grounds are pretty, and you can't argue with those gorgeous ocean views. *Intersection of PCH and Malibu Canyon Rd.*

## SELF-REALIZATION FELLOWSHIP LAKE SHRINE

Although the name is a bit of a mouthful to use as a mantra, the Self-Realization Fellowship Lake Shrine is just the place to focus on your Christ center (the area between your eyes) and to forget your earthly woes for a while. The inexperienced meditator may find the crowded conditions a little distracting, but whether you achieve self-realization or not (it is, after all, a tall order for one afternoon), you will probably enjoy the walk around the lake, where you will find representations of Christianity, Judaism, Islam, Buddhism, and Hinduism, as well as some structures that defy explanation, like a replica of a Dutch windmill. Throughout there are benches with people at various stages of achieving their own bliss, and there is an indoor meditation chapel if you find that all that nature and sunshine takes your mind off your maker. The Self-Realization Fellowship was founded in 1920 by Paramahansa Yogananda, who came to the United States to spread meditation for the purpose of "attaining direct personal experience of God." Today his work is continued by a white American disciple known as Sri Daya Mata. Even if meditation is not your cup of dharma, the shrine provides an interesting historical perspective on California's New Age movement. *17190 Sunset Blvd., ½ mi north of PCH, Pacific Palisades, tel. 310/454–4114. Admission free. Open Tues.–Sat. 9–4:30, Sun. 12:30–4:30.*

## WILL ROGERS STATE PARK

Come discover why cowboy-philosopher Will Rogers was one of the most beloved public figures of his day by visiting the museum that was once his Pacific Palisades ranch. Start your tour by watching a 12-minute movie on his life, including his early years in Oklahoma, where he learned to rope steers so well that Hollywood later deemed his skills worthy of whole motion pictures. Indeed, the footage of Rogers doing a figure-eight loop around a galloping horse and its rider is impressive. Although Rogers made several silent movies, they were not the right vehicle to display his full talents, because it was ultimately his witticisms that made him most famous. It is hard to imagine people believing a star who said, "I never met a man I didn't like," but Rogers made it sound credible. Proceed from the screening room to the Rogers family home, where you can either embark on a one-hour recorded tour of the house and grounds or wait for one of the elderly volunteer docents to explain the significance of all the furnishings. He reportedly raised the roof several feet to accommodate his penchant for practicing his roping techniques indoors. You can also view the still-in-operation polo grounds (games weekends only). One of the park's nicest features is the 2-mi loop **Inspiration Point Trail** (*see* Hiking *in* Chapter 6), which begins behind the stables and gives you a view of the ocean. *1501 Will Rogers State Park Rd., off Sunset Blvd., Pacific Palisades, tel. 310/454–8212. Admission $6 per vehicle. Open daily 8–sunset. House tours daily, hourly on the half hour 10:30–4:30.*

# SANTA MONICA

Santa Monica is an ironic mixture of beach town and urban blight. On Main Street crowds of cappuccino drinkers read the *New York Times* and bask in the glow of their own success, but on strips of beach near the pier, a scruffier throng makes the potential for getting mugged almost as good as that for getting a tan. The pedestrian-only Third Street Promenade is a major magnet; it's easy to fritter away a few hours by shopping, snacking, and people-gawking.

Luckily, there are plenty of parking lots, though you may have to fork over $10 or more on weekends. There's also metered parking near the Third Street Promenade. If you've got to rely on public transportation, you can take buses 20 or 320 from downtown to Santa Monica. Within Santa Monica and Venice the Santa Monica Municipal Bus Lines, commonly known as the Big Blue Buses (tel. 310/451–5444) operate a comprehensive local service. *See also* Bus Travel within Los Angeles *in* Chapter 1.

*See the Santa Monica and Venice map.*

## BERGAMOT STATION

Where can you find more than 30 world-class galleries and design studios clustered together? Behind the Santa Monica city recycling and toxic waste recovery headquarters in a restored railroad depot, of course. Most avant-garde studios here are open Tuesday–Saturday from about 10 to 6. They often collaborate to curate shows expanding on current exhibitions showing in the county museums. Some more notable spaces include: the **Craig Krull** photo gallery (tel. 310/828–6410), the **Shoshana Wayne Gallery** (tel. 310/453–7535) and performance space, the ingenious **Gallery of Functional Art** (tel. 310/829–6990), **Track 16** (tel. 310/264–4678), and the **Robert Berman Gallery** (tel. 310/315–9506). It's also the home of the **Santa Monica Museum of Art** (tel. 310/586– 6488), which mounts unusual exhibits of contemporary paintings and video art, not to mention interactive performance art shows. On Friday evening, the museum hosts a salon, where artists lecture on contemporary art issues, and every Wednesday night throughout the summer, free movies are screened in the parking lot. The museum admission is

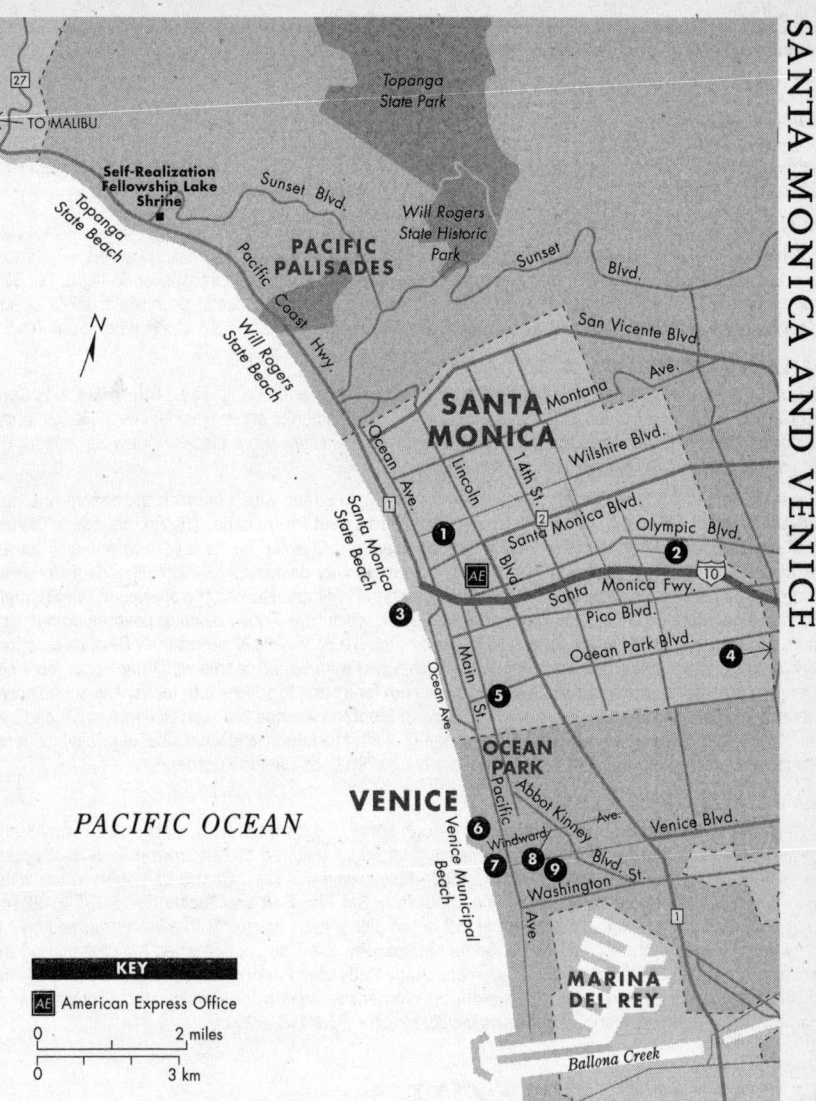

**SANTA MONICA AND VENICE**

**KEY**

AE American Express Office

0 — 2 miles
0 — 3 km

Bergamot
Station, **2**

California Heritage
Museum, **5**

Canals, **9**

Muscle Beach, **6**

Museum of
Flying, **4**

Santa Monica
Pier, **3**

Third Street
Promenade, **1**

Venice
Boardwalk, **7**

Windward Ave., **8**

67

$3. *2525 Michigan Ave., at Cloverfield Blvd., north of I–10, Santa Monica, tel. 310/829–5854. Admission free. Museum open Tues.–Sat. 11–6.*

## CALIFORNIA HERITAGE MUSEUM

If you're interested in Golden State history, step into this 1894 American colonial revival home. Rotating displays of California history are on the second floor; the first floor has rooms furnished in turn-of-the-century styles. *2612 Main St., at Ocean Park Blvd., tel. 310/392–8537. Admission $3. Open Wed.–Sat. 11–4, Sun. noon–4.*

## MUSEUM OF FLYING

If fighter planes get your blood pumping, here you can check out Spitfires, Sopwith Camels, jet fighters, and the 1986 *Voyager,* the first plane to make a nonstop, unrefueled around-the-world flight. For $2 a shot you can fly in a simulation ride; the stomach-turning Tornado is not to be missed. *2772 Donald Douglas Loop N, at Santa Monica Airport, tel. 310/392–8822. Admission $7. Open Wed.–Sun. 10–5.*

## MAIN STREET AND INLAND

Beyond the beach Santa Monica is a mecca of small galleries and shops. The **18th Street Arts Complex** (1639 18th St., at Olympic Blvd., tel. 310/453–3711) includes artists' residences, galleries, and a performance space that often hosts gay and lesbian events. A few more blocks northwest, look for the art gallery complex **Bergamot Station** (*see above*).

Two inland areas lend themselves to people-watching. Main Street, which parallels the beachfront, runs into Santa Monica Place, a mall which leads to the **Third Street Promenade.** The Promenade, a Disney-fied version of hip, is worth a quick walk-through (*see also* Chapter 7). It's a pedestrians-only bazaar between Wilshire Boulevard and Broadway, lined with topiary dinosaurs that look like giant Chia Pets and Generation X chain stores like Z Gallerie and Urban Outfitters. Browse the shelves in the **Midnight Special Bookstore** (1318 3rd St., tel. 310/393–2923), which has Friday-evening poetry readings (*see* Cheap Thrills, *below*). **Benita's Frites** (1437 3rd St., tel. 310/458–2889) serves tasty Belgian-style fries with dipping sauces like peanut curry satay. Within two minutes of people-watching here, you'll see everyone from sunburned tourists to older couples out for a stroll to sullen Goth teens. The scene grows increasingly sophisticated as you move north toward **Montana Avenue** between Ocean Avenue and Lincoln Boulevard. Shops here sell artsy jewelry, one-of-a-kind furniture, and whimsical (if pricey) clothing. Montana's intersection with 7th Street is popularly referred to as Caffeine Corner.

## SANTA MONICA PIER

This is one of the main tourist destinations, though some find the popularity of its arcade games and greasy fast-food stands unfathomable. Here you can ride a restored 1922 carousel for 50¢; it's open June–September, Tuesday–Sunday and October–May, weekends only. Or you can stare at the water while holding a fishing pole rented for $3 an hour from **SM Pier Bait and Tackle** (tel. 310/576–2014). In the Pacific Park amusement area at the foot of the pier, a roller coaster with a 30-ft drop and an 11-story Ferris wheel afford a great view of Santa Monica Bay. Exercise caution when hanging around the pier after dark. You also can stroll the adjacent shady **Palisades Park** or rent Rollerblades (*see* In-Line Skating *in* Chapter 6) and cruise the waterfront promenade. Watch for people with clipboards—they may be studio flunkies distributing free movie tickets. *Tel. 310/458–8900.*

# VENICE BEACH

The world's greatest free freak show and amorphous open-air carnival runs daily at Venice Beach, just south of Santa Monica. Exhibitionists of all stripes strut their stuff for fun or for profit along the Venice Boardwalk. Chain-saw juggling and bench pressing mix with a little roller disco, while one brave (or is he crazy?) soul walks on broken glass. Street musicians compete with psychics for your money and attention, and you can always don your Lycra and Rollerblades and join the show. To enter the thick of it (which is, after all, why you go to Venice in the first place), start at the Windward Avenue murals and head south along Ocean Front Walk (also known as the Boardwalk) past the palm readers and one-man bands. Continue down toward 18th Street to witness the well-toned and the wanna-bes grunt and pump iron for the audience of passersby at Muscle Beach. If you're there on a Saturday, take the winding bike path a bit away from the boardwalk proper to listen to the gathering of bongo drummers and watch the impromptu roller-disco show. A few blocks inland are the famous canals for which the city is named.

Although you won't start hallucinating that you've entered Italy, the paths along the waterways are a placid retreat from the high-intensity boardwalk scene.

Like Santa Monica, Venice is very much a city, and more than Santa Monica, it has city problems. Inland from the beach are working-class and low-income neighborhoods, where people go about their daily business quite apart from the beach. At night the boardwalk area sees its share of gang activity, so exercise caution if you decide to explore Venice after dark. Parking can be tricky, especially on weekends, but it's worth a drive through the city streets to look for a free spot before you pay $5–$7 at one of the all-too-convenient pay lots. On the upside, the Boardwalk was under renovation at press time; resurfacing, new lighting, and extra elbow room were in the works. As for public transit, Venice shares the Santa Monica Municipal Bus Lines, a.k.a. the Big Blue Buses (tel. 310/451–5444).

*See the Santa Monica and Venice map.*

## CANALS

They don't call it Venice for nothing. East of Ocean Avenue and south of Venice Boulevard, a few canals are all that remain of Abbot Kinney's attempt to bring a little bit of Italy to southern California. What was once 16 mi of canals and a replica of St. Mark's Cathedral is now a few blocks of beautiful, very pricey real estate. Back when Jim Morrison used to roam the neighborhood, the canals were choked with algae and a bit smelly. Today they lend the area a quirky touch of class and make for a nice, quiet stroll.

*In Venice look for the offices of the Chiat/Day advertising agency (340 Main St.), designed by Frank Gehry. The conference rooms, which constitute the building's facade, are in the shape of giant four-story binoculars.*

## MUSCLE BEACH

Long before there was liposuction, Angelenos have been fighting fat in style and in public at Muscle Beach. If you've seen photos from the '50s, you'll expect a grungy barbell scene here, but the Muscle Beach of the '90s is more like an open-air 24-hour Nautilus, with sleek machines replacing the rougher free weights. Lifters face the crowd as they strive to press their maximum weight. Although you'll see more than a few flabby weaklings, this is definitely the prime spot to view the ripped and oiled. It's a symbiotic relationship of free mutual pleasure between those who like to watch and those who like to be watched. *Ocean Park Walk, between 17th and 18th Sts.*

## THE STRAND

Parallel to the Boardwalk and several yards closer to the beach is the Strand, one of L.A.'s prime spots for biking or 'blading (*see* Chapter 6). Venice is at the heart of this 19-mi paved stretch, which extends from Redondo Beach north past Malibu. Even if you don't care to indulge in biking or 'blading, the path in Venice affords yet another opportunity for spectatorship. Every Saturday the space due west of Muscle Beach becomes an outdoor roller *Solid Gold,* complete with DJ and big loudspeakers. On occasion the path adjacent to the disco area hosts some outrageous Evel Knievel–type activity, with 'bladers and bikers jumping barrels and rails.

## VENICE BEACH AND BOARDWALK

Venice Beach's famous Boardwalk, officially known as Ocean Park Walk, adds a bizarre, often fascinating, mix of humanity to the usual boardwalk attractions of T-shirt vendors and pizza stands. Street performers reach new heights of outrage in order to outcompete one another for your buck. One gentleman's entire act consists of his ability to walk on broken glass, which he does either unscathed or with a G. Gordon Liddy air of stoicism. Another performer starts his act by taking a chain saw to a bedraggled stuffed (by a taxidermist) dog. If this fails to win him sufficient attention, he will run among passersby flailing his weapon in a manner none too safe. Once he gets going, he is not content merely to juggle the chain saw against an apple and a bowling ball. To augment his act, he juggles over the prone body of a hapless volunteer, shrieking jokes that border on or cross the line of offensive. If this is all a bit much for you, there's usually a one-man band, a collection of Andean musicians, or an a-cappella group. Near the intersection with Windward Avenue you can avail yourself of any number of occult services. In addition to garden-variety palm readers and psychics, there are "specialists"—ranging from Cherokee aura readers to channelers of the dead. Finally, the spectators themselves are spectacle. Although you can see a fair amount of flesh in L.A. miles from the beach, body culture reaches its apex here, and it's always fun to try to spot the silicon in the bikinis.

## WINDWARD AVENUE

Venice's main street is decorated by a number of interesting murals; the most noteworthy is Venus on a shell thinking the aptly Los Angeles thought: "History is myth." Also featured in the painting is one of Venice's famous free-roaming freaks, a bearded gentleman in a turban who rollerblades along Ocean Front Walk playing electric guitar (the amp is strapped to his belt). Besides the murals, Windward Avenue offers a few pleasant places to drink coffee and take in the scene (*see* Cafés and Coffeehouses *in* Chapter 3). Most important, it provides the most central access to Venice's main attraction: the Boardwalk.

# SOUTH BAY

The three beach towns that make up the majority of the South Bay—Manhattan, Hermosa, and Redondo—embody most people's preconceptions about southern California. The local attitude is noticeably more laid-back and the pace of life less frenetic than that found inland. If you cruise through on PCH, you'll see nothing but commuters, car dealerships, and minimalls, but as you approach the water, the distinctive features of each town emerge.

Manhattan is the most upscale and yuppified of the lot. You'll find more professionals, million-dollar homes, and fewer unemployed surfers per capita than most beach towns. As you proceed south through Hermosa and Redondo, the residents become younger, less upwardly mobile, and more prone to party. Redondo is home to more strip malls and stroller-toting families, while Hermosa hosts the majority of the bachelor pads. East of PCH, which borders on Torrance and suburbia, may as well be a different world. A comparative tour of the continuum is easily executed by rollerblading, bicycling, or walking along the cement strand that separates all three cities from the sand. Call 310/372-2166 to speak to an aspiring *Baywatch* lifeguard about beach conditions.

Many residents argue that the beach cities of the South Bay are the choicest spots to reside in Los Angeles. Endless summer days, well-groomed stretches of sand, and a stream of well-endowed bodies exercising along the beach suffice to convince many visitors the locals are right. It's said that when you decide to settle here, you first rent east of PCH—the unofficial cutoff point of the surf-cat lifestyle—and gravitate toward the ocean with each successive move. When you finally arrive on the beach, having climbed the social and rental ladder, you stay put as long as you can afford the monthly payments.

## HERMOSA BEACH

Hermosa Beach is of the last generation of the archetypal southern California seaside town, and an anti-establishment don't-worry-be-happy feel still lingers; even the Mercedes Benzes sport Grateful Dead stickers. But one look at all the construction along Pier Avenue and at the successive waves of new multimillion-dollar houses that keep replacing torn-down beachfront bungalows will tell you where Hermosa is headed. To reach the main jumble of shops and restaurants from PCH, look for Pier Avenue, 2 mi south of Manhattan Beach (it leads, naturally, to the municipal pier). Restaurants and equipment rental shops dot the beachfront. Head out to the tip of the 1,320-ft pier for great views of the coastline. Call 310/379-8471 to hear surf and weather reports, updated three times a day.

## MANHATTAN BEACH

Manhattan Beach Boulevard leads into the heart of the low-lying downtown, intersecting PCH 3 mi south of the airport and dead-ending at the pier. Part family neighborhood, part upwardly mobile singles capital, Manhattan is where successful surfers come to settle down. The Strand, a two-lane beachfront thoroughfare open to bicyclists, skaters, and pedestrians, is *the* place to gawk and be gawked. Manhattan's gloriously clean sand hosts a seemingly endless string of volleyball nets and practicing pros.

## REDONDO BEACH

The most family oriented of the South Bay communities, Redondo is caught between becoming like the suburban-mall hell of Torrance and the beckoning tranquillity and party-inducing sunshine of the beach. Perhaps because it is removed from the beach by bluffs and substantially impinged on by the commercialization of PCH, it lacks the character of Manhattan and Hermosa. Still, the breezy beachfront along Esplanade Avenue (the street that parallels Redondo State Beach) remains one of the premier spots to stroll and watch the sun set. From PCH take Torrance Boulevard west to Veterans Park, where you can picnic on the grass overlooking King Harbor and the Pacific; there's a farmers' market here every Thursday morning.

## MONSTAD PIER

On this privately owned, touristy 200-ft-long pier you can rent fishing gear and buy live bait as well as. eat the catch of the day for lunch or dinner in **Tony's Fish Market Restaurant** (Coral Way, at end of pier, tel. 310/515–2275), which is open daily 11–11. Or warm up with fishermen at the **Redondo Coffee Shop** (tel. 310/318–1044), open daily 7 AM–midnight.

# PALOS VERDES

Just south of Redondo Beach, the Palos Verdes peninsula (home to both Palos Verdes and the more southern Rancho Palos Verdes) rises dramatically from the Pacific Ocean: a relatively uncommercialized mass of rolling hills and steep cliffs dotted by elegant estates and horse stables. Once a vast, treeless ranch owned by José Dolores Sepúlveda—whose name graces one of the longest boulevards in Los Angeles—the peninsula was purchased for $1 million by financier Frank Vanderlip in 1913 and subsequently subdivided into exclusive residential communities. Today it remains a conservative enclave where residents pay top dollar to escape the smog and hustle of the surrounding metropolis. Its pocket-size coves and tide pools, though difficult to reach, are well worth a visit.

*Amid the tourist clutter of the Monstad Pier, look for the simple bust of George Freeth, southern California's first lifeguard and a surfing pioneer.*

Parking on the street is generally easy in Palos Verdes, which is just as well since the commuter trains don't make it over here.

*See the Palos Verdes, San Pedro, and Long Beach map.*

## COMING AND GOING AND GETTING AROUND

From the 110 (Harbor Freeway), exit west on PCH, turn left on Crenshaw or Hawthorne boulevards, and head uphill to Palos Verdes Drive North. From the South Bay beach cities, follow PCH south, parallel the ocean through Redondo Beach until you hit Palos Verdes Boulevard, and turn right. You can circumnavigate the peninsula in a fantastic 26-mi drive (or bicycle ride) by following Palos Verdes Drive, which goes in all four directions (*see* Bicycling *in* Chapter 6).

## BEACHES AND TIDE POOLS

The severe terraces and rocky cliffs that characterize the peninsula don't allow for wide, sandy beaches; however, if you don't mind scrambling down a steep incline, you'll find several picture-perfect patches of sand. **Malaga Cove,** or **RAT** (for "Right after Torrance") **Beach** as it's more commonly known, is a surfer hangout and trove of tide pools, accessible via Paseo del la Playa from Torrance Beach. The narrow **Bluff Cove,** in Palos Verdes Estates, is accessible to the nimble via a winding trail from Paseo del Mar, beginning at Flat Rock Point. Once at sea level, hike 2 mi south along the rocky shore, around Rocky Point to Lunada Bay, where the rusty remains of the Greek freighter *Dominator* are often visible against the looming, almost perpendicular cliffs. It is possible to keep trekking south to Point Vicente during low tide. **Abalone Cove** is a secluded county beach and tide-pool preserve, accessible from a parking lot ($5 fee) off Palos Verdes Drive South, near Wayfarers Chapel (*see below*).

## POINT VICENTE LIGHTHOUSE AND INTERPRETIVE CENTER

Whales pass Point Vicente twice yearly, traveling south from December through February and north from February through April, as they migrate between the Arctic and Baja California. The center's exhibits highlight the geology, cultural history, and coastal life of the peninsula, and the outdoor whale observation areas are ideal for panoramic picnicking during off-season. The lighthouse is open sporadically for guided tours by reservation only. Call for seasonal whale information. *31501 Palos Verdes Dr. W, near Hawthorne Blvd., tel. 310/377–5370 or 310/541–0334. Admission $2. Open June–Sept., daily 10–7; Oct.–May, daily 10–5.*

# PALOS VERDES, SAN PEDRO, AND LONG BEACH

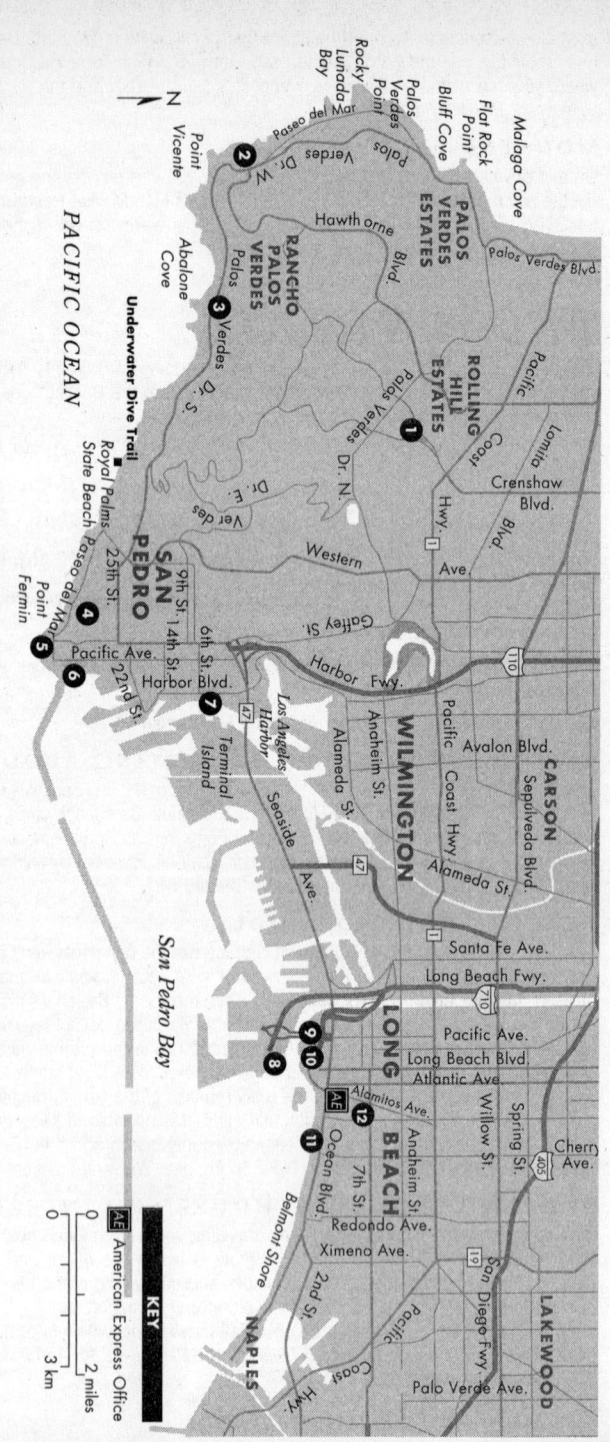

Cabrillo Marine
Aquarium, **6**
Long Beach
Aquarium of the
Pacific, **9**

Long Beach
Museum of Art, **11**
L.A. Maritime
Museum, **7**

Museum of Latin
American Artists, **12**
Point Fermin Park, **5**

Point Vicente
Lighthouse and
Interpretive Center, **2**
Queen Mary, **8**
Shoreline Village, **10**

South Coast Botanic
Garden, **1**
Wayfarers Chapel, **3**

## SOUTH COAST BOTANIC GARDEN

Previously a garbage dump, this prime piece of real estate was expertly transformed in 1959 by the alchemists at the L.A. County Arboreta Department into a series of lush gardens. Several vibrant collections are organized by color, and species from every continent except Antarctica are represented. Visitors wander serendipitously through a self-guided walking tour, past fragrant flower and herb gardens, rare cacti, and a duck-filled lake. On a clear day the highest elevations in the garden offer superb views of the city basin below. *26300 S. Crenshaw Blvd., at Palos Verdes Dr. N, Rancho Palos Verdes, tel. 310/ 544–6815. Admission $5. Open daily 9–5.*

## WAYFARERS CHAPEL

This unusual house of worship was commissioned by the Swedenborgian church, designed by Lloyd Wright, the son of famed architect Frank Lloyd Wright, and erected in 1949. Inspired by the cathedral-like majesty of the native redwoods, Wright intended the chapel, made almost entirely of glass, to blend in with the surrounding forest. Most of the original redwoods vanished (murdered by smog), but another stand of trees (mostly pines but some redwoods, too) and lush ferns and azaleas have taken root. Pick up a 12-step self-guided walking tour brochure (25¢) from the information kiosk for detailed descriptions of the architectural intricacies and the peaceful surrounding grounds. The chapel's glass panes were joined together only at 30-degree or 60-degree angles, the same angles found in snowflakes. *5755 Palos Verdes Dr. S, Rancho Palos Verdes, tel. 310/377- -1650. Admission free. Open daily 7–5.*

# SAN PEDRO

Poised at the end of the Harbor Freeway (I–110) like the bait at the end of the line, San Pedro is everything big-screen Hollywood is not: honest, hardworking, and rough around the edges. It is also home to the **Los Angeles Harbor,** which hosts film crews but also functions as the largest container port on the Pacific Rim. Longshoremen, naval enlistees, and Portuguese fishermen all call Pedro (*Pee*-droh) home, as did the disgruntled postal workers' poet laureate, Charles Bukowski. You might recognize the wharf from a cameo in the movie *The Usual Suspects.*

For a slice of the real San Pedro, cruise real slow down **Gaffey Street,** the terminus of the Harbor Freeway, past the naval installation to the panoramic vista at **Angels Gate Park** (3601 S. Gaffey St., tel. 310/ 519–0936). This is the windswept home of the **Korean Friendship Bell**; the **Fort MacArthur Military Museum,** which is free and open Tuesday, Thursday, Saturday, and Sunday noon–5; and an AYH hostel (*see* Hostels *in* Chapter 4). East of Pacific Avenue, **6th Street,** locally "downtown," you'll find a flourishing local arts community and several excellent restaurants, cafés, and bars. At the harbor's edge, **Ports O'Call Village** (tel. 310/831–0287) is a 15-acre cluster of pier- side shops gussied up for tourists to look like a 19th-century New England fishing village. At the Village's **Boat House** (Fisherman's Wharf, Berth 78, tel. 310/831–0996), you can catch a daily harbor cruise; times and prices vary seasonally. Visit on a Thursday to peruse the expansive farmers' market (6th St. and Mesa, 3–7). Ferries to Santa Catalina Island (*see* Chapter 8) run from Berth 95 regularly. Stop by the **Chamber of Commerce** (390 W. 7th St., tel. 310/832–7272), which is open weekdays 9–5, or the AYH hostel and pick up a visitor's guide, a trolley schedule, or a detailed city map ($1).

*See the Palos Verdes, San Pedro, and Long Beach map.*

## COMING AND GOING AND GETTING AROUND

To reach San Pedro from downtown L.A., take I–110 south, past the fumy industrial belt south of LAX. In town, the **Electric Trolley** runs Thursday–Monday 10–6 in summer, 11–5 in winter, between the Catalina Air and Sea Terminal and Cabrillo Beach, stopping at Ports O'Call Village, downtown San Pedro, the Cabrillo Marine Aquarium, and other points of tourist interest. The fare is 25¢; routes and schedules are available at the Chamber of Commerce (*see above*) and the AYH hostel (*see* Hostels *in* Chapter 4).

## CABRILLO MARINE AQUARIUM

The 35 saltwater aquariums here range in size from 5 to more than 1,000 gallons and display the indigenous marine life that flourishes off the southern California coast. Frank Gehry designed the building in 1981; it sits right on Cabrillo Beach. On the seaward patio you can get up close and personal with starfish and sea anemones who live in the tide-pool touch tanks. If time allows, consider making the short walk west from the aquarium to **White Point** and **Royal Palms State Beach,** where Japanese-American settlers built a health spa in the Roaring '20s. Beach parking is $6.50, or you can park for free

# FISH ON A
# LUNAR CYCLE

*Gloria Steinem once observed that women need men about as much as fish need bicycles; take one look at the hundreds of Schwinn-less grunions struggling to spawn on the beaches of southern California and make the call yourself. The silvery fish, which bear a strong resemblance to angry anchovies, voluntarily beach themselves twice monthly from March through August, in accordance with the lunar cycle. As full and new moons arise, the grunions appear on the beach like clockwork, burrowing determinedly into the fecund sands, dying to procreate (their eggs hatch about two weeks later). You need a license (available at the aquarium) to catch during spawning season, and you may only use your hands as you fish. For further information on how to join an organized grunion run ($1), contact the Cabrillo Marine Aquarium in San Pedro (see above).*

if you find street parking in the surrounding neighborhood. *See also box* Fish on a Lunar Cycle, *below. 3720 Stephen White Dr., tel. 310/548–7562. From I–110, exit south on Gaffey St., left on 22nd St., right on Pacific Ave., left on 36th St., and left at bottom of hill. Admission free. Open weekdays noon–5, weekends 10–5.*

## L.A. MARITIME MUSEUM

This impressive collection, chronicling the nautical facets of San Pedro's history, along with miscellaneous seafaring tidbits, sits in a former ferry building. The 700 models are definitely worth a gander; look for Sir Francis Drake's *Golden Hind* and *Sirius,* the first steam-powered ship to cross the Atlantic. There are also interesting WWII documents, such as a copy of the Japanese surrender. *Fisherman's Wharf, Berth 84, at end of 6th St., tel. 310/548–7618. Donation requested. Open Tues.–Sun. 10–5.*

## POINT FERMIN PARK

Home to a handsome Victorian-style lighthouse built in 1874, this breezy bluff-top park is an ideal refuge for picnicking and daydreaming. The 37 landscaped acres and coin-operated telescopes afford great views of the harbor and Pacific Ocean. To the east, between the park and the aquarium below the bluffs, you'll find the bountiful Point Fermin Marine Life Refuge tide pools. *End of Gaffey St., at Paseo del Mar, tel. 310/548– 7756. Open daily 5:30 AM–10:30 PM.*

## UNDERWATER DIVE TRAIL

Certified scuba divers should explore the Underwater Dive Trail, just east of Royal Palms State Beach on Western Avenue at South Paseo Del Mar, which winds by rope through kelp beds, sulfurous hot springs, and underwater coves (*see* Snorkeling and Scuba Diving *in* Chapter 6).

# LONG BEACH

Just across the harbor and the Vincent Thomas Bridge from San Pedro, Long Beach seems like a contradiction in terms—a seaside resort amid towering oil refineries and massive natural-gas processing plants. Yet somehow, parts of the city—once known as the Coney Island of the West—keep industrialization at bay. There's plenty to explore here, from the miles of sandy beaches to the landmark art deco buildings of downtown to the new Aquarium of the Pacific. The population is one of southern California's most socially diverse, a place where blue-collar workers, conservative suits, gays, and tawny beach bums peacefully coexist.

Within Long Beach are two smaller communities: Belmont Shore and Naples. If you get a kick out of architecture, head to the small residential community of **Belmont Shore,** at the east end of Ocean Boulevard. Developed in the 1940s, it has some of the town's oldest beach homes and bungalows. The unofficial inland boardwalk is **1st Street** (between Livingston Drive and Bay Shore Avenue), a commercial strip chockablock with bars, cafés, and nightspots where twenty-somethings drunkenly shed job angst. Across from Belmont Shore in man-made Alamitos Bay is the upscale island community of **Naples,** an ersatz attempt to re-create the ambience of its authentic Italian counterpart. Second Street crosses Naples's main island on its way to PCH. The two tinier islands hugged by Naples Island are cheerfully lined with a series of alleys, canals, and footbridges that make for pleasant walking, especially during the annual **Boat Parade,** held around Christmastime.

Ocean Boulevard is the main thoroughfare along part of the coast—in Long Beach, north over the bridge to San Pedro, and south into Belmont Shore and Seal Beach. Downtown Long Beach is made up of five districts: quaint **Shoreline Village,** with an old seaport feel (*see below*); **East Village**'s arts community; the financial district of **West Side;** the residential North End; and busy **Pine Avenue.** At the bottom of Pine Avenue, the major **Queensway Bay** waterfront development pushes ahead, anchored by the aquarium. These areas are bordered by Shoreline Drive in the far northwest corner, 10th Street on the easternmost side, Golden Avenue to the west, and Lime Street to the south. The best way to appreciate the crowded commercial district downtown is by taking a stroll along the **Promenade,** a six-block brick walkway stretching from 3rd Street south to the waterfront.

To get a feel for Long Beach's funkier side, explore **Broadway Avenue,** the alternative downtown drag, between Pacific and Cherry avenues. The art deco feel is authentic; if you have any doubts, check out the terra-cotta detailing and vibrant colors of the **Dr. Rowan Building** (201 Pine St.). Other landmarks include **Villa Riviera** (800 E. Ocean Blvd.), a 16-story high-rise built in 1929 with a schizophrenic mix of Gothic, Tudor, French, and Italianate architectural styles; and the **Breakers Hotel** (210 E. Ocean Blvd.), a Spanish Revival–style former resort built in 1926. Covering the entire exterior of the Long Beach Arena (300 E. Ocean Blvd., at Pine Ave.) is **Planet Ocean,** whose life-size depiction of whales and other frolicsome sea creatures helps it qualify as the world's largest mural.

Cruise along Harbor Scenic Drive and watch longshoremen do their thing (handle cargo) around the **Port Administration Building** (925 Harbor Plaza, tel. 562/590–4123) weekdays 7:30–4:30.

*See the Palos Verdes, San Pedro, and Long Beach map.*

## VISITOR INFORMATION

As is fitting in a city eager for tourist dollars, the **Long Beach Area Convention and Visitors Bureau** delights in distributing a comprehensive area map and guide, info on ferries to Santa Catalina Island (*see* Chapter 8), and the extremely helpful handout "Quick Guide to Long Beach and South Bay." The staff is knowledgeable about San Pedro and Palos Verdes, too. If you're just looking to pick up a brochure or map, they're also available at a kiosk at the Aquarium of the Pacific (*see below*). *1 World Trade Center, Suite 300, between Magnolia Ave. and Ocean Blvd., tel. 562/436–3645 or 800/452–7829. Open weekdays 8–5.*

## COMING AND GOING

To get to Long Beach from L.A., take I–710 south. From the south take I–405 to I–710 or I–110. **Greyhound Lines** (tel. 800/231–2222) has a station in downtown Long Beach (464 W. 3rd St., at Magnolia Ave., tel. 562/432–1842) with service to L.A. (one hour, $8). The Metro's **Blue Line** runs between L.A. and downtown Long Beach every 10–20 minutes, stopping at the Long Beach Transit Mall (*see* Getting Around, *below*) and 1st Street; the ride costs $1.35 each way. For more information call 800/266–6883.

**Long Beach Airport** (4100 E. Donald Douglas Dr., tel. 562/570–2600) is served by America West (tel. 800/235–9292) and several charter services. Unfortunately, there's no public transportation to the airport; private shuttles will take you to your hotel or downtown for about $15, and **Yellow Cab** (tel. 562/421–7180) can do the same for $18– $20.

## GETTING AROUND

Public buses (90¢) are operated by **Long Beach Transit** (tel. 562/591–2301). Obtain schedules and catch most bus lines at the **Transit Mall** (1st St. between Long Beach Blvd. and Pacific Ave.). The **Passport Shuttle** (no phone) offers frequent free service from downtown (Ocean or Pine Boulevard) to the ferry terminal and the *Queen Mary.* Shuttles run 7–6 weekdays and 10–5 weekends. For a 90¢ fare it will connect you with Belmont Shore. The **Aquabus** water taxi (tel. 800/995–4386) shuttles between the

Aquarium and the Queen Mary, the Catalina Express Port, and Shoreline Village. It costs $1 a pop. The brightly decorated **Village Tour D'Art** buses zip between the Long Beach Performing Arts Center, the Oceanic Art Museum Gallery, the Museum of Latin American Art, the World Trade Center, Pine Avenue, and the Broadway Corridor. These run 10–7:30 Sunday–Thursday and 10–9:20 on Friday and Saturday; a ride costs 90 ¢.

If you plan on visiting several places in one day, consider snagging a $5 **"DayTripper" pass.** This gives you unlimited rides on all Passport Shuttles, the Tour D'Art shuttle, and all local bus routes, plus two tickets for the Aquabus water taxi and some attraction discount coupons. You can get the pass from Long Beach Transit, local attractions, and some local hotels.

## LONG BEACH AQUARIUM OF THE PACIFIC

Smack on the Pacific, this gleaming new (1998) aquarium focuses on the sealife of the ocean it faces. Walk in and you'll confront a giant model of a blue whale; then move on to the seventeen habitats and more than two dozen other exhibits. The inhabitants run from toothy predators (sharks, barracuda) and six-ft-wide Japanese spider crabs to awww–cute sea otters and seals. There's also a deep-reef tank, a kids' area, and a skate-and-ray touch pool should you want to get your hands on something slimy. They use a timed ticketing system, so try to get here early. *100 Aquarium Way, off Shoreline Dr., tel. 562/590–3100. Admission $14.95. Open daily 9–6.*

## LONG BEACH MUSEUM OF ART

On a beautifully landscaped patch in a 1912 Craftsman-style house, this avant-garde museum highlights the work of southern California artists. The videotape archive here is the largest on the West Coast, and the galleries host a wide variety of traveling modern exhibits. *2300 E. Ocean Blvd., between Junipero and Temple Aves., tel. 562/439–2119. Admission $2. Open Wed.–Thurs. and weekends 10–5, Fri. 10–8.*

## MUSEUM OF LATIN AMERICAN ART

One of the feel-good experiences of exploring a large city is an unexpected find such as this fantastic museum. The former skating rink is now filled with a rich, fascinating collection of contemporary work by artists from Mexico, the Caribbean, and Central and South America. Paintings by should-be-famous artists like Gerardo Chávez, Gonzalo Cienfuegos, and Margarita Canton join works by internationally prominent artists such as Fernando Botero and Diego Rivera. You can follow strains of Cubism, Dadaism, Surrealism, and muralism—but the bottom line is that this opens an exhilarating window into modern Latin American artistic expression. *628 Alamitos Ave., at Martin Luther King Blvd., tel. 562/437–1689. Admission $5. Open Tues.–Sat. 11:30–7:30, Sun. noon–6.*

## QUEEN MARY

Exploring the *Queen Mary,* once the most luxurious and largest passenger ship in the world, can be both overwhelming and expensive. The 80,000-ton, 1,000-ft liner was a floating masterpiece of art deco splendor when first launched in 1934. Thirty-three years later, the city of Long Beach bought, grounded, and converted the ship into a veritable city at sea, adding restaurants, shops, and a ritzy hotel to the refurbished interior. Walking tours lead visitors through the ins and outs of shipboard life. Parking costs $8 on top of admission. *Pier H, at end of I–710, tel. 562/435–3511. Admission $12. Guided 1-hr tour $4 additional. Open daily 10–6.*

## SHORELINE VILLAGE

A mock-up of a historical fishing village aimed at tourists, the only thing original here is the 1906 Charles Looff carousel. The boardwalk proves fertile ground for a pleasant stroll and great views of the harbor both day and night. Shoreline Village Cruises (tel. 562/495–5884) offers one-hour harbor ($6) and three-hour dinner cruises ($49.50 per person); call for daily departure times. *Shoreline Dr. and Pine Ave., tel. 562/435–2668. Carousel admission $1. Open winter–spring, daily 10–10; summer, daily 10 AM–11 PM.*

# OUT THERE

Not only is this museum off of the beaten L.A. path, it's also a rather offbeat experience . . .but if you've got the right mindset, it's more than worth the trip. If you don't have your own set of wheels, you can take MTA bus line 33, 333, or 436 or Santa Monica Municipal Bus line 12.

## MUSEUM OF JURASSIC TECHNOLOGY

The complete absence of exhibits on Jurassic anything is the first clue that things are not what they seem at the Museum of Jurassic Technology. Although the abundance of taxidermy may lull you into thinking you're back on an elementary school field trip to the local museum of natural history, listen carefully to the hypnotic taped voices you hear on those familiar exhibit-side telephones. You will learn of bats that can fly through solid matter, though you will eventually realize that the convincing descriptions are 100% fictitious. Well, maybe not 100%—and therein lies the brilliance of what may be the world's only meta-museum. The challenge exists not so much in separating fact from fiction, but rather in rethinking the function and form of the museum as institution. A mounted human horn, a display on hypersymbolic cognition, pronged ants—all pique curiosity and perhaps disbelief. Decide for yourself in the musty darkness of one of L.A.'s most remarkable cultural institutions. If you need help getting in the mood, read Lawrence Weschler's *Mr. Wilson's Cabinet of Wonders*, inspired by this museum. *9341 Venice Blvd., 4 blocks west of Robertson Blvd., Culver City, tel. 310/836–6131. From L.A., take the I–10 (Santa Monica Freeway) west and exit at Robertson Blvd. Suggested donation $4. Open Thurs. 2–8, Fri.–Sun. noon–6.*

# STUDIOS

*The early 20th-century influx of migrant workers from the Midwest earned Long Beach the moniker Iowa by the Sea.*

Hooray for Burbank? Although it lacks the former poetry of Hollywood, Burbank has become the actual center of movie production, with nearly every major studio player set up in its immediate environs. When the motion picture industry got its start, at the turn of the century, land in L.A. was cheap—a prime reason, along with the endless sunshine, the city became the capital of the entertainment world. The rapid growth of the movie business was responsible for Los Angeles's second and defining boom, but the prosperity the movies helped create soon forced the industry out of L.A. proper. As early as the 1920s rising property values (accompanied by the studios' need for more and more space) prompted an industry migration northeast to the San Fernando Valley.

Although movies made Los Angeles the metropolis it is today, early citizens did not have the foresight to welcome the new art form; instead they saw it as a new means to promote sin. Anti-Semitism was also responsible for some of the poor reception to the studios and their product—all the major studio founders, from Samuel Goldwyn to the Warner Brothers, were Jewish. In fact, anti-Semitism was a factor in the founding of the industry: It forced Jewish businessmen to look for new, wide-open fields for investment because the ownership of nearly all established businesses was closed off to all but the most wealthy white Anglo-Saxon Protestants. Today, of course, moviemakers of all religions are L.A. royalty, and to see their fiefdoms firsthand, you should take a trip to the studios of Burbank.

Studios themselves are not the autonomous powerhouses they were in the golden days of Hollywood. For years studios practically owned their stars, keeping them on contract for a set time and a certain number of movies. Now all stars are free agents of sorts, a development that has changed the look of the studios. Once upon a time actors and actresses had their dressing rooms in buildings on the studio lot. Today, these rooms have become offices, and celebs have trailers; they make movies for whatever studio they please, and their dressing rooms on wheels put them right on the set. Another change in the studio system is cooperation between competitors. A director might shoot some scenes at Paramount and then rent lots at Warner if the need arises. (If you take more than one tour, you might hear about the same movies and television shows over and over, giving you an eerie sense of collusion.) Finally, in recent years the rise of computer technology has begun to change the studio workplace again. Huge construction lots where artists once erected life-size dinosaurs out of chicken wire and plaster are today giving way to rooms full of young computer artists using state-of-the-art 3-D, multimedia, and other software to create movie scenes. Nonetheless, the studio tours are still a good show. Most everyone has been influenced in one way or another by the movie industry, so visiting a studio is not only a Los Angeles must-do, it is also a necessary component of your development as an entertainment consumer.

Picking the studio tour on which to spend your money requires some thought. Each tour has its own strong points, and prices vary a lot. Universal is both the most expensive and the least informative of all the tours. Set up like a theme park, with a back-lot tour that seems tacked on as an afterthought, you come here to "feel" the movies rather than understand their production. Universal should be your choice if you like spectacle and thrill and prefer to keep the mystery of the movies sacred. To make the

$39 admission worth your while, come early or stay late and make sure you hit all the important rides. Warner Bros., Paramount, and NBC all provide more traditional and interesting tours. All take you to see sets, costumes, and construction areas, and all will dazzle you with tales of movie mishaps and star sightings. NBC is the cheapest and shortest: only $7 for a one-hour tour. If you watch a lot of television, this might be your ticket, as you can ask your guide about all your favorite NBC shows. Paramount's two-hour tour ($15) is the only one to take place in Hollywood proper. Like the NBC tour, it gives you a standard view of the production process accompanied by a few revealing anecdotes about your favorite movies or stars. Although Warner Bros. charges twice as much for the same length of tour ($30 for two hours), they do put on a better show. Because of Burbank's cheaper real estate, there is literally a lot more to see: fake cities, fake towns, and fake backwaters. Greater size also means more goes on at Warner, and you are more likely to run into movie action here than at Paramount. Another plus is its movie museum, containing such artifacts as James Dean's motorcycle and dresses worn by Bette Davis. Ultimately, however, these three tours are fairly similar. You should make your decision based on the amount of time and money you wish to spend, or you could do some research and figure out where your favorite shows and movies were made. Certainly, if you are stalking a particular celebrity, you will have to do some careful homework to figure out the best time and place to stumble upon him or her—keeping in mind, of course, that it's a tour no-no to actually speak to a star unless spoken to. If you'd like a deeper look into moviemaking, try the Academy of Motion Pictures Arts and Sciences exhibits (see Beverly Hills, above).

## FOX TELEVISION

Those hoping to be discovered as the next Jennifer Love Hewitt will be deeply disappointed to learn Fox TV does not offer back-lot tours. The consolation prize: You can pick up free tickets to various TV programs taped here (although in the dog-eat-dog world that is filmed entertainment, who knows when your favorite show will get the ax). The box office is open weekdays 8:30–6. Tickets are available beginning each Wednesday for the following week on a first-come, first-served basis. *5746 Sunset Blvd., 1 block west of U.S. 101, Hollywood, tel. 818/506–0043.*

## NBC STUDIOS

The only TV studio open to tourists, NBC puts on a good show for a relatively cheap admission ticket. You start in the screening room, where more than 70 years of NBC history (they started as a radio station in 1926) come flying at you with more cuts than an Oliver Stone film and with a narrator straight out of a game show. If you've taken a movie studio tour, you'll learn not much is different in the world of television: These are the sound sets, here are some facades, et cetera. That many NBC shows are actually taped at other studios, mainly Warner Bros., will add to your sense of déjà vu, so you may find yourself listening to the same anecdotes about *Friends* or *ER*. On the bright side, you'll see a display of hairstyles from popular NBC shows and learn that Robin Williams had to sit for seven hours a day to apply his make-up for *Mrs. Doubtfire*—and then wait two hours at the end of the day to have it removed. Although you will be wise not to mention former NBC employee David Letterman, you will hear an earful about his competitor, Jay Leno, and there's always the chance you'll see him in the midst of his famously long workday. If not, you can at least see one of his 40 cars (he keeps the rest in a hangar at the Burbank airport) as well as the seat in the *Tonight Show* audience reserved nightly for his auto mechanic. Even though it's the least expensive of the studio tours, NBC's gets you the most involved. You can "fly" on camera (via a special-effects chroma-key blue screen), and you can participate in the end-of-tour quiz show, animated by familiar sounds for the right and wrong answer. Tours leave hourly between 9 and 3 and last about an hour, but you might want to arrive at 8 to pick up free *Tonight Show* tickets. Reservations are unavailable, and tours sell out early in the day in summer. *3000 W. Alameda Ave., Burbank, tel. 818/840–3537. Admission $7. Ticket office open weekdays 8–5. Tours weekdays 9–3 on the hr (and 10–2 some summer Sat.).*

## PARAMOUNT PICTURES

The only major motion picture studio still in Hollywood proper, Paramount offers the cheapest and the most low-key of the movie studio tours. Like the tour at Warner Brothers, the Paramount tour is a straightforward look at the mechanics of film and TV production. The lot is smaller than the one at Warner, so there is less to see—only one street of facades instead of three—and you walk your way through rather than ride a tram. Depending on the shooting schedule, you can see the soundstages from Paramount's TV shows, notably *Star Trek* and a long list of talk shows, as well as whatever movie is in production on site. Perhaps its setting in old Hollywood gives Paramount incentive to focus more on the golden age of movies; you will hear a lot of anecdotes about such silent stars as Mary Pickford and Rudolph Valentino. Reservations are not available nor are they generally necessary, although you may want to show up early to make sure you get a slot on the day you want to go. Tours generally take up to 15 people and last about two hours. Tickets to shows filmed at Paramount are free, available on a first-come, first-served basis. There's parking in the lot on South Bronson. *5555 Melrose Ave., tel. 323/ 956–5000. Admission $15. Tours weekdays every half hr 9–2.*

## UNIVERSAL STUDIOS

What started as a simple tour of the Universal Pictures studio lots has evolved into a pricey theme-park experience comparable to Disneyland or hell, depending on your vantage point. Unlike Disneyland, which transports you to simulated new worlds, Universal Studios transports you to simulated movie sets, that is, simulated simulations. Don't think about this too hard or you will need to read a volume of French deconstructionist philosophy, which will give you motion sickness on some of the more turbulent rides. The effects are still pretty neat, and there's always the threat of some explosion going tremendously awry to keep you on your toes. The *Terminator 2: 3-D* ride drops you into a computer-generated cyber war, while the *Backdraft* setup simulates a burning warehouse. The *Jurassic Park* water ride (watch out for the big drop) gets you close to animated dinosaurs, including a *T. rex.* Less menacing is the *E.T.* ride, which brings one lucky visitor via flying bicycle to E.T.'s home turf, a magical planet with grinning fungi and floras, while everyone else watches. And for another back-to-the-'80s experience, there's the virtual-reality ride *Back to the Future,* where a stationary DeLorean pitches violently but goes nowhere while a high-definition video screen makes passengers feel like they are flying 80 mph into the mouth of a volcano. The attitude of Universal Studios becomes clearest on the Tram Backlot Tour, which promises that you will "not only see the world of movies, you'll feel it." The tram takes you by the Bates Motel and home from *Psycho,* the shark from *Jaws,* and dozens of other props and sets from famous Universal pictures, but these sights are apparently not interesting enough unto themselves. As the guide rattles off the history behind the making of *Jaws,* the creature lurches from the water, and at another point, King Kong threatens to pull passengers into his gaping maw while violently shaking the tram.

*Only in L.A. could a Bob's Big Boy (4211 Riverside Dr., Burbank) be a historic landmark. The restaurant won its status in the early '90s, saving it from destruction. Good thing, too: this is the last remaining Big Boy statue – all 35 feet of him.*

Clumped together with the park are the **Universal Amphitheatre** (*see* Major Venues *in* Chapter 5), the **CityWalk,** which is lined with all kinds of eats, and, of course, a movie theater. Come early or plan on staying late to avoid the worst of the crowds. The last tram tours are given several hours before the park closes. *100 Universal City Plaza, just off the 101 freeway, Universal City, tel. 818/508–9600. Admission $39. Open summer, daily 8–10; winter, daily 9–7. Park opening hrs. vary so call ahead.*

## WARNER BROS.

Set up as if to counteract the Universal experience, the Warner Bros. tour is a straightforward, literal, behind-the-scenes look at the movies, demystifying the magic their competitor seeks to maintain. Unlike Universal's, their tram does not pitch into seeming abysses or veer into the mouths of movie monsters, and visitors are allowed to disembark frequently and poke around the costumes and sets and inside a museum of movie artifacts. Even if you have never visited Warner Bros. before, the guide assures you, visiting the front and back lots will be like a "homecoming," because thanks to movies and television, "we all grew up here," along with the Waltons and Batman. The tour begins with a movie packed with the greatest moments of Warner Bros. history. Although a Universal tour steers you far from the working sets, Warner Bros. takes you past costumers, set designers, and even the occasional star going about his or her daily routine. You can run your hands over the fake brick of the hospital from *ER,* walk into the saloon from *Blazing Saddles,* and even observe that the apartment where Jim Carrey lived in *The Mask* is across the simulated street from his home in *Batman III.* You will learn that the set called "Midwest Street" served as the locale for such diverse productions as *The Dukes of Hazzard* and *The Music Man,* and you can see the piano played again by Sam in *Casablanca.* With no more than a dozen visitors per tour, Warner Bros. gives the sense you are privy to some of moviemaking's most intimate secrets, and you can even ask the guide questions along the way. If you prefer technical explanations and endless movie trivia to 30-ft free falls and dry ice, the Warner Bros. lot is the best way to spend your studio wad. A tour lasts about two hours. *4000 Warner Blvd., at Olive Ave., Burbank, tel. 818/954– 1744. Admission $30. Tours on the hour weekdays 9–3. Reservations required.*

# CHEAP THRILLS

For an expensive city, Los Angeles offers a wide range of cheap activities for the perpetually broke and the frugal. The metropolis's visible contingent of punk-bohemians, starving artists, and newly arrived immigrants always manages to keep the low-cost spectrum of things interesting. In addition to the tight-fisted thrills listed below, consider some of the cheap forms of entertainment discussed in other sections, such as author readings, open-mike nights at cafés and coffeehouses, free concerts and free museum days (usually Thursday), gallery hopping, spiritual fulfillment on a Sunday morn, and the glut of annual festivals and street fairs, especially during summer (*see* Festivals *in* Chapter 1)—not to mention the ubiquitous people who beg to be watched and flamboyant characters who yearn to be studied. In a bind, you can always spring for that quintessential free show: sunset at the beach.

**AUDIENCES UNLIMITED** • TV shows taped live need bodies to fill the audience, and these guys are there to help. Pick up free tickets at Fox Television Studios (*see* Studios, *above*) or write in advance. *100 Universal Plaza, Bldg. 153, Universal City 91608, tel. 818/506– 0043.*

**CALIFORNIA INSTITUTE OF THE ARTS** • Admission is free to the student films and video show-cases here, which are usually held at the end of each school year (early May). *24700 McBean Pkwy., Valencia, tel. 805/253–7825.*

**FLOWER MARKET** • This block-long series of stalls comes alive in the middle of the night, as whole-sale flower brokers hawk their fragrant wares to flower shop proprietors. The public is officially welcome to shop after 9 AM, but who can resist a 5 AM stroll through this urban flower forest? *See also* Downtown, *above.. 700 block of Wall St., east of downtown.*

**FREE SUMMERTIME TUNES** • Besides practice sessions at the Hollywood Bowl (*see* Hollywood, *above*), you'll find free summer concerts at the **UCLA Summer Chamber Music Festival,** in the university's Schoenberg Auditorium (tel. 310/825–4401). Musicians from the L.A. Philharmonic, L.A. Chamber Orchestra, and UCLA's Music Department perform on Monday and Thursday afternoons. **Jazz at the Wadsworth** (tel. 310/825–2278), a series of free concerts that take place the first Sunday of each month at UCLA's Veterans Wadsworth Theatre, has featured such artists as Tito Puente, Branford Marsalis, and Maceo Parker. The Santa Monica Pier's **Twilight Dance Concerts** (tel. 310/458–8900) feature a different sound each week, from big band to reggae; bands play Thursday evening 7:30–9:30. At downtown's **California Plaza** (350 S. Grand, at Olive St.), you can catch local and international musicians Wednesday, Friday, and Sunday afternoons or Friday and Saturday evenings. Past performers have included the Japanese group Shoukichi Kina, and El Vez (known as the Mexican Elvis) and his Memphis Mariachis. The free **Summer Nights at MOCA** (tel. 213/621–1749), Thursday 5–8, consist of jazz and gallery tours tastefully paired with wine and microbrew sampling.

**MOTION PICTURE COORDINATION OFFICE** • Here's where you find out where flicks are filmed each day if you're desperate to hear the sound of the clapboard. *See also* Hollywood, *above. 7083 Hollywood Blvd., 5th fl., tel. 323/957–1000. Open weekdays 8- -6.*

**THE MUTUAL UFO NETWORK OF LA** • You know them from *The X Files.* E-mail them at mufonla@aol.com for info on local talks and conferences.

**OPEN-MIKE NIGHTS** • Poetry readings draw the new beatniks of L.A.'s café society. They're usually freewheeling (and free) affairs—audience members stand up and read their own work while Wordsworth spins in his grave. On Santa Monica's Third Street Promenade, the **Midnight Special Bookstore** (1318 3rd St., tel. 310/393–2923) has open readings every Friday starting at 8. And in Hollywood the folks at **Highland Grounds** (*see* Cafés and Coffeehouses *in* Chapter 3) open their café to musicians and poets at 7:30 PM on Wednesday. Participation is never required, but if you've composed a modern *Iliad* or even just an ode to sweat socks, arrive half an hour early to sign up for a reading time.

# STARS, SETS, AND DEATH SITES

Although maps of the stars' homes sold by street hawkers are notoriously inaccurate, their existence points to an abundant L.A. cheap thrill: Driving around and gazing at places where celebrities have lived, acted, and died. We've gathered eight tours for voyeurs with empty pockets. But note: When you're gawking at Marilyn's death site, use your head: Real people live in the homes we've listed, and they have no qualms about getting the aggressive LAPD or the Beverly Hills PD to throw trespassers in jail.

## DO ANDROIDS DREAM OF ELECTRIC SHEEP?

**UNION STATION** • *Blade Runner,* Ridley Scott's apocalyptic vision of a future when people would live in nightmarish urban centers and wouldn't be sure if they were even human, was set in—where else?— Los Angeles. A tour of hero Harrison Ford's world should begin at the movie's police headquarters, or Union Station (*see* Downtown, *above*). *800 N. Alameda St.*

**ENNIS-BROWN HOUSE** • In the film Rick Deckard lived in this hillside Mayan-style concrete-block house, actually built by Frank Lloyd Wright in the 1920s. To see the interior, you'll need to make a prior reservation for a tour. *2607 Glendower Ave., Hollywood. For reservations, contact Trust for Preservation of Cultural Heritage, 2655 Glendower Ave., tel. 323/668–0234. Admission $10.*

**BRADBURY BUILDING** • The Bradbury Building was genetic designer Sebastian's futuristic home (*see* Downtown, *above*). *304 S. Broadway.*

## FAST TIMES AT MANY HIGHS

**BEVERLY HILLS HIGH SCHOOL** • The force is with the students at Bev Hills High: They have their own cable TV channel, oil wells, a gym floor that slides open to reveal a swimming pool, plus a slew of famous grads including Burt Ward, Carrie Fisher, Nora Ephron, Rob Reiner, Shawn and Patrick Cassidy, Richard Dreyfuss, and Barry Diller. Holy Lockers, Batman! But Beverly Hills High was not the site of *90210,* which was shot at the more banal Torrance High, in South Bay. *241 S. Moreno Dr., Beverly Hills.*

*Don't forget to stop by Charlie Chaplin's house at 1085 Summit Drive in Beverly Hills. It was well known for its poor construction; Chaplin hired studio carpenters to build it.*

**HOLLYWOOD HIGH SCHOOL** • Publisher Norman Chandler, as well as Lana Turner, Carol Burnett, Mike Farrell, Jason Robards, and John Ritter, passed notes in these hallowed halls. *1521 N. Highland Ave., Hollywood.*

**JOHN MARSHALL HIGH SCHOOL** • The angst-ridden teens of Rydell High (*Grease*) and Dawson High (*Rebel Without a Cause*) romped here. *3939 Tracy St., Hollywood.*

## MOVIE SETS

**NIGHTMARE ON ELM STREET HOUSE** • *1428 N. Genesee Ave., West Hollywood.*

**CASABLANCA AIRPORT** • Bogart and Bacall said their final good-byes not in Africa but at the Van Nuys Airport. *Backside of hangar at 16217 Lindbergh St.*

**SUNSET BOULEVARD APARTMENT BUILDING** • Unemployed screenwriter Joe Gillis sacked out here. *Alto-Nido Apartments, 1851 North Ivar Ave., Hollywood.*

**DOUBLE INDEMNITY HOUSE** • Hard to find without a map, this was the home where Barbara Stanwyck plotted the insurance-scam demise of her poor husband. *6301 Quebec Dr., at El Contento.*

**PAN PACIFIC AUDITORIUM** • Olivia Newton-John's roller-disco *Xanadu* and one of Elvis Presley's last pre-Army gigs. *7600 Beverly Blvd., Wilshire.*

**WHATEVER HAPPENED TO BABY JANE'S HOUSE** • Where Bette Davis tortured Joan Crawford. *172 S. McCadden Pl., Wilshire.*

**9 TO 5 HOUSE** • Where working women Dolly Parton, Jane Fonda, and Lily Tomlin helped Dabney Coleman realize that feminism is the remarkable theory that women are not doormats. *10431 Bellagio Rd.*

## MONKEY BUSINESS

**ERROL FLYNN'S HOUSE AND ALLEGED SEX PALACE** • The sword man supposedly had special one-way mirrors instead of ceilings built into the bedrooms of this estate. *Nichols Canyon, off Mulholland Dr.*

**BEVERLY HILLS HOTEL** • Although every hotel in the L.A. area has probably been the site of some illicit trysts, JFK allegedly spent some time sans Jackie here, and Marilyn and Yves Montand supposedly took the title of their film *Let's Make Love* seriously here in 1959. *9641 Sunset Blvd., Beverly Hills.*

## TV SHOW SETS

**DYNASTY'S CARRINGTON ESTATE** • *1145 Arden Rd., Pasadena.*

**FANTASY ISLAND GUEST HOUSE** • *Los Angeles State and County Arboretum, 301 N. Baldwin Ave., Arcadia.*

**BEVERLY HILLBILLIES' MANSION** • *750 Bel Air Rd., at St. Cloud, Bel Air.*

**HAPPY DAYS HOUSE** • Home of the Cunninghams of Milwaukee, Wisconsin. *565 N. Cahuenga Ave., Wilshire.*

**OZZIE AND HARRIET HOUSE** • Where Ozzie and Harriet Nelson really lived, and used for exterior shots in the show. *1822 Camino Palmero Dr., Hollywood.*

**MALIBU CREEK STATE PARK** • This park has been used repeatedly as an alien world in *Star Trek* and was also the *Planet of the Apes.* Devoted *M*A*S*H* fans could find remnants of the show's set among the overgrowth. The park charges a $5 admission fee per vehicle. *1925 Las Virgenes Rd., 4 mi south of U.S. 101, Calabasas, tel. 818/880–0367.*

## MARILYN MONROE'S LIFE

**LOS ANGELES GENERAL HOSPITAL** • Where Norma Jean Mortenson was born in 1926. She was promptly tossed into a foster home. *1200 S. State St., downtown.*

**LOS ANGELES ORPHANS HOME** • Norma Jean lived here for years, even though her mother was alive (Gladys Mortenson was in a mental institution). *815 N. El Centro Ave., Hollywood.*

**FLORENTINE GARDENS** • Where Norma Jean Baker and a 20-year-old factory worker named Jim Dougherty celebrated their wedding; their marriage ended four years later, when Marilyn Monroe was just 20 and well on her way to being eaten alive by the star-making factory. *5951 Hollywood Blvd., Hollywood.*

**MARILYN AND JOE DIMAGGIO'S HOUSE** • The unhappy couple lived here from April through September in 1954. *508 N. Palm Dr., Beverly Hills.*

**THE GRANVILLE** • Where Marilyn hid out in 1954 while waiting for her divorce from Joe DiMaggio to become final. *1424 N. Crescent Heights Blvd., West Hollywood.*

**MARILYN'S LAST HOUSE** • Where Marilyn took the last of many Nembutal on August 4, 1962. *12305 5th Helena Dr., between Sunset and San Vicente, Brentwood.*

## MACABRE LOS ANGELES

Skip the pricey Grave Line Tour of famous death sites. Just throw some black, pop organ music in the tape deck, and conduct your own sinister, spooky tour of the famous dead.

**CHARLES MANSON CULT MURDER ESTATE** • On August 9, 1969, four Mason followers slaughtered Sharon Tate (who was eight months pregnant with Roman Polanski's baby), coffee heiress Abigail Folger, Folger's lover Wojtek Frywoski, hairstylist Jay Sebring, and college student Steve Parent, who was visiting the estate caretaker. The murderers scrawled PIGS on the wall with the victims' blood. Gruesome. The house has been torn down. *10050 Cielo Dr., in Benedict Canyon.*

**SUPERMAN SUICIDE HOUSE** • George Reeves (a.k.a. television's Superman) was found dead here on June 16, 1969. Officials ruled his death a suicide, but his mother insisted he was murdered. *1579 Benedict Canyon Dr., in Benedict Canyon.*

**BUGSY SIEGEL MURDER SITE** • Benjamin "Bugsy" Siegel (referred to by J. Edgar Hoover as "the most dangerous man in America") was murdered here on June 20, 1947, reportedly by the Mafia. Bugsy could be considered the father of modern Las Vegas; he was the first to build a luxury hotel there. *810 Linden Dr., Beverly Hills.*

**JOHNNY STOMPANATO MURDER SITE** • Actress Lana Turner's abusive (and Mob-connected) boyfriend was stabbed to death in her bedroom on April 4, 1958. The culprit? Her 14-year-old daughter, who was trying to protect her mother. *730 N. Bedford Dr., Beverly Hills.*

**MARILYN MONROE HOME** • Marilyn ended her life (or as some theorists purport, was murdered because of her affairs with John and Robert Kennedy) here on August 4, 1962. *12305 5th Helena Dr., between Sunset and San Vicente, Brentwood.*

**NICOLE BROWN SIMPSON HOME** • The slashed corpses of Nicole and struggling actor Ron Goldman were found outside this house on June 12, 1994. As most of us know all too well, Nicole's ex-husband, football player and B-movie actor O. J. Simpson, was acquitted of the murders on October 3, 1995. *875 S. Bundy Dr., Brentwood.*

**JANIS JOPLIN DEATH SITE** • Joplin died of an overdose at the Landmark Hotel (now the Highland Gardens) on October 4, 1970. *7047 Franklin Ave., Hollywood.*

**SAL MINEO MURDER SITE** • Actor Mineo was stabbed to death by a pizza deliveryman in the carport of this apartment building on February 12, 1976. Mineo played the vulnerable Plato in *Rebel With-*

*out a Cause,* and mysteriously, the other stars of the film died in unusual ways, too (Natalie Wood by drowning, James Dean in a car wreck). *8569 Holloway Dr., West Hollywood.*

**JOHN BELUSHI OVERDOSE HOTEL** • Belushi overdosed on heroin and cocaine at the Chateau Marmont in 1982. *8221 Sunset Blvd., West Hollywood.*

**RIVER PHOENIX'S LAST DANCE** • Poor Phoenix was bashed as a hypocrite after this self-described clean-living advocate died of a drug overdose at the Viper Room on Halloween 1993. *8852 Sunset Blvd., Hollywood, tel. 310/358–1881.*

# CEMETERIES

Let's face it, L.A. is a great place to die. The sometimes-cursed City of Angels also happens to be home to several enclaves of heaven on earth. Visit the area's most prominent final resting grounds to enjoy an idyllic respite from hectic daily life. Many Angelenos enjoy pleasant afternoons picnicking in the parklike cemeteries described below. Join them and you might even stumble on some famous grave sites as well.

## FOREST LAWN GLENDALE MEMORIAL PARK

More than a home to dead types, these 300 landscaped acres of greenery constitute a heavenly park worthy of an afternoon of prolonged exploration. Historical replicas abound: Leonardo da Vinci's *Last Supper,* in the Great Mausoleum in the Memorial Court of Honor, is reproduced entirely in stained glass. The Hall of Crucifixion/Resurrection hosts the world's largest religious-theme oil painting, Jan Styka's *The Crucifixion,* along with Robert Clark's behemoth *The Resurrection.* The doors to

*The address at Ron and Nancy Reagan's Bel Air house, 668 St. Cloud, used to be the devilish 666, but nervous Nancy had it changed.*

this hall are open every half hour. The Court of Freedom includes a huge mosaic rendition of the *Signing of the Declaration of Independence.* Buried among all the ersatz art are luminaries like Nat King Cole, Clark Gable, Carole Lombard, Jean Harlow, W. C. Fields, and Humphrey Bogart. *1712 S. Glendale Ave., Glendale, tel. 323/254–3131 or 800/204–3131. Open daily 8–5.*

## FOREST LAWN HOLLYWOOD HILLS MEMORIAL PARK

The 340-acre sister park to Forest Lawn Glendale is just west of Griffith Park, on the north slope of the Hollywood Hills. It's replete with wacky buildings with historic themes, like the Liberty Hall, which celebrates the legacy of the Revolution and sets the tone for a rather selective history of North America played out in the rest of the grounds' decadent statuary and murals. Replicas of Boston's Old North Church and Longfellow's Church of the Hills sit at opposite ends of the grounds. Pick up a free visitor's guide at the drive-up information booth at the entrance, and be sure to visit the Plaza of Mexican History for the Aztec sun-stone replica, and the mural *The Birth of Liberty,* supposedly the largest mosaic in the world. Liberace, Buster Keaton, and Freddie Prinze, among a cast of famous others, were laid to rest here. *6300 Forest Lawn Dr., off Ventura Fwy. (Hwy. 134), Hollywood, tel. 323/254–7251 or 800/204–3131. Open daily 8–6.*

## HILLSIDE MEMORIAL PARK

Many of the entertainment industry's biggest behind-the-scenes players are interred in this Jewish cemetery. Al Jolson, who starred in the first talkie, is memorialized with a white marble structure and waterfall. Besides offering a panoramic view of the bumper-to-bumper I–405 traffic, the gentle green slopes prove fertile ground for enjoying a French dip from nearby Johnnie's Pastrami (*see* South-Central *in* Chapter 3). *6001 Centinela Ave., Culver City, tel. 310/641–0707. 2 blocks east of Sepulveda Blvd. and I–405. Open weekdays and Sun. 8–5.*

## HOLLYWOOD MEMORIAL PARK CEMETERY

Fame *is* immortal. Just ask the groundskeepers here, who've seen countless tourists drive up in rented convertibles, stand on the grave sites of their favorite stars, and take snapshots of the hallowed tombstones with disposable cameras. Charlie Chaplin, Douglas Fairbanks, Sr., Marion Davies, and other notables are buried here, denied anonymity and privacy even in death by a tour-of-the-dead-stars map available free in the cemetery office. Walk from the entrance to the lake area, and you'll find the crypt of seminal filmmaker Cecil B. DeMille. Mel Blanc's stone is etched with his signature farewell, "That's all, folks." Inside the Cathedral Mausoleum lies Rudolph Valentino's crypt, where fans, the press, and the famous Lady in Black once turned up every August 23, the anniversary of his death. *6000 Santa Monica Blvd., between Gower St. and Van Ness Ave., tel. 323/469–1181. Open daily 8–5.*

## WESTWOOD VILLAGE MEMORIAL PARK

Buried behind the behemoth office buildings along Wilshire Boulevard is one of the most famous graves in the city. Marilyn Monroe was put to rest here in a simply marked wall crypt after she died of a drug overdose in August 1962. For the first 25 years following her death, her former husband and baseball great Joe DiMaggio had a half-dozen red roses placed on her grave three times a week. Also present are the remains of femme fatales Natalie Wood, playmate Dorothy Stratten (murdered by a jealous ex-husband), and Heather O'Rourke (the child star of *Poltergeist*). *1218 Glendon Ave., at Wilshire Blvd., tel. 310/474–1579. Look for driveway southeast of intersection beside Avco Theater. Open daily 8–5.*

## LOS ANGELES CORONER'S DEPARTMENT GIFT SHOP

If it's body bags and toe tags you need to complete that outfit, look no further. Call and request their morbid mail-order catalog or visit the undertakers in person. Proceeds from these gruesome gifts go to help convicted drunk drivers realize the tragic errors of their ways. *1104 N. Mission Rd., off I–5, Lincoln Heights, tel. 323/343–0760. Open weekdays 8–4:30.*

## LOS ANGELES PET MEMORIAL PARK

Even your pooch or pussycat can rest in peace. "Are you unsure about the guidelines for euthanizing a pet?" they ask thoughtfully: The stated goal of the nonprofit Save Our Pets' History In Eternity (SOPHIE) is to treat the deceased as humanely as possible. Steven Spielberg's cat, Hopalong Cassidy's horse, and other pampered celebrity companions are buried here without the least bit of irony. There's 24-hour pickup service. *5068 N. Old Scandia La., Calabasas Pkwy. exit off Hwy. 134, Calabasas, tel. 818/591–7037. Open summer, Mon.–Sat. 8–5, Sun. 8–7; fall–spring, daily 8–5.*

# FOOD

BY CATHERINE BELONOGOFF, ANDREW DEAN NYSTROM,

AND ELIZA ENGELBERG

REVISED BY BILL STERN

C alifornia cuisine is easy to come by in Los Angeles, but in a city where the foods of many nations are so well represented, it would be a shame to limit your taste buds to run-of-the-mill menus. Now even Westside communities—including Santa Monica, Westwood, Beverly Hills, West Hollywood, Melrose, and the Wilshire District—have ethnic delights along with the designer food of their fashionable restaurants. Santa Monica and the coastal towns afford sea breezes and cooler weather, and the eateries there tend to serve more seafood. Try the Santa Monica Pier, the Malibu Pier, Third Street Promenade in Santa Monica, or Ocean Front Walk in Venice for convenient and affordable eating. In Beverly Hills expect valets, later dinners, and an older crowd; flattering attention and compliments are included with the cost of the meal. In Hollywood, tables are a mix of movie and record industryites and tourists, while in Westwood, around UCLA, you'll find students, professors, and cubical farmers ducking into casual eateries.

Grocery stores and delis shouldn't be overlooked as places to buy a nourishing meal. And most cafés offer at least cheap, simple basics, such as soups, bagels, and baked goods, if not a whole lot more. Splurging on a big breakfast or lunch and having a smaller snack later is one way to alleviate the bite eating out takes out of your wallet. But don't forget that Los Angeles is a romantic and tempting place to treat your sweetie to a heavenly and expensive meal. If you want to splurge, crack open *Zagat* (*see below*) to get the latest scoop on the hot new restaurants. Nice restaurants with table service generally seat diners for an early lunch (around 11) and a late dinner (around 8).

Most L.A. restaurants follow the same formula: Expect outdoor patios and indoor air-conditioned seating. Smoking is not allowed in restaurants, but it's not illegal to light up on patios, even when surrounded by diners. People generally dress casually to eat out, so unless you're in Beverly Hills or an expensive restaurant (indicated by more than five valets), you won't have to worry about open-toe shoes, jeans, or lacking a coat and tie. Many restaurants post a notice from the city Department of Health near the doorway; these display the establishment's health grade.

If you're in L.A. for an extended period of time, consider obtaining the annual *Zagat Survey* ($11) for L.A. and southern California, which lists restaurants with rankings and commentary by L.A. residents. It's available at most bookstores. You could also hit the L.A. listings in its website, *www.zagat.com.* Some final notes: The price categories in this chapter refer to the cost of a main course, including a nonalcoholic drink. If you insist on a glass of vino or ending your meal with flaming bananas Foster, all bets are off. Also, in reviews we won't mention a restaurant's credit card acceptance policy unless it doesn't

# FRESH AND FRIENDLY FAST FOOD

*Two fast-food places you shouldn't miss are Koo-Koo-Roo (citywide) and In-N-Out Burger (citywide, tel. 800/786–1000); at both you can stuff yourself for under $8. At spic-and-span, poultry-only Koo-Koo-Roo you get freshly prepared potatoes and seasonal veggies along with the first-rate bird. In-N-Out Burger, the first drive-thru in California, opened in 1948, and the menu at this family-owned chain hasn't changed much since (visit the original at 13766 Francisquito Ave., near the I–10 in Baldwin Park). It's known for its fresh-cut french fries, the "double-double" (a two-patty cheeseburger), and free bumper stickers.*

accept credit cards at all, in which case we'll say "no credit cards." Otherwise, you can assume that the establishment takes some or all major credit cards. Likewise, unless otherwise noted, all establishments are open seven days a week.

# DOWNTOWN

Even though downtown hasn't been the center of L.A. life for decades, it's long been a good place for reasonably priced ethnic eats, notably in **Chinatown, Little Tokyo,** and the mostly Hispanic **Grand Central Market** on Broadway (*see* Farmers' Markets, *below*). But some recent openings—both large and small—have added depth to the Downtown scene.

*See the Downtown Los Angeles Dining map.*

**UNDER $5 • Clifton's Brookdale Cafeteria.** Clifton's dorm- style food and curious interior (a waterfall and a wallpaper redwood forest) give it cult status among young locals. The typical diner fare (fried chicken or roast beef with choice of vegetables) at this 1930s relic generally runs less than $5. If you're really broke, try the macaroni and cheese for about $1—guaranteed to leave a greasy feeling in your mouth for at least a week. *648 S. Broadway, at 7th St., tel. 213/627–1673.*

**Cole's French Dipped Sandwiches.** Cole's and Philippe's (*see below*) are waging an unspoken war over who can legitimately call themselves the originator of the French-dip sandwich. Sample both and bring along your Hi-8 camera for a surefire Oscar-winning short film. Although the food and prices are nearly identical (very satisfying French-dip turkey, ham, roast beef, etc.), the ambience at Cole's is considerably mellower, and you're likely to be the only tourist present. *118 E. 6th St., at Los Angeles St., tel. 213/622–4090. Closed Sun.*

**La Luz del Dia.** This hacienda-style restaurant is Mexico to the nth degree. Cheap, excellent, fresh, and authentic Mexican dishes are turned out in the beautifully tiled kitchen, where women make tortillas from scratch. Expect serenades from Mexican bands and lots of Mexican families. The taco and tamale with beans and rice is especially good. Every Friday they make chili rellenos. *1 W. Olvera St., near Main St., tel. 213/628–7495. No credit cards. Closed Mon.*

**Lucky Deli.** A real Chinatown deli, this busy, loud joint sells duck feet, spicy shrimp with little beady eyes, and pork buns. You will be hard-pressed to spend more than a few bucks since it's all so cheap. The squeamish and MSG-allergic should stay away; for all others this is a feast for the senses and easy on the purse. *706 N. Broadway, at Ord St., Chinatown, tel. 213/625– 7847. No credit cards.*

**Philippe the Original.** Cater corner from Union Station, Philippe's (established 1908) is another beloved downtown institution, with faded photographs, communal tables, and sawdust on the floor. It's also the reputed birthplace of the French-dip sandwich. You'll find all sorts lunching here, from bankers to beggars (and plenty of tourists). A cup o' joe is still just a dime. *1001 N. Alameda St., at Ord St., tel. 213/628–3781. No credit cards.*

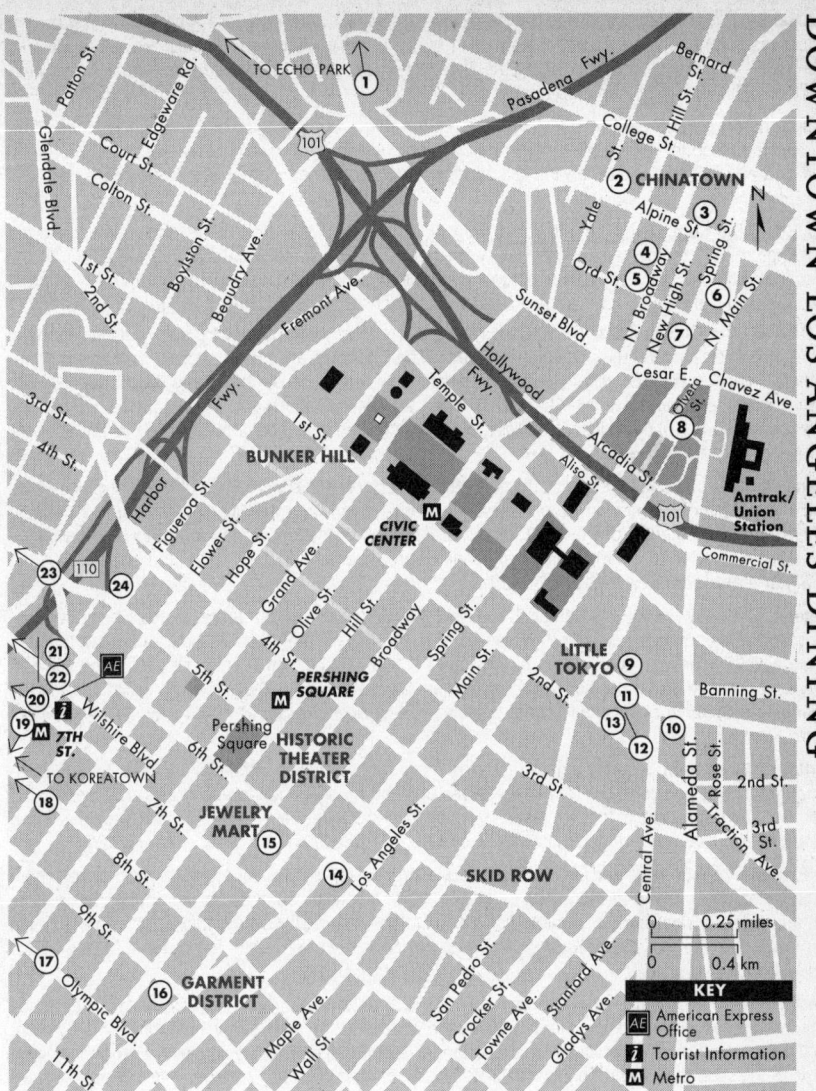

TO ECHO PARK

① Paru's Indian Vegetarian

101

Pasadena Fwy.

Bernard St.

College St.

Hill St.

② CHINATOWN

③

Yale

Alpine St.

④

⑤ Ord St.

N. Broadway

New High St.

Spring St.

⑥

N. Main St.

⑦

Sunset Blvd.

Cesar E. Chavez Ave.

Hollywood Fwy.

Temple St.

Olvera St.

⑧

Arcadia St.

Aliso St.

BUNKER HILL

Fremont Ave.

1st St.

CIVIC CENTER

M

Amtrak/ Union Station

101

Commercial St.

Glendale Blvd.

Patton St.

Court St.

Edgeware Rd.

Colton St.

Boylston St.

Beaudry Ave.

1st St.

2nd St.

3rd St.

4th St.

Fwy.

Harbor

Figueroa St.

Flower St.

Hope St.

Grand Ave.

Olive St.

4th St.

Hill St.

Broadway

Spring St.

Main St.

LITTLE TOKYO ⑨

Banning St.

⑪

⑬

⑩

⑫

Alameda St.

Rose St.

2nd St.

3rd St.

Traction Ave.

⑳③ 110

⑳④

㉑

㉒ AE

⑳

i

⑲ M 7TH ST.

Wilshire Blvd.

5th St.

6th St.

Pershing Square

M

PERSHING SQUARE

HISTORIC THEATER DISTRICT

3rd St.

Central Ave.

TO KOREATOWN

⑱

7th St.

JEWELRY MART

⑮

Los Angeles St.

⑭

SKID ROW

0.25 miles

0.4 km

⑰

8th St.

9th St.

Olympic Blvd.

11th St.

⑯ GARMENT DISTRICT

Maple Ave.

Wall St.

San Pedro St.

Crocker St.

Towne Ave.

Stanford Ave.

Gladys Ave.

2nd St.

3rd Ave.

N

KEY

AE American Express Office

i Tourist Information

M Metro

Atlas Bar and Grill, **21**

Ciudad, **24**

Clifton's Brookdale Cafeteria, **15**

Cole's French Dipped Sandwiches, **14**

El Cholo, **17**

Guelaguetza, **18**

Jeepney Grill, **23**

La Luz del Dia, **8**

Langer's, **20**

Lucky Deli, **5**

Mayflower Restaurant, **2**

Mr. Ramen, **9**

Mon Kee's Seafood Restaurant, **7**

New Moon, **16**

Original Pantry Café, **19**

Paru's Indian Vegetarian, **1**

Philippe the Original, **6**

Rascals, **11**

Señor Fish, **10**

Shabu Shabu House, **13**

Sushi and Teri, **12**

Won Kok Dim Sum, **3**

Woo Lae Oak, **22**

Yang Chow, **4**

**Rascals.** Set in the Japanese Village in Little Tokyo, across from the Japanese American Museum, this outdoor restaurant serves a variety of tasty morsels, including cheeseburger meals, teriyaki bowls, and chow mein, to a touristy crowd enjoying the Japanese street scene. *103 Japanese Village Plaza, Little Tokyo, tel. 213/687–4811. No credit cards.*

**Sushi and Teri.** Cheap eats in Little Tokyo are not the norm, but this modest restaurant offers no-frills Japanese fast food for reasonable prices. Specials include sesame-teriyaki chicken with rice and green salad and an even tastier deal on the red snapper. *116 Japanese Village Plaza, Little Tokyo, tel. 213/687–8368.*

**Won Kok Dim Sum.** Right off the main drag of Chinatown, Won Kok offers cheap and delicious dumplings, often steamed, minus the fancy presentation. The waiter will have you look through the steamer to pick out your tasty treats: barbecued chicken or pork buns, steamed shrimp rolls, and taro cake. Taste it all and fill up for a song. *210 Alpine St., at New High St., Chinatown, tel. 213/613–0700.*

**UNDER $10 • Guelaguetza.** The kitchen here prepares the lively (but not too spicy) dishes of one of Mexico's most respected culinary regions, Oaxaca. The standouts are the red, yellow, and brown *moles* (sauces), intensely flavored with intricate combinations of nuts, spices, chiles, and bitter chocolate. Be sure to order the *clayudas* (similar to pizza) topped with white cheese and *tasajo* (dried beef), *cecino* (chile marinated pork), or *chorizo* (sausage), plus a barbecued goat taco or two. *3337½ W. 8th St., near Bundy Dr., tel. 323/427–0601.*

**Jeepney Grill.** A minimall filled with upscale Korean restaurants is probably not the first place you'd think of looking for Filipino food. Nonetheless, here it is—and with a gaudily painted Jeep from Manila parked right in the center of the small dining area. Many of the traditional pork and beef barbecue dishes are marinated in a surprisingly tasty concoction of banana sauce, honey, and spices. *3470 W. 6th St., at Alexandria Ave., tel. 213/739–2971.*

**Langer's.** If you like the food at Canter's (*see* West Hollywood, *below*) but prefer to avoid beautiful people, head to this emptier, spookier deli right on MacArthur Park. The food and prices are comparable (pastrami with coleslaw, sauce, and a pickle), but the potato pancakes at Langer's could feed you and a traveling companion for the better part of a week. Sit at the bar for the added bonus of hearing the cooks talk in Spanish about their kosher cuisine. *704 S. Alvarado St., at 7th St., tel. 213/483–8050. Closed Sun.*

**Mayflower Restaurant.** Literally a mom-and-pop restaurant (sometimes the owners wear T-shirts identifying themselves as such), the Mayflower serves up good Chinese food for low prices. You can keep it under $5 by ordering one of the rice plates, such as roast duck or beef with tomato over rice, or you can try a more exotic item like dried squid with spicy salt. *800 Yale St., at Alpine St., tel. 213/626–7113.*

**Mr. Ramen.** For late-night grub in a rather strange space, stop by this Japanese *ramen* house, where the tablecloths are vinyl and the music is reggae. Order a special, such as chicken cutlet, miso soup, rice, and salad, a rice bowl, or ramen. Don't expect Japanese high cuisine; this is just a place to eat downtown after the sun has set. *341½ E. 1st St., at San Pedro St., Little Tokyo, tel. 213/626–4252. Closed Mon.*

**New Moon.** The Garment District building may be old and industrial, but this Asian restaurant's space is modern and airy- –a good place for lunch. Try the velvet chicken (with straw mushrooms, young corn, and Chinese snow peas in white sauce). Vegetarians can indulge in stir-fry vegetables, and there's the requisite selection of rice and noodles. *102 W. 9th St., at Main St., tel. 213/624–0186. Closed Sun.*

**Original Pantry Café.** This classic American greasy spoon isn't the place to drag a vegetarian friend: They've been carving up about 7,200 cows a year since 1924. Pot roast, stewed chicken, and creamed tuna are menu staples. With red-vinyl stools, stainless-steel countertops, and employees with names like Vera, Flo, Mel, and Alice, the whole joint could qualify as a living museum. Next door, the **Pantry Bake Shoppe** is a less greasy alternative serving decent, moderately priced sandwiches, soups, and salads. *875–877 S. Figueroa St., at 9th St., tel. 213/972–9279 for Original Café or 213/627–6879 for Bake Shoppe.*

**Paru's Indian Vegetarian.** Don't be intimidated by the prison- style fence or the need to be buzzed in. You'll enter a beautiful garden patio and then a restaurant decorated with tapestries and photos of Indian temples. The food is tasty and plentiful. Try the Delhi Durbar (Indian bread, chickpea curry, and sauces). Shave a few bucks off your meal by ordering a main dish without the bread, rice, and chutneys. *5140 Sunset Blvd., at Normandie Ave., tel. 323/661–7600.*

**Señor Fish.** Zip in here for a speedy, fresh Mexican meal. This branch of the small, well-run chain sits on the edge of Little Tokyo, close to the Geffen Contemporary and the Japanese-American Museum; it has an inviting patio. Try a fish taco, or, if you're not into marine life, a tostada. *422 E. 1st St., at Alameda St., tel. 213/625–0566.*

**Shabu Shabu House.** There's only one dish on this menu: Japanese *shabu shabu.* You cook the parchment-thin slices of beef yourself in a broth of vegetables and noodles. Though it's at the center of touristy Japanese Village, it's far from a tourist trap. *127 Japanese Village Plaza Mall, between San Pedro and Center Sts., Little Tokyo, tel. 213/680–3890. Closed Mon.*

**UNDER $15 • El Cholo.** Tasty Mexican food and attentive service make this festive, decades-old restaurant well worth the drive. Try the cheese-filled enchilada *suiza* or the *carne asada* (steak). To make your wait for a table fly by in a veritable blur, grab a margarita at the bar. *1121 S. Western Ave., between Pico and Olympic Blvds. (2 mi west of downtown), tel. 323/734–2773.*

**Mon Kee's Seafood Restaurant.** Residents from all over the city will make the trip to the heart of Chinatown for Mon Kee's seafood—from such exotics as sea cucumber and abalone to more familiar dishes like oyster and crab. Reasonably priced Cantonese poultry, pork, beef, and vegetable dishes are also served. *679 N. Spring St., between Ord St. and Cesar E. Chavez Ave., tel. 213/628–6717.*

*For the premier on-line foodie resource in L.A., point your browser to www.calendarlive.com's restaurant section. You can search restaurants by cuisine, location, name, and price range, check recent reviews, or hit the editor's pick.*

**Woo Lae Oak.** At this classic Korean barbecue, you grill your dinner at the table, choosing from chicken, squid, beef, pork, and other meats. If you choose a noodle dish, however, you won't have to use your cooking skills. Cavernous ceilings and a fountain add a touch of grandeur. *623 S. Western Ave., between Wilshire Blvd. and 6th St., tel. 213/384–2244.*

**UNDER $20 • Atlas Bar and Grill.** Incredibly high ceilings with hanging lightning bolt and star-burst lighting fixtures, flickering candlelight, soft jazz and Latin music, and crisp white tablecloths add atmosphere to this sensational place where you don't merely eat, you *dine.* Try the exotica salad (shrimp, avocado, hearts of palm, artichoke, and passion fruit vinaigrette) or a heftier dish such as spicy jerk chicken. For vegetarians there are a few items, including grilled seasonal vegetables with tomatoes and smoked mozzarella. *3760 Wilshire Blvd., at Western Ave., tel. 213/380–8400. Closed Sun.*

**Yang Chow.** There hasn't been an empty table at this Chinatown restaurant in years, thanks to the addictive power of the slippery shrimp (crisp, juicy, sweet, hot, and sour all at once), fiery Szechuan dumplings, dried-fried (spicy, sautéed) string beans, and pan-fried dumplings. Booths are comfortable, and the service is crackerjack and friendly. *379 N. Broadway, tel. 213/625–0811.*

**SPLURGE • Ciudad.** Famed chefs Susan Fenniger and Mary Sue Millican conjure up their spins on Latin American dishes in a retro setting. Lunch sandwiches are about $10 while midday entrées, like Peruvian poached shrimp or Cuban fried chicken salad, are in the $10 to $14 range. Dinner entrées could include tamarind-glazed salmon or Argentinean gaucho steak; they normally run $12.50 to $22. *445 S. Figueroa St., between 4th and 5th Sts., tel. 213/486–5171.*

# SOUTH-CENTRAL

You won't find fancy presentations in the void between the Santa Monica, San Diego, Century, and Harbor freeways, but there is plenty of straightforward, satisfying food served to real people.

**UNDER $5 • Good Life Health Centre.** This is *the* purveyor of organic food, fresh vegetarian eats, and music in South-Central. By day the amiable staff serves salads and soups, as well as wheat grass, smoothies, coffee, and herbal tea from the juice bar. When the kitchen closes at 7, crowds pour in for the entertainment. Monday night hums with jazz; reggae starts early on Saturday at 5, and lectures and poetry fill the other slots. The cover is never more than $5; call to see what's on. *3631 S. Crenshaw Blvd., at Exposition Blvd., tel. 323/731–0588.*

**Randy's Donuts.** With the notable exception of the monumental Programmatic Do-Nut-Hole in La Puente, this is the last great 24-hour drive-thru doughnut shop in the Southland. A dozen glazed zingers and some gourmet coffee will keep you going all day. There is also a drive-thru ice-cream joint in the same lot. *La Cienega Blvd. at Manchester Blvd., just west of I-405, Inglewood, no phone.*

**Tito's Tacos.** Famished families and carpoolers who would rather wait out the traffic with a crispy taco or huge burrito swear by Tito's no-nonsense grub. Tax is included in prices, but cheese is extra. This particular corner is an ideal spot for midtown people-watching. Next door, **Lucy's Drive-In** serves cheap Mexican and American fare and fresh juices. *11222 Washington Pl., 1 block west of Sepulveda, Culver City, tel. 310/391–5780.*

**UNDER $10 • Johnnie's Pastrami.** Johnnie's has been serving the best non-Jewish French dip in L.A. since 1952. The tableside jukeboxes—and even some of the waitresses—are original staples of this local institution. A fascinating crowd of locals, crosstown commuters, and club goers all frequent this hot spot for the same reasons: friendly, efficient service and mounds of piping-hot salty pastrami. *4017 S. Sepulveda Blvd., between Washington Pl. and Washington Blvd., Culver City, tel. 310/397–6654. No credit cards.*

**Toucan.** You'll need a major-league appetite for the *raino* (a thick, gumbolike brew with oxtail) or the riotous *boil up* (hearty Belizean mulligan stew served Saturday only). All entrées come with fried plantains and with rice and beans stewed in coconut milk. Don't even think of passing on dessert; try the bread, rice, or sweet potato pudding *before* your meal if you have to. *3854 Crenshaw Blvd., in Crenshaw Sq. Center, tel. 323/293– 9490. No credit cards. Closed Sun.*

**UNDER $15 • Stevie's on the Strip.** This happening Creole diner brews up the best high-viscosity gumbo in L.A.; it's thick with shrimp, smoked chicken, sausage, and sweet crab legs poured over rice. Among the weekday lunch specials is the house specialty: smoky fried chicken. Don't leave without a dollop of banana pudding. *5730 W. Adams Blvd., near La Cienega Blvd., tel. 323/734–6975.*

# EAST L.A.

You will have no problem finding good, cheap Mexican food anywhere in East L.A.; the only difficulty will be deciding between taco trucks and restaurants. The taco trucks that line Cesar E. Chavez Avenue and Olympic Boulevard offer consistently good tacos and burritos, and the better trucks offer a choice of garnishes, from fresh radishes to pickled jalapeños and carrots. You can find similarly cheap Mexican grub in the smaller *taquerías* throughout the neighborhood. If you spend slightly more, you get a nicer place, with table service and, often, live music.

**UNDER $5 • King Taco.** If you are unsure which taquería to enter, try one of the many King Taco locales in East L.A.; you'll get reliably tasty tacos, burritos, tostadas, and the like. Dependability has a price—tacos here are 99(rather than the standard 50), and a burrito filling enough for a week will put you out $2.99. Most locations have indoor and outdoor seating, usually filled with happy diners. *2400 Cesar E. Chavez Ave., at Soto St., tel. 323/268–2267; call for other locations.*

**Siete Mares Seafood Express.** They serve wonderful Mexican seafood at this simple sit-down taquería. Fish tacos (tortillas with deep-fried white fish, onions, and salsa) are just $2, while a seviche tostada (crisp tortilla with tangy raw fish salad) is a mere $1.50. The decor is part maritime mural, part boxing memorabilia; the crowd comes from both within and outside the neighborhood. *1912 Cesar E. Chavez Ave., at State St., tel. 323/267–9748.*

**UNDER $10 • El Tarasco.** East L.A.'s liveliest dining ambience can be found at this restaurant atop El Mercado de Los Angeles (*see* East L.A. *in* Chapter 2). Not one, but two full mariachi bands trade songs and even play over one another—one band takes the stage at El Tarasco, the other band less than 20 yards away at a competing restaurant. No wall separates the two dining establishments, so as you enjoy your chimichangas or enchiladas (combinations include rice, beans, and salad) you will be treated either to beautiful music or cacophony. Either way there's always a crowd, and it's tons of fun. *3425 E. 1st St., at Lorena St., tel. 323/262–4507.*

**UNDER $15 • La Parilla.** This festive restaurant is best known for its celebrated guacamole, made right at your table. You can stick to the plain grilled meat specialties (*parilla* means grill), like the *carne asada* (steak), or branch out to fancier fare, like chicken *mole* (with a spicy chocolate-based sauce). The busy visual decor is accompanied by live mariachi music, and the restaurant is popular with Latinos and gringos alike. *2126 Cesar E. Chavez Ave., between St. Louis and Chicago Sts., tel. 323/262–3434.*

**La Serenata de Garibaldi.** Probably the fanciest restaurant in East L.A., La Serenata is so popular among the young power-lunch set they had to open a Westside branch to satisfy customers who think the city ends east of the Los Angeles River. You can get the famed seafood specialties for under $15 during lunch, but dinner might run you more. Try the fish enchiladas in green tomatillo sauce or a chicken quesadilla, like no quesadilla you've ever seen. *1842 E. 1st St., between Boyle and State Sts., tel. 323/265–2887. Closed Mon.*

# HOLLYWOOD AND SILVER LAKE

Budget travelers can choose from an ample selection of quirky, inexpensive eateries along Hollywood Boulevard (between Highland and La Brea avenues) or succumb to one of the burger joints and taco stands along Santa Monica Boulevard. F. Scott Fitzgerald was once a regular customer at the **Musso & Frank Grill** (6667 Hollywood Blvd., at Cherokee Ave., tel. 323/467–7788), but don't let that tempt you into eating at "the oldest restaurant in Hollywood." Instead, make like Gatsby: Pass up the overpriced food (corned beef sandwiches for $10 and steaks for $20) and head straight for the cocktails. On Sunday from 8:30 AM to 1 PM, pick up organic produce at the **Hollywood Farmers' Market** (Ivar Ave. between Hollywood Blvd. and Selma Ave., tel. 323/463–3171).

East of Hollywood lies the once-sleepy **Silver Lake** neighborhood. Now, with its growing gay community and packs of movie-industry staffers and writers, it's begun to attract interesting eateries like Fred 62 and Paio. Hot-to-trot eateries are popping up in nearby **Los Feliz,** too, joining the ethnic favorites.

*The Original Pantry Café is owned by L.A. businessman and (at press time) Republican mayor Richard Riordan—so if something's wrong with your order, go right to the top and ask for Dick.*

*See the Western Los Angeles Dining map.*

**UNDER $5 • Al Wazir Chicken.** This Middle Eastern rotisserie serves tender and delicious chicken, lamb, and beef. The basic white dining room, snug in a minimall, has no apparent ventilation and is quite hot. The chicken salad and the chicken kebabs are succulent, but they tend to overdo the mayonnaise-based sauces, especially on the salads. *6051 Hollywood Blvd., at Gower St., Hollywood, tel. 323/856–0660.*

**Larchmont Deli.** Just south of Hollywood, you'll find the charming, small Larchmont Village neighborhood. Around the corner from its Main Street—Larchmont Boulevard—sits this Greek deli where a fat half-sandwich and a soda cost only $4.95. The Greek salads and whole sandwiches are big enough for two. *5210 Beverly Blvd., at Larchmont Blvd., tel. 323/466–1193.*

**Los Tacos.** Tacos, enchiladas, and other Mexican standbys are served here late into the night. The food won't rock your world, but talk about convenience! You could get your car detailed while you nosh. *1043 N. La Brea, at Santa Monica Blvd., at the Bel-Air Car Wash, Hollywood, tel. 323/850–9346.*

**Yuca's Hut.** Long a local favorite, this parking lot stand makes some of the tastiest burritos, tacos, and *carnitas* (shredded pork) in the area. Sit outside with a bottle of Corona from the nearby liquor store and you'll be doing the real L.A. thing. It may not be fancy, but this was one of food critic Ruth Reichl's favorite spots. *2056 N. Hillhurst Ave., at Price St., Los Feliz, tel. 323/662–1214. No credit cards. Closed Sun.*

**Zankou Chicken.** For rotisserie chicken that leaves the colonel in the dust, head to this modest Armenian restaurant tucked away in a strip mall. Try the half chicken with bread, tomatoes, and some exceptional garlic sauce. They also serve beef and chicken *shawarma* (straight off the spit) and falafel sandwiches. *5065 Sunset Blvd., at Normandie Ave., Hollywood, tel. 323/665–7842. No credit cards.*

**UNDER $10 • Csárdás.** The television drones on at this Hungarian restaurant while patrons eat delicious bowls of beef bouillon with noodles or a good plate of Wiener schnitzel. The waiters—as though a living testament to the authenticity of this Hungarian experience—speak little or no English. Don't expect fancy service or fancy digs, but you will get delicious, hearty meals only a grandmother could execute as well. *5820 Melrose Ave., at Vine St., Hollywood, tel. 323/962–6434.*

**Fabiolus Cafe.** Vegetarians will be happy here—most dishes have no meat. Try the rigatoni *salsa rosa* (in red sauce) or the Asiago sandwich while basking on the calm back patio filled with a wild assortment of cacti, palms, and trees. *6270 Sunset Blvd., at Vine St., Hollywood, tel. 323/467–2882; 5750 Melrose Ave., at Lucerne Blvd., tel. 323/461–1549; 5255 Melrose Ave., at N. Van Ness Ave., tel. 323/464–5857. Closed weekends.*

**Hollywood Canteen.** Dimly lighted, elegant, yet relaxed, this 1940s-style diner is jam-packed at lunch with execs and gofers from the nearby studios. Try the baby artichoke salad with sliced Parmesan or the swordfish sandwich with tartar sauce for lunch. Come dinnertime, the place is quiet and the food more

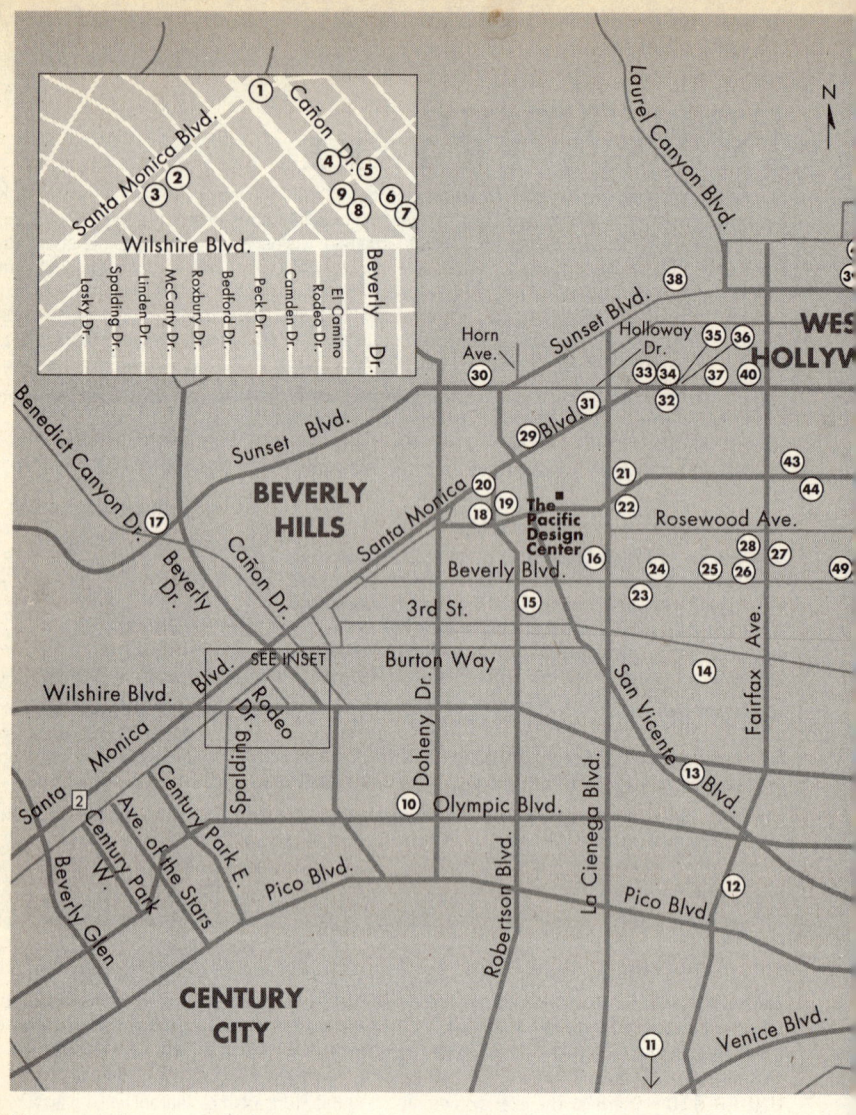

Al Wazir
Chicken, **66**
Authentic Café, **49**
Baja Fresh, **9**
Basix Cafe, **33**
Benvenuto
Caffe, **31**
Birds, **69**
Bossa Nova, **20**
Bourbon Street
Shrimp, **22**
Cadillac Cafe, **16**

Caffe Latte, **13**
Caffè Luna, **43**
California Chicken
Café, **47**
Canter's, **28**
Carney's, **38**
Chan Dara, **62**
Chang's, **3**
Cobalt Cantina, **19**
Crazy Fish, **10**
Csárdás, **53**

Da Pasquale, **2**
Damiano's, **27**
Duke's, **30**
Eat Well, **32**
El Coyote Café, **50**
Fabiolus
Cafe, **56, 57, 63**
Flora Kitchen, **52**
Flowering Tree, **37**
Fred 62, **74**
French Quarter, **40**

Greenwich
Village, **29**
Hollywood
Canteen, **58**
Hollywood Hills
Coffee Shop, **67**
Hugo's, **34**
Intermezzo, **46**
Ipanema Grill, **26**
Jacopo's, **1**
Jan's Family
Restaurant, **23**

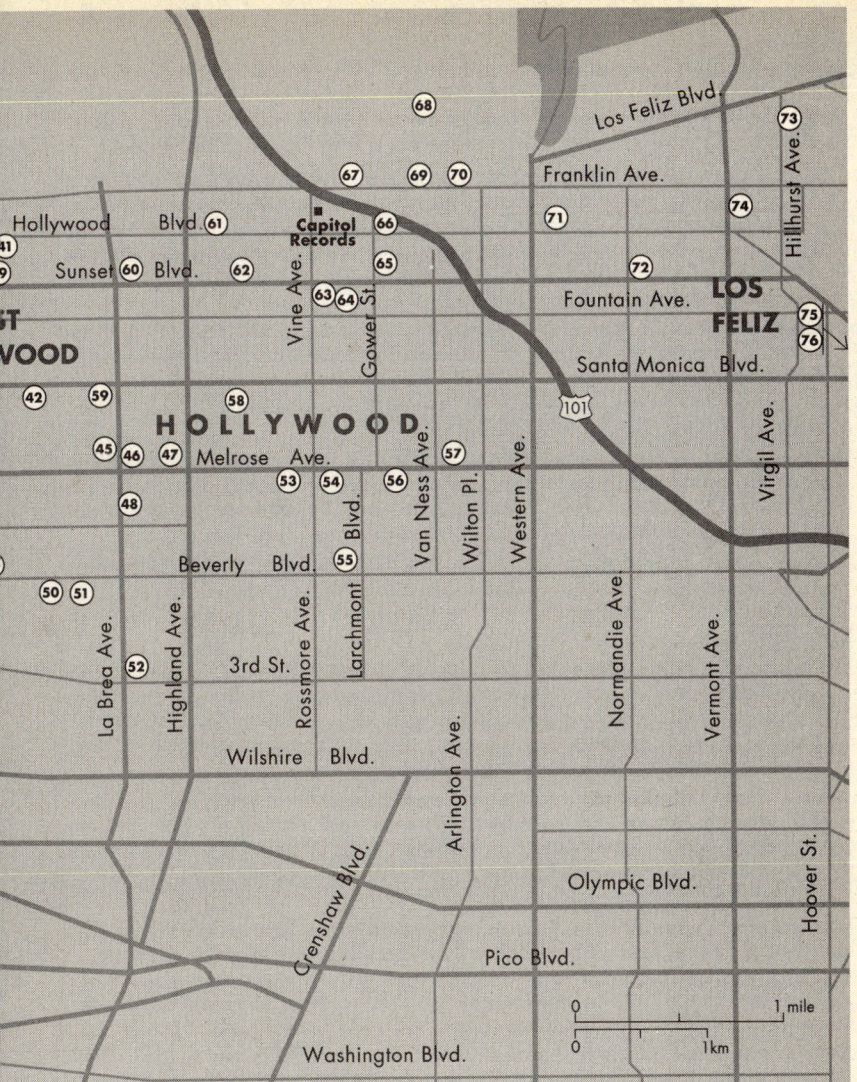

King's Road Cafe, **24**

La Bottega, **35**

Larchmont Deli, **55**

Los Tacos, **59**

Louis XIV, **48**

Marino Pizzeria, **36**

Mario's Peruvian Seafood, **54**

Moun of Tunis, **41**

Mulberry Street Pizzeria, **7**

Nate 'n' Al's, **8**

Netty's, **75**

Newsroom Café, **15**

Noura Café, **21**

Nyala, **12**

Off Vine, **64**

Paio, **76**

Pink's Famous Chili Dogs, **45**

Polo Lounge, **17**

Porta Via, **5**

Prizzi's Piazza, **70**

Red, **51**

Roscoe's House of Chicken 'n' Waffles, **65**

Snow White Cafe, **61**

Sofi, **14**

Spago, **4**

Starlight Cafe, **11**

Swingers Diner, **25**

Tavola Calda, **18**

Thailand Plaza, **71**

Toi on Sunset, **39**

Uzbekistan, **60**

Vienna Café, **44**

Village Coffee Shop, **68**

Yuca's Hut, **73**

Yukon Mining Co., **42**

Zankou Chicken, **72**

expensive. *1006 Seward St., between Santa Monica Blvd. and Romaine St., Hollywood, tel. 323/465–0961. Closed Sun.*

**King's Road Café.** This popular establishment is part coffeehouse, part outdoor café, and part restaurant. You can tuck into an omelet and a strong cup of coffee for breakfast, lunch on inventive pizza or a sandwich (like the spicy rock-shrimp panini), or support the L.A. rotisserie chicken fad (half a chicken, garlic mashed potatoes, and green salad). *8361 Beverly Blvd., at Kings Rd., tel. 323/655–9044.*

**Prizzi's Piazza.** Pick up some bottled poetry from the corner liquor store before going to Prizzi's, a charming restaurant serving giant portions of pasta. (Choose your vino wisely, as there's an $8 corkage fee.) This place is justifiably famous for its garlic bread sticks. Sidewalk tables provide excellent people-watching opportunities, with the Scientology Center across the street and the Bourgeois Pig (*see* Cafés and Coffeehouses, *below*) nearby. *5923 Franklin Ave., between Bronson and Tamarind Aves., Hollywood, tel. 323/467–0168.*

**Roscoe's House of Chicken 'n' Waffles.** Don't be fooled by the strange combination of foods in the name of this casual eatery: It is *the* place to go for real down-home Southern cooking. Just ask the people who drive from all over the L.A. basin for Roscoe's fried chicken, waffles, grits, and potatoes at bargain prices. And you can start your day with a glass of sunrise (a mix of orange juice and lemonade). *1514 N. Gower St., at Sunset Blvd., Hollywood, tel. 323/466–9329.*

**Snow White Cafe.** Whistle while you wallow in this whimsical world where dwarfs peek through faux windows above sleigh-shape booths. Pop in for beer or wine at night or for an omelet, burger, or plate of pasta during the day, or just order a Coke, rest your dogs, and count the weirdos passing by the "castle" windows. *6769 Hollywood Blvd., at Highland Ave., Hollywood, tel. 323/465–4444.*

**Swingers Diner.** This '50s-style diner enjoyed a stint as a late- night hangout for cast members of *Beverly Hills 90210*. With the Spelling brats gone, what remains is better-than-average diner fare and smart drinks with names like Thermite Bomb and Female Love. *8020 Beverly Blvd., at Laurel Ave., Hollywood, tel. 323/653–5858.*

**Thailand Plaza.** Above the Silom supermarket, this food-court-like restaurant offers Thai delicacies from eight minirestaurants, whose menus have been consolidated into one for easy ordering. Curry and rice dishes or seafood plates are among the more ordinary things served. On weekend nights a band plays Thai music to a full house. Be prepared to point and pantomime, as English is not a top priority here. *5321 Hollywood Blvd., at Western Ave., Hollywood, tel. 323/993–9000.*

**Toi on Sunset.** Toi offers Thai food as it's never been seen in Thailand. The creative menu caters to a vegetarian diet; the vegetable curries come highly recommended, and most dishes can be prepared meat-free. The decor is definitely avant-grunge (note the giant papier-mâché cat suspended from the ceiling). Patrons with pierced body parts complete the scene. *7505½ Sunset Blvd., at Gardner St., Hollywood, tel. 323/874–8062.*

**Village Coffee Shop.** There's a nice view of the HOLLYWOOD sign on the way up to this Swiss chalet–style diner. Regular good ole American breakfast fare is served all day, along with other deli favorites such as patty melts and chef salads. But even amidst this country kitsch, you can never really escape the city's consciousness—the menu includes low-cal and vegetarian plates and Perrier. *2695 N. Beachwood Dr., at Westshire St., tel. 323/467–5398. Closed Sun.*

**UNDER $15 • Birds.** Go ahead, pick at some marinated rotisserie chicken parts—and try to forget the menacing bird pictures and paraphernalia surrounding you. Perhaps the most disconcerting booth is the one with the larger-than-life photo of Alfred Hitchcock with two big birds on his shoulders hanging above it. The roll-up sandwiches are scrumptious and have chicken (of course) nestled in lots of veggies. *5925 Franklin Ave., at Tamarind and Bronson Aves., Hollywood, tel. 323/465–0175.*

**Chan Dara.** The rock and rap music, '80s decor, and new-wave silver-and-black design set Chan Dara apart from the run-of-the-mill Thai places. The waitresses are not only beautiful; they are also incredibly helpful. Try the vegetable curry or the crab-claw and shrimp pot. The portions are big enough to feed two, especially if you load up on rice. All the stir-fry and noodle dishes can be ordered vegetarian or with chicken, beef, pork, shrimp, or scallops. *1511 N. Cahuenga Blvd., at Sunset Blvd., Hollywood, tel. 323/464–8585.*

**Fred 62.** You can wear anything to this 24-hour diner—if it's black. Its round-the-clock convenience pulls both club kids and neighbors into its vintage-style dining room. The menu may sound goofy but once past the bad jokes you can choose from a mix of Japanese noodle dishes and American classics like tuna melts, macaroni and cheese, and veggie burgers. *1850 N. Vermont Ave., at Russell St., Silver Lake, tel. 323/667–0062.*

**Hollywood Hills Coffee Shop.** It may not look like much, but this little café turns out surprisingly good food for your money. Breakfast covers classics like huevos rancheros, cheese blintzes, and even a whole grilled salmon trout. For dinner, there are vegetarian choices as well as their perennial favorite, chicken-fried steak. You could find yourself sharing the dining room with a troupe of green-haired rockers or the entire Jeanette MacDonald International Fan Club—or both. *6145 Franklin Ave., between Gower and Vine Sts., Hollywood, tel. 323/467–7678.*

**Netty's.** At this unpretentious eatery, movie-industry types keep their sunglasses on in the shaded patio while making and breaking deals. The daily specials run from Cajun to contemporary; linger over choices such as shrimp and crayfish etoufée, yellowtail with ginger-lime-basil butter, vegetable ravioli, or gazpacho while eavesdropping on the execs. And don't let the flan pass you by. Call 323/665–3474 to hear the daily menu. *1700 Silver Lake Blvd., at Effie St., Silver Lake, tel. 323/662–8655. Closed Sun.*

**Uzbekistan.** This cheerful restaurant with lavender tablecloths, blue glass, and colorful murals offers both Uzbeki and Russian specialties. Especially interesting are the *manti* (steamed lamb dumplings) and the *shashlik* (tender and juicy shish kebab). Russian dishes include oxtail stew and chicken Kiev. On the weekends a band plays international pop music. *7077 Sunset Blvd., at La Brea Ave., Hollywood, tel. 323/464–3663.*

**UNDER $20 • Moun of Tunis.** Roaming belly dancers entertain diners indulging in one of eight prix fixe options, ranging from soup and couscous to a five-item Moroccan or Tunisian feast. Every inch of the restaurant is covered with tapestries, pillows, and rugs. *7445½ Sunset Blvd., between Fairfax and Gardner Aves., Hollywood, tel. 323/874–3333.*

**Off Vine.** This adorable restaurant is in an old bungalow with huge hedges separating the intimate patio from the street. For lunch, try the Southwestern fettuccine with shrimp, the frittata *tuscana* (with vegetables and olives) or one of the many salads. Dinner entrées, such as the pecan-breaded chicken and the pasta broccoli, are delightfully different. *6263 Leland Way, at Vine St., 1 block south of Sunset Blvd., Hollywood, tel. 323/962–1900.*

**SPLURGE • Paio.** The young chef of this small, smart restaurant has helped propel Silver Lake's culinary trajectory. Start with white-bean soup or deep-fried salmon wontons, then move on to something like roasted quail or barbecued fried chicken. (Most entrées are in the $15–$24 range.) The pecan-crusted apple tart is not to be missed. Bringing your own wine helps keep the tab down *and* there's no corkage fee. *2520 Hyperion Ave., near Tracy St., Silver Lake, tel. 323/953–1973.*

# WEST HOLLYWOOD

Santa Monica Boulevard (from La Cienega Boulevard to Doheny Drive) is host to a bevy of restaurants, cafés, and stands. For cheap, fast eats, try **Hamburger Haven** (8954 Santa Monica Blvd., at Robertson Blvd., tel. 310/659–8796) or **L.A. Buns** (8787 Santa Monica Blvd., at Palm Ave., tel. 310/659–3745). West Hollywood also has more than its fair share of luxurious bistros and restaurants, including the original Spago, which put chef Wolfgang Puck on the map.

*See the West Los Angeles Dining map.*

**UNDER $5 • Carney's.** For low-price, high-viscosity chili concoctions, burgers, or hot dogs, find a seat in this former train caboose. It's open until midnight Sunday–Thursday, 'til 2 AM on Friday and Saturday. *8351 Sunset Blvd., at Sweetzer Ave., tel. 323/654–8300.*

**Eat Well.** This white-box, blond-wood hangout serves breakfast and lunch every day and dinner weekdays to a mostly gay crowd. The menu relies heavily on American comfort food like hamburgers, sandwiches, and pancakes. *8252 Santa Monica Blvd., at Harper Ave., tel. 323/656–1383.*

**Greenwich Village.** Join some overzealous and underfed club goers and order a slice of pizza at the counter. As they know all too well, it will add just $2 to your night out. *8937 Santa Monica Blvd., at San Vicente Blvd., tel. 310/278–2003.*

**Ipanema Grill.** This crisply casual Brazilian café offers great lunch values, like the $4.95 marinated chicken or beef served with green salad, platanos, rice and beans, and fluffy manioc root. Drinks include caffeine-packed *guarana*. *7912 Beverly Blvd., at Fairfax Ave., tel. 323/933–7254.*

**Marino Pizzeria.** Besides delicious, fancy pizzas like the Vaticano (yellow tomatoes, mozzarella, and basil), Marino's also cooks up a variety of focaccia, including the Atomico (tomatoes, crushed red chili, and spicy grated cheese). *8274 Santa Monica Blvd., at Sweetzer Ave., tel. 323/654–6075.*

**UNDER $10 • Basix Café.** The restaurant's porch feels like the patio of a gay man's Italian coast home—breezy, simple, austere, and filled with gay-friendly friends and neighbors. The *panzanella* salad (with cucumbers, tomatoes, and croutons, but no lettuce) is a refreshing snack on a hot day. Grab a sandwich at lunch; for dinner try one of the tasty thin-crust grilled pizzas, pasta dishes, or mesquite-grilled chicken, beef, and veggies. *8333 Santa Monica Blvd., at Flores St., tel. 323/848–2460.*

**Benvenuto Caffè.** This conscientious, gay-friendly Italian restaurant has a dim, recessed interior and a cheery, street-side terrace. The pizzas and pastas stay close to authentic—try the penne *al pomodoro* or the pizza *rustica.* For a light meal, consider the *panini vegetali. 8512 Santa Monica Blvd., at La Cienega Blvd., tel. 310/659–8635.*

**Bossa Nova.** The sunny mood in this Brazilian restaurant is infectious; even the bathroom looks chipper with its wall-size sunflowers. Try the sautéed black tiger shrimp served with rice, black beans, plantains, and yucca flower or the mushroom appetizer, which is big enough for a meal. FYI: Mix the yucca flower with the beans and rice to add texture. *685 N. Robertson Blvd., at Santa Monica Blvd., tel. 310/657–5070.*

**Cadillac Café.** A fun alternative to the food chains in the nearby Beverly Center, this Jetsons-inspired spot serves weird-sounding but good-tasting dishes such as Original Turkey Sundae and Burnt Meatloaf Marinara. Or stay on more familiar turf with a smoked salmon and brie sandwich, grilled ahi tuna salad Niçoise, or angel hair pasta with shrimp. Weekend breakfasts include a bacon, eggs, and cheese pasta. *359 N. La Cienega Blvd., at Oakwood Ave., tel. 310/657–6591.*

**Canter's.** Since 1948 waitresses of a certain age have served up Reuben sandwiches, chips, and a pickle to the neighborhood folks and those willing to drive the distance for New York City–style deli grub. Enjoy the sight of vinyl booths filled with seniors or club kids. For an after-meal drink, pop into the attached music venue, the **Kibitz Room.** *419 N. Fairfax Ave., between Beverly Blvd. and Melrose Ave., Fairfax, tel. 323/651–2030.*

**Flowering Tree.** Focusing on organic, no-artificial-anything dishes—from wheat-free waffles to sugarless chocolate mousse pie—this tiny, Formica-counter joint hands you an inventive and surprisingly affordable menu, including turkey and tempeh burgers and turkey-chili burritos. It's a friendly place where the staff greets longtime customers by name. *8253 Santa Monica Blvd., between La Cienega and N. Crescent Heights Blvds., tel. 323/654–4332.*

**French Quarter.** Entirely indoors, this market-square restaurant falls somewhere between Disneyland's New Orleans Square and the real Louisiana deal, with its koi pond, small shops, and clusters of café seating. The wait to get a table can be long, but the staff will provide you with a beeper so you can wander about the "market." The large menu of salads, sandwiches, entrées, and breakfast items tends toward the healthy West Coast rather than the deep-fried South. Try the fresh strawberry crepes or the crab-cake sandwich. Lucky for you late risers, breakfast is always served. *7985 Santa Monica Blvd., between Crescent Heights Blvd. and Fairfax Ave., tel. 323/654–0898.*

**Hugo's.** You can breakfast with the stars, or so rumor has it, sampling creative cooking such as pumpkin pancakes in a pleasant, sunny atmosphere. The clientele is mostly a well-groomed West Hollywood and movie-industry crowd. *8401 Santa Monica Blvd., at King's Rd., tel. 323/654–3993.*

**La Bottega.** Euro-waiters scoot around this small deli serving such Italian dishes as gnocchi and *insalate tricolore.* The sandwiches, combined with some deli salads and sweets from the minuscule grocery section, are perfect for an upscale picnic. *8301 Santa Monica Blvd., at Sweetzer Ave., tel. 323/654–1214.*

**Noura Café.** The *oliveh* salad (Middle Eastern chicken and potato salad) and the *shawarma* plate (rotisserie lamb and beef with salad, hummus, and potatoes) are out-of-this-world delicious. Don't hesitate to ask for a sample to help you decide. Be aware that the sandwiches can be dry, so you might want to order yogurt sauce or hummus to accompany them. For added exotic ambience, sit on a pillow in lieu of a chair. *8479 Melrose Ave., at La Cienega Blvd., tel. 323/651–4581.*

**Yukon Mining Co.** To passersby this may seem like any other American coffee shop, with its green-vinyl booths and its pathetic attempt at a mining theme. But after midnight it takes on a whole new identity—just like the drag queens who show up for a quick, surprisingly ungreasy bite to eat after hours of clubbing. The waitresses are of the jaded-but-sweet variety and can be heard yelling things like, "I feel like a chicken with my head cut off tonight" (supply a twang for full effect). The menu is a predictable collection of sandwiches, omelets, and burgers. The BLT with avocado hits the late-night snack spot. *7328 Santa Monica Blvd., between La Brea and Fairfax Aves., tel. 323/851–8833.*

**UNDER $15 • Bourbon Street Shrimp.** Night is the perfect time for gumbo or shrimp and rice on a patio lush with bougainvillea and sparkling with red Christmas lights. Finish dinner off with a small slice of pecan pie. Of course, the live rhythm and blues every Sunday afternoon should be accompanied by a tall, cold beer. Inside at the bar, the music is louder and the air hotter. *8454 Melrose Ave., at La Cienega Blvd., tel. 323/653–2640.*

**Cobalt Cantina.** Everything except the food is blue at this party place too cobalt cool even for itself. The interesting menu is based on Mexican cuisine, with variations on Spanish and Italian food; try the baja tomatillo chicken (with pumpkin seeds and tomatillo salsa) or Cal-Mex pasta. *616 N. Robertson Blvd., at Santa Monica Blvd., tel. 310/659–8691.*

**Duke's.** The food is nothing special, but your chances of dining with rockers and character actors at this Sunset Boulevard burger joint are great. Eat your BLT under the gleaming head shots of famous past diners or try a gourmet burger. *8909 Sunset Blvd., at San Vicente Blvd., tel. 310/652–3100. No dinner weekends.*

**Tavola Calda.** This low-tech Italian nirvana draws the budget- watching crowd, who are attracted to the inexpensive entrées. Cabaret tables are scattered about the roomy place, with the piano player and the high ceilings and intimate lighting all working together to set the upbeat tone—don't be surprised if one of the customers gets up to do a rendition from a popular opera. Best bets on the limited menu are unusual gourmet pizzas, like the vegetarian, cheeseless pie, and risotto that's reminiscent of Milan. *7371 Melrose Ave., at Robertson Blvd., tel. 323/658–6340.*

**UNDER $20 • Sofi.** Hidden down a narrow passageway is this friendly little taverna that makes you feel like you've been transported straight to Mykonos. Enjoy your meal in the stone-wall dining room or under a vine-shaded patio. The food is authentic Greek cuisine: *dolmas* (stuffed grape leaves), lamb gyros, a sampling of traditional salads, phyllo pies, spanakopita, and souvlakia. *8030¾ W. 3rd St., between Crescent Heights Blvd. and Fairfax Ave., tel. 323/651–0346. No lunch Sun.*

# MELROSE, WILSHIRE, AND CULVER CITY

In this neck of the woods you can graze among glam cafés, strip-mall finds, or bare-bones takeout stands. There are plenty of options west of La Brea Avenue between Santa Monica Boulevard and the Santa Monica Freeway (I–10). Chic and casual restaurants are also strung along trendy Melrose Avenue and down La Brea Avenue.

*See the Western Los Angeles Dining map.*

**UNDER $5 • Pink's Famous Chili Dogs.** For the absolute best chili creations in town, keep your eyes peeled for the landmark neon sign. They've been stuffing buns daily 9:30 AM–2 AM (Friday and Saturday until 3 AM) since 1939. *709 N. La Brea Ave., at Melrose Ave., tel. 323/931–4223.*

**Damiano's.** Pick up hero sandwiches or a slice of New York–style pizza for a snack or a late-night meal in this long, dark, Italian restaurant. They deliver until 6 AM. *412 N. Fairfax Ave., between Beverly and Melrose Aves., tel. 310/658–7611.*

**India Sweets & Spices.** Many Indian food markets also serve amazingly inexpensive, delicious, vegetarian meals in plastic containers. Here you sit at one of the four tables out front and savor your $3.99 multicourse meal of *chana* (chickpeas), *pakora* (fritter), spinach, rice, bread and *papadum* (a crispy, chickpea- flour crepe), rounded off, if you like, with a mango *lassi* (a yogurt drink). And it's barely a block from the Museum of Jurassic Technology (*see* Chapter 2). *9409 Venice Blvd., at Bagley Ave., Culver City, tel. 310/837–5286.*

**UNDER $10 • California Chicken Café.** This casual restaurant is a lunch favorite with the office crowd and stray café types. Chicken—pita chicken sandwiches, chicken salad, and rotisserie chicken—dominates the menu, but vegetarians can choose from a few nonmeat salads. *6805 Melrose Ave., between La Brea and Highland Aves., tel. 323/935–5877. No credit cards. Closed Sun.*

**El Coyote Café.** The only way to explain the enormous popularity of El Coyote—site of the last meal of Manson victims Sharon Tate and company—is the abundance of cheap liquor and way tasty margaritas. The food borders on awful, the decor a tacky Tinseltown approximation of Mexican. Nonetheless, it continually draws a crowd from every walk of life, including a fair number of celebrities. Try a combination plate (select from enchiladas, tacos, tamales, and the like). *7312 Beverly Blvd., just west of Poinsettia Pl., tel. 323/939–2255.*

**Flora Kitchen.** This corner café is a popular place to pick up the makings for a gourmet picnic to enjoy at the Hollywood Bowl. It's also an ideal spot for a sit-down lunch at tables surrounded by buckets of

# BEYOND MICKEY D'S

*If the thought of dining at a chain restaurant makes you break out in hives, reconsider when visiting Los Angeles. A number of locally owned chains keep residents coming back for great, reliable eats.*

**California Pizza Kitchen.** *The main event is pizza with unusual toppings like Peking duck, Thai chicken, guacamole, and smoked salmon. 330 S. Hope St., between 3rd and 4th Sts., downtown, tel. 213/626–2616; 121 N. La Cienega Blvd., in Beverly Center, West Hollywood, tel. 310/854–6555; 1815 Hawthorne Blvd., at Artesia Blvd., Redondo Beach, tel. 310/370–9931.*

**Chin Chin.** *L.A.'s hip come here for Chinese food California style. The Chinese chicken salad is a favorite. 8618 Sunset Blvd., between La Cienega Blvd. and Doheny Dr., West Hollywood, tel. 310/652–1818; 13455 Maxella Ave., at Lincoln Blvd., Marina del Rey, tel. 310/823–9999.*

**Gaucho Grill.** *This sparse but stylish nouveau Argentinean restaurant features moderately priced grilled chicken and beef dishes as well as sandwiches and salads. 7980 Sunset Blvd., at Laurel Ave., West Hollywood, tel. 213/656–4152; 1253 Third St. Promenade, Santa Monica, tel. 310/394–4966.*

**Jerry's Famous Deli.** *This 24-hour deli, popular after hours with the clubbing crowd, serves massive sandwiches. 8701 Beverly Blvd., at San Vicente Blvd., West Hollywood, tel. 310/289–1811; 10925 Weyburn Ave., between Broxton Ave. and Westwood Blvd., Westwood, tel. 310/208–3354.*

**Louise's Trattoria.** *Sizable Italian dishes are served alfresco with a California twist. 7505 Melrose Ave., at Gardner St., West Hollywood, tel. 213/651–3880; 1008 Montana Ave., between 10th and 11th Sts., Santa Monica, tel. 310/394–8888; 1430 PCH, at Ave. G, Redondo Beach, tel. 310/316–5236.*

**Tommy's.** *This 24-hour shack is notorious for its chili burgers. 2575 Beverly Blvd., at Rampart Blvd., downtown, tel. 213/389–9060; 1900 Lincoln Blvd., at Pico Blvd., Santa Monica, tel. 310/392–4820; 1310 N. San Fernando Rd., at Burbank Blvd., Burbank, tel. 818/843–9150.*

fresh-picked flowers from the adjacent florist. The quasi–California cuisine menu includes sandwiches, salads, and sinful desserts. *460 S. La Brea Ave., at 6th St., tel. 323/931– 9900. Closed Sun.*

**Intermezzo.** The sweet scent of garlic, basil, and tomato and the clang of pots and pans are perceptible before you reach the door. Not as trendy as its western Melrose cousins, this Italian *ristorante* still dishes up calzone, fettuccine *pomodoro,* and tiramisu with the best of them. French quiche and sandwiches have sneaked onto the copious menu, too. To watch the chef at work, sit at the bar in the front; for romance, park it in the back garden. *6919 Melrose Ave., ½ block east of La Brea Ave., tel. 323/937–2875. Closed Sun.*

**Jan's Family Restaurant.** Not far from the Miracle Mile, this coffeehouse retains its original L.A. drive-up look, with big windows, a long counter, and cozy booths for two or more. The food is absolutely average, but if you crave a BLT or veal parmigiana, the ambience beats Denny's by a long shot. Much of the crowd is either over 65 or—true to its name—moms, dads, and little ones. *8424 Beverly Blvd., at Orlando Ave., tel. 323/651–2866.*

**Mario's Peruvian Seafood.** In an unassuming strip mall near Paramount Pictures studios (*see* Studios *in* Chapter 2), Mario's serves excellent, generous portions of sautéed or fried red snapper, shrimp, and squid, with side orders of Peruvian-style rice and vegetables. *5786 Melrose Ave., at Vine St., tel. 323/466–4181.*

**Starlight Café.** This trattoria is as *très* L.A. as it gets. Lulled by the sun, surrounded by white lattice and bougainvillea, you may almost forget you're basically in a parking lot as you consume a savory seafood salad or a grilled vegetable sandwich at lunch or a colorful spinach and ricotta omelet for a weekend brunch. *10445 Venice Blvd., near Overland Ave., Culver City, 310/559–9325. Closed Mon.*

**UNDER $15 • Authentic Café.** The eclectic menu at this popular eatery combines Southwestern, Latin American, Asian, and Middle Eastern cuisines; the results can be inspired. Try the zesty, wood-grilled Yucatán-style marinated chicken breast with citrus and Mexican spices or the fresh corn tamales. Be prepared to wait for a table in the company of a young, clean-cut, casual crowd. *7605 Beverly Blvd., at N. Curson Ave., tel. 323/939–4626.*

**Caffè Latte.** The location may be nondescript—it's in a strip mall—but the menu pulls out a few stops for budget-minded diners. A dinner like blackened turkey loaf might be a bit out of your price range, but you can get interesting breakfast items, like cappuccino pancakes, for a relative song. The interior is tastefully done in pale oak and coffee sacks, and the tables are often filled with a youngish movie-business crowd. *6254 Wilshire Blvd., at San Vicente Blvd., tel. 323/936–5213.*

**Caffè Luna.** Caffè Luna keeps late hours for a good reason: There's always a crowd (including the occasional hoping-not-to-be-noticed celebrity). The menu includes a wide selection of pastas (buckwheat fettuccine) and pizzas that feed two. The best tables are on an outdoor patio meant to look like an Italian village square, and all come equipped with crayons for between- course scribbling. *7463 Melrose Ave., at Gardner St., tel. 323/655–8647.*

**Louis XIV.** The softly lit, narrow interior is furnished in mock grandeur with majestic carved chairs, gilt mirrors, and chandeliers. The cuisine has a certain amount of flair (tuna carpaccio, papaya salad, rack of lamb), and a cool bar scene develops in late evening after the neighboring movie theater lets out. *606 N. La Brea Ave., at Melrose Ave., tel. 323/934–5102.*

**Nyala.** Though it's surrounded by a bunch of other African eateries, this Ethiopian restaurant stands out, with burnished orange-and-red sponge-painted walls, courteous help, and finger-licking-good food. Lunch and dinner menus are identical. For lunch try the *yedoro tibs* (cubes of chicken sautéed with onions, hot red-pepper paste, and butter) or *yemiser wot* (red lentil stew). On Friday and Saturday stop in for some Ethiopian music. *1076 S. Fairfax Ave., between Olympic and Pico Blvds., tel. 213/936–5918.*

**Vienna Café.** A swank Euro atmosphere pervades this sidewalk café complete with marble tables and foreign tourists. On a hot day the cold pasta-and-vegetable salad hits the spot and can feed two medium-hungry people, or try the potato and spinach frittata with green salad. The breakfast fare consists of egg creations, raisin brioche French toast, and cereals. *7356 Melrose Ave., between La Brea and Fairfax Aves., tel. 323/651–3822.*

**UNDER $20 • Red.** A young, too-attractive crew congregates to enjoy the pretentious, bright red color scheme. You can't help but feel a bit smug while sitting at the sidewalk tables. Tips to blend in: Bring a cute small dog, wear black, and take a long time to eat. The breakfast *bruschetta* (honey-sweetened ricotta with caramelized apples) is mouthwatering. The lunch is a dizzying selection of soups, salads, and sandwiches—all with an original spin on a traditional recipe. Dinner can be very romantic at the small tables; share some linguine *checca* (with chopped tomatoes, roasted garlic, and basil) or *orechiette* (ear- shape pasta) with rapini and chicken sausage. *7450 Beverly Blvd., at Vista St. between Fairfax and La Brea Aves., tel. 323/937–0331.*

# BEVERLY HILLS

Dining in Beverly Hills's Golden Triangle (bounded by Wilshire Boulevard, Little Santa Monica Boulevard, and Rexford Avenue) is fascinating. The food, of course, is more than acceptable, but it's the locals who add a distinctive flavor to the restaurant scene. Smoking divorcées complain about alimony while sitting next to "enhanced" young women dining with older men. Rich grandmothers with outlandishly flashy sunglasses eat Sunday dinner with their families. And the tourists, well, they often stand out all the more.

*See the Western Los Angeles Dining map.*

**UNDER $5 • Baja Fresh.** If you can get past the accolades they give themselves all over the menu and the store, you will be in for a treat. The burritos and tacos are scrumptious. *475 N. Beverly Dr., at Santa Monica Blvd., tel. 310/858–6690. No credit cards.*

**UNDER $10 • Cañon Liquor Café.** It's really a liquor store with a deli—though they say they don't have those nasty liquor stores in Beverly Hills, darling. Grab a sandwich or a salad and sit on the homey patio in front. The wine selection is extensive. Though the liquor store is open Saturday, they don't serve food. *338 N. Cañon Dr., between Brighton and Dayton Ways, tel. 310/246–9463. Closed Sun.*

**Chang's.** This white-tile and pink-tablecloth dot of a restaurant is a total anomaly in snazzy Beverly Hills. A bunch of Chinese guys serve to-go and stay-in chow mein, Mandarin crispy beef, and other Chinese specialties. Stop by for lunch (11–3:30) and take advantage of the lunch specials (one entrée, rice, an egg roll, and fortune cookie, all sans MSG). *9747 Little Santa Monica Blvd., between Linden and Roxbury Drs., tel. 310/274–8720.*

**Da Pasquale.** Italian restaurants are a dime a dozen here, but this one stands out because of its cool, modern wooden tables, stone floor, great staff, and well-priced food. Try pizza Pasquale (tomato sauce, smoked cheese, basil, and garlic) or penne *all'arrabiata* (pasta with spicy tomato sauce). They even have osso buco. *9749 Little Santa Monica Blvd., between Linden and Roxbury Drs., tel. 310/859–3884. Closed Sun.*

**Jacopo's.** This small, dark, cozy restaurant is a real Italian- American experience, heavy on the Italian, with red-and-white-checked tablecloths, a heady smell of tomato and parmigiana, and red-vinyl booths. You can't go wrong with the delicious pizzas, calzones, and pastas. *490 N. Beverly Dr., at Santa Monica Blvd., tel. 310/858–6446. West L.A.: 11676 Olympic Blvd., at Barrington Ave., tel. 310/477–2111. West Hollywood: 8166 Sunset Blvd., at Crescent Heights, tel. 323/650–8128. Pacific Palisades: 15415 Sunset Blvd., at Via de la Paz, tel. 310/454–8494.*

**Mulberry Street Pizzeria.** This New York–style pizza shop, owned by Cathy Moriarty (of *Raging Bull* fame) and staffed by teenagers, is a Beverly Hills favorite. The thin-crust pizza smells fab and tastes even better. They also have hefty meatball sandwiches and pasta dishes. *347 N. Cañon Dr., between Brighton and Dayton Ways, tel. 310/247–8998; 240 S. Beverly Dr., between Charleville Blvd. and Gregory Way, tel. 310/247–8100.*

**Nate 'n' Al's.** In 1945 this deli, this institution, this pinnacle of Beverly Hills's slumming-it eating was born. All walks of Beverly Hills life cross here; weekend mornings can be prime star-spotting times. The menu has regular items like sandwiches, as well as more exotic stuff like turkey-mushroom chow mein. Beverly Hills residents swear by this smallish place and don't take kindly to those comparing Nate 'n' Al's with Canter's deli in Fairfax (*see* West Hollywood, *above*). *414 N. Beverly Dr., between Brighton Way and Little Santa Monica Blvd., tel. 310/274–0101.*

**Porta Via.** A little slice of Italy in Beverly Hills isn't surprising, but this place takes the cake and serves it to you at outdoor tables. The European waiters are apt to call you "mademoiselle" and tend you as if you were their only customer all day. The turkey sandwich is superior, as is the arugula salad. No need to have a meal though—an espresso will still get you a seat and a doting waiter. *424 Cañon Dr., between Little Santa Monica Blvd. and Brighton Way, tel. 310/274–6534.*

**UNDER $15 • Crazy Fish.** The sushi chefs at Crazy Fish mold giant rolls as big as footballs, filled with unusual combinations of fish, chicken teriyaki, asparagus, and Cajun spices. The names of dishes are equally strange: Crazy Rock 'n' Roll, Baked Hawaiian Volcano, and Oy Vey Salmon Sashimi. There's usually a wait for a seat in the small, brightly lighted restaurant, which is extremely popular with L.A.'s sushi-mad populace. *9105 W. Olympic Blvd., at Doheny Dr., tel. 310/550–8547.*

**Newsroom Café.** If you can't work up the nerve or the finances to eat at Ivy you can at least spy on the goings-on from the Newsroom Café across the street, which offers similar food for substantially less. Sit inside near the newsstand or on the patio for better people-watching. Breakfast tends toward the creative, like a scramble of eggs, sun-dried tomatoes, and red-chili pesto, while dinner relies on comfort foods, such as chicken potpie and baked penne. *120 N. Robertson Blvd., just south of Beverly Blvd., tel. 310/652–4444.*

**SPLURGE • Polo Lounge.** Glamour junkies and old Hollywood aficionados will find $25 for breakfast a small price to pay to see the splendor of the Beverly Hills Hotel, site of the famous Polo Lounge. For some, the thought of eating beside a movie star in an entirely pink-and-green setting might make $4.50 seem like a reasonable price to pay for coffee. Sure, you could find corned beef hash for cheaper than $13, but it wouldn't be half the fun. *9641 Sunset Blvd., in Beverly Hills Hotel at Crescent Dr., tel. 310/276–2251.*

**Spago.** This tourist destination has to be taken with a grain of salt. Chef Wolfgang Puck serves similarly delicious food at his Wolfgang Puck Cafés at lower prices. But who cares about the food? Diners comes here to see the many Rolls-Royces and Bentleys parked in the lot (your nasty car will be carefully placed in the darkest corner), along with the occasional famous face and a permanent collection of important people (editors, producers) whom only a motion picture industry fanatic would recognize. The service is very familiar and the maitre' d straight out of your Hollywood dreams. Although casual business attire is the rule here, shorts- and jeans-wearing men and women have been spotted. Reservations are a must, as is requesting a table by the window. Pizzas and appetizers are about $14, and entrées are about $25. *176 N. Cañon Dr., near Wilshire Blvd., tel. 310/385– 0880.*

# WESTWOOD AND WEST L.A.

Check out Westwood Village (the area at the western base of UCLA, bounded by Wilshire Boulevard, Veteran Avenue, and Westwood Boulevard) for an international array of cheap meals. Restaurants here cater to students, most of whom soundly refuse to drop more than a five spot on food; many swear by the grub found in the shacks on Gayley Avenue at Weyburn. Walk southeast from the UCLA campus along Broxton Avenue, and you'll pass the majority of Westwood's cheapest eats. A collection of Persian restaurants lines Westwood Boulevard between Wilshire Boulevard and Santa Monica Boulevard.

Farther south and east are a sprinkling of eclectic eateries worth the extra drive. For groceries, stop by the large **farmers' market** held every Thursday (2 PM–7 PM) on Weyburn Avenue, between Glendon Avenue and Westwood Boulevard, just south of campus.

West L.A. covers a lot of turf—all of L.A. between Century City and Santa Monica, north of the 10 Freeway, south of Sunset. It's mostly residential, with fast-food and doughnut shops.

*See the Coastal Los Angeles Dining map.*

**UNDER $5 • Cafe 50's.** Green high school lockers and outdated movie posters add to the 1950s high-school-straight-out-of-*Grease* feel of this diner. Accordingly, the food is still living in the '50s, with an attendant aftertaste of grease. On the last Wednesday of the month from 6 PM to 10 PM, wear your "traditional" PJs and eat for free. Omelets, hamburgers, and sandwiches permeate the menu. Vegetarians will have to settle for a veggie burger or a PB&J sandwich. *11623 Santa Monica Blvd., 2 blocks east of Barrington Ave., West L.A., tel. 310/479–1955.*

**Falafel King.** This Westwood favorite dishes out *shawarma* (rotisserie beef or chicken), falafel, lamb shish kebab, and other Middle Eastern dishes in a cafeteria-style atmosphere. Lunchtime finds the local suits munching happily; students occupy the place at all hours. *1059 Broxton Ave., at Kinross Ave., Westwood, tel. 310/208–4444. No credit cards.*

**Feast from the East.** This postage-stamp-size eatery serves up Chinese chicken salad, egg rolls, and other Asian vegetable and meat dishes, all without MSG! *1949 Westwood Blvd., between Santa Monica and Olympic Blvds., West L.A., tel. 310/475–0400. Closed Sun.*

**Sepi's.** If you can put up with a frat/jock atmosphere, fortify yourself with submarine sandwiches; during happy hour (2–9) pitchers of beer are $4.50. *10968 Le Conte Ave., at Gayley Ave., tel. 310/208–7171.*

**UNDER $10 • The Apple Pan.** The menu hasn't changed one iota since the Pan opened in 1947— why bother, since it's widely considered the city's best burger joint? They serve up fries and homemade apple pie in addition to the much-loved burgers. *10801 W. Pico Blvd., at Westwood Blvd., West L.A., tel. 310/475–3585. No credit cards. Closed Mon.*

**Hurry Curry of Tokyo.** This clean, modern restaurant serves all things curry—and all dishes can be ordered mild, medium, or hot. Try the mushroom and spinach curry or the sautéed shrimp curry, both of which come with rice or noodles. Garlic lovers take note: The salad dressing is packed with this glorious vampire poison. *2131 Sawtelle Blvd., at Olympic Blvd., West L.A., tel. 310/473–1640. No credit cards.*

**John O'Groats.** If Laura Ashley got her hands on a 1950s diner, the result would be Rancho Park's John O'Groats, a popular breakfast and lunch spot for the usual L.A. important types. The food reflects the decor's blend of elegance and Americana. Try the Huevos O'Groats, a gentrified version of huevos rancheros. The lunch menu sports a snazzy selection of sandwiches and salads. *10516 Pico Blvd., at Patricia Ave., West L.A., tel. 310/204–0692. No dinner Sun.–Tues.*

**Mishima.** Friendly waiters and beautifully arranged dishes make this Japanese noodle house an oasis in a strip mall. Portions are generous and delicious. Try the *tanin don* (beef and egg cooked in a special sauce over rice) for a taste of Japanese comfort food. They also serve an extensive variety of *udon* (rice noodles) and *soba* (buckwheat noodles) dishes. *11301 Olympic Blvd., at Sawtelle Blvd., West L.A., tel. 310/473–5297. Wilshire: 8474 W. 3rd St., at La Cienega Blvd., tel. 213/782–0181.*

**Mongols BBQ.** This cafeteria-style joint is always mobbed by students who know a good deal when they eat one. You can order your choice of meats, vegetables, or noodles, all grilled Mongolian style with a variety of spicy oils and served with rice, soup, and a sesame bun. *1064 Gayley Ave., between Weyburn and Kinross Aves., Westwood, tel. 310/824–3377. No credit cards.*

**Sunnin.** Some of the best Near Eastern food in town lurks just south of Westwood in this homey Lebanese café. Look for the owner sitting outside preparing fresh herbs for such dishes as *hommos* (with or without beef), tabouleh, and *shish tawook* (marinated chicken). *1779 Westwood Blvd., at Santa Monica Blvd., West L.A., tel. 310/477–2358.*

**Versailles.** As you drive by, the perennial long line and delicious smells should tip you off that this is a local favorite, with cordial Cuban waiters serving up a taste of Old Havana. The house special, roasted garlic chicken, comes with generous portions of rice, black beans, and fried plantains. And make sure to order a robust *café cubana* (espresso). *1415 S. La Cienega Blvd., south of Pico Blvd., West L.A. (near Beverly Hills), tel. 310/289–0392. Venice: 10319 Venice Blvd., tel. 310/558–3168.*

**Yum Yum Dim Sum.** There are flavor-packed, MSG-free dim sum and Chinese noodle and meat dishes in this lunch hot spot, so excuse the pink and tacky decor and the requisite fish tank. Try the won ton soup or Szechuan broccoli. *1108 Gayley Ave., at Kinross Ave., Westwood, tel. 310/824–6566.*

**UNDER $15 • Bombay Cafe.** If another meal of tandoori chicken sounds dull, head to this lively mini-imall café, where you'll discover the wonderful tastes of Indian street food prepared with a modern L.A. twist. Regulars return for the chili-laden lamb frankies (sausages), the various chutneys, and the *sev puri* (little crackers topped with onions, potatoes, and chutneys). The *uttapam* (a thick semolina pancake) is spectacular. Some of L.A.'s best chefs come here on a night off. *12021 Pico Blvd., near Bundy Dr., West L.A., tel. 310/473—3388. Closed Mon.*

**O-Sho.** The Sawtelle Avenue strip south of Santa Monica Boulevard in West L.A. offers cheaper Japanese food than downtown's Little Tokyo and in a setting less reminiscent of a theme park. An example is O-Sho, where amid modest decor you can get a full dinner of sashimi (raw fish), tempura (deep fried vegetables and shrimp), miso soup, salad, and rice. *2021 Sawtelle Ave., at La Grange Ave., tel. 310/478–6404. Closed Sun.*

# SANTA MONICA, VENICE, AND MARINA DEL REY

You won't have a hard time finding cheap eats in these beach towns, but if you want to spend a bit more, there are also plenty of nicer options beyond the usual shoreline pizza and hot dogs. There are lots of meals to be had for under $5 along the boardwalks in Venice and Santa Monica, though much is of the deep-fried persuasion. The Third Street Promenade in Santa Monica has two budget food courts; both Santa Monica Place, at the Broadway end of the promenade, and the Gallery Gourmet food court, about one block in, offer dozens of inexpensive international options.

*See the Coastal Los Angeles Dining map.*

**UNDER $5 • Abbot's Pizza Company.** Ninety-nine-cent pizza stands are a dime a dozen along the Venice Boardwalk, but you get what you pay for. So fork out an extra dollar for a more gourmet slice at Abbot's, where you can get such California toppings as pesto or artichoke hearts. *1407 Abbot Kinney Blvd., at California Ave., Venice, tel. 310/396–7334.*

**Dory's Deli Station.** Pass up the zillions of Subways in favor of Dory's, where the decor is dull but the sandwiches are more than adequate. You can fill up easily on the special: a sub, chips, and a large drink. *1215 Third St. Promenade, at Wilshire Blvd., Santa Monica, tel. 310/395–9599. Closed Sun.*

**Falafel King.** Standard Middle Eastern fast food gets spiced up with an exciting array of free condiments. Salad plates (like tahini and hummus) are more filling than they appear, and although the decor is bland, the food is lively. *1315 Third St. Promenade, near Arizona Ave., Santa Monica, tel. 310/587–2551.*

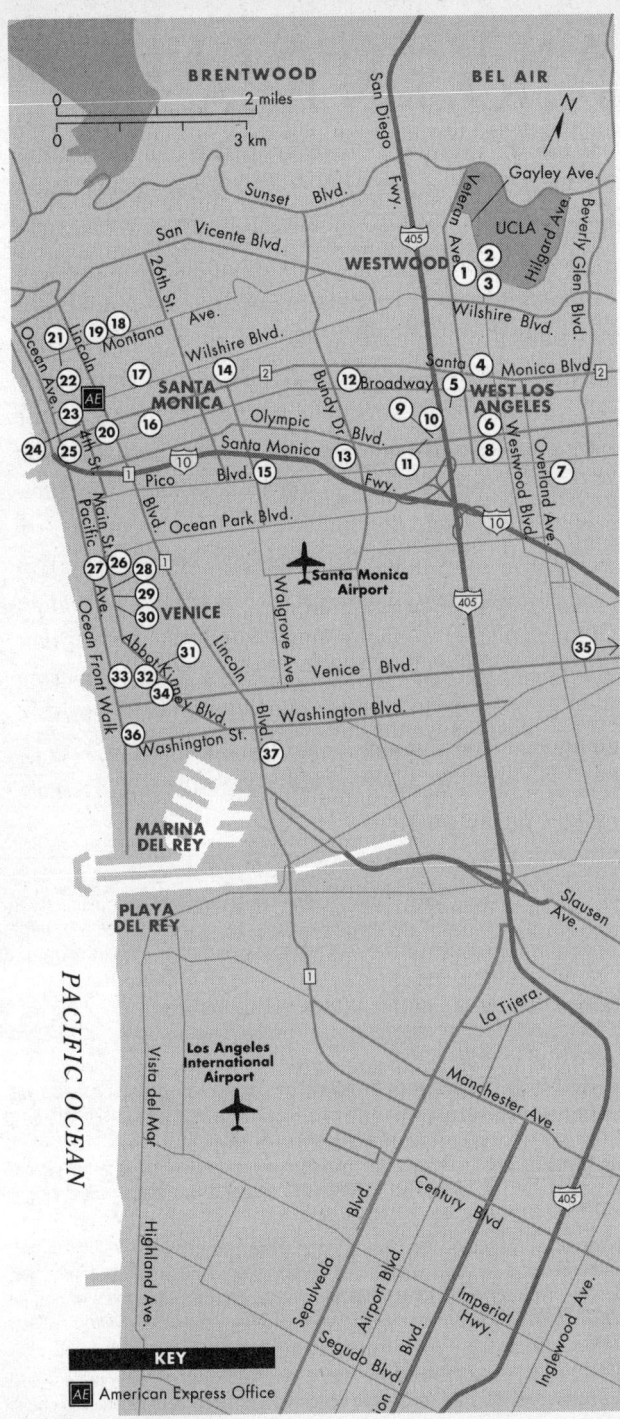

Abbot's Pizza Company, **32**

Alejo Presto Trattoria, **37**

The Apple Pan, **8**

Bombay Cafe, **13**

Cafe 50's, **12**

C&O Trattoria, **36**

Dory's Deli Station, **24**

Falafel King, **2, 21**

Feast from the East, **6**

The Firehouse, **28**

Fritto Misto, **20**

Gallegos Mexican Deli, **16**

George's Bistro, **22**

Hal's, **31**

Hurry Curry of Tokyo, **9**

Ivy at the Shore, **25**

Jody Maroni's Sausage Kingdom, **33**

John O'Groats, **7**

La Vecchia Cucina, **26**

Mishima, **11**

Mongols BBQ, **5**

Nawab of India, **17**

O-Sho, **10**

Rae's, **15**

Rose Café, **29**

Rosti, **19**

St. Urbain St. Bagels, **23**

Sepl's, **1**

The Shack, **14**

Sunnin, **4**

Van Go's Ear, **30**

Venus of Venice, **34**

Versailles, **35**

Wildflour Boston Pizza, **27**

Wolfgang Puck Cafe, **18**

Yum Yum Dim Sum, **3**

# WANT TO SELL A SCREENPLAY?

*Or be discovered as an actor? A musician? Years ago writers and starlets from Ohio hung around Schwab's Drugstore (made famous in the movie* Sunset Boulevard*), waiting to be noticed by the big movie execs who'd occasionally sweep in for aspirin. But since Schwab's no longer exists, a modern assault on the Hollywood elite requires a bit more cunning. A large number of celebrities and behind-the-scenes power brokers frequent Mortons (8764 Melrose Ave., West Hollywood, tel. 310/276-5205) and Spago (176 N. Cañon Dr., Beverly Hills, tel. 310/385-0880). You may not be able to afford the food at these places, but you can down drinks at the bar, provided you act nonchalant and keep that dog-eared copy of* Entertainment Weekly's *annual "100 Most Powerful People in Hollywood" issue hidden. For a low-key encounter, try Dalt's Grill (3500 W. Olive Blvd., in Union Bank Bldg., tel. 818/953-7752), in Burbank. You'll find affordable Mexican food, peons from the nearby studios, and DJs from KROQ (106.7 FM), a popular alternative radio station that broadcasts from upstairs—so try slipping that long-haired dude your demo tape. If you just want to gawk at a celebrity (not become one), Patrick's Roadhouse, in Santa Monica (106 Entrada Dr., at PCH, tel. 310/459-4544), offers mediocre grill food but folks like Zsa Zsa Gabor, Sean Penn, and Arnold Schwarzenegger have been sighted there.*

**Gallegos Mexican Deli.** Stop by for delicious, filling Mexican dishes served on a breezy patio. Try the chicken chili *verde* and green corn tamales, the enormous burritos, or combination plates with refried beans and rice. And while you're here, you might as well stock up on pork rinds. *1424 Broadway, at 14th St., Santa Monica, tel. 310/395-0162. Closed Sun.*

**Jody Maroni's Sausage Kingdom.** Meat eaters should head to the self-proclaimed "home of the haute dog" for all-natural and original variations on the frankfurter, such as the Toulouse Garlic. *2011 Ocean Front Walk, at Venice Blvd., Venice, tel. 310/822-5639.*

**St. Urbain St. Bagels.** This small chain offers simple, reliably good bagels. You can get a bagel with cream cheese and a salad, or you can upgrade to lox spread. Sit inside or out among a consistently large crowd. *1232 Third St. Promenade, at Wilshire Blvd., Santa Monica, tel. 310/260-1511.*

**UNDER $10 • Alejo Presto Trattoria.** The line forms early at this mini-mall restaurant, a temple to garlic. Basic Italian dishes are served. Go the old-school route—spaghetti and meatballs. *4002 Lincoln Blvd., at Washington Pl., near Marina del Rey, tel. 310/822-0095.*

**The Firehouse.** Built in 1902 as an actual firehouse, this historic building on the Venice/Santa Monica border serves diner food for the health conscious. You can get a tasty Cajun mahimahi burger, a vegetable burger, or a turkey burger—or you can go for traditional burgers. You can sit indoors or out, eat or just drink, and while away the display of antique fire toys. *213 Rose Ave., near Main St., Santa Monica, tel. 310/396-6810.*

**George's Bistro.** Enjoy an elegant ambience and fancy Italian food here for surprisingly low prices. Tasty pastas, like linguini *pescatore* (with mussels and fish), come accompanied by soup or salad. You can sit outside and watch the promenade scene or plant yourself in the artistically rendered cavelike interior for a more intimate meal. *1321 Third St. Promenade, at Arizona Ave., Santa Monica, tel. 310/451–8823.*

**Rae's.** Get quality comfort food for cheap in this pleasant, genuine '50s coffeehouse (its authenticity verified by a framed cover of an early '60s hot rod magazine with Rae's in the background). Try the hot turkey sandwich or their renowned tapioca. *2901 Pico Blvd., at 29th St., Santa Monica, tel. 310/828–7937.*

**Rose Café.** More than a restaurant, the Rose is part of the daily routine for most Venice natives. You'll see bodybuilders and unemployed scriptwriters taking coffee at 10, actors showing up for a bite around noon; and artists hunkering down for a meal after dark (a gallery displays local work). From croissants to chicken tacos, the kitchen and bakery crank out a wide range of fresh, reasonably priced food in an open, social atmosphere. *220 Rose Ave., at Main St., Venice, tel. 310/399–0711.*

**Rosti.** Enjoy economical Tuscan cooking with an emphasis on healthy fare. Although famous for its chicken with olive oil, garlic, and rosemary potatoes, Rosti also has good pastas. *931 Montana Ave., at 10th St., Santa Monica, tel. 310/393–3236.*

**The Shack.** Just throw something over your swimsuit and head over to the Shack, a genuinely casual hangout, ideal for a postbeach burger or pizza and beer. There are a pool table and a TV broadcasting the hot sports events of the moment. The service is superfriendly, and the crowd is pleasantly mellow. *2518 Wilshire Blvd., at 26th St., Santa Monica, tel. 310/449–1171.*

**Van Go's Ear.** A visit to the Ear can provide unexpected entertainment: Mornings, bodybuilders fuel up before hitting Muscle Beach, and café types filter in after midnight. There are omelets, sandwiches, salads, plenty of vegetarian options, and desserts baked in-house daily. *796 Main St., between Rose and Brooks Aves., Venice, tel. 310/396–1987. No credit cards.*

**Venus of Venice.** Venus is worth more as a flashback to Venice's hippie days than for its vegan cuisine, but if you've been hitting the burger stands one too many times, you might want to purify yourself with one of the many faux meat offerings. For example, there's lasagna with soy cheese and some kind of simulated sausage, which comes with a salad. You can sit outside on the patio or inside amid the stuffed animals and scented candles. Service can be on the slow and surly side. *1202 Abbot Kinney Blvd., at San Juan Ave., Venice, tel. 310/392–1987. Closed Mon.–Wed.*

**Wildflour Boston Pizza.** Come here if you crave traditional pizza in a city where guacamole often replaces pepperoni as the topping of choice. It's a great choice for a 15-inch thin-crust pie or a slice. Inexpensive sandwiches and pastas round out the menu. *2807 Main St., near Ocean Park Blvd., Santa Monica, tel. 310/392–3300.*

**UNDER $15 • C&O Trattoria.** The crowds at this restaurant come for the lively atmosphere and the blaring Frank Sinatra tunes. The pastas are simple but satisfying, and the famed freshly baked garlic rolls come to your table for free. The attractive patio makes a nice place to enjoy a glass of wine if you just want to take in the ambience. *31 Washington Blvd., at Pacific Ave., Marina del Rey, tel. 310/823–9491.*

**Fritto Misto.** This simple restaurant offers piles of pasta, from the plain to the peculiar. You can create your own dish, choosing the noodle shape, sauce, and extras (veggies, sausages, the usual). If decision making overwhelms you, the ultrafriendly waitstaff recommends their vegetarian Mediterranean dish (artichoke hearts, sun-dried tomatoes, mushrooms, and pesto over lemon-pepper fettuccine). *601 Colorado Ave., at 6th St., Santa Monica, tel. 310/458–2829.*

**Nawab of India.** One of the best, most affordable Indian restaurants in L.A. is a short drive inland from Santa Monica Beach. Nawab offers tasty tandoori dishes, vegetarian plates, and delicious curries; particularly good is the tandoori chicken *makhanwala*. Though it's nothing fancy, the dining room is pleasantly serene. *1621 Wilshire Blvd., between 16th and 17th Sts., Santa Monica, tel. 310/829–1106.*

**Wolfgang Puck Café.** Colorful tiles create a jumbled mosaic on the walls and floors of this busy, slightly noisy California-Italian restaurant. The service can be somewhat disorganized, but savory entrées such as mushroom tortellini and calzones more than compensate. Bring a cell phone and order Perrier to blend in. *8000 Sunset Blvd., at Crescent Heights Blvd., West Hollywood, tel. 323/650–7300. Santa Monica: 1323 Montana Ave., west of 14th St., tel. 310/393–0290.*

**UNDER $20 • Hal's.** This artsy-chic SoHo-esque restaurant serves tasty entrées such as petrale sole and New York steak plus a nicely varied weekend brunch menu. The decor may be more interesting than the food: Oil paintings of Joni Mitchell and other local celebrities line the walls. You can always forgo the food and drink at the bar. *1349 Abbot Kinney Blvd., between Venice Blvd. and Main St., Venice, tel. 310/396–3105.*

**La Vecchia Cucina.** The salads, pastas, and thin-crust pizzas here look fancier than you would expect from their price—along the lines of eggplant stuffed with goat cheese and veal with porcini mushrooms. The dining room is beautifully lighted, and the huge bouquets of fresh flowers make you feel like more of a big spender than you actually are. *2654 Main St., at Ocean Park Blvd., Santa Monica, tel. 310/399–7979. No lunch.*

**SPLURGE • Ivy at the Shore.** See celebrities or people who just look like celebrities at the Santa Monica branch of Ivy. The food is consistently superior, though expensive—the ever-popular gourmet meat loaf is a steep $23.75. Make reservations, and even then expect to wait. Don't take the snotty service personally: The burden of serving people more important than you has taken its toll on the waitstaff. But there's a beautiful dining room and easily an evening's worth of people-watching entertainment. *1541 Ocean Ave., at Colorado Ave., Santa Monica, tel. 310/393–3113.*

# PACIFIC PALISADES AND MALIBU

Restaurants in both Pacific Palisades and Malibu exude so much charm and peacefulness you may feel as though you are on a vacation from your vacation. Pacific Palisades's restaurants are concentrated around Sunset Boulevard in Pacific Palisades village (from I–405 go east on Sunset Boulevard through Brentwood). Malibu restaurants, like the rest of commercial Malibu, flank PCH. Oceanside restaurants are inevitably more expensive than those inland, so budget diners need to decide between more view or more food. Shopping at grocery stores or importing your own picnic are the only real ways to cut costs here.

**UNDER $5 • La Salsa.** Inhale a few tacos and quesadillas without ingesting too much grease. As an offshoot of a local chain, the space is a little cleaner and the food healthier than an authentic Mexican dive. *22800 PCH, between Carbon Canyon and Cross Creek Rds., Malibu, tel. 310/456–6299.*

**UNDER $10 • Gourmet Gala.** This European café-deli is small and charming, with a red-and-white checkered floor and tiny marble tables. Besides tea and coffee, you can pick up soup, simple salads, and sandwiches (try the black on black—Black Forest ham, brie, honey mustard, tomato, and lettuce on wheat). Those who want to splurge and have a picnic packed for them can order one of five picnic baskets. If you linger over a cappuccino, you may just run into the whole neighborhood— *everyone* stops by for lunch and afternoon snacks. *15324 Antioch St., between Swarthmore Ave. and Via de la Paz, Pacific Palisades, tel. 310/459–7419. Closed Sun.*

**Greg's Grill.** The interior may be bland, but this is one of the cheapest places to sit down and nosh in fancy-schmancy Pacific Palisades. Besides the diner staples (sandwiches, soups, and salads), there are a few nods to Mediterranean food, such as spanakopita and souvlakia sandwiches. *15317 Antioch St., between Swarthmore Ave. and Via de la Paz, Pacific Palisades, tel. 310/459–0396. No credit cards.*

**Kay & Dave's.** You could get out of here with just a bean-and- cheese burrito, but you won't want to after you've entered the small brick-and-wood cantina and smelled the delicious cooking. Try the *pollo mole poblano* (chicken in Mexican chocolate sauce) or a veggie tamale plate. These gringo *gatos* (cats) don't use lard and serve big portions. *15246 Sunset Blvd., at Swarthmore Ave., Pacific Palisades, tel. 310/459–8118. Santa Monica: 262 26th St., tel. 310/260–1355.*

**Malibu Seafood Patio Cafe.** On the Pacific Coast Highway (PCH), the all-outdoor seating here affords you a view of Malibu's beautiful coast while you enjoy no-nonsense fish—consider ordering the fried fish sandwich. Also recommended are the fried seafood platters and the especially good spicy tuna burger. *25653 PCH, west of Malibu Canyon Rd., across from Puerco Beach, Malibu, tel. 310/456–3430.*

**Mort's Palisades Deli.** Just like a real New York City deli, this place has a mind-meltingly huge menu, including the standard variety of sandwiches, melts, salads, breakfast items, hamburgers, and fish; treats like whitefish with cream cheese and a bagel; and unconventional lunches like the Sunset sandwich (ham, Swiss cheese, coleslaw, and Russian dressing). You can serve yourself cafeteria style, get it to go, or sit outside on a tree-lined, suburban street. *1035 Swarthmore Ave., at Sunset Blvd., Pacific Palisades, tel. 310/454–5511.*

**Pacific Coast Greens.** In the back of this full-service grocery store is a delectable deli where you can pick up lip-smacking concoctions such as confetti black-bean salad and chicken salad or meat or veggie sandwiches for a day at the beach. *22601 PCH, between Carbon Canyon Rd. and the Serra Retreat Center, Malibu, tel. 310/456–0353.*

**Terri's.** They want you to feel at home at this white-walled restaurant with butcher paper and crayons on every table. The selection, which could include a grilled vegetable sandwich, barbecued chicken salad, or French toast and bacon for breakfast, is swell. *1028 Swarthmore Ave., at Sunset Blvd., Pacific Palisades, tel. 310/454–6467.*

**Village Natural Food.** Health-food freaks can happily slurp fresh- squeezed juice or smoothies as a snack on the patio of this strip mall deli. The sandwiches and salads are healthy, and some are even vegetarian, like the falafel and tofu picks. *15200 Sunset Blvd., at La Cruz Dr., Pacific Palisades, tel. 310/459–1010. No credit cards. Closed Sun.*

**UNDER $15 • Il Sogno.** This café-restaurant's brick patio surrounded by wrought iron and hanging vines is the perfect place to enjoy Spanish paella or a grilled eggplant and feta sandwich for dinner or a simple soup and sandwich for lunch. Of course, you are more than welcome to sip some coffee and nibble a cherry tart or slice of chocolate marble cake anytime. *863 Swarthmore Ave., at Antioch St., Pacific Palisades, tel. 310/454–6522.*

# SOUTH BAY

The towns of the South Bay are close together, and you will inevitably drive to a dinner spot, so it doesn't matter if a restaurant is in Hermosa or Redondo or whatever. Manhattan, Hermosa, and Redondo beaches have excellent food, but you'll never find it if you stay on PCH. As you move closer to the shore, generic spots give way to locally owned kitchens offering fresh seafood and inexpensive California cuisine, particularly in health-conscious Hermosa Beach.

Expect additional cheap and entertaining grub in Torrance (which is inland from Hermosa) and San Pedro (on the southern tip of the Palos Verdes Peninsula), all within a stone's throw of the Pacific Ocean.

*See the South Bay Dining map.*

**UNDER $5 • Beach Hut.** Hawaiian-style treats like *chow fun* (wide noodles) and Big Island Steak (actually two slabs of Spam) are served up fresh out of the microwave to a loyal crowd of burly surfers. All orders include salad, rice, and the all-important teriyaki sauce. *3920 Highland Ave., Manhattan Beach, tel. 310/545–8911; 1342 Hermosa Ave., Hermosa Beach, tel. 310/376–4252. No credit cards.*

**Cozy Cafe.** Cheap, no-fuss eats like pastrami sandwiches and tuna melts are dished out to the folks who frequent the bus stop outside (including the driver-gourmands, all quite large in size). *307 S. PCH, at Torrance Blvd., Redondo Beach, tel. 310/316–1414.*

**El Burrito Jr.** If there isn't a line outside this take-out Mexican joint, it probably isn't open. Fresh tacos and huge burritos are served up as fast as locals can eat them. If you're not headed for the beach, lounge outside on the benches and watch the world go by. There are other locations in Lomita and Seal Beach. *919 S. PCH, at Ave. A, Redondo Beach, tel. 310/316–5058. No credit cards.*

**Rosa's.** For over 25 years, people have feasted on Rosa's traditional Mexican dishes; try the pork tacos *adobadas* (barbecued) or the bean-and-cheese burrito. *322 PCH, at 3rd St., Hermosa Beach, tel. 310/374–9094.*

**Sion's.** This friendly establishment serves good Mexican and American meals in a clean diner setting. The lunch specials, like the big veggie burrito covered in ranchero sauce and cheese, draw a loyal business crowd. Many locals come for breakfast and return with heartburn for dinner and a cheap beer. *235 N. Sepulveda Blvd. (PCH), Manhattan Beach, tel. 310/372–4504.*

**UNDER $10 • Big Wok Mongolian BBQ.** You select the meats, noodles, veggies, and sauces from the buffet-style bar, and the sweaty chefs stir-fry it up before your eyes. All-you-can eat lunch and dinner deals include rice, sesame biscuits, and hot tea. Single servings and vegetarian options cost a few bucks less. *1200 PCH, south of Pier Ave., Hermosa Beach, tel. 310/798– 1155.*

**CJ's Pantry.** A sociable breakfast spot favored by families and beachgoers, CJ's serves delectable daily specials such as French toast stuffed with seasonal fruits and cream cheese. All orders come with a choice of home-baked muffins or breads, and the Breakfast Bang specials are only $3.95 until 11 AM. *324 S. Catalina Ave., at Pearl St., just west of PCH, Redondo Beach, tel. 310/318–2411.*

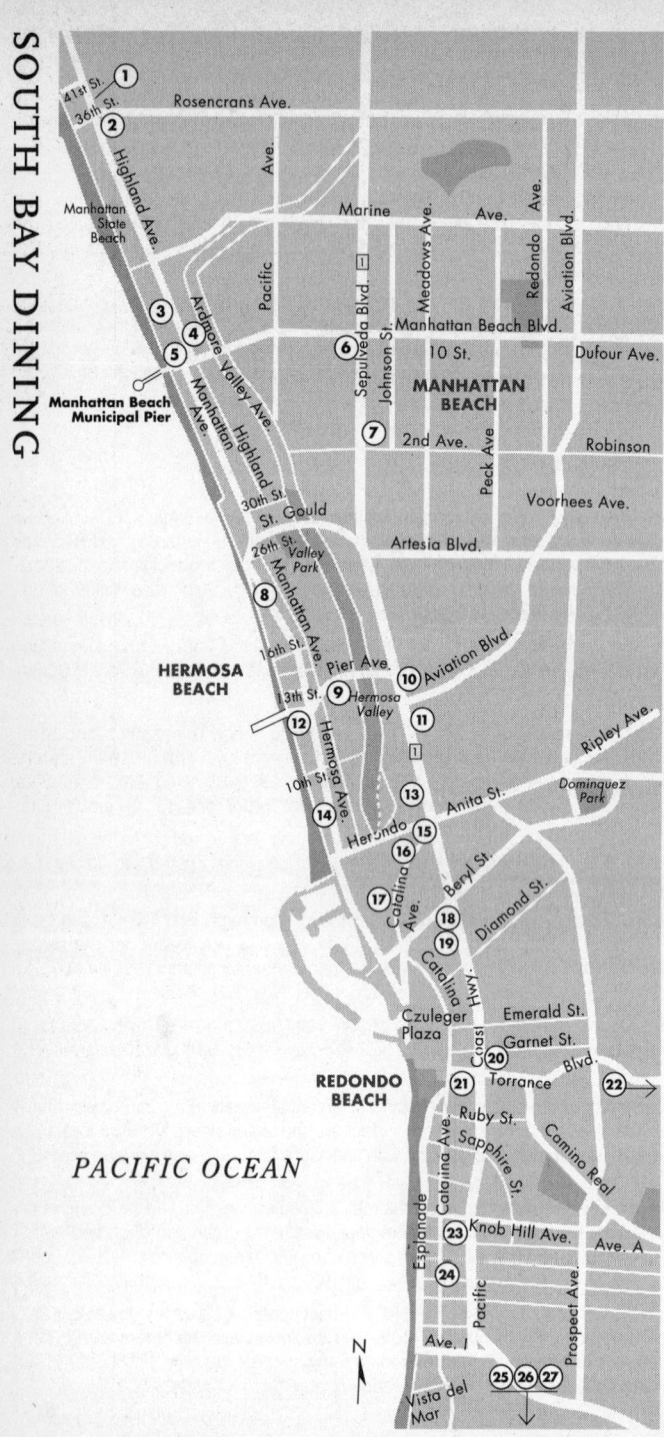

Alpine Village Inn
and Market, **22**
Beach Hut, **1**
Big Wok Mongolian
BBQ, **10**
CJ's Pantry, **15**
Cozy Cafe, **21**
El Burrito Jr., **23**
El Pollo Inka, **11**
Good Stuff, **12**
Greens at the
Beach, **16**
Hennessey's
Tavern, **5, 17**
Italy's Little
Kitchen, **6**
Joe's, **20**
The Kettle, **4**
Killer Shrimp, **19**
La Salsa, **18**
Martha's 22nd
Street Grill, **8**
Ocean View Café, **3**
Papadakis
Taverna, **27**
Ragin' Cajun Café, **9**
Rosa's, **13**
Sion's, **7**
Sixth Street
Bistro, **25**
Utro's, **26**
Sloopy's, **2**
The Spot, **14**
Thai Thani, **24**

**El Pollo Inka.** Peruvians come out of the woodwork for the *lomo saltado* (sautéed beef), a garlicky mix with tomatoes and french fries tossed in for good measure. The half rotisserie chicken, served with salad and a choice of fluffy rice or fries, is the best deal going at $4.25. The extended family that runs each location provides extraordinarily friendly service. Live music accompanies meals most weekends; call for schedule. *1110 PCH, at Aviation Blvd., Hermosa Beach, tel. 310/372–1433; 1425 W. Artesia Blvd., Gardena, tel. 310/516–7378; 15400 S. Hawthorne Blvd., Lawndale, tel. 310/676–6665; 23705 Hawthorne Blvd., Torrance, tel. 310/373–0062.*

**Good Stuff.** Home-cooked food California style (vegetarian burgers, massive burritos, omelets) tastes even better when served right on the beach. On weekend mornings the line for brunch can be formidable, but locals never seem to mind—it's just one more opportunity to tan. *1286 The Strand, at Pier Ave., Hermosa Beach, tel. 310/374–2334; 1300 Highland Ave., Manhattan Beach, tel. 310/545–4775.*

**Greens at the Beach.** From the former owners of the Spot (*see below*) come less pretentious but still stylish veggie and vegan offerings, this time accompanied by live jazz on Sunday night from 7 to 9. There are no cover and no minimum, but you might want to try a jazzy combo like the Beany Goodman (brown rice and beans in a savory sauce) or the Al Greens (brown rice and beans dancing in collard or mustard greens). The apple cobbler ain't bad, either. *247 Avenida del Norte, between Catalina Ave. and PCH, Redondo Beach, tel. 310/316–9451.*

**Hennessey's Tavern.** A late breakfast segues into a pub-grub lunch, then the rowdy happy hour (4–7), and before you know it, it's time for the last call—1:30 AM! Where *do* the days go? Hennessey's loyal and fun-loving crowd is more familiar with this routine than they'd like to admit. For California cuisine in a more mellow setting, hop over to the H. T. Grill, next door. *1712 S. Catalina Ave., just west of PCH, Redondo Beach, tel. 310/540–8443; 8 Pier Ave., Hermosa, tel. 310/372–5759; 313 Manhattan Beach Blvd., Manhattan, tel. 310/546–4813.*

**Italy's Little Kitchen.** Turn up in this bistro to settle down to pizzas big enough for two and pasta dishes prepared with a touch of virgin olive oil and more than a touch of finesse. The service is good and the tiramisu delicious. *921 Sepulveda Blvd., at 10th St., Manhattan Beach, tel. 310/374–9905; 8516 Lincoln Blvd., Playa del Rey, tel. 310/645–4423.*

**Joe's.** This classic blue-plate-special diner is famous for its John Wayne Special: eggs over hash browns, all smothered with cheese and enchilada sauce and surrounded by sausages. Vegetarians can substitute tomatoes for the links and will find plenty else to tide them over. Breakfast and meaty lunch specials are served all day to a hardworking crowd who enjoy sharing mess-hall-style tables. *400 N. PCH, Redondo Beach, tel. 310/376– 9570.*

**The Kettle.** Just one block up from the pier and a slew of bars, this all-hours eatery is a local institution. On weekends drunken revelers stumble in after 2 AM for giant burgers like the broiled Jonathan B (sautéed mushrooms, grilled onions, ham, lettuce, tomato, and Swiss and cheddar cheese). Many return the next morning for the "hangover breakfast club," which unofficially convenes on the flowery patio. Everything on the menu is huge and comes with a choice of homemade soup, fries, fruit, or pasta salad. *1138 Highland Ave., at Manhattan Beach Blvd., Manhattan Beach, tel. 310/545–8511.*

**La Salsa.** Here you'll find some of the healthiest fast Mexican food in the city, food that doesn't rely on can openers and lard. Tacos, burritos, and quesadillas all come accompanied by an assortment of fresh vegetables and homemade salsas. *1759 S. Elena Ave., Redondo Beach, tel. 310/543–2448; 2790 Manhattan Beach Blvd., Redondo Beach, tel. 310/793–9444; 24223 Crenshaw Blvd., at Lomita Blvd., Torrance Crossroads, Torrance, tel. 310/326–1444; 245 Pine Ave., at AMC Pine Sq., Long Beach, tel. 562/ 491–1104.*

**Martha's 22nd Street Grill.** Breakfast on the heavenly patio here is a tradition among laid-back locals. There's frequently a wait to get in, but don't despair: The healthy soups and hearty sandwiches are also available to go from **Martha's Corner,** next door. *25 22nd St., at Hermosa Ave., Hermosa Beach, tel. 310/376– 7786 for Martha's 22nd Street Grill or 310/379–0070 for Martha's Corner. No dinner.*

**Ocean View Café.** A cross between a coffeehouse and a restaurant, the Ocean View serves excellent salads and sandwiches, light breakfasts, and wonderful espresso drinks. Try the soup du jour with a baguette and freshly squeezed orange juice. Both the view of the Pacific from the outdoor patio and the staff's mellow attitude are big bonuses. *229 13th St., off Highland Ave., Manhattan Beach, tel. 310/ 545–6770. No credit cards. Closed Mon.*

**Ragin' Cajun Café.** Mobbed by visitors and locals alike, this tiny restaurant dishes up authentic Cajun food—*boudin*, crawfish, red beans and rice, gumbo, and jambalaya—cooked by a Lafayette, Louisiana, native. Coffee and beignets (square doughnuts) are served every Sunday morning 8–11:30. *422 Pier Ave., between PCH and Hermosa Ave., Hermosa Beach, tel. 310/376–7878. Closed Mon.*

**Sloopy's.** On the overgrown garden patio near the open fireplace, friendly regulars put their feet up on tables fashioned from old wagon wheels and beer barrels while they wait on big breakfasts, ground salmon burgers, and thick peanut butter milk shakes. Although freshly squeezed juices and shots of wheat-grass juice are served, this is no health food joint. Don't miss the hodgepodge of oddities along the walls. *3416 N. Highland Ave., at 35th St., Manhattan Beach, tel. 310/545–1373. No credit cards.*

**The Spot.** You don't need to be a vegetarian to enjoy this very popular health food restaurant. Everything—from fresh-baked bread to soups, lasagna, and Mexican food—is made in-house without refined sugar or animal products and using purified water. *110 2nd St., at Hermosa Ave., Hermosa Beach, tel. 310/376- -2355.*

**Thai Thani.** The subtly spicy lunch specials, served with rice and soup or salad, attract a business lunch crowd. The *pad thai* (noodles tossed with sprouts, egg, and crushed peanut sauce) is always a reliable bet. Top off whatever you order with a sweet Thai iced tea or coffee. *1109 S. PCH, at Ave. C, Redondo Beach, tel. 310/316–1580.*

**UNDER \$15 • Alpine Village Inn and Market.** Excellent sausages, wursts, and microbrews are all made on the premises of this decidedly German deli. There are also prime rib specials, a champagne brunch, live oompah entertainment, and bingo three nights a week in the adjoining restaurant. Don your lederhosen and polka on down for the epic Oktoberfest celebrations come autumn (September–October). Swappers meet on Sunday 8–2:30 in the huge parking lot to trade bric-a-brac at the weekly flea market, which charges a 50¢ admission. *833 W. Torrance Blvd., off I–110, near Torrance, tel. 310/327– 2483 or 310/327–4384.*

**Killer Shrimp.** They only prepare one dish here, but they do it with gusto. For \$12, you can gorge yourself on a dozen fresh, never frozen, Louisiana shrimp, served with a hunk of bread to soak up the spicy broth. *403 N. PCH, between Beryl and Carnelian Sts., Redondo Beach, tel. 310/798–0008; 523 Washington St., at Ocean Ave., Marina del Rey, tel. 310/578–2293.*

**Sixth Street Bistro.** Mediterranean food successfully meets California cuisine at this romantic bistro. Dine inside to the sounds of live jazz or sit under the stars and enjoy such utterly unique dishes as chocolate pesto pasta served over a bed of Grand Marnier–accented rice. *354 W. 6th St., Centre and Nelson Sts., San Pedro, tel. 310/521–8818.*

**Utro's.** The catch o' the day comes in fresh with the fishermen who stop by and drop anchor for a beer. Huge burgers like the half-pound Devine, served with avocado and bacon, draw a hardworking (and hard-drinking) crowd of train engineers and longshoremen during lunch. *Berth 73, on Fisherman's Wharf, San Pedro, tel. 310/547–5022.*

**SPLURGE • Papadakis Taverna.** A fun-loving Greek family sparks an overwhelmingly festive atmosphere. The singing waiters have been known to kiss bald men on their chrome dome, chug glasses of ouzo, and dance chorus-line-style, à la the Rockettes. The meaty main dishes are impeccable; many are over \$20, but it is possible to construct a hearty meal for less by sampling authentic appetizers like dolmas or by sticking to the all-inclusive dinner specials. Come prepared for a party and blaring bouzouki music. *301 W. 6th St., at Center St., San Pedro, tel. 310/548–1186.*

# LONG BEACH

In the area known as Belmont Shore, 2nd Street is lined with sports bars and restaurants catering to the young but not necessarily rich. A lively crowd also fills the cluster of restaurants near the intersection of Pine Avenue and Broadway downtown.

**UNDER \$10 • Alegria.** Tapas (literally "little lids," or appetizers) and sangria draw a lively crowd to this cozy Latin restaurant and bar. For variety try splitting a few dishes; good choices include the *salmón y aceitunas* (olives and roasted bell peppers wrapped with salmon sashimi) and the *gambas y alcachofas* (marinated artichoke hearts with ham, prawns, and Parmesan cheese in a cayenne sauce). *115 Pine Ave., at Broadway, tel. 562/436–3388.*

**M Bar and Grill.** A young crowd filters into this coffeehouse/café for an eclectic calendar of live music and rotating art exhibits. Try the sautéed red snapper sandwich or Peruvian chicken paired with curried peas and potatoes. *213A Pine Ave., between Broadway and 3rd St. in Pine Sq., tel. 562/435–2525. Closed Sun.*

**UNDER $15 • Johnny Rebs Southern Smokehouse.** You won't find General Lee's horse parked outside this transplanted Southern roadhouse, but don't be surprised if you're called "Honey" by the sweet wait-staff of Beaus and Daisy Dukes. There's always plenty of free peanuts and Dixie beer to tide you over during the inevitable wait for a table. The mouthwatering menu includes Kiss My Grits breakfast specials, green tomatoes, and barbecued beef ribs. Thursdays are all-you-can-eat catfish nights. *4663 Long Beach Blvd., at PCH, North Long Beach, tel. 562/423–7327; 16639 Bellflower Blvd., Bellflower, tel. 562/866–6455.*

# CAFÉS AND COFFEEHOUSES

Los Angeles bristles with quirky coffee bars offering a variety of entertainment to patrons quaffing espresso drinks strong enough to peel paint. But as you might expect, few Angelenos are the type to fret over a volume of existential poetry. Instead, the café has been woven nicely into the fabric of the city's nightlife, a hip addition to clubbing in the era of Alcoholics Anonymous. The celeb-spotting opportunities at the Coffee Bean & Tea Leaf aren't too shabby either. Many cafés stay open after bars and clubs close, offering live music and poetry readings as well as backgammon boards, magazines, used paperbacks, and free local weeklies. And they generally don't give a damn how long you sit on that overstuffed couch. *Caffeine,* the café scene's own (free) magazine, prints poetry, art, fiction, and the praise of coffeehouses. Pick it up at any café.

Caffiends can always get their java fuel to go at the coffee spots around town; however, some cafés deserve more attention. Lurking about a café for longer than it takes to steam some milk can afford riveting conversation with L.A. natives or allow some downtime in an environment bristling with people-watching opportunities. So before you take your paper cup of hot java to your car and head back onto the freeway, ask yourself, "Do I want to sip all alone behind the wheel or do I want sit down and check out L.A.'s version of community?"

*Craving a meal but can't bring yourself to make the drive? Call the Takeout Taxi delivery service, which contracts with numerous South Bay restaurants. Call in your order (tel. 310/301–7074), and they'll have it to you in an hour.*

## HOLLYWOOD

**All-Star Theatre Café and Speakeasy.** In the Hollywood Knickerbocker Hotel, the self-proclaimed "ultimate 1920s coffeehouse" has comfortably overstuffed club chairs and oversize drinks. Come for the Art Deco decor and the speakeasy atmosphere, but stay for a glimpse of the oft-seen ghost of Valentino. *1714 N. Ivar Ave., ½ block north of Hollywood Blvd., tel. 323/962–8898.*

**The Bourgeois Pig.** With red lights illuminating the erotic- political paintings on the black walls and thrift-store-clad patrons at the pool table, this is an achingly hip caffeine outlet. Despite the lack of alcohol, it's got a barlike social quality, and its denizens are engaging in their own studied way. Recommended reading: *The Long Dark Tea Time of the Soul,* by Douglas Adams. *5931 Franklin Ave., at Beachwood Dr., tel. 323/962–6366.*

## WEST HOLLYWOOD

West Hollywood's cafés are often particularly gay- and lesbian-friendly; the younger men seem to prefer The Abbey (*see below*). But regardless of orientation, these spots are great places to hunker down with a local paper. Santa Monica Boulevard and the surrounding streets have plenty of places to caf up.

**The Abbey.** The classical statues of robust young men provide inspiration for the members of the gay community who gather here; the massive outdoor patio can be a bit of a pickup joint. The tea selection is more than adequate—yogi healing tea, Male N*R*G, and Women's Moon Cycle, to name a few. Breakfast egg dishes, pasta salads, and sandwiches round out the menu. Of course, there's also lots of java to fuel your jive. *692 N. Robertson Blvd., at Santa Monica Blvd., tel. 310/289–8410.*

**Chado.** The sweet smell of tea seeps from this cozy, dark tearoom. Soups, salads, sandwiches (try the Scottish smoked salmon with cream cheese and dill), and scones pepper the menu, but you could simply sit back, raise your pinkie as you sip, and read *Tea Magazine. 8422½ W. 3rd St., between Orlando Ave. and La Cienega Blvd., tel. 323/655–2056.*

**Sweet Lady Jane.** It's almost impossible to come here for a mere caf-fix. Instead, your sweet tooth will clamor for some heavenly chocolate cake, fresh baked pie, or lemon bars. The desserts are all baked on the premises. The space itself is perfectly refined, with stained glass on the ceiling, wood paneling, a glimmering deli case, and doilies on every marble tabletop. *8360 Melrose Ave., 2 blocks east of La Cienega Blvd., tel. 323/653–7145. Closed Sun.*

**Swing Cafe.** Down to the glass and silver cups, this place is civilized. The outside patio is extremely pleasant, with a flagstone floor, a fountain, hanging vines, and opera and swing music on the dial. Sandwiches and delectable pastries make up the menu. On Friday and Saturday bands play; call for other special events. *8545 Santa Monica Blvd., at La Cienega Blvd., tel. 310/652–8838.*

# WILSHIRE AND MELROSE

Melrose and Wilshire are not coffee-and-atmosphere fiends' prime destinations. But weary shoppers will find plenty of cafés where they can stop, quaff, and continue to shop.

**Highland Grounds.** Don't let the graffiti-covered exterior frighten you: This café is mellow and friendly, with excellent breakfasts (omelets and pancakes), and lunch and dinner items available after 11 AM. Come nightfall, it transforms into a demiclub, with art openings, open-mike poetry, and live music. There's an occasional small cover charge for some entertainment. *742 N. Highland Ave., ½ block north of Melrose Ave., tel. 323/466–1507.*

**Nova Express.** Flip through a tattered sci-fi novel and slurp a Galaxy 69 (banana smoothie with a shot of espresso) at this black, silver, and lava-orange space-age hideout. They also serve simple eats. DJs spin atmospheric tunes Tuesday and Sunday from midnight to 4 AM. *426 N. Fairfax Ave., between Melrose Ave. and Beverly Blvd., tel. 323/658–7533.*

**Stir Crazy.** You'll be so damn cozy within this café's faux log walls and low ceilings, you'll want to camp out for a few hours, maybe play a board game, or snuggle up on a couch to read. You won't even have to lift a finger as your cup o' joe is refilled for free. They'll lend you a *New Yorker* or a copy of *Los Angeles* magazine. *6917 Melrose Ave., east of La Brea Ave., tel. 213/934–4656.*

# BEVERLY HILLS

This area is low on cafés. Seriously low. Remember, this is the neighborhood where they can charge $4.50 for a cup of joe (*see* Polo Lounge *in* Beverly Hills and Century City, *above*).

**Caffè del Arte.** It's sleek, it's modern, and it's the only café in the Golden Triangle. The mood here is closer to Starbucks and other chains than it is to a neighborhood hangout. But you can still hang out on the teeny-weeny patio with a sandwich or a smoothie and watch the beautiful people sashay by. *428 N. Bedford Dr., between Wilshire and Little Santa Monica Blvds., tel. 310/271–6842. Closed Sun.*

# WESTWOOD AND WEST L.A.

**Cacao.** A little piece of mod lounge culture lingers in this bamboo bar with atmospheric music and tiki motif. Coffee up, chomp on a bagel sandwich, tap your toes to the groovy sounds, and feel happy that someone has created something so good. *11609 Santa Monica Blvd., at Federal Ave., West L.A., tel. 310/473–7283.*

**Elysée.** An assortment of delectable French pastries and desserts make this a good spot to get an afternoon refuel of sugar and coffee. The inside is generic—a deli case and boring white walls—but outside, the modern metal tables and people-watching opportunities make for a great place to rest your dogs. Sandwiches are also available. *1099 Gayley Ave., at Kinross Ave., Westwood, tel. 310/208–6505.*

**Lulu's Alibi.** Small and cheerful, Lulu's is a popular meeting place for those catching a show at the nearby Nuart Theater. Stop by on weekdays 5–7 for happy hour, when prices are slashed by half on caffeinated drinks. Brazilian appetizers and entrées dominate the food menu. *1640 Sawtelle Blvd., at Santa Monica Blvd., West L.A., tel. 310/479–6007.*

# SANTA MONICA, VENICE, AND MARINA DEL REY

Santa Monica, Venice, and Marina del Rey offer the best café scene in the city (with the possible exception of Santa Monica Boulevard in West Hollywood). You can caffeinate yourself in a variety of atmospheres, from a funky surf shop to a more elegant French bakery. You're welcome to bring a book and camp out for the day, and many cafés offer food tasty enough to persuade you to stay for a snack.

**Abbot's Habit.** Although history is unclear on whether Venice canal-builder Abbot Kinney had a yen for espresso drinks, his famed waterways at least prove his appreciation of Italian culture. This café has a plain wooden interior, with artwork that changes monthly and pretty tapestries on the tables. *1401 Abbot Kinney Blvd., at California Ave., Venice, tel. 310/399–1171.*

**Anastasia's Asylum.** Check out the shrine in the blood-red bathroom and pray for deliverance from the smog of the city. Among the perks here are the almost completely vegetarian menu, the free live music or open mike every night, and the 10% discount on all coffee drinks before 6 PM. *1028 Wilshire Blvd., at 11th St., Santa Monica, tel. 310/394–7113.*

**Café Collage.** Come here to get away from the Venice Beach circus. Modernist interpretations of Renaissance paintings hang on the terra-cotta walls, and wrought-iron furnishings add to the funky atmosphere. There's the regular café cuisine as well as original espresso concoctions like the Palermo (chocolate, espresso, orange peel, and nutmeg). *1518 Pacific Ave., at Windward Ave., Venice, tel. 310/399–0632.*

**Coffee Bean and Tea Leaf Company.** Okay, okay, it *is* a local chain, but at some point or another you will have to enter and learn just why it is so darn popular. The outdoor seating is always filled with a glamorous crowd here to enjoy fancy twists on the usual espresso drinks. You may as well splurge and discover for yourself why such treats as Caffe Vanilla keep them coming back for more. *2901 Main St., at Ashland Ave., Santa Monica, tel. 310/392–1406.*

**The Cow's End.** It is a tragedy of the modern era that a vapid Starbucks can survive across the street from one of Los Angeles's wackiest cafés. Cow lovers will enjoy the many bovine artifacts that decorate this busy hangout. You can browse at the adjoining newsstand or enjoy ice cream and a variety of rich pastries. Your daily horoscope is always available at the front counter. *34 Washington St., at Pacific Ave., Venice, tel. 310/574–1080.*

**Joni's Coffee Roastery.** Like many L.A. hot spots, Joni's is in a nondescript strip mall, but it's the place to go if you find yourself in Marina del Rey at 5:30 AM in dire need of coffee. (On the flip side, you can't come here for an after-dinner espresso; it closes at 4 PM.) Lots of knickknacks give the place a homey atmosphere. *550 Washington St., at Via Marina, Marina del Rey, tel. 310/305–7147.*

**Mani's Bakery and Espresso Bar.** This is southern California, so there's no need to ingest harmful fats to satisfy your sweet tooth. With a few locations around L.A., Mani's serves up healthy desserts, like nondairy mousses. At this branch, you can sit outside and watch the Main Street traffic stream by. *2507 Main St., at Ocean Park Blvd., Santa Monica, tel. 310/396–7700.*

**Metro Rags and Java.** The collection of used clothing being sold at this café gives it a youthful spirit. Coffee drinks are $1–$2. Lots of the neighborhood hangs out here, so expect some moms, kids, and old guys. Run next door to Cool City Comics for reading material. *1630 Ocean Park Blvd., between 16th and 17th Sts., Santa Monica, tel. 310/396–8356. Closed Sun.*

**Napoleon French Bakery and Café.** True to its name, Napoleon provides some delicious sweets in a convincingly European ambience. You'll find a well-attired crowd enjoying the simple decor and the flowers on the tables. *2301 Main St., at Strand St., Santa Monica, tel. 310/399–9511.*

**Newsroom Espresso Café.** Only at Newsroom can you catch CNN updates while sipping Bolt Coke, a mix of espresso and cola. In other words, this is a habitat for tightly wired media junkies. Normal, well-adjusted types will enjoy the large magazine rack and tasty range of entrées, including tandoori chicken and pesto pizza. *530 Wilshire Blvd., at 6th St., Santa Monica, tel. 310/319–9100.*

**Novel Café.** This is where the literati of Venice and Santa Monica congregate. Elegant, aging couches and floor-to-ceiling shelves of used hardbacks give the café-bookstore a clubby feel. Nosh on inexpensive soups, salads, and sandwiches while attempting to plow through Joyce or Faulkner. Bonus for insomniacs: it's open 24 hours. *212 Pier Ave., at Main St., Santa Monica, tel. 310/396–8566.*

# IT'S THE CHEESE!

*For great deals and free samples of all cheeses on the globe, stop by one of these shops.*

*Beverly Hills Cheese Store. Inside a little mall is the cheese capital of the Southland. The selection is dizzying and the quality is impeccable; look for artisanal varieties like creamy Reblochon. 419 N. Beverly Dr., near Brighton Way, Beverly Hills, tel. 310/278–2855. Closed Sun.*

*Say Cheese. Smaller than the Beverly Hills Cheese Store but still with a wide variety, this is a good place to avoid the crowds and be with the cheese. 2800 Hyperion Ave., between Griffith Park Blvd. and Rowena Ave., Los Feliz, tel. 323/665–0545.*

**Wednesday's House.** Its proximity to the Main Street art strip makes this the perfect place to do the post-gallery java-and-art-criticism thing. The outlandish collection of overstuffed furniture and the display of velvet Elvis paintings could only be the work of a gifted postmodernist decorator. On some evenings musical friends of the owner drop by to jam. Recommended reading: *Maus*, by Art Spiegelman. *2409 Main St., at Hollister Ave., Santa Monica, tel. 310/452–4486.*

**Un Urban Coffee House.** Sweetie pies run this cozy café, where you can hear blues or jazz, storytelling, poetry, or comedy on different nights of the week (call for a schedule or check the *L.A. Weekly*). Not only do they serve luscious *chai* (spiced tea) and strong coffee, but they also make sandwiches and a cheap breakfast (three scrambled eggs, tomatoes, and toast). Knickknacks from eras past line the walls and sit in the old Frigidaire in the back room. Bring a journal or sketchpad. *3301 Pico Blvd., at Urban St., 1½ blocks west of Centinela, Santa Monica, tel. 310/315–0056.*

## SOUTH BAY AND LONG BEACH

Bookworms and cybersurfers comfortably rub elbows at the laid-back, well-lighted fuel stations in the South Bay and Long Beach. For a quick morning fix, look for drive-thru java joints in former one-hour photo kiosks along PCH.

Bypass Starbucks and pick up a sobering drink at **Java Man,** in a Victorian home two blocks from the beach. Strong cups of joe can be refilled twice for only 25¢ before 6 PM daily; salads and sandwiches are about $6. The café also functions as a gallery, displaying works by local artists. *157 Pier Ave., at Manhattan Ave., Hermosa Beach, tel. 310/379–7209.*

**The Library.** Curl up with the old standbys—a book and a steaming cup of coffee—at this intimate roost, which draws a friendly, mixed crowd of the how-am-I-going-to-pay-off-the-student-loans and the not-quite-ready-to-admit-art-school-is-over-and-I-am-settling-down types. There's live music every Wednesday, Friday, and Sunday at 8. *3418 E. Broadway, Long Beach, tel. 562/433–2393.*

**Sacred Grounds.** Bring your dominoes, harmonica, or poetry for sharing: This intimate space houses a performance stage and is the locus of San Pedro's thriving art scene. Live music or spoken-word entertainment begins nightly around 8. Cover is $2–$5. *399 W. 6th St., at Mesa St., San Pedro, tel. 310/514–0800.*

**Yesterdays Coffeehouse and Bookstore.** A comfortable retro feel permeates this café, where families with dogs mingle with bored skate brats. Enjoy a book from the collection of used romance, mystery, sci-fi, and pulp fiction while sitting on rec-room couches. *126 N. Catalina Ave., Redondo Beach, tel. 310/318– 2499.*

# GROCERS AND SPECIALTY STORES

Most grocery and specialty stores are open from early morning until late evening, and a few in Hollywood and West Hollywood are open 24 hours, generally in areas where there is late-night activity. **Vons** (11674 Santa Monica Blvd., at Barrington Ave., West L.A., tel. 310/820–1012, and other locations) is by far the most ubiquitous grocery store in L.A. and one of the oldest. **Pavilions** (8969 Santa Monica Blvd., at Robertson Blvd., West Hollywood, tel. 310/273–0977), an upscale arm of Vons, has more international and gourmet selections and slightly higher prices; it is also found all over the L.A. area, as is the larger **Ralph's** (7257 Hollywood Blvd., between La Brea and Fairfax Aves., tel. 323/874–6333, and other locations). Zagat's annual *Survey Marketplace,* available at most bookstores, is a good source for finding everything food except restaurants. It lists the best buys and best places to find things like bagels and bialys, ethnic food sources, cooking schools, delis, and more.

**Bristol Farms.** This pricey shop brings together the best in gourmet bakery, deli, butchery, produce, and dairy offerings. Samples from every department create the atmosphere of an indoor picnicker's paradise. Come here for hard-to-find imported and boutique items or when preparing dinner for someone you want to impress. *1570 Rosecrans Ave., at PCH, Manhattan Beach, tel. 310/643–5229; 837 Silver Spur Rd., Palos Verdes, tel. 310/541–9157; 606 Fair Oaks Ave., South Pasadena, tel. 626/441–5450; 6627 Topanga Canyon Blvd., Woodland Hills, tel. 818/227–8400.*

*You can get free tickets to various CBS tapings at the Farmers' Market Office (upstairs, inside Gate 1). The best time to pick them up is Monday in the late-morning hours.*

**Co-Opportunity.** This natural foods store and grocery may look like the rest of them, but it's fundamentally different, because it is owned by its employees (please note clever name). Stop by the deli for some scrumptious salads with a vegetarian emphasis or drink up at the juice bar while getting groceries the PC way. *1525 Broadway, at 16th St., Santa Monica, tel. 310/451–8902.*

**Erewhon Natural Foods.** Besides hosting macrobiotic lectures and cooking classes, this mecca of health food and obscure natural products offers a full-service deli, a soup and salad bar, and a grocery store. *7660 Beverly Blvd., at Stanley Ave., Fairfax, tel. 323/937–0777.*

**Noah's Bagels.** This New York–style bagel shop of increasing popularity is favored for its flavored cream-cheese schmears. A bagel with your choice of schmear (except lox) and a cup of coffee is $2. *200 S. Beverly Dr., 1 block south of Wilshire Blvd., Beverly Hills, tel. 310/550–7392; 2710 Main St., at Hill St., Santa Monica, tel. 310/396–4339; 320 Santa Monica Blvd., between 3rd and 4th Sts., Santa Monica, tel. 310/394—3557; 11911 San Vicente Blvd., at Montana, Brentwood, tel. 310/472–5651; 8919 Santa Monica Blvd., at San Vicente Blvd., West Hollywood, tel. 310/289–1795.*

**One Life Natural Foods.** This grocery store has a complete fruit and vegetable section, bulk foods, and other health-food-nut favorites. In the back is a deli and the de rigueur juice bar. *3001 Main St., at Pier Ave., Santa Monica, tel. 310/392–4501.*

**Trader Joe's.** Based in South Pasadena, this steadily growing chain will leave cheapskates with a smile on their little faces. The wine and beer six-packs here are inexpensive, and you'll appreciate the abundant selection. You can also pick up a vast array of inexpensive frozen food, nuts, cereals, soy milk, trail mix, pastas, and cheese. *1821 Manhattan Beach Blvd., at Aviation, Manhattan Beach, tel. 310/372–1274; 1761 S. Elena Ave., at Ave. I in Hollywood Riviera shopping area, Redondo Beach, tel. 310/316–1745; 2738 Hyperion Ave., at Griffith Park Blvd., Silver Lake, tel. 323/665–6774; 7304 Santa Monica Blvd., at Poinsettia, West Hollywood, tel. 323/851–9772; 10850 National Blvd., West Los Angeles, tel. 310/470–1917. Call 800/746-7857 for closest location.*

**Whole Foods Market.** This upscale grocery chain specializes in organic and macrobiotic products. Most locations have full deli, fish, and meat counters, as well as sushi bars and a wide assortment of locally grown produce. Weekends mean lots of free samples from every department. They also stock an extensive selection of vitamins, health products, and nontoxic household goods. *405 N. PCH, Redondo Beach, tel. 310/376–6931; 826 N. Glendale Ave., Glendale, tel. 818/240–9350; call for other locations.*

# FARMERS' MARKETS

Sure, Angelenos flock to farmers' markets for luscious farm-fresh produce, glorious baked goods, and other specialty items (jams, sausages, plants, and crafts) sold directly by the growers and manufacturers, but the real attraction is the opportunity to shop outside. Prices are competitive with supermarket chains, and the quality and selection of the goods (often organic) are unsurpassed. Samples of most products are de rigueur, and it is possible to picnic without making a purchase. Take the opportunity to ask farmers how they prepare their products. Marketing is usually best in the early morning, when selection is best, or just before closing, when merchants are eager to bargain. Most markets are more like minifestivals, where street musicians croon for the crowds.

**Farmers' Market.** This collection of permanent vendors stands is a good place to eat—the more, the better. The site was originally a gathering place for farmers and their produce. Over the years it has become an assortment of stalls selling cheap and yummy eats and shoddy souvenirs from all over the world. The Gumbo Pot (tel. 323/933–0358) is the local favorite, with its New Orleans jambalaya, gumbo, beignets, and chicory coffee. To get the real Angeleno experience, grab an *L.A. Times,* a few snacks, and a shady table. There's three hours free parking here. The market is open Monday–Saturday 9–6:30, Sunday 10–5. *6333 W. 3rd St., at Fairfax Ave., Fairfax, tel. 323/933–9211.*

**Grand Central Market.** It's busy, busy, busy at this farmers' market, where you can buy your own raw foodstuffs to prepare back at the hostel or eat at a variety of Mexican, Chinese, and Italian stands. Maria's Fresh Seafood stand is especially good, with inexpensive tacos and tortas. Geraldine's Let's Get Juiced serves—yep—juice; stop by Lil Orbit's Donut Shop for superfresh sugar-and-grease balls to eradicate that healthy OJ taste. The market is open Monday–Saturday 9–6, Sunday 10–5:30. After the culinary fun take a ride on Angels Flight Railway (*see* Downtown *in* Chapter 2) across the street. *317 S. Broadway, between 3rd and 4th Sts., downtown, tel. 213/624–2378. Take the Red Line to Pershing Sq. metro station, exit at 4th St.*

## OTHER MARKETS

**Hermosa Beach.** *13th St. and Hermosa Ave., no phone. Open Fri. noon–4.*

**Hollywood.** *Ivar Ave. between Hollywood Blvd. and Selma Ave., tel. 323/463–3171. Open Sun. 8:30–1.*

**Long Beach.** *The Promenade between 3rd St. and Broadway, tel. 562/433–3881. Open Fri. 10–4.*

**North Long Beach.** *Dooley's, 51st St. and Long Beach Blvd., tel. 562/433–3881. Open Sat. 7:30–11:30.*

**San Pedro.** *Ports O'Call Village parking lot, tel. 562/433–3881. Open Thurs. 10–2.*

**Santa Monica.** *Main Street: 2640 Main St., at Ocean Park Blvd., in California Heritage Museum parking lot. Open Sun. 9:30–1. Others: 2nd St. and Arizona Ave., open Wed. 9:30–2; Pico Blvd. and Cloverfield Ave., open Sat. 8–1; Arizona Ave. between 2nd and 3rd Sts., open Sat. 8:30–1. Tel. 310/458–8712.*

**Torrance.** *Torrance Blvd. at Redondo Pier, tel. 310/375–5900. Open Thurs. 9–1.*

**Westwood.** *Weyburn Ave. at Westwood Blvd., tel. 310/208–6115. Open Thurs. 2–7.*

# REFERENCE LISTINGS

## BY TYPE OF CUISINE

### AFRICAN

**Under $15**

Nyala *(Wilshire)*

**Under $20**

Moun of Tunis *(Hollywood)*

### AMERICAN

**Under $10**

Basix Café *(West Hollywood)*

Cadillac Café *(West Hollywood)*

California Chicken Café *(Melrose)*

CJ's Pantry *(Redondo Beach)*

Fabiolus Café *(Hollywood, Melrose)*

Flora Kitchen *(Wilshire)*

French Quarter *(West Hollywood)*

Good Stuff *(Hermosa Beach, Manhattan Beach)*

Hennessey's Tavern *(Redondo Beach, Hermosa Beach, Manhattan Beach)*

Hugo's *(West Hollywood)*

King's Road Café *(Hollywood)*

M Bar and Grill *(Long Beach)*

Malibu Seafood Patio Café *(Malibu)*

Ocean View Café *(Manhattan Beach)*

Rose Café *(Venice)*

Sloopy's *(Manhattan Beach)*

Snow White Café *(Hollywood)*

Starlight Café *(Culver City)*

Terri's *(Pacific Palisades)*

Venus of Venice *(Venice)*

**Under $15**

Birds *(Hollywood)*

Caffè Latte *(Wilshire)*

Fred 62 *(Silver Lake)*

Hollywood Hills Coffee Shop *(Hollywood)*

Il Sogno *(Pacific Palisades)*

Louis XIV *(Melrose)*

Newsroom Café *(Beverly Hills)*

Netty's *(Hollywood)*

Sixth Street Bistro *(San Pedro)*

Vienna Café *(Melrose)*

Wolfgang Puck Cafe *(West Hollywood, Santa Monica)*

**Under $20**

Atlas Bar and Grill *(Downtown)*

Hal's *(Venice)*

Off Vine *(Hollywood)*

**Splurge**

Ivy at the Shore *(Santa Monica)*

Paio *(Hollywood)*

Polo Lounge *(Beverly Hills)*

Spago *(Beverly Hills)*

### AMERICAN DINER/ DELI FOOD

**Under $5**

Abbot's Pizza Company *(Venice)*

Café 50's *(West L.A.)*

Carney's *(West Hollywood)*

Clifton"s Brookdale Cafeteria *(Downtown)*

Cole's French Dipped Sandwiches *(Downtown)*

Cozy Café *(Redondo Beach)*

Dory's Deli Station *(Santa Monica)*

Eat Well *(West Hollywood)*

Greenwich Village *(West Hollywood)*

Jody Maroni's Sausage Kingdom *(Venice)*

Larchmont Deli *(Hollywood)*

Philippe the Original *(Downtown)*

Pink's Famous Chili Dogs *(Melrose)*

Randy's Donuts *(South-Central)*

Sepi's *(Westwood)*

Sion's *(Manhattan Beach)*

St. Urbain St. Bagels *(Santa Monica)*

**Under $10**

The Apple Pan *(West L.A.)*

Canter's *(West Hollywood)*

Cañon Liquor Café *(Beverly Hills)*

Hollywood Canteen *(Hollywood)*

The Firehouse *(Santa Monica)*

Gourmet Gala *(Pacific Palisades)*

Greg's Grill *(Pacific Palisades)*

Jan's Family Restaurant *(Wilshire)*

Joe's *(Redondo Beach)*

Johnnie's Pastrami *(South-Central)*

John O'Groats *(West L.A.)*

The Kettle *(Manhattan Beach)*

Langer's *(Downtown)*

Martha's 22nd Street Grill *(Hermosa Beach)*

Mort's Palisades Deli *(Pacific Palisades)*

Nate 'n' Al's *(Beverly Hills)*

Original Pantry Café *(Downtown)*

Pacific Coast Greens *(Malibu)*

Rae's *(Santa Monica)*

The Shack *(Santa Monica)*

Swingers Diner *(Hollywood)*

Van Go's Ear *(Venice)*

Village Coffee Shop *(Hollywood)*

Wildflour Boston Pizza *(Santa Monica)*

Yukon Mining Co. *(West Hollywood)*

**Under $15**

Alpine Village Inn and Market *(Torrance)*

Duke's *(West Hollywood)*

Utro's *(San Pedro)*

## ARMENIAN

**Under $5**

Zankou Chicken *(Hollywood)*

## BELIZEAN

**Under $10**

Toucan *(South-Central)*

## BRAZILIAN

**Under $5**

Ipanema *(West Hollywood)*

**Under $10**

Bossa Nova *(West Hollywood)*

## CHINESE

**Under $5**

Feast from the East *(West L.A.)*

Lucky Deli *(Downtown)*

Rascals *(Downtown)*

Won Kok Dim Sum *(Downtown)*

**Under $10**

Big Wok Mongolian BBQ *(Hermosa Beach)*

Chang's *(Beverly Hills)*

Mayflower Restaurant *(Downtown)*

Mongols BBQ *(Westwood)*

New Moon *(Downtown)*

Yum Yum Dim Sum *(Westwood)*

**Under $15**

Mon Kee's Seafood Restaurant *(Downtown)*

**Under $20**

Yang Chow *(Downtown)*

## CREOLE/CAJUN

**Under $10**

Ragin' Cajun Café *(Hermosa Beach)*

**Under $15**

Bourbon Street Shrimp *(West Hollywood)*

Killer Shrimp *(Redondo Beach, Marina del Rey)*

Stevie's on the Strip *(South-Central)*

## CUBAN

**Under $10**

Versailles *(West L.A. and Venice)*

## GREEK

**Under $20**

Sofi *(West Hollywood)*

**Splurge**

Papadakis Taverna *(San Pedro)*

## ECLECTIC

**Under $5**

Beach Hut *(Hermosa Beach, Manhattan Beach)*

**Under $15**

Authentic Café *(Melrose)*

## HEALTH FOOD

**Under $5**

Good Life Health Centre *(South Central)*

**Under $10**

Flowering Tree *(West Hollywood)*

Greens at the Beach *(Redondo Beach)*

The Spot *(Hermosa Beach)*

Village Natural Food *(Pacific Palisades)*

## HUNGARIAN

**Under $10**

Csárdás *(Hollywood)*

## INDIAN

**Under $5**

India Sweets & Spices *(Culver City)*

**Under $10**

Paru's Indian Vegetarian *(Downtown)*

**Under $15**

Bombay Café *(West L.A.)*

Nawab of India *(Santa Monica)*

## ITALIAN

**Under $5**

Alejo Presto Trattoria *(Marina del Rey)*

Damiano's *(Melrose)*

Marino Pizzeria *(West Hollywood)*

**Under $10**

Benvenuto Caffè *(West Hollywood)*

Da Pasquale *(Beverly Hills)*

George's Bistro *(Santa Monica)*

Italy's Little Kitchen *(Manhattan Beach)*

Intermezzo *(Melrose)*

Jacopo's *(Beverly Hills)*

La Bottega *(West Hollywood)*

Mulberry Street Pizzeria *(Beverly Hills)*

Porta Via *(Beverly Hills)*

Prizzi's Piazza *(Hollywood)*

Rosti *(Santa Monica)*

**Under $15**

C&O Trattoria *(Marina del Rey)*

Caffè Luna *(Melrose)*

Fritto Misto *(Santa Monica)*

Tavola Calda *(West Hollywood)*

**Under $20**

Red *(Melrose)*

La Vecchia Cucina *(Santa Monica)*

## JAPANESE

**Under $5**

Sushi and Teri *(Downtown)*

**Under $10**

Hurry Curry of Tokyo *(West L.A.)*

Mishima *(West L.A. and Wilshire)*

Mr. Ramen *(Downtown)*

Shabu Shabu House *(Downtown)*

**Under $15**

Crazy Fish *(Beverly Hills)*

O-Sho *(West L.A.)*

## KOREAN

**Under $10**

Jeepney Grill *(Downtown)*

**Under $15**

Woo Lae Oak *(Downtown)*

## LATIN AMERICAN

**Under $20**

Ciudad *(Downtown)*

## MEXICAN

**Under $5**

Baja Fresh *(Beverly Hills)*

El Burrito Jr. *(Redondo Beach)*

Gallegos Mexican Deli *(Santa Monica)*

King Taco *(East L.A.)*

La Luz del Dia *(Downtown)*

La Salsa (*Malibu, Redondo Beach, Torrance, Long Beach*)

Los Tacos *(Hollywood)*

Rosa's *(Hermosa Beach)*

Siete Mares Seafood Express *(East L.A.)*

Tito's Tacos and Lucy's Drive-In *(South-Central)*

Yuca's Hut *(Los Feliz)*

**Under $10**

El Coyote Café *(Melrose)*

Guelaguetza *(Downtown)*

El Tarasco *(East L.A.)*

Kay & Dave's (*Pacific Palisades, Santa Monica*)

Señor Fish *(Downtown)*

**Under $15**

Cobalt Cantina *(West Hollywood)*

El Cholo *(Downtown)*

La Parilla *(East L.A.)*

La Serenata de Garibaldi *(East L.A.)*

## MIDDLE EASTERN

**Under $5**

Al Wazir Chicken *(Hollywood)*

Falafel King *(Westwood, Santa Monica)*

**Under $10**

Noura Café *(West Hollywood)*

Sunnin *(Westwood)*

## PERUVIAN

**Under $10**

El Pollo Inka *(Hermosa Beach, Lawndale, Gardena, Torrance)*

Mario's Peruvian Seafood *(Melrose)*

## SOUTHERN

**Under $10**

Roscoe's House of Chicken 'n' Waffles *(Hollywood)*

Johnny Rebs Southern Smokehouse *(Long Beach)*

## SPANISH

**Under $10**

Alegria *(Long Beach)*

## THAI

**Under $10**

Thai Thani *(Redondo Beach)*

Thailand Plaza *(Hollywood)*

Toi on Sunset *(Hollywood)*

**Under $15**

Chan Dara *(Hollywood)*

## UZBEKI AND RUSSIAN

**Under $15**

Uzbekistan *(Hollywood)*

# WHERE TO SLEEP

## 4

BY CATHERINE BELONOGOFF

UPDATED BY BOBBI ZANE

**M**ost important in determining where to sleep in L.A. is deciding where you want to be when you wake up the next day. The city's sprawl will force you to spend a lot of time in transit, and naturally you'll want to keep your time stuck in traffic to a minimum. You'll need to strategize, keeping in mind the old refrain "location, location, location." For instance, if you've got a yen to see Hollywood, Melrose Avenue, and the Sunset Strip, make one of the nearby, inexpensive Hollywood motels your base.

A double room at a motel (with furnishings that have probably not changed since the first decade of the motel's existence) will cost $50–$65. Most motels in L.A. are just a place to sleep and wash and flee from as soon as day breaks, since they offer little more than a room, a parking space (usually), and an occasional Continental breakfast. Bed-and-breakfasts tend to cost more but they may suit you better; you'll get a hearty breakfast, the amenities of a whole house, and an innkeeper acting as a concierge.

Both Venice and Hollywood have the largest concentration of hostels, which are the cheapest way to go for solo explorers; a bed will cost only $12–$20. The hostels can feel like a mini language program, since they're favored by European budget travelers.

While there are campgrounds in the L.A. area—in the mountains east of the city and along the beaches north and south of the city—camping is not an appealing option. You'll spend more money on gas getting to and from town than you'd save in lodging costs. And if you're looking for a pristine slice of Mother Nature, you'll have to look elsewhere. Also, mountain campgrounds may not be safe. If you'll be heading out of the city and are set on roughing it, check out the campground listings in Chapter 8.

Spending a night or two in one of L.A.'s university dorms is next to impossible unless you are somehow connected to the school: a prospective student or staff member, an alumnus, or a student's parent. If you fit one of these categories, check with the university's housing department.

With a little extra effort, you can often find bargain rates at hotels. In summer many hotel chains that cater to weekday business travelers drop their weekend rates and add extras such as a free breakfast, free stays for kids, or late check-out. You'll find the best deals on these in nontouristy areas such as mid-Wilshire and downtown. Rates also drop during the off-season, which is generally January through March, when rain is most likely. Before you sniff at the idea of an off-season visit, consider this: With the exception of occasional rainy days, you'll encounter warm days and cool nights. And there will be fewer tourists to compete with for parking space.

Hotels and motels are arranged under our price categories according to the cost of a double room excluding tax—14 percent in the city of Los Angeles, somewhat less elsewhere. Unless stated otherwise, all lodgings listed in this book have air-conditioning as well as free parking, and all accept major credit cards. All rooms have their own bathrooms unless otherwise noted. If you're concerned about luggage storage, be sure to ask.

# DOWNTOWN

Although downtown is smack in the middle of five freeways and has at least as many museums, it's not necessarily the best place to stay. Walking around at night may be a scary proposition, some restaurants close early, and the area resembles a ghost town on weekends. However, the late-1999 opening of the Staples Center arena should breathe new life into the southern part of downtown over the next couple of years, encouraging cleaner and safer streets and an upswing in business. In the meantime, if you're looking for some bona-fide Hollywood action, this is a good place to be at night and on weekends, when many film studios set up shop on the mostly deserted streets.

The sketchiest areas are generally just west of the Harbor freeway and south of the University of Southern California—look elsewhere for a roof over your head. Another tip: hotels near the Convention Center tend to fill up early at inflated rates in spring and fall, when most trade shows and conventions hit town. To get exact dates so that you can avoid mobs of convention goers, call ahead (213/741–1151) for an events schedule.

*See the Downtown Los Angeles Lodging map.*

**UNDER $50 • Orchid Hotel.** Amid a sea of pricey Sheraton types, the Orchid is a welcome respite. Clean, comfortable doubles are a refreshing $38 ($246 a week). If one person in your group can produce a student ID, you'll receive a 15% discount. The clientele includes an odd mix of backpackers and pensioners; the 24-hour reception desk keeps the place safe and orderly 'round the clock. *819 S. Flower St., between W. 8th and W. 9th Sts., 90017, tel. 213/624–5855 or 800/874–5855, fax 213/624–8740. 62 rooms. Laundry.*

**UNDER $75 • Hotel Stillwell.** East Indian prints line the halls of this 10-story hotel near the heart of downtown, and the rooms have tastefully matched curtains and linens. The management can be effusively friendly, and you'll even find some families staying here, a testimony to the building's excellent security. Doubles are $59; a student ID will net you a 10% discount. *838 S. Grand Ave., between W. 8th and W. 9th Sts., 90017, tel. 213/627–1151 or 800/553–4774, fax 213/622–8940. 250 rooms. Laundry.*

**UNDER $100 • Best Western Dragon Gate Inn.** This Chinatown hotel, just a few blocks north of Civic Center, was renovated in 1999. Simply furnished rooms come with refrigerators, coffeemakers, and TVs. Doubles run $79–$99 including Continental breakfast; student, senior, and corporate discounts are available. Keeping your car overnight in their secured underground parking lot is just an extra $2.50. *818 N. Hill St., at Alpine St., 90012, tel. 213/617–3077 or 800/282–9999, fax 213/680–3753. 57 rooms.*

**Figueroa Hotel.** Nearby hotels pale in comparison to this breezy, Southwestern-style, high-rise hotel. Lots of Europeans lounge around the back patio bar and pool area filled with magenta flowers and tropical greenery. The decorator was unable to reconcile the Southwest with Mexico and the Mediterranean, judging from the color schemes and the wacky assortment of chandeliers. Still, the place is nice and makes a mighty fine spot to stay. Doubles start at $95. Since the hotel is just steps away from the Convention Center, it's little wonder it books up months in advance of major events. *939 S. Figueroa St., between Olympic and W. 9th Sts., 90015, tel. 213/627–8971 or 800/421–9092, fax 213/689–0305. 285 rooms. Restaurant.*

**Inn at 657.** Patsy will be your charming, nonintrusive hostess at this bed-and-breakfast in a residential neighborhood. The patios, fountain, beautiful flowers, and Jacuzzi take a back seat to the spacious 1940s apartments with private entrances. All are beautifully decorated with silks and luxurious furniture. There's a palpable spirit of generosity: The fridges in the immaculate kitchens are stocked with juices and coffee, the homemade breakfast is more than ample, and all local phone calls are free. Rooms start at $95. *657 W. 23rd St., 1 block west of Figueroa St., 90007, tel. 213/741–2200 or 800/347–7512. 5 rooms. Laundry. Cash only.*

**Kawada Hotel.** The old, office-like exterior of this hotel belies the bright, modern rooms inside. The rooms may not set off fireworks in the decor department, but they've got TVs and refrigerators; some

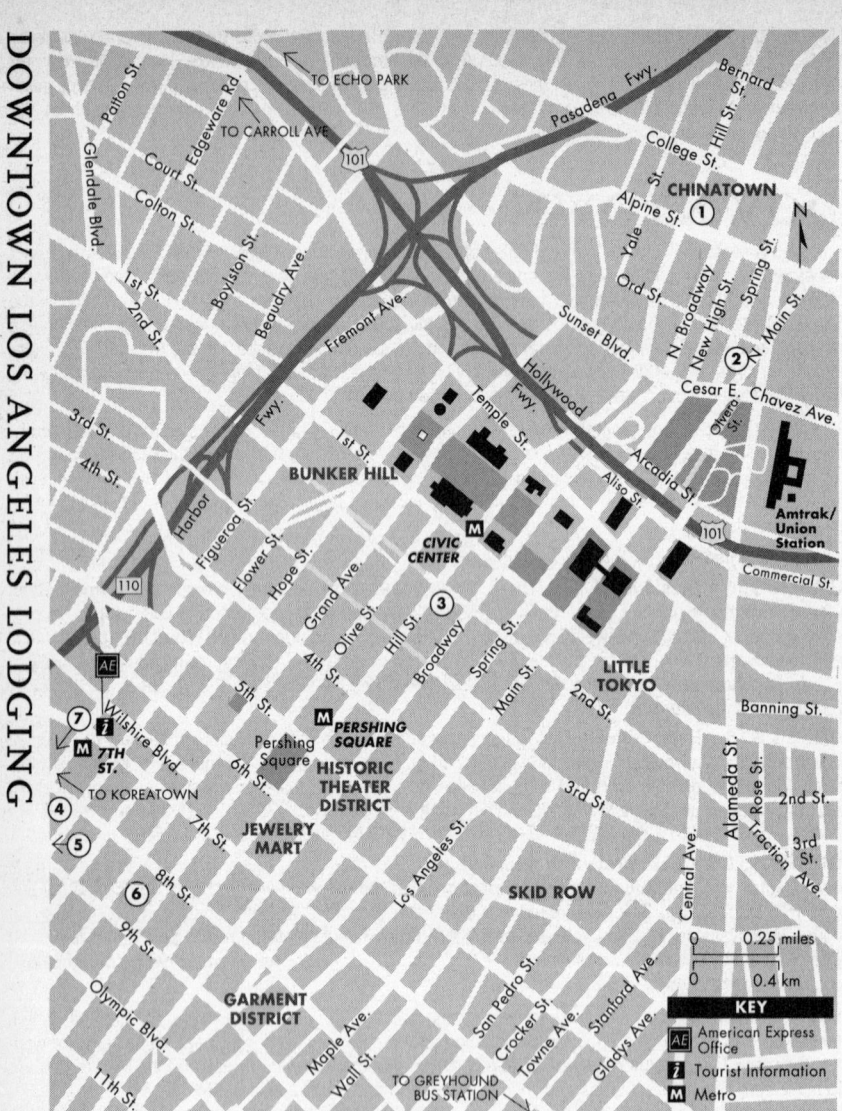

TO ECHO PARK

TO CARROLL AVE

101

Patton St.

Glendale Blvd.

Edgeware Rd.

Court St.

Colton St.

Boylston Ave.

Beaudry Ave.

Fremont Ave.

1st St.

2nd St.

3rd St.

4th St.

Pasadena Fwy.

College St.

Bernard St.

Hill St.

Alpine St.

Yale St.

Ord St.

Sunset Blvd.

**CHINATOWN**

①

N. Broadway

New High St.

Spring St.

N. Main St.

N

②

Cesar E. Chavez Ave.

Ord St.

Olvera St.

**Amtrak/ Union Station**

101

Commercial St.

Harbor

Fwy.

1st St.

Temple St.

Hollywood Fwy.

**BUNKER HILL**

Arcadia St.

Aliso St.

**CIVIC CENTER**

M

110

Figueroa St.

Flower St.

Hope St.

Grand Ave.

Olive St.

Hill St.

Broadway

Spring St.

Main St.

2nd St.

**LITTLE TOKYO**

Banning St.

③

AE

Wilshire Blvd.

5th St.

6th St.

M

**PERSHING SQUARE**

Pershing Square

**HISTORIC THEATER DISTRICT**

3rd St.

Alameda St.

Rose St.

2nd St.

⑦

i

M

**7TH ST.**

TO KOREATOWN

④

⑤

7th St.

8th St.

9th St.

**JEWELRY MART**

**GARMENT DISTRICT**

Los Angeles St.

**SKID ROW**

Central Ave.

3rd St. Ave.

Traction Ave.

⑥

Olympic Blvd.

11th St.

Maple Ave.

Wall St.

San Pedro St.

Crocker St.

Towne Ave.

Gladys Ave.

Stanford Ave.

TO GREYHOUND BUS STATION

0        0.25 miles

0        0.4 km

**KEY**

AE  American Express Office

i  Tourist Information

M  Metro

Best Western
Dragon Gate Inn, **1**

Figueroa Hotel, **5**

Hotel Stillwell, **6**

Inn at 657, **7**

Kawada Hotel, **3**

Metro Plaza Hotel, **2**

Orchid Hotel, **4**

even have kitchenettes. Check on their discount rates; besides 10% discounts for AAA and AARP members, they could have a promotion, like a deal for Amtrak passengers. Parking is about $10 extra. It's a short walk from here to the Music Center and Civic Center, and a Metro station. *200 S. Hill St., between 2nd and 3rd Sts., 90012, tel. 213/621–4455, fax 213/687–4455. 116 rooms. Restaurant, coffee shop.*

**Metro Plaza Hotel.** Smack between bustling Chinatown and kitschy, carnivalesque Olvera Street, this hotel is also just a short walk from Union Station. Doubles, equipped with refrigerators and TVs, cost $75; AAA members get a 20% discount. *711 N. Main St., at Cesar E. Chavez Ave., 90012, tel. 213/680–0200 or 800/223–2223, fax 213/620–0200. 80 rooms.*

# WILSHIRE, FAIRFAX, AND MELROSE

What a difference a few blocks make. A string of ridiculously priced hotels lines Sunset Boulevard west of Crescent Heights Boulevard, straddling the Hollywood/West Hollywood border. Two of the top addresses are the Chateau Marmont, long a favorite of the rich and famous, and the Mondrian Hotel, redesigned by Philippe Starck, who painted the building white, covering the brightly colored Mondrian-like facade and rendering the name meaningless. Admire and move on; you'll find much cheaper lodgings a few blocks south, around the intersection of Beverly Boulevard and Fairfax Avenue. Prices are a bit higher than in Hollywood or downtown L.A., but you're paying for comfort, security, and prime locale. Enjoy the Melrose café scene, visit museums and the La Brea Tar Pits, or drive 20 minutes to downtown or Santa Monica Beach.

*See the West L.A. Lodging map.*

**UNDER $50 • Bevonshire Lodge Motel.** This is a small and unremarkable motel with a Chihuahua-size pool and fatigued furnishings. It's close to CBS and the Farmer's Market, an excellent place to nosh (*see* Wilshire District *in* Chapter 2). Doubles, all with refrigerators, are $50. *7575 Beverly Blvd., between Fairfax Ave. and Gardner St., Fairfax, 90036, tel. 323/936–6154, fax 323/934–6640. 25 rooms.*

**UNDER $75 • Beverly Laurel Motor Hotel.** Take a deep breath and relax in the tastefully furnished, spacious rooms at this well-situated, three-story motel. Extras include refrigerators and microwaves in every room, a downstairs coffee shop, and a pleasant pool. Doubles are $73, $85 with a full kitchenette (with cookware and dishes). *8018 Beverly Blvd., 2 blocks west of Fairfax Ave., Fairfax, 90048, tel. 323/651–2441, fax 323/651–5225. 52 rooms. Coffee shop.*

**Farmer's Daughter Motel.** This three-story motel across from the Farmers' Market (*see* Wilshire District *in* Chapter 2) hasn't seen any real farmers—or their daughters—for decades. Large, immaculate doubles, complete with refrigerators, usually start at $69. There are also a pool and a sundeck. *115 S. Fairfax Ave., between Beverly Blvd. and 3rd St., Fairfax, 90036, tel. 323/937–3930 or 800/334–1658, fax 323/932–1608. 66 rooms.*

**Park Plaza Lodge.** The name is more swank than the hotel itself, but who can complain about the enormous and spectacularly clean rooms? Rooms are done in muted pastels, each with a nice table, pair of chairs, and a king-size bed. It's just a short walk to the Farmers' Market and a little farther to the Los Angeles County Museum of Art and the La Brea Tar Pits. Doubles run $60. *6001 W. 3rd St., between Fairfax and La Brea Aves., Wilshire, 90036, tel. 323/931–1501, fax 323/931–5863. 50 rooms.*

**Wilshire Dunes Motor Hotel.** The peach-and-brown rooms of this quiet hotel look out to a pool just big enough to splash around in with all the other tourists. The aroma of cleaning products nearly masks the faint cigarette odor—but hey, at least it's evidence of housekeeping. Double rooms are $62. *4300 Wilshire Blvd., between La Brea and Wilton Aves., Wilshire, 90010, tel. 323/938–3616 or 800/443–8637, fax 323/938-8661. 63 rooms. Laundry.*

# HOLLYWOOD

Hollywood is a swirl of punk kids, Midwesterners, European tourists with big cameras, and angry and disturbed homeless sorts. It's hard to find an L.A. native. The area is heavily touristy, bordering on ridiculous (how many T-shirt shops and tattoo parlors can you squeeze into one block?). If you stay here, expect a carnival atmosphere at the front desk and on the streets. That said, this old (for Los Angeles) neighborhood has some breathtaking historic buildings, especially from the art deco era. Accordingly, the hotels range from classically elegant (like the Hollywood Roosevelt Hotel) to classically kitschy (such as the Saharan Motor Hotel). Also, change is afoot—new developments like the Hollywood and Highland complex and restorations like the Egyptian Theatre (*see* Hollywood *in* Chapter 2) will likely rustle up some civic improvements.

*See the Hollywood Lodging map.*

**UNDER $50 • Liberty Hotel.** Quiet, charming, and unlike anything you'd expect to see in Hollywood, this low-rise hotel is the place to stay if you have high standards of personal hygiene. Though it's on a tree-lined side street, it's only a block north of the everlasting sideshow surrounding Mann's Chinese Theater (*see* Hollywood *in* Chapter 2). Doubles start at $45. *1770 Orchid Ave., near Franklin Ave., 90028, tel. 323/962–1788, fax 323/463–1705. 20 rooms.*

**Saharan Motor Hotel.** The aggressively orange doors remind you this hotel was built in the 1960s, and it probably hasn't changed much since then. The 9-ft-deep pool is practically the only one deep enough to dive in without killing yourself in all of motel L.A. Pretend the street noise is just, um, urban ambience. Doubles are $49; if you need to wash your socks, there's a laundry next door. *7212 Sunset Blvd., at Poinsettia Pl., 90028, tel. 323/874–6700, fax 323/874–5163. 62 rooms.*

**UNDER $75 • Dunes Sunset Motel.** You wouldn't guess by looking at it, but this motel, right off U.S. 101, is related to the Wilshire Dunes Motor Hotel (*see* Wilshire, Fairfax, and Melrose, *above*). The rooms here are clean and even smell fresh. Be prepared for lots of stark concrete, plenty of gray-haired patrons, and rooms with decor to match. Doubles start at $60. *5625 Sunset Blvd., between Western and Wilton Aves., 90029, tel. 323/467–5171 or 800/452–3863, 800/443–8637 in CA, fax 323/461–1720. 53 rooms.*

**Hollywood Celebrity Hotel.** The relaxed mood of the twenty-something management has permeated this art deco hotel's atmosphere. Everything is gray and burgundy, including the murals of Hollywood icons like Charlie Chaplin, the Tin Man, and Will Rogers painted over every bed. A luxurious perk is the Continental breakfast waiting at your door each morning; there's also a free shuttle to Universal Studios. Doubles are $65. *1775 Orchid Ave., near Franklin Ave., 90028, tel. 323/850–6464 or 800/222–7017, 800/222–7090 in CA, fax 323/850–7667. 38 rooms.*

**La Mirage Inn.** The dark brown shag carpets and big beds draped in '70s comforters don't detract too much from this passably clean and very quiet motel. It's a bit of a trek to the main Hollywood drag from here, but the Bourgeois Pig café (*see* Cafés and Coffeehouses *in* Chapter 3) is within walking distance. Doubles are $50 plus a $5 key deposit. *6020 Franklin Ave., at N. Beachwood Dr., 90028, tel. 323/464–1824, no fax. 20 rooms.*

**Magic Hotel.** Magical? Maybe not, but the rooms in this former apartment building are humongous and some have balconies. Plants spill out over the patio and pool area, and a few blocks away is the madness of Hollywood Boulevard. The downside is that the housekeeping leaves something to be desired. Doubles start at $60. *7025 Franklin Ave., between Highland and La Brea Aves., 90028, tel. 323/851–0800 or 800/741–4915, fax 323/467–7649. 40 rooms. Kitchenettes, laundry.*

**Orchid Suites Hotel.** This one-time apartment building has three types of accommodations: junior suites (large rooms); executive suites with separate kitchen and dining room; and deluxe one-bedroom suites, which sleep up to four. Furnishings are simple and functional, but some units have private balconies. There's an attractive rooftop sundeck plus a heated swimming pool. Doubles run $60–$89. *1753 N. Orchid Ave., near Franklin Ave., 90028, tel. 323/874–9678 or 800/537–3052, fax 323/874–5246. 39 rooms. Laundry.*

**Travel Inn.** Anyone wishing to avoid Christian Science pamphlets and paraphernalia should steer clear of this '50s motel, but everyone else will enjoy the spacious, colorful rooms, the pool, and the profusion of flowering tropical plants. Doubles start at $50. *7370 Sunset Blvd., at Vista St., 90046, tel. 323/876–0330. 40 rooms. Cash only.*

**UNDER $100 • Highland Gardens Hotel.** This hotel feels akin to the Magic up the street (*see above*), but its large, clean rooms and attractive courtyard are a step above. The decor is nothing special and the lighting is dim but the multilingual staff, the large, sparkling pool, and the lush, if somewhat overgrown, tropical garden may make it worth paying the additional bucks. Doubles are $73, $84 with a kitchen. *7047 Franklin Ave., at Sycamore Ave., 90028, tel. 323/850–0536 or 800/404–5472, fax 323/850–1712. 70 rooms. Laundry.*

**SPLURGE • Hollywood Roosevelt Hotel.** Built in 1927, this splendid, restored, art deco hotel is an unofficial historic landmark. It's reputedly haunted by Marilyn Monroe and Montgomery Clift—and on a less spectral note, it also provided a trysting spot for Clark Gable and Carole Lombard and was a hang-

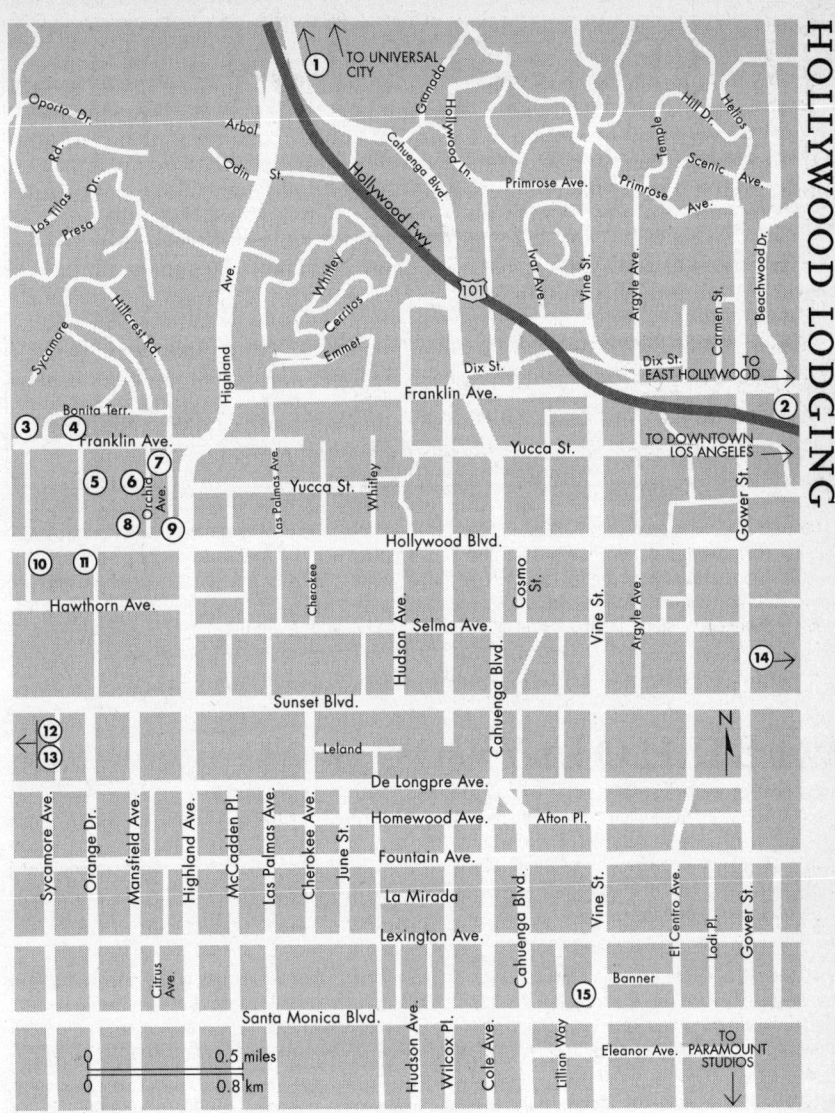

TO UNIVERSAL CITY

Oporto Dr.
Arbol
Odin St.
Granada
Hollywood Ln.
Cahuenga Blvd.
Primrose Ave.
Primrose Ave.
Hill Dr.
Temple
Scenic Ave.
Helios
Beachwood Dr.
Rd.
Los Tilas
Dr.
Presa
Hillcrest Rd.
Whitley
Cerritos
Emmet
Highland Ave.
Hollywood Fwy.
101
Ivar Ave.
Vine St.
Argyle Ave.
Carmen St.
Sycamore
Bonita Terr.
Franklin Ave.
Orchid Ave.
Las Palmas Ave.
Yucca St.
Whitley
Dix St.
Franklin Ave.
Yucca St.
Dix St. TO EAST HOLLYWOOD
TO DOWNTOWN LOS ANGELES
Gower St.
Hollywood Blvd.
Cherokee
Hawthorn Ave.
Hudson Ave.
Selma Ave.
Cosmo St.
Cahuenga Blvd.
Vine St.
Argyle Ave.
Sunset Blvd.
Leland
De Longpre Ave.
N
Sycamore Ave.
Orange Dr.
Mansfield Ave.
Highland Ave.
McCadden Pl.
Las Palmas Ave.
Cherokee Ave.
June St.
Homewood Ave.
Afton Pl.
Fountain Ave.
La Mirada
Cahuenga Blvd.
Vine St.
El Centro Ave.
Lodi Pl.
Gower St.
Lexington Ave.
Citrus Ave.
Banner
Santa Monica Blvd.
Hudson Ave.
Wilcox Pl.
Cole Ave.
Lillian Way
Eleanor Ave.
TO PARAMOUNT STUDIOS

0    0.5 miles
0    0.8 km

Banana Bungalow Hotel and Hostel, **1**

Dunes Sunset Motel, **14**

Highland Gardens Hotel, **3**

Hollywood Celebrity Hotel, **6**

Hollywood International Guest House and Hostel, **9**

Hollywood International Hotel and Hostel, **15**

Hollywood Roosevelt Hotel, **11**

La Mirage Inn, **2**

Liberty Hotel, **7**

Magic Hotel, **4**

Orange Drive Manor, **5**

Orchid Suites Hotel, **8**

Saharan Motor Hotel, **12**

Student Inn International Hostel, **10**

Travel Inn, **13**

# THEY DON'T MIND
# IF YOU'RE STRAIGHT

*The San Vicente Inn, a gay-owned and -operated bed-and-breakfast, is magnificent, private, and right near the hustle and bustle of Santa Monica Boulevard. As soon as you step through the gate, it's as though you were staying with friends—friends with a very nice house and a pool who serve a healthy Continental breakfast. Some rooms have shared bathrooms (from $59 for a single). Bigger bucks—$144—will get you a cottage with a kitchenette right at the pool. Everyone is welcome; the owner, Rocky Farren, jokes, "We don't mind if you're straight." 845 N. San Vicente Blvd., between Santa Monica and Sunset Blvds., West Hollywood, tel. 310/854–6915, fax 310/289–5929. 28 rooms.*

out for Ernest Hemingway and F. Scott Fitzgerald. The first Academy Awards were held here in 1929. The Spanish Colonial architecture, lushly landscaped gardens, and David Hockney–painted pool make for a luxurious retreat from the grime of Hollywood. If you're motivated, take advantage of the exercise room, pool, and Jacuzzi. And to extend the sweet life fantasy, head to the Cinegrill nightclub, which regularly presents jazz stars. Doubles start at $133, but call ahead to get the dope on special seasonal deals, mostly in winter. *7000 Hollywood Blvd., between La Brea Ave. and Orange Dr., 90028, tel. 323/466–7000 or 800/252–7466. 300 rooms, 20 suites. Restaurant, coffee shop, bar.*

# WEST HOLLYWOOD

Aside from being the gayest 'hood in L.A., West Hollywood is also the center of the local dance-club universe. If you want to be near boys and girls shaking their booties till the wee hours, you should park it here and walk up to the Sunset Strip or to Santa Monica Boulevard. Beverly Hills and art museums are both a 15-minute drive away, and Santa Monica is 25 minutes. The abundance of eats strung along Santa Monica Boulevard from Fairfax Avenue to Robertson Boulevard complement the decent selection of fabulously located motels.

*See the West L.A. Lodging map.*

**UNDER $50 • Alta Cienega Motel.** Run by an older couple, this bare-bones motel is in the heart of the West Hollywood action and below the Sunset Strip. If you're planning to do the night swing thing, it would make a good headquarters, but you wouldn't want to spend much time hanging out in the small brown rooms. Doubles are $43. *1005 N. La Cienega Blvd., at Santa Monica Blvd., 90069, tel. 310/652–5797, no fax. 32 rooms. Cash only.*

**UNDER $75 • Holloway Motel.** In the thick of the gay West Hollywood action, this apartment-style motel has clean rooms, some with kitchens, and a 1940s aesthetic. The manager is a sweetheart and very helpful. Tourists and some long-term residents park it here because it's so convenient to Beverly Hills, Santa Monica, and Hollywood. Doubles start at $75. *8465 Santa Monica Blvd., at Holloway Dr., 90069, tel. 323/654–2454, fax 323/654–2454, ext. 260. 22 rooms.*

**UNDER $100 • The Standard.** This new dashingly hip hotel in the heart of the Sunset Strip is anything but what the name implies. Rooms, starting at $95, are outfitted in inflatable sofas, metallic-silver beanbag chairs, royal blue carpeting, and Andy Warhol flower-print drapes. You could even get some work done, what with the built-in desks and T-1 modem lines. If you want to be seen, hit the 24-hour restaurant or bar (*see also* Bars *in* Chapter 5), the barber shop, tattoo parlor, or the outdoor pool surrounded by bright blue Astroturf. If not, order up something from the video and CD library. There are plenty of hotel services, including room service, voicemail, dry cleaning, and the like. *8300 Sunset Blvd., at Sweetzer Ave., 90069, tel. 323/650–9090, fax 323/650–2820. 138 rooms.*

# WEST L.A. LODGING

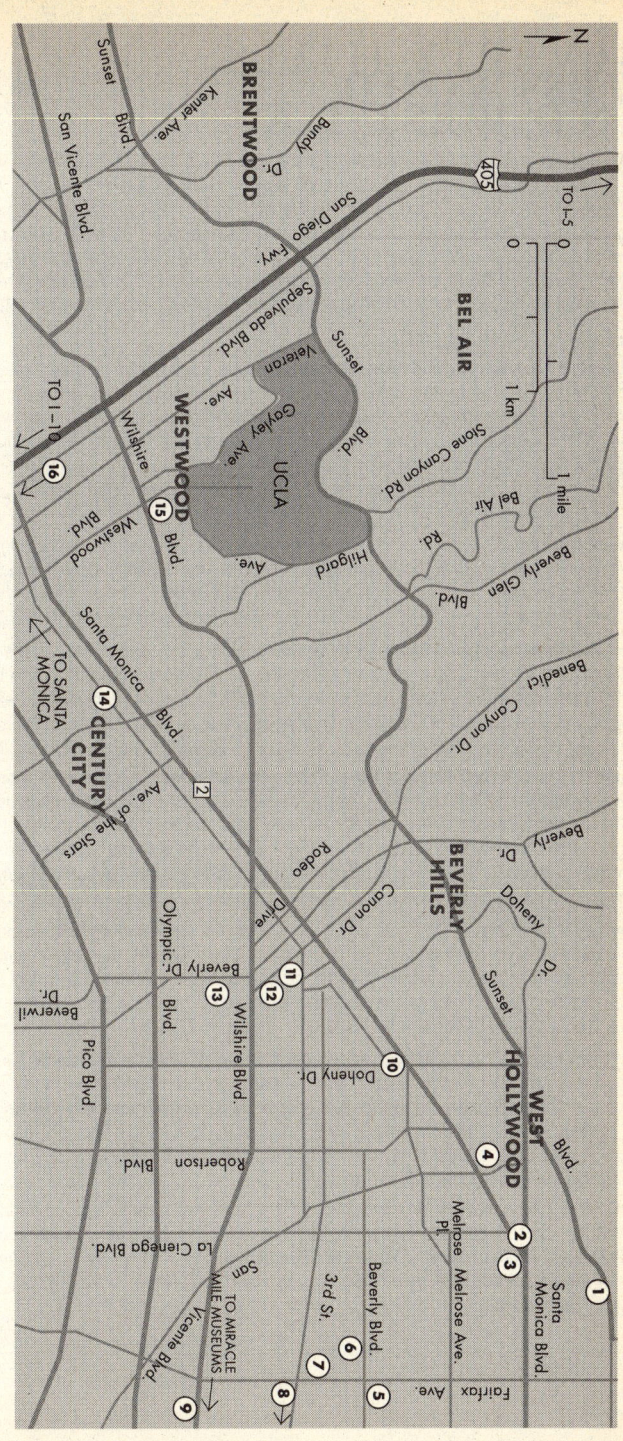

Alta Cienega Motel, **2**
Best Western Royal
Palace Inn &
Suites, **16**
Beverly Crescent
Hotel, **11**

Beverly Hills Reeves
Hotel, **13**
Beverly Laurel
Motor Hotel, **6**
Beverly Terrace
Hotel, **4**

Bevonshire Lodge
Motel, **5**
Claremont Hotel, **15**
Farmer's Daughter
Motel, **7**
Holloway Motel, **3**

Hotel del Flores, **11**
The Little Inn, **14**
Park Plaza Lodge, **8**
San Vicente Inn, **4**
The Standard, **1**

Wilshire Dunes
Motor Hotel, **9**

# BEVERLY HILLS, WESTWOOD, AND WEST L.A.

Rich. Picky. Pampered. If you are all of these, Beverly Hills is a perfect place for you to stay. If you're not, be prepared for the chosen few to look down their surgically enhanced noses at you. The properties here, like the "Pink Palace" a.k.a. the Beverly Hills Hotel, are some of the best in Los Angeles, and if you can afford them, you're in for a pleasantly controlled environment. If not, the budget options here have limited appeal unless you're visiting UCLA or doing business in the neighborhood. One area to avoid is Westwood Boulevard south of Wilshire Boulevard. But in Westwood, near the UCLA campus, you can eat at the plentiful and cheap restaurants and watch students slack off.

*See the West L.A. Lodging map.*

**UNDER $75 • Beverly Hills Reeves Hotel.** Built in 1926, this charming hotel on a quiet, shady, residential street used to be the Beverly Wilshire's staff quarters. Now it's the cheapest place to sleep in Beverly Hills. The rooms are all equipped with a minirefrigerator and furnished with old but pleasant furniture. Only some have air-conditioning, so be sure to ask if it matters to you. From the minuscule rooftop sundeck there is a good view of the hills and palm trees. Rooms with shared bathrooms are $50; doubles start at $65. *120 S. Reeves Dr., at Wilshire Blvd., Beverly Hills, 90212, tel. 310/271–3006, fax 310/271–2278. 50 rooms, 25 with bath. Laundry.*

**Claremont Hotel.** The draw here is a great location: It's on a residential street close to UCLA. The clean, quiet rooms have simple wooden furniture, but summertime visitors be warned: Most of the rooms have ceiling fans instead of air-conditioning. Doubles start at $55. *1044 Tiverton Ave., 1½ blocks north of Wilshire Blvd., Westwood, 90024, tel. 310/208–5957 or 800/266–5957, fax 310/208–2386. 54 rooms.*

**The Little Inn.** Lots of Europeans stay at this spectacularly clean and, as the name indicates, small motel close to Century City and Beverly Hills. The rooms are smallish, the beds big, and the bathrooms tiled. The manager is a sweetie pie and very helpful. Doubles are $50–$60 (weekly $399); doubles with a kitchen start at $60. *10604 Little Santa Monica Blvd., between Overland Ave. and Beverly Glen Blvd., West L.A., 90025, tel. 310/475–4422, fax 310/475–3236. 15 rooms. Refrigerators, laundry.*

**UNDER $100 • Best Western Royal Palace Inn & Suites.** This small hotel doesn't offer much in the way of location (it's right off I–405), but what it lacks in atmosphere it makes up for in elbow room. All rooms are actually suites with cooking facilities, including microwaves, refrigerators, and coffeemakers. Each unit also has two queen-size beds and a queen-size sofa bed. Distract yourself at the pool, exercise room, sauna, or billiard table. Rooms start at $85. *2528 S. Sepulveda Blvd., at Exposition Blvd., West L.A., 90064, tel. 310/477–9066 or 800/528–1234, fax 310/478–4133. 23 rooms. Laundry.*

**Beverly Crescent Hotel.** Lush and green on the outside, stark and white on the inside, this strange hotel has rooms with teensy-weensy TVs and closets that look like the orgasmatron from Woody Allen's *Sleeper*. To really get your money's worth, be sure to stealthily stock up on the pastries and fruit in the lobby. Doubles are $90, including Continental breakfast. *403 N. Crescent Dr., at Brighton Way, Beverly Hills, 90210, tel. 310/247–0505 or 800/451– 1566, fax 310/247–9053. 39 rooms.*

**Hotel Del Flores.** This 1926 hotel is just steps from Rodeo Drive and seems as if it hasn't changed an iota since it was built (except perhaps for the bedding, circa 1970). The rooms are heavy on the peach paint and not particularly clean, but $79 a night for a double in Beverly Hills is as good as it's going to get, darling. Keep in mind there is no air-conditioning—just fans. If you can share a bathroom, you'll pay only $60 for a double. *409 N. Crescent Dr., at Burton Way, Beverly Hills, 90212, tel. 310/274–5115, fax 310/550–0374. 37 rooms, 17 with bath.*

**UNDER $125 • Beverly Terrace Hotel.** On the border of West Hollywood and Beverly Hills, this motel is centrally located, decently furnished, clean, and welcoming. The clientele consists mainly of families and couples. There's a pool here, and doubles start at $105. Rates include a Continental breakfast. *469 N. Doheny Dr., at Santa Monica Blvd., Beverly Hills, 90210, tel. 310/274–8141, fax 310/385–1998. 39 rooms. Restaurant.*

# SANTA MONICA

Like Hollywood, Santa Monica is a huge tourist destination, especially for Europeans. However, Santa Monica is much cleaner, breezier, and nicer than Hollywood, mostly because beach life seems to make the folks here tanned, relaxed, and suspiciously content. For the most enjoyable stay, choose a place near the beach; the Hotel California (*see below*) is by far the most outstanding of this lot. Santa Monica also has the best public transportation system and walking opportunities in L.A. County.

*See the Santa Monica and Venice Lodging map.*

**UNDER $50 • Palm Motel.** Palm trees, flowerpots, and painted flags cheer up this bungalow-style motel. The rooms are airy and relatively clean, and doubles are only $45. There's no air-conditioning, but since it's close to the beach you should be able to catch a breeze. The clientele ranges from gregarious elderly residents to young hip-hop types. *2020 14th St., at Pico Blvd., 90405, tel. 310/452–3861, fax 310/396–1000. 26 rooms.*

**UNDER $75 • Ocean Park Inn.** As far as motels go, this is one of the more modern and less sketchy of the lot. It's obsessively clean, and the rooms are comfortable. The beach is a short drive away. Doubles are $55. *2452 Lincoln Blvd., between Ocean Park and Pico Blvds., 90405, tel. 310/392–3966 or 800/605–5005, fax 310/399–0502. 29 rooms.*

**Resthaven Motel.** This adorable little gray-and-blue motel is old, but well-kept with flower-filled planters everywhere. The rooms are small and just on the good side of clean; they also lack air-conditioning. But, heck, what have you got to complain about when a double is just $60 and you're just a few blocks from the beach? *815 Grant St., at Lincoln Blvd., 90405, tel. 310/452–3977, fax 310/396–8107. 12 rooms.*

*Even if you don't have $130 burning a hole in your pocket (and therefore can't afford a room at the Roosevelt), a subtle cruise through the hotel's lobby and pool area will give you a taste of a legendary but long-gone Hollywood.*

**UNDER $100 • Bayside Hotel.** The colored tiles in the bathrooms might trigger a flashback, but you can't beat the location of this attractively landscaped motel, just across the street from the beach. Comfortable doubles go for $89–$134 depending on the season; some have kitchens, and all have in-room coffee. If cool temperatures are a must, request one of the seven rooms with air-conditioning. *2001 Ocean Ave., south of Pico Blvd., 90405, tel. 310/396–6000, fax 310/396–1000. 45 rooms.*

**Hotel Carmel.** One of Santa Monica's original grand hotels, the Carmel is now just plain and serviceable. Rooms are basic, with TVs and phones but not much else in the way of amenities. It's just two blocks from the beach and around the corner from the Third Street Promenade (*see* Santa Monica *in* Chapter 2). Double rooms start at $95. *201 Broadway, at 2nd St., 90401, tel. 310/451–2469 or 800/445–8695, fax 310/393–4180. 102 rooms.*

**Ocean Lodge Traveler's Motel.** Less than a block from the Santa Monica Pier, this motel is a reasonable choice but lacks the charm of the Hotel California across the street (*see below*). Businesspeople and young tourists stay in the well-maintained rooms. Doubles are around $80. *1667 Ocean Ave., between Colorado and Pico Blvds., 90401, tel. 310/451–4146, fax 310/393–9621. 20 rooms.*

**Pacific Sands Motel.** Peeling in places and patched in others, this motel is still clean and comfortable overall. The property has two sections, one with a pool (which can be tricky to find from the other section). The motel is between the beach and Third Street Promenade, directly across from the Santa Monica Pier. You may need the ocean breezes since there's no air-conditioning. Doubles range from $90 to $125. *1515 Ocean Ave., between Broadway and Colorado Ave., 90401, tel. 310/395–6133, fax 310/395–7206. 40 rooms, 52 during summer.*

**Village Motel.** This place isn't anything to write home about, but the simply furnished rooms come with cable TV. Doubles are normally $85 but drop to just $60 in winter. *2624 Santa Monica Blvd., between 26th and Princeton Sts., 90404, tel. 310/828–0515, no fax. 7 rooms.*

**SPLURGE • Hotel California.** Go ahead, hum the Eagles song. For years it was known as the Belle Blue Inn to legions of cost-conscious visitors, but in 1998/99 this little gem changed hands, underwent a general face-lift, and raised its rates to splurge level. Its collection of cute bungalows is intact; all still have hardwood floors and eclectic decor. The new owner has added a phone system, TVs, and some handmade furnishings, like the hand-carved headboards and mirrors. The garden rooms and ocean-view rooms are gated, steps from the beach, and on an alley surrounded by residential homes. Doubles

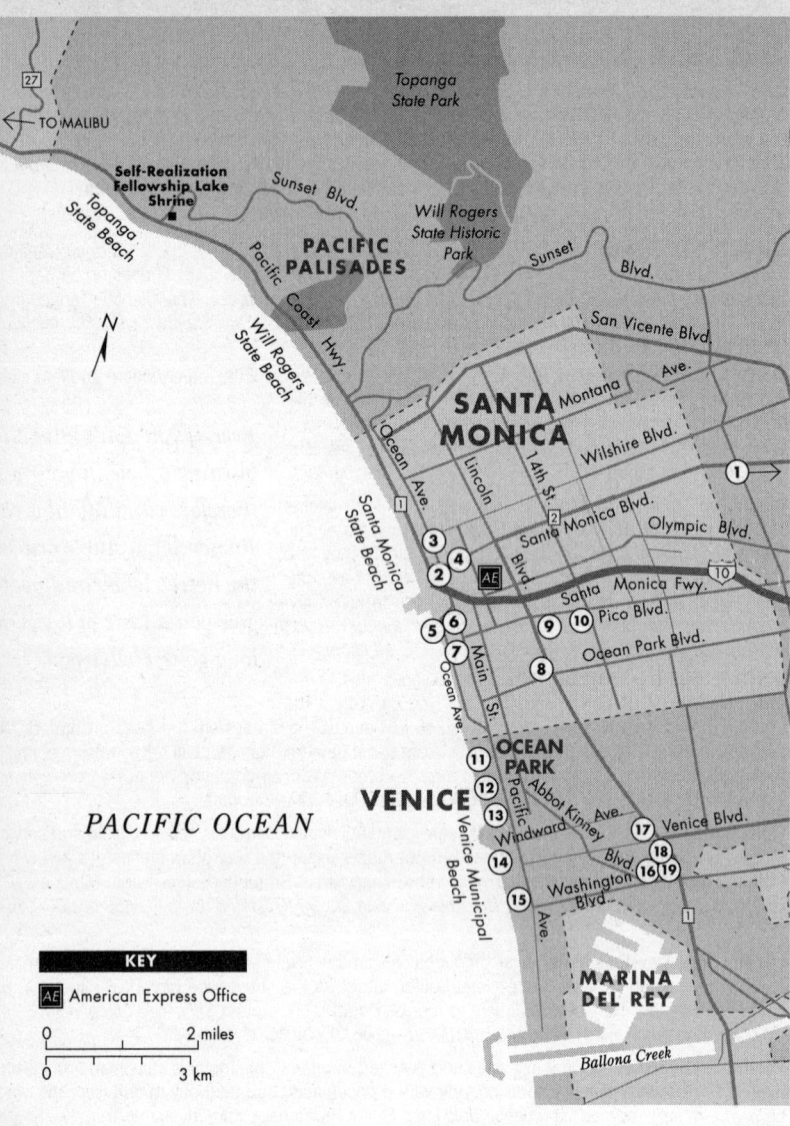

TO MALIBU

Self-Realization
Fellowship Lake
Shrine

Topanga
State Park

Sunset Blvd.

Will Rogers
State Historic
Park

PACIFIC
PALISADES

Topanga
State Beach

Pacific Coast Hwy.

Will Rogers
State Beach

Sunset Blvd.

San Vicente Blvd.

SANTA
MONICA

Montana Ave.

Ocean Ave.

Santa Monica
State Beach

Lincoln

14th St.

Wilshire Blvd.

Santa Monica Blvd.

Olympic Blvd.

Santa Monica Fwy.

Pico Blvd.

Ocean Park Blvd.

Main St.

Ocean Ave.

OCEAN
PARK

VENICE

Abbot Kinney Ave.

Pacific

Windward

Venice Blvd.

Washington Blvd.

Venice Municipal Beach

PACIFIC OCEAN

MARINA
DEL REY

Ballona Creek

**KEY**

AE American Express Office

0        2 miles
0        3 km

Bayside Hotel, **7**

Cadillac Hotel, **11**

Hostel
California, **17**

Hotel California, **5**

Hotel Carmel, **3**

Jim's at the
Beach, **12**

Jolly Roger
Hotel, **16**

Lincoln Inn, **18**

Ocean Lodge
Traveler's Motel, **6**

Ocean Park Inn, **8**

Pacific Sands
Motel, **2**

Palm Motel, **10**

Ramada
Limited, **19**

Resthaven Motel, **9**

Santa Monica
American Youth
Hostel, **4**

Share Tel
Apartments, **13**

Venice Beach
Cotel, **14**

Venice Beach
House, **15**

Village Motel, **1**

cost $125–$275, depending upon season. *1670 Ocean Ave., between Colorado and Pico Blvds., 90404, tel. 310/393–2363, fax 310/393–1063. 26 rooms.*

# VENICE

Staying in a Venice beach motel requires a car even for the most energetic of walkers, since most places (with the exception of the Venice Beach House) are more than a 10-minute drive from the surf and fun of Ocean Front Walk. For younger travelers, hostels tend to be a better choice, especially if you're into raucous nights with foreigners and can forsake your privacy for an ocean view. Be forewarned that Venice is a somewhat seedy place, and any motel or hotel under $50 is likely to be either a drug den or just plain awful.

*See the Santa Monica and Venice Lodging map.*

**UNDER $75 • Jolly Roger Hotel.** Despite its colorful name, this three-story hotel is a bit on the bland side, with a decor that sticks close to a beige-and-brown theme. But the price (doubles are $55) and location (a five-minute drive from Venice Beach) are bonuses. So are the pool and Jacuzzi. *2904 Washington Blvd., between Lincoln and Abbot Kinney Blvds., Marina del Rey, 90291, tel. 310/822–2904 or 800/822–2904, fax 310/301–9561. 82 rooms.*

**Lincoln Inn.** This peach-stucco motel has modern, clean rooms like you might find at one of the chain motels. The managers are very pleasant and helpful. Double rooms are $65, $60 with a AAA discount. Continental breakfast is included. *2447 Lincoln Blvd., between Venice and Washington Blvds., 90291, tel. 310/822–0686, fax 310/822–3136. 30 rooms.*

*Miss your mom? Stay at the Resthaven Motel, where the manager will call you "dear" at every opportunity.*

**UNDER $100 • Ramada Limited.** If you want some peace and quiet after enduring the madness of the sands, this is just the place—and it's only 1½ mi from Venice Beach. The clean, basic roadside motel is a fave of old-timer tourists. Doubles start at $89, including Continental breakfast. AAA members get a 10% discount. *3130 Washington Blvd., ½ block west of Lincoln Blvd., 90291, tel. 310/821–5086, fax 310/821–6167. 32 rooms.*

**Venice Beach House.** This turn-of-the-century, Craftsman-style bed- and-breakfast on a pedestrian street near the beach is a marvelous place to relax. Each room is dedicated to a local historical figure, including one named for evangelist Aimee Semple McPherson, who once lived here (*see* Echo Park *in* Chapter 2). Double rooms are $95 if you're willing to share a bath; a double with its own bath starts at $130. The breakfast is more Continental than stick-to-your-ribs. There's no air-conditioning, and though there's no specific parking area, you can find a space on 29th Avenue between Pacific and Speedway avenues. *15 30th Ave., between Pacific and Speedway Aves., 90291, tel. 310/823–1966, fax 310/823–1842. 9 rooms, 5 with bath.*

# MALIBU

Malibu is practically synonymous with secluded private mansions and gorgeous public beaches. Luckily, you can crash the party without taking out a loan by staying in one of the mellow motels strung along the Pacific Coast Highway (PCH) with a dramatic mountain backdrop. Despite the riches (both natural and Industry), there's still a laid-back, small-town atmosphere. If you're the outdoors type, you can hit one of the excellent trails (*see* Hiking *in* Chapter 6). But because the drive from Malibu inland is unpleasantly slow, it's best to consider these seaside spots as a destination in themselves and not use them as a home base for visiting the rest of the city.

**UNDER $75 • Topanga Ranch Motel.** Mountains provide the backdrop for this collection of small red-and-white cottages. The rooms are clean and cozy—reminiscent of a ship's quarters. Refreshing ocean air blows in from Topanga State Beach, which is just across the road; this is especially important in summer since there's no A/C. Doubles start at $65 ($350 a week). *18711 PCH, near Topanga Canyon Blvd., 90265, tel. 310/456–5486 or 800/200–0019, fax 310/456–1447. 30 rooms. Refrigerators.*

**UNDER $100 • Malibu Riviera Motel.** Make the most of this small motel's location; it's just a mile from Zuma State Beach. Rooms are passably clean if retro-ish, with 1950s wooden furniture and fans (read: no air-conditioning). A common deck runs along the side of the motel and ends with a big patio and Jacuzzi. Unfortunately, the deck faces the PCH, but from the Jacuzzi all you can see are mountains and flowers. Doubles are $80 ($90 on weekends), including Continental breakfast. *28920 PCH, at Kanan Dune Rd., 90265, tel. 310/457–9503, no fax. 13 rooms.*

**Malibu Surfer Motel.** This charming, blue-and-white stucco motel has bright, clean rooms with refrigerators, king-size beds, and balconies. You won't have to haul your beach gear far; it's just one mile south of Surfrider State Beach. If you don't feel like getting sandy, take advantage of the small pool, sundeck, hilltop patio, or picnic area. Singles and doubles start at $89. *22541 PCH, between Carbon Canyon and Malibu Canyon Rds., 90265, tel. 310/456–6169, fax 310/456–5410. 17 rooms.*

**UNDER $125 • Malibu Shores Motel.** If you're itching to surf, you can't beat this location: right across the street from Surfrider State Beach. The motel was renovated in 1999; it now has new, though standard-issue, furnishings and colorful landscaping. Though there isn't any air-conditioning, rooms do have fans. Doubles start at $119 ($169 on weekends) with a 10% discount for AAA members. *23033 PCH, between Los Flores Canyon and Cross Creek Rd., 90265, tel. 310/456–6559, fax 310/456–6549. 18 rooms. Laundry.*

# SOUTH BAY

The South Bay includes Manhattan Beach, Hermosa Beach, and Redondo Beach, all linked to the rest of Los Angeles by the Pacific Coast Highway (also known as PCH, Highway 1, or sometimes Sepulveda or Lincoln Boulevard). Budget lodgings here line the highway, and room rates get progressively higher as you near the water. Presumably, you're here for the beaches, so it might be worth it to fork over a few extra bucks to watch the waves from your room. Manhattan and Redondo beaches are more commercialized than their quirky small-town neighbor Hermosa. Regardless of where you stay, the other beach towns will be either a short, short drive by car or an easy bike ride away.

*See the South Bay Lodging map.*

**UNDER $50 • Budget 9 Motel.** Lots of students stay in these airy, pastel rooms. The motel is just a few blocks from the beach and a 15-minute walk to the pier. The beds are very firm, if you care about that sort of thing. Doubles run $40–$48. *711 S. PCH, at Nob Hill, Redondo Beach, 90277, tel. 310/540–1888, fax 310/540–7260. 36 rooms.*

**East West Inn.** A great bargain considering it's only a five-minute walk from the beach, the East-West lets doubles for $45 a night or $275 for the week. Crisp rooms (with microwaves and fridges) and scattered tubs of small palm trees save the hotel from total blandness. *435 S. PCH, at Guadalupe St., Redondo Beach, south of Torrance Blvd., 90277, tel. 310/540–5998, fax 310/543–9828. 40 rooms.*

**Moonlite Inn.** This hotel has been around a while; its greatest virtue is its location: The beach is a five-minute walk away. Some rooms come with a minirefrigerator, microwave, or balcony. Doubles are $45. There's a Laundromat next door if you need to do a load. *625 S. PCH, near Nob Hill Ave., Redondo Beach, 90271, tel. 310/540- -4058. 23 rooms.*

**UNDER $75 • Hi View Motel.** A nice couple runs this immaculate motel. The rooms have sloped ceilings, a nice break from the usual shoebox feeling; most are equipped with refrigerators and microwaves. Doubles start at $50. It's about a mile from the beach. *100 S. Sepulveda Blvd., between Manhattan Beach and Artesia Blvds., Manhattan Beach, 90266, tel. 310/374–4608, fax 310/937–9542. 22 rooms.*

**Manhattan Beach Motel.** This basic motel is a stone's throw from the beach. If you like your privacy, you'll appreciate the layout; double rooms with two beds are really two rooms, each with one bed. Although they're showing their age, the rooms are clean and they come with minirefrigerators, phones, and TV/VCRs. One important thing they *don't* have is air-conditioning. Doubles start at $70. *4017 Highland Ave., between Rosecrans Ave. and 41st St., Manhattan Beach, 90266, tel. 310/545–9020, fax 310/545–5055. 15 rooms.*

**Seahorse Motel.** Don't let the *Miami Vice* pink-and-aqua pastel exterior dissuade you: The rooms here are large, clean, pleasantly furnished, and equipped with refrigerators and HBO. It's a five-minute drive to the ocean and the Manhattan Beach Pier; there's a pool on the premises should you prefer chlorine to saltwater. Double rooms are $59–$69. *233 N. Sepulveda Blvd., between 2nd St. and Manhattan Beach Blvd., Manhattan Beach, 90266, tel. 310/376–7951 or 800/233–8057, fax 310/379–6721. 33 rooms.*

**Sea Sprite Motel.** It lacks character, but the Sea Sprite is nirvana for beach-seeking travelers: If it were any closer to the ocean, you'd need a life raft. All rooms have a microwave and a refrigerator, and rates vary from $64 for economy one-bed rooms to $149 for ocean-view doubles. Amenities in this family-oriented place include a swimming pool, a playground, and a volleyball court. *1016 The Strand, at 10th St., Hermosa Beach, 90254, tel. 310/376–6933, fax 310/376–4107. 70 rooms. Laundry.*

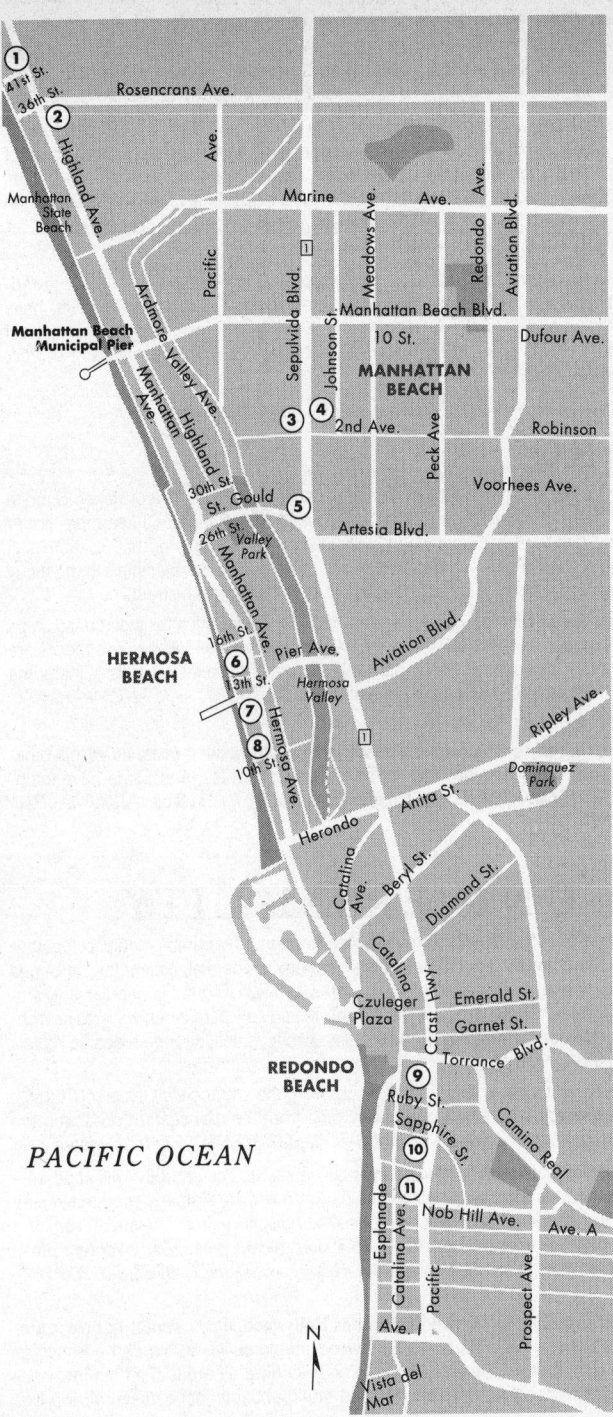

Budget 9 Motel, **11**
East West Inn, **9**
Grandview Motor Hotel, **6**
Hi View Motel, **4**
Hotel Hermosa, **5**
Manhattan Beach Motel, **1**
Moonlite Inn, **10**
Seahorse Motel, **3**
Sea Sprite Motel, **8**
Sea View Inn at the Beach, **2**
Surf City Hostel, **7**

PACIFIC OCEAN

**UNDER $100 • Grandview Motor Hotel.** This tiny, modern, three- story hotel sits steps from the beach. Spacious rooms come complete with refrigerator and private balcony, and friendly managers give the place a homey feel. Doubles start at $95; weekly rates are available in winter. *55 14th St., off Hermosa Ave., Hermosa Beach, 90254, tel. 310/374–8981, fax 310/374–8983. 17 rooms.*

**Hotel Hermosa.** This is one of the best-looking places in Hermosa Beach, and it's just a 15-minute walk from the beach to boot. The pastel decor gives you the weird impression a renegade Easter-egg painter got a hold of the place for just a little too long. Perks include free Continental breakfast, a heated pool, a Jacuzzi, and—drum roll, please—an exercise room (just what you need on a vacation!). Doubles on the "city side" are $79, "ocean side" $89. *2515 PCH, at Artesia Blvd., Hermosa Beach, 90254, tel. 310/318– 6000 or 800/331–9979, fax 310/318–6936. 82 rooms. Laundry.*

**Sea View Inn at the Beach.** Quiet, secure, and crisply comfortable, this motel is the type of place grandparents might pick. It's two blocks up the hill from the beach. Most rooms (doubles at $80–$95) have ocean views; all have refrigerators and some have microwaves. A string of cafés along the same street gives you plenty of choices for breakfast. *3400 Highland Ave., at 34th St., Manhattan Beach, 90266, tel. 310/545–1504, fax 310/545–4052. 23 rooms.*

# SAN PEDRO

If you're into ocean sports or perhaps shopping for everything kitsch, San Pedro is your ticket. Cabrillo Beach and the Underwater Dive Trail near Royal Palms State Beach (*see* Chapter 6) keep the flipper crowd happy, while the Ports O'Call Village, on the wharf, will satisfy your yearning for that plastic Hollywood sign or cheesy T-shirt. When looking for a room, avoid at all costs the residential hotels in the dicey area bordered by Centre Street and Harbor Boulevard, between O'Farrell and 9th streets.

**UNDER $75 • Best Western Sunrise Hotel.** Businesspeople and tourists waiting for their cruise ships to sail stay at this high-rise hotel across the street from the touristy Ports O'Call Village. The rooms are spacious and clean, and the hotel is equipped with a pool and Jacuzzi. Doubles start at $68, including Continental breakfast. *525 S. Harbor Blvd., between 5th and 6th Sts., 90731, tel. 310/548–1080 or 800/356–9609, fax 310/519–0380. 110 rooms.*

**Pacific Inn.** Both Cabrillo Beach and Fort McArthur Museum are within walking distance of this pink-and-green motel. The rooms are clean and big, with deep burgundy carpets, and some have kitchenettes. Doubles are $69–$89. *516 W. 38th St., at Pacific Ave., 90731, tel. 310/514–1247, fax 310/ 831–5538. 24 rooms. Laundry.*

# AROUND UNIVERSAL CITY

If you plan on concentrating on the studios and nothing else, stay here. This area—cobbled together from parts of North Hollywood, Studio City, and Toluca Lake—is pretty residential, except for Cahuenga Boulevard and Riverside Drive, where there are some restaurants and watering holes popular with studio workers. Hollywood is a 10-minute drive over the hill. Of course, adventurers can always go searching for nightlife in San Fernando Valley after a day at the studios. Expect small, strange roadside motels with both a shady and a tourist clientele.

**UNDER $75 • Nite Inn.** Okay, so it's bland, but it's two blocks from the entrance to Universal Studios. The vaguely clean, small doubles are $62. Don't expect any help from the managers. *10612 Ventura Blvd., at Lankershim Blvd., Studio City, 91604, tel. 818/508–8022, fax 818/980–2721. 19 rooms.*

**Universal City Inn.** This motel puts you close to the action at Universal Studios and CityWalk at about a third of the price of the high-rise hotels adjacent to the theme park. Rooms are simple, decorated in pink and green; rates range from $70 to $90. If you want to reduce the noise level from the street, ask for a room in the back. Though it's far away from the beach, the hotel does have a pool. *10730 Ventura Blvd., between Lankershim Blvd. and Vineland Ave., Studio City, 91604, tel. 818/760–8737, fax 808/762– 5159. 37 rooms.*

**SPLURGE • Beverly Garland's Holiday Inn Universal Studios Hollywood.** If you want to dabble in star residue, check in here. The walls are decorated with Hollywood memorabilia: studio portraits, scrapbook items, and such. Many rooms have private courtyards or balconies; all are tricked out in blond-wood furniture and plenty of amenities (hair dryers, irons and ironing boards, coffeemakers). Dip into the sweet life by lounging around the swimming pool, sauna, and tennis courts, or meander along the paths through the tropical gardens. On the walls of the lobby you can follow the filmdom career of Beverly Garland herself (she was a hard-working, B-movie actress in the 1950s). Rates are about $130, with discounts available for AAA and AARP members. The staff is notably attentive. *4222 Vineland Ave., at the Vineland exit of the 101, North Hollywood, 91602, tel. 818/980–8000 or 800/238–3759, fax 818/ 766–5230. 252 rooms. Restaurant, bar.*

# BURBANK

Burbank might be considered a "real" destination if it weren't for those pesky Hollywood Hills, which create a natural border between it and the rest of Los Angeles. Burbank has its share of Americana kitsch diners and is amusing in its own way. It's extremely safe and quiet, with wide streets and a plethora of nice police officers. Early birds craving the sights and sounds of the Media District (the area where studios are—between Riverside Drive, Verdugo Avenue, Pass Avenue, and Buena Vista Street) will appreciate it most.

**UNDER $100 • Holiday Lodge.** If you want to mingle with the players, this may be the perfect headquarters. The motel sits in the shadow of the Disney tower, close to NBC and Disney studios—and it's surrounded by shops and restaurants rife with studio workers. Though it's getting a bit worn and showing its '60s roots, the rooms are well kept. Doubles are $65 to $90. There's a quiet atomosphere in that there's not a lot of activity, but expect to hear a certain amount of street noise. Pass on the small, unappealing swimming pool and hold out for a beach. *3901 Riverside Dr., between Hollywood Way and Pass Ave., 91505, tel. 818/843–1121, fax 818/843– 1121. 30 rooms.*

*Would-be hostelers should be prepared to prove they don't live in L.A. or southern California by presenting a passport or driver's license. Hostel managers enforce this policy in order to discourage clever youth from making a hostel a permanent residence.*

**Safari Inn.** Site of a bloodbath and lovers on the run in *True Romance,* this hotel charms Hollywood guys looking for a 1950s period set. Unfortunately, there are no leopard-print rooms here like in the movie—instead, the aqua and orange rooms are geared for business travelers, with phones, data ports, desks, and cable TV. There's a swimming pool and fitness room, plus a laundry and dry cleaning service should you get a spot on your suit. Doubles start at $99; AAA members get a 10% discount. *1911 W. Olive Ave., at Parish Pl. near Buena Vista St., 91506, tel. 818/845–8586 or 800/782–4373, fax 818/845–0054. 105 rooms.*

# NEAR THE AIRPORT

**UNDER $75 • Hacienda Hotel.** If you're determined to stay near LAX, head straight for this labyrinthine, business-oriented hotel on the south side of the airport. Rooms (doubles starting at $77) are almost antiseptically clean, with data ports and movie channels. If you'd like a refrigerator, request one in advance. Extras include free wine and hors d'oeuvres during happy hour (weekdays 4:30–6:30), free 24-hour airport shuttle service, and—if you're the type—free country-and-western dance lessons on Friday and Saturday nights. You can soak in the pool or Jacuzzi if you're antsy from—or anticipating—the plane ride. *525 N. Sepulveda Blvd., at Mariposa Ave., El Segundo, 90245, tel. 310/615–0015 or 800/262–1314, fax 310/615–0217. 630 rooms. Coffee shop, laundry.*

**SPLURGE • Inn at Playa del Rey.** To pamper yourself before or after a flight, this is a swell place to stay. The bed-and-breakfast is just five minutes north of LAX, overlooking Marina del Rey—in fact, from some windows you can watch the sailboats glide along the Main Channel. Rooms, starting at $125, have nicely varied decor; behind your door could be a fireplace, a whirlpool tub, painted pine furniture, or (in the best rooms) antiques or repros. They're also well equipped for business travelers, with data ports, voice mail, and TV/VCRs. To stretch your legs, hit the exercise room or the Ballona Wetlands nature trails, which are just out the back door; the attentive, knowledgeable innkeepers will be happy to point the way. *435 Culver Blvd., at Jefferson Blvd., Playa del Rey, 90293, tel. 310/574–1920, fax 310/574– 9920. 19 rooms, 2 suites.*

# HOSTELS

Hosteling in Los Angeles is a great way to meet other travelers, drink copious amounts of alcohol, work on murals, and stay up late; however, hostels are often reserved for those holding a foreign passport. The hostels in L.A. are typically fun-loving places resembling college dorms, with lax residential assistants rather than traditional wardens who enforce draconian lockouts and curfews and petty little rules. Nobody requires sleep sheets here—instead, they provide you with clean bed linens. Most places have a kitchen, a lounge, and freebie excursions and airport pickups. The sleeping options are varied; dorms usually don't house more than eight people (usually of the same sex), and singles and doubles, though more expensive, are often available. Most places will cut a deal with you for week and longer stays. There is no age limit at hostels in L.A., and almost all accept credit cards and traveler's checks. A membership with Hostelling International/American Youth Hostels could lower your fee a bit, but it's not required to get a bed. To keep wannabe actors from moving in semipermanently, L.A. hostels require you to show passports and airline tickets.

*See the Hollywood Lodging, Santa Monica and Venice Lodging, and South Bay Lodging maps.*

## HERMOSA BEACH

**Surf City Hostel.** Do you have an artistic bent and a lack of cash? If you have good negotiation skills, this should be the first place you stop—you can paint a mural in lieu of paying for the night. This boisterous hostel is just a few years old, and these cats spring spontaneous parties sloshing with beer and margaritas. You must be up to joining in and resign yourself to not getting much sleep. Somehow, they manage to keep the place clean. A bed in a cramped dorm room of four to six people costs $15–$17, depending on the bathroom and ocean-view situation. A double room is $35–$45 per night. Breakfast is included; tea and coffee are available all day. You can sack out in the TV lounge or look for a ride or sign up for an outing ($15) to Universal Studios, Disneyland, or Magic Mountain at the bulletin board. And let's not forget the beach, which is just a stone's throw away. Air Shuttle provides service to and from the airport for $5 by arrangement through the hostel. *26 Pier Ave., at Hermosa Blvd., 90254, tel. 310/798–2323 or 800/305–2901. 56 beds. Reception and check-in 8 AM–10 PM, checkout 8 AM–11 AM, no lockout. Kitchen, laundry.*

## HOLLYWOOD

**Banana Bungalow Hotel and Hostel.** Near U.S. 101 and the Hollywood Bowl (*see* Hollywood *in* Chapter 2), this well-run hotel-hostel offers so much you may forget to venture down to frothy Hollywood Boulevard for fun. Dorms sleeping four to six people are $18 per person; doubles are $45. There's always a crowd floating among the pool, weight room, basketball courts, sundeck, and arcade. Other extras include free airport pickup; free breakfast; free movie nights; free shuttles to the beach, studios, and amusement parks; and a reasonably priced café-restaurant. A passport (foreign or U.S.) and proof of international travel is required for dormitory space so they can be sure you will actually leave. *2775 Cahuenga Blvd. W, 1 mi north of Franklin Ave., 90068, tel. 323/851–1129 or 800/446–7835. 250 beds. Reception and check-in open 24 hrs., check-out by 10:30 AM, no lockout. Kitchen, laundry.*

**Hollywood International Guest House and Hostel.** A stay here puts you in the heart of Hollywood insanity—it's just two blocks east of Mann's Chinese Theater, hard by the Hollywood and Highland development. Dorms sleep two to four people ($15 per person); there are also seven doubles at $35 a night. Free movie nights, the occasional barbecue, a lounge area with a pool table, free breakfast, and a common-use kitchen are perks. *6820 Hollywood Blvd., at Highland Ave., 90028, tel. 323/463–0797 or 800/750–6561. 158 beds. Reception and check-in open 24 hrs., checkout by 10 AM, no lockout. Kitchen, laundry.*

**Hollywood International Hotel and Hostel.** This sparkling new hostel, opened in 1999, sets you up with plenty of amenities for cheap. Both the dorm rooms ($15) and the ten private rooms ($37 for two) have private bathrooms. You'll also get free breakfast, access to the kitchen, free movie nights, and Internet access. Chill out with a game of pool in the lounge area or hit the rooftop sundeck and bar (read: party space). As a guest here, you can snag a discount sightseeing tour or a cut-rate car rental from Universal. *1057 Vine St., at Santa Monica Blvd., 90038, tel. 323/462–6351 or 800/750–1233. 130 beds. Reception and check-in open 24 hrs., checkout 10 AM, no lockout.*

**Orange Drive Manor.** This 1918 boardinghouse, right behind Mann's Chinese Theater, is the perfect spot to relax after a hard day of touring Hollywood Boulevard. The rooms are big and clean and have charming antique furnishings. Dorms with four beds are $17.50 per person. Single rooms are $29.95, and doubles are $37.50–$43.50. Five rooms have private baths; the rest share. *1764 N. Orange Dr., between Hollywood and Franklin Blvds., 90028, tel. 323/850–0350. 30 beds. Reception and check-in 9 AM–midnight, checkout 10 AM, no lockout. Kitchen. Cash only.*

**Student Inn International Hostel.** If you've got an international passport and want to stay with other non-Americans, park it here. The staff will pick you up from the Amtrak and Greyhound stations; if you're coming from LAX, you'll be reimbursed $5 if you take the American Shuttle. Dorms have four beds, each for $15 per person. Doubles are $32 per couple. The key deposit will put you back $5. Free doughnuts and coffee for breakfast ensure that you'll have enough caffeine and sugar to last all day. *7038½ Hollywood Blvd., at Sycamore Ave., 90028, tel. 323/469–6781. 44 beds. Reception and check-in 7 AM–midnight, checkout 10 AM, no lockout. Kitchen.*

# SAN PEDRO

**AYH-San Pedro.** It doesn't get much more panoramic than this—these converted army barracks perched atop a bluff give you a gorgeous view out to sea. If for some reason you'd rather watch the idiot box, there's a TV lounge and videos for the VCR. Or get motivated by the loads of information on public transportation and things to do in the area. The aquarium and tide pools are a short walk away, as are a few restaurants. A bed in a five- to 16-bed dorm room is $13.75; in a three-bed room $15.50; in a double room $33. A private room is $29. Non-members add $3 to all listed prices. Sleep sheets are $2. The reception hours change seasonally, so call ahead if you'll be arriving at an odd hour. *3601 S. Gaffey St., at 36th St. in Angels Gate Park, 90731, tel. 310/831–2836. 60 beds. Check-in 7 AM–11:30 PM, checkout 11 AM, no lockout. Laundry.*

*The Korean Friendship Bell in front of the San Pedro Hostel was donated by the South Korean government in commemoration of the U.S. Bicentennial. More recently it was used as scenery in the movie* The Usual Suspects.

# SANTA MONICA

**Santa Monica American Youth Hostel.** Perhaps the best hostel in L.A., this place is almost a self-sufficient community; its amenities include laundry machines, a spacious courtyard, kitchen facilities, and a travel store. The proprietors have preserved the brick-and-wood charm of the historic building, a former town hall. (It's quite a contrast to the neighboring Pussycat Adult Movie Theater, the only blemish in an otherwise respectable neighborhood.) The hostel, one block from the Third Street Promenade (*see* Santa Monica *in* Chapter 2), is open year-round to both AYH members and nonmembers. Single-sex dorm rooms are $19–$24 per person, and doubles are $26–$29 a person. Add $3 if you are not a Hostelling International member. Call for free airport pickup. *1436 2nd St., south of Santa Monica Blvd., 90401, tel. 310/393–9913. 200 beds. Reception and check-in open 24 hrs., checkout 11 AM, no lockout. Kitchen, laundry.*

# VENICE

**Cadillac Hotel.** The Cadillac is a stylishly renovated art deco hostel-hotel less than a block from Venice Beach. Most rooms are of the standard hotel type, while a few dorm-style rooms pack in four beds each. Dorms are $25 per person; double rooms with bathrooms go for $69–$120. They offer airport pickup for $7, and you'll have access to a sauna, sundeck, gym, pool table, and laundry facilities. You can also turn up discount car rentals and studio tours. *8 Dudley Ave., at Ocean Front Walk, 90291, tel. 310/399–8876. 37 rooms. Reception and check-in open 24 hrs., checkout 11 AM, no lockout.*

**Hostel California.** Recognizable from the road as the two-story structure with a perpetual string of drying laundry suspended from the balcony, this hostel provides a cheap place to sleep, free airport pickup, discount rentals on cars and bikes, and a reasonable standard of hygiene. There's one 30-bed dorm and several smaller ones that run $12–$14 a night; a handful of double rooms go for $34. The common room has the hangout standards: a pool table and TV. The management gives preference to foreign and out-of-state visitors, particularly in summer; a passport is required. *2221 Lincoln Blvd., near Venice Blvd., 90291, tel. 310/305–0250. 70 beds. Reception and check-in open 24 hrs., checkout 10:30 AM, no lockout. Kitchen, laundry.*

**Jim's at the Beach.** Crash near the beach in this laid-back, small- scale spot. Beds in six-person dorm rooms go for $20, including breakfast; there are bargain weekly and monthly rates. A U.S. or foreign passport is required. The hostel will reimburse up to $5 for a shuttle ride from LAX. *17 Brooks Ave., at Pacific Ave., 90291, tel. 310/399–4018. 30 beds. Reception open 10 AM–midnight, check-in 10 AM–11 PM, checkout 10 AM–noon, no lockout. Kitchen, laundry.*

**Share Tel Apartments.** This former apartment building is a pretty good deal—if you have the required foreign passport. Dorm rooms with six to eight beds cost $20 per night or $110 per week; doubles (bathrooms down the hall) range from $46 to $50 a night. Dinner and breakfast are usually included in the rate. *20 Brooks Ave., at Pacific Ave., 90291, tel. 310/392–0325. 125 beds. Reception open 8 AM–11 PM, check-in 24 hours, checkout 11 AM, no lockout. Kitchen, laundry. Cash or traveler's checks only.*

**Venice Beach Cotel.** Well-scrubbed and literally steps from the beach, this high-rise layers dorm- and hotel-style accommodations. Dorm rooms sleep three to four people; the basic beds with a shared bath down the hall cost $15, a few bucks extra for an adjoining private bath and/or an ocean view. Double rooms with ocean views are $34.25–$48.25. There's a BYOB bar, and coffee and tea are served all day. You can save on entertainment, too; they help out with studio tours, an inexpensive weekly shuttle to San Diego, and discount car rentals. Try to get there soon after checkout to get a bed; a foreign or U.S. passport is required. *25 Windward Ave., 1 block west of Pacific Ave., 90291, tel. 310/399–7649. 70 beds. Reception and check-in open 24 hrs., checkout 11 AM, no lockout.*

# AFTER
# DARK

BY CATHERINE BELONOGOFF, ANDREW DEAN NYSTROM,

AND ELIZA ENGELBERG

UPDATED BY LINA LECARO

While Los Angeles's reputation as the city of bars, cars, and stars is well deserved, its nightlife offerings are much more diverse than all the glossy PR might lead you to believe. The city's multicultural makeup and its role as the home of the entertainment industry make going out a never-ending adventure, whether you enjoy intimate watering holes, loud rock clubs, louche dives, wild techno dance spots, or the trendy hangouts of the rich and famous.

Turn to the *L.A. Weekly* (published every Thursday and found in cafés and book and record stores throughout town) for the definitive guide to dance clubs, live music, spoken-word, theater, and even more highbrow evening entertainment. The "Calendar" section of the Thursday and Sunday *Los Angeles Times* has extensive listings, too. You should also keep your eyes peeled for flyers in such popular shopping areas as Melrose and Vermont avenues in Hollywood and Third Street Promenade in Santa Monica. Just as in any major city, going out in L.A. begets more going out, and with so many different scenes to explore, you're bound to find plenty of lively sounds and colorful sights to suit your every mood. Keep in mind that most clubs in L.A. have a shelf life shorter than Danny Devito's trousers and places listed below may have undergone a reincarnation or four by the time you read this.

Bars and clubs run from elitist glamour to casual grunge, and covers range from free to $20. If you choose a spot popular with the upper crust (look for a rope outside the door and lots of fancy cars in the parking lot), be prepared for attitude from the bouncers and other patrons if you aren't dressed to the nines. Those lacking the money and inclination to wear their stylist's name on their sleeve may want to avoid posh Westside locales like Beverly Hills in favor of Hollywood establishments, where you will find a more open-minded crowd and security guards who pay little attention to the make of your shoes.

As this is an early-to-bed city (last call is just before 2 AM), it's smart to get going around 9 or 10 PM, although most clubs aren't at their fullest until about 11 PM. The legal drinking age of 21 is strictly enforced, and when a place says it's "18 and over," they mean it. Due to the city's smoking ban, indoor puffing is strictly prohibited even in bars, but the more popular establishments offer "ins and outs" or special roped-off areas outside where smokers can puff away. Although you may be tempted to drive yourself home after a few nightcaps, it's not a smart idea. LAPD often wait outside of popular nightspots hoping to catch intoxicated drivers (more than two drinks in a short period of time and you could be a candidate for a DUI citation). Play it safe and call one of the countless cab companies in town (*see* Taxis *in* Chapter 1). Most bars and clubs will even do it for you.

Some of the city's biggest and best dance clubs can be found in the rainbow-flag part of town, along Santa Monica Boulevard in West Hollywood. The young straight crowd can be found mostly in Hollywood and its surrounding areas. You can find a live-music venue in any L.A. neighborhood, with West Hollywood's Sunset Strip firmly entrenched as the historic center of loud rock music. But to push deeper into the music scene, head to the pint-sized neighborhoods tucked north of the 101 freeway: Silver Lake, Los Feliz, and Atwater Village. This quirky area is the place to see rising musical talent—its bars and clubs launch unexpected stars like Beck and L7. The young and the funky have also rediscovered some of old Hollywood's celebrity haunts, and often it's the hidden hangout that becomes the "It-spot" of the moment—that is, until every Joe in search of cool finds out about it. Bars run the range from swank to scary in all corners of the city, providing scores of backdrops for flirting, networking, gossip, and of course, liquid meals.

As you should have learned by now, you don't need alcohol to have fun, and if loud music and blood-shot eyes aren't your cup of tea, consider checking out one of the city's many fine repertoire film houses or cafés (*see* Cafés and Coffeehouses *in* Chapter 3). The unlucky among you who haven't yet had a star sighting can cheat by checking out the local theater—film and TV faces often spend their off-seasons on the L.A. stage. Think about heading downtown to snag rush tickets for the opera or symphony or swinging into South-Central for some jazz. In a city with this much to see and do, the only wrong choice is staying in your motel in front of the tube.

# BARS

In L.A., each neighborhood's bar scene is, well, representative of that neighborhood (what did you expect?). Posh folks take to the Westside, gay men chat and drink in West Hollywood, and hip twenty-somethings warm bar stools all over Hollywood. Most bars open early in the afternoon and close their doors to new patrons at 1:30 AM. Generally, if you want to hang out somewhere comfortably, get there early and secure a table, especially on weekend nights (which means Thursday–Saturday in this town). Bars usually don't charge a cover unless they've lined up live entertainment.

In the South Bay party goers rarely stray far from the beach, even after dark, and the bar scene centers around several groups of drinking establishments near the ocean. Things usually start to heat up around 10, except for weekends, when late-afternoon happy hours (4–7) attract a typically rowdy, tawny, and upwardly mobile crowd of recent grads. The piers in each town are the locus of all liquid activity, with a slew of bars packed in each area. Walk or take a cab between hops, especially if hitting more than one town. The area is known for frequent 502s (drunk-driving arrests).

## DOWNTOWN

**Koma Cocktails and Piano Bar.** This Japanese bar is usually pleasantly empty, with just a few patrons and friends of the bartender. The piano bar's duo—one plays, the other sings Japanese songs—kicks in Wednesday–Saturday. This is a place to lounge and think about the glamour of the olden days. *333 E. 1st St., at San Pedro St., Little Tokyo, tel. 213/625–9111.*

**Redwood Second Street Saloon.** Drink among those who know how: reporters from the *Los Angeles Times,* who pack this gaudy, gabby place after 5 to trade war stories. *316 W. 2nd St., between Broadway and Hill St., tel. 213/617–2867.*

**The Tower.** This bar atop the 32-story Transamerica Building provides a terrific view, if not the hippest environment—it's more of an older-and-wiser, suit-clad crowd. *1150 S. Olive St., at 12th St., tel. 213/746–1554.*

## WILSHIRE AND MELROSE

**Louis XIV.** Europeans and wanna-bes frequent this bi-level bar, where Gothic ironwork is juxtaposed against acid-video projections. You can sit inside or out, upstairs or down, depending on your preferred proximity to the pulsating house music. *606 N. La Brea Blvd., at Melrose Ave., Melrose, tel. 323/934–5102.*

**Molly Malone's Irish Pub.** Don't worry about finding the perfect, fashionable club getup for this Irish neighborhood pub—no one else does. "England: Get out of Ireland" posters and Guinness paraphernalia cover the walls. Live rock music (mostly Irish) happens nightly. Pub grub is available weekdays 10:30–2:30. A pint o' Guinness will set you back $4. *575 S. Fairfax Ave., at Wilshire Blvd. near Miracle Mile, Wilshire, tel. 323/935–1577. Cover: $3–$5.*

# HOLLYWOOD

**Boardner's.** At this slightly rumpled, friendly alternative to the surrounding glitz of Hollywood, the drinks are cheaper and the clientele more down-to-earth than at other watering holes in the 'hood. They've been serving reliable grub to free spirits since 1942, and in recent years they've added a couple of DJ nights. The music ranges from gothic to funk, depending on the promoter and night. *1652 N. Cherokee Ave., between Hollywood Blvd. and Selma Ave., tel. 323/462–9621. Cover: Free–$6.*

**Burgundy Room.** This small bar is a fun neighborhood hangout where old and young congregate to swill and jabber. Expect bad air circulation, high tables and stools, and if you're lucky, endless Cure on the stereo. If your date is dull, there are always the rock posters and sexy cowgirl pictures to stare at. *1621½ Cahuenga Blvd., between Selma and Hollywood Blvds., tel. 323/465–7530.*

**Cat & Fiddle Pub.** It's a restaurant, too, but the food is unremarkable, so order a pint and lean back in the plastic patio furniture on the beautiful Spanish hacienda–style patio or listen to live music (Sunday is jazz, Monday blues, Tuesday open mike) inside the dark-wood pub. Lots of local industry types (big surprise!) hang around after work. On weekdays you can munch on free nibbles, and pints are $2.50 instead of $3.75. *6530 Sunset Blvd., at Seward between Highland Ave. and Cahuenga Blvd., tel. 323/468–3800.*

**Frolic Room.** Another old Hollywood hangout rediscovered by twenty-somethings, the Frolic Room has one of L.A.'s best neon signs outside and a fabulous mural of the golden age of movies within. You are likely to find a barstool, and the jukebox plays a good mix of tunes. *6245 Hollywood Blvd., at Vine St., tel. 323/462–5890.*

**Jones.** Get up close and personal with Hollywood hipsters at Jones, where they pack 'em in like sardines. It's too dark and crowded for you to be able to tell, but this is an authentically preserved old showbiz haunt, with secluded booths, scrumptious food, and very loud music. *7205 Santa Monica Blvd., at Formosa Ave., tel. 323/850–1727.*

**Kane.** This hangout across the way from Paramount Studios recently morphed from a dark rock dive to a polished dance club/bar. The drinks are stiff, the sounds are funky, and the crowd looks like the cast of *Friends. 5574 Melrose Ave., tel. 323/469–8258.*

**Lava Lounge.** Occupying a two-tier strip mall, this is one of L.A.'s favorite dimly lit dens of Polynesian pleasure. Look for the faux lava-rock fountain and a variety of weird lounge acts (was that a xylophonist?). *1533 N. La Brea Ave., between Sunset and Hollywood Blvds., tel. 323/876–6612. Cover: $1–$3.*

**Three Clubs.** This casually hip lounge is furtively located in a strip mall (beneath the fantastic Bargain Clown Mart and next door to an AA meeting center). The music bumps from funny martini-party music to potent grooves to hep-cat lounge sounds depending on the night. Between the soundtrack, the dark-wood paneling, and the lamp-lighted tables, you could be in a basement rec room from decades past— no fancy dress required, but fashionable looks suggested. *1123 N. Vine St., at Santa Monica Blvd., tel. 323/462–6441.*

**Yamashiro.** Kimonoed waitresses glide through this expensive, elegant Japanese restaurant. Lucky for penny-pinchers yearning for the good life, this palacelike place has a lounge from which there's a spectacular view of Los Angeles. The mandatory valet parking costs $3, and the cheapest drink is Perrier ($2.50). Hungry? The sake and kamikazes go well with the *edamame* (steamed, salted soy beans). *1999 N. Sycamore Ave., between La Brea and Highland, ¼ mi north of Franklin Ave., tel. 323/466–5125.*

# WEST HOLLYWOOD

**Barney's Beanery.** Half bar, half restaurant, and home to what they call "L.A.'s second-best chili" (don't ask about the first), the Beanery serves more than 300 different beers, including a few of their own. Janis Joplin used to hang here, though the story of her brandishing a Southern Comfort bottle cannot be confirmed. The crowd clustered at the long bar is hip but not haughty, just like the decor. *8447 Santa Monica Blvd., between La Cienega and Crescent Heights Blvds., tel. 323/654–2287.*

# CONSPICUOUS CONSUMPTION

*Actors, models, rockers, and other perpetually cool L.A. types usually frequent a tight circle of trendy bars, which morphs at least every year. These cosmo-zones can charge over $10 for a drink, but hey, it's cheaper than celebrity-hunting over an expensive meal. Getting past the velvet rope can be a hurdle. The rules of thumb: look great, act like you're supposed to be there, and if all else fails ply the doorman with a fib or two (i.e., "I work for . . .," "I'm meeting . . .inside") or a little flattery ("Weren't you in that Calvin Klein ad?").*

*Bar Marmont (8171 Sunset Blvd., West Hollywood, tel. 323/650–0575). Leonardo DiCaprio called this swanky bar his favorite hangout not too long ago, but that was before his fans started frequenting the place. Still, this eclectic restaurant–cocktail lounge is still the cat's meow for plenty of celebutantes and their entourages. If you plan to go on a weekend, get there early before the line reaches ridiculous lengths.*

*Barfly (8730 Sunset Blvd., West Hollywood, tel. 310/360–9490). Pouty models in Gucci, moguls in Italian suits, and the odd TV personality pepper this restaurant–nightclub. Settle in for a luscious drink and perhaps an entrée (the menu's heavy on the sushi) while the DJs spin the latest.*

*Les Deux Cafés (1638 N. Las Palmas Ave., Hollywood, tel. 323/465–0509). Hidden on a grungy street off of Hollywood Boulevard, this high-end restaurant has a bar where megastars like Madonna and Tom Cruise camouflage themselves somewhat in its dark, elegant environment. The purr of a lounge singer occasionally winds through the buzz.*

*North (8029 Sunset Blvd., West Hollywood, tel. 323/654– 1313). This upscale restaurant-bar has a woodsy, lodge-style décor and a massive celebrity clientele. Even when the star wattage dims, it's still a great place to people-watch.*

*Sky Bar (Mondrian Hotel, 8440 Sunset Blvd., West Hollywood, tel. 323/650–8999). This poolside bar is notoriously one of the hardest hangouts in the city to get into—you must have a key to prove you're a hotel guest or be exceptionally fabulous to make it past security.*

*The Standard (8300 Sunset Blvd., West Hollywood, tel. 323/650–9090). Between the ringing of cell phones and the giggles and air-kisses of starlets, there's no wonder this hotel bar hums. There's a strong entertainment industry bigwig presence, which not suprisingly raises its aspiring actress/actor quotient, too.*

**Blades.** Enjoy karaoke, show tunes, and occasional comedy at this mostly male West Hollywood gay bar. The ceiling is hung with cherubs and pink triangles, and the slightly older crowd is festive and friendly. *801 Larrabee St., at Santa Monica Blvd., tel. 310/659-6693.*

**Formosa Café.** This Chinese restaurant and bar are partially housed in a converted railroad car decorated with a photographic shrine to Hollywood's movie legends, many of whom were patrons. The fun crowd is fittingly eccentric, and the good kitchen smells may whet your appetite. *7156 Santa Monica Blvd., at Formosa Ave., tel. 323/850-9050.*

**H.M.S. Bounty.** L.A.'s cocktail-marinated crowd cyclically embraces this unlikely mix of the nautical and futuristic. Its popularity stems from its potent drinks and its excellent (and free!) jukebox. *3357 Wilshire Blvd., between Normandie and Vermont Aves., tel. 213/385-7275.*

**J. Sloan's.** Since 1919 people have been donning beer goggles in this bar, where trees are used for furniture and dead animals for decorations. The Budweiser paraphernalia lends a tacky touch. *8623 Melrose Ave., at Huntley Dr., tel. 310/659-0250.*

**Micky's.** Bartenders at this packed and popular gay bar are more than occasionally bare-chested, and video screens dominate the walls. *8857 Santa Monica Blvd., between La Cienega and San Vicente Blvds., tel. 310/657-1176.*

**Rafters.** This mellow gay bar has a pool table, pinball, and a jukebox filled with house music. The crowd is predominantly thirty-something guys, and the decor suggests an elegant Old West saloon. *7994 Santa Monica Blvd., at Laurel Ave., tel. 323/654-0396.*

# SILVER LAKE, LOS FELIZ AND ATWATER VILLAGE

**Akbar.** A low-key, Indian-mosque-like décor, dim lighting, and an excellent jukebox add up to a comfy local spot. It's packed each night with a mixed gay/hetero crowd. *4356 Sunset Blvd., at Fountain Ave., Silver Lake, tel. 323/665-6810.*

**Dresden Room.** Though its kitsch-cool was exposed in the film *Swingers,* the Dresden Room continues on its dark and campy way, and the senior citizens who live for the happy-hour buffet as well as the teenage lounge lizards who filter in after dark like it like that. Aged but glamorous crooners Marty and Elayne hold forth on the piano Monday–Saturday among furnishings unchanged since the '60s. *1760 N. Vermont Ave., near Hollywood Blvd., Los Feliz, tel. 323/665-4294.*

**Good Luck Bar.** Chinese lanterns, cushy sofas, funky music, and a crowd that's willing to line up outside are sure signs this is a hot hangout. They stock powerful Chinese rose and melon whiskeys, meant for sipping. *1514 Hillhurst Ave., at Hollywood Blvd., Los Feliz, tel. 323/666-3524.*

**Pro Billiard Club.** You can play pool morning, noon, and night in this well-lighted bar the size of a gymnasium. Mingle with Silver Lake locals who take their billiards seriously and try not to take offense at the metal-detector search at the door. Game prices vary according to time of day and number in your party. Doors open at 11 AM. *3126 Los Feliz Blvd., at Glen Feliz Blvd., Atwater Village, tel. 323/644-1444.*

**The Roost.** Those who like to drink without distractions should head to this petite bar where Christmas lights and mirrors provide decoration and the neighborhood provides the atmosphere. Throw some quarters in the jukebox to liven it up. *3100 Los Feliz Blvd., at Glen Feliz Blvd., Atwater Village, tel. 323/664-7272.*

**Smog Cutter.** Take the karaoke plunge at Silver Lake's favorite no-nonsense dive. The artsy crowd of habitués knows how to follow the bouncing ball no matter how many mai tais they've had. The neighborhood's sketchy, so park in the adjacent lot. *864 Virgil Ave., between Melrose Ave. and Santa Monica Blvd., Silver Lake, tel. 323/667-9832.*

**Tiki Ti.** In a small, lusciously tacky Hawaiian setting, these guys serve up huge, potent cocktails. The bartenders create drinks from rum, vodka, or gin. You just order your poison, and they'll make it to their own specifications—different every time but always delicious. Call ahead—vacationing is a regular activity for the proprietors, and patrons frequently find the bar doors securely locked. *4427 W. Sunset Blvd., east of Hillhurst Ave., Los Feliz, tel. 323/669-9381.*

# HOW TO DRESS
# FOR THE SCENE

When clubbing in L.A., more important than your destination is how you dress. The good news is that L.A.'s brutal mandate to look good or else is an equal opportunity oppressor. In this city known for its abundance of "beautiful people," appearances are your biggest selling point. However, despite what Joan Rivers and her fashion police might lead you to believe, "who you're wearing" is less important than having your own personal style, at least among the non-famous. There is no one uniform, unlike the all-black designer ensemble favored in New York. Instead, you'll need to pitch your look to the audience, putting in serious prep time or leaving your hair uncombed depending on where you're going.

First of all, the purpose of club clothing is not to cover up but to reveal what you've got—getups that would get you arrested for prostitution in other parts of the country won't even win you a second glance in most Los Angeles nightspots. If your club-going outfit makes you feel self-conscious or cold, you are probably on the right track. In a city where implants are a dime a dozen, the natural look isn't too common. Swank evening looks have the sheen of high-maintenance: sleek clothing that shows off frequent trips to the gym, shiny, well-coiffed hair, and impeccable makeup. Street style often involves tattoos, piercings, and other body modifications. Remember that cosmeticians on movie sets are called makeup "artists"; there's no need to limit yourself to what you actually look like.

If you head to an expensive dance spot on the Westside, consider a little black dress—little being the operative word. Men should do well in dark, subdued threads, preferably by Armani, Gucci, or other boldface designers. In seedier Hollywood, there's more of an anything-goes attitude. Kids at electronic music clubs gravitate toward extra-baggy pants and, for women, tiny tops. At rock venues, you'll see a lot of glittery fabrics, miniskirts, hip huggers, faux fur jackets, and slip dresses on women and dark denim, retro-style shirts, work boots, and leather on men. Swing nights call for vintage dresses and two-tone shoes. Feeling paralyzed by indecision? Flip through a couple of L.A.-based magazines like Bikini, Raygun, or Glue for inspiration.

## WESTWOOD AND WEST L.A.

**The Arsenal.** Although the military decor here is mind-blowing, cocktail hour is the only real draw—get toasted on $1.50 well drinks between 4 and 6. *12012 W. Pico Blvd., between Bundy Dr. and Barrington Ave., West L.A., tel. 310/479–9782.*

**Liquid Kitty.** A flashing neon sign of a martini glass and a cigarette mark the door of this dimly lighted, smoky bar filled with disaffected youth trying desperately and unsuccessfully to re-create the glamorous aura their parents and grandparents enjoyed here. Drop in for almost comically serious cocktail drinking and cigar smoking. *11780 W. Pico Blvd., between Bundy Dr. and Barrington Ave., West L.A., tel. 310/473–3707.*

**Monty's.** This popular steak house offers a panoramic view of the city from its upstairs bar. Throngs of amiable students are in attendance weekends for performances by the versatile house band, which accommodates requests for everything from James Brown to Tom Jones. *1100 Glendon Ave., north of Wilshire, Westwood, tel. 310/208–8787.*

**San Francisco Saloon and Grille.** Although Bay Area natives may scratch their heads at the name, this rambling West L.A. bar is a popular spot with clean-cut Angelenos. You can watch TV and munch on potato skins while knocking back an Anchor Steam or some other northern California brewski. *11501 W. Pico Blvd., at Exposition Blvd., West L.A., tel. 310/478–0152.*

## SANTA MONICA AND VENICE

**Babe Brandelli's Brig.** The action centers around two pool tables at this comfortable neighborhood dive. There's an equal chance you'll find yourself pitted against a peroxide blonde Gen-Xer, an indigent hustler, or an Aussie expat. No attitude here, just cheap brew and a friendly, hard-drinking crowd. Check out the mural outside. *1515 Abbot Kinney Blvd., at Palms Blvd., Venice, no phone.*

**Buffalo Club.** No bull—there's studded red-leather bar stools, peach walls with oak paneling, and chicken potpie on the menu. Macaroni and cheese with your vodka martini—why not? If the atmosphere of celebs going incognito is too strong, you can always escape to the authentic dives just down the street. *1520 Olympic Blvd., at 15th St., Santa Monica, tel. 310/450–8600.*

**Daily Pint.** Pool tables, darts, shuffleboard, and beer on tap draw the neighborhood into this sports bar/pub where young folks rock out to Lynyrd Skynyrd. *2310 Pico Blvd., between 22nd and 23rd Sts., Santa Monica, tel. 310/450–7631.*

**Oar House.** Relive all those fabulous frat parties of your lost college years at this rowdy bar. The decor is much funkier than is the collegiate crowd, with old-fashioned advertisements and rusty old automobiles hanging from the ceiling. Come before 10 PM on Friday to get $2 well drinks; the more you have, the better you will fit in with the regular clientele. *2941 Main St., at Pier Ave., Santa Monica, tel. 310/396–4725.*

**O'Brien's Pub.** Attached to the Oar House (*see above*), this pub entices the local British and Irish community to come in for a pint and some Irish rock music (Friday and Saturday, with a $5 cover) or comedy (Thursday at 8). *2941 Main St., at Kinney St., Santa Monica, tel. 310/396–4725.*

**Round Table.** This piano bar is where retired types meet to trade insights ("Frank Sinatra is the greatest communicator of the 20th century") and hear great old songs like "Goody Goody" belted out by somebody's grandma. Expect some stares, a heavy assortment of Christmas decor, and pictures from the Kama Sutra in the men's bathroom and pink paint in the women's. *2460 Wilshire Blvd., at 25th St., Santa Monica, tel. 310/828–2217.*

**Ye Olde King's Head.** Guinness is on tap at this fish-and- chips refuge for Irish and British expats and other Anglophiles. On Saturday night the crowds are as thick as the accents. *116 Santa Monica Blvd., between Ocean Ave. and 2nd St., Santa Monica, tel. 310/451–1402.*

## SOUTH BAY

**Bestie's.** Soccer fans say this British pub, named after English football legend George Best, is the top sports bar in the South Bay. The greasy grub and imported beers on tap will undoubtedly make you feel like a champ. Darts, pool, live music on weekends, and 17 TVs round out the lineup. *1332 Hermosa Ave., at 14th St., Hermosa Beach, tel. 310/318- -3818.*

**H₂O.** This is a happening bar and lofty cigar club where hoards of upwardly mobile beachgoers eat international dinners and dance to DJ grooves after hours. *401 Manhattan Beach Blvd., between Highland Ave. and Valley Dr., Manhattan Beach, tel. 310/545–6220.*

**Hennessey's Tavern.** The loyal locals are far more accustomed to Hennessey's pub grub and good beer selection than is probably healthy (*see also* South Bay *in* Chapter 3). *1712 S. Catalina Ave., west of PCH*

*Redondo Beach, tel. 310/540–8443; 8 Pier Ave., at Hermosa Ave., Hermosa, tel. 310/372–5759; 313 Manhattan Beach Blvd., at Highland Ave., Manhattan Beach, tel. 310/546–4813.*

**Manhattan Beach Brewing Company.** As the beach (two blocks away) empties in the late afternoon, this place fills with salty characters. The home-brewed ales, bitters, and stouts go for $3.50 a pint, or you can sample them in shot-glass "tasters." *124 Manhattan Beach Blvd., at Ocean Dr., Manhattan Beach, tel. 310/798–2744.*

**Pitcher House.** Don't let the row of Harleys out front scare you off: This friendly, anachronistic, 1950s roadhouse is a real hoot. It has spawned many fruitful burly-biker-meets-barefoot-beach-babe relationships. The hodgepodge interior decor is an experience unto itself—think sign graveyard meets Elks lodge. There's sawdust afoot as well as plenty of pool tables, Foosball, darts, and cheap Bud. *150 PCH, between 1st and 2nd Sts., Hermosa Beach, no phone.*

**Toes Tavern.** It's a classic surf bar, dude. Don't hit your head on a skag as you play pool and sway to the live surf rhythms on weekends. And don't mix up your blue-plastic party cup with the one belonging to that blond, tanned guy during the 50¢ happy hour (daily 4–7). Long-boarders drop in for their Big Beer Wednesday, for free pizza on Thursday, and to watch killer vintage video reels. *732 N. Catalina Ave., at Elena Ave., Redondo Beach, tel. 310/374–4628. Cover: $3 (weekends).*

# DANCE CLUBS

If you're looking to shake it, L.A. has no end of options, but it may take some forethought to hit your favored music/crowd combination. The term *club* can denote a specific venue, but more often than not, it refers to the promotion—a night dedicated to specific DJs and music genres. One club venue can have different club promotions every night of the week, which means you could go a particular space to hear techno one night and reggae the next. A night of club-hopping will run up your odometer and deplete your funds (expect to pay $5–$15 per establishment). Most club doors don't open until 9 PM, and they keep swinging until dawn. It's a good idea to take what's called a "disco nap" in the late afternoon if you're not used to dancing all night so that you don't start fading too soon. Due to the scene's erratic nature, some of the clubs listed below have undoubtedly folded, so call ahead. Check the *L.A. Weekly* for a detailed guide of a club's promotions for each night of the week. All clubs below are 21-and-over unless otherwise noted; expect to have your identification checked on a regular basis.

*See also* Dragonfly, Gabah, Fais Do-Do, LunaPark, Key Club, and Martini Lounge in Live Music, *below.*

**Arena.** A favorite among the hip gay men of Hollywood, this huge former ice-making factory literally thumps with house music Thursday–Sunday. A straight Asian crowd takes over on Thursday, while all ages bounce around to deep house and old school on Friday. Latin music takes center stage Saturday, with a drag show around midnight; on Sunday families show up for more live Latin rhythms. 18-and-up except on Friday and Sunday. *6655 Santa Monica Blvd., between Highland Ave. and Vine St., Hollywood, tel. 323/462–0714. Cover: $6–$10.*

**Century Club.** Be a beautiful person or just look at one in this posh restaurant, which also serves as a dance spot. Every Friday they spin Latin house, salsa, and hip-hop; there's a $10 cover for those who arrive before 10, $15 for those cool and rich enough to come after. Saturday's music is more of a mix, including '70s soul and funk as well as hip-hop, while Sunday is an R&B dance party. If you arrive after 10 for either of these nights, you'll be coughing up $20. *10131 Constellation Blvd., between Century Park East and Ave. of the Stars, Century City, tel. 310/553–6000. Cover: $10–$20.*

**Crush Bar.** This '60s–'80s dance club draws mostly casually dressed older San Fernando Valley people and tourists. Come for the music, as the space itself is slightly run-down. If shaking your butt and flailing your arms to soul, disco, and reggae (on Sunday) is your idea of fun, this relaxed spot is for you. *1743 N. Cahuenga Blvd., at Hollywood Blvd., Hollywood, tel. 323/461–9017. Cover: $8–$10.*

**El Rey.** This beautiful art deco building not only hosts big-name live acts but also the most unique and colorful dance promotions you're likely to find in Los Angeles. On the first Saturday of the month it puts on the fabulous Makeup, which glitters with live drag performances and an equally delish crowd prancing to glam rock and retro trash. On the second Saturday of the month, a '60s shindig called Shout pumps out soul, mod, and Brit pop for a young, scooter-riding crowd. On first and third Sundays, it morphs into the bewitching Coven 13, a Goth club; on the last Saturday of the month, it becomes Beat It, an 80s night. All club nights are 21-and-over. *5515 Wilshire Blvd., at Fairfax Ave., Miracle Mile, tel. 323/769–5500.*

**Florentine Gardens.** Here you can get down to techno-salsa, house, or some other brutally repetitive dance music until 5 AM—if you are not put off by the pink and green neon, the small squadron of security guards, or the remarkably unfriendly staff. The trendy, racially mixed crowd is the club's strong point. It's an 18-and-over venue, and much of the crowd seems to have barely made that criterion. *5951 Hollywood Blvd., at Bronson Ave., entrance in the back, Hollywood, tel. 323/464–0706. Cover: $12.*

**Garden of Eden.** A funk-with-money crowd rocks to old school, hip-hop, and house spun by top notch turntablists Wednesday–Saturday nights at this enchanting dance club. *7080 Hollywood Blvd., La Brea Ave., Hollywood, tel. 323/465–3336. Cover: $10–$15.*

**The Gate.** Spotting a celebrity among the well-dressed, cell-phone types here is a gratifyingly common occurrence. Dance sounds range from '70s and '80s hits to European electronica. Ladies who dress sexily are virtually guaranteed VIP treatment. *643 La Cienega Blvd., at Melrose Ave., Hollywood, tel. 310/289–8808. Cover: $10–$15.*

**Grand Avenue.** Dress to impress for this fantastic Latin dance club featuring rock *en Español*, salsa, funk, hip-hop, and R&B. The fish tanks in the coat-check area are interesting, but wait until you hit the dance floor and spot the naked woman dancing behind a multicolor screen. Park in a secured lot and be careful, as downtown is very dicey at night. *1024 S. Grand Ave., between 10th and 11th Sts., downtown, tel. 213/747–0999. Cover: $10–$12.*

**ID.** Formerly Club Lingerie, this well-known, long-running Sunset Boulevard venue has a circular stage, spacious dance floor, and a private, VIP, upstairs lounge. On Tuesday, DJs spin soulful sounds; on Thursday hip-hop reigns. Friday is devoted to electronica, and on Saturday Prada-philes hit the Eurohouse fave High Society. *6507 Sunset Blvd., at Wilcox St., Hollywood, tel. 323/466–8557. Cover: $10–$12.*

**Mayan.** This Friday- and Saturday-night venue is utterly dedicated to the dithyrambic powers of disco, retro, hip-hop, and salsa. Dress your best, or the powers that be may not let you over the threshold of this renovated art deco former movie house. The club has secure parking; take advantage and be careful walking around here at night, as it is not a safe neighborhood. *1038 S. Hill St., near 11th St., downtown, tel. 213/746–4287. Cover: $12.*

**Opium Den.** Occasional live bands and diverse crowds spark this exotic venue. Thursday draws a gay crowd; on Friday and Saturday, swarms of cute Hollywooders bop to Brit pop, funk, and old school. *1605½ N. Ivar Blvd., at Selma Ave., Hollywood, tel.323/466–7800. Cover: $5–$10.*

*Late-night bowlers should try the 28-lane Mar Vista Bowl (12125 Venice Blvd., at Grand View Blvd., Mar Vista, tel. 310/391–5288), open Sunday–Thursday until midnight, Friday and Saturday until 1 AM. If you need to bowl even later, head over to the 24-hour Hollywood Star Lanes (5227 Santa Monica Blvd., between Western and Normandie Aves., Hollywood, tel. 213/665–4111).*

**The Palms.** L.A.'s oldest exclusively women's nightclub rotates DJs nightly; the pool tables and cheap-drink nights (50¢ Wednesday, $1 Thursday) also lure many of the fair sex. Music runs the gamut from live blues, rock, and jazz (Tuesday) to house and dance mixes (Wednesday–Monday). *8572 Santa Monica Blvd., at N. La Cienega Blvd., West Hollywood, tel. 310/652–6188. Cover: $3–$5, free Mon. and Thurs.*

**The Pink.** This small club is fleshed out with colorful projected images, tiny tables, and a dance floor for getting hot and heavy to electronic sounds like drum n' bass, speed garage, jungle, and trip hop. *2810 Main St., at Ashland, Santa Monica, tel. 310/392–1077. Cover: $5–$10.*

**Rage.** Come on Wednesday before 11 PM to watch the Troupers perform fine transvestite cabaret (with signed translation for the hearing impaired). On Monday they play alternative music, but every other night it's straight-ahead dance music, with a spacious floor where you can get down with droves of boys' boys. *8911 Santa Monica Blvd., at San Vicente Blvd., West Hollywood, tel. 310/652–7055. Cover: Free–$5.*

**The Ruby.** You can't miss the congress of goggle-eyed rave kids waiting to get in on Wednesday's Magic 2000 night, or the pale-faced, black leather–and–latex youth who line up for Thursday's Perversion. Be ready for go-go dancers, alternative and techno dance tunes, and frenzies of a sexual kind on Friday and Saturday. It's 18-and-over except Wednesday, when it's open to all ages. *7070 Hollywood Blvd., 1 block east of La Brea Ave., Hollywood, tel. 323/467–7070. Cover: $7–$15.*

**Rudolpho's.** You can salsa and swing with abandon in this easygoing restaurant. Most nights it's a mixed crowd, but on the first Saturday of each month gays shake it until the wee hours. The venue also hosts Dragstrip 66, the legendary dance spot where guys can be queens for an evening on the second Saturday of every month (tel. 323/969–2596). There's always a dress-up theme, such as cave women, space girls, or women of rock. On Monday and Wednesday stop by for salsa classes at 8:15 PM. *2500 Riverside Dr., Silver Lake, tel. 323/669–1226. Cover: $6–$10.*

**7969.** Ignore the haughty bouncers and check out the impressive parade of transvestites pouring into this West Hollywood dance club. Most nights are dancing nights, with Friday's drag show and Saturday's fetish/S&M spot Sin-a-matic the most popular. The whole exterior is bathed in pink neon, and inside you will see a most remarkable display of cleavage, sequins, and corsets on boys, girls, and those in between. *7969 Santa Monica Blvd., at Edinburgh Ave., West Hollywood, tel. 323/654–0280. Cover: $6–$10.*

**Sugar.** An ultra-cool, Hollywood-like dance spot for the Westside, Sugar satisfies beachside natives' craving for a more alternative scene. It blasts funky house on Wednesday, soul on Thursday, '60s and '70s soul and funk classics on Friday, and trance on Saturday. *814 Broadway, Lincoln Blvd., Santa Monica, tel. 310/899–1989. Cover: $10.*

**Tantra Bar.** Another of Santa Monica's more youthful dance clubs, dewy fresh faces boogie to soul and old school on Thursday and Friday, and electronic grooves (till 5 AM) on Sunday. This is one of the rare Westside places where the young and not-so commingle. *23 Windward Ave., near Venice Blvd., Santa Monica, tel. 310/452–2222.*

**Tempest.** After the dinner dishes are cleared from this restaurant, it becomes an intimate dance hangout. On Monday chicks in platforms and guys in makeup dance to glam rock spun by local DJ faves Jason Lavitt and K-ROQ radio star Rodney "on the Rock" Bingenheimer. Thursday becomes a mod, mod world at 1960s-style Café Bleu. *7323 Santa Monica Blvd., West Hollywood, at Fuller St., tel. 323/850–5115. Cover: $3–$7.*

**360.** It's all about the view at this classy restaurant and club. It flaunts two of the city's hottest spots: Tuesday's Beige, where head-shot-worthy gays and wanna-be actors mingle, and Thursday's Quick Fix, which is even harder to get into than Beige. There's one room for dancing and another for dining. *6290 Sunset Blvd., at Vine St., Hollywood, tel. 323/871–2995. Cover: Free–$10.*

**The West End.** You're practically guaranteed a good time here, especially on Friday night, when there's a disco show with a band fully attired in Afros, jumpsuits, and tube tops. On Saturday night there's an '80s show and dancing. Sunday's promotion, Deluxe, imports house DJs from all around the world. *1301 5th St., at Arizona Ave., Santa Monica, tel. 323/313–3293. Cover: $5–$10.*

# LIVE MUSIC

L.A. is an epicenter of the music industry; the number of music transplants surely approaches that of movie hopefuls. With an innovative scene that flourished decades before Seattle became wired for sound, L.A. isn't just the home of the country's most exciting rock bands. It also remains one of the best cities in the world to catch promising punk, pop, hip hop, and folk acts—if you're hanging at one of the smaller clubs, you're likely in the company of talent scouts. The jazz, blues, and classical scenes are no slouch either; concerts here can reveal musicians at their most passionate. Major venues offer the biggest talents on tour, but it can be far more interesting to check out the city's smaller spaces, where you can catch local favorites who just may break into the bigtime. Rappers like Snoop Dogg and Coolio, electro-heads like The Crystal Method, and alternative acts like Orgy all got their starts here, and all of these styles continue to flourish in clubs throughout town.

As it does in most large U.S. cities, Ticketmaster has a virtual monopoly on tickets for shows at major venues (*see below*). Smaller venues (bars, cafés, and clubs) usually sell tickets (free–$20) in advance at their own box offices or at the door. Opening bands start up around 8 or 9, with headliners taking the stage around 10 or later. Shows in smaller venues are 21-and-over unless otherwise noted.

## MAJOR VENUES

**Ticketmaster** outlets (commonly found in record stores) have a headlock on advance sales for larger venues. Be prepared to surrender a service charge of up to $6 per ticket. *6243 Hollywood Blvd., tel. 213/480–3232 or 714/740–2000.*

**Greek Theater.** This open-air amphitheater in Griffith Park (*see* Griffith Park *in* Chapter 2) hosts big-name rock, pop, and jazz acts like R.E.M., the Gypsy Kings, and Al Green from June through October. *See also* Classical Music, Dance, and Opera, *below*. *2700 N. Vermont Ave., Los Feliz, tel. 323/665–1927. Tickets: $10–$30.*

**Hollywood Bowl.** A concert here is a sigh-worthy experience. The outdoor amphitheater, nestled in the Hollywood Hills, hosts the L.A. Philharmonic in summer but makes room for other music ranging from gospel to movie scores. To milk it for all it's worth, get there early and bring a picnic. Also, don't forget a sweater to fend off a chill after sunset. *See also* Classical Music, Dance, and Opera, *below*. *2301 N. Highland Ave., ¾ mi north of Hollywood Blvd., Hollywood Hills, tel. 323/850–2000.*

**Hollywood Palladium.** Formerly a swing-era dance hall, the Palladium now hosts all variety of live shows in a restored '40s interior. Check the *L.A. Weekly* for specific shows—it's more complete than their info line. *6215 Sunset Blvd., at Argyle St., Hollywood, tel. 323/962–7600. Tickets: $10–$25.*

**John Anson Ford Amphitheater.** Soak in the sun at this outdoor amphitheater in the Hollywood Hills. Its summer series embraces everything from bluegrass musicians to jazz ensembles to local dance troupes. Though it closes after Labor Day, it does host the Annual World Festival of Sacred Music in October. *See also* Theater, *below*. *2580 Cahuenga Blvd., near the 101 freeway, Hollywood, tel. 323/461–3673. Tickets: $7–$30. Open mid-June–Labor Day.*

**Santa Monica Civic Auditorium.** Come here for music and food festivals, such as Brews and Blues and Festa Italia. Parking is $5.50. *1855 Main St., at Pico Blvd., Santa Monica, tel. 310/393–9961. Tickets: Free–$24.*

**Staples Center.** This new, 20,000-seat stadium is not only the home of the Lakers, Clippers, and Kings sports teams, but also an occasional mega-concert venue for big names like Bruce Springsteen and Ricky Martin. *1111 S. Figueroa St., at 11th St., downtown, tel. 213/624–3100.*

**Universal Amphitheatre.** This subdued corporate venue hosts all manner of mainstream artists (read: Whitney Houston and her ilk), yet manages a standing-room-only mosh pit during livelier shows. *On Universal Studios lot, tel. 818/622–4440 or 818/777–3931. Tickets: $15–$35.*

**Wiltern Theater.** This restored art deco venue is home to the L.A. Opera Theater and is listed in the National Register of Historic Places. *See also* Classical Music, Dance, and Opera, *below*. *Wilshire Blvd. and Western Ave., Wilshire, tel. 213/380–5005. Tickets: $20–$100.*

## CLUBS AND OTHER VENUES

### ALL SORTS OF MUSIC

**Alligator Lounge.** Cool cats play their rhythms and tunes at this blood-red club, which admits all ages. Biggies like Frank Black and the Melvins have played here, as well as punk and surf rock bands of various levels of fame. *3321 Pico Blvd., between Urban Ave. and 33rd St., Santa Monica, tel. 310/449–1844. Cover: $5–$8, free Tues.*

**Crooked Bar.** This subterranean venue features soothing acoustic sets by folk and rock bands in an intimate, dark room filled with long-haired rockers nodding gently to the strum of the guitar. Their idea of physical activity is a game of eight ball upstairs. Call to hear a sample of the upcoming acts. You must be over 21 to enter, except Sunday–Wednesday when the minimum is 18. *8121 Sunset Blvd., at Crescent Heights, West Hollywood, tel. 323/654–4773. Cover: $5–$10, free Mon.*

**The Derby.** This swank retro club is housed in an impressive, domed room and comes complete with private booths, an oval-shape bar, and plush furnishings. There's always live jazz, blues, rockabilly, and swing. *4500 Los Feliz Blvd., at Hillhurst Ave., south of Griffith Park, Los Feliz, tel. 323/663–8979. Cover: $5.*

**Dragonfly.** The live music here is different each night, with everything from quirky alterna-pop to heavy metal to rhythmic hip hop, but Dragonfly is always at the cutting edge of L.A.'s club scene. Attractive twenty-somethings congregate, smoke cigarettes, and flirt on the outdoor patio. *6510 Santa Monica Blvd., between Highland Ave. and Vine St., Hollywood, tel. 323/466–6111. Cover: $5–$10.*

**El Rey Theater.** This enchanting, two-level theater offers big-name rock, pop, reggae, and Latin bands as well as some steamy dance nights (*see* Dance Clubs, *above*). *5515 Wilshire Blvd., at Fairfax Ave., Miracle Mile, tel. 323/769–5500.*

**Fais Do-Do.** The Creole name may instruct you to go to sleep, but the luscious music, dancing, and food will have just the opposite effect. This historic rooming house–turned–soulful dance café has an under-appreciated pool table (and a kitchen sink!) in the loft, zesty Cajun bites, and good beer and wine on tap. Prepare to party with a wide cross section of all-age Angelenos drawn together by this Mid City location. *5257 W. Adams Blvd., between La Brea and Fairfax Aves., south of I-10, Mid City, tel. 213/954–8080. Cover: usually $5.*

**Foothill Club.** Punk, surf, and soul-funk rule here—at least when country-and-western nights are not in swing. This happening honky-tonk is one of the oldest dance halls on the West Coast. *1922 Cherry Ave., on Signal Hill, at Long Beach city limits, tel. 562/494–5196. Cover: $3–$7.*

**The Garage.** Painted flames crawl up the walls in this intimate spot, which rocks with alternatunes several nights a week. Thursday's Cadillac Club is a blast; on other nights you can hear examples of bold local talent along with the refreshingly dressed-down clientele. *4519 Santa Monica Blvd., at Virgil Ave., Silver Lake, tel. 323/662–6802. Cover: $3–$7.*

**Genghis Cohen Cantina.** Even if kosher Chinese food is not your idea of fine dining, you can enjoy music and heavy drinking at the bar later in the evening. The dimly lighted pink interior is a good backdrop for acoustic bands eager to impress the record-company agents rumored to lurk about the premises. All ages are welcome. *740 N. Fairfax Ave., near Melrose Ave., Melrose, tel. 323/653–0640. Cover: $7–$10.*

**Key Club.** The new kid on the block of West Hollywood's hard-rocking Sunset Boulevard clubs, the Key Club presents acts of all musical stripes. Come here to see your favorite music-industry execs basking in their own glory. Covers vary depending on how fabulous the evening's show is, and there's dancing nightly after the shows. In its previous life it was Billboard Live and before that, the legendary "hair band" metal club Gazzarri's. *9039 Sunset Blvd., at San Vicente Blvd., West Hollywood, tel. 310/274–5800. Cover: $10–$22.50.*

**Largo.** It's not often you get to experience L.A. unplugged, but if you need a break from the throbbing house music or hard-rocking bands of Hollywood, come to this Fairfax Avenue nightspot, open to all ages, to hear a variety of acoustic music in an appropriately mellow setting. The adult crowd tends to dress for the occasion, and covers vary, but there's an act of one kind or another most Tuesdays through Saturdays. *432 N. Fairfax, at Beverly Blvd., Fairfax, tel. 323/852–1073. Cover: $2–$12.*

**LunaPark.** Classy without being too obnoxious, this venue stages an intelligent mix of mambo, blues, alternative, and acid jazz acts. *665 N. Robertson Blvd., between Melrose Ave. and Santa Monica Blvd., West Hollywood, tel. 310/652–0611. Cover: $5–$12.*

**Martini Lounge.** A fabulously frocked crowd shows up for hip-hop or rock, depending on the night. Live bands range from pop to electro-rock and dance nights have DJs spinning everything from Duran Duran to Fatboy Slim. Security is tight, so don't make them mad unless you don't want to get in. Look for the giant neon martini glass outside. *5657 Melrose Ave., at El Centro Ave., Hollywood, tel. 213/467–4068. Cover: $3–$8.*

**McCabe's Guitar Shop.** This guitar shop presents mostly live acoustic folk, country, and blues every weekend. Expect music fanatics in small quarters with light refreshments. The place is devoid of pretension and blessed with a self-serve coffee bar; tickets for this intimate venue, open to all ages, sell out quickly. *3101 Pico Blvd., at 31st St., Santa Monica, tel. 310/828–4403 for concert info hot line or 310/828–4497 for charges. Cover: Free–$22.*

**Rusty's Surf Ranch.** Part sports bar, part live-music club, and 100% beach culture, the Surf Ranch is a convenient place for a beer after your long night of bumper cars on the Santa Monica Pier. There's a pool table if you don't care to concentrate on the rock band du jour. Every Monday is karaoke, and Tuesday–Saturday you can hear live music. *256 Santa Monica Pier, tel. 310/393–7386. Cover: Free–$6.*

**Troubadour.** You won't find any strolling minstrels singing about courtly love, but this is an excellent place to catch budding and established alternative bands—from folksingers to head-bangers—and it admits all ages. *9081 Santa Monica Blvd., between Doheny Dr. and San Vicente Blvd., West Hollywood, tel. 310/276–6168. Cover: $6–$12.*

**Viper Room.** The tragic death of actor River Phoenix on the sidewalk outside the Viper Room has, for better or for worse, *made* Johnny Depp's Sunset Strip nightclub. Although you may not see an actual celebrity unless you can convince the beefy security you are significant enough to enter the VIP back room, many nights you can see a range of live acts, mostly of the young, hard-rocking variety. *8852 Sunset Blvd., at Larrabee St., West Hollywood, tel. 310/358–1880. Cover: $10 and up.*

## ROCK AND POP

**Al's Bar.** Every so often an unknown punk, jazz, or neo-pop band shows up in this large brick warehouse downtown and blows people away. A popular hangout for the pierced and tattooed set and local loft-dwelling artists, the bar hosts live music on Thursday, Friday, and Saturday nights and an occasional Sunday barbecue. Al's rough charm is worth the trek to its sketchy neighborhood. *305 S. Hewitt St., at Traction Ave., downtown, tel. 213/625–9703. Cover: $5.*

**Canter's Kibitz Room.** Adjoining the landmark kosher deli Canter's (*see* Restaurants *in* Chapter 3) is the all-ages Kibitz Room, which often has jazz and blues in addition to rock acts. Intoxicated punkers sit next to hip members of AA, and CBS executives and Hasidic Jews share the space-age Formica tables. *419 N. Fairfax Ave., between Melrose Ave. and Beverly Blvd., Fairfax, tel. 323/651–2030. No cover.*

**Gabah.** Formerly the Anti Club, this space was once the vanguard of L.A.'s music scene—Henry Rollins, the Red Hot Chili Peppers, and Dwight Yoakam all played here early in their careers. It now offers sub-thrash and rock bands, plus a few dance nights. *4658 Melrose Ave., between Western and Normandie Aves., Hollywood, tel. 323/661–8913. Cover: $5–$10.*

**The Gig.** Formerly the Gem, this space was absorbed by the owners of Westside live music venue The Gig; it's now a sister club. Meet beautiful people with attitude, and that's before you even make it past the rope. But hey, you didn't come to L.A. to hang out with the humble. You must pay at least $5 to be treated to the fashion show within, which is accompanied by a variety of live rock, pop, and funk acts. *7302 Melrose Ave., at Poinsettia St., Melrose, tel. 323/936–4440. Cover: $5–$10. West L.A. location: 11637 W. Pico Blvd., near Barrington Ave., tel. 310/444–9870.*

*For tips on free (often random, sometimes good) shows, cheap beer nights, off-beat art openings, and the occasional apartment for rent, call the community-supported hotline 310/288–3668.*

**The Roxy.** A metal haven in the '80s, this Sunset Strip club now books local rock, pop, and punk acts and occasional big-name bands on tour stops in L.A. The excellent PA system means you'll hear every last chord. *9009 Sunset Blvd., near Doheny Dr., West Hollywood, tel. 310/276–2222. Cover: $6–$15.*

**Spaceland.** An adventurous booking policy and dazzling decor attract a happening crowd of local artists and musicians. The digs are less than roomy, but when the right band blasts off, the scene is out of this world. *1717 Silver Lake Blvd., Silver Lake, tel. 213/413–4442. Cover: Free–$7.*

**Whisky A Go Go.** In past years this club was *the* venue of the L.A. punk scene; it was home to the Min-utemen, Black Flag, and, of course, X. (Not to mention the days of the Doors.) Some of the city's best alternative rock bands still play here, hoping to impress scouts, but more often than not you'll find strug-gling metal and pop bands whose audience has a disproportionate ratio of friends and family. All ages. *8901 Sunset Blvd., near San Vicente Blvd., West Hollywood, tel. 310/652–4202. Cover: $3–$15.*

## BLUES

For the best detailed club listings, grab a copy of *Southland Blues,* a free monthly magazine, at a record store or any club listed below. Or call the recorded KLON 88.1 FM blues hot line (tel. 562/985–5566) for tips on where to weep in your beer. Don't forget to also check out the blues listings in the *L.A. Weekly.*

**Babe and Ricky's Inn.** Charles Mingus and other jazz and bluesmen honed their craft in the early years on Central Avenue, L.A.'s original strip. At its current location, the Inn still whines with blues, and there are plenty of pool tables, too. *4339 Leimert, near Leimert Park, tel. 323/295–9112. No cover.*

**Blues Cafe.** Nothin' but the blues six nights a week at 9 on the waterfront in Long Beach. There are also plenty of pool tables, afternoon jam sessions, and deli fare. *210 The Promenade, Long Beach, tel. 562/983–7111. Cover: $2–$10.*

**Café Boogaloo.** The locals packing this bar know it's hard to beat the nightly live blues, the California-Cajun food, and the selection of 27 microbrews here. There's a full bar, a happy hour (3–7), and break-fast on weekends. *1238 Hermosa Ave., at Pier Ave., Hermosa Beach, tel. 310/318–2324. Cover: $5.*

**Harvelle's.** Smoke and thick crowds are de rigueur for a great blues house, and Harvelle's is no excep-tion. Nightly sessions start at 8:30 and last until 2 AM. *1432 4th St., at Santa Monica Blvd., Santa Mon-ica, tel. 310/395–1676. Cover: $3–$7, free Mon.*

**House of Blues.** Actor Dan Aykroyd's $9 million plaything offers such a glitzy interpretation of the South that it's hard to concentrate on the quality blues, funk, and rock acts. Some shows are open to all ages.

*8430 Sunset Blvd., east of La Cienega Blvd., West Hollywood, tel. 323/650–1451 for information or 323/ 848–5100 for box office. Cover: $10 and up.*

**Jack's Sugar Shack.** Is it a blues bar or a beach bungalow? The Sugar Shack has an all-out faux-tropical decor, with bamboo trellises, plastic birds, and beach landscapes painted on the walls. There are also 16 beers on tap (in addition to live music nightly). *1707 N. Vine St., at Hollywood Blvd., Hollywood, tel. 323/466–7005. Cover: $5.*

**Mint Lounge.** Drinks are cheap and "soft" (beer and wine only), the music hard and furious. This very un-L.A. hole-in-the-wall plays gritty blues and some indie rock. Shows happen every night, but Wednesday's performances are considered best. *6010 W. Pico Blvd., between Fairfax Ave. and La Cienega Blvd., West L.A., tel. 323/954–9630. Cover: $5–$10.*

## JAZZ

Cal State Long Beach's listener-supported KLON 88.1 FM sponsors two annual club caravans (July and August), which visit 10 of the area's premier clubs in one evening, and the blockbuster **Long Beach Blues Festival** (tel. 562/985–1686), held around Labor Day weekend.

**Fifth Street Dick's Coffee Company.** The caffeine-fueled, hot-buttered-jazz jam sessions start at 9 or 10 and typically keep burning until the wee hours. For more information on this place and its neighbors, *see* South-Central *in* Chapter 2. *3347½ W. 43rd Pl., near Crenshaw Blvd., Leimert Park, tel. 323/296–3970. Cover: Free–$5.*

**Jazz Bakery.** The music and the baked goods run the gamut here, from sweet-tooth standards to fine fusion and globally influenced contemporary platters. This concert house–cum–concert hall manages to maintain an intimate atmosphere, with every seat and set a good one. *3233 Helms Ave., at Venice Blvd., Culver City, tel. 310/271–9039. Cover: $12–$20.*

**World Stage.** Around the corner from Fifth Street Dick's Coffee Company (*see above*), drummer Billy Higgins's spartan Leimert Park performance space is home to many young artists who hang here because they often get to jam with greats like Max Roach and Cedar Walton. No food or drink is served, but the music will nourish your soul. *4344 Degnan Blvd., at Crenshaw Blvd., Leimert Park, tel. 323/ 293–2451. Cover: $5.*

## LATIN AND WORLD

**Cava.** Limber up your joints in the upstairs room of this restaurant; it's easy to let loose since the live flamenco and salsa bands play their hearts out. There are three ways to get in: You can make reservations and eat some Spanish/Caribbean food ($15 minimum per person), you can hang out at the bar and order a drink ($5–$6), or you can come after 11 and slip right onto the dance floor. Don't show up in shorts, sandals, or sneakers—the bouncers are a little picky about your look, though not your birth date (it's all-ages). *8384 W. 3rd St., at Orlando Ave., West Hollywood, tel. 323/658–8898. No cover.*

**The Conga Room.** Celebrity co-owners Jimmy Smits, Jennifer Lopez, and Paul Rodriguez reel you in with the finest salsa, merengue, and Latin jazz bands around. If you feel unprepared for the dancing, get there at 8 for a lesson, usually free on selected nights. If you're somehow not hot enough, try the spicy, flavor-packed cuisine. *5364 Wilshire Blvd., near La Brea Ave., Miracle Mile, tel. 323/938–1696. Cover: $10–$50.*

**El Floridita.** Enjoy scandalously good Cuban food and sizzling live salsa rhythms nightly. Reservations are recommended for dinner, especially for the Monday-night jam sessions. *1253 N. Vine St., between Sunset and Santa Monica Blvds., Hollywood, tel. 323/871–8612. Cover: $8, free with dinner.*

**Rudolpho's.** Salsa is king at this Mexican restaurant in Silver Lake. Orchestras and DJs take turns laying down the grooves nightly for a young, downwardly mobile crowd (*see also* Dance Clubs, *above*). *2500 Riverside Dr., Silver Lake, tel. 323/669–1226. Cover: $6–$10.*

**Zabumba.** South American rhythms set the tempo at this Latin eatery. The Brazilian beats will make you want to shake your bootie all night long, especially on samba Saturdays. *10717 Venice Blvd., West L.A., tel. 310/841–6525. Cover: $5, free some weekdays.*

# MOVIE HOUSES

It's no surprise that movie houses are a big part of life in L.A. Multiplexes may be blimping out in their game of size one-upmanship, but there are plenty of unique theaters to hit when you don't want to stand in line with what feels like half the city's teenage population. One of L.A.'s niftiest theater treats is the L.A. Conservancy's (tel. 213/623–2489) **Last Seats** series in June, during which classic flicks are shown at the gorgeous old movie palaces downtown (*see* Downtown *in* Chapter 2).

Call 777–3456 in the 323 or 310 area codes for recorded information on movie times, locations, previews, and to charge advance tickets. General admission tickets are normally in the $8 range, with bargain matinees a few bucks cheaper. Exceptions are noted. Most theaters give a bargain rate to students with valid ID, seniors, and children as well.

**Bing Theater.** The exterior isn't much to look at, but within is one of the most expensive and state-of-the-art movie sound systems in L.A. (and therefore probably the world). Essential and artsy flicks shine on this screen at the L.A. County Museum of Art. For a cheap date, check out the $2 classic film matinee on Tuesday. *5905 Wilshire Blvd., at Ogden Dr., Miracle Mile, tel. 323/857–6010. Tickets: $5–$7.*

**Cinerama Dome.** The theater resembles a golf ball from the outside and a beehive from within. In keeping with 1950s Cinerama philosophy, the screen is enormous and rounded, so you feel virtually surrounded by the audiovisual experience. Take a stand against those ubiquitous multiplex theaters and check out first-run movies here. *6360 Sunset Blvd., near Vine St., Hollywood, tel. 323/466–3401.*

**Egyptian Theatre.** It opened with Douglas Fairbanks' *Robin Hood* and premiered films for decades, but by the '90s the Egyptian was another Hollywood casualty. A few years ago it was rescued and stunningly restored, from the pharaoh sculptures to the sunburst ceiling, and now it's the home of American Cinematheque, a nonprofit film exhibition group. Besides showing vintage classics, silents, foreign films, retrospective series, and eclectic new works, they host panel discussions and workshops thick with past and present Industry members. *6712 Hollywood Blvd., at Las Palmas Ave., Hollywood, tel. 323/466–3456. Tickets: $7.*

*Splurge ($45–$55) on murder and dinner during "Murder by Night" or "Medium Murder" (tel. 310/278–7712), mysteries staged and solved as you dine.*

**El Capitan.** This masterpiece was one of the trio of magical, themed movie palaces developed by Sid Grauman in the 1920s (the other two being Mann's Chinese Theatre, *below,* and the Egyptian Theatre, *above*). Reopened by Disney in the early '90s, its Spanish Colonial exterior and East Indian–theme interior are now swankily restored. Disney runs the show, screening its own first-run films and tacking on a stage show before the flick, accompanied by a mighty Wurlitzer. The bad news? You pay through the nose. Tickets cost $18 for general admission and $28 for VIP status (free popcorn and drink, early admission, best seats, and no waiting in line). *6838 Hollywood Blvd., near Highland Ave., Hollywood, tel. 323/467–7674.*

**Fairfax.** They probably are showing movies you didn't much like the first time you saw them, but for $2.75 any time, it's worth double-checking. *7907 Beverly Blvd., at Fairfax Ave., Fairfax, tel. 323/653–3117.*

**IMAX Theater.** A film on the IMAX seven-story monster screen with its spectacular sound system can be breathtaking—or a bit of a yawn. Both 3-D and 2-D films are screened daily; if it's something with aerial footage, like *Wildfire: Feel the Heat,* chances are it's a good bet. *At the California Science Center, 700 State Dr., Exposition Park, tel. 213/744–2014. Tickets: $7.50 for 3-D films, $6.50 for 2-D.*

**Laemmle Theaters.** Ignore your gag reflex to chain theaters and consider one of the Laemmle branches in your quest for quality film. A family business since 1938, the Laemmle theaters show documentaries, retrospectives, indie flicks, and Academy-nominated foreign films. If you are in town just before the Oscars, you can view some of the nominated shorts at their Sunset location. Only the Grande Fourplex shows run-of-the-mill Hollywood releases. Check the *Los Angeles Times* or *L.A. Weekly* for the Laemmle location nearest you or call the general information number. *Tel. 310/478–1041. Tickets: $6.50–$8.*

**Mann's Chinese Theatre.** Possibly the most famous movie theater in the world, the Chinese is another Grauman fantasy, this one with a pagoda-like roof. Its cement courtyard marked with movie stars' foot- and hand-prints is still growing, and its main theater is also one of the best places to see new blockbusters. *See also* Hollywood *in* Chapter 2. *6925 Hollywood Blvd., near Highland Ave., Hollywood, tel. 323/464–8111.*

**Melnitz Theater.** This UCLA theater screens the offbeat, the classic, and the neglected, including choice cuts from the university's Film and Television Archive. *405 Hilgard Ave., at Sunset Blvd., Westwood, tel. 310/206–3456 or 310/206–8013. Tickets: usually $6.*

**New Beverly Cinema.** Film festivals, classics, documentaries, and cool foreign films are the fare at this theater. There is usually a double bill. *7165 Beverly Blvd., 1 block west of La Brea Ave., near West Hollywood, tel. 323/938-4038. Tickets: $5.*

**NuArt.** Although most of the art deco theaters along Broadway downtown are closed or in disrepair (*see* Downtown *in* Chapter 2), West L.A.'s NuArt is still up and running in its full 1920s glory. Specializing in cult and independent films, it also offers a regular showing of the *Rocky Horror Picture Show. 11272 Santa Monica Blvd., at Sawtelle Blvd., West L.A., tel. 310/478-6379.*

**Old Town Music Hall.** This old-time revival house in sleepy downtown El Segundo attracts flocks of families for its weekend screenings of '20s through '50s flicks, including an occasional silent film. All shows are accompanied by live overtures from a giant fluorescent pipe organ and sing-alongs. Don't miss out on the homemade macaroons. *140 Richmond St., at El Segundo Blvd., El Segundo, tel. 310/322-2592. Tickets: $6.*

**Vista Theater.** Once Bard's Hollywood Theater, where both moving pictures and vaudeville took the stage, this movie house presents first-run art and blockbuster films. The Spanish-style facade gives way to an ornate Egyptian interior. *4473 Sunset Dr., near Vermont Ave., Los Feliz, tel. 323/660-6639.*

# THEATER

The strip of Santa Monica Boulevard between Cole and Seward streets in Hollywood promotes itself as Theater Row. Here, a loose federation of microtheaters hosts an eclectic and usually obscure range of one-act and experimental plays with cheap ticket prices. **Actors' Gang** (6209 Santa Monica Blvd., 1 block east of Vine St., tel. 323/465-0566) was founded by actor Tim Robbins and is well known for both its original productions and its innovative adaptations of established plays; tickets cost $5–$15. In Santa Monica, **Highways** (1651 18th St., near Olympic Blvd., tel. 310/453-1755) presents performance art, dance, theater, comedy, and any combination thereof; it's always avant-garde, wild, weird, and affordable ($10–$15). If you feel like splurging on a big Broadway-style production, check out the downtown Music Center's **Ahmanson Theatre** (*see below*).

Flip through the *Daily News, Drama-Logue, L.A. Weekly, Los Angeles* magazine, the *L.A. Times* (especially the Sunday and Thursday "Calendar" sections), and *L.A. New Times* for reviews and information on specific performances around town. **Check out Theatre L.A.'s website at www.theatrela.org., which offers information on all things staged and artsy, including how to get discount tickets. You can get advance tickets through Ticketmaster** (tel. 213/365-3500), but it's cheaper to get them at the individual theater box offices. Of course, student ID will almost always get you a discount on performances.

**Cast Theater and Cast-at-the-Circle.** This is one of the oldest theaters in the city—the stage and director's chair have seen the likes of Charlie Chaplin. If you're lucky, you'll get to see Justin Tanner's weird and wacky *Zombie Attack*, which has played for years. The theater mostly showcases avant-garde improv pieces in addition to some musicals and revivals. *804 N. El Centro Ave., between Santa Monica Blvd. and Melrose Ave., 1 block east of Vine, Hollywood, tel. 323/462-0265. Tickets: $15.*

**Celebration Theater.** This 55-seat gay and lesbian theater stages weekly performances Thursday–Sunday. *7051 Santa Monica Blvd., ½ block east of La Brea Ave., near West Hollywood, tel. 323/957-1884. Tickets: $12–$15.*

**Fountain Theater.** This small theater (with a whopping 80 seats) hosts the occasional flamenco dance show, in addition to original American dramas. Marian Mercer and Rob Reiner got their starts here. The theater has also won numerous awards for its outstanding dedication to "the ethnic diversity and varied citizenry of Los Angeles," with occasional Armenian works and children's plays in *Español,* and shows starring actors with disabilities. *5060 Fountain Ave., ½ block east of Normandie Ave., Los Feliz, tel. 323/ 663-1525. Tickets: $15–$18.*

**Geffen Playhouse.** An acoustically superior theater with great sight lines, the 498-seat playhouse showcases new plays, primarily musicals and comedies. Many productions here are on their way to or from Broadway. Jason Robards and Nick Nolte got their starts here. *10886 Le Conte Ave., ½ block east of Westwood Blvd., Westwood Village, tel. 310/208-6500 or 310/208-5454. Tickets: $30–$40.*

**Globe Playhouse.** This 99-seat house is a small-scale replica of Shakespeare's Old Globe Theater. The company is one of the nation's best Shakespearean acting groups and shouldn't be missed. *1107 N. Kings Rd., ½ block north of Santa Monica Blvd., West Hollywood, tel. 323/654-5623. Tickets: $10–$25.*

**Groundling Theater.** This is where Pee-Wee Herman and many *Saturday Night Live* cast members got their starts. The Groundling puts on several shows a week, from scripted sketches to improvisational and audience-interaction pieces. *7307 Melrose Ave., near La Brea Ave., West Hollywood, tel. 323/934–9700. Tickets: $7–$17.50.*

**James A. Doolittle Theater.** In the heart of Hollywood, this house seems intimate despite its 1,038-seat capacity. New plays, dramas, comedies, and musicals are presented here year-round. *1615 Vine St., between Hollywood and Sunset Blvds., Hollywood, tel. 323/462–6666. Tickets: $30–$40.*

**Japan American Theater.** This community-oriented 880-seat theater at the Japan Cultural Arts Center is home to local theater, dance troupes, and the L.A. Chamber Orchestra, plus numerous children's theater groups. *244 S. San Pedro St., between 2nd and 3rd Sts., Little Tokyo, tel. 213/628–2725 or 213/680–3700. Tickets: Free–$100.*

**John Anson Ford Amphitheater.** This 1,300-seat outdoor house in the Hollywood Hills is best known for its Shakespeare and summer jazz, dance, and cabaret concerts. *2580 Cahuenga Blvd., Hollywood, tel. 323/461–3673. Tickets: $7–$30. Open mid-June–Labor Day.*

**Music Center.** Yup, this is where people walk the red carpet for that most L.A. of ceremonies, the Academy Awards. The downtown complex includes three theaters, which host everything from orchestral performances to ballet to cutting-edge dramas. The 1,600-seat **Ahmanson Theatre** presents classics and Broadway warhorse musicals. When not mounting the Oscars, the 3,200-seat **Dorothy Chandler Pavilion** offers a smattering of plays in between performances of the L.A. Philharmonic, L.A. Master Chorale, and L.A. Opera. Between these two sits the round, 760-seat **Mark Taper Forum** (tel. 213/972–0700), which hosts newer and more experimental theater. Shows often go on to New York City's Broadway; on the roster for 2000 are Neil Simon's *The Dinner Party* and Alan Alda as *Richard Feynman*. The theater triumvirate is slated to be joined by a fourth in 2002, as plans are afoot for a new Walt Disney Concert Hall designed by Frank Gehry. There are a couple of ways to get a bargain for a performance. Public rush tickets are available for productions at the Taper and the Ahmanson, which have banded together as the Center Theatre Group (tel. 213/628–2772). The Taper issues rush tickets nightly, except Saturday and opening nights, during the first five weeks of a given run. The tickets go on sale two hours before curtain time. Public rush tickets at the Ahmanson are a chancier deal; though they have the same arrangement as the Taper, they don't offer them for every production. The Chandler is more restricted, providing $10 discount tickets only for students and seniors. *135 N. Grand Ave., at 1st St., downtown, tel. 213/972–7211. Tickets: $10–$45.*

**Pantages.** Once the home of the Academy Awards telecast and Hollywood premieres, this house is massive (nearly 2,700 seats) and a splendid example of high-style Hollywood art deco, although the acoustics could use some work. Large-scale musicals from Broadway, such as *Jekyll & Hyde*, are usually presented here. *6233 Hollywood Blvd., at Vine St., Hollywood, tel. 323/468–1700 or 323/468–1716. Tickets: $15–$55.*

**Santa Monica Playhouse.** With just under 100 seats, this house is worth visiting for its cozy, librarylike atmosphere and its good comedies, dramas, and children's programs. *1211 4th St., at Wilshire Blvd., Santa Monica, tel. 310/394–9779. Tickets: $8–$20.*

**Skylight.** Many highly inventive productions have been hosted in this 99-seat theater. Different companies rent the house, so the fare varies. *1816½ N. Vermont Ave., Los Feliz, tel. 323/666–2202. Tickets: $10–$15.*

**Theatre/Theater.** Angelenos and anyone craving new and sensational theater productions crowd into this 70-seat house to view original works by local authors and international playwrights. The troupe here can always be counted on to come up with something witty and weird. Recent efforts include *The Dysfunctional Show*, which lampooned daytime talk shows. Audience participation is integral. *6425 Hollywood Blvd., near Cahuenga Blvd., Hollywood, tel. 323/871–0210. Tickets: $10–$20.*

**Wilshire Theater.** Built in the 1920s as a movie theater, this 1,900-seat art deco house usually stages Broadway musicals. Keep in mind that you can only get specific seats guaranteed if you actually go to the box office. *8440 Wilshire Blvd., east of La Cienega Blvd., Beverly Hills, tel. 323/468–1700, 323/468–1716, or 323/480–3232 for reservations. Tickets: $20–$45.*

# MULTIMEDIA, PERFORMANCE ART, AND SPOKEN WORD

The clever, wacky, and creative minds of Angelenos are evident in the city's abundant offerings of non-standard theater. Check out the *L.A. Weekly* for listings and specific reviews. Cafés and coffeehouses (*see* Chapter 3) usually have something cooking in the way of open mikes and readings, as does **Midnight Special Bookstore** on Santa Monica's Third Street Promenade (*see* Books *in* Chapter 7). Your best bet for finding out about readings and performance art around town is to check with the **Beyond Baroque Literary/Arts Center** and the **Highways Performance Space** (*see below*). These guys are generally not part of the Ticketmaster crew; in most cases you'll need to go to the box office to get a ticket.

**Beverly Hills Library Theater.** This 190-seat house above the library offers readings, dramatic monologues, storytelling, and mime. *444 N. Rexford Dr., between Santa Monica Blvd. and Burton Way, Beverly Hills, tel. 310/288–2201. Tickets: Free–$5.*

**Beyond Baroque Literary/Arts Center.** In Venice's former city hall, this center hosts theater, readings, performance art, film presentations, and music. Amy Tan and Andrei Codrescu have read here at the Friday-night Reading and Performance Series, and Raymond Carver once performed. On Wednesday night there are free poetry workshops, Sunday night is open-reading night. Check out their **Small Press Bookstore and Library** for a splendid selection of literature. *681 Venice Blvd., ½ mi west of Lincoln Blvd., Venice, tel. 310/822–3006. Tickets: $3–$10.*

**Bilingual Foundation for the Arts.** This center alternately puts on Spanish- and English-language productions of classic Latin American plays and musicals like Lorca's *Blood Wedding*. The 99-seat theater is the usual venue, but call to find out about other possibilities. *421 N. Avenue 19, between San Fernando and Pasadena Aves., Echo Park, tel. 323/225–4044. Tickets: $15–$20.*

**Getty Center.** The free "Friday Nights at the Getty" series includes lectures, concerts, and readings, plus occasional performances in conjunction with whatever new exhibition that passes through. *See also* the Westside *in* Chapter 2. *1200 Getty Center Dr., Brentwood, tel. 310/440–7300.*

**Highways Performance Space.** This inclusive arts center stages intimate performances and experimental shows from unconventional artists such as sex-pert Annie Sprinkle and body manipulator Ron Athey. *1651 18th St., at Olympic Blvd., Santa Monica, tel. 310/453–1755 or 213/660–8587. Tickets: $10–$15.*

# CLASSICAL MUSIC, DANCE, AND OPERA

Although smaller theaters shake their heads in disbelief as they lose public funding, highbrow treats like operas and symphonies are going strong. And as the gap between the rich and the poor widens in this country, so does the gap between the cost of small-theater tickets and tickets for lavish productions at L.A.'s most influential venues: You can watch unknown actors for $1–$10 or be overwhelmed by the L.A. Opera for $35–$150. Keep in mind, however, that most big-shot houses do offer student and senior rush tickets—little gems you can snag for $10 or $15 in cash right before curtain (though the seats are often terrible).

Check the *L.A. Times* Sunday and Thursday "Calendar" sections or the current issue of *Los Angeles* magazine for the most complete listings of weekly events. Freebies worth checking out include: the **UCLA Summer Chamber Music Festival,** held in the university's Schoenberg Auditorium (tel. 310/206–8552), where moonlighting musicians on furlough from the Philharmonic, Chamber Orchestra, and the school's music department perform on Monday and Thursday afternoons; and the **Symphony in the Glen** series, a run of outdoor classical concerts put on every summer in Griffith Park. There are usually at least two daytime programs per month; call 213/955–6976 for schedule info and directions to the glen. The Veterans Wadsworth Theater hosts the well-attended **Jazz at the Wadsworth** (tel. 310/825–5706) series, with free performances on the first Sunday of every month in the winter, spring, and fall.

## CLASSICAL MUSIC AND OPERA

**Dorothy Chandler Pavilion.** This 3,200-seat theater in the Music Center complex is home to the L.A. Opera, L.A. Master Chorale, and L.A. Philharmonic (when it's not playing the Hollywood Bowl during the summer; *see below*). Regular tickets aren't cheap ($10–$150), but it's definitely worth trying to get student rush tickets ($10) for them. All foreign-language productions are now accompanied by the projection above the stage of supertitles, the operatic equivalent of cinema's subtitles. The opera season usually runs September–June. Plácido Domingo (one of those Three Tenors) will take over the company's artistic directorship in summer 2000. *135 N. Grand Ave., at 1st. St., downtown, tel. 213/972–8000 for information or 213/972–7211 for tickets.*

**Greek Theater.** A few classical performances find their way into the less sophisticated summer (June–October) lineup at this open-air amphitheater in Griffith Park, where tickets go for $17–$70. *2700 N. Vermont Ave., Los Feliz, tel. 323/665–1927.*

**Hollywood Bowl.** Alfresco cultural events don't get much better than this. The Bowl is beautifully fitted into the natural hillsides of Bolton Canyon, and you can bring in a picnic dinner to devour at sunset. The L.A. Philharmonic spends the summer (July–mid-September) here. There are a variety of performances daily (except Monday), and many groups hold free open rehearsals weekday mornings—call ahead to be sure. Student and senior rush tickets ($10) are often available at the box office for Sunday–Thursday events; otherwise, expect to fork over up to $25 for decent seats. Consider taking advantage of the Park-and-Ride shuttles ($2.50), which leave from 15 locations around town, or an MTA Bus (163 or 420) to avoid the gnarly parking scene. Bringing a sweater is a good idea, as it can get chilly after dark—or your tush might need some cushioning. *See also* Hollywood *in* Chapter 2 *and* Live Music, *above. 2301 N. Highland Ave., ¾ mi north of Hollywood Blvd., Hollywood Hills, tel. 323/850–2000 or 213/480–3232 for tickets.*

**Japan America Theater.** The L.A. Chamber Orchestra occasionally appears in this community-oriented theater best known for its rousing Kabuki presentations. Tickets cost $10–$50, but there are student discounts. *244 S. San Pedro St., in Japan Cultural Arts Center, downtown, tel. 213/680–3700.*

**Shrine Auditorium.** Erected in 1926 by the Al Malaikah Temple, this one-of-a-kind 6,200-seat auditorium welcomes touring companies from all over the world, as well as local gospel and choral groups. Tickets run $5–$50. It also shares hosting duties for the Academy Awards with the Dorothy Chandler Pavilion; the statuettes will be doled out here in 2000. *665 W. Jefferson Blvd., 1 block west of Figueroa St. across street from USC campus, South-Central, tel. 213/749–5123.*

**UCLA Center for the Performing Arts.** This center presents a year-long run of world-class performing arts events, including dance, choral, folk, cabaret, and theatrical groups at a number of venues in the Westwood area. (Caliber-wise, think: White Oak Dance Project, vocalist Bobby Short, and violinist Anne-Sophie Mutter.) Tickets for the classical concerts and world-music performances start at around $15, with student discounts for selected events. Events run during the school year (September–May). *10920 Wilshire Blvd., tel. 310/825–2101.*

*For info on shows around town, tune in to KLOS at 5 PM for the Five O'clock Funnies or call KROQ's Rockline 818/566–7625.*

**Veterans Wadsworth Theater.** This plush theater is rented out to top touring groups (sometimes classical and sometimes opera) and also hosts many UCLA performing arts events, including a free monthly jazz series. *Wilshire Blvd., west of I–405, off San Vicente Blvd., on Veterans Administration grounds, West L.A., tel. 310/825–2101.*

**Wilshire Ebell Theater.** The L.A. Opera Theater performs in this 1924 Spanish-style building, along with a broad spectrum of other musical acts. Tickets cost $22–$28. *4401 W. 8th St., 1 block south of Wilshire Blvd., off Miracle Mile, tel. 323/939–1128.*

**Wiltern Theater.** Reopened in 1985 as a venue for the L.A. Opera (though they no longer perform here), this plush art deco structure was built in 1930 and is listed on the National Register of Historic Places. It now runs devoted-fan acts like Beck, Tom Waits, and Johnny Cash. Tickets run $20–$100. *3790 Wilshire Blvd., at Western Ave., Koreatown, tel. 213/388–1400 or 213/380–5005.*

## DANCE PERFORMANCES

L.A. has not been able to keep hold of a major dance company, but fortunately what it lacks in quantity it makes up for in quality and imagination. Interesting troupes, including exciting, unconventional dancers and ethnic ensembles, can be found here even if high-profile companies like the Joffrey Ballet only pass through on tour. Large-scale performances are commonly held at the **UCLA Center for the Performing Arts** and **Shrine Auditorium** (*see* Classical Music and Opera, *above*). Local publications, including the *L.A. Weekly,* the *Los Angeles Times,* and *Los Angeles* magazine, cover dance performances in their calendar listings. If you're visiting in July, look into the Dance Kaleidoscope Festival (*see* Arts Festivals, *below*).

**Jazz Tap Ensemble.** This local group has been playing with the marriage of two dance genres for over 20 years. They have been so successful with their innovative style it's hard to catch them in L.A.— they're always busy dancing around the world. Locations and ticket prices vary. *Tel. 310/475-4412.*

**Los Angeles Chamber Ballet.** The more experimental counterpart to the Classical Ballet, the Los Angeles Chamber Ballet pushes the envelope on classical dance. Recent acts of innovation have included "Cocktails With Joey," a collaborative ballet set to the music of loungester Joey Altruda, and "Where Are You My Love?," danced to Raiford Rogers and jazz legend Charlie Haden. Locations vary, and ticket prices range from free to $20. *Tel. 310/453-4952.*

**Lula Washington Dance Studio.** This modern dance troupe performs the works of their founder, Lula Washington, along with other contemporary African-American choreographers. The studio serves as a base for the group, and the company performs here and at venues around town. Call ahead for a local performance schedule, as they're constantly touring. *5041 W. Pico Blvd., near La Brea Ave., Culver City, tel. 323/936-6591.*

# COMEDY CLUBS

Countless big-name comedians—from Roseanne to Jim Carrey—were discovered in L.A.'s comedy clubs. They're wonderful, if sometimes pricey, places to enjoy up-and-coming comics and the occasional star performer. At most large clubs you must buy two drinks on top of paying the admission price; accordingly, most check IDs at the door. Most also strongly recommend or require a reservation.

**Comedy & Magic Club.** Some of the biggest names from the late-night TV and cable circuit try their new material on for size here, accompanied by at least one offbeat magic act. *1018 Hermosa Ave., at Pier Ave., Hermosa Beach, tel. 310/372-1193. Cover: $10-$20.*

**Comedysportz.** This improv group hosts serious Friday- and Saturday-night battles between improv teams, utilizing sports lingo like *penalty, referee, scores,* and *first ball* (the beginning of a skit). *Tamarind Theater, 5919 Franklin Ave., at Bronson Ave., Hollywood, tel. 323/871-1193 or 323/856-4796. Tickets: $10 in advance, $12 at the door.*

**Comedy Store.** Los Angeles's premier comedy showcase has been going strong for more than a decade, and remains a great place to see up-and-coming funny men and ladies. Famous comedians occasionally make unannounced appearances. *8433 Sunset Blvd., La Cienega Blvd., West Hollywood, tel. 323/656-6225. Cover: $6-$20.*

**Fifth Street Dick's Coffee Company.** Robust coffee and well-steeped humor are served up every Monday around 9. The club also sponsors jazz nights (*see* Jazz *in* Live Music, *above*). *3347½ W. 43rd Pl., near Crenshaw Blvd., Leimert Park, tel. 323/296-3970. Cover: $3.*

**Groundling Theater.** Home of the best improv in town, Groundling rivals Chicago's Second City as a breeding ground for *Saturday Night Live* players like Jon Lovitz, the late Phil Hartman, and Julia Sweeney. Audience participation is an integral part of the inevitably hilarious experience, and all ages are welcome. *7307 Melrose Ave., Hollywood, tel. 323/934-9700. Cover: $7-$17.50. Closed Tues.–Wed.*

**Ice House Comedy Club and Restaurant.** Enjoy the riotous three-act shows at this Pasadena comedy fave. Featuring comedians, celebrity impressionists, ventriloquists, and magicians from Las Vegas, as well as from television shows, this place has it all. Shows take place Tuesday–Sunday. *24 N. Mentor Ave., Pasadena, tel. 626/577-1894. Cover: $5-$12 (2-drink minimum).*

**Improvisation.** This transplanted New York establishment showcasing comedians and occasional vocalists is the place where Richard Pryor got his start; occasional drop-ins have included Jerry Seinfeld. You can dine in Hell's Kitchen, inside the Improv. *8162 Melrose Ave., near Crescent Heights Blvd., West Hollywood, tel. 323/651-2583. Cover: $8-$11 (2-drink minimum).*

**Laugh Factory.** Look for comedy acts and improvisation seven nights a week at this popular comedy hangout. Hot-cha comedians make special appearances; Monday is Latino night. *8001 Sunset Blvd., near Fairfax Ave., West Hollywood, tel. 323/656-1336. Cover: $9-$10.*

**Mice.** An established improv troupe holds forth every Saturday at 10 PM and conducts free therapeutic comedy workshops every Monday at 8 PM. Bring your therapist and your split personality. *West Hollywood Playhouse, 666 N. Robertson Ave., at Santa Monica Blvd., West Hollywood, tel. 818/762–7547. No cover.*

# ARTS FESTIVALS

Below are festivals that focus on more than drinking, shopping, and gawking (for those shindigs, *see* When to Go *in* Chapter 1). To get a copy of the comprehensive *Festivals of Los Angeles* calendar, which contains over 150 in-depth listings, stop by the L.A. Cultural Affairs Department (433 S. Spring St., 10th floor, between 4th and 5th Sts., downtown, tel. 213/485–2433).

The free two-day **UCLA Jazz and Reggae Fest** (tel. 310/825–9912) blows up over Memorial Day weekend on the intramural field in Westwood.

The free summer **Celebrations!** concert series (350 S. Grand Ave., downtown, tel. 213/687–2159) features a different array of entertainment Friday and Saturday evenings and Sunday afternoon. The outdoor performances include circus troupes, dance, theater, and classical music. Free weekday noontime concerts continue from June through October. Call for detailed listings and parking information.

A great concentration of L.A.'s dance resources can be sampled at the annual **Dance Kaleidoscope Festival** (tel. 323/343–6683), which is held on two weekends in July. With 30 companies performing at several venues throughout town (often including the John Anson Ford and Cal State L.A.'s Luckman theaters), this festival showcases a diverse range of styles including ballet, modern, and world.

**Outfest: The LA Gay & Lesbian Film Festival** (Directors Guild of America, 7920 Sunset Blvd., tel. 323/960–9200) has been presenting the best in independent gay film every July since 1982. It has become an anticipated event for movie lovers of all sexual preferences.

The two-day **Sunset Junction Street Fair** (3600–4400 Sunset Blvd., Silver Lake, tel. 323/661–7771) happens every August (usually the third weekend of the month), attracting crowds of trendy gays and straights. The music performances are all over the map—Latin, folk, punk, soul—and there are craft booths, games, and multi-culti food stands.

# OUTDOOR ACTIVITIES AND SPORTS

BY ANDREW DEAN NYSTROM AND ELIZA ENGELBERG

UPDATED BY SUE ALEXANDER

Southern California *is* an outdoor activity. Whether you are cruising the coast in a convertible with the top down, taking in a sporting event at one of many open-air venues, spying on a beachfront movie shoot, or simply walking your dog down Main Street, you'll soon realize that Angelenos have as many reasons year-round for heading to the sunny outdoors as they do excuses for speeding on the freeway. In fact, part of the reason you'll run into so many people speeding in Los Angeles is that they are scurrying to flee the urban sprawl. To escape weekend crowds, avoid both the Pacific Coast Highway anywhere north of Santa Monica and the road to Palm Springs and Vegas, especially during holidays. Fortunately, the L.A. basin is something of an outdoor enthusiast's paradise, surrounded on three sides by golden beaches, hikable and skiable mountains, and desert solitude. The weather on the coast is always cooler than inland, and with so many beaches to choose from, you'll never have trouble finding an empty patch of sand. Before you head out for a jog or bike ride, check the *Los Angeles Times* weather page or the South Coast's Air Quality Management District's **smog report** (tel. 800/CUT–SMOG [288–7664]) to find out whether exercising might actually do your lungs more damage than good, especially during hot summer months. Bugs aren't usually a problem, but don't forget waterproof sunscreen.

For those who like to mix business with pleasure, there are a number of good resources for information on where you can schmooze while maintaining your fitness. Get off your duff and get in the game with the **South Bay Sport and Social Club** (tel. 310/546–1121), which runs a variety of mostly coed non-contact leagues; or talk to the folks at the **Athletic Singles Association** (tel. 310/302–9332) about the smorgasbord of sporting, social, and cultural events that they put on for members throughout L.A. The **Greater Los Angeles Sports Association** was created in 1978 as an arena for gay athletes to play together. Today, gay teams still play on the softball diamonds of Hollywood, but all the group's other leagues are now defunct. The newer **Gay and Lesbian Sports Alliance** (tel. 310/515–3337) sponsors more than 30 recreational and competitive sports; or contact **Christopher Street West** (tel. 323/969–8302) for more gay-team sporting ideas. For the final word on sporting opportunities, contact the **City of Los Angeles Recreation and Parks Department** (200 N. Main St., Room 1350 CHE, Los Angeles 90012, tel. 213/473–7070) or the **County of Los Angeles Department of Parks and Recreation** (433 S. Vermont Ave., Los Angeles 90020, tel. 213/738–2961), which administers well over 100 open spaces.

The best place to stock up on pamphlets, books, and equipment is **Adventure 16** (11161 W. Pico Blvd., between Sepulveda Blvd. and I-405, tel. 310/473–4574), a well-stocked though expensive outdoor outfitter. This store maintains a good library of guidebooks and topographical maps for local attractions, employs a knowledgeable staff, and sponsors frequent wilderness outings, hikes, and slide shows. It also stocks free magazines about local outdoor opportunities. Serious multisport athletes will want to grab a free copy of the monthly magazine *Competitor* while you're here.

# SPECTATOR SPORTS

Los Angeles sports fans have the luxury of being fickle and demanding. With so many sports and so many teams from which to choose, loyalties are often short-lived. The number of Hollywood celebrities at a game is always a good indication of the Southland team's popularity. Using that litmus test, L.A. Lakers basketball (*see below*) leads the pack. During intermissions you can amuse yourself by scanning the crowd for season-ticket holder Jack Nicholson—look for the smirk and sunglasses. Or you might find yourself sharing an aisle with a lip-smacking, peanut-packing, wisecracking Jon Lovitz. The shiny new **Staples Center,** which opened in fall 1999, will be the new home for not only the Lakers but also the Clippers (more b-ball) and the Kings (ice hockey).

For cheaper admission and less celebrity-packed venues, catch some minor-league action or look for ads in the *Los Angeles Times* for brutal boxing and wrestling at the Forum and the Olympic Auditorium downtown.

For the best up-to-the-minute scores and sports coverage, check in with the *L.A. Times* daily. Buy tickets in person at the box office to avoid a service charge or pay additional for the convenience of phone ordering by credit card through Ticketmaster (tel. 213/480–3232 or 714/740–2000).

## BASEBALL

Bundle up—preferably in Dodger blue—if you are headed to a night game. All the overpriced beer and spicy Farmer John hot dogs in the world can't keep you warm if the fog rolls into Chavez Ravine, beloved home of the **Los Angeles Dodgers.** The stadium is northwest of downtown, off I–110 (Harbor Freeway), just north of U.S. 101. Seats start at $6 if you don't mind a nosebleed, and the regular season runs from April through early October. Games rarely sell out, but the best bet for good seats is to befriend loyal season-ticket holders, who are infamous for habitually leaving after the seventh-inning stretch. *Tel. 323/224–1400 for game information, 323/224–1448 for tickets.*

At the other end of town, the **Anaheim Angels** entertain Orange County in Edison International Field (2000 Gene Autry Way, near Disneyland, tel. 888/796–4256 or 714/634–2000 for ticket information, 714/940–2201 for directions to stadium). With the team as pennant-chasing contenders the last few seasons and the renovated stadium—complete with a theme-park-like waterfall over the outfield fence and baseball-related carnival games in the tunnels—fans have been flocking. The Angels still clash with rival Dodgers just before the regular season starts during the crosstown Freeway Series. The cheapest seats (left-field pavilion) cost $6.

## BASKETBALL

The **Los Angeles Lakers** are worshiped in their hometown (with or without the mercurial Dennis Rodman), and at press time their future is looking even brighter as they hit L.A.'s spanking new, state-of-the-art Staples Center. The Laker faithful are sitting pretty with 20,000 seats, 160 luxury suites, and 2,500 premier-level chairs—all the better to see Shaquille O'Neal and Kobe Bryant with, my dear. While the Lakers have never done quite as well since the retirement of their universally loved Magic Johnson, with the former Bulls coach Phil Jackson at the helm and their new digs beckoning, their rung at the top of the Southland's professional sports ladder is a sure bet. The Staples Center is located at 1111 S. Figueroa St., at the intersection of the I–110 (Harbor Freeway) and the I–10 (Santa Monica Freeway). Tickets start at $21 for individual games; the season runs October–April. *Tel. 213/742–7333 or 213/624–3100 for tickets and information.*

The **Clippers** are L.A.'s "other" basketball team. The city hasn't yet decided whether to love 'em or hate 'em, and this won't change until they win a championship (which they haven't come close to doing since fleeing San Diego years ago). Perhaps their move to L.A.'s new Staples Center (*see* the Lakers, *above*) will change all that, but don't hold your breath. Seats at the new venue start at $10 for individual games. *Tel. 213/742–7333 or 213/624–3100 for tickets and information.*

With the coming of the WNBA in 1997, the **Los Angeles Sparks** joined the professional roundball roster in southern California. While their records haven't been that memorable, the high-energy performances of stars like center Lisa Leslie and guard Tamecka Dixon keep their June–August season exciting. The Sparks play at the Great Western Forum (3900 W. Manchester Blvd., off the I–405 at Century Blvd.). *Tel. 310/330–2434 for information, 213/480– 3232 or 714/740–2000 (Ticketmaster) for tickets.*

There's also plenty of collegiate action in L.A. The **USC Trojans** (tel. 213/740–4672) slam their dunks at the L.A. Sports Arena, near their campus in Los Angeles. The **UCLA Bruins** (tel. 310/825– 2101) hoop it up at Pauley Pavilion, on the campus; both teams compete in the Pac 10 conference and regularly advance to the NCAA tourney. The high-flying, top-five-ranked **Loyola Marymount Lions** (tel. 310/338–4532) run and gun for coach Charles Bradley on their Westchester campus.

## BEACH VOLLEYBALL

If you spend enough time in L.A., you can be sure to catch one of the professional, take-no-prisoners volleyball competitions that take place April–September on the sand in Manhattan Beach and Hermosa Beach. Tournament dates and sites change year to year; call the **Association of Volleyball Professionals** (tel. 310/577– 0772) for more information.

If you are not going to be in town for a scheduled tourney, you can always head down to the South Bay, the home of most top U.S. players, and watch them practice their serves and spikes near the piers in Manhattan and Hermosa.

## FOOTBALL

Now that the Rams have transplanted their franchise to St. Louis and Al Davis's Raiders and their tattooed tailgaters have jumped ship for Oakland, Angelenos have to rely on college pigskin for their kicks. Luckily, one of the most heated college rivalries in the country—between the **USC Trojans** and the **UCLA Bruins**— provides ample entertainment. The competition alternates between the L.A. Coliseum and Pasadena's Rose Bowl and culminates on the Saturday before Thanksgiving, when the two teams clash and the winner walks away with a year's worth of bruises and bragging rights. Tickets to see either team play cost about $20–$30. To reach the UCLA ticket office call 310/825–2101; the USC ticket office answers at 213/740–4672; or call the Coliseum directly at 213/748–6131.

The winner of the Pac 10 conference and the Big 10 champs meet annually in the mother of all bowls, the Rose Bowl, in Pasadena on New Year's Day. Tickets for this blockbuster are traditionally hard to come by, but local scalpers never seem to be in short supply, especially if you have hundreds of bucks to shell out (look in the *L.A. Times* classifieds or in the *Yellow Pages* under "Ticket Brokers"). Perhaps more entertaining is the Beef Bowl, held every year at Lawry's steak house in Pasadena, where beefy linemen go head to head in a no-holds-barred prime-rib-eating competition.

## HORSE RACING

**Santa Anita Race Track** (Huntington Dr. and Colorado Pl., Arcadia, tel. 626/574–7223) is a great if out-of-the-way site to catch world-class Thoroughbred racing. It's open when Hollywood Park isn't (all of October and December 26–April 17). **Hollywood Park** (Century Blvd. and Prairie Ave., Inglewood, tel. 310/419–1500) is another favorite track, known for its occasional $1 Friday-night racing sessions and tacky giveaways. It's open from mid-April through mid-July and from mid-November until December 24 (*see* Inglewood *in* Chapter 2). For more restrained competition, check out the day (by satellite) and night (live) harness racing at **Los Alamitos** (4961 Katella Ave., just east of I–605, Anaheim, tel. 714/236–4400) year-round.

## ICE HOCKEY

Blood, gore, and random acts of violence are a **Los Angeles Kings** tradition. Since losing in the Stanley Cup finals in 1993 and subsequently losing recently retired superstar Wayne Gretzky, the team has fallen on hard times but still knows how to put up a good fight. In the Staples Center, the Kings's new home (*see* Basketball, *above*), they have 2,000 more hockey seats to fill than in their former Forum digs and thus 2,000 more fans to please. Tickets for home games, held October–April, start at $18.50. For tickets and schedule information, call 888/KINGSLA, *213/742–7333,* or 213/624–3100. Disney's professional promotional vehicle on skates, the **Mighty Ducks,** have overcome their laughable status as Mickey Mouse marketing tools and emerged as a halfway decent team. They push the puck around at the Pond (2695 E. Katella Ave., just off the I–57, Anaheim, tel. 714/704–2701 for information, 213/480–3232 or 714/740–2000 for tickets) October–April. Tickets start at $23.50.

For a look at the minor league, hit a slippery **Long Beach Ice Dogs** hockey game at the Long Beach Arena (300 E. Ocean Blvd., at the end of the I–701, tel. 562/423–3647). Their season runs from October through April, and tickets start at just $10.

## POLO

Long ago haute-culture cowboy Will Rogers built a polo field so his friends could enjoy an afternoon chukker and barbecue. The field is still in use at **Will Rogers State Historic Park** (1501 Will Rogers State Park Rd., tel. 310/454–8212), where you can pay $6 to park near the grounds or park on the street outside for free and walk in. Either way, make like Julia Roberts and Richard Gere in *Pretty Woman* and bring a picnic for maximal luxuriating on the sidelines. Games are played from April or May until September, Saturday 2–5 and Sunday 10–1 (weather permitting). The polo field is in the hills of Pacific Palisades, just off the 14000 block of Sunset Boulevard. *See* Hiking, *below,* for more information.

*Taka Radi, a combo of soccer and beach volleyball that may soon become a nonmedal Olympic sport, and capoiera, a rhythmic mix of music and combat, are often demonstrated on Venice Beach by bronzed Brazilian bicycle-kicking wonders.*

## ROLLER HOCKEY

When the ice melts, the Roller Hockey International season hits the composite rink, from early June to mid-August, featuring a fast-paced, hard-hitting, higher-scoring version of the original. While the L.A. Blades are no longer with us, the **Anaheim Bullfrogs** (The Pond, 2695 E. Katella Ave., tel. 714/704–2500) face off against eight other semiprofessional squads, comprised mostly of NHL minor leaguers who aren't afraid of a few fisticuffs. Tickets run $10–$30 and are available from the Pond box office window or Ticketmaster (tel. 213/480–3232 or 714/740–2000).

## SOCCER

Professional *fútbol* rolled into town in 1996, as the sport was still riding the local wave of excitement generated by the final match of the 1994 World Cup between Brazil and Italy, held in Pasadena. In 1999, in front of another sold-out Rose Bowl crowd, the U.S. women's team beat out China (in a penalty-kick shootout, no less) to capture their own World Cup. All this attention has only helped southern California's Major League Soccer (MLS) team, the **L.A. Galaxy,** which took the competition by storm in its inaugural year and has remained a formidable force from its home at the Rose Bowl, going all the way to the Western Conference Finals and posting some of the best records in the league. Dial 626/432–1540 for general information, or contact Ticketmaster (213/480–3232 or 714/740–2000) to purchase advance tickets. The season runs from April through October, and tickets are $8–$30.

The minor league **Orange County Zodiac** team plays fast-paced matches at the Santa Ana Bowl (602 N. Flower St., Santa Ana, off Flower St. and Civic Center Dr., tel. 714/479–0880). Their season runs from April through September, and tickets cost $5–$10.

# LEAGUE SPORTS AND PICKUP GAMES

For urban folk, pickup games and organized sports leagues are a convenient way to get the blood pumping without having to trek too far to do it. You can join pickup games on just about every public court and field in the Southland, though skill levels vary from place to place. Weekends and holidays draw the largest crowds, but temperate weekdays and long summer evenings generally guarantee activity. Get in touch with the local community center, parks department, or YMCA to get involved with programs in each neighborhood. When looking to break a sweat, the possibilities are only limited by your imagination: **Lawn bowling** with someone's grandparents at Recreation Park (home of the 1999 U.S. championships), at 1109 Federation Drive in Long Beach; an intense **chess** match on the outdoor boards near the Santa Monica Pier; or some zany avant-garde endeavor at Venice Beach all beckon.

# BASKETBALL

Coed pickup games are few and far between, and intensity levels vary dramatically. Women looking for same-gender competition should look around UCLA, USC, and Loyola Marymount. Peruse the courts in your 'hood carefully before you lace up those high-tops. Hoop activity on the following courts usually picks up weekday afternoons for the after-work crowd and on weekend mornings after 10. Almost every medium-to-large park and beach has a couple of hoops.

**WHERE TO PLAY** • Fierce competition and a veritable freak show of muscle-bound spectators and college-bound cagers congregate on the courts in **Venice Beach** for endless games. The lighted courts at Hermosa Beach's **Clark Park** are a good place to find a frisky postgrad crowd playing low-key full-court games until about 9 PM. **Polliwog Park,** on Manhattan Beach Boulevard just west of Aviation Boulevard in Manhattan Beach, sees lots of sweaty thirty-something action on weekends. **UCLA's men's gym** (tel. 310/825–1135 or 310/206–8307 for schedule) has three courts open to the public for free pickup games. The catch is that the schedule changes every week, so you'll need to call ahead to check availability. To find out about men's leagues in the city, contact the local Parks and Recreation Department (*see above*) or the YMCA (in Hollywood, 1553 Schrader Blvd., at Sunset, tel. 323/467–4161).

On the two lighted courts at **Marine Avenue Park,** at Aviation Boulevard in Manhattan Beach, angst-ridden investment brokers are often pitted against scrawny, tawny surfers who never wear watches, while real gym rats like to strut their stuff in Gardena's dank **Rush Gym** (1651 W. 162nd St., at La Salle Ave., tel. 310/217–9598) during free-for-all weekday afternoon (3–6) and Saturday (noon–4) jam sessions.

# BEACH VOLLEYBALL

Volleyball is *huge* in southern California. As regularly as the sun shines, tanned spikers of both sexes make the daily pilgrimage to the South Bay coast for some peppering and world-class competition. Permanent nets line the pristine sands near the piers in **Manhattan** and **Hermosa Beach,** with many other clusters scattered in between. Farther up the coastline, the courts on **State Beach,** in Santa Monica, are home to some of the best twosomes in the world. The skill level on all beaches runs the gamut from clumsy family reunions to top pros, and even with the abundance of courts, waits are still common. Contact the **California Beach Volleyball Association** (tel. 800/350–2282) for membership information and a schedule of its weekly weekend amateur tournaments. The association sponsors groovy grass-court events, too.

# RACQUET SPORTS

Most public parks have at least one tennis court, though many are not lighted. It costs $3–$7.50 per hour to play. Griffith Park maintains a dozen lighted courts at their **Riverside Pay Tennis Center** (3401 Riverside Dr., tel. 323/661–5318) as well as 12 unlighted at the **Vermont Pay Tennis Center** (2715 Commonwealth, tel. 323/664–3521). Both are free weekdays till 4; $6 per hour evenings and weekends. On the Westside, **La Cienega Tennis Center** (325 South La Cienega Blvd., across from La Cienega Park, tel. 310/550–4767) rents 16 lighted courts for $7.50 per hour prime time, $6.50 per hour off-peak. (Prime time is generally after 5 PM weekdays and in the mornings and evenings on weekends.) For about $10 an hour you can lead the club life at the **Racquet Center** (20 Lohman La., South Pasadena, tel. 323/258–4178), where lighted tennis and indoor racquetball courts are open to the public. **Studio City Golf and Tennis** (4141 Whitsett Ave., tel. 818/769–5263) offers 20 lighted courts for $5 per hour off-peak and $12 per hour prime time. For more information about clubs and local tournaments, contact the **Southern California Tennis Association** (Box 240015, Los Angeles, CA 90024, tel. 310/208– 3838).

# ROLLER HOCKEY

The rink at **Charles H. Wilson Community Park** (corner of Crenshaw Blvd. and Jefferson St., Torrance, tel. 310/320–9529) is ground zero for organized roller hockey. Call for league schedules and information; pickup games start every Friday night at 10:30 and each player chips in $7. Contact the **Torrance Skate Association** (tel. 310/320–9529) or stop by a **Golden Bear Skate Shop** (2383 W. Lomita Blvd., Lomita, tel. 310/534–3100; 10725 Washington Blvd., Culver City, tel. 310/838–6611) or **Skatey's Sports** (102 Washington Blvd., Venice, tel. 310/823–7971) for expert advice on leagues, clinics, and where to find pickup games to match your skill level.

**WHERE TO PLAY** • Vacant beachfront parking lots stretching from Newport Beach to Santa Monica are regularly appropriated as concrete rinks on weekday afternoons and all day on weekends. The empty upended trashcans in the **Ocean Park** beach lots in Santa Monica attract the best players in the city on a daily basis. In the Valley, **Rollerplex** (8345-C Hayvenhurst Pl., North Hills, tel. 818/830–4170) is the premier in-line venue, with a 14,000-square-ft indoor surface. Pickup games are played weekdays 1:30–3:30. Orange County's bandits on wheels, the Bullfrogs (*see* Spectator Sports, *above*), train at the **In-line Hockey and Sports Club of Tustin** (2681 Walnut Ave., right off I–241, tel. 714/508- -9999). They have just about everything you need; two rinks plus a mini warm-up rink, leagues, lessons, pickup games, and a pro shop.

## SOCCER

Soccer, like music, is truly an international language, and no recreational activity brings together a larger cross section of Angelenos. Every Sunday morning year-round, multicultural crowds gather citywide on any empty pitch area for impromptu games. League teams usually form along ethnic lines, but don't be surprised if you discover an Ethiopian goalkeeping for an Iranian side. **Offside Sport** (11710 Santa Monica Blvd., West L.A., tel. 310/207–4226) supplies the Westside with top-notch gear and information on citywide sporting opportunities. **Edward's Soccer** (5027 PCH, Torrance, tel. 310/375–7110) has been outfitting South Bay kickers for as long as owner Mary can remember. While you're here, check out the bulletin board and pick up a free copy of the *Soccer America Yellow Pages* for a nationwide listing of clubs, leagues, and some tournaments.

**WHERE TO PLAY** • Most sides are sponsored by sports bars and are made up of regular patrons, so if you are interested in signing on, your best bet is to patronize sporty watering holes, talk shop, and make friends. Expansive **Balboa Sports Center** (corner of Balboa and Burbank Blvds., just off the Ventura Freeway, Encino) fields lots of spirited competition on several lighted fields. For the occasional barefooted match, head to **Venice Beach,** where a no-hands Brazilian variation of soccer- volleyball is also often demonstrated by limber high-kicking spikers. For more coed pickup competition, look to the intramural fields on the UCLA, USC, and Loyola Marymount campuses on weekends.

# BICYCLING

Despite the local addiction to autos, you'll find several worthwhile biking areas. Riding conditions are best in outlying areas during the week and around deserted downtown on weekends. However, the combined foot, horse, and bicycle traffic in some of the state parks on weekends can make the I–405 Friday commute look like a walk in the park. The relatively level Strand, or Santa Monica Bikeway/South Bay Bicycle Trail (*see below*), which parallels some 45 mi of sandy coastline, is a good bet for sun and scenery anytime. There are three basic types of bike routes: designated paths away from vehicular roads; lanes that run on city streets but are marked with painted stripes along the shoulders; and lanes that are not separated from vehicular traffic but are marked with bike route signs and have wide, safe shoulders. At press time, the city was reassessing its bike paths; call 213/485–9957 to find out if they've issued corresponding maps. Wherever you ride, follow traffic rules and be especially wary of motorists—you're on their turf.

Unfortunately, getting to your starting point usually requires some type of fuel-injected personal transport; while some buses are fitted with racks, it's a hit-or-miss proposition. To take your bike on an MTA train or subway, you have to request a free Metro permit, which allows you to ride the trains anytime except weekdays 6–9 AM and 3–7 PM. Call 800/COMMUTE or 213/626–4455 to request the permit; it will arrive by mail.

Fortunately, fellow bicyclists realize they need to stick together when navigating the internal-combustion-dominated Southland: Look for the biannual **Bicycling Event Guide** at local bike shops and contact the **San Fernando Valley Bicycle Club** (tel. 818/787–2788) for support from fellow pedal revolutionaries. Gay folks: Call **Different Spokes** (tel. 213/896–8235) for information on organized recreational rides

# TARGET PRACTICE WITH THE LAPD

*Although the shooting range at the Los Angeles Police Revolver and Athletic Club (1880 Academy Dr., across from Dodger Stadium, Elysian Park, tel. 323/ 221–3101) is private, the café and training grounds—immortalized in the slapstick "Police Academy" flicks—are open to the public. The cocktail lounge opens on paydays to sworn-in members and their guests, and you can hold your next (well-armed?) wedding reception here.*

*If you're really interested in target practice, however, head to the Angeles Shooting Range (12651 Little Tujunga Canyon Rd., San Fernando Valley, tel. 800/499–4486), an outdoor rifle, pistol, and shotgun range that caters to all types of well-rounded firearm owners. It sponsors special days for women (Wednesday) and senior citizens (Tuesday). The L.A. Gun Club (1375 E. 6th St., downtown, tel. 213/612–0931) is an indoor range offering rentals, an extensive sales department, multilingual instruction, and loads of free parking.*

of a different bent in the L.A. county area. **Bikecology** (9006 W. Pico Blvd., near Beverly Hills, tel. 310/ 278–0915; 4220 Lincoln Blvd., Marina del Rey, tel. 310/821–0766) stocks a good selection of parts and accessories in several locations.

## EQUIPMENT RENTAL

Rentals aren't cheap, but they do run less than cars and allow for more hassle-free sightseeing and active sunbathing. Make sure the shop you choose includes with your bike rental a lock, a pump, spare tire tubes (or roadside service), and a helmet. You should also take a water bottle. When choosing your duds, keep in mind that most places in L.A. have relaxed dress codes that allow sporting attire. Consider what kind of riding you'll be doing (cruising the Strand, climbing the hills, or surveying the city streets) when selecting a bicycle. Generally speaking, a mountain bike will get you anywhere, but cruisers and street bikes can be more cost effective. Rental places in touristy areas tend to charge the same amount for mountain bikes or street bikes, but more serious bike shops may charge more for a mountain bike.

Bike rentals cost $5–$8 per hour ($14–$30 per day) at **Rental on the Beach** (3100 Ocean Front Walk, at Washington Blvd., Venice, tel. 310/821–9047) and **Spokes and Stuff** (1715 Ocean Front Walk, at Loews Hotel, Santa Monica, tel. 310/395–4748). Both spots have mountain bikes, cruisers, and tandem bikes. You can't miss **Perry's Beach Café and Rentals**'s five shops (tel. 310/372– 3138), which are sprinkled right along the Strand between Santa Monica and Venice. Both mountain bikes and cruisers rent for $6 per hour, $18 per day; tandems cost $30 for 10 hours. Near Griffith Park's southeast entrance, **Woody's Bicycle World** (3157 Los Feliz Blvd., just east of I–5, tel. 323/661–6665) rents mountain bikes by the day ($15) and the week ($65). On the weekends, bikes are available in the park at a rental place right next to the Ranger Headquarters (4730 Crystal Spring Dr., tel. 323/662–6573) for $5.50 an hour, $25 all day.

## WHERE TO BIKE

Rides can be divided into three types: coastal cruises, inland exploration, and outlying canyon and mountain climbing. You're best off sticking to one genre per day. If you only have time for one ride, make a beeline for any point along the autoless Strand—which runs north along the coast from the base of the

Palos Verdes Peninsula, through the South Bay, Venice, and Santa Monica—and cruise for the day. Inland, the areas around Hollywood, the Hollywood Hills, and downtown provide ample opportunity to sightsee while getting some exercise, albeit often in heavy auto traffic. To get away from the urban underbelly, you will need a mountain bike and a willingness to ascend. The proximity of Griffith Park (*see* Chapter 2) to the city, coupled with its numerous attractions and paved trails, makes it the favorite destination of cyclists in need of a respite from street-level smog. And the flat, paved path around the Hollywood Reservoir is an ideal escape from the traffic-clogged streets (*see* Hiking, *below*). Riding from Malibu and the Palos Verdes Peninsula offers mile after mile of scenic views along the Pacific Ocean but involves considerably more hills than the Strand. For in-depth and opinionated descriptions of possible rides, pick up a copy of *Short Bike Rides in and Around Los Angeles* (Globe Pequot Press; $12), by Robert Winning, or stop in a local bike shop and seek counsel from a fellow two-wheel traveler.

## THE PACIFIC COAST

The best riding L.A. has to offer is along the coast at either end of the city. Malibu's stretch of Pacific Coast Highway is heavenly but can become clogged with traffic on weekends; fortunately, the good shoulders and pavement provide ample room for passing stalled cars. You can begin anywhere along the 44-mi strip demarcated by **Topanga Canyon** to the east and the **Mulholland Highway** and Ventura county line to the west. The hilly tract parallels pristine sands and inviting surf. Parking is easiest to come by in Topanga Canyon or way up the coast, near the supermarket at **Trancas Canyon,** across the road from fabled **Zuma Beach.** In between you'll pass Pepperdine University, lots of great deserted beaches, and many stars' homes.

Above the other end of the smoggy spectrum, 26 mi of winding hills and clear ocean views beckon on the relatively untrammeled **Palos Verdes Peninsula.** On-street parking is in ample supply at the base of the peninsula near the intersection of **Palos Verdes Boulevard** and **Palos Verdes Drive North.** From here you can head out around the peninsula and not see one bit of commercial development, save for a few luxury condo developments. The circumnavigation, which includes a few steep ascents and takes at least three hours, is best attempted on a temperate morning when fog isn't obscuring the ocean-side views. Simply follow the four cardinal incarnations of Palos Verdes Drive clockwise while making a series of right-hand turns: north to east to south to west around the dramatic outcropping. Defined bike lanes come and go along the way, but drivers are generally considerate and accustomed to cyclists along this route (*see also* Palos Verdes *in* Chapter 2).

## THE STRAND

The popular paths paralleling the winding Pacific Coast offer some of the best riding in the region. The most entertaining is the cement Strand, a glorious 22-mi path (from Topanga Canyon in Malibu south to Palos Verdes), open year-round to cyclists of all levels of seriousness. Two-wheelers share the path with joggers, skateboarders, in-line skaters, walkers, and other nonvehicular traffic. The sunny beach scenery is uninterrupted, save for a couple of short city-street detours around the Marina del Rey Harbor and the Redondo Beach Pier. The ride can be done in a long leisurely afternoon, with plenty of time for stops along the way in various beachfront towns.

From north to south your Strand sights will include: **Will Rogers State Beach,** at Temescal Canyon; inland at Sunset Boulevard, the 22-acre **Temescal Canyon State Park,** which provides free parking, swimming, and good hiking; **Palisades Park,** on the bluff in Santa Monica, a great place to stop for refreshments; the **Ocean Front Walk** in Venice, packed with the proverbial people who make the world go 'round; the undesirable scenery (and smell) of El Segundo (beware the sewage treatment plant); the piers in **Manhattan** and **Hermosa,** which both provide nice views of beach volleyball courts and the breezy ocean; and finally, the bluffs of the **Palos Verdes Peninsula.** Unless you have someone meet you at one end of the ride, a round-trip journey is imminent, but don't fret—the scenery looks completely different in the opposite direction. Keep in mind that parking is expensive on the beach, so it is best to ditch your car inland and bike out to the Strand.

## GRIFFITH PARK

**Travel Town,** a collection of old trains in the northeast corner of the park, is the best place to park your car for making forays into the surrounding hills. Bicyclists are officially restricted to paved byways within the park. There are two unmaintained roads that are closed to vehicular traffic: the 5-mi Mt. Hollywood Road, which branches off Griffith Park Drive near the Travel Town Museum, and the 5-mi Vista del Valle Drive, which you pick up from Commonwealth Canyon Drive near the Roosevelt Golf Course. Both are easy rides that offer good views and plenty of solitude.

For an overview of the park's main attractions, head out of the Travel Town parking lot onto Zoo Drive and continue east for a mile and a half, where the road becomes Crystal Springs Drive. A little more than a mile past the zoo the road intersects with Griffith Park Drive (across from the visitor center); take a right at the stop sign and follow the road around to the left. Here you have the option of heading into the hills past the Wilson Golf Course to the Mineral Wells picnic area, perched a steep, panoramic couple of miles atop the hill approaching Mt. Hollywood. The descent toward Travel Town follows Griffith Park Drive down the north side of what is known colloquially to cyclists as Trash Truck Hill, which takes you past, not surprisingly, oncoming dump trucks and the local landfill. If you bypass the climb and stick to the lowlands, you'll hit busy Los Feliz Boulevard a mile and a half later. Here it's time to turn around, unless you dare dash across the street to check out the ebullient **William Mulholland Memorial Fountain** (only worth a look if it is spurting, which is not often). Back on Crystal Springs Drive, heading north after a U-turn, you'll pass lots of children's amusements and 2 mi later come upon a fork, at which you make a sharp right, leading to the **Autry Museum of Western Heritage,** a worthwhile stopover (see Griffith Park in Chapter 2). Bear left out of the museum parking lot and pedal about 2 mi west back toward Travel Town. If you opt to continue past Travel Town, you can make a 4-mi loop on Forest Lawn Drive to Barham Boulevard and back, traveling past two behemoth cemeteries (**Forest Lawn Memorial Park** and **Mount Sinai Memorial Park**), while enjoying views of the Los Angeles River and the **Disney** and **Warner Bros.** studios on its northern bank (see Studios in Chapter 2).

Another noteworthy ride departs Travel Town for the **Griffith Observatory.** It requires an extended, gradual climb, but spectacular views should help take your mind off the pain. Burst left (south) out of the Travel Town lot uphill onto Griffith Park Drive. Less than a mile later, resist the temptation to continue downhill over Trash Truck Hill and steel yourself for a winding Tour de France–esque climb as you turn right onto Mount Hollywood Drive. Four leg-burning miles later you'll have passed lots of fantastic scenery and be ready to take a refreshing right on Observatory Drive. Okay, there's one more short climb, but the Observatory is only a half mile ahead. From here you can backtrack quickly to Travel Town or press forward for another hour or so and make a loop of the entire park, heading out of the Observatory parking lot down the same Observatory Drive, making a left on scenic Western Canyon Drive, continuing onto Fern Dell Drive, and making a left onto traffic-laden Los Feliz Boulevard 1 mi later. Two congested miles to the east you'll want to cut a hectic left onto Crystal Springs Drive, which leads 4 mi north back to Zoo Drive and the familiarity of Travel Town.

## HOLLYWOOD

This 11-mi ride takes you sightseeing through the heart of old Hollywood, the ethnic Fairfax enclave, along the Miracle Mile of museums, through the posh Hancock Park neighborhood, past Hollywood Memorial Cemetery, and back to ground zero. It should only be attempted during the day by those with a strong tolerance for inconsiderate auto traffic. Start from the parking lot next to the **Capitol Records Tower** (1750 N. Vine St.; see Hollywood in Chapter 2). (For a quick 2-mi side trip to the Hollywood Bowl, you can ride up Vine Street to Franklin Avenue, take a left and then a right on Highland Avenue, and follow the signs while watching out for heavy traffic.) To begin the big trip, though, head right (uphill) out of the lot on Vine toward Franklin and make a right, another quick right on Argyle Avenue, and yet another right on Hollywood Boulevard. Cruise for a mile past all the requisite tourist traps until you hit La Brea Avenue, where you make a left and then another left onto Sunset Boulevard, where you'll find the **Hollywood High School** campus. Turn back and go 1 mi westward, turning left onto Fairfax Avenue to enter the most kosher quarter of the city. You'll pass Fairfax High School on your left. A mile and a half south of Melrose Avenue, look for **CBS Television City** and the **Farmers' Market,** between Beverly Boulevard and 3rd Street. Keep heading south on Fairfax for another mile until Wilshire Boulevard, hang a left, and look for the **L.A. County Museum of Art** and farther along, the **La Brea Tar Pits,** both on your left. Peddle another 1½ mi east on Wilshire as you enter residential Hancock Park and turn left on Rossmore Avenue. Ahead 1 mi, between Beverly Boulevard and Melrose Avenue, lies the ritzy Wilshire Country Club. Veer right on Melrose, roll past **Paramount Studios** on your left, and execute a left on Van Ness Avenue, where you'll soon pass the **Hollywood Memorial Park** cemetery, behind Paramount on the left-hand side. On the home stretch orchestrate a left onto Santa Monica Boulevard, cross Gower Street, and head right up Vine. After crossing Sunset half a mile later, you'll find yourself safely at home under the towering stack of Capitol Records.

## FARTHER AFIELD

For some serious solitude and rural terrain, your best bet is to head for the **Angeles National Forest,** in the northern reaches of L.A. County. There is little traffic and no smog to speak of, but the weather can be extreme, and the hills pose a serious challenge. The rustic region north and east of the I–5 (Golden State Freeway) and Highway 14 (Antelope Valley Freeway) interchange is ripe for exploration. The Carl's Jr. parking lot, just off the San Fernando Road exit in Santa Clarita, is a favorite stop for cyclists headed for the **Canyon Country** area. Contact the **Placerita Canyon Nature Center** (tel. 805/259–7721) office for more information on rides through the National Forest and environs. And remember: don't stay here after dark.

# HIKING

One of Los Angeles's many amazing attributes is the proximity of natural beauty to its sprawling urban blight. Ignore the famous X song "Nobody Walks in L.A.": Replace your platforms with a pair of sensible shoes and check out one of the many worthwhile hikes in and around the city. If you don't have access to a car, you can find rambling retreats as close as the Hollywood Hills. Even in a car, though, there's no need to travel more than an hour to scale massive mountains or descend craggy canyons in search of waterfalls, rock pools, and—smog notwithstanding—scenic views. Keep in mind that Los Angeles is a desert, and even a short walk in the hot summer months can tax your system, so make sure you always carry a lot of water. Avoid the temptation to work on your tan while you hike: A hat will help keep you hydrated, and you'll appreciate the sunblock when you hit the shower later that evening.

*Models and musclemen, unicyclers and disco-dancing roller skaters, break-dancers and sidewalk surfers: Every type of person employing every imaginable kind of locomotive device passes through Venice on the Strand during the course of a sunny Saturday.*

## WHERE TO HIKE

If you have come to Los Angeles to do a lot of hiking (which isn't as peculiar as it may sound), you should look into Dennis Gagnon's *Hike Los Angeles, Volumes I and II* (Western Tanager Press; $9.95 each), Jerry Schad's *Afoot and Afield in Los Angeles County* (Wilderness Press, $14.95), or Robert Stone's *Day Hikes in Los Angeles, Malibu and Hollywood* (Ics Books, $9.95) for a wide variety of well-detailed treks. Should you want to stay close to central Los Angeles, you'll find the Hollywood Hills, the Santa Monica Mountains, and the coast the most convenient getaways. If you're in the Pasadena area, you'll have easy access to the surprisingly wild San Gabriel Mountains and the gentler San Gabriel Valley. Put the gnarly images of Moon Unit Zappa's "Valley Girl" behind you and enjoy scenic beauty in the suburbia of the San Fernando Valley. Farther afield, look into some more extensive hikes in the Verdugo or Santa Susana mountains.

### THE HOLLYWOOD HILLS

Head for the hills when the throngs of undiscovered starlets in the Hollywood flats start to get you down. Walking north from Franklin Avenue (between La Brea and Highland avenues) will put you in lovely residential neighborhoods near such sights as the Hollywood Reservoir, the HOLLYWOOD sign, and Runyon Canyon. Driving to the base of your hike is not a bad idea, if you have the option, so you can save your energy for the vistas of the less-developed highlands.

**THE HOLLYWOOD SIGN** • Due to vandalism and starlet suicide, the HOLLYWOOD sign is now off-limits, but the Mt. Lee Trail will take you right by the famous cockeyed letters and give you some lovely views along the way. The sign was first put up in 1923 to advertise Harry Chandler's Hollywoodland real estate development. When the last four letters fell down in an earthquake, it was considered just as well, and the sign has stuck around as the symbol of the neighborhood and the massive industry it spawned. To reach the Mt. Lee trailhead, drive north up Beachwood Drive from Franklin Avenue. When you reach Hollyridge Drive (1¾ mi later), park and walk 50 yards up Hollyridge, until you find the wide trail on your left. The walk is approximately 3 mi round-trip and has a steady incline, but nothing too strenuous. In the course of your walk, you will be able to view the HOLLYWOOD sign from many angles, as well as the flats of Burbank below. Early in your walk look to your right to see the dome of the Griffith Park Observatory. Keep going straight and uphill until you reach an unmarked intersection, where you will turn left on a fire road (actually Mulholland Highway), which will lead you to the paved Mt. Lee Drive. Take Mt. Lee Drive until you reach the fence that seals the sign from the public. Climbing the fence is strictly illegal and probably not worth the risk.

**HOLLYWOOD RESERVOIR TRAIL** • As a walk, run, or bike ride, the reservoir (a.k.a. **Lake Holly-wood**) trail is probably one of the best spots to shake your bones in all L.A. The 4-mi flat walk around the reservoir provides great views of hillside mansions (including the spread once owned by Madonna and its controversial striped retaining wall), the HOLLYWOOD sign, and, of course, the reservoir itself. The park opens around 6:30 AM. Make sure you finish up your walk by sunset, as the majority of the path is locked after dark, and it's possible to get stuck inside if you don't leave by the time posted on the sign at the reservoir entrance. The reservoir is on Lake Hollywood Drive, which you can reach by exiting U.S. 101 at Barham Boulevard (near Universal City) and going north. Head east on Lake Hollywood Drive, making sure you stay the course as it makes some tricky turns. Park when you see the gate to the reservoir and enter to begin your power walk or stroll. No sight in L.A. is worth its salt unless it's been featured in a major motion picture, and this area has a particularly whopping credit: Roman Polanski's *China-town*. In reality (for what *that's* worth in Los Angeles), the reservoir was built by the god of Los Angeles water, William Mulholland. Although high fences and trees will obscure your view of the water for much of the walk, when you do catch a glimpse, you will be glad that L.A. residents have put up a fight to keep the lake uncovered despite the city's fear of vandalism and evaporation. Even though you can't reach the reservoir, the walk is worthwhile just to see a large amount of fresh, clean water in the midst of the desert. The foliage will shield you from the worst of the Hollywood sunshine.

**RUNYON CANYON** • Take this hike for a comprehensive view of Hollywood and the surrounding areas; it's also a strenuous run. Be aware that you'll have plenty of canine company; in 1999 Runyon Canyon was designated an official off-leash dog park and its trails runneth over with man's best friend, particularly on the weekends. Go north (uphill) on Fuller Avenue from Hollywood Boulevard (Fuller is between La Brea and Fairfax avenues) until you see the gated entrance to Runyon Park. Like the reservoir, the access to this walk can be locked up after dark, so make sure you allow time to get up and down before sunset. Now-forgotten movie star John McCormick owned the canyon in 1929 and built a mansion there that has since been razed: The area is more worthwhile for its views and invigorating uphill climb than for its historical importance. If you are ambitious and healthy, the path is smooth and wide enough for running, and if you don't mind a steep downhill stretch, you can make a 3-mi loop of the trail. Otherwise, you will have to turn around when you round the corner from the west wall to the east wall of the canyon. Either way, you begin your hike by going straight from the entrance to the park until you see a wide dirt path to your left. Take this trail up until it meets a concrete road, which will bring you up the canyon's west side. You can turn around at the top, or you can look for a steep downhill path that will take you down the canyon's east side. If you do the loop, you will end up at the ruins of a tennis court from which you will have a marvelous view of Hollywood, Century City, and even downtown L.A. If you forego the loop and backtrack down, you can still reach the tennis courts by taking a left at one of the many westward trails at the bottom of the canyon. If you're running, look for the one that is wide and gentle.

## SANTA MONICA MOUNTAINS

The Santa Monica Mountains are an unlikely swath of natural beauty that extend right into the heart of Los Angeles. Although the climate is Mediterranean, the plants suggest more of a prairie, with golden grasses and gnarled live oak. Some of Los Angeles's best-known natural beauty spots, such as Topanga Canyon and Leo Carrillo State Park, are within the bounds of the Santa Monicas, or you can head farther out of the city to the wilder terrain of Point Mugu State Park.

**WILL ROGERS STATE HISTORIC PARK: INSPIRATION POINT** • Who knows how many of Will Rogers's famed witticisms came to him while he and his wife hiked or rode horses along the well-marked Inspiration Point Trail from their Pacific Palisades ranch. If you pay the $6 entrance fee to enter the park and investigate the Will Rogers home (*see* Malibu *in* Chapter 2), save some time for this beautiful 2-mi loop trail, which takes you gently to the highest point in West Los Angeles. Designed by Rogers as a riding path for the family, it makes for a peaceful, scenic walk. On an average smoggy day you can still see the Santa Monica Bay and the San Gabriel Mountains, and if divine Providence makes the air unusually clear, you can see as far as Catalina Island. To reach the park, take Sunset Boulevard 4½ mi east from PCH and turn left when you see the brown sign marking the road to the park. The walk begins and ends behind the riding stables. If you're looking for a longer trip, the path meets up with Backbone Trail, which connects to Topanga State Park (*see* Rustic Canyon Trail, *below*).

**RUSTIC CANYON TRAIL** • Lots of greenery and the Rustic Creek make this a nice trip for the more serious hiker. Start along the Will Rogers Inspiration Point Trail described above, but after you've enjoyed your view and descended a ways, follow the path marked as the Backbone Trail. When you reach a three-way junction, you'll leave the Backbone by taking a sharp right, descending steeply down to the bottom of Rustic Canyon. You will come to a white barn and an unmarked intersection where you will bear right (the trail remains at the bottom of the canyon for a while). Continue along the trail past a dam and over a bridge until you see the Rogers home, where you began. This is a 6-mi loop with some rough downhill sections, and the poorly preserved trail can be muddy or even underwater. So if you're not interested in a rugged experience, stick to the Inspiration Point Trail. Abbot Kinney, the man whose vision created the canals and identity of Venice Beach, also left his mark on Rustic Canyon, this time using ideas from Australia. He planted the canyon with eucalyptus, which, sadly for him, only gave the area its distinctive odor, not the massive timber profits he anticipated.

**MALIBU CREEK STATE PARK ROCK POOL** • Bring your bathing suit—the Rock Pool will be a welcome sight at the end of what can be a very hot and dusty trail. Despite the heat, the walk is gentle, almost level, and about 3½ mi round-trip from the parking lot. To reach the park, exit U.S. 101 at Las Virgenes Road and go south 4 mi to the park entrance (about a quarter mile south of Mulholland Highway), where you will have to pay a $5-per-vehicle entrance fee. The trail is marked by a sign below the parking lot, and following it should be pretty straightforward. Just go right along the high road when you reach an intersection, and before long you'll see a sign directing you to the Rock Pool. The wide path makes a gentle curve through golden grass and live oak, then descends into the dramatic gorge that forms the Rock Pool. Like much of L.A., Malibu Creek State Park has achieved most of its historical significance from its relation to the movies. The tracts of land that now make up the park were formerly owned by Ronald Reagan (his pre–Santa Barbara ranch), Bob Hope, and 20th Century Fox, and of course the area has been used in several movies. If you were to take the trail past the Rock Pool, you would see the site where parts of the *M*A*S*H* television series, including the eternally replayed opening scene, were filmed. The Rock Pool itself was a location in *Swiss Family Robinson* and a handful of Tarzan movies. You have to appreciate a piece of land that can pass for Korea, Switzerland, and the African jungle, despite its own status as a coastal semidesert, or you have to chuckle at us moviegoers who can't tell the difference. You can make your visit into a nice day trip by driving south on Las Virgenes Road (which becomes Malibu Canyon Road) when you exit the park. This is one of the most spectacular short drives in L.A., and it gives you a chance to see some of the rugged beauty of Malibu's interior. When you hit PCH, take a right and consider replenishing at the Malibu Seafood Patio Cafe (*see* Pacific Palisades and Malibu *in* Chapter 3) and then heading across the highway to lounge about on Coral Beach.

*The cluttered bulletin board toward the front of the REI sporting goods store (18605 Devonshire St., Reseda Blvd., Northridge, tel. 818/ 831–5555) is a singles hot spot—an ideal place to hook up with your next climbing partner, some used gear, or a free dog.*

## THE COAST

If you spend too much time in Burbank or downtown, you may forget that Los Angeles is one enormous beach town. Although the beaches in the South Bay, Venice, and Santa Monica are urban and developed, head up the coast to Malibu for some beautiful coastal walks that can be downright pristine.

**MALIBU LAGOON AT SURFRIDER STATE BEACH** • You can walk a mile or so around the lagoon and down to the Malibu Pier or, tide permitting, 2–3 mi up the coast where the beach narrows. Start your walk at Malibu Lagoon State Beach, at the intersection of PCH and Cross Creek Road. You can avoid the $6 park entrance fee by parking on PCH, an easier feat early on a weekday but always worth a try. This is a mellow walk that allows you to look at the birds and wetland vegetation on the lagoon side and the surfers in the ocean. If you come Wednesday–Saturday (11–3), you can also check out the **Malibu Lagoon Museum** at Adamson House (*see* Malibu *in* Chapter 2). If not, you will still walk by the house's beautifully landscaped lawns and gardens, which form a welcome contrast to the sand and marsh of the Malibu Lagoon. Walking around the lagoon and down the coast brings you to the Malibu Pier, a ghostly contrast to Santa Monica's bustling Pacific Ocean Park. If the tide is out, you can walk up the coast from the lagoon as far as the gated (and hence exclusive) Malibu Colony, home of real-life movie stars and fictional Raymond Chandler characters.

**ZUMA–DUME TRAIL** • Bring your bathing suit to enjoy one of Malibu's most secluded beaches, inaccessible by car. Take PCH to Westward Beach Road. Head toward the water and either park along the road or in the parking lot ($6) at **Point Dume State Beach.** Walk either through the parking lot or along the more scenic beach until the pavement ends and you see a trail heading up the point. There will be many trails off to the side, but you want to continue until you reach the top of the hill, where you will see water on all sides. If it is whale migration season (*see* Whale-Watching, *below*), this is an ideal place to spot the giant mammals. Head down the trail toward the cove on the other side of the point. You can make a day of it in relative isolation at the beach or continue walking around the point to Paradise Cove, where there are a pier and a restaurant. Retrace your steps to the parking lot when you're done for the day.

## SAN GABRIEL MOUNTAINS AND VALLEY

In the eastern part of Los Angeles stand the majestic San Gabriel Mountains, so pretty it's hard to believe they're to blame for trapping smog in the city. Many hikes in the mountains are rugged and provide backcountry views. Valley walks tend more toward the gentle and the landscaped, but both are worth the drive, especially if your sightseeing has brought you to the Pasadena area.

**CHANTRY FLAT TO STURTEVANT FALLS •** This is not the hike to take if you'd like to fancy yourself in the wilderness, as the presence of 80 or so cabins in the canyon reminds you of humanity's stewardship over the land. The trail itself starts off fully exposed to the sun, but as you descend into the canyon, you will be protected by trees that provide not only shade but a very pleasant scent; bring a bathing suit so you can stand beneath the cascading water of the impressive waterfall or swim in the pool it forms below. Take I–210 to Arcadia and exit at Santa Anita Avenue. Go north (uphill) to the road's end, at the Chantry Flats parking lot. The clearly marked trail begins downhill from the lot and continues along and across the creek to the falls. If you want peace and quiet, go during the week; on weekends the falls are a hot spot for locals. The trail makes for a 3½-mi round-trip and is steep in places but well maintained. Alas, since you are hiking to a canyon, you will experience the bliss of downhill first and will have a somewhat strenuous and potentially very hot return hike.

**EATON CANYON FALLS •** It's a 3-mi round-trip journey to Eaton Canyon Falls, named for a judge who cultivated a vineyard on this land. The easy terrain makes it a popular hike, so if you want to avoid crowds, try to come on a weekday. Take I–210 to the Altadena Drive exit in Pasadena. Go north for 1¾ mi along Altadena until you see the first entrance to Eaton Canyon Park on your right. The trail begins north of the parking lot (head toward the mountains). Just follow the wide dirt road along the dry, rocky creek bed winding for a while beneath a stretch of oak trees. After a mile of easy walking, you will see a bridge. (If you want to forgo the falls in favor of a more strenuous 8-mi hike up Mt. Wilson, take the trail to the bridge and swing a sharp right.) At this point you will probably be sufficiently hot and dusty to appreciate a waterfall, so take the narrow trail that splits off to the left and takes you underneath the bridge. Here, the concept of a trail is a bit dubious, as you will be following the stream. You should be able to navigate your way with dry feet by sticking to the bank, but you will be forced to cross several times before reaching Eaton Canyon Falls. Naturalist John Muir felt these were the finest falls in the San Gabriels, and he may just have been right. Although they don't have as deep a swimming hole as nearby Sturtevant Falls (*see above*), they cascade from a greater height and with a more impressive force. You can wade in the water or just meditate a while before backtracking to your car.

**LOS ANGELES COUNTY AND STATE ARBORETUM •** While taking in the fantasyland that is L.A., it would only be appropriate to hike through one entirely simulated environment. At the Los Angeles County and State Arboretum, you can wander from a piece of South Africa to the Australian outback and even through a bit of tropical forest. Throughout the park beautiful indigo peacocks with the temperament of street pigeons give you a surly eye as they wait for food (feeding them, however, is against the rules). Perhaps the highlight of the arboretum is the tropical greenhouse, with carnivorous-looking orchids and a pond full of brilliant Chinese goldfish. Although there is more than one logical way to wend through the gardens, if you go everywhere, you will probably only walk just more than a mile. Some paths are paved, others are sanded, and even though the entire area is only 40 acres, it's easy to spend the better part of a day here, strolling or sitting on a bench. To get to the arboretum, go east from Pasadena on I–210, exit in Arcadia on Baldwin Avenue and go south, and you will soon see the entrance.

## SAN FERNANDO VALLEY

"Grody to the max," an old phrase brought to the provinces by the song "Valley Girl," is not a bad turn of phrase to describe the San Fernando Valley, the birthplace of the infamous lingo. Nonetheless, when stuck among the smog and malls of L.A. suburbia, seeking out a little nature will make you feel better.

**SEPULVEDA DAM RECREATION AREA •** You can take an easy 3-mi round-trip walk here, during which you'll see plants beyond the lawn life of the suburbs and—even more spectacular—a section of the Los Angeles River that actually looks like a river. Exit U.S. 101 at Balboa Boulevard in Encino and go north a half mile until you cross a bridge over the river and see a sign to your right signaling the recreation area. Walk along a dirt path that runs beside the river, taking note of the actual water therein and the plant and bird life that makes the area their home. When you hit the Burbank Boulevard bridge, cross over and continue your walk along the opposite bank. After passing two golf courses (this is not wilderness hiking), you will wind your way back to the Burbank bridge and your car. Although this hike doesn't merit a long trip out of your way, it's a nice excursion if you happen to be in the Valley.

# VERDUGO MOUNTAINS

Although smack in the center of metropolitan Los Angeles above Burbank, the Verdugo Mountains are among the least known of local getaways. Their relative obscurity is a result in part of the ruggedness of their terrain. Although the highest mountain in the range is less than 3,500 ft, the peaks get steep toward the top. Hikes in the Verdugos are on the long and strenuous side. Save these walks for a day when you have a lot of time and energy to spend.

**BEAUDRY CANYON LOOP** • This is a strenuous 6-mi hike that will take you by a small creek and past vistas of the Valley. Take I–210 to the Verdugo Boulevard exit and go south. Stay right when the road forks, putting you on La Cañada Boulevard. When you reach Santa Maria Avenue, take a right, then another right on Country Club Drive. Take a left on Beaudry Boulevard and park near the intersection of Beaudry Terrace, where you will see the trailhead. The paved beginning of the trail will take you past a vehicle barrier where the asphalt ends. When you reach a fork, bear right and begin the climb. In a mile take a left on Verdugo Fire Road, which takes you up and then down again to another fork, where you will head left to a point a quarter mile from the trailhead. Go back the way you came to find your car.

**LA TUNA CANYON TRAIL** • In the course of this relatively steep 6-mi trip, you will climb in and out of canyons to the top of ridges affording impressive views of the San Fernando Valley below. To reach the trailhead, take I–210 to the La Tuna Canyon Road exit in Tujunga. Go west for 1 mi past a sign for the Santa Monica Mountains Conservancy. After another 3/10 of a mile, take the turnout to your left and park. The trail takes you in and out of two canyons. At the bottom of the second canyon, take a steep dirt road up and away to the ridge top and a junction with Verdugo Fire Road. Take a left and continue your ascent, making sure to enjoy the views on your way up. After passing the second-highest peak in the Verdugos, you will reach another junction where you'll take a left and begin your trip downward along (unmarked) Hostetter Fire Road. Eventually the road becomes paved; continue along it until reaching La Tuna Canyon Road. Go west for another 1.3 mi until you return to the trailhead.

# SANTA MONICA MOUNTAINS

From the peaks of the Santa Monicas (north of L.A.), there are gorgeous views of the ocean and surrounding ranges. Although we list just one trail, the area has a lot of hiking potential; call the Santa Monica Mountains Conservancy (tel. 310/589–3200) for more information.

**ZUMA LOOP TRAIL** • One of the prettiest hikes in L.A. is the Zuma Loop Trail, which takes you on a 2½-mi journey around the mouth of the only undeveloped canyon in the Malibu area. Take PCH north 1 mi past Kanan-Dume Road to Bonsall Drive, where you will take a right. Follow the road for a mile past where the pavement ends; you'll see a parking area and a trailhead. Walk a short distance until you reach a junction; turn left. The first portion of the trail is well marked. Follow the signs for the Zuma Loop Trail to the top of the ridge, enjoying the vista and the views of Zuma Canyon below. The signs disappear as you make your descent, but when you reach the bottom of the canyon, cross the creek bed, take the creek-side trail to your right, and head south out of the canyon. If you take only one hike in L.A., this should be it. You will see very few people, lots of fat and frisky lizards, and some of the finest scenery in the area.

# SANTA SUSANA MOUNTAINS

The Santa Susana Mountains look like a piece of Arizona in the middle of the San Fernando Valley. You can hike among precarious rock structures and mesas in a very desertlike climate. Some of the best views are from the road, so keep your eyes peeled as you drive from suburbia into the sands beyond.

**DEVIL CANYON TRAIL** • Despite its ominous name, Devil Canyon is a creek-side oasis in the midst of the severe desert landscape. Take Highway 118 to the Topanga Canyon Boulevard exit. Just north of the freeway you will see a small unpaved parking lot; leave your car and begin your trek. Walk west from the parking lot along a narrow trail until you see a wide asphalt road. Continue down the pavement until it gives way to a wide dirt path, which takes you directly into the bottom of the canyon. The cool shade of the canyon bottom will surprise you after the severe heat above. Enjoy the foliage as you head up the creek. You can continue along until the trail ends at a gate, then retrace your path to your car. If you go the entire way, the round-trip distance is 4½ mi, and it's never very steep.

# FANCY FOOTWORK

*If you can read a map while running at breakneck speed, dodging tree limbs, and leaping over fallen logs, you've got what it takes to go orienteering with the Los Angeles Orienteering Club. Once a month they lay out obstacle-laden courses around the greater L.A. area and leave participants to find their way to a series of checkpoints in the wilderness as fast as their feet can carry them, armed only with a compass, a topographical map, and their wits. For more information contact Clare Durand at 818/769–0906 or write c/o Joel Thompson, 5131 W. 134th Place, Hawthorne, 90250.*

**SANTA SUSANA PASS STAGECOACH TRAIL** • The most challenging part of this hike is finding the trailhead and then sticking with it amid all the confusing unsigned junctions. If you succeed in staying on the path, you will be rewarded by a plaque marking the site of one of the westward trail's trickiest stretches: Devil's Slide. But even if you don't find the historic site, you will be rewarded with views of the spectacular rocky landscape and the incongruous suburbia below. Take U.S. 101 to the Topanga Canyon Boulevard exit in Woodland Hills. Go north 6½ mi on Topanga Canyon and take a left on Devonshire Street. You will enter Chatsworth Park after ¾ of a mile. Park and walk toward the mountains, navigating a course roughly down the center of the green lawn. You will come to a gravel path with a rusty water tower above you to the right. Ascend the path until you reach the paved road. Go right for a few hundred feet until you see a break in the picket fence marked by two telephone poles. Take the dirt path to the left of the telephone poles and do your best to stay centered, going up when in doubt. Even if you don't meet this goal, you can scramble on the rocks and poke around the many side paths that lead around the various mesalike formations. Continue down the way you came: The park should be visible below, making your return trip easier to navigate. The trip to the top of Devil's Slide and back is 2½ mi.

# HORSEBACK RIDING

With miles of bridle trails in Los Angeles, most notably in Griffith Park and in the coastal mountains, renting a horse can be a fun way to kill an afternoon—especially if you've got secret cowpoke aspirations. Griffith Park is a great place to ride, with 54 mi of trails offering beautiful views of the Hollywood Hills and below. Nearby rentals include the **Los Angeles Equestrian Center** (480 Riverside Dr., Burbank, tel. 818/840– 8401), which will rent you a steed starting at $15 an hour and provide lessons for considerably more. Other options are **Sunset Stables** (3400 N. Beechwood Dr., Hollywood, tel. 323/464–9612) and **J.P. Stables** (1914 Mariposa St., Burbank, tel. 818/843– 9890), both of which rent horses starting at $15 an hour. In Malibu, **Adventures on Horseback** (31811 Mulholland Hwy., Malibu, tel. 818/706–0888) offers horse rentals along with guided tours for about $25 per hour and up; they also give lessons. At **The Connemara Ranch** (5904 Bonsall Dr., Malibu, tel. 310/457–5838) knowledgeable guides lead you through the Santa Monica Mountains on horses outfitted with orthopedic saddles for the animals' comfort; it costs about $60 for a 1½ hour tour. Lessons in both English and Western riding are available, too.

# IN-LINE SKATING

Arguably the best rollerblade experience on earth can be found along the beach path known as the **Strand,** which stretches from Pacific Palisades to Manhattan Beach and provides nearly 22 mi of perfectly paved flat surface with a view. Hillier options exist inland at **Griffith Park,** and you can always take the urban guerrilla option of striking out on the city streets. If you are serious about seeing L.A. from your blades, you might want to look into Liz Miller's exhaustive guide, *California In-Line Skating* (Foghorn Press; $19.95).

If you're into distance skating, hook up with Santa Monica's **Friday Night Skate** (tel. 310/577–5283). On the first and third Friday of every month, skaters gather at Ocean and Colorado boulevards near the entrance of the Santa Monica Pier at 8 PM. From this starting point, everyone zips off on a 10-mi route through the city streets—you just follow the pack, behind the guy with the huge boom box strapped to his body.

## EQUIPMENT RENTAL

**Sea Mist Rentals** (1619 Ocean Front Walk, across from Santa Monica Pier, tel. 310/395–7076), open daily 9–8 in summer, rents blades for $5 for the first hour, $4 each additional hour. The maximum daily price is $14. **Perry's Beach Café and Rentals** (tel. 310/372–3138) has five shops along the Strand from Santa Monica to Venice and rents skates for $6 an hour, $18 a day. If you want to start inland at Griffith Park, you can rent blades at the park's **Ranger Headquarters** (*see* Bicycling, *above*) on the weekends for $5 an hour, $12 all day. All of these outfitters include protective gear (helmets, kneepads, etc.) in the cost of the rental.

## WHERE TO SKATE

You can enjoy the beauty of the Pacific as well as the splendor of some freakish and fine humanity along the 22-mi **Strand,** between Pacific Palisades and Manhattan Beach. Head for the area north of Santa Monica for minimum crowds, but save the Venice strip for optimal people-watching. On Saturday you can observe the experts roller disco and pull some rad stunts near Muscle Beach (*see* Venice Beach *in* Chapter 2). Closer to Manhattan Beach, there are more hard bodies in Lycra, so if you like to scope wholesome athletic types, start your trip there. Be warned, however, that the whole Strand gets very crowded on weekends and may provide the beginner with a few too many moving obstacles for comfort. But with its con-

*Skateboarders can hit an awesome combination of curbs, rails, ramps, and bowls at the Vans Skate Park (tel. 714/769–3800) at The Block mall in Orange. They provide safety equipment but you'll need your own skateboard; a two-hour session runs $11–$14.*

sistently flat and smooth surface, it is otherwise an ideal place to get your skate legs. If the occasional hill doesn't frighten you, head to the bike paths of **Griffith Park** (*see* Bicycling, *above*). Here you can enjoy more than 6 mi of trail utilized by serious speed skaters for training. You will be far from the cooling winds of the ocean, so you might want to come early in the day and pack plenty of water. Past the zoo you will encounter a relatively large hill. The southbound lane is tamer than the north if your T stops aren't up to par.

Another good 'blading locale is the **UCLA campus,** which offers flat or hilly options, depending on your ability and ambition. Finally, you can take advantage of the ghostly quality that descends on **downtown** on the weekends to skate the relatively deserted postapocalyptic streets. If you decide to hit the roads of Los Angeles on 'blades, you will be in good company. Cars are used to seeing 'bladers and bikers, but you should gauge traffic, hills, lights, and your own abilities just as you would in any urban jungle before taking undue risks.

# RUNNING

Runners are a very common sight in the more affluent areas on the west side of Los Angeles, but if you want to branch out into the less body-conscious sections of town, exercise the usual cautions: going out during daylight hours and/or taking a companion. Probably the best running in L.A. exists at any of the beaches, either on the sand or on the Strand (*see* Bicycling, *above*).

## WHERE TO RUN

There is a nice unpaved track circling **La Cienega Park,** on La Cienega Boulevard between Olympic Boulevard and Gregory Way in Beverly Hills. Along Santa Monica Boulevard between Doheny and Wilshire boulevards, you'll find a nearly 2-mi runner's trail through a long and narrow but pretty park. Flatter pastoral possibilities can be found in the lower parts of Beverly Hills, between Sunset and Santa Monica boulevards south of Doheny Road, but you should wear your best warm-up suit or be prepared to explain yourself to the roaming Westec private security force on the lookout for low-life intruders. There's also the **Hollywood Reservoir Trail** (*see* Hiking, *above*), a great, flat 4-miler; just remember to beat it before dark.

If you prefer to avoid the bigger streets, there are some nice trails in the Hollywood Hills—the **Runyon Canyon** trail (*see* Hiking, *above*) is popular for its views, and the rugged runner can speed along any of the listed hikes. Take note: The trails are now an off-leash dog area.

# SAILING AND SEA KAYAKING

High insurance liability makes it difficult for the short-term traveler to rent a sailboat. Most places require a membership fee and proof of sailing proficiency before they will let you near one of their crafts. Sea kayaking is much more user-friendly and widely available. Marina del Rey is the prime spot for boating of all kinds, although you can always load your sea kayak on your car and try your luck elsewhere.

## EQUIPMENT RENTAL

You can rent small crafts like Holder 14s, Coronado 15s, and catamarans by joining the **UCLA Marina Aquatic Center** (membership fee $45) and passing its sailing-proficiency test. Beginners can bolster their chance of passing the exam by taking a class for $65–144. Once you are a member, sailboats go for $12 an hour and sea kayaks for $10. *14001 Fiji Way, off Lincoln Blvd., Marina del Rey, tel. 310/823–0048.*

In Long Beach you can rent sea kayaks at the **Long Beach Windsurf Center** (*see* Windsurfing, *below*) for $15 a half day, $25 a full day for singles. **Malibu Ocean Sports** (22935 PCH, 50 yards south of Malibu Pier, tel. 310/456–6302; 511 Washington Blvd., at Ocean, Marina del Rey, tel. 310/823–1972) specializes in ocean kayaks for $15 an hour, $25 for 2 hours, $35 a day, for singles. **Marina Boat Rentals** (13719 Fiji Way, Marina del Rey, tel. 310/574–2822) will rent you anything that floats, from paddleboats to powerboats to sailboats, for $10–$75 an hour. **Action Water Sports** (4144 Lincoln Blvd., Marina del Rey, tel. 310/306–9539) rents kayaks for about $40 a day.

# SNORKELING AND SCUBA DIVING

You'll have to show proof of scuba certification to touch an air tank, but anyone who can swim can snorkel. L.A. is probably not the best place to start learning scuba—the water's rough—but if you like, you can get certified at one of the dive centers listed under Equipment Rental below. Snorkeling and scuba diving require calm waters, and despite its misleading name, the Pacific Ocean does not quite fit the bill. Although conditions can permit some diving off Malibu, you're better off leaving L.A. for Santa Catalina Island, the Channel Islands, Palos Verdes, or Laguna Beach if you hope to see anything besides swirling sand (*see* Santa Catalina Island and Laguna Beach *in* Chapter 8).

If you or your diving partner are seriously injured in a diving-related accident, the 24-hour staff at the U.S. National Diving Accident Network can help you find a doctor trained to treat divers; call 919/684–8111.

## EQUIPMENT RENTAL

**Divers Discount** claims scuba rentals and sales for 10–70 percent off average retail rates and guarantees the lowest prices. A full scuba package costs $35 a day; beginner lessons run $225 for two weekends, and advanced classes will siphon off $135 for six dives over two days. *3575 Cahuenga Blvd., east of Lankershim, tel. 323/850–5050.*

**Pacific Wilderness and Ocean Sports** rents scuba gear for $40 a day, half-price each additional day, and is a great source of information regarding local diving opportunities. *1719 S. Pacific Ave., San Pedro, tel. 310/833–2422.*

**Reef Seekers Dive Company** rents gear and offers scuba certification classes. A full scuba package will run you $55 for the weekend or $45 for a weekday. Lessons cost $250 plus the boat rental fee, so you might want to put this toward a trip to Belize and try snorkeling instead. *8612 Wilshire Blvd., between La Cienega and Robertson Blvds., tel. 310/652–4990.*

You can also get scuba (but not snorkeling) equipment closer to the water at **Scubahaus,** where a full package will run you $47 a day. Lessons toward certification cost $325 for two weekends. *2501 Wilshire, at 25th St., Santa Monica, tel. 310/828–2916.*

## WHERE TO SNORKEL AND DIVE

If you are determined to dive off L.A. County, people have been known to dive near **Will Rogers State Beach** (16000 block of PCH, Pacific Palisades, tel. 310/394–3261), **Torrance County Beach** (along Paseo de la Playa, Torrance, tel. 310/372–2166), **Palos Verdes Estates Shoreline Preserve** (entire shore of Palos Verdes Estates), **Bluff Cove** (path to cove starts at Flat Rock Point, 600 block of Paseo del Mar, Palos Verdes Estates), **Point Vicente** (off Palos Verdes Dr., Rancho Palos Verdes), **Abalone Cove Beach** (Palos Verdes Dr. S, west of Narcissa Dr., Rancho Palos Verdes, tel. 310/372–2166), **Christmas Tree Cove** (between Point Vicente and Abalone Cove Beach), and **Cabrillo Beach** (40th St. and Stephen M. White Dr., San Pedro, tel. 310/832–1179).

Divers should definitely consider exploring the **Underwater Dive Trail at White's Point,** just east of Royal Palms State Beach (Western Ave. at S. Paseo del Mar, San Pedro), which winds by rope through kelp beds, sulfurous hot springs, and underwater coves.

# SURFING

Those with impaired balance or hydrophobia may not agree with the Beach Boys' claim that "if everybody had an ocean across the U.S.A., then everybody'd be surfing, like Californ-I-A," but even if you never don a wet suit, checking out the surf scene is a must. If you do surf or wish to try, you've come to the right place. Angelenos will tell you that Malibu is the place to go for the killer swells, while Orange County loyalists laud Huntington Beach and San Clemente. Either way, when the surf gods smile, you can't miss in the greater L.A. area. If you've never been able to stay on a skateboard for more than a few seconds, you may want to stick to dry land, but watching the beautiful guys and gals shoot the curl and wipe out is an aesthetic treat on a par with anything you'll see at the L.A. County Museum of Art. Besides, you can always brush up on surf music, surf fashion, and surf lingo, and then your friends at home will never know whether you did or you didn't hit the waves.

## EQUIPMENT RENTAL

When you hit the surfing hot spots, surf shops will be in long supply. Competition keeps prices comparable, but below are a few starting suggestions. If you are in Huntington Beach to check out the International Museum of Surfing (*see* Chapter 8) and you become inspired to give it a whirl, head to the friendly folks at **Huntington Surf and Sport** (300 PCH, tel. 714/377–9191). They can set you up with a wet suit for $6 an hour or $10 a day, a softboard for $6 an hour or $20 a day, or a boogie board for $3 an hour or $10 a day. They can also point you toward lessons. If you stick to the L.A. area, try **Malibu Ocean Sports** (*see* Sailing and Sea Kayaking, *above*). Here you can get a hard surfboard for $25 a day, a wet suit for $8 a day, or a boogie board for $12 a day. They regularly offer two-hour lessons for $72, and their staff is happy to advise you. In Venice, **Rental on the Beach** (*see* Bicycling, *above*) rents boogie boards for $4 an hour or $12 a day. **Spokes and Stuff** (*see* Bicycling, *above*), in Santa Monica, has boogie boards for $3.50 an hour or $14 a day. If you want to try a different locale, like Trestles in San Clemente or Sunset Beach in the South Bay, just head to the prime surfing area or nearby commercial district: You'll have no trouble finding a rental shop.

## WHERE TO SURF

Don't try surfing at all if you are not a strong swimmer, as going against the tide to get to where the waves break is a strenuous proposition. Beginning female surfers should expect encouragement and support from local hotshots. A hapless male, however, should expect a few sneers, if not outright ridicule. For the best results, be as polite and mellow as possible. Give other surfers plenty of space—do *not* cut them off—and avoid swimmers. Surfing calls for caution: That huge piece of flying fiberglass beneath you could kill someone.

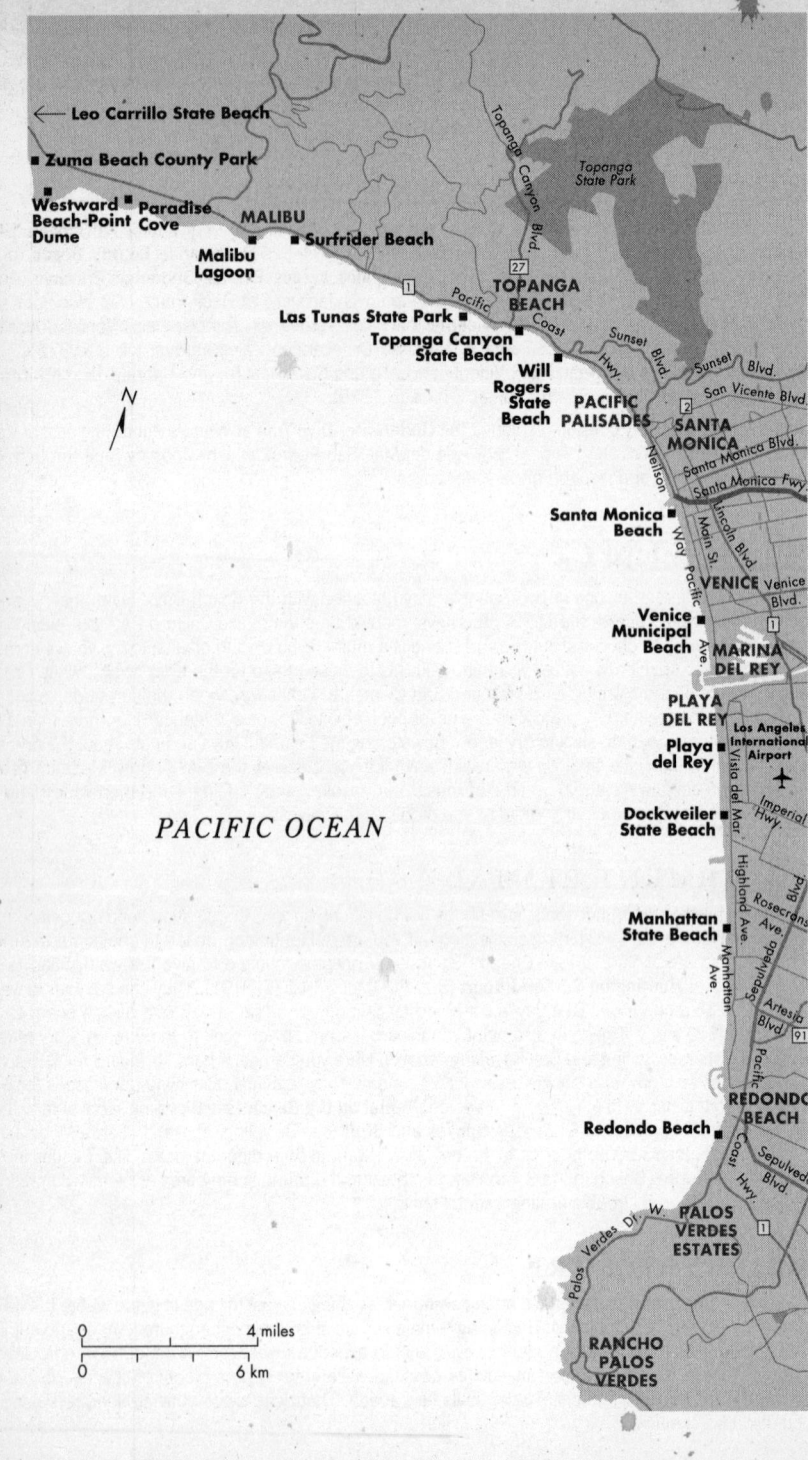

LOS ANGELES AREA BEACHES

← Leo Carrillo State Beach

■ Zuma Beach County Park

Westward ■ Paradise
Beach-Point   Cove
Dume         MALIBU
        Malibu       ■ Surfrider Beach
        Lagoon

                              Topanga
                              State Park

                    1        Pacific
        Las Tunas State Park ■        Coast    27   TOPANGA
                                                    BEACH
            Topanga Canyon ■
            State Beach          Will    Sunset
                                 Rogers   Hwy.    Sunset   Blvd.
                                 State            San Vicente Blvd.
                                 Beach   PACIFIC
                                         PALISADES  2   SANTA
                                                       MONICA
                                              Santa Monica Blvd.
                                                  Santa Monica Fwy.

                            Santa Monica ■
                            Beach                Lincoln Blvd.
                                            Main St.              VENICE
                                                         Way Pacific          Venice
                                                                     VENICE    Blvd.
                            Venice ■                          1
                            Municipal                    MARINA
                            Beach                         DEL REY
                                 PLAYA
                                 DEL REY
                                         Los Angeles
                            Playa ■      International
                            del Rey      Airport
                                              Vista del Mar    Imperial
                                                               Hwy.
                            Dockweiler ■
                            State Beach                 Highland Ave.  Rosecrans Ave.
                                                                       Aviation Blvd.
                            Manhattan ■                              Artesia
PACIFIC OCEAN               State Beach         Manhattan            Blvd.   91
                                               Ave.
                                                                  Pacific
                                                       REDONDO
                                                       BEACH
                            Redondo Beach ■              Coast
                                                         Hwy.   Sepulveda
                                                                Blvd.
                                              W.  PALOS
                                         Verdes Dr.  VERDES
                                    Palos            ESTATES   1

0 _____ 4 miles                    RANCHO
0 _____ 6 km                       PALOS
                                         VERDES

## BEGINNERS

If you think "swell" is an adjective from the '50s, you are a novice, and you need help. Experienced surfers are impressive amateur oceanographers who begin their day of surfing by studying the sea's terrain. You might want to shell out the big bucks on a lesson so you understand whether you are looking at a "break," a "peak," or something "tubular" and so you can figure out what you are supposed to do about it. The **Malibu Ocean Sports** (*see above*) lesson will keep you on the sand for at least 45 minutes explaining these important points to you. If you have a mind to strike out alone, there are a few options. Some surfers recommend a day on a boogie board—which they claim anyone can handle—to get the feel of the water without the risk of cracking your skull on a long, hard surfboard. You might also consider going on a calm day, when the tiny waves won't tempt experienced surfers. In kinder, gentler waters, you can practice balance and steering, and you won't have to work so hard to paddle out to the action. But even difficult waves will not be as much of a barrier to the beginner as are crowded waters and the infamous surfer attitude. Avoid the beaches where the pros go, opting for the mellower shores and less judgmental spectators of the South Bay's **Sunset Beach** (west of Pacific Avenue, in Huntington Beach) or **County Line Beach** (west of Highway 1 at Yerba Buena Road, in Malibu). If the surf is less than 4 ft, **El Porto**, in Manhattan Beach (north from 35th Street), is a good place for beginners. You might also want to try the waves at **Gladstones,** in Santa Monica (1 mi north of Sunset on PCH; look for Gladstones restaurant), during midtide. Beginners should avoid Palos Verdes; surfers there are notoriously territorial and have been known to verbally harass outsiders and vandalize nonnatives' cars.

## EXPERIENCED

If you've done this before and want to catch the best waves, call the L.A. County Lifeguards' prerecorded surf conditions hotlines: 310/457–9701 for Malibu, 310/578–0478 for Santa Monica, or 310/379–8471 for Manhattan, Redondo, and Hermosa beaches. If you don't mind a little raw sewage in your swells, there are many options in the immediate Los Angeles area. Foremost of these is **Malibu Surfrider Beach** (in Malibu Lagoon State Beach, tel. 310/457–9891), considered by some the ideal summer surf locale. Breaks are consistently 2–4 ft, sometimes approaching 8 ft. **Point Dume** has good conditions year-round, although the word is that locals resent outsiders with even more than the standard degree of surf tribalism. In the South Bay go to the **Manhattan Beach Pier** for steep peaks and good bodysurfing. The **Redondo Break Wall** is another favorite spot, with especially good winter conditions.

The cleanest water around can be found in Orange County. You should investigate the **Huntington Beach Pier,** in Huntington Beach, home to the International Surfing Competition every September (winners make the Surfer Walk of Fame—*see* the International Museum of Surfing *in* Chapter 8) and **Trestles Beach,** in San Clemente, consistently rated the best surfing in the continental United States. **Seal Beach** (south of Long Beach; tel. 562/430–2613) is also worth a try. Farther south, **Newport Beach** (between 40th and 44th streets) has good breaks for both beginning and experienced surfers, although when the water is crowded with swimmers, it's "blackballed" by lifeguards (look for yellow flags with black balls, which indicates surfing is not allowed). Of course, you can always drive along the coast and look for where the surf truly is up.

# SWIMMING

Whether you want to take a quick dip or swim some serious laps, there are plenty of places to get your feet wet in Los Angeles. The city's most popular swimming hole is hard to miss. The cool, blue Pacific Ocean is great for swimming, and the 75 mi of L.A. County coastline give you plenty of space to spread your towel. Ocean swimming is best in the summer and early fall; the water is generally a tad too cold during other times of the year. If you'd prefer chlorine to salt, there are numerous pools open to the public for small admission fees; these have both general and lap swimming times.

## BEACHES

### SANTA MONICA STATE BEACH

Probably L.A.'s most famous beach, Santa Monica is a wide, white sand strip with fine swimming on either side of the Santa Monica Pier. Its high profile and easy access from the I-10 freeway make this beach extremely popular with natives and tourists alike, and sunny summer weekends can be a mob scene of joggers, bicyclists, swimmers, boogie boarders, and posers of all kinds. *Parking, lifeguard, rest rooms, showers. 1642 Promenade, PCH at California Incline, Santa Monica, tel. 310/394–3266.*

## VENICE CITY BEACH

Venice Beach itself is frequently all but forgotten in the frenzy of activity that happens on shore along the Boulevard. However, the beach here is wide and white and the swimming is nice and easy. The water is great for a serious workout or simply to bob and float. *Parking, lifeguard, rest rooms, showers, food concessions, playground, volleyball. West of Pacific Ave., Venice, tel. 310/394–3266.*

## WESTWARD BEACH/POINT DUME

Interesting sandstone cliffs and tidepools mark this southern extension of Zuma, and the trails leading out to the bluffs above offer great views—you can whale-watch here from November through May. The swimming area is decent, and much less crowded than others in the area, but beware of the strong currents. On the eastern side of the bluffs is a relatively quiet area where people are known to sun and swim in the buff (unofficially, of course). *Parking, lifeguard, rest rooms, food concessions. South end of Westward Beach Rd., Malibu, tel. 310/457–9891.*

## WILL ROGERS STATE BEACH

Will Rogers is generally considered a good place to swim since the surf is gentle and the ocean is easily accessible from the relatively wide beach; it's very popular with local families. Unfortunately, the water here also has the distinction of being some of the most polluted in the area. Run-off from the hills on the other side of the PCH reaches the Pacific via drains located along the beach; conditions are particularly soupy after storms. However, on any given summer weekend, when storms are almost unheard of, there are hordes of folks bobbing in the water with no apparent ill affects. *Parking, lifeguard, rest rooms, volleyball. 15100 PCH, 2 mi north of Santa Monica Pier, tel. 310/394–3266.*

## ZUMA BEACH

Located in Malibu, Zuma is a quintessential 2-mi stretch of southern California coastline with wide, white-sand beaches, calm waters that are ideal for swimming, and plenty of beachside amenities. (You can't help but expect to see David Hasselhoff jog by.) Zuma is one of L.A.'s most popular beaches, so it gets extremely crowded on summer weekends. Tourists, San Fernando Valley teens, surfers, and bronzed sun worshippers all vie for towel space on the sand and elbow room in the water. *Parking, lifeguard, rest rooms, showers, food concessions, playground, volleyball. 30050 PCH, Malibu, tel. 310/ 457–9891.*

# POOLS

If you have an overwhelming urge to swim in a waveless, sandless, controlled environment and your hotel lacks the facilities, there are several relatively inexpensive options. The City of Los Angeles Department of Recreation and Parks operates several **public year-round pools.** Admittance is free for those 17 and under, 65 and over, and the disabled. The fee for adults is a very reasonable $1.25. Hours of operation as well as designated general swimming and lap swimming times vary with the season. Call for a current schedule. The Echo Park Pool (1419 Colton St., tel. 213/481–2640) is a 25-yard indoor facility located a few blocks south of the park. If you're staying on the Westside, check out the Venice Pool (2490 Walgrove Ave., Venice, tel. 310/575–8260), a popular indoor swimming pool located next to the high school, or the indoor Westwood Park Pool (1350 Sepulveda Blvd., tel. 310/478–7019), located near Westwood Village and the UCLA campus.

For other year-round as well as seasonal summer pools, call the **Aquatics Section of the Department of Recreation and Parks** for information: San Fernando Valley (tel. 818/765–0284); Pacific Region, the Westside, and coast (tel. 213/765–5390); Griffith-Metro Region, the rest of the metro area, including downtown and Hollywood (tel. 213/485–5559).

Another swimming option is the **YMCA** (there are more than 20 in the Los Angeles area). The Hollywood Wilshire YMCA (553 N. Schrader Blvd., tel. 323/993–0876) has both a lap pool and a training pool open daily. A day pass costs $20. For $12, you can visit the lap pool at the Beverly Hills YMCA (9930 Santa Monica Blvd., tel. 310/553–0731), which is open Monday–Saturday. The large Temescal Canyon outdoor pool of the Palisades-Malibu YMCA (821 Via del la Paz, Pacific Palisades, tel. 310/454–5591) has varying lap and general swim times that vary by day and season; call for a current schedule. A day pass runs $15. The Santa Monica YMCA (1332 6th St., Santa Monica, tel. 310/393–2721) has a lap pool that's open daily; their day pass costs $10. If you'd like more information on other L.A. area YMCA pool facilities, call the YMCA of Metropolitan Los Angeles at 213/380–6448.

# WHALE-WATCHING

All winter and spring, the Pacific gray whales pass by the Palos Verdes Peninsula during their annual 5,000- to 7,000-mi migration from the Arctic to the warm lagoons of Baja California, where females eventually give birth. Along the headlands of Rancho Palos Verdes, at the Point Vicente Interpretive Center (*see* Palos Verdes *in* Chapter 2), open daily 10–5, you can witness these magnificent mammals spy-hopping (peaking above the water) and breaching (jumping). Naturalists and volunteer census takers from the Whalewatch Society congregate at this hot spot during the whale-watching season, from late December to early April.

The **Cabrillo Marine Aquarium** (*see* San Pedro *in* Chapter 2) coordinates whale-watching expeditions and trains volunteer tour narrators. Call the aquarium's Whalewatch Line (tel. 310/832–4444) in season for recorded information on the variety of whale-related activities it sponsors.

**Los Angeles Harbor Cruise** offers 2-hour whale-watching cruises December–April; hitting the deck costs $12. *Village Boat House, Berth 78, Ports O'Call Village, San Pedro, tel. 310/831–0996.*

**Redondo Sport Fishing,** on the pier at the Redondo Beach Marina, sends out two whale-watching boats a day during the season. Trips last about three hours and cost $7–$10 per person ($12 on weekends). *233 N. Harbor Dr., Redondo Beach, tel. 310/372–2111.*

# WINDSURFING

Less-than-ideal wind conditions and the fickle interests of Angelenos have reduced the amount of windsurfing that goes on in the L.A. area. San Pedro claims the best conditions, but you can also give it a go in Marina del Rey or Long Beach. Locals say the best place by far is **Cabrillo Beach** (40th St. and Stephen M. White Dr., San Pedro, tel. 310/832–1179).

## EQUIPMENT RENTAL

At **Captain Kirk's** in San Pedro you can get a basic beginner's setup for $45 a day. More advanced gear will run you up to $60 a day, and beginner lessons start at $75, which includes equipment and two hours of instruction. *525 N. Harbor Blvd., near Hwy. 47, San Pedro, tel. 310/833–3397.*

Cheaper rates are available at **Long Beach Windsurf Center.** Windsurfers go for $25 a half day, $35 for a full day. Small group lessons (including equipment) are given on Saturday morning and cost $95. For ultimate windsurf knowledge, pick up Scott Carter's self-published book, *Southern California Windsurfing Sites* ($9.95), at the center. *3850 E. Ocean Blvd., between Termino and Redondo Sts., Long Beach, tel. 562/433–1014.*If you plan on spending a lot of time in L.A. or making multiple windsurfing excursions, you might want to pay the membership fee at **UCLA Marina Aquatic Center** (*see* Sailing and Sea Kayaking, *above*). After the initial $45 fee, you can get a windsurfing setup for only $10 an hour. However, you have to show your ability on the board before you can rent; testing costs $15.

**Wind & Wave** in West L.A. rents equipment for about $75 a day; they don't give lessons. *11910 Pico Blvd., just east of Bundy Dr., tel. 310/478–7537.*

BY CATHERINE BELONOGOFF

UPDATED BY NANCY RONES

In Los Angeles shopping is more than just the acquisition of some necessary object. Rather, it has become the way most of society relaxes. Indoor malls bundle shops, eating establishments, gyms, movie theaters, and public seating areas all under one roof. Outdoor pedestrian streets (like the Third Street Promenade in Santa Monica) struggle to recapture the intimate feeling of a village lost in modern L.A. It doesn't work—you can't re-create community by bunching together chain stores like the Gap, Crate and Barrel, and Starbucks with a few benches on a street corner. But, hell, add L.A.'s endless sunshine to these areas, and you've got a relatively pleasant shopping experience, though not always a cheap one.

L.A. is an ideal place to drop loads of cash on music, clothes, movie paraphernalia, and books. Ethnic shopping opportunities extend far beyond the kitschy Mexican knickknacks on Olvera Street; in Fairfax Russian and Jewish shops abound, while Koreatown, Little Tokyo, and Chinatown have all things Asian for sale. Inveterate shoppers shouldn't stay locked into the major neighborhoods; Los Feliz Village (on Vermont Avenue from Los Feliz Boulevard to Hollywood Boulevard) and Sunset Boulevard in Silver Lake are great places to shop for ultrafringe gifts.

Scan advertisements in the *L.A. Weekly* and *The New Times* for clues on where to find some cool clothes and accessories. Most clothing shops keep shorter hours (from about 10 to 6) than record stores and big bookstores, which are open until 10 PM or 11 PM. Of course, in areas where shops are concentrated, like Santa Monica's Third Street Promenade, the hours are later for all types of stores (usually until 9). Weekend hours are almost always shorter than weekday hours. Sales at most stores occur in July and after Christmas, especially at mall stores. You can use credit cards at virtually every consumer establishment in L.A., including grocery and liquor stores and some fast-food restaurants. Most shops also accept ATM debit cards.

# SHOPPING BY NEIGHBORHOOD

## WEST HOLLYWOOD AND MELROSE AVENUE

Picture a Venn diagram of punk, trendy, and vintage—where all three overlap sums up what you'll find on Melrose between La Brea and Fairfax avenues. On this stretch, you'll find stores that stock extremely trendy clothes at wide-ranging prices, from multi-hundreds to downright dirt-cheap. Many of Melrose's mostly indistinguishable stores are white-tiled, long, narrow rooms with supertrendy clothes of poor quality sold for unwarranted prices ($30–$50). So if you see that white tile or a tall, thin, bored saleswoman dressed in tight black Spandex—flee. Instead, try **My Closet** (705 N. Sierra Bonita, at Melrose Ave., tel. 323/658- -8765) or one of the many establishments listed below, where the clothes are unique approximations of the trendy garbage on Melrose, but the prices are low enough to allow you some fun. If you're dressing for another decade, dig into the heaps of vintagewear at places like **The Wasteland** (*see* Secondhand Clothes, *below*). Melrose east of Fairfax, on the other hand, has sprouted decadent places like Miu Miu and Maxfield, where quadruple-digit price tags are commonplace. A stone's throw from the too-too Beverly Center mall lies West 3rd Street; the section between La Cienega and Crescent Heights boulevards is the up-and-coming place to be seen and spend money. A mix of hip clothing boutiques, like **Noodle Stories** (8317 W. 3rd St., at Flores St., tel. 323/651– 1782), and quality gift shops such as **Illume** (*see* Miscellaneous, *below*) make it worth a few quarters for the parking meter. Nearby on Beverly Boulevard between La Brea and Fairfax is a strip of stores more for gawking than buying, including designer Tom Mark's **Mark Wong Nark Collection** (7384 Beverly Blvd., at Martel Ave., tel. 323/939–9710) and **Tyler Trafficante,** the studio for L.A. über-designer Richard Tyler (7290 Beverly Blvd., at Poinsetta Pl., tel. 323/931–9678). Think of them as art galleries for fashion.

## WEST L.A. AND WESTWOOD

The student population determines the shopping experience in Westwood, especially around UCLA. Kitsch shops are ubiquitous, probably because students are dumb enough to repeatedly drop small amounts of cash on instant (albeit temporary) objets de gratification. West L.A.'s shopping streets (like San Vicente Boulevard south of I–405) are a collection of expensive stores filled with the same sort of tchotchkes as Westwood Village, just on a finer, more costly scale. Of course, two of L.A.'s best establishments—**Rhino Records** (*see* Music, *below*) and **Sisterhood Bookstore** (*see* Books, *below*)—call West L.A. home; so the shopping scene is not completely hopeless here—it's just not great.

## BEVERLY HILLS

**Rodeo Drive** lures visitors with promises of clean streets, faux European niches, and famous designers. It delivers, but it also delivers overpriced merch and throngs of tourists. You should go just for the hollow, overblown experience and the possibility of a celeb sighting; afterwards, with a knowing sigh, you can wonder aloud why people flock to where they are obviously not wanted. If you want to breathe a rarefied atmosphere, you'll have your pick of jewelers (Cartier, Harry Winston, Tiffany & Co.) and designers (Chanel, Prada, Polo/Ralph Lauren, Versace). If you really need to shop Beverly Hills, try **Victoria's Secret** (330 N. Beverly Dr., at Dayton Way, tel. 310/288–0862), the **Gap** (370 N. Beverly Dr., at Brighton Way, tel. 310/274–0461), **Banana Republic** (357 N. Beverly Dr., at Brighton Way, tel. 310/858-7900), and **Club Monaco** (401 N. Beverly Dr., at Brighton Way, tel. 310/858–0204), all chains but with a special appeal in these upscale digs. The Canadian leather and sportswear retailer **Roots** (371 N. Beverly Dr., at Brighton Way, tel. 310/858–8343) is worth a once-around. Searching for sales can net you a relative bargain. **BCBG** (201C N. Rodeo Dr., at Dayton Way, tel. 310/278–3263) has an excellent sale rack for its hip women's fashions; **Tag Rag** (363 N. Beverly Dr., at Brighton Way, tel. 310/275–2131) stations a $24.95 sale rack right by the front door (that's guts in this zip code). **Barneys New York** (9570 Wilshire Blvd., at Beverly Dr., tel. 310/276–4400) has infrequent but hugely popular sales, although the superstylish clothing is already so expensive, sales don't help much.

## HOLLYWOOD AND LOS FELIZ

Shopping in Hollywood is a great way to waste money on souvenirs and the like, which will undoubtedly be rotting in your closet by year's end. Movie maniacs will find choice items like movie posters, books about film, and screenplays for sale at **Larry Edmund's** (*see* Specialty Items, *below*) or **Book City** and **Samuel French's** (*see* Books, *below*). Otherwise, shopping in Hollywood is one of the worst ways to spend your time in the area.

Venture east to Los Feliz's **Vermont Avenue** between Hollywood Boulevard and Franklin Avenue, however, and you'll find yourself on one of the hippest strips in town. Along with **Koma Books** (*see* Books, *below*) and the Dresden Room (*see* Bars *in* Chapter 5) are several tempting clothing shops and bookstores, including X-Large and X-Girl, partly owned by the Beastie Boys' Mike Diamond, and the Half-Off Clothing Company, a good place to pick up discounted Lucky jeans and flowing skirts.

## DOWNTOWN

Downtown's claim to shopping fame is The Los Angeles Fashion District, formerly dubbed the Garment District. In the heart of this district is the **Cooper Building** (860 S. Los Angeles St., at 8th St., tel. 213/

622–1139). This building is described in ads as "extraordinary." Perhaps extra ordinary would be more fitting. The Cooper's shops carry brand names at substantially reduced prices, but the atmosphere is weary and dull. The Rampage and Guess? outlets are the Cooper's high points, and they're nothing to write home about. The shops in the surrounding area (between Santee Street, Maple Avenue, 12th Street, and Pico Boulevard) carry repetitive stock at similar prices; even an industrious shopper will find only cheap accessories and trendy but poorly made clothing.

More lively shopping sections of downtown include **Olvera Street** (*see* Flea Markets and Street Markets, *below*), and the **Grand Central Market** (317 S. Broadway, between 3rd and 4th Sts., tel. 213/624–2378), a block-long strip of produce purveyors, butchers, and herb hawkers. **Little Tokyo** and **Chinatown** are also in the downtown area but have mostly small groceries and overpriced tchotchke shops (*see* Downtown *in* Chapter 2).

## SOUTH-CENTRAL

The neighborhood surrounding Leimert Park, at the corner of Crenshaw Boulevard and Vernon Avenue, is an oasis of African-American shops in an otherwise blighted area. Around the park and along 43rd Place and Degnan Boulevard, you'll find shops selling African jewelry, clothing, and art. *See* Leimert Park *in* South-Central *in* Chapter 2 for details.

## VENICE AND SANTA MONICA

Shopping at the beach is savory compared to being trapped in an environmentally controlled mall. Hours of fresh sea air and sunshine with breaks to take a swim—just watch out for seagull poop. **Ocean Walk** in Venice is great for inexpensive, quality sunglasses, handmade jewelry, and touristy T-shirts. You do, however, need patience for the accompanying quantities of schlock. In Santa Monica, the **Third Street Promenade** is the place to be when you want to be surrounded by people—and lots of 'em. Locals and tourists alike flock to this outdoor pedestrian zone to shop, eat, and soak up the lively street scene. The stores, however, are mostly just another serving of the usual chains: Pottery Barn, J. Crew, Banana Republic. If you'd like a mall with a roof, you can get another fix at Santa Monica Place, on the south end of the Promenade, and Sears is just down the street. Santa Monica's **Main Street** has the cozy feel of a small town, except that people parade around in all states of beach undress during the weekend and sip overpriced coffee drinks. **Montana Avenue** from about 9th Street to 17th Street is a great place to walk around and stare at celebrities out with their kids, but beware the cute little boutiques that line the street: They know they're cute, and they make you pay.

# NEW CLOTHES

Between the city's gorgeous weather and its mandate to look good or else, typical Angelenos are ultra-fashionable, if not half naked. They also know it takes cash to look that slick. For the budget-conscious, there are Gaps to be found on every corner, if you must, but there are also plenty of places unique to L.A. that are somewhat affordable. Melrose Avenue between Highland Avenue and Crescent Heights Boulevard should be your starting point if you want the L.A. look; you can park on surrounding residential streets, but pay close attention to posted restrictions. The Third Street Promenade in Santa Monica is runner-up for pleasant (albeit touristy) shopping, and the city parking structures peppered around the area are free.

**A.B.S. Clothing Collection Inc.** (1533 Montana Ave., at 16th St., Santa Monica, tel. 310/393–8770; 55 W. Colorado Blvd., at Fair Oaks Ave., Pasadena, tel. 626/577–8505). Love the gown Gwyneth Paltrow or Calista Flockhart wore to the Oscars? You may just stumble upon a pretty close knockoff here among the Hollywood-"inspired" lines, which run $270–$500. There are some simple separates, too, if you're not in the market for an evening gown.

**Anthropologie** (1402 Third St. Promenade, Santa Monica, tel. 310/393–4763; 320 N. Beverly Dr., Beverly Hills, tel. 310/385–7390). Enter this airy space and convince yourself you need some of the mellowed women's trends and home accents. Most things are under $100, like a hand-painted cardigan for $78, an embroidered handbag for $68, or pairs of floral drawer pulls for $16. Check out the great sale racks.

**Betsey Johnson** (8052 Melrose Ave., at Laurel Ave., Melrose, tel. 323/852–1534; 2929 Main St., at Pier Ave., Santa Monica, tel. 310/452–7911; Beverly Center, at Beverly and La Cienega Blvds., tel. 310/652–8391). With the opening of her new flagship store on Melrose, Betsey has saturated La-La land. Head straight to the back of the store for the sale rack and don't look back unless you want to daydream about where you might be going and what the hell you might be doing in those expensive yet delicious dresses.

**Fred Segal** (8118 Melrose Ave., at Crescent Heights Blvd., Melrose, tel. 323/651–1935; 500 Broadway, at 5th St., Santa Monica, tel. 310/458–1160). He's so, so hip and so, so expensive. His stores (actually a bunch of connected boutiques) are the favorite haunts of everyone—from Beverly Hills high school students to young movie stars—for pricey, stylish clothes and accessories, and they're credited with launching the careers of many young L.A. designers. At the end of September there's a huge sale, and for 50% to 75% off, you may be able to find a cute, affordable T-shirt. If you can avoid getting bitter, they're a fun browsing and people-watching spot, even in nonsale season.

**Frederick's of Hollywood** (6608 Hollywood Blvd., between Highland and Cahuenga Aves., Hollywood, tel. 323/466–8506). You may be surprised to see how predominately unraunchy—in fact, almost sweet—the styles are in this famous lingerie store. But not to worry, naughty black getups and thongs are still sprinkled throughout. If you're just sightseeing here, check out the free Celebrity Lingerie Museum in back, where bloomers of the stars, from Lana Turner to Madonna, are on display.

**French Connection** (1418 Third St. Promenade, Santa Monica, tel. 310/393–4484; 420 N. Beverly Dr., between Brighton Way and Little Santa Monica Blvd., tel. 310/248–2632; Beverly Center, at Beverly and La Cienega Blvds., tel. 310/854–1965). The threads at this stylish men's and women's chain are mostly classic clothes with a bit of stretch—perfect for casual urban wear, if a tad expensive. The sale rack in the back can ease the pain a bit. The best part is you could actually be caught dead in these clothes back home. How refreshing.

**Heaven 27** (6316 Yucca St., at Ivar Ave., Hollywood, tel. 323/871–9044). Filmmaker Sophia Coppola owns this tiny store that carries her Milk Fed line. Prices can be a bit on the steep side, at about $90 for a cotton sheath dress and $80 for a short-sleeve nylon jacket, but sales strike frequently. You can also snap up goodies that Coppola finds on film shoots, like Japanese bath products.

**Industrial Shoe Warehouse** (5176 Santa Monica Blvd., between Normandie and Western Aves., Hollywood, tel. 323/663–3984; 8801 Santa Monica Blvd., 4 blks. west of La Cienega Blvd., West Hollywood, tel. 310/659–9893). This store talks the trendy talk in its advertising but barely walks the walk in reality. It's stocked with mostly comfy shoes, including a good selection of tennis shoes. Still, if you want some Docs or Skechers at reasonable prices, step right up.

**L.A. Eyestyle** (2356 Cotner Ave., 2 blks. west of Sepulveda Blvd., West L.A., tel. 310/477–6708). This store is locally famous for its discounted designer sunglasses—everything from Calvin Klein to Versace.

**L.A. Sporting Club** (8000 Sunset Blvd., at Crescent Heights Blvd., West Hollywood, tel. 323/650–1166). Getting buff is important to Angelenos and so is what they wear when they're doing it. Hit this popular source for fitness wear and gear and tamper with the neat arrangements of cargo pants, cool sweatshirts, and quality tees. Clearance sales happen in the fall and winter. For even cooler cotton-and-Lycra (and for a peek at where everyone who's anyone works out), head up the escalator to **Crunch** (tel. 323/654–4550). You don't have to be a member to buy, and all of their workout wear is emblazoned with the Crunch logo, so you can walk around with an attitude like everyone else there.

**Na Na** (1245 Third St. Promenade, Santa Monica, tel. 310/394- -9690). Small doses of new and used hipster clothes and shoes may lure you in, not to mention trinkets like fuzzy handcuffs and Elvis toys.

**O'My Sole** (1354 Third St. Promenade, Santa Monica, tel. 310/393–7278). This is a small store that stocks shoes. That's right—*shoes,* not fashion statements or ankle twisters or blister makers, but straightforward, good-looking, rugged walking shoes. So walk this way and buy shoes you can use at prices you can afford—be they $20 flip-flops or a mean pair of hiking boots for $200.

**Polka Dots & Moonbeams Modern Wear** (8379 W. 3rd St., at Orlando Ave., West Hollywood, tel. 323/655–3880). You're bound to find something among the small but thorough hodgepodge of comfy weekend clothes and dresses packed into this store. The styles sometimes look vintage, like the $14 antiqued rhinestone earrings, sometimes unexpected, like the cotton pants edged with kimono fabric for $78. They'll never be taken for mass-produced.

**Sacks SFO** (8936 Santa Monica Blvd., at Robertson Blvd., West Hollywood, tel. 310/659–1771; 652 N. La Brea Ave., at Melrose Ave., Hollywood, tel. 323/939–3993). Don't come here with a purpose; instead, settle into browsing and you may discover something you didn't know you needed. Men's and women's clothes are 40%–80% off retail, and though you'll have to dig for the brand-names, you'll uncover a few, like DKNY and Vertigo.

**Slave** (1223 Abbot Kinney Blvd., at Santa Clara Ave., Venice, tel. 310/314–7016). Before hitting L.A.'s swing clubs, surf scene, or velvet-rope bars, do some retail therapy in this hip store, run by a charming South African and French couple. It's the place to go for the latest to-be-seen-in styles for men and women. Submit to the fashions here and save yourself from pricier, snootier stores.

**Trashy Lingerie** (402 N. La Cienega Blvd., between Beverly Blvd. and Melrose Ave., West Hollywood, tel. 310/652–4543). Its name and the eye-raising panties pinned to the wall notwithstanding, this is a friendly family-run establishment. They will happily whip you up a custom bra or anything else you have in mind. Of course, there's a whole rack of Officer Naughty police uniforms in the back. Trashy will charge you a $2 "annual membership fee" to get in, apparently with the aim of somehow keeping out cross- dressers and riffraff.

**Urban Outfitters** (1440 Third St. Promenade, Santa Monica, tel. 310/394–1404; 7650 Melrose Ave., at Stanley Ave., Melrose, tel. 323/653-3231). Sort of a left-of-center, pay-to-look-poor Gap, this store is part of a chain and like the other stores, offers a wild assortment of urban wear, jewelry, shoes, and apartment furnishings. Accessories are cheap and sometimes unique, but a T-shirt could run you $30.

**Warehouse Shoe Sale** (4935 McConnell Ave., No. 7, at Culver Blvd., near Marina del Rey, tel. 310/827–8024). This store has a wide selection of men's and women's brand-name shoes, with a great stock of tennis and athletic shoes at low prices ($10–$40). The setup is serve yourself, which completely eliminates those pesky salespeople. If you're out to be pampered, this isn't the place.

# SECONDHAND CLOTHES

In Los Angeles used clothes are either high-end vintage duds, '70s clothes revived, or old ladies' and men's closets set out for sale at the charitable thrift shops. Used clothing stores are ubiquitous on Melrose Avenue.

**Aardvark's Odd Ark** (7579 Melrose Ave., at Curson Ave., Melrose, tel. 323/655–6769; 810 Hermosa Ave., at 8th St., Hermosa Beach, tel. 310/376–3688; 85 Market St., at Pacific Ave., Venice, tel. 310/392–2996). Deck yourself out in the clothing casualties of the '70s. And if you're sick of spending a bundle on garb for formal affairs, try the vintage dresses and tuxedos (starting at about $45).

**American Rag Cie** (150 S. La Brea Ave., between 1st and 2nd Sts., Melrose, tel. 323/935–3154). Unless you want to plunk down wads of cash on the new clothes here, don't even bother walking toward the left side of this popular shop. Stay to your right to encounter a handsome stash of Euro vintage dresses, tanks, and jackets, with some Asian items (mandarin collars, Chinese silk jackets) tossed in. The semiannual sale brings savings of 50%–65%. While you're here, wander into **Maison Midi,** a charming housewares annex. You'll find pretty (and pricey) Provençal pottery to go with your French frocks.

**Golyester Antiques** (136 S. La Brea Ave., between 1st and 2nd Sts., Melrose, tel. 323/931–1339). If you have $100 burning a hole in your gabardine suit, step right up to this emporium of exquisite vintage dresses, suits, shoes, shirts, and accessories. They have an array of antique textiles and notions that will definitely interest dressmakers. If you're not flush with cash or you can't see paying 10 times the original price for a phenomenally elegant crepe dress with hand-sewn beadwork, then move on.

**It's A Wrap** (3315 W. Magnolia Blvd., at California St., Burbank, tel. 818/567–7366). Are you just dying for that red spaghetti-strap dress with the "L" monogram that Laverne wore on *Laverne and Shirley* or the custom-tailored Bernini suit donned by John Travolta in *She's So Lovely*? Well, look no further than this clearinghouse chock-full of wardrobes from tons of films, TV shows, and commercials. The clothes are in excellent condition, of excellent quality, and are substantially cheaper than they would be off the designer rack. If you need an extremely fancy dress or suit or just want some designer duds so you can look as cool as the folks on TV, it's worth the trip.

**Jet Rag** (825 N. La Brea Ave., between Willoughby and Melrose Aves., Hollywood, tel. 323/939–0528). Here's the stuff that designers are copying and selling for three times the price. It's obvious that the folks running this bi-level warehouse, filled with dresses (starting at $12), shirts, leather jackets (a car coat, $28), hats, and fun vintage fabrics, are picky about their selection. Go for their $1 sales, every Thursday and Sunday from 11:30 to 6.

**Slow** (7474 Melrose Ave., at Gardner St., Melrose, tel. 323/655–3725). "Original clothing" is what they sell, but the extraordinarily original digs in which they sell their vintage and contemporary used clothes for men and women is what sets them apart from all the others. Cruise through the pleasantly unmusty warehouse-type space, chock-full of lush greenery, to find some outstanding, attention-grabbing clothes.

**The Wasteland** (7428 Melrose Ave., at Vista St., Melrose, tel. 323/653–4028). Everything from baseball jerseys to '60s cocktail dresses is stashed in here somewhere, and the celebs can't stay away. (Johnny Depp's been spied sorting through the vintage denim.) Take your cues from the funky staff here; they obviously dig into the stock.

# BOOKS

Despite its reputation as an intellectual vacuum, Los Angeles has a fine assortment of bookstores selling new and used books for every political bent, cultural interest, or curiosity. Don't forget to patronize some of the smaller local bookstores while you're here, or someday there won't be any.

## NEW BOOKS

**Bodhi Tree Bookstore** (8585 Melrose Ave., at Westbourne Dr., West Hollywood, tel. 310/659–1733). Pungent smells of incense accost the senses as you enter this store (really two stores in one) rife with new and used books on topics such as goddesses, Judaica, Shamanism, Tantra, writing, and Zen Buddhism. Lecturers and authors regularly come by to speak on topics such as Vedic astrology and Ayureveda or the spiritual tarot. Visit the annex next store and splurge on a 15-minute tarot card reading for $20.

**Book Soup** (8818 Sunset Blvd., at Holloway Dr., West Hollywood, tel. 310/659–3110). It's mmm-mmm good at this store crammed full of books and celebrity shoppers. The selection of magazines is ferocious, as are the authors they lure for readings and signings (like Walter Mosley, Tom Stoppard, and Alex Garland). Don't hesitate to get tips from the well-read and friendly clerks.

**The Cook's Library** (8373 W. Third St., at Kings Rd. between La Cienega and Crescent Heights Blvd., West Hollywood, tel. 323/655–3141). It's like your living room away from home, except this one is stuffed to the gills with cookbooks. Settle down on the worn couch or rocking chair and page through Julia Child's biography or Mollie Katzen's *Vegetable Heaven.*

**A Different Light Bookstore** (8853 Santa Monica Blvd., between San Vicente Blvd. and Larrabee St., West Hollywood, tel. 310/854–6601). The books (new and used) here are primarily about, by, and for gays, bisexuals, and lesbians. Periodically, the store hosts book signings and readings. Besides gay and lesbian fiction, erotica, women's studies, lit crit, and gay theory, it also stocks gay and lesbian domestic and international periodicals.

**Either/Or Bookstore** (950 Aviation Blvd., at Ocean Drive, Hermosa Beach, tel. 310/374–2060). This small, new-agey store houses things you need to read, things you want to read, and some things you didn't know you could read. For its size, the selection, dedicated to topics like metaphysics, travel, and sci-fi, is amazing. The magazine selection is not huge, but they have most of the big-name rags. The staff has picks for best new and not-so-new fiction and nonfiction, but the "Non-essential Reading" shelf is by far the most curious and enticing collection.

**Midnight Special** (1318 Third St. Promenade, Santa Monica, tel. 310/393–2923). This is the best general bookstore on the Third Street Promenade, if not in Santa Monica. These guys haven't just stocked the bestseller list, they've created a meaningful, important space. Every Friday at 8 PM, open-mike and featured poetry readings take over. If you want to read your sonnets, stop by at 7:30 to sign up. Besides these positive poetry programs, the store sponsors liberal-leaning lectures and frequently invites authors to read. Everyone should care so much.

**Samuel French Theatre & Film Bookshop** (7623 Sunset Blvd., at Stanley Ave., Hollywood, tel. 323/876–0570). Lots of brawny and beautiful hopefuls mill around the many aisles of books for cinephiles and theater buffs alike. Amateurs might want to stick with books like McFarland's *Famous Hollywood Locations* or pick up a play to read with a friend on your next long train trip through Europe.

**Small World of Books** (1407 Ocean Front Walk, Venice, tel. 310/399–2360). This Venice Beach bookstore has a corner dedicated to crime and mystery books, and a few times a month a crime/mystery or local writer stops by to read and sign books. There is also a decent selection of other books perfect for picking up on your way to the beach. The staff will do acrobatics to get the book you want.

# OUT-OF-PRINT

*The folks at these bookstores will hunt down that out-of-print book for you with a smile. Eric Chaim Kline, Bookseller (5200 W. Century Blvd., near LAX, tel. 310/395– 4747), specializes in Judaica, art and architecture, German language, scholarly, and unusual books. Moondance (11633 Santa Monica Blvd., at Barry Ave., West L.A., tel. 310/996–2665), an African-American– and Native American–owned bookstore, is stocked with literature about the experiences of their people as well as more general reads. Sam Johnson's Bookshop (12310 Venice Blvd., Mar Vista, tel. 310/391–5047) specializes in literary, scholarly, mystery, and fantasy books. West L.A. Book Center (1650 Sawtelle Blvd., West L.A., tel. 310/473–4442) has a good selection of general new and used books, with an emphasis on art, literature, and poetry.*

**Traveler's Bookcase** (8375 W. Third St., at Kings Rd., West Hollywood, tel. 323/655–0575). Duck in here to dream about a future trip or plan it with their seemingly small but actually choice selection of guides, narratives, and maps. The owner is a fount of good advice.

## USED BOOKS
*See also* Bodhi Tree Bookstore *and* A Different Light Bookstore *in* New Books, *above."*

**Arcana** (1229 Third St. Promenade, Santa Monica, tel. 310/458–1499). A gold mine for art freaks, the stock here includes new, out-of-print, and rare books on the arts of the 20th century. The helpful staff will try to obtain your heart's desire, as long as that desire is art-book related—not a bad deal.

**Bayside Books** (1234 Third St. Promenade, Santa Monica, tel. 310/394–8311). This tiny, Dickensian general bookshop is crowded with books, and the owners keep thousands more in "storage" (also known as their home). If you can't find what you need, ask at the counter, and they can probably get it for you by the next day.

**Book City** (6627 Hollywood Blvd., at Cherokee Ave., Hollywood, tel. 323/466–2525). Besides being the best resource for general used books in L.A., this store also stocks a hefty supply of screenplays and film books. There are so many books it's a good idea to ask for some help, which they will graciously give.

**Hennessey+Ingalls** (1254 Third St. Promenade, Santa Monica, tel. 310/458–9074). New and used art and architecture publications, including technical books, coffee table books, and magazines, are the focus of this large, airy bookstore. They also buy used art and architecture books for cash or credit. For the best deals, swing by for the 20%-off annual sale from the first Saturday in November through the second.

**Koma Books** (1764 N. Vermont Ave., between Franklin St. and Hollywood Blvd., Hollywood, tel. 323/665–0956). The sign over the door reads "Amok," and that's about as straightforward as this store gets. Esoteric to the bone, these folks delve into fringe works of all sorts. Conspiracy, the occult, and exotica, Nietzsche, Kerouac, and cheesy '50s paperbacks—you can never second-guess what you'll find here. The record and fringe magazine selections are equally, wonderfully peculiar. Check the crates by the door for $1 tomes.

**Michael R. Thompson Books** (8312 W. 3rd St., between Sweetzer Ave. and La Cienega Blvd., West Hollywood, tel. 323/658–1901). This museumlike antiquarian and scholarly bookstore has hardbacks on such titillating subjects as history, philosophy, literature in translation, and art. If antique books are your gig, stop by for a chat with the helpful staff and get some beauts for the shelves back home.

**Nations** (500–504 Pier Ave., at Cypress Ave., Hermosa Beach, tel. 310/318–9915). This mother of all travel stores (it takes up four storefronts) has travel books, travel videos, a map center, language tapes, travel accessories, and a travel agency. And you can't beat this: For every $35 you spend, you get back $5 in store credit.

**Psychic Eye Book Shop** (218 Main St., at Rose Ave., Venice, tel. 310/396–0110). New age paraphernalia and books are what this cozy, slightly creepy bookstore stocks. There is always a clairvoyant on hand (tarot card readings run $20 for 15 minutes, appointment recommended). New and used book topics range from witchcraft to Eastern religions, and you can pick some crystals or candles to help you portend the future or torture that worthless ex.

**Sisterhood Bookstore** (1351 Westwood Blvd., at Rochester Ave., Westwood, tel. 310/477–7300). Girls, what an atmosphere! It's cozy, inviting, and the books and music are all by, about, and for women. On the third Thursday of each month from 6:30 to 8, women gather here to discuss books like Simone de Beauvoir's *The Mandarins* and Nora Keller's *Comfort Woman*. The back room is resource central, with a want ads board, free newspapers, and flyers. The books span the literary galaxy, with sections devoted to topics ranging from feminist studies to travel guides.

# MUSIC

Record shopping in L.A. is a great way to blow cash in a flash. Even the most discriminating collector will be amazed at the quality and selection of sounds found in the city's main music stores. There are big chain stores like Virgin Megastore and Tower as well as small independent shops. Music stores are also excellent places to pick up information about who's playing where.

*For new books in San Pedro, head to Williams' Bookstore (443 W. 6th St., between Pacific and Mesa Sts., tel. 310/832–3631), a books, magazines, and comics store.*

**Go Boy Records** (1310 S. PCH, at Ave. F, Redondo Beach, tel. 310/316–1957). Yeah, dude, they've got a whole section just for surf rock—way cool. Come by to check the live music listings or to rifle through the rows of new and used records, CDs, and tapes. The emphasis is on mainstream rock, but if you're a good boy, you may find that rockabilly or jazz recording you've been jonesing for.

**Hatikvah** (436 N. Fairfax Ave., between Melrose Ave. and Beverly Blvd., Fairfax, tel. 323/655–7083). All international, all music, all the time—this small music store chiefly stocks Israeli and Jewish music, but you can also pick up Russian and Italian recordings.

**McCabe's Guitar Shop** (3101 Pico Blvd., at 31st St., Santa Monica, tel. 310/828–4403 for concert info, 310/828–4497 for ticket charges). This shop sells instruments and music-instruction books, CDs, and cassettes. It has a huge selection of acoustic and electric guitars, and even some Pakistani tambourines, African log drums, and porcelain flutes. It offers classes and workshops on banjo, rockabilly guitar, and the like. Come here for live acoustic folk, country, and blues on weekends (*see* Live Music *in* Chapter 5).

**Penny Lane** (1349-B Third St. Promenade, Santa Monica, tel. 310/319–5333; 1080 Gayley Ave., Westwood, tel. 310/208–5611; 7563 Melrose Ave., at Curson Ave., Melrose, tel. 323/651–3000). The massive listening stations are the appeal of this small chain of stores selling new and used LPs, CDs, and tapes. The selection is diverse, and they also stock music mags.

**Rhino Records** (1720 Westwood Blvd., at Massachusetts Ave., Westwood, tel. 310/474–8685). You can practically hear the beating pulse of the city's music scene here. The general selection is strong in international, jazz, indie, and alternative discs, vinyl, and tapes. Prices for CDs hover around $15. Check the store for a calendar of its upcoming in-store shows (free) and for flyers on the L.A. music scene.

**Ritmo Latino** (5515 Santa Monica Blvd., at Western Ave., Hollywood, tel. 323/962–0555). This music store is a warehouse of Latin grooves and sounds. It has CDs and tapes that are hard to find anywhere else in this country, as well as an almighty Ticketmaster desk.

**Virgin Megastore** (8000 Sunset Blvd., at Crescent Heights Blvd., West Hollywood, tel. 323/650–8666). This is one of those stores that threatens the existence of the small, independent music store. You can plug into one of the many listening stations to hear that new album all the kids are raving about. Sale CDs go for about $12. If you don't mind standing, call to find out if any in-store performances will be happening while you're here.

# FLEA MARKETS AND STREET MARKETS

Ads for garage sales are published in *The Recycler,* available at newspaper stands and corner stores around town. Also check the classifieds section of the Sunday *Los Angeles Times* for garage and estate-sale addresses. On sunny weekends (which are most weekends) impromptu yard sales abound, especially in the residential areas of the Wilshire and Mid City districts. Yard sales are rare in the hills, so don't even bother looking up there—you're better off sticking to flat land. The most outstanding flea market by far is in Pasadena (*see below*).

**Alameda Swapmeet** (4501 Alameda St., at 45th St., Central L.A., tel. 323/233–2764). Flee indoors to this smallish market, with free admission, where you can pick up an assortment of all-new merchandise from socks to headphones. About 200 vendors sell their wares here Monday through Friday from 10 until 7 and weekends from 8 until 7.

**Alpine Village Swapmeet** (833 W. Torrance Blvd., between Main and Vermont Sts., Torrance, tel. 323/770–1961). Even if you don't find something at one of the almost 100 booths, you can always lunch on German food at the restaurant. The vendors sell new and used goods in this indoor and outdoor market, open Tuesday through Sunday from 6 until 3:30 PM. Admission is 50.

**Melrose Trading Post** (Melrose Ave. and Fairfax Ave., at Fairfax High School, Melrose, tel. 323/655–7678). Every Sunday at 9 neighborhood folks circle around antiques and collectibles stands that shack up in a high school parking lot. Your $2 admission may be worth it or it may be a waste—it's a hit or miss experience.

**Olvera Street** (in El Pueblo de Los Angeles Historic Park). Come here for Mexican kitsch up the wazoo. Check out the velvet paintings (mostly Christian-themed) at **Casa Carolina** (W-21 Olvera St.). For authentic fashions for little *dinero,* visit **Bazaar De Mexico** (W-7 Olvera St.). Given that these guys are selling the same stuff they would in Mexico, prices can sometimes seem a bit steep, but keep in mind they've saved you miles of traveling. Besides Virgin Mary candles, wooden figurines, sandals, woven bags, and crucifixes, the pedestrian street has got many *muy delicioso* taco and sweets kiosks. Don't leave without munching a *churro* and listening to some Mexican bands play. It's cheesy, it's fun, it's free, and it's a great place to practice your Spanish.

**Pasadena Rose Bowl Flea Market** (1001 Rosebowl Dr., near intersection of I–210, Hwy. 134, and I–110, tel. 323/560–7469). This gargantuan gathering could leave your bank account begging for mercy. On the second Sunday of each month, rain or shine, vendors sell antiques, art and crafts, and new and old merchandise. The box office is open from 9 to 3; admission is $5. For early risers and the very best selection, you can get in at 7:30 for $10 admission. Most merchants leave shortly after the box office closes, but up until 4:30 stubborn shoppers can still find some last-minute sales.

# SPECIALTY ITEMS

Los Angeles attracts a great deal of weird goods. Maybe it's because the city harbors such an abundance of special-interest groups and eccentric and creative individuals; maybe it's because people come here to "create" a lifestyle for themselves and need the proper accessories. For terminally hip items head to Melrose Avenue, while complements to gay life can be found in West Hollywood. Art stores pepper the city, as do toy stores.

## ART AND PHOTOGRAPHY

**Bel Air Camera and Video** (10925 Kinross Ave., at Gayley Ave., Westwood, tel. 310/208–5150). Here at the largest camera store on the West Coast, the employees are wacko about cameras. They'll sell yours, fix it, or help you choose just the right one to buy. They'll even meet other stores' advertised prices, as long as it's not a closeout or discontinued item.

**Flax** (10852 Lindbrook Dr., at Glendon Ave., Westwood, tel. 310/208–3529). Notoriously pricey, this large art store has supplies for the serious artist or hobbyist and all-in-one kits for the dilettante. The staff is extremely eager to help, so bring a big stick or be prepared to give in to their excellent salesmanship.

**The Folk Tree** (217 S. Fair Oaks Ave., Pasadena, tel. 626/795–8733) This store stocks Latin American objets d'art such as Mexican pottery, handmade tin-frame mirrors, and Oaxacan carved wooden animals. Browsing is the name of the game, especially in the gallery in back. Next door, **Soda Jerks** (219 S. Fair Oaks Ave., tel. 626/583–8031) whips up the best fountain drinks this side of the 1950s.

**Frank's Highland Park Camera** (5715 N. Figueroa St., at Ave. 57, Highland Park, tel. 323/255–0123). This huge store has been selling, trading, buying, and fixing cameras since 1969. They even sell darkroom equipment and paraphernalia. Their prices are low, so shutterbugs may want to start their search here.

**La Luz de Jesus** (4633 Hollywood Blvd., at Rodney Dr., Los Feliz, tel. 323/666–7667). Tucked inside a whirligig store called Wacko, which itself promises "nutty & nasty novelty," La Luz provokes and titillates the underground art scene. The monthly exhibits mainly show paintings and prints, ranging from the loungy, '60s-influenced works by Shag to Tony Fitzpatrick's gritty etchings. Price tags can be too hefty to allow for acquisition, but a viewing is definitely worthwhile.

**Ten Women** (2651 Main St., Santa Monica, tel. 310/314–9152). This teeny-weeny gallery-store is filled with jewelry, furniture, and other arts and crafts made by a co-op of nine women and one man. You probably won't be able to afford anything, but the artists take turns minding the counter, and they are always willing to chat about their work or about other art resources in L.A. Call to find out when they'll be open.

## KITSCH

**aahs** (1090 Westwood Blvd., at Broxton Ave., Westwood, tel. 310/824–1688). There's a slew of writing paper, cards, and postcards—enough to leave any letter writer in a state of ecstasy. What's left over is a clutter of objets d'effort in futility, like mindless plastic figurines and dumb party paraphernalia, but you can also find some beautiful candelabras, glow-in-the-dark-kitsch, and gag gifts.

**ga•ga** (8362 W. 3rd. St., at Kings Rd. between La Cienega and Crescent Heights Blvds., West Hollywood, tel. 323/653–3388). The front window gives the definition of the store's name: senseless and crazy. Functional and crazy would be more apropos. Rummage among flower-ladened flip-flops, '50s-themed chalkboards, and decoupage photo boxes, then dive into one of the old-fashioned candy canisters on the counter.

**Hippocampus** (8870 Sunset Blvd., at San Vicente Blvd., West Hollywood, tel. 310/652–3245). They call themselves a general store, but this is true only in the sense they stock things generally not available elsewhere—like their small yet dazzling collection of replicas of turn-of-the-century greeting cards or the upstairs loft of antique bric-a-brac. This may be the place to find something fab for that lady or gent who has everything.

**Pickett Fences** (111 N. Larchmont Blvd., between 1st. St. and Beverly Blvd., Hancock Park, tel. 323/467–2140). Chocolate bar soap, baseball caps, fridge magnets, Hawaiian shirts, Western-motif tees, and so on fill the front of this small mom-and-pop shop. The higher-priced clothes take a backseat to the fun doodads here, but you may get lucky with the sale rack in the rear.

**Powwow** (8868 Sunset Blvd., at Clark St., West Hollywood, tel. 310/854–0668). Grab a cup of java and meander around this coffeebar slash knickknack shop. With the selection of Beanie Babies, retro clocks, and ceramic miniatures, anyone who calls themselves a collector will score here.

**Y-Que Trading Post** (1770 N. Vermont Ave., at Melbourne Ave., Los Feliz, tel. 323/664–0021). This might just be the most fun clutter-selling store in all L.A. Pick up a vintage lunch box, a trendy logo-tee, a '70s-themed poster, or vintage postcards.

## MOVIE MEMORABILIA

*See also* Book City *in* Books, *above.*

**Chic-a-Boom** (6817 Melrose Ave., between Highland and La Brea Aves., Melrose, tel. 323/931–7441). Step into the past and relish media flotsam dating from the 1930s through the 1970s. Old magazines and posters abound. Search out a copy of your long-lost lunch box on the shelf or just daydream about the stories behind the old photos and postcards sitting in a box on the counter.

**Collector's Bookshop** (6225 Hollywood Blvd., at Argyle Ave., Hollywood, tel. 323/467–3296). This is the place to find legitimate Hollywood souvenirs like movie posters, film books, and other cinema paraphernalia. The staff is helpful, so go ahead and ask.

**Fantasies Come True** (8012 Melrose Ave., between Fairfax Ave. and Crescent Heights Blvd., West Hollywood, tel. 323/655–2636). Be their guest. This store delivers Disney figurines and memorabilia for souvenir freaks. Avoid the park, the heat, the lines, and the outrageous prices by picking up a useless

# IT'S A MALL WORLD
## AFTER ALL

*L.A.'s suburbs might have spawned the world's first shopping malls, but did you really travel all this way to visit chain stores you could find anywhere? In case you did, here are three of your better options.*

**Beverly Center** *(Beverly and La Cienega Blvds., Beverly Hills, tel. 310/854–0070). This gigantic, fancy-pants shopping center shelters an exhausting consumer fest (the anchor stores are Macy's, Bloomingdale's, and Bed, Bath, and Beyond). Finally, a mall that really caters to women and men—that's why the benches outside the stores are usually empty. Whatever you do, don't go to the movies here, unless you want to watch the latest release on a screen the size of a television. Stop by the customer service center (sixth floor) for free tickets to a CBS taping.*

**Century City Shopping Center** *(10250 Santa Monica Blvd., Century City, tel. 310/553–5300). This large, outdoor maze is more than the sum of its parts. Paths link the usual chains (Pottery Barn, the Gap, Benetton) with the anchors (Bloomingdale's and Macy's) and plenty of specialty spots. The variety of stores, the all-ages crowd, and the thumbs-up movie theater and food court make this the city's best outdoor mall.*

**Westside Pavilion** *(10800 and 10850 W. Pico Blvd., between Veteran and Overland Aves., West L.A., tel. 310/474–6255). You shouldn't have any qualms about wearing a wrinkled flannel shirt to this casual, unintimidating mall—celeb run-ins are usually reserved for the Bev Center. Robinson's May and Nordstrom bookend the three-level complex; in between are national chains where you can get the latest uniform. The requisite cineplex is on the third floor.*

(but aesthetically pleasing) figurine (like a Quasimodo magnet for $4) without ever leaving L.A. They're closed Sunday–Monday and some Tuesdays, so call ahead.

**Larry Edmund's** (6644 Hollywood Blvd., at Cherokee St., Hollywood, tel. 323/463–3273). Movie stills and posters round out the incredible stock of books on film and theater here.

**Star Wares on Main** (2817 Main St., at Ashland St., Santa Monica, tel. 310/399–0224). Be a star (or look just like one)! Well, sort of. This eccentric shop sells things like Cher's plastic pants and leopard-print shirt, Bruce Willis's space training suit from *Armageddon*, or Angela Bassett's bikinis ($150 each) from *How Stella Got Her Groove Back*. Some of the wilder movie costumes are displayed on the wall so all can ooh and ahh over them. All clothes are marked with a (sometimes) reasonable price and the former owner's famous name.

## OUTDOOR EQUIPMENT

**Adventure 16** (11161 W. Pico Blvd., at Sepulveda Blvd., West L.A., tel. 310/473–4574). Outdoors people get slightly bug-eyed with desire here. They rent sleeping bags, packs, stoves, and ice axes for cheap; for instance, two-person tents are $15 for the first day, $3 each day thereafter. There's a small climbing wall for trying out climbing shoes. They're also a good source for info on local outdoor activities. Try to make it to their big annual sale May 1–9.

**Oshman's Sporting Goods** (11110 W. Pico Blvd., at Sepulveda Blvd., West L.A., tel. 310/478–0446). No matter what your game, chances are they've got the gear—unless it's fishing or bicycling, which they've left out of their repertoire. Be on the alert: They run sales every week.

**Surplus Value Center** (3828 W. Sunset Blvd., at Hyperion Ave., Silver Lake, tel. 323/662–8132). This store has a huge selection of genuine government surplus items at reasonable prices. Stop by to pick up a tent, sleeping bag, tarp, stove, rain gear, or clothes.

**ZJ Boarding House** (2619 Main St., at Ocean Park Blvd., Santa Monica, tel. 310/392–5646). When the surf's up, this fine establishment can provide the proper getup and instruction. Serious surfers, skaters, and snowboarders can stock up on gear at steep to reasonable prices. Novices might want to rent: Surfboards are $25 a day, body boards $15, snowboards with boots $30. Half-day rentals are also available. Private lessons cost about $80 for two hours. In their next-door-over annex they sell boardshorts, bikinis, sundresses and the like, so you'll look good even if you wipe out.

## TOYS AND GAMES

**Hollywood Toys and Costumes** (6600 Hollywood Blvd., between Whitley and Hudson Aves., Hollywood, tel. 323/464–4444). So you want to be a stripper? Pick up a sequined bikini, a long-haired wig, and maybe even some fake plastic body parts to prepare yourself. On the tamer side, choose from hundreds of costumes, wigs, and accessories for Halloween or props for your big movie. The store also carries children's toys and games. A zombie and skeleton are encased in the glass floor of the spooky entryway.

**Puzzle Zoo** (1413 Third St. Promenade, Santa Monica, tel. 310/393–9201). Puzzles, teddy bears, and plastic figurines are strewn about for you to play with and purchase. If you are serious about playing, make this your first stop—though you'll have to dodge a huge number of kids spazzing out. Ask for a free magic demonstration.

**The Wound and Wound Toy Co.** (7374 Melrose Ave., between Martel and Fuller Sts., Melrose, tel. 323/653–6703). The motto here is, "We do not stop playing because we grow old; we grow old because we stop playing." This small, friendly store is a good place to pick up a windup toy, a flip book, or a battery-powered dog to de-stress with on a Monday morning, during exams, before that big job interview, or whenever you realize you're starting to act like your parents.

## WINES AND SPIRITS

**Beverage Warehouse** (4935 McConnell Ave., at Culver Blvd., near Marina del Rey, tel. 310/306–2822). This mega–liquor store in a mini-mall has the largest selection at the lowest prices in all L.A. They have wine, spirits, beer, soda, water, and even tea.

**Los Angeles Wine Co.** (4935 McConnell Ave., at Culver Blvd., near Marina del Rey, tel. 310/306–9463). This small shop only sells reasonably priced wine; there's a great selection of bottles for under $10. Don't expect too much direction on what to buy, as the sales staff has better things to do. However, when you're good and ready, they will help you decide between a heavy Barolo and a complicated California red.

**The Wine House** (2311 Cotner Ave., between Olympic and Pico Blvds., West L.A., tel. 310/479–3731). These folks take themselves very seriously, which is okay if you are not easily intimidated or are actually a wine aficionado. They have an international variety of wine and liquor ranging from low to outrageously high prices. Some bottles have staff descriptions, and there are many wine guidebooks lying about that can help.

## MISCELLANEOUS

**Baha Coca** (7556 Melrose Ave., at Sierra Bonita Ave., Melrose, tel. 323/966–0096). Dramatic imports from Indonesia, Bali, and Morocco crowd this very zen home furnishings store. Iron candleholders, lanterns, mirrors, and furniture all have surprisingly low price tags. If your purchase is too large for your suitcase, the staff will hook you up with their shipper. With the blessing of good timing, you'll visit during one of their three huge two-for-one sales; call ahead to see if it's happening.

**Bouvardia** (8317 Beverly Blvd., at Sweetzer Ave. between La Cienega and Crescent Heights Blvds., West Hollywood, tel. 323/782–1800). The gigantic sunflower hanging over the door makes it easy to spot this small garden shop/full-service florist. Come here for indoor/outdoor accessories like shaped wire planters, rustic watering cans, and fresh potpourri for $3.50 a bag. The owner is so sweet he may even offer you a chocolate kiss.

**The Daily Planet** (5931½ Franklin Ave., at Tamarind Ave., Hollywood, tel. 323/957–0061). Of course, you can pick up newspapers at this neighborhood corner store attached to Bourgeois Pig (*see* Cafés and Coffeehouses *in* Chapter 3), but they also have local artists' wares, like decorative candles and jewelry. The collections of unique, erotic, and gay and lesbian magazines set this mishmash of print media apart.

**Greeko's Sandals** (1120 Hermosa Ave., at Pier Ave., Hermosa Beach, tel. 310/374–9040). Unlike many L.A. establishments, this is the real deal. Established in 1966 (and judging from the decor, still living in 1966), this house of hippie is the place to grab some tarot cards, incense, and a tie-dyed shirt. Never mind the name—you won't find any footwear here.

**Illume** (8302 W. Third St., at Sweetzer Ave., West Hollywood, tel. 323/782–0342). Just walking into this intimate candle shop can bliss you out. A cocktail of fruit-scented pillars ($8 and up), aromatic bath products, and friendly service keeps customers—including Melanie Griffith and James Cameron—coming back for more.

**L.A. County Coroner's Gift Shop** (1104 N. Mission Rd., at Marengo St., Lincoln Heights, tel. 323/343–0760). This is the perfect place to grab a trinket for Ma and Pa back in Nebraska. They sell beach towels, T-shirts, and toe-tag key chains, all emblazoned with the coroner's official emblem.

**Necromance** (7220 Melrose Ave., between Formosa and Alta Vista Sts., Melrose, tel. 323/934–8684). If you have ever been fascinated with natural history, Gothic jewelry, preserved bird heads, human femur bones as furniture accents, actual death notices of babies, or replicas of shrunken heads, this small gallery-type store will tickle you. The proprietress is charming and well versed in subjects of the curious kind.

**New Stone Age** (8407 W. Third St., at Orlando Ave., West Hollywood, tel. 323/658–5969). Peruse the interesting jumble of handcrafted pottery, jewelry, journals, frames, and coatracks (look for the one of JFK and Jackie O) in this artsy store. Say hello to the pet parakeets when you browse in the back.

**Restoration Hardware** (Beverly Center, Beverly and La Cienega Blvds., Beverly Hills, tel. 310/360–9651; Century City Shopping Center, 10250 Santa Monica Blvd., Century City, tel. 310/551–4995; Third St. Promenade, Santa Monica, tel. 310/458–7992). At first glance, this chain may seem like a glorified Pottery Barn, but their hardware and furnishings reproductions are tantalizingly unique. The repros cover a range of periods, from Victorian to 20th century. Prices vary, from $300 for an old-fashioned wooden teacher's chair to $12 for a mining lantern. No matter what, a stop here is great for nostalgia's sake.

**Skinmarket** (Beverly Center, at Beverly and La Cienega Blvds., tel. 877/777–5576). "Don't touch" is the exact opposite of this cosmetic and body care store's concept. Try on nail polish ($7.50), get a makeover, and if you dare, come face-to-face with a SuperNatural Fresh Face Mask in Coconut, Mango, or Blackberry ($9.95). If occasional groups of giddy teens don't bug you too much, you'll have a blast.

**Soolip Paperie & Press** (8646 Melrose Ave., at Robertson Blvd., West Hollywood, tel. 310/360–0545). When your card is doubling as a gift, here's where to get it. The handmade greetings in this service-with-a-smile shop elicit lots of oohs and aahs, as does the stationery (boxed and loose). Don't miss the art gallery and bungalow filled with sometimes-pricey personal accessories in back.

**Spice Co. Sunset Smoke Shop** (7558 Sunset Blvd., between Curson and Sierra Bonita Aves., Hollywood, tel. 323/874–4130). Sift through the deluxe selection of legal stimulants (from coffee beans to tobacco), along with accessories for illegal depressants (stone, wooden, glass, and ceramic pipes and bongs). Stop by for that necessary accoutrement or just to admire the graffiti walls.

**Sur la Table** (161 W. Colorado Blvd., at Pasadena Ave., Pasadena, tel. 626/744–9987). For anyone who's happiest in the kitchen, this store is a goldmine—and it's a great place to pick up a foodie gift. Besides the Le Creuset cookware, utensils from spatulas to oyster knives, and the extensive cookbook selection, there are unusual finds like Moroccan mini tajines ($5.95), four-bottle fine oil tester sets (just under $10), and funnily shaped cookie cutters ($1). Get inspired during their Friday night cooking demos.

**Three Dog Bakery** (8733 Santa Monica Blvd., at Hancock Ave., West Hollywood, tel. 310/657–1645). For the person who has everything: fresh-baked goodies for their pooch. Choose from assorted boxed samplers, or create your own gift with the pupcakes, boxer brownies, and beagle bagels in the display case. Oversized pillows, chic food bowls, and other canine-friendly stuff brings doggie heaven to earth.

**Zipper** (8316 W. 3rd St., at Sweetzer Ave., West Hollywood, tel. 323/951–0620). Lined with photographs from American road trips, this bright, airy space feels like a gallery but is actually just a fabulous place to pick up gifts for your loved ones (or more realistically, yourself). The unifying theme here is cool—the minimalist brand of cool. Check out the recycled vintage milk bottles etched with words like "love" and "be," or thumb through one of the design books by Herman Miller. Cocktail necessities and Asian tableware make up most of the interesting gift items. A twenty-spot should do the trick for something modish.

# NEAR LOS ANGELES

UPDATED BY LISA OPPENHEIMER

**P**opular wisdom has it that almost everything south of San Francisco is part of Los Ange-les—just ask beleaguered tourism workers here who strive to convince visitors that San Diego is *not* in L.A. In fact, many of the famous "L.A." sights aren't in Los Angeles at all; Disneyland, for one, is in Anaheim. But the umbrella term persists, and it's undeniably more glam, if not geographically correct, to say you're vacationing in L.A. rather than Orange County.

L.A.'s dual identity as both city and county accounts for much of the confusion. Where Los Angeles proper is just a blip (467 square miles), Los Angeles county is ten times larger, with 81 cities sprawling in every direction, encompassing cool movie capital-I-industry enclaves like chichi Malibu, hardworking Burbank, and Hollywood itself. The communities are distinct, but with show biz spreading and com-muters criss-crossing everywhere, it's getting hard to keep track of the cities' bedroom community sta-tus.

As you move farther from L.A., the magnetic pull of Tinseltown weakens a bit, allowing glimpses into other ways of life. Other industries include aerospace, health and biomedical services, and, in a nod to the area's mercurial rapport with Mother Nature, disaster-relief enterprises. Oil rigs and port facilities line the shore near Long Beach; in characteristic style, they're so nicely packaged that tourists often mistake them for attractions. Long Beach and San Pedro are also convenient departure points for Santa Catalina Island. Just 22 mi off the coast, Catalina is a world apart from La-La Land; the majority of it is undevel-oped and ruggedly beautiful.

Heading south from San Pedro brings you over into Orange County, a stretch of coast with pristine beaches, dramatic hillsides . . .and voracious development. But despite the miles of lookalike housing tracts, the area still has pockets of surfers, artists, and musicians. Galleries fill the streets of progressive Laguna Beach, a great place to spend some time on your way south toward San Diego or Mexico. The Pacific Coast Highway (PCH) is often congested with traffic during summer, so if you're in a hurry to reach San Diego you'll want to take I–5. But the coast road is the best way to discover southern Califor-nia's golden beaches firsthand, from healing ocean vistas to the tacky bric-a-brac of the tourist trail.

Going "behind the Orange curtain" doesn't mean you'll leave showmanship behind. Inland Anaheim, after all, is home to the first house that Walt built, Disneyland. As if the Magic Kingdom weren't enough, there's also Knott's Berry Farm theme park in Buena Park, a couple of nifty water parks, and kitschy tourist spots like the Movieland Wax Museum and "Wild West" dinner theaters.

Forget what you may have heard about Orange County's inaccessibility. While the inland expanses are unwieldy and the freeways often clogged, a trip here isn't nearly as bad as Angelenos make it out to be. Though locals may tell you different, most sights are easily within reach of L.A., as long as you don't mind traveling over half an hour. So blaze your own trail. But nondrivers, take note: Although public transportation is improving, it can suck up a lot of time and be a true test of patience. If you plan to use the MTA, you'll be happy to know that buses take bills as well as coins. You're best off carrying a combination of both as drivers *don't* make change. If you're going to be in town for a while, consider a weekly pass, which costs $11 for a Sunday–Saturday week (freeway charges are extra). *See* Bus Travel within Los Angeles *in* Chapter 1.

# PASADENA AREA

Your mental picture of Pasadena may be a mishmash of blurred images from New Year's Day television: the Rose Parade and the Rose Bowl. There's much more to this burg than flowers and football, though. For starters, there are several incredible museums, including the Norton Simon and, in nearby San Marino, the Huntington Library, Art Collections, and Botanical Gardens. The Old Pasadena historic district has been a tremendously successful example of urban renewal; it's now crowded with young people out to dent their credit cards. From the Pasadena Freeway, you can spot the Southwest Museum up on Mt. Washington, a cache of Native American art. The Rose Bowl hosts one of the best flea markets on the west coast every month, and on Thanksgiving the goofy Doo Dah Parade spoofs the Tournament of Roses. And as for that proverbial little old lady, she probably just nabbed your parking space.

For lodging and dining tips, plus schedules of current area events, pick up *Pasadena Weekly,* available free at most bookstores, cafés, restaurants, and supermarkets. The best way to get to Pasadena from downtown is to drive north on the 110 (Pasadena Freeway). Old Town Pasadena is anchored by Colorado Boulevard; California Boulevard, which runs parallel to Colorado, takes you to San Marino and the Huntington.

## VISITOR INFORMATION

The **Pasadena Convention & Visitor's Bureau** (171 South Los Robles Ave., tel. 626/795–9311, www.pasadenacal.com) supplies free maps, visitor guides and brochures, and events calendars; you can either pick some up or have them mailed to you in advance. The office is open daily except Sunday.

## COMING AND GOING

The most convenient way to get to Pasadena is—surprise—by car. From downtown Los Angeles, take Hwy. 110 north. From Orange County, take I–5 north to I–605 north to I–210 west. From the San Fernando Valley, take U.S. 101 east to Hwy. 134 east.

Commuter rail plans for the area are in the works but won't be up and running until 2002. In the meantime, the **Metro Transit Authority** (MTA; tel. 213/626–4455) provides frequent bus service from downtown L.A. to Old Pasadena daily 6 AM–midnight. Catch Pasadena-bound Bus 483 at Olive Street between 6th and 7th streets; the fare is $1.85 for the 45-minute ride. Look for schedules at the MTA Customer Center on level C of the Arco Plaza, on Flower Street between 5th and 6th streets. **Greyhound** buses run between 7th Street and Alameda in downtown L.A. and the Pasadena Greyhound station (645 E. Walnut St., at the corner of El Molino Ave., tel. 626/792–5116). They've got only three buses daily from Pasadena to L.A.: one in the morning, one around lunchtime, and one in the late afternoon. Buses from L.A. to Pasadena run five times a day between 7 AM and 1:30 PM. Rides take as long as the MTA buses, but they're more expensive; the fare is $9 from Friday to Sunday, $8 the rest of the week.

## GETTING AROUND

Like most of the L.A. area, Pasadena is much too spread out to cover on foot. Luckily, it's a pretty car-friendly town. There are several parking garages in the Old Town area, or you could snag a free space in the lots behind the restaurants and shops along South Lake Avenue.

Getting to Pasadena's primary attractions can be accomplished, in most cases, by bus. Local bus routes can drop you right by some attractions (the Norton Simon, for example) and within a few blocks of others. On the other hand, it's not terribly convenient time-wise; you could find yourself waiting over half an hour for a bus. The **MTA** provides bus service around town; the fare is $1.35, plus an extra quarter for transfers. For local routes, pick up a schedule at the Pasadena public library (285 E. Walnut St., tel. 626/744–4052) or the Arco Plaza customer center in downtown L.A. (*see* Coming and Going, *above*).

**Foothill Transit Bus Lines** (tel. 800/743–3463 or 626/967–3147) service goes from Pasadena to the San Gabriel Valley and Pomona, but you could also grab a ride down Colorado Boulevard. Bus 187 includes Colorado on its route, and the fare is just 90¢. Though Foothill's service in Pasadena is limited, locals generally prefer it to the MTA, if not for their cleaner buses then for their lower price and more frequent schedule (Foothill buses travel about every 15 minutes apart as opposed to 40 minutes or longer).

Pasadena's **ARTS buses** (tel. 626/744–4055) literally mobilize the concept of public art. There are 10 theme buses, including the Tournament of Roses bus and the Peace bus. Each loops around either the downtown or uptown routes. The downtown route hits the three major shopping districts: Old Pasadena, the Pasadena Playhouse district, and South Lake Avenue. The uptown route covers mostly residential areas. Times of operation for the downtown route roughly mirror shopping hours: 11–7 Monday through Thursday, 11–11 on Friday, and noon–8 on weekends. The uptown route has somewhat shorter hours. The good news is that they're free; however, they're not always punctual. The buses share some of the MTA stops; these stops are marked with pink triangles. You can pick up a route map at the CVB (*see* Visitor Information, *above*) or City Hall (100 N. Garfield Ave.).

## WHERE TO SLEEP

Most of Pasadena's budget motels lie along East Colorado Boulevard, just east of the city's happening area. Accommodations get more expensive as you head toward Fair Oaks Avenue and the heart of Old Pasadena. Rates are comparable to much of L.A., except during the week surrounding the January 1 Rose Bowl, when prices soar and vacancy signs disappear.

Despite being a wide, safe, palm-lined avenue, Colorado Boulevard is quite ugly in places. You can always head for the safety of **Pasadena Travelodge** (2131 E. Colorado Blvd., west of Sierra Madre Blvd., tel. 626/796–3121), with doubles for $50 per night. An even better bet lies so far east it borders the neighboring town of Arcadia: The **Regal Inn Motel** (3800 E. Colorado Blvd., at Rosemead Blvd., tel. 626/449–4743). It's extremely clean, with doubles for $35 ($180 per week) and kitchenettes for $5 extra per night. Closer to the action is the **Saga Motor Hotel** (1633 E. Colorado Blvd., tel. 626/795–0431 or 800/793–7242), which has 70 spacious rooms and a heated pool. Doubles here cost $63.

## FOOD

The number of restaurants here has jumped exponentially in the past few years, and Old Pasadena has surely reached a zenith in its gustatory renaissance. People not only flock from L.A. to dine here, they actually wait in line to do so. Prowl around the blocks surrounding Fair Oaks Avenue and Colorado Boulevard when your stomach starts growling. The Italian kitchen and bakery **Mi Piace** (25 E. Colorado Blvd., near Fair Oaks Ave., tel. 626/795–3131) is reasonably priced, but if you're a walk-in you may face a long wait. (Mondays are quieter.) If there are four or more of you, plan ahead and make reservations. Try the penne *all'arabbiata* (pasta with crushed red pepper and mushrooms in a spicy marinara sauce; $8.25) or the ravioli *al burro salvia* (filled with ricotta and pumpkin in brown butter with sage and parmesan cheese; $8.95). Across from Mi Piace is the more authentic and less crowded **Sorriso** (46 E. Colorado Blvd., tel. 626/793–2233), where you'll pay $13–$18 for dishes ranging from pasta and risotto to seafood. For more splurging, head for the shaded patio, cool interiors, and stocked bar of the **Clearwater Café** (168 W. Colorado Blvd., at Pasadena Ave., tel. 626/356–0959), where seafood entrées start at $12.

Another crop of restaurants lies just south of Colorado, along Lake Avenue. **Green Street Restaurant** (146 South Shoppers Lane, off South Lake Ave., tel. 626/577–7170) is a friendly local haunt with new twists on old comfort-food favorites. Menu items share the names of the owner's friends and family; one good choice is "Stephen's" grilled chicken sandwich with sautéed mushrooms, onions, avocado, and sour cream ($7.95). The boisterous, thickly accented voice on the information line at **Bucha di Beppo** (80 W. Green St., at De Lacey Ave., tel. 626/792–7272) is a hint of what's in store. This fun, family-style place has curious rooms with monikers like the Pope Room (look for a throne at the head of the table). Think big portions—dishes serve five to seven people each. The *macaroni rosa* (macaroni with chicken, broccoli, and mushrooms in a pink cream sauce; $18.95) is a big seller, as is the pizza. Part bar, part restaurant, and part belly-dancing venue (on most nights, anyway), **Burger Continental** (535 S. Lake Ave., at California Ave., tel. 626/792–6634) is popular with almost everyone in Pasadena. Besides cheap pitchers of beer, you'll find an excellent selection of Middle Eastern dishes; justifiably famous is the delicious chicken Corinthian ($9), baked in phyllo dough with spinach and feta cheese. Most nights, a quartet of Greek musicians plays on the outdoor patio.

# WORTH SEEING

If you tire of museums, check out the kitsch for sale at Pasadena's two well-known flea markets. **Pasadena City College** (1570 E. Colorado Blvd., at Hill St., tel. 626/585–7906) holds one the first Sunday of each month from 8 AM to 3 PM; admission is free. The mother of all swap meets, though, takes place at the **Rose Bowl** (1001 Rosebowl Dr., tel. 626/577–3100 or 213/560–7469) the second Sunday of each month. Admission is $5.

**GAMBLE HOUSE** • From its roofline to its art glass doorway, the Gamble House is an incredible example of Craftsman style architecture. In 1908, when Pasadena was little more than a small town next door to L.A., architects Charles and Henry Greene created this fabulous, 8,400-square-ft house for David and Mary Gamble (of Procter and Gamble fame). The historic landmark shows off the designers' trademark love of open space and elaborately carved wood, as well as the turn-of-the-century furnishings they designed especially for the structure. If you like what you see, keep exploring the neighborhood. Next door at 2 Westmoreland Place is another Greene and Greene structure, **The Neighborhood Church,** a former residential home and now a Unitarian place of worship. Nearby is **Arroyo Terrace,** a curved street full of bungalows designed by the famous duo. Only the Gamble House gives tours (and these are necessary to see the interior); it tends to get crowded, so plan to arrive early as reservations are not taken. *4 Westmoreland Pl., tel. 626/793–3334. From Hwy. 134, take Orange Grove Blvd. exit north, first left after Walnut St., first right onto Westmoreland Pl. Admission: $5. Tours several times an hr., Thurs.–Sun. noon–3.*

**HUNTINGTON LIBRARY, ART COLLECTIONS, AND BOTANICAL GARDENS** • For a full-day culture immersion, the Huntington is hard to top. The basis for the complex was established in 1919 through a trust of Henry and Arabella Huntington. (Henry had a railroad fortune; Arabella, the brains behind the art collection, was first his aunt and later, when widowed, his wife.) The center now includes three art galleries, the library, and the expansive gardens. If you've got a taste for 18th- and 19th-century British and French art, you can sate it here with paintings like Gainsborough's *Blue Boy,* which generally gets too-cutely paired with Lawrence's *Pinkie.* Even the setting is carefully calibrated; these main galleries are mostly designed after French and British 18th-century style. There are notable Renaissance works as well and, in the Scott Gallery, American paintings that range from a colonial Copley portrait to Hopper and Cassatt. On to the library's rare books and manuscripts—ensconced here are a Gutenberg Bible, the Ellesmere manuscript of Chaucer's *Canterbury Tales,* a fantastic William Blake collection, and several early editions of Shakespeare.

Unlike most museums, you shouldn't pick a rainy day for a visit here—you wouldn't get the full effect of the 15 botanical gardens. You can walk through the 12-acre desert garden with the largest group of mature cacti and other succulents in North America, rose, camellia, and herb gardens, Japanese and jungle gardens, and, should you get overwhelmed, a Zen garden. The Pavilion, built in 1980, affords unmatched (albeit often smoggy) views of the surrounding mountains. Opt out of the several guided tours and wander serendipitously to your heart's content. The best time to visit is in the spring, when the cacti are in bloom, and the smog—which can smother Pasadena in summer—is in check. *1151 Oxford Rd., San Marino, tel. 626/405–2100 or 626/405–2141 for recorded information. Admission $8.50, free 1st Thurs. of month. Open June–Aug., Tues.–Sun. 10:30–4:30; Sept.–May, Tues.–Fri. noon–4:30, weekends 10:30–4:30.*

# NORTON SIMON MUSEUM

Like the Getty, this museum is a tribute to the connoisseurship of a deep-pocketed businessman. The building may be more modest than the look-at-me Getty Center, but Mr. Norton Simon's excellent eye is clearly in evidence and the collections are wonderfully satisfying. After he saved the failing Pasadena Art Museum in 1974, the eccentric and very particular Simon used to rework his museum's displays to his liking. For instance, he might put every flower painting in one room, lavishing that room with dozens of fresh tulips from the gardens. Even though he is no longer around to curate the displays, the museum retains a personal, intimate charm.

As you walk in you're greeted with a smile—from a towering Thai Buddha statue positioned under an oculus skylight. The wings on the main level span centuries of European art, with room after room of exceptional holdings. In the 19th- and 20th-century rooms, you could compare a wiry Giacometti statue with Brancusi's sleek "Bird in Space." Groups of Degas's bronzes (the museum owns a complete set) perch on pedestals, including a cast of "The Little Fourteen Year Old Dancer." The Impressionist and post-Impressionist roster also includes Cézanne, van Gogh, Monet, Renoir, and Matisse. Galleries for the 14th–18th centuries span fleshy Rubens portraits, Botticelli and Raphael Madonnas, and gold-leaf altarpiece panels. There are pastel Fragonards of cooing lovers and touching Rembrandt portraits, a glowing Tiepolo ceiling painting and a series of giant tapestry cartoons depicting the story of Dido and Aeneas.

Downstairs, the phenomenal Southeast Asian collection takes you back centuries. Two rows of stone pillars are studded with statues and reliefs, and the surrounding galleries are filled with graceful stone and bronze sculptures: smiling Buddhas and serpent kings, dancing Shivas and elephant-headed Ganesh figures. The lower level also has a few rooms for special exhibitions, often with a modern bent.

In fall 1999, the museum finished up a few years' worth of renovations. The sculpture garden was relandscaped, and the gallery spaces were redesigned (by Frank Gehry, no less). Don't worry if you didn't take art history in school—throughout the museum there are informative plaques discussing each work's significance, technique, imagery, etc. *411 W. Colorado Blvd., at Orange Grove Blvd., near intersection of I–210 (Foothill Fwy.) and Hwy. 134 (Ventura Fwy.), tel. 626/449–6840. Admission $6. Open Wed.–Sun. noon–6, Fri. noon–9.*

**OLD PASADENA** • This historic neighborhood is still basking in its successful revival. The 20-block area is bordered by Pasadena Avenue, Arroyo Parkway, Walnut Street, and Del Mar Boulevard; its heart lies at the intersection of Colorado Boulevard and Fair Oaks Avenue. The rows of two-story buildings and warehouses were the city's business district at the turn of the century—now you'll find restaurants, bars, shops, and guilty-looking L.A. natives enjoying the scene. Though plenty of chains (J. Crew, Starbucks) have muscled their way in, there are still some fun individual places to browse, like Sur la Table (*see* Miscellaneous *in* Chapter 7). Because Old Pasadena knows it's charming, expect to pay for parking at meters (until 11 PM, midnight on weekends) or at city-owned lots. To get to know its history in-depth, try a walking tour through Pasadena Heritage (tel. 626/441–6333), given on the second Saturday of every month.

**PACIFIC ASIA MUSEUM** • Not only is this one of the few museums in California that specialize in arts and crafts from Asia and the Pacific Islands, it's also housed in one of the gaudiest Chinese-style buildings outside Chinatown. Designed in the mode of a northern Chinese imperial palace, it has a central courtyard garden and a pond filled with koi the size of schnauzers. Enlightening exhibits on loan from other museums and private collections include Japanese and Chinese woodwork, illuminated manuscripts, and pottery. *46 N. Los Robles Ave., north of Colorado Blvd., Pasadena, tel. 626/449–2742. Admission $5, free 3rd Sat. of month. Open Wed.–Sun. 10–5.*

**SOUTHWEST MUSEUM** • From the Pasadena Freeway, you can spot this huge mission revival structure halfway up Mt. Washington. Its focus is Native American art, with a special emphasis on artifacts from the tribes of the Great Plains, the northwest coast, the southwest, and California. Check out the painted pottery, clothing, blankets, and especially the outstanding basket collection; there's also an 18-ft tepee. Just below the main building is the Casa de Adobe, based on a 19th-century, Spanish California adobe rancho. Deliciously authentic, cheap Mexican food is easy to come by along Figueroa Street in the friendly surrounding neighborhood. The museum has another branch at the LACMA West building in downtown L.A. (*see* Chapter 2) where it mounts rotating exhibits. *234 Museum Dr., east of I–110 off Ave. 43 exit, Highland Park, tel. 323/221–2163. Admission $5. Open Tues.–Sun. 10–5.*

# AFTER DARK

Old Pasadena is where several alternate universes collide. Weekend nights, the streets clog with everything from the white stretch limos of the nouveau riche to the Kustom Klass low riders of visiting gangstas. Various nightspots cater to the entertainment palates of upscale wine tasters and jazz aficionados as well as the rowdy partiers of discos and pool halls. Slick sorts queue up at Q's Billiard Club (99 E. Colorado Blvd., one block west of Arroyo Pkwy., tel. 626/405–9777), where it costs up to $16 an hour just to play pool—*if* they find your attire suitable (no tees, baggy pants, jeans, or tennis shoes, much less tank tops or torn items). If you don't fit the dress code, head across the street to **Freddie's 35er Bar** (12 E. Colorado Blvd., tel. 626/356–9315), a longtime working man's establishment, which has billiards and beer for less. **Moose McGillicuddy's** (119 E. Colorado Blvd., at Arroyo Pkwy., tel. 626/304–9955) draws a youngish crowd looking for sports scores and action on the dance floor. South of Colorado Boulevard is **Crown City Brewery** (300 S. Raymond Ave., at Del Mar Blvd., tel. 626/577–5548), which pours over 170 kinds of beer ($2–$7, but mostly in the middle).

If you're more interested in live theater than 16-ounce curls, consider the well-known **Pasadena Playhouse** (39 S. El Molino Ave., at Colorado Blvd., tel. 626/356–7529), which offers both revivals and new works. Look for laughs at the **Ice House** comedy club (24 N. Mentor Ave., at Colorado Blvd., tel. 626/

577–1894). It's been famous since the 1960s; some of the country's best-known comics (Steve Martin, Jay Leno, Robin Williams) honed their craft here. The place still hosts some excellent up-and-comers; call ahead for reservations.

# BIG BEAR LAKE

L.A. County's suburbs would probably continue to multiply were it not for the abrupt mountain ranges demarcating the Angeles and San Bernardino national forests (the two are divided by the ribbon of I–15). Though you may not believe it as you stand in smog-filled Los Angeles, an entirely different world awaits just two to three hours northeast and 5,000–10,000 ft above sea level. Within this vast acreage lies Big Bear Lake, a one-time refuge of cattle ranches and gold mines, now a source of year-round diversions for generations of grateful L.A. residents.

Though visitors swarm up here in winter to ski, Big Bear residents swear by the summers here as well—the fresh air rarely tops 90 degrees. "We're so spoiled, we'd all wilt in hotter," quips a local. Home base for most vacationers is on the south shore in the city of Big Bear Lake, where nature coexists with motels and homey restaurants. There's also the small village of Fawnskin on the north shore, which has a couple of inns and some quiet fishing spots.

## VISITOR INFORMATION

The **Big Bear Chamber of Commerce and Visitor Center** (630 Bartlett Rd., tel. 909/866–7000, www.bigbearinfo.com) has an excellent visitor's guide, many brochures, and limited information on campgrounds and hiking. The **Big Bear Ranger Station** (North Shore Dr., 3 mi east of Fawnskin, tel. 909/866–3437) has maps and detailed information on campgrounds and trails. The station also dispenses permits required for camping at undeveloped sites. About ⅛ mi away from the ranger station is the **Big Bear Discovery Center** (North Shore

*If Pasadena's heat becomes oppressive, cool off at the ice skating rink in Pasadena Center (310 E. Green St., tel. 626/578–0801). Lessons are available, just call the rink (preferably 24 hours ahead) and ask for the skating school.*

Drive, tel. 909/866–3437), manned by the San Bernardino National Forestry Association. It offers historical and natural information about the area, plus an extensive list of activities like mining tours, canoe trips, nature walks, and mountain bike jaunts.

## COMING AND GOING

To get to Big Bear, you've simply got to drive; there are no direct bus routes. From L.A., take I–10 east to Redlands and pick up Hwy. 30 north; it becomes Hwy. 330 and then turns into Hwy. 18 at Running Springs. Here, turn right onto Hwy. 18 east, which takes you to Big Bear Lake city. The lake's north shore can be reached via Hwy. 38 (North Shore Dr.), which meets Hwy. 18 at the dam. The drive will take at least 2 ½–3 hours. Winter weather in the area can be extreme; before venturing out, call Cal Trans (tel. 800/427–7623) for current road conditions, and don't forget a set of tire chains.

Many adventuring spots in Big Bear are forestry land, meaning you'll need a Forest Adventure Pass to park there. These cost $5 for a day pass, or $30 annually; both are available through the Discovery Center (*see* Visitor Information, *above*) as well as at most sporting goods stores and gas stations.

## WHERE TO SLEEP

Big Bear Lake city is chock-full of expensive matchbox cottages tucked between pines, with names like Snuggler's Cove and Cuddly Inn. A few budget options exist: The nearby **Hillcrest Lodge** (40241 Big Bear Blvd., tel. 909/866–6040 or 800/843–4449) is an appealing mountain cabin with 12 unique, clean, and comfortable rooms for $35–$45 in summer ($39–$59 in winter) and a soothing spa to relax in. **Motel 6** (42899 Big Bear Blvd., at Division Rd., tel. 909/585–6666) offers some of the cheapest lodging in the area, with doubles for $46 weekdays and $56 weekends.

Camping at one of Big Bear's six campgrounds is your best option during summer months. **Pineknot** (south on Summit Blvd., near Snow Summit ski area, tel. 800/280–2267 for reservations) has 48 pine-studded spots ($15) available from mid-May through the end of September. Two miles east of Fawnskin, **Serrano** (North Shore La., off Hwy. 38, tel. 800/280–2267 for reservations) has 132 sites ($15–$24) open May–November and more amenities than Pineknot, including showers and electrical hookups. The sparse foliage here means that privacy will be minimal. These two campgrounds fill up quickly, so

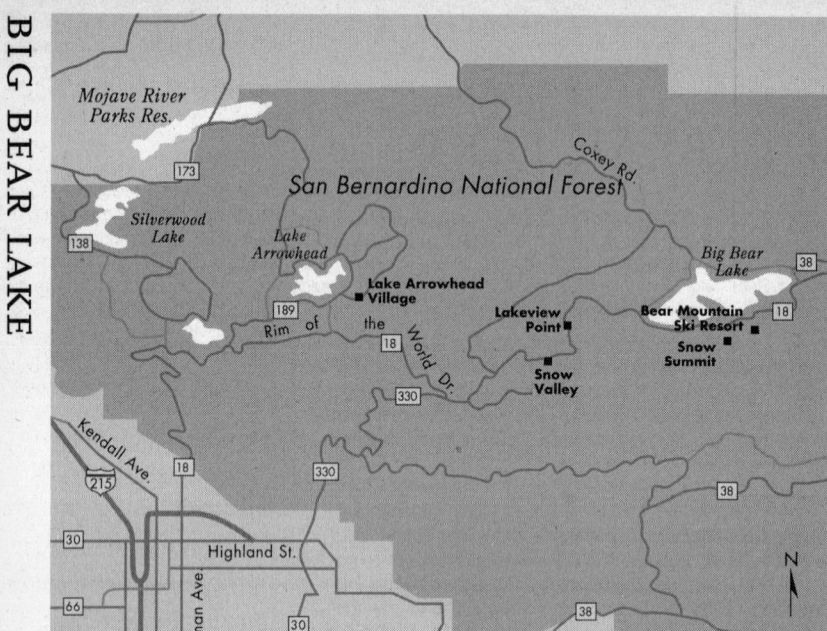

although you technically need to call for a reservation only five days in advance, you're safer calling three or four weeks ahead. It is possible to camp during the off-season, but it's only for the hardy. Off-season sites have no water and no fire pits—an important consideration since temperatures can drop into the 20s at night. For more information, contact the ranger station or Chamber of Commerce (*see* Visitor Information, *above*).

## FOOD

Local restaurants must rely on the appetite-inducing fresh mountain air to increase the appeal of their fare, as less-than-remarkable cuisine abounds. If you're jonesing for carbs, head for **Maggio's** (42160 Big Bear Blvd., in the Interlaken Shopping Center, tel. 909/866–8815), where the smell of homemade garlic bread lures people inside. Pasta dishes start at about $4.75. **Mongolian Palace** (40797 Lakeview Dr., west of Pine Knot Blvd., tel. 909/866–6678) lets carnivores and vegetarians alike fill up on all-you-can-eat Mongolian barbecue for lunch ($6) and dinner ($8). **Thelma's Twin Pines Restaurant** (337 West Big Bear Blvd., near Hwy. 38, tel. 909/585–7005), a local favorite in Big Bear City, offers a hearty breakfast special ($2.75) that includes two slices of thick french toast, two eggs, and bacon or sausage weekdays 6 AM–3 PM and weekends 6 AM–8 AM. In addition to being the area's most convenient and well-stocked market, **Vons** (Interlaken Shopping Center, Hwy. 18 near Stanfield Rd., tel. 909/866–8459) can also set you up with sandwiches and other provisions to go.

## OUTDOOR ACTIVITIES

Look for the monthly newspaper *Big Bear Today* at motels and restaurants; it's a handy resource for Big Bear's many outdoor activities.

**FISHING AND BOATING** • During summer, you can fish for trout, bass, and silver salmon from any secluded spot along the shore; a California fishing license is required for all fishing in the area. (You can get these at local sporting goods stores or convenience stores.) Struggle for casting space at **Dana Point** in the tiny north-shore community of Fawnskin, where some swear the fish bite better. The congenial owner at **Jack's Tackle Shop** (39730 Big Bear Blvd., at Iris St., tel. 909/866–6525) will set you up with rental gear ($10 a day, $35 deposit), bait (about $4), and the required permit ($10 for two days, $27.55 per season). You can rent a fishing boat or a pontoon at any of the lake's marinas, including **Pleasure Point Boat Landing** at Metcalf Bay (603 Landlock Landing Rd., at Cienega Rd., tel. 909/866–2455), where rates start at $14 an hour ($30 for up to 5 hours). The **Get Wet Water Sports Center** (38573 North Shore Dr., tel. 909/878–4386) rents Jet Skis and Waverunners (about $45–$65 an hour, plus deposit) and offers waterskiing packages ($87 an hour) that include optional instruction. If you pay cash here, you'll get a nominal discount.

**HIKING** • A compass and a good map are essential for any hike; **Franko's Map of Big Bear** ($3), hand drawn by local Frank Nielsen and complete with anecdotes on the back, is one of the best. It's available at the ranger station and the Discovery Center (*see* Visitor Information, *above*) if they haven't run out of copies, that is. On the easy, .3-mi **Champion Lodgepole Trail,** maps and signposts designate landmarks and greenery. It begins at the end of Forest Service Road 2N11 and meanders through subalpine forest. To get to the starting point, take Mill Creek Road to Forest Service Road 2N10 (a dirt road). Go 4½ mi, turn right on 2N11; the Champion Lodgepole Trail is 1 mi down on the right. The walk itself will take you along a small stream; it's perfect for novice hikers. The **Cougar Crest Trail** is a 2-mi, moderately difficult trail that begins a half-mile west of the ranger station on Hwy. 38. The trailhead is at the north end of the parking area, just off the highway. It traverses a mixed conifer forest of juniper, Jeffrey pine, and piñon, and provides beautiful views of the lake. You'll also get a gander at the remains of an old limestone mine. For a more in-depth look at the area's bygone gold mining trade, pick up the **Gold Fever Trail** handouts at the ranger station. The 13-mi, self-guided driving tour takes you through the late 1880s mining community of Holcomb Valley, while giving those tired dogs a rest—though ambitious souls can tough out the hike. Bring a flashlight, and you could take a peek into one of the mines.

**MOUNTAIN BIKING** • Mountain biking is popular in summer; purchase a map of bike trails ($4) at the Big Bear Ranger Station (*see* Visitor Information, *above*) or at a local sporting goods store. For $7, a ride up the **Snow Summit** ski lift (Summit Blvd., south of Big Bear Blvd., tel. 909/866–5766) puts you and your bike on top of 40 mi of roads and trails. A full-day pass gives you unlimited runs for $19; bike rentals are an additional $6.50 an hour ($22 a half day, $32 all day). The trails vary in difficulty but there's always a backdrop of spectacular scenery. The 2-mi **Cougar Crest Trail** (*see* Hiking, *above*) is a popular, moderately challenging trail. For bike rentals and information about bike trails, contact local mountain-biking gurus **Team Big Bear** (tel. 909/866–4565).

**SNOW SPORTS** • During winter, Big Bear fills up with those eager to shred the slopes of **Big Bear Mountain Resort** (43101 Goldmine Dr., east of Big Bear Lake City, tel. 909/585–2519), **Snow Summit Mountain Resort** (880 Summit Blvd., south of Big Bear Blvd., tel. 909/866–5766), and **Snow Valley Mountain Resort** (Hwy. 18, 5 mi east of Running Springs, tel. 909/867–2751). Though they'll never be mistaken for the Swiss Alps, all three resorts offer downhill runs ranging in difficulty from novice to expert. Bear Mountain has the highest elevation, as well as several ungroomed, experts-only canyons (snow conditions permitting). Lift tickets sometimes sell out on weekends, so consider purchasing in advance by telephone; the smallest resort, Snow Valley, is least likely to have crowds. Snowboarders may want to head straight for Snow Summit; locals claim it has the best hills for catching air. They'll rent you a snowboard for $28 (plus $300 deposit). Lift tickets at all three places will set you back about $40, with equipment an extra $25. It's wise to call for snow conditions: Get the Big Bear Mountain ski report (tel. 909/585–2519) or county weather and road conditions (tel. 909/866–7669). Cross-country skiers should pick up the cross-country skiing brochure at any of the ranger stations. It outlines some favorite local spots and includes a handy map. Most of the spots are off Forest Service Roads and require a four-wheel-drive to get to. On Big Bear Boulevard, rental shops sprout as soon as the first snowflake falls.

# SAN FERNANDO VALLEY

There are plenty of valleys snaking out from Los Angeles. But if locals are talking about *The* Valley, they're undoubtedly pointing you to that land of once ubiquitous "valley speak," the San Fernando Valley. It's been nearly two decades since the 1981 *Valley Girl* flick introduced us all to the gag-me-with-a-spoon vernacular. Grateful residents are happy to tell you that a lot has changed since then. The Galleria

Shopping Mall, once the center of the Valley Girl universe, is now defunct. Even original Val-queen Moon Unit Zappa (daughter of the late Frank) wouldn't, like, be caught *dead* talking that way. Local image makers looking to rise above the dated designation have hopefully slapped a new moniker on their homeland: Valley of the Stars.

The new name is at least partly accurate. Though there are lots of strip mall– and tract house–filled 'burbs here, Burbank, in the eastern Valley, has a bumper crop of TV and film studios. Drive north along Barham from the 101 and you can't miss the sprawl of sound stages making up the Warner Bros. back-lot. NBC, Universal, and Disney are also here (*see* Studios *in* Chapter 2). Apart from the entertainment industry, however, there's not much of a draw. Just north of the Valley is where you'll find most of the non-studio attractions, including Six Flags Magic Mountain (*see* Worth Seeing, *below*), with its gut-wrenchingly swift roller coasters.

## VISITOR INFORMATION

The **San Fernando Valley Conference and Visitors Bureau** (tel. 818/782–7282, www.valleyofthes-tars.org) has plenty of information and brochures. Make your requests ahead of time, however (by phone or via their website), since at press time the organization did not yet have a drop-in center.

## COMING AND GOING

**BY BUS • MTA** (tel. 213/626–4455 or 800/266–6883) runs to almost every part of the Valley, but avoid the bus unless you have hours to kill (no joke). Pick up the bus on Hill and 7th streets in downtown L.A. The local fare is $1.35; added freeway charges will make it a $2.35 trip. You can pick up schedules at the MTA Customer Center on level C of the Arco Plaza, on Flower Street between 5th and 6th streets, or at the MTA customer center branch in Van Nuys (14435 Sherman Way). For long-distance travel, **Grey-hound** has three stations in the Valley: North Hollywood (11239 Magnolia Blvd.), Glendale (400 W. Cer-ritos Ave.), and San Fernando (1441 Truman St.). Call the general information number (tel. 800/231–2222) for tickets and timetables.

**BY CAR •** The Valley's main streets are **Ventura Boulevard,** which runs east–west, and **Van Nuys Boulevard,** which runs north–south. Traffic is worst 7–10 AM and 3–7 PM, but even at nonpeak hours the highways look much like parking lots. The main freeways are the north–south **I–5** and **I–405,** which fol-low the coast to San Diego. **U.S. 101** runs east–west through the southern edge of the Valley, eventu-ally leading north to San Francisco. To get to the Valley from West L.A., take I–405 north or follow **Coldwater Canyon Boulevard, Laurel Canyon Boulevard,** or **Beverly Glen Boulevard.** These three streets can be accessed from Sunset Boulevard, and all eventually lead to Ventura Boulevard.

**BY METRO • Metrolink** (tel. 800/371–5465) offers service to greater L.A. weekdays from stations throughout the Valley. The trip from Burbank (201 N. Front St., at Olive St.) takes 20 minutes and costs $3.50; from Van Nuys (7720 Van Nuys Blvd., at Keswick St.) it takes 30 minutes and costs $4.50; and from Northridge (8775 Wilbur Ave., at Parthenia St.) it takes 40 minutes and costs $5.50.

**BY PLANE •** The **Burbank-Glendale-Pasadena Airport** (2627 N. Hollywood Way, at Thornton Ave., tel. 818/840–8847) offers service within and outside California. All international flights are handled by LAX (*see* Airports & Transfers *in* Chapter 1).

**BY TRAIN • Amtrak** (tel. 800/872–7245) has two stations that serve the Valley. In Glendale (400 W. Cerritos Ave., at San Fernando Rd., no phone) you can catch trains departing for all points along the Pacific coast; prices and travel times are similar to those from Los Angeles's Union Station (*see* Train Travel *in* Chapter 1). From Burbank (3750 Empire Ave., near airport at Hollywood Way, no phone) trains run only to Santa Barbara (2½ hrs, $12) and San Diego (3½ hrs, $17).

## WHERE TO SLEEP

Unless you're doing business in the Valley, there aren't many incentives to stay here, especially if you want to stay cheap. The term "budget accommodations" in this neck of the woods can be misleading, since many Valley lodgings thus advertising charge well into triple digits. Of the truly low-priced haunts that do exist, you may well have to contend with the sleaze factor. If you must stay in the Valley, your budget options will lie along Sepulveda Boulevard, north of Ventura Boulevard. But keep in mind, if it's under $35 it's probably dodgy.

The Studio City **Days Inn** (12933 Ventura Blvd., at Coldwater Canyon Ave., tel. 818/789–6900) may not be a palace, but for fairly reasonable rates you can call it home. Decor is vintage for the chain—the Bland Contemporary school—but you'll be close to whatever action there is. Rooms start at $59. The combination of baroque headboards, tropical bedspreads, and garish carpets in the **777 Motor Inn**

(4781 Sepulveda Blvd., 1 block north of Ventura Blvd., Sherman Oaks, tel. 818/788–3200) could make you dizzy, but the rooms are clean and in good repair. Doubles go for $49; they charge an additional $5 for a third or fourth person. Continental breakfast is included. The English country-style **Starlite Cottage** (5450 Sepulveda Blvd., between Magnolia Ave. and Burbank Blvd., Sherman Oaks, tel. 818/997–9754) seems like a fish out of water on Sepulveda Boulevard. The promise of its manicured shrubs, gentle pastel colors, and neatly painted trim is carried out in the fresh, carefully furnished rooms. Basic doubles go for $40–$45; $10 extra puts you in a theme room (French cottage, safari, Ralph Lauren Polo). All room rates go up $5 for Friday and Saturday night; there's no check-in at all on Sunday. If you're a nic freak, you may want to look elsewhere since all 11 rooms are no-smoking.

## FOOD

The Valley is blighted by countless indistinguishable chain eateries, many of them expensive. In the eastern part of the Valley, however, it is possible to eat cheaply and well. In Van Nuys, head to **Dr. Hogly Wogly's Tyler Texas BBQ** (8136 Sepulveda Blvd., south of Roscoe Blvd., tel. 818/782–2480) for L.A.'s undisputed best barbecue sandwiches ($6.45) on home-baked bread. If you can ignore the plastic booths, mirrored walls, and framed pictures of food in the window, **ZanKou Chicken** (5658 Sepulveda Blvd., at Burbank Blvd., tel. 818/781–0615) is a splendid place for falafel sandwiches ($2.75) or spicy roast chicken and pita ($3.75 for a half chicken).

For splurges, try one of the nicer eateries along Ventura Boulevard's budding "restaurant row." It's easy to spot the black and yellow awning of **La Frite Cafe** (15013 Ventura Blvd., at Lemona Ave., tel. 818/990–1791), which offers a scrumptious array of French and Italian dishes ($10 and up). You may have to wait for a shaded table on the front patio. The marvelous food at **The Great Greek** (13362 Ventura Blvd., near Woodman Ave., tel. 818/905–5250) is almost beside the point; it's the singing and dancing waiters that draw the crowds. Try the Macedonia shrimp pasta ($16) or a few appetizers ($4–$9) while you inspect the Greek newspapers that line the walls. Over at **Sushi on Tap** (11056 Ventura Blvd., at Vineland Ave., Studio City, tel. 818/985–2254), the chefs themselves do the dancing. On Friday and Saturday nights, sushi chefs step out from behind their ginsus and perform some lively tap routines. The food (about $15 for a meal) isn't bad either.

# WORTH SEEING

Several of the major studios, including **Universal** and **Warner Bros.,** lie at the eastern end of the Valley. For more information, see Studios in Chapter 2. You can even bring home a wearable memento of the experience from It's a Wrap! Production Wardrobe Sales (see Secondhand Clothes in Chapter 7), where you can snag threads from the sets of films, TV series, and soaps for a small fraction of their original designer prices.

**LOS ANGELES PET MEMORIAL PARK** • If you're unsatisfied by a dead-celebrity fix at the Hollywood Memorial Park Cemetery, there is, thankfully, a celebrity pet cemetery. See Stars, Sets, and Death Sites in Chapter 2.

**MISSION SAN FERNANDO REY DE ESPAÑA** • When you think of visiting southern California, historic buildings don't exactly spring to mind. However, this carefully restored mission at the northern edge of the Valley is well worth the trip. The 1797 structure is small, but its 35-bell carillon casts an enchanting spell over the surrounding gardens. The church's interior is decorated with Native American designs and Spanish–Californian artifacts. 15151 San Fernando Mission Blvd., Mission Hills, tel. 818/361–0186. From I–405, Mission Blvd. exit east. From I–5, Mission Blvd. exit west. Admission: $4. Open Mon.–Sat. 9–4:15, Sun. 10–4.

**SIX FLAGS MAGIC MOUNTAIN** • On 260 acres in Valencia, north of the Valley off I–5, await more than 100 roller coasters, rides, shows, and attractions. Magic Mountain's coasters are fast and wicked, in some cases turning the corner of questionable sanity. Among the newest is The Riddler's Revenge, an achingly fast stand-up coaster. The G-forces rack up as you zoom through loops and barrel rolls. **Superman, the Escape** takes you on a 40-story vertical trip up and, more importantly, back down— faster, and backwards. Eight other "monster coasters," with names like **Viper, Colossus,** and **Psyclone,** should reduce you to a quivering, jelly-kneed lump. If not, you're a prime candidate for **Dive Devil,** a bungee- jumping/skydiving experience where people dole out an extra $28–$48 to free fall 150 ft. Dive Devil is so popular, you'll need to make a reservation. Several of the other thrill rides get you wet, which could be a good thing on a scorching day. The faint of heart might do better at **Bugs Bunny World,** a Looney Tunes–themed area geared for young kids. When you've had enough of roller coasters, and if you remembered your swimsuit, head to the adjacent **Hurricane Harbor** ($19; discounted, dual-park

ORANGE COUNTY

South Gate
Downey
Lynwood
Rosecrans Ave.
Bellflower
Compton
North Long Beach
Dominguez
San Gabriel River
Los Angeles River
7th St.
Long Beach

Santa Fe Springs
Norwalk N8
La Mirada
Artesia
Cerritos
Lincoln Ave.
Cypress
Hawaiian Gardens
Katella Ave.
Los Alamitos

East Whittier
La Habra
Fullerton
Buena Park
Beach Blvd.
Anaheim

Brea 142
90
1
Placentia
Olive
Orange

Stanton
Garden Grove
5
6
5

TO PALOS VERDES, SAN PEDRO

Seal Beach
Warner
Sunset Beach
Westminster
3rd Ave.
Goldenwest St.
San Diego Fwy
Fountain Valley
Main St.
Pacific Coast Hwy.

Santa Ana R.
Harbor Blvd.
Main St.
Jamboree
55
8
Costa Mesa
10
73
Co de

TO SANTA CATALINA ISLAND

Huntington Beach
Newport Harbor
9
Newport Beach
Balboa

*PACIFIC OCEAN*

KEY
- - - - Ferry Lines

0                    10 miles
0                    15 km

Balboa Island, **9**
Bowers Museum, **6**
Crystal Cathedral, **5**
Disneyland, **4**
International
Surfing Museum, **7**
Knott's Berry
Farm, **2**
Laguna Art
Museum, **11**
Mission San Juan
Capistrano, **12**
Movieland Wax
Museum, **3**
Orange County
Museum of Art, **10**
Richard M. Nixon
Library and
Birthplace, **1**
Upper Newport Bay
Ecological
Reserve, **8**

Olinda
Village
Yorba
Linda
Home
Gardens
Corona
El Cerrito
Villa
Park
Cleveland
National
Forest
Santiago Canyon Rd.
Silverado
Canyon
Tustin
Irvine Blvd.
Santa
Ana
Irvine
Santa Ana Fwy.
Trabuco
Canyon
El Toro
Laguna
Hills
Mission
Viejo
na
Mar
Laguna
Beach
Pacific Coast Hwy.
Laguna
Niguel
San Juan
Capistrano
South
Laguna
Dana
Point
Capistrano
Beach
San
Clemente
San
Onofre

passes are available) and hit the water slides and rides. Look for coupons worth $2–$12 off the admission price in Six Flags brochures, available at L.A.-area tourist offices and some motels. *Magic Mountain Pkwy., off I–5 in Valencia, tel. 661/255–4100 or 818/367–5965 from L.A. From L.A., I–405 north to I–5 north to Valencia. Admission: $39, parking $7. Open year-round (Nov.–Mar., weekends and holidays only); hrs vary, so call ahead.*

**TELEVISION TAPINGS** • One of L.A.'s most money-glutted industries can give you an afternoon's activity—gratis. Television tapings are done in many Burbank studios, including NBC, Warner Bros., Paramount, and Universal. **Audiences Unlimited** (tel. 818/753–3470) supplies free tickets for most shows (*see also* Cheap Thrills *in* Chapter 2). If you're interested in coveted sitcoms like *Friends,* order ahead—way ahead—as those shows fill up fast. If you haven't planned ahead, you're not completely out of luck. You can sometimes get same-day tickets to Jay Leno's *Tonight Show.* Or fill a seat for a new, lesser-known show that's eager to recruit an audience. Of course, you may end up with something dreadful, but it could be a laugh. Either way, heed a few warnings: Arrive early, even if you have a ticket, as producers oversell to ensure a full house; and expect to stay a while as half-hour shows can take up to five hours to tape.

## AFTER DARK

The crop of nightspots in the San Fernando Valley has improved since the days of the Valley Girl. These days you're apt to find grownups roaming the streets, as opposed to just restless teens. One big draw is the neon-lit Universal CityWalk (100 Universal City Plaza, tel. 818/508–9600), where you can pick from a bunch of restaurants (Hard Rock and Wolfgang Puck cafés, for instance), catch a flick, slip into B.B. King's Blues Club, or simply people-watch. Unlike the adjacent Universal Studios theme park, there is no admission to get in, but you'll have to pay $7 for parking. In good ol' coffeehouse fashion, **Coffee Junction** (19221 Ventura Blvd., near Tampa Ave., Tarzana, tel. 818/342–3405) hosts a wide variety of live music. Players go to it on Thursday (5 PM– 8 PM) and Friday and Saturday nights (8 PM–11 PM), when there's a one-drink minimum. The daring can audition during open-mike afternoons on Sunday 3PM– 5PM. On the other end of the spectrum, **Mexicala Cocina Cantina** (12161 Ventura Blvd., at Laurel Canyon Blvd., Studio City, tel. 818/985–1744) soaks up the sports-bar atmosphere. It's got to-die-for margaritas as well as a house specialty, the Margatini. Food here is worth a try as well—authentically Mexican as opposed to the hokey, chain-restaurant variety. There's a nightly party at the **Sagebrush Cantina** (23527 Calabasas Rd., near Mulholland Dr., Calabasas, tel. 818/222–6062) where almost-nightly live music brings out a lively crowd, with everyone from bikers to corporate execs.

# DISNEYLAND AND INLAND

Far and away the most popular attraction that inland Orange County has to offer is Disneyland. Walt's original, utopic vision has expanded far beyond the classic towers of Sleeping Beauty's Castle. The park has upped itself to resort status, drastically revamped Tomorrowland, and continues to add attractions, often based on Disney animated films. However, there's more to the area than the mouse—other noteworthy destinations include Knott's Berry Farm, with its ghost town complete with authentic, relocated buildings; the Crystal Cathedral, one of the world's largest churches; and the Richard M. Nixon Library and Birthplace. Disney and Knott's lie in Anaheim and Buena Park, respectively, while the other sights are in surrounding suburbs easily reached by car. Accommodations are cheaper here than along the shore, but what you save in dollars you certainly lose in beauty—for the most part, this is a ghastly panorama of tedious suburbs, tightly buckled to the ailing defense industry.

## VISITOR INFORMATION

The **Anaheim/Orange County Visitor & Convention Bureau** (800 W. Katella Ave., Anaheim, tel. 714/999–8999 or 714/765–8899, www.anaheimoc.org) provides information about local attractions, events, visitor facilities, and so forth. The **Buena Park Convention & Visitors Office** (6280 Manchester Blvd., Ste. 103, tel.714/562– 3560 or 800/541–3953, www.buenapark.com) can also be helpful.

## COMING AND GOING

**BY BUS** • Greyhound (tel. 800/231–2222) has a station in Anaheim (100 W. Winston Rd., at Anaheim Blvd., tel. 714/999–1256), across I–5 from Disneyland. Service runs several times daily from the downtown L.A. station (1716 E. 7th St., at Alameda St.) for $15 round-trip, $8 one-way. **MTA** (tel. 213/626–4455) offers limited service to Orange County from L.A.; Bus 460 leaves downtown L.A.(pick it up at 6th and Hill streets) for Anaheim, Disneyland, and Knott's Berry Farm ($3.35 one-way). Within Orange County, call the **Orange County Transportation Authority** (OCTA; tel. 714/636– 7433, ext. 10) for information about routes and schedules. The local bus routes hit all the main communities and big draws, like Disneyland, but using the system can eat up a lot of time. The basic fare is $1; you must have exact change. There are no transfers, so if you plan on making more than a couple of trips, you should get a day pass ($2.50). There are two express OCTA bus routes that go to downtown L.A.: 701, which goes from Huntington Beach, and 721, which goes from Fullerton. The fare for these routes is $3, $2 with a day pass.

**BY CAR** • The easiest way to reach Anaheim from L.A. is via I–5 (a.k.a. Golden State Fwy. or Santa Ana Fwy.). There are hundreds of signs once you get near Disneyland and Knott's Berry Farm. Traffic can be particularly troublesome during rush hour (7–10 AM and 3–7 PM), but at press time, things were perpetually messy due to construction reconfiguring highway exits and routes. The Caltrans transportation help line (tel. 800/724–0353) can direct you around the construction. In a best-case scenario, it shouldn't take you more than an hour by car from downtown L.A.

**BY TRAIN** • All **Amtrak** trains (tel. 800/872–7245) between Los Angeles and San Diego stop at Anaheim Station (2150 E. Katella Ave., tel. 714/385–1448). Travel between L.A. and Anaheim costs $8–$10.50 one way. From the Anaheim station, OCTA Bus 50 heads to Disneyland every half hour. It takes only nine minutes to shuttle you to the Magic Kingdom. The buses travel between roughly the hours of 5 AM and 10 PM weekdays, until about 9 PM on weekends. Fare is $1. Amtrak also serves Fullerton Station (120 E. Santa Fe Ave., at Harbor Blvd., tel. 714/992–0530), which is 6 mi from Knott's Berry Farm and the city of Buena Park. From the Fullerton Station, OCTA Bus 43 (southbound) connects to Disneyland. The bus runs about every 8 minutes from roughly 4 AM to 10 PM weekdays. On weekends, service is every 20–30 minutes and goes until 9 PM. From the Fullerton Station to Knott's Berry Farm, take OCTA Bus 47 to Anaheim and transfer to Bus 42 heading west. Bus 47 runs about every 30 minutes. The fare is $1.

## WHERE TO SLEEP

You'll find ample lodging around Disneyland (Katella Ave. and Harbor Blvd. in Anaheim) and Knott's Berry Farm (south of Hwy. 91 on Beach Blvd. in Buena Park). However, many accommodations are rundown, and even so-called budget properties can be priced maddeningly like nicer hotels (up to $100 a night). It's hard to make a spontaneous trip—you'll need to reserve a room at least a week in advance, especially during summer, when hordes of tourists invade the area. Your best bet for a low-cost crash pad is the area's lone hostel (*see below*), but if you do opt for a hotel, remember that an AAA card can often get you a discount.

**NEAR DISNEYLAND • Alpine Motel.** The outside is admittedly cutesy (the "snow"-encrusted lodge smacks of *Heidi*), but the Alpine has clean rooms, a friendly staff, and a superb location for about $36 to $49 per night. This is about as close as you can get to the Magic Kingdom without paying a premium for a Disney hotel. *715 W. Katella Ave., at Harbor Blvd., Anaheim, 92802, tel. 714/535–2186, fax 714/535–3714. 41 rooms. Pool.*

**Anaheim Fairfield Inn by Marriott.** A rarity among chain hotels, the Fairfield stands out by its cleanliness, great service, and a relatively low price tag, with rooms starting at $59 per night. The hotel is across the street from Disneyland but runs a free shuttle that will get you around the construction. If you need to unwind after a day in line for the Matterhorn, you can loll in the outdoor hot tub. *1460 S. Harbor Blvd, near Katella Ave., Anaheim, 92802, tel. 714/772–6777, fax 714/999–1727. 467 rooms. Pool.*

**Desert Palm Suites.** This comfy hotel offers spacious, clean rooms with plenty of conveniences: refrigerators, microwaves, and Continental breakfast. Rooms run about $79; they often fill with corporate types from the Convention Center across the street, so reservations are advised year-round. It's hard by Disneyland, but its free shuttle means you won't have to hoof it. *631 W. Katella Ave., at Harbor Blvd., Anaheim, 92802, tel. 714/535–1133 or 800/635–5423, fax 714/491–7409. 105 rooms.*

**NEAR KNOTT'S BERRY FARM • Colony Inn.** This spankin' clean blue- and-white inn feels fresher than most budget places. Doubles start at $45; for $60 you can get a minisuite that sleeps up to six. The pool-sauna complex and a location across from Knott's Berry Farm attract colonies of families. *7800 Crescent Ave., at Beach Blvd. (Hwy. 39), Buena Park, 90620, tel. 714/527–2201 or 800/982–6566, fax 714/826–3826. 130 rooms. Laundry.*

**HOSTEL • Fullerton-Hacienda AYH-Hostel.** For price and location, the Fullerton-Hacienda is your best value. One mile from Amtrak's Fullerton Station (*see* Coming and Going, *above*), it's served by numerous public buses and is only a short car ride from both Disneyland and Knott's Berry Farm. Lockout is noon–4 PM, but there's no curfew. The rate for members is $13.45, for nonmembers $16.75. To reach Disneyland from here, take OCTA Bus 41 south to Chapman and transfer to OCTA Bus 43 south. To get here from Fullerton Station, take Bus 41 west (sign says La Habra) to Brea Dam Park. Reservations for a bed are next to necessary. *1700 N. Harbor Blvd., tel. 714/738–3721. 3 mi north of Hwy. 91 on Harbor Blvd., in Brea Dam Park. 20 beds. Check-in 4–10:30 PM, checkout anytime. Laundry, linen ($2), lockers.*

## FOOD

Most restaurants and food stands within the theme parks are overrated and overpriced—as in $3 ice-cream cones and $15 plates of leathery chicken and cold potatoes. The one exception is **Mrs. Knott's Chicken Dinner Restaurant** (8039 Beach Blvd., on Hwy. 39, tel. 714/220–5225), in the Berry Farm parking lot, where enormous six-course meals including fresh-baked berry pies and fried chicken ($10.95) still taste homemade and smell heavenly. If you'd rather pack your lunch, the **K&C Market** (8465 Western Ave., at Crescent Ave., tel. 714/828–9141) near Knott's has basic items; near Disney, the behemoth **Food 4 Less** (1616 W. Katella Ave., at Euclid St., tel. 714/539–7497) is open 24 hours and carries whatever you desire in numbing quantities.

**PoFolks** (7701 Beach Blvd. [Hwy. 39], between Hwy. 91 and La Palma Ave., Buena Park, tel. 714/521–8955) is your place if you're in the mood for a hearty homestyle meal in a slightly hokey setting (a sticker in the window boasts, "I'm Po but I'm Proud"). Country-fried steak, barbecued ribs, and Southern-style catfish are all under $10. Finish your meal with a scrumptious Mississippi mud pie ($3).

Don't be dismayed by the unassuming exterior of **Restaurant Ararad** (1827A W. Katella Ave., between Euclid and Brookhurst Sts. in Anaheim, tel. 714/778–5667); you can't go wrong with its delicious Armenian and Middle Eastern dishes. Pick out a few appetizers ($2–$4.50) to share, or go for the generous kabob combo dinner ($8.75). Vegetarians should try the creamy smooth metabbal appetizer, a tantalizing mix of blended eggplant, sesame, and garlic, which is superb slathered on pita bread ($2.25). Call ahead on weekend evenings to make sure the restaurant isn't closed for a private party. They don't serve lunch, and are closed Monday and Wednesday.

You'll feel like a kid again at **Tiffy's** (1060 W. Katella Ave., at West St., Anaheim, tel. 714/635–1801), a comfort-food mecca where the lure of homemade ice cream will make you want to clean your plate. This might be a challenge considering the heaping helpings. Entrées average around $6.

## WORTH SEEING

**BOWERS MUSEUM •** In an attractive, Pueblo-style building, the Bowers Museum mounts ethnographic exhibits from the Americas, the Pacific Rim, and Africa. Displays cover Native American arts and crafts, traditional African costumes, clothing, and artifacts, as well as a first-rate display of international photography. Visit the museum's Topaz Cafe (tel. 714/835–2002) for Southwestern cuisine with unique spices; lunch runs about $6–$10. *2002 N. Main St., Santa Ana, tel. 714/567–3600. Exit I–5 at Main St., go ½ mi south. Admission: $6. Open Tues.–Sun. 10–4 (Thurs. until 9 PM).*

**CRYSTAL CATHEDRAL •** It's been called a spectacular religious edifice, as well an excerpt from a bad science-fiction flick—take a gander and cast your vote. Either way, architects Philip Johnson and John Burgee certainly designed a unique house of worship; the glass-and-steel structure looms over surrounding Garden Grove in peculiar majesty. Home to Dr. Robert Schuller and his *Hour of Power* ministry, the cathedral also hosts Christmas and Easter pageants that are reminiscent of glitzy Broadway shows. Tours are available (a donation is suggested), or you could go for a Sunday service and hear the gigantic pipe organ. Keep in mind this is a working church—conservative dress is recommended. *12141 Lewis St., at Chapman Ave., Garden Grove, tel. 714/971–4013. Admission free.*

**DISNEYLAND •** Ever since it opened in 1955, the "Happiest Place on Earth" has been the childhood mecca of the West. If you haven't been here for a few years, you'll still find some of the old favorites: Swans swim in the moat around **Sleeping Beauty's Castle**; the **Haunted Mansion** continues to look for its "1,000th ghost"; the abominable snowman roars in the **Matterhorn**; and the **Mad Tea Party** keeps spinning over-gorged youngsters wildly about. Of course, the nostalgia is half the fun, but over the past few years several attractions have been yanked up to speed, so you're certainly not in for a museum experience.

One of the biggest changes is the revamped **Tomorrowland,** punctuated by the gilded Astro Orbiter. The '60s-style, once-futuristic rides have made way for up-and-coming technology in the **Innoventions** pavilion and interactive 3-D effects in the **"Honey, I Shrunk the Audience"** show. **Space Mountain** is still here, and with its updated sound effects, it's still one of the park's coolest coasters. Over in Adventureland, the **Indiana Jones Adventure** bounces you around the Temple of the Forbidden Eye—hold on to your hats. The newest "land" to date is **Mickey's Toontown,** which draws scads of little kids to meet the famous rodent. And even more change is afoot: Maddening construction outside the park's gates is the groundwork for a second Disneyland theme park, scheduled to open in 2001.

Once past one of the dozens of entrance-ticket booths, you'll ease into the park along Main Street, U.S.A., a section modeled on Walt's idea of the classic, turn-of-the-century American town. Study a map, get your bearings, and then plunge into the half-a- dozen theme "lands." Long lines—sometimes *really* long lines—can be a real problem at virtually all Disneyland attractions. Though some queue areas are attractions in and of themselves (like those at Indiana Jones and Rocket Rods, for example), it's a long, boring, sweaty wait at others where there's no shade, much less distraction. Your best bet is to visit the park weekdays during off season, like late fall or winter, when the primary audience is ostensibly in school. If you're intent on braving the summer rush, head to the most popular rides early in the morning, late at night, or during popular shows or parades. As for the park's food, Rocket Rods Pizza Port and Blue Bayou offer meals that are a cut above the standard, overpriced, hamburger-and-hotdog fare. For the Blue Bayou, however, you'll need to make a reservation as early in the day as possible. *1313 Harbor Blvd., Anaheim, tel. 714/781–4565. Admission: $39. Hrs vary, so call ahead.*

*In case you ever questioned southern California's devotion to the automobile: The Crystal Cathedral has a drive-in worship area, and the service is broadcast while you stay behind the wheel.*

**KNOTT'S BERRY FARM** • If the world knows Disneyland for fantasy, locals know Knott's Berry Farm for thrill rides. Once a diversion for customers waiting for one of Mrs. Knott's famed chicken dinners (*see Food, above*), Knott's, the oldest theme park in America, has grown into six different areas spread over 300 acres. Although the Knott family sold out in 1997 to amusement behemoth Cedar Fair LP, the folksy, friendly vibe remains. The good news is that the infusion of corporate cash has sparked the addition of more hair-raising rides, including **Hammerhead,** the **Supreme Scream,** and **GhostRider,** a fantastic wooden coaster. The company recently purchased the adjacent Buena Park Hotel, which marks the beginning of Knott's Berry Farm's future as a full-fledged resort.

The park's **Ghost Town,** modeled after an 1890's Old West mining town, is studded with authentic buildings, uprooted and moved from spots such as Prescott, Arizona. Activities here are linked to mining, like panning for gold, a gold-mine train ride, and the like. In the Wild Water Wilderness area, check out **Bigfoot Rapids** if you're hot and willing to get wet; the whitewater ride is guaranteed to soak you. If you need to rest, head to **Mystery Lodge,** full of weird special effects including a time-traveling Native American storyteller. The strong-stomached will enjoy constitution challengers throughout the park: **Boomerang,** which flips you upside down six times in less than a minute; **Jaguar,** which whips past a Mayan temple, and **Montezooma's Revenge,** which catapults you from zero to 65 mph in less than five seconds.

In October, Knott's Berry Farm becomes **Knott's Scary Farm** with disorienting special effects, 1,000-plus monsters, and lots of fog and chainsaws. Come December, it transforms into **Knott's Merry Farm,** a Victorian Christmas village with costumed characters and live performances of *Gift of the Magi* and Dickens's *A Christmas Carol.* In 2000, look for a birthday celebration for the world's most famous beagle as Snoopy turns 50. Like Disneyland, Knott's is prone to ridiculously long lines so plan accordingly: Pick nonpeak times to visit and hit the most popular rides early or late in the day. *8039 Beach Blvd., (Hwy. 39), ½ mi south of Hwy. 91, Buena Park, tel. 714/220–5200. Admission $36.00, $16.95 after 4 PM. Hrs vary so call ahead.*

**MOVIELAND WAX MUSEUM** • If you somehow feel that you haven't made your kitsch quota, try a visit to this celebrity homage. Covering the spectrum of Hollywood history from silent stars to action heroes, the museum showcases the likenesses of Michael Jackson, Little Richard, Bruce and Brandon Lee, Marilyn Monroe, and James Dean, among others. Figures are displayed in a maze of realistic sets from films such as *Star Trek, The Wizard of Oz,* and *Home Alone.* Believe it or not, there are more bizarre exhibits across the street at the Ripley's "odditorium" (7850 Beach Blvd., tel. 714/522–7045). Buy tickets for both and get a discount. *7711 Beach Blvd., tel. 714/522–1155. Admission $12.95. Open daily 9–7.*

# TIMES CHANGE, EVEN AT DISNEY

*In a nod to the politically correct '90s, the new-and-improved Pirates of the Caribbean ride shows the lascivious pirates chasing food instead of women. In 1998 Disneyland's Tomorrowland was dramatically modernized, ditching the old B-movie, sci-fi look that had earned it the nickname "Yesterdayland." (Breathe a sigh of relief that "Captain E.O." is no more.) In 1999, Tarzan took over the Swiss Family Robinson's treehouse. And there's more on the construction-filled horizon, as a second theme park, the California Adventure, will open next to Disneyland in 2001.*

**RICHARD M. NIXON LIBRARY AND BIRTHPLACE** • Built on the grounds of Nixon's childhood home, this 9-acre tribute to the life and times of the late 37th president was opened by Presidents Bush, Reagan, Ford, and Nixon on July 19, 1990. There are several things that are easy to mock: the 30-minute film *Never Give Up*; the "World Leaders" exhibit (littered with life-size bronze statues of Nixon's picks for the 20th century's greatest leaders); and carefully chosen snippets from the infamous Watergate tapes. There's even a gift shop (think of the souvenir possibilities!). But there's something both sad and stirring about the shiny marble headstone at the base of the Rose Garden. *18001 Yorba Linda Blvd., Yorba Linda, tel. 714/993–3393. Follow signs from Hwy. 91. Admission: $5.95. Open Mon.–Sat. 10–5, Sun. 11–5.*

## AFTER DARK

Inland Orange County isn't known for its exciting nightlife. Except for a few dance clubs and Top 40 hangouts, you'll find your options sorely limited; pick up the *O.C. Weekly* (at record stores and cafés) to scrounge some ideas. One happy exception is **Linda's Doll Hut** (107 S. Adams, tel. 714/533–1286) in Anaheim. This awesome live music club has broken many an act, from rockabilly to punk. If you're looking for something other than a movie and can stomach the idea of hanging out at a mall, try the **Block at Orange** (The City Drive, Orange, tel. 714/769–4001). This latest retail shrine is actually mostly entertainment, with high-tech playgrounds like GameWorks (owned by Steven Spielberg) and Dave & Busters offering a bar alongside souped-up arcade games. Or risk breaking your behind on the indoor/outdoor Vans Skateboard Park. If you want to wet your whistle, **The Olde Ship** (709 N. Harbor Blvd., Fullerton, tel. 714/871–7447) is a traditional British pub and a laid-back local watering hole. Be sure to check out the loo, where British tabloids line the walls.

If you don't mind driving a while, you could head over to Irvine; there's a University of California campus there, with the accompanying collegiate hangouts. The **Improv** (4255 Campus Dr., tel. 949/854–5455) offers live stand-up comedy nightly; the best acts appear on Friday and Saturday.

The pickings can be better on the arts front. Find out what's playing at the **Orange County Performing Arts Center** (600 Town Center Dr., Costa Mesa, tel. 714/556–2787); it frequently hosts the American Ballet Theatre, the L.A. Philharmonic, the New York Opera, and other impressive companies. Performances can be steep ($30–$70), but student and senior discounts are available one hour before some shows. Just across the way is **South Coast Reperatory** (655 Town Center Dr., Costa Mesa, tel. 714/708–5500), a two-stage venue that often premieres excellent new plays. Seasons here can span classics (George Bernard Shaw) and modern works (Sam Shepard), and often earn raves from all over the country. Anaheim's new (1999) **Sun Theatre** (2200 E. Katella Ave., tel. 714/712–2700) has some funky headliners, from Brian Wilson to Tito Puente to the Cramps. It's a midsize, soundstage style venue, so it's got a more hands-on feel. Over at the University of California Irvine campus, the **Irvine Barclay Theater** (4242 Campus Dr., tel. 949/854–4646) presents a wide range of performers, from soprano Dawn Upshaw to actor Spalding Gray.

# In case you want to see the world.

At American Express, we're here to make your journey

a smooth one. So we have over 1,700 travel service loca-

tions in over 130 countries ready to help. What else

would you expect from the world's largest travel agency?

do more

**Travel**

Call 1 800 AXP-3429 or visit
www.americanexpress.com/travel

# In case you want to be welcomed there.

**We're here to see that you're always welcomed at establishments everywhere. That's why millions of people carry the American Express® Card – for peace of mind, confidence, and security, around the world or just around the corner.**

do more    AMERICAN EXPRESS

Cards

**To apply, call 1 800 THE-CARD
or visit www.americanexpress.com**

# In case you're running low.

We're here to help with more than 190,000 Express Cash locations around the world. In order to enroll, just call American Express at 1 800 CASH-NOW before you start your vacation.

do more AMERICAN EXPRESS

Express Cash

# And in case you'd rather be safe than sorry.

We're here with American Express® Travelers Cheques. They're the safe way to carry money on your vacation, because if they're ever lost or stolen you can get a refund, practically anywhere or anytime. To find the nearest place to buy Travelers Cheques, call 1 800 495-1153. Another way we help you do more.

do more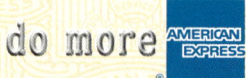

**Travelers Cheques**

# SANTA CATALINA ISLAND

Just a couple of hours' sail away from L.A.'s coastal communities, Santa Catalina (known here as simply Catalina) is the perfect spot for a weekend escape. The pristine shores lure over yachters and backpackers, divers and day-trippers.

Long before the pleasure-cruise set arrived, Catalina was home to Native Americans. The first European explorers, led by Don Juan Rodriguez Cabrillo, arrived in 1542, followed by Don Sebastian Viscaino of Spain, who named the island after St. Catherine of Alexandria. The centuries that followed brought a mixed bag of visitors—aggressive otter hunters and whalers, smugglers, miners, and Civil War troops—until the late 19th century when developers got the idea to turn the island into a resort.

Avalon, Catalina's main town, was developed early in this century by the Wrigley family of Chicago (as in the chewing gum), who acquired majority ownership in the Santa Catalina Island development company in 1919. The Wrigleys made the mountainous island into a tourist resort and a spring training ground for their baseball team, the Chicago Cubs. By the 1930s, the island had become a celebrity haunt as Hollywood stars—Mary Pickford, Norma Shearer, James Cagney—came to swing to the big bands. Not surprisingly, moviemakers found Catalina as well, making the island a backdrop for films like *The Sea Wolf, Captains Courageous,* and Clark Gable's version of *Mutiny on the Bounty.*

Things have quieted down since then; the Cubs no longer train here, and ballroom dancing in the Casino is but an occasional diversion. Still, the island's renown as a first-class playground endures, though with less fanfare, which suits the locals just fine. In 1975, the Santa Catalina Island Conservancy bought the title to 88% of Catalina so as to preserve and protect the land, ensuring that it would retain its rugged beauty. Luxury yachts, sailboats, and cruise ships still crowd the marina, but Catalina welcomes average Joes as well, giving you the chance to get in some snorkeling, scuba diving, and backpacking at reasonable prices.

The island has two hubs: Avalon, the larger and more populated, sees the heaviest traffic and is where you'll find all the food, shops, souvenir hawkers, and nightlife. The more rustic Two Harbors (23 mi northwest of Avalon by road, 13 by boat) has limited food and facilities but is quieter, equally (if not more) scenic, and offers seaside and beach camping at secluded Parson's Landing as well as access to the island's five wilderness campgrounds (*see* Where to Sleep, *below*). The extra time and effort required to reach this remote but attractive village means that it's less likely to be overrun by day-trippers.

## VISITOR INFORMATION

The **Catalina Island Chamber of Commerce** (tel. 310/510–1520, www.catalina.com), on Avalon's green Pleasure Pier, has maps, brochures, a visitor's guide, and information on hotel availability; either drop in during your stay, or ask to have the information mailed in advance. The **Catalina Island Interpretative Center** (1202 Avalon Canyon Rd., tel. 310/510–2514) focuses on the island's natural habitats and history. In Two Harbors, the **visitor center** (tel. 310/510–0303) at the end of the pier can advise you on that town's activities and amenities.

## COMING AND GOING

How fast you get to Catalina depends on how much you're willing to spend. The deep-pocketed can zip over in 15 minutes via helicopter—that is, if you're not cruising over on your yacht. The rest of us will have to make do with ferries, departing regularly to Avalon from Long Beach, San Pedro, Newport, and Dana Point. The least expensive of the lot, **Catalina Cruises** (320 Golden Shore Blvd., Long Beach, tel. 800/228–2546), will take you the longest. The two-hour ride costs $25 round-trip to Avalon. Boats depart from Catalina Landing in downtown Long Beach. Their service to Two Harbors is the same price, but requires an additional hour of travel time. Several ferries a day head to Avalon in summer, with less frequent service to Two Harbors; call ahead for the schedule. For a few extra bucks, **Catalina Express** (tel. 310/519–1212) speeds over to Avalon in about an hour from Berth 95 in San Pedro (follow signs from I–110) or from the Queen Mary in Long Beach (off Queen's Way Dr.). The company recently launched service from Dana Point (the Dana Wharf Sports Fishing Pier, off Golden Lantern St), but expect to be at sea for an extra half hour. They also have direct ferries to Two Harbors from San Pedro

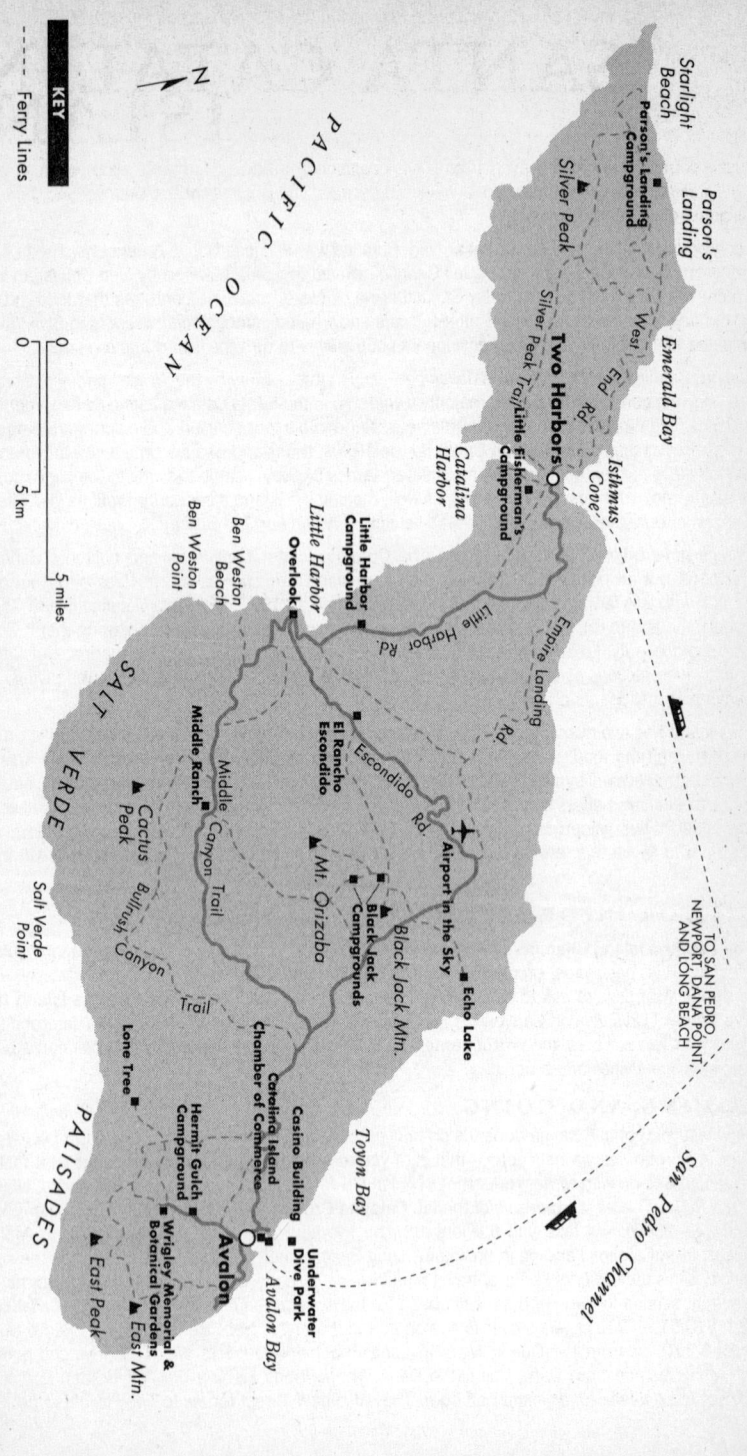

SANTA CATALINA ISLAND

only; call ahead for the (erratic) schedule. Round-trip tickets from all locations cost $38. From Newport Beach, pick up **Catalina Passenger Service** at the Balboa Pier (400 Main St., Balboa, tel. 949/673–5245); it goes only to Avalon, and the 75-minute ride costs $36 round-trip. Excessive baggage is not allowed, and reservations are required. All three ferry lines charge extra if you bring bicycles and surfboards. Boats have both indoor and outdoor seating and snack bars. Reserving two weeks ahead is a must, especially during summer. Since the waters around Santa Catalina can get rough, you may want to bring along some seasickness pills.

## GETTING AROUND

Motor traffic on the island is strictly limited; only residents are allowed to have cars here, and there's a ten-year waiting list. Those who do have cars require an electronic key card to drive through the gates of Avalon to outlying areas. Inside Avalon, the town is small enough to explore on foot—a true rarity in California. This makes the notion of renting a **golf cart** ($30 per hour plus $30 deposit) seem ridiculous, but nonetheless they're quite popular, so distracted pedestrians beware. **Bicycles** are another option, though you'll need a $50 permit to ride outside the town limits of Avalon and Two Harbors (see Outdoor Activities, below).

Bus and boat service can get you around outside of Avalon. In season, the **Catalina Safari Bus** (tel. 310/510–2800) offers twice- daily transportation between Avalon, Two Harbors, and several campgrounds for $36 round-trip; check schedules as bus service decreases off season. Buses depart from Island Tour Plaza in Avalon and from the bus station just inside town in Two Harbors. In summers past, **Two Harbors** (tel. 310/510–0303) has run an express boat shuttling between Avalon and Two Harbors, but the boat's future was in question at press time, so call ahead to check on its status. To actually learn about what you're driving through, **Discovery Tours** (tel. 310/510–2800) offers tours of the island's undeveloped interior. (Keep an eye out for those bison.) Trips cost $19 for a two-hour jaunt, $34.50 for a 3½-hour tour. The company also offers several cruises for viewing sea lions and other aquatic wildlife.

## WHERE TO SLEEP

If you want to stay overnight without camping, prepare to lay down a lot of cash. Not only that, but most lodgings have two-night minimums in season. In Avalon, your cheapest option is the **Hermosa Hotel and Catalina Cottages** (131 Metropole St., between Crescent Ave. and Beacon St., tel. 310/510–1010 or 800/666–3383), where you can get tidy, sparse rooms with shared bath for $45–$65 in summer, or private cottages with kitchen and bath for $70–$95. At **Hotel Atwater** (125 Sumner Ave., ½ block inland from Crescent Ave., tel. 800/851–0217), decent doubles in the unrenovated section of the building go for $61 weekdays and $80 weekends during summer. It closes from mid-November to mid-February; from mid-February to mid-March it takes guests on weekends only. The cheerful, yellow **Catalina Lodge** (235 Sumner Ave., at Beacon St., tel. 310/510–1070) has only 15 rooms ($89 weekdays, $94 weekends in season), but it's clean and cozy and a jovial proprietor keeps things lively. It closes between mid-November and mid-January. If you're scrounging for a room off-season, be sure to ask about discounts; many places lower their rates.

**CAMPING •** Avalon's only campground is **Hermit Gulch,** 1 mi southwest of town at the end of Avalon Canyon Road. With room for 240 people in 68 sites, this could hardly be classified as "getting away from it all"; the campground is usually filled with families and large groups. However, it's an easy walk into town (summer tram service available, $1 one-way), and it's cheaper than any Avalon inn.

If you can, experience the island's rugged outback and secluded coves. Inland **Black Jack Campground,** midway between Avalon and Two Harbors, offers stunning mountain vistas, while **Little Harbor Campground,** 7 mi south of Two Harbors on the opposite coast, overlooks a serene beach. Both can be reached by shuttle (see Getting Around, above) or hiking (you can bike to Little Harbor as well), and both have cold showers and chemical toilets. The **Two Harbors Campground** sits ¼ mile from the eponymous village; it has cold showers, chemical toilets, and, from many sites, ocean views.

Rates for all campgrounds (except Parson's Landing, below) run $12 per person. Hermit Gulch and Two Harbors also rent tents and tepees of various sizes ($10–$25 per night), as well as other camping gear; tent rental is seasonal at Two Harbors. Reservations for space and equipment are recommended in summer and required in July and August; call the Santa Catalina Island Company's central reservations line (tel. 310/510–2800).

If you really want to get away from it all, bring everything you'll need to survive—this includes food and water—and hike on out to **Parson's Landing.** Parson's is 7 mi west of Two Harbors on the island's northwest shore. In summer, a scheduled shoreboat shuttles from Two Harbors to Emerald Bay; from Emer-

# WHERE THE
# BUFFALO ROAM

*Zane Grey—the writer who put the western novel on the map—spent a lot of time on Catalina, and his influence is still evident in a peculiar way. When the movie version of Grey's book* The Vanishing American *was filmed here in the 1920s, buffalo were ferried across from the mainland. (Pigs, goats, and deer were also shipped over, but they lost out on the starring roles.) A small herd of buffalo remains, grazing Santa Catalina's interior. As for population control . . . well, there's a buffalo burger shack in Avalon.*

ald Bay, it's a 1½-mi hike to Parson's. Off-season you'll have to hoof it the entire way. There are six sites, and each can hold up to six people. All sites are located on the beach and include picnic table, fire ring, and barbecue. The price supposedly includes 2½ gallons of water and a bundle of firewood daily, but to be on the safe side, especially off-season, bring your own. Unfortunately, the pristine scenery comes at a premium, and at $21 for the first person and $12 for each additional person, Parson's is no bargain. If you plan to hike to your campground, you must also pick up a free hiking permit in Avalon or Two Harbors (*see* Outdoor Activities, *below*).

## FOOD
Santa Catalina's eateries are secure in the knowledge that they play to a captive audience; the food ranges from decent to awful and will sit best with those who enjoy a dose of grease. Fortunately, all restaurants keep menus and prices out front, allowing you to make a relatively informed decision. And you can take heart in the fact that fresh sea air almost always makes food taste better. The **Catalina Cantina** (311 Crescent Ave., tel. 310/510–0100) serves good Mexican cuisine at moderate prices; try an enormous "big and wet" burrito for around $8 and wash it down with a beer or a fresh-fruit margarita from the bar. Live bands play here on weekends. The **Blue Parrot** (205½ Crescent Ave., tel. 310/510–2465), on the second level in the Metropole Marketplace, has a decent spread of steaks, seafood, and pasta; entrées start at about $12. Tropical drinks from the bar, views from all tables, and whimsical decor almost make the prices worthwhile. After hours, don your favorite aloha shirt and slip into **Luau Larry's** (509 Crescent Ave., tel. 310/510–1919) for a fantastic variety of tropical drinks. If you're on a tight budget, hit the **Vons** supermarket on Metropole Avenue, a half block inland from Crescent Avenue.

## WORTH SEEING
**CASINO BUILDING** • The name might conjure up visions of roulette wheels, but Avalon's most famous sight has absolutely nothing to do with gambling—the name comes from the Italian word for "entertainment." The circular building is an art deco masterpiece; as you near Avalon on one of the ferries, you can't miss its white curves on the north side of the bay. Built in 1929, it played host to top-notch big bands of the '30s and '40s. Now it's home to a renovated movie theater, a historical museum (tel. 310/510–2414, admission $1.50), and a tiny, free art gallery showcasing local talent. For nostalgia buffs longing to relive the golden age, ballroom and swing dancing and evening concerts are still held here occasionally; check the Chamber of Commerce for schedules (*see* Visitor Information, *above*). In the hills above the building, look for the Zane Grey Pueblo (a tan building with a flat roof), once home to the writer and now a luxury hotel. *Casino Way.*

**WRIGLEY MANSION** • Chewing gum magnate William Wrigley Jr. and his wife, Ada, were the driving force behind Catalina's development; this was their family home for over a decade. They say Mr. Wrigley chose the hilltop site since it got every last ray of daylight. The 1920s building is now the Inn on Mt. Ada bed and breakfast. Unless you're staying there or enjoying a pricey breakfast, however, you'll have to appreciate the Inn from the outside, as tours are not available. *398 Wrigley Rd., tel.310/510–2030 or 800/608–7669.*

**WRIGLEY MEMORIAL AND BOTANICAL GARDENS** • Here you can visit Ada Wrigley's acres of gardens, which now focus on California island endemic plants, especially the six plants that grow naturally only on Catalina. There's also the monument to William—a tower made with as many Catalina-native materials as possible. *1½ mi southwest of Avalon, at the end of Avalon Canyon Rd., tel. 310/510–2288. Open daily 8–5. Admission $1.*

## OUTDOOR ACTIVITIES

Santa Catalina's varied terrain makes it an enticing place to hike, bike, and get your feet wet; however, efforts to preserve the island have led to costly permits and limited trail access. If the listings below sound too tame for you, you could line up a jet ski at **Wave Runner Rentals** (101 Pebbly Beach Rd., Avalon, tel. 310/510- -1922) or sign up for a rafting tour at **Catalina Ocean Rafting** (103 Pebbly Beach Rd., Avalon, tel. 310/510–0211); prices at both begin under $40.

**BIKING** • Mountain biking on the island can be a blast, but you'll need to buy a $50 permit to ride outside Avalon or Two Harbors. In Avalon, permits are available at the **Catalina Island Conservancy** (125 Claressa St., at 3rd St., tel. 310/510–2595). Permits are valid from May 1 until April 30 of each year, and applicants must have a mountain bike and helmet. You can rent both at **Brown's Bikes** (107 Pebbly Beach Rd., near ferry landing, tel. 310/510–0986) for about $20 a day. They also rent tandems and six-speed bikes ($6–$12 per hr) for in-town cruising. In Two Harbors, biking permits are available at the visitor center (tel. 310/510–0303) at the end of the pier. The Conservancy can dish out general advice and information on biking around the island.

**BOATING** • Joe's Rent-a-Boat (*see* Fishing, *below*) rents single ($10 per hr) and double ($17 per hr) kayaks. **Wet Spot Rentals** (120 Pebbly Beach Rd., Avalon, tel. 310/510–2229), next to the ferry landing, rents kayaks and pedal boats from $10 per hour. Kayaks can also be rented by the half- or full day ($30 and $45, respectively).

**FISHING** • Year-round, the sport fishing is tremendous in the waters off Catalina, with an abundance of yellowtail, calico bass, and barracuda. The once-large shark population, however, is rapidly diminishing. You can rent fishing equipment ($5 plus for 4 hrs) at **Joe's Rent-a-Boat** (tel. 310/510–0455) on Avalon's Pleasure Pier. **Earl and Rose's Seafood,** at the pier's end, sells bait ($1–$2). For a small fee, they'll also fillet and freeze whatever you catch. No permit is necessary to fish off Pleasure Pier or from the end of the cement ferry landing. While barracuda, bonito, and mackerel bite at either location, some say the larger fish are found at the ferry landing.

**HIKING** • It's possible to hike or bike between Avalon and Two Harbors, starting at the Hogsback gate above Avalon, though the 28-mi journey has an elevation gain of 3,000 ft and is not for the weak. For a pleasant 4-mi hike out of Avalon, take Avalon Canyon Road to Wrigley Gardens and follow the trail to Lone Pine. At the top you'll have an amazing view of the Palisades cliffs and, beyond them, the sea. A hiking permit is required anywhere outside of Avalon, but luckily, they're free. In Avalon, permits are available at the Catalina Island Conservancy (125 Claressa St., at 3rd St., tel. 310/510–2595) or at Hermit Gulch Campground (*see* Where to Sleep, *above*); you can pick up hiking maps at the Conservancy, the Interpretive Center, and the Wrigley Botanical Gardens. In Two Harbors, pick up a permit at the visitor center (tel. 310/510–0303) on the pier. Two general reminders: Bring plenty of water and watch out for poison oak. Also, during hunting season (roughly late fall to early winter) you'll be limited to hiking the main roads only.

**HORSEBACK RIDING** • You can wrangle four-legged transportation at **Catalina Stables** (600 Avalon Canyon Rd., Avalon, tel. 310/510– 0478) where scenic, guided trail rides start at about $20.

**SNORKELING AND SCUBA DIVING** • At the foot of the Casino building is the **Underwater Dive Park,** a marine preserve with two shipwrecks, kelp forests, and school after school of fish. It's a terrific site for scuba diving, with some shallow areas suitable for snorkeling. You can rent scuba (certification required) and snorkeling gear in Avalon at **Catalina Diver's Supply** (end of Pleasure Pier, tel. 310/510–0330) for $50 and $23, respectively, for a full day's usage in summer. Noncertified divers can scuba with the aid of an instructor for $85 for two hours. Snorkelers should head to the shallow waters of **Lover's Cove Marine Preserve,** a short walk east past the Avalon ferry landing; this is also a good spot to swim, since it's free of the boat traffic that jams Avalon Bay. Masks, snorkels, and fins can be rented by the hour or the day ($4–$10) at **Wet Spot Rentals** (*see* Boating, *above*).

# ORANGE COUNTY COAST

The 50-mi stretch of coast between Seal Beach and San Clemente is fondly known as the "American Riviera," (one of them, anyway), a scenic and lively seaside region of California's coast. Seal Beach, only 10 mi south of Long Beach, is a quirky, uncommercial small town—the perfect place to begin your coastal odyssey. The adjacent Sunset Beach offers no-frills sand and surf and budget motels. A little farther south you'll come across Huntington Beach, a trendy enclave filled with bleached-blond surfers and their suntanned groupies. The average age here seems to be 18–25. Sprawling Newport Beach, one of southern California's most exclusive seaside playgrounds, is just 40 mi south of downtown Los Angeles; its size makes it the unofficial coastal capital, particularly for boat trips of all types. At rugged Laguna Beach, the coast earns its Riviera nickname—it's beginning to resemble Prince Rainier's cliffside Monaco. Laguna has also been a colorful coastal stop since the '60s, when Timothy Leary and his hippie cronies hung out in the town's fast-food joints. The final two stops are San Juan Capistrano and San Clemente, both worth a short visit—the former for its historic mission and the latter for its narrow, crowd-free beaches. Wherever you go, pay attention to the brown COASTAL ACCESS signs; they may lead you to a completely untouristed stretch of sand.

Nothing comes cheap on this part of California's coast, including lodging. There is a youth hostel in San Clemente, and you'll find excellent campgrounds near San Juan Capistrano, but otherwise be prepared to spend upward of $40 for lodging along the coast. You'll also pay anywhere from $2 to $10 for daytime parking at most beaches.

## VISITOR INFORMATION

Though the **Anaheim/Orange County Visitor & Convention Bureau** (800 W. Katella Ave., Anaheim, tel. 714/999–8999 or 714/765–8899, www.anaheimoc.org) specializes in inland towns, they can certainly help with questions on the coastal towns.

## COMING AND GOING

**BY BUS** • The **Santa Ana Greyhound Station** (1000 E. Santa Ana Blvd., at Santiago Blvd., tel. 714/542–2215 or 800/231–2222) lies in the Transit Center just off the Santa Ana Freeway, 10 mi north of Newport Beach and the coast. Daily connections from this station include San Diego (2 hrs, $11 one-way), Riverside (2 hrs, $7.50 one-way), Los Angeles (1½ hrs, $8.50 one-way), Santa Barbara (4 hrs, $11 one-way), San Luis Obispo (8 hrs, $59 one-way), and San Francisco (10 hrs, $69 one-way). To reach the coast from here you need to take OCTA Bus 85 to Main Street and Santa Ana Boulevard and then Bus 53 south to Newport Beach; a taxi will run you about $25.

In **San Clemente,** Greyhound picks up and drops off passengers in front of Dad's Liquor and Deli (2421 S. El Camino Real). Buses head north from here to Santa Ana (45 min, $7.50 one-way), L.A. (2½ hrs, $11 one-way) and beyond, and south to Oceanside (40 min, $5 one-way) and San Diego (1½ hrs, $12 one-way). You pay for the trip at the next station along your route.

Call the **Orange County Transportation Authority** (OCTA; tel. 714/636–7433, ext. 10) for routes, schedules, and public bus information for all of Orange County.

**BY CAR** • Driving is hands-down the most convenient way to explore Orange County. In some cases, just getting to a town's public transportation center virtually requires a car unless you have lots of time to spare. The scenic stretch of **Hwy. 1** called Pacific Coast Hwy., or PCH for short, traverses the coast from L.A. to San Juan Capistrano, where it merges with I–5. To save some time and still see some of Orange County's most rugged beachfront, you can take I–405 south from L.A., cross to the coast on Hwy. 55 (to Newport Beach) or Hwy. 133 (to Laguna), and continue south. If you're planning a trip to the OC coast on Friday, try leaving by noon at the latest to beat traffic—or better yet, leave on Thursday night.

**BY TRAIN** • Between Los Angeles and San Diego, the main stop for Amtrak trains is the **San Juan Capistrano Depot** (26701 Verdugo St., west of Camino Capistrano, tel. 949/240–2972). You can head to L.A. (1½ hrs, $11 one-way) and to San Diego (1½ hrs, $11.50 one-way). Public buses run between this depot, Laguna Beach, and San Clemente hourly 9–7.

Otherwise, you can get off the train at the **San Clemente Auxiliary Amtrak Station** (1850 Avenida Estacion at El Camino Real). There's no staff here, and outgoing passengers can't purchase tickets at the station; you must either already have a ticket or be prepared to pay for one in cash when you step on board. Call **Amtrak** (tel. 800/872–7245) for more information. To reach Laguna Beach from the San Clemente station, take OCTA Bus 91 south to the last stop, then hop on Bus 1 heading north.

A couple of **Metrolink** (tel. 800/371–5465) lines snake through the area: the Orange County line and the Inland Empire/Orange County line. The Orange County line goes from L.A.'s Union Station south to Oceanside, stopping at the San Juan Capistrano and San Clemente stations mentioned above, among others. The Inland Empire line starts inland from San Bernardino and goes south to San Juan Capistrano. The fare depends on how many zones you pass through. Starting from L.A., a one-way ticket south will cost in the $4.75–$7.75 range. Tickets are cheaper if you get them during off-peak times, between 8:30–3:30 on weekdays or all day Saturday.

## GETTING AROUND

**BY BUS** • The **Orange County Transportation Authority** (OCTA; tel. 714/636–7433, ext. 10) buses run pretty frequently and go to all the main communities, but they do take a lot of time. The basic fare is $1; you must have exact change. There are no transfers, so if you plan on making more than a couple of trips, buy a day pass ($2.50).

**BY CAR** • Highways and freeways snake throughout the area; because of the distances involved and spotty public transportation, driving is the most convenient way to get around. You will have to contend with rush hours (6:30–9:30 AM and 3–6 PM) and a certain amount of construction (highways in the Anaheim area are particularly snarly). For main roads, see Coming and Going, *above*.

**BY TRAIN** • Stops along the **Metrolink** (tel. 800/371–5465) Orange County and Inland Empire/Orange County lines include Anaheim, San Juan Capistrano, and San Clemente. The fare depends on how many zones you go through; a one-way ticket should be under $8. Tickets are cheaper if you get them during off-peak times, between 8:30–3:30 on weekdays or all day Saturday. *See also* Coming and Going, *above*.

# SEAL BEACH

If you blink, you could easily miss this mellow seaside community 10 mi south of Long Beach. Named for the sea lions that once populated the shores (Sea Lion Beach was too long for the mellow locals, so they abbreviated), the quiet cove has a wonderfully quirky, 1950s beach-town feel. **Main Street** has managed to ward off most of the evils of tourism (only two shops sell Seal Beach T-shirts). In the simply named **Book Store** (213 Main St., tel. 562/598–1818), you can browse among haphazard stacks of used books; behind one of them you may even uncover the proprietor. The **municipal pier,** Seal Beach's pride and joy, sits in the center of a wide, sandy half-shell of beach, bordered by enormous houses. Though the view of oil rigs is less than inspiring, it's fun to stroll along the pier or pause to fish for rock cod. The sportfishing shop at the pier's end rents rods ($10) and sells bait ($3). The beach itself is fantastic for swimming, with its calm waves and sandy shore. Surfers will probably want to head elsewhere. To get even closer to nature, take a guided walk through the local **National Wildlife Refuge.** Free tours of the 1,000-acre preserve, on the grounds of a naval station, can be arranged by contacting the local chamber of commerce (see Visitor Information, *below*) at least a day in advance.

The town's appeal notwithstanding, you'll probably have to stay elsewhere as accommodations are scarce and cater to the wealthy. You're better off in nearby Sunset or Huntington beaches (*see below*), where rooms go for about half the price.

## VISITOR INFORMATION

For information on local events, contact the **Seal Beach Chamber of Commerce** (311 Main St., #14A, off PCH, tel. 562/799–0179, www.sealbeachchamber.com), open only on weekdays.

## FOOD

Seal Beach has roughly two dozen eateries spread primarily along the short, three-block span of Main Street, the PCH, and Marina Drive. Regular patronage by now-legendary slugger Mark McGwire has made **The Abbey** (306 Main St., tel. 562/799–4246) a local hit. Tuck into large burgers for around $8, or sandwiches and tasty pizzas starting at $6. Contrary to what the name suggests, **Kandi Lahaina Broiler** (901 Ocean Ave., tel. 562/596–3864) does not serve Hawaiian food. But the good old American staples (burgers, salads, etc.) at reasonable prices ($7 and up) go nicely with the oceanfront view. Line up at longtime local fave **Nick's Deli** (223 Main St., tel. 562/598–5072), where beach fuel includes the tasty breakfast burrito ($3) and the vegetarian sandwich ($3.50). Otherwise, head to **Ruby's** (tel. 562/431–7829), at the end of Seal Beach's pier. This '50s-style diner (part of an Orange County chain) has hefty burgers (beef, turkey, veggie, or chicken) starting at $4, thick shakes, and drop-dead views.

# SUNSET BEACH

Barely 2 mi long, this no-frills town is bordered by **Seal Beach Boulevard** (to the north) and **Warner Boulevard** (to the south). It's got the same sand and lifeguard towers you'll find in Huntington Beach in a more residential, less crowded setting. While the surf isn't up to par with Huntington, it's a fabulous place to swim. The shores are lined with a trim collection of two-story cottages, and you'll find free parking along North and South Pacific avenues, parallel to PCH.

## WHERE TO SLEEP

You can't camp on the beach, but you can stay a mere half block from it at the reasonably clean, slightly seedy **Islander Motel** (16545 Pacific Coast Hwy., at 21st St., tel. 562/592–1993) for as little as $59 (off season) a night for a room with a small kitchenette. To register, head next door to the Econo Lodge (16555 Pacific Coast Highway). An even better bet is the **Harbour Inn** (16912 Pacific Coast Highway, tel. 562/592–4770) where large, well-kept rooms start at $69. You can virtually roll out of bed and hit the beach; the hotel is just across the street from the sand.

## FOOD

Indulge yourself at the **Harbor House Café** (16341 Pacific Coast Hwy., at Anderson St., tel. 562/592–5404), which serves the best omelets in Orange County ($7) 24 hours a day.

# HUNTINGTON BEACH

Huntington Beach *is* Surf City U.S.A. Twelve miles south of Seal Beach on the PCH, this was once a quiet town, but a building and renovation boom has created a bustling Main Street lined with glittery shops and restaurants. A shiny new music and art-fair venue, the Pier Plaza amphitheater, opened in 1998, and at press time the Plaza Almería restaurant/retail complex was under construction. These, plus the inevitable sprawling housing developments, are adding to the city's resort popularity.

The town is a haven for recently graduated working stiffs clinging to their youth—at any moment of the day, a steady stream of them can be found jaywalking across PCH with surfboards, in-line skates, and overexcited Labradors. At night the same throng packs into Main Street bars. Fourth of July festivities are notorious here, with the largest parade west of the Mississippi and drunken revelers whooping it up. The booze flows again from mid-September until mid-November (but especially weekends in October), when locals exhaustively celebrate Oktoberfest with German food, music, and, of course, beer. Lots of it. Call the Old World German Restaurant (tel. 714/895–8020) for more details.

Once you hit the 8½ mi of wide beaches, that lackadaisical lifestyle might sound pretty good. You can get sun and a little exercise playing pickup sand volleyball on the courts next to the pier. (Be warned, though, that locals take their volleyball pretty seriously.) The beaches are thick with conveniences, including tons of stands hawking slushies, soft tacos, firewood, boogie boards, and beach umbrellas. Two paths mirror the coast, one for rollerbladers and bikers, the other for skittish pedestrians. You can either pay $5–$6 for the privilege of parking near the action, or park for free on Beach Boulevard and walk.

## VISITOR INFORMATION

The staff of the **Huntington Beach Conference and Visitors Bureau** (101 Main St., Suite 2A, at PCH, tel. 800/729–6232 or 714/969–3492, www.hbvisit.com) will ply you with glossy material on restaurants, lodging, and activities. The office is only open on weekdays.

## WHERE TO SLEEP

If you're willing to forgo beachside digs, reasonably priced motels abound along **Beach Boulevard (Hwy. 39),** about a mi inland. The visitor's bureau (*see* Visitor Information, *above*) can refer you to several.

There are also a couple of good bets right across the PCH from the beach. At the **Huntington Shores Motel** (21002 PCH, between Huntington St. and 1st St., tel. 714/536–8861 or 800/554–6799) you can mess around with the Ping-Pong or horseshoes, or swim a few laps in the pool. Doubles cost $88 in summer; prices drop $20 or so off-season. If you're itching to hang with the surfing migrators, head to the **Huntington Surf Inn** (720 PCH, north of 8th St. pier, tel. 714/536–2444). Doubles run $74 to $79 with a $5 charge per extra person. Other than a few stray surfing stickers, rooms are well-kept, and the management aims to keep them that way. "Unregistered guests" (read: parties) are forbidden after 10 PM. There's a second-story sundeck, plus a laundry for sending your boardshorts through the spin cycle. To get into either of these places in summer, you'll need to make reservations a couple of weeks in advance.

## FOOD

**The Huntington Beach Brewing Company** (201 Main St., at Walnut Ave., tel. 714/960–5343) has live jazz and blues and views of the beach, not to mention "armadillo eggs" (deep-fried, stuffed jalapeños, $5.45) and other fillers for less than $10. When the kitchen closes at 10, the pub becomes a nice place to socialize. **Jan's Health Bar** (501 Main St., at 6th St., tel. 714/536–4856) is known for healthy sandwiches, salads, and fruit and vegetables drinks, all homemade. The Surf Shop special comes with a half sandwich, chips, and soup or salad for $5.25. At **Wahoo's Fish Tacos** (120 Main St., at PCH, tel. 714/536–2050) you can get an utterly healthy lunch or dinner for about $5—think tacos and burritos with grilled or blackened fish, cheese, and cilantro-y salsa. There are also meat and vegetarian choices if you're not into *pescado*.

## WORTH SEEING

**INTERNATIONAL SURFING MUSEUM** • Billed as the "world's only museum where it's okay to call the curator dude," the International Surfing Museum looks like a pack rat's labor of love. The two tiny rooms are jammed with a hodgepodge of surfing memorabilia, starting with a shrinelike exhibit on the father of U.S. surfing, Duke Kahanamoku. Credited with popularizing surfing in Huntington Beach in the 1920s, Duke has his image plastered all over the museum—from a bust to several photographs to his famous surfing hood ornament. Other permanent exhibits include a wall of surfing albums and a display on women surfers. The all-volunteer staff is friendly and happy to educate neophytes on surfing rituals. *411 Olive Ave., at Main St., tel. 714/960–3483. $2 suggested donation. Open Wed.–Sun. noon–5.*

**SURFING WALK OF FAME** • After you wipe out on a massive swell, be sure to pay your respects along this strip of Main Street, which is modeled after the Walk of Fame in Hollywood. Every August surfers who have made significant contributions to the culture of surfing receive a golden stone on the walk of fame. To see the stars, begin at the corner of PCH and Main Street.

## OUTDOOR ACTIVITIES

Nature lovers—especially bird watchers—will want to check out the **Bolsa Chica Ecological Reserve** (tel. 714/840–1575). A 1½- mi loop trail traverses the Bolsa Bay, highlighting the archaeology, ecology, and biology of the reserve. Explore on your own, or take a free guided tour; these are offered 9 AM–10:30 AM on the first Saturday of the month from September through April. The reserve is located at Huntington Harbor, off PCH.

**SURFING** • Wannabe surfers can sign up at **Corky Carroll's Surf School** (tel. 714/841–0253) for a lesson with a pro. The $50-per- hour private lesson cost includes board and wetsuit, as well as a follow-up coached practice session. **Robert August** (301 5th St., at Olive St., tel. 714/960–2266) rents surfboards for $20 per day.

# NEWPORT BEACH

Newport Beach, about 5 mi south of Huntington Beach on PCH, has something of a split personality. There's the high-society side, evidenced by the multimillion-dollar beachfront homes and gleaming boats, and then there's the tousled, looser side, as shown by the scattering of tattoo parlors, the low-key beach bungalows, and a branch of Hooters. As you'd expect, the city's beaches are regularly swamped with summer visitors, who transform its quiet boardwalk into a crowded promenade. But Newport's graciousness keeps the upper hand during its seasonal upheaval; this largest of Orange County's beachfront communities offers plenty of organized scuba-diving, sport fishing, and whale-watching possibilities. There's also a daily ferry to Catalina Island (*see above*).

You can explore the happening parts of the city on foot, starting on the beach near the rather austere Newport Pier. To blend in with the locals, rent a bicycle or a pair of in-line skates from any of the shops along the waterfront. Otherwise, head for the FunZone, a small amusement park in Balboa Pavilion with an old-fashioned Ferris wheel ($2) and penny arcades. From here it's only a 5-minute walk to the town's liveliest nightspot—the stretch of beach and bars between Balboa Boulevard and Ocean Front Avenue. The minipalazzos of the city's wealthy are shoehorned onto Lido Island in the center of Newport Harbor. Farther inland lies Fashion Island, the second largest mall in Orange County, and the Orange County Museum of Art (*see* Worth Seeing, *below*).

## VISITOR INFORMATION

**Newport Beach Visitors and Conference Bureau** (3300A W. Coast Hwy., at Newport Blvd., tel. 949/722–1611 or 800/942–6278, www.newport-beach.ca.us) offers the usual: tourist brochures, maps, and sound advice. It's open weekdays, and adds limited weekend hours in summer.

## WHERE TO SLEEP

You'll find a string of reasonably priced (though occasionally unreasonably shabby) motels ($25–$40) along Newport Boulevard in **Costa Mesa.** You won't have an ocean view (more likely a view of the highway), but Costa Mesa is only a 15-minute drive from the beach up the 55. The **Sandpiper Motel** (1967 Newport Blvd., near 19th St., tel. 949/645–9137), where doubles start at $50, is probably the best of the bunch. The only two affordable hotels in Newport proper are the **Newport Channel Inn** (6030 W. PCH, between Brookhurst and Superior Aves., tel. 949/642–3030), with rooms starting at $89 (higher on weekends); and the **Newport Classic Inn** (2300 W. PCH, at Tustin Ave., tel. 800/633–3199), with rates from $65. Both are well-maintained, clean, and seconds from the beach. They're also popular with summer crowds, so reservations are advised.

**CAMPING •** The privately owned **Newport Dunes** (1131 Back Bay Dr., off Jamboree Rd., tel. 949/729–3863 or 800/765–7611) facility is primarily an RV trailer park, but a limited number of tent sites go for a brutal $30–$120 a night (the latter for a prime beachfront site during summer weekends). Don't expect the great outdoors, either: The gravel sites don't have a tree or verdant hillside in sight. However, it's got plenty of facilities, including barbecues, drinking water, fire grates, flush toilets, picnic tables, and showers. It's only minutes away from Balboa Island and the peninsula, Newport Beach's hot spot—and it's very self-sufficient, with its own grocery store, restaurant, boat rentals, and recreational areas with a swimming lagoon.

## FOOD

Newport's cheap eats lie between **Balboa Boulevard** and **Ocean Front Avenue,** one block from the beach and pier. Along with ice-cream parlors and the good old Orange Julius spot, there's a decent selection of breakfast and burger joints, as well as a healthy sampling of bars.

For casual dining, you can't beat **The Crab Cooker** (2200 Newport Blvd., at 22nd St., tel. 949/673–0100). This no-frills place serves tasty seafood on paper plates. Dinner entrées range from skewered scallops with bacon ($12) to cracked crab ($14.25); there's also an unbeatable clam chowder ($3.95 for a large bowl). You can sit down in the restaurant or get your food to go from the adjoining market. For food with a view, try **Muttlynch's** (2300 W. Ocean Front, tel. 949/675–1556) in the parking lot of the Newport Pier. The bar-and-grill's menu is standard fare, but the prices aren't bad—like shrimp and chips for $8.75, overstuffed pizzas starting at $10.50—and you'll get to gaze at the ocean while you eat. Get even closer to the water at **Ruby's** '50s-style burger joint on the end of the pier. Grab a burger and one of their specialty shakes (like mocha or peanut butter cup), then watch people cast fishing lines and fight off the seagulls. Tiny hole-in-the-wall **Taquería Tía Rosa** (2307 Balboa Blvd., at 23rd St., tel. 949/675–6574) serves up excellent Mexican food. A hefty carne asada burrito fetches $3.49; a veggie burrito with beans, rice, cilantro, onions, salsa, cheese, and guacamole is $2.89. They don't serve chips, but you won't miss 'em. Be sure to bring cash; they don't take credit cards.

## WORTH SEEING

**BALBOA ISLAND** • Other than the beach, Newport's main attraction is Balboa, which is connected to the mainland by Jamboree Road. You can catch a ferry that shuttles between island and peninsula, docking on the peninsula at the end of Palm Street (follow BALBOA FERRY signs from PCH). The fun five-minute ride is a bargain at $1 per car, 50¢ per bike, or 35¢ per passenger. Marine Avenue is Balboa Island's main drag, with more than 70 shops, art galleries, and restaurants. It's touristy, but it still has a seaside charm that most of California's overdeveloped beach towns lost years ago.

**BALBOA PAVILION** • Despite the name, this Victorian pavilion is on the peninsula—and it's a knock-out. Built in 1906 as a bathhouse, it became a haven for big-band sounds in the 1940s. Today, it's the place to pick up deep-sea fishing charters ($23 a half day) and whale-watching tours (*see* Outdoor Activities, *below*). To really get into the retro seaside moment, take a ride on the Ferris wheel ($2) in the FunZone arcade area. *400 Main St., off Balboa Blvd.*

**ORANGE COUNTY MUSEUM OF ART** • An old library building near Fashion Island is now the second largest museum in the county (first place goes to Santa Ana's Bowers Museum). The OCMA focuses on art from the mid-1900s on, including the works of post–World War II California artists. Besides shows drawn from their own collections, they sometimes exhibit works from other museums, like a selection of urban paintings from New York's Whitney Museum. The Plein Air Cafe (open weekdays only) is a nice place to grab lunch for $10 or less. They've also got a small branch with free admission at the South Coast Plaza Mall (3333 Bristol St., Costa Mesa). *850 San Clemente Dr., tel. 949/759–1122. From PCH, Jamboree Rd. north and follow signs. Admission: $5, free Tues. Open Tues.–Sun. 11–5.*

*One of Newport's edible attractions is the Balboa Bar—a frozen, chocolate-dipped creation that was invented here (so locals claim) in the 1940s.*

**UPPER NEWPORT BAY ECOLOGICAL RESERVE** • If you're curious about what the California coast looked like before all the raging development, you'll get a strong sense of it here. The protected, natural wetland habitat is rich with flora and fauna, all within earshot of the peaceful rumble of the sea. There are some pretty impressive birds—about 30 species in all—including herons, egrets, and the occasional pelican. Kayak tours can be taken on your own, or with a knowledgeable guide ($20 per person, including kayak rental). Either way, expect to get your exercise, as the full tour entails about 5 mi of paddling. The road that follows the shore is popular among bicyclists, joggers, and in-line skaters. To get to the preserve from PCH, turn inland onto Jamboree Road, veer left on Back Bay Drive, and follow it to the end. *End of Back Bay Dr., tel. 949/640–6746 or 800/585–0747 for kayak reservations.*

## AFTER DARK

Newport Beach has long had a reputation as *the* oceanside playground of Orange County's young and available. Though many have defected lately for the crush of new bars in Huntington Beach, Newport will always be King. Most of the late-night action takes place on the Balboa peninsula, particularly in the strip of restaurants and bars near Newport Pier and in Lido Village.

Locals flock to **The Blue Beat** (107 21st St., at the base of the pier, tel. 949/675–2338), where crowds of all kinds enjoy the laid-back atmosphere and nightly live music. Across the street from the Newport Pier, **Blackies by the Sea, Inc.** (2118 W. Ocean Front, tel. 949/675–1074), the apotheosis of all things Californian, dispenses cheap beer with an attitude; the sign on the door reads SORRY—WE'RE OPEN. On the other side of the peninsula and a world apart, **The Cannery** (3010 Lafayette Ave., at Newport Blvd., tel. 949/675–5777) draws crowds into its maw for the thrice-weekly happy hour (Tuesday, Wednesday, and Thursday, 4–7) and weekend live music.

Jazz lovers should make a beeline for **Studio Café** (100 Main St., at Balboa Blvd., tel. 949/675–7760), which presents top-rate jazz and blues musicians on Thursday and Saturday nights; there's no cover. The café has a full-service bar and dining room; try the savory shrimp scampi ($15.50) or the barbecued ribs ($11.50). The **Alta Coffee Warehouse and Roasting Co.** (506 31st St., off Newport Blvd., tel. 949/675–0233) has jazz, folk, and blues singers weekly (no cover). The food is simple, the coffee strong.

## OUTDOOR ACTIVITIES

Newport Beach seems to revolve around sporting activities, most of which take advantage of the town's prime coastal location. **Balboa Bikes 'n' Beach Stuff** (601 E. Balboa Blvd., Balboa, tel. 949/723–1516) rents skates for about $5 an hour, and bikes for as little as $10 a day. If these guys don't have what you're looking for, just keep walking down the street; there's no shortage of rental places.

**BODY SURFING** • Thrill seekers (or lunatics, depending on your perspective) may want to check out **The Wedge** (end of Balboa Blvd.), one of the most famous—and dangerous—bodysurfing breakwaters in the world. Be warned: The Wedge is for experienced swimmers only, and surfboards are not allowed. Waves range anywhere from 8 to 12 ft, although they loom larger if you're looking up at them. The water here is also extremely shallow. If you'd prefer to save life and limb, get a vicarious buzz by watching the local body surfers getting knocked silly by the infamous swells.

**FISHING** • Fishing is allowed from either of Newport's two piers without a permit. Both **Davey's Locker** (400 Main St., tel. 949/673–1434; bait is available here as well) and **Newport Landing** (309 Palm St., Ste. F, tel. 949/675–0550) organize fishing trips year-round for rock cod, mackerel, bonito, barracuda, or whatever else is biting (from about $25 per half-day). Both are located in the Balboa Pavilion (*see* Worth Seeing, *above*).

**SNORKELING AND SCUBA DIVING** • In Newport Beach, the **Aquatic Center** (4537 W. Coast Hwy., at Balboa Blvd., tel. 949/650–5440) rents scuba gear (from $35 a day) and snorkeling equipment ($10 a day). Photo ID and a deposit are required, and scuba divers must bring certification papers. Call their 24-hour hotline (tel. 949/650–5783) for diving conditions. But the best dive spots along this stretch of coastline are not in Newport; they're farther south in Corona del Mar and Laguna Beach.

**WHALE-WATCHING** • If you're in the area between December and March, check out the gray-whale migration, during which herds of grays head from Alaska to Mexico and back along the California coast. Whale-watching boats ($14 per person) are run by Davey's Locker (*see* Fishing, *above*) at the Balboa Pavilion.

# CORONA DEL MAR

At this small coastal community, take advantage of the exceptional beach—search for starfish and anemones in the tide pools around the breakwater, or walk clear out into the bay on a rough-and-tumble rock jetty and watch local anglers reel in barracuda and perch. Corona del Mar is off-limits to boats *and* it has two colorful reefs, making it an ideal place for snorkeling and diving. Unfortunately, no one rents gear, so bring your own or stop first in Newport Beach's Aquatic Center (*see above*); Newport is just 3 mi up the coast. When the blinding sun on the beach gets to you, retreat to the **Sherman Library and Gardens** (2647 E. Coast Hwy., near MacArthur Blvd., tel. 949/673–2261). Both the botanical garden and library focus on Southwestern flora; you can have pastries and coffee in the tea garden. Admission is $3.

Corona del Mar's golden beaches are ideal for a late-afternoon walk, but past sunset there isn't much to do. Unless you're prepared to pay $50 for a suit-and-tie meal in one of the town's swank restaurants, you're better off stopping here for an hour or two on your way somewhere else.

# LAGUNA BEACH

The expanse of beach between Newport Beach and Dana Point has long been a haven for up-and-coming artists—in fact, fine art infiltrates the entire community. The California Plein-Air movement—landscapes painted in the great outdoors—was born here at the turn of the century. Today, nearly 100 art galleries pepper the streets, showing everything from traditional seascapes to contemporary and abstract work; on the first Thursday of every month, there's an evening gallery art walk. Famous artworks become tableaux vivants during the wonderfully wacky Pageant of the Masters (*see* Festivals, *below*), just one of several arts-related events. Public art pieces are scattered throughout the town. And on any given day, you're likely to find Heisler Park—a city park on a bluff overlooking the ocean—abrim with painters at work.

The steady stream of artistic inspiration makes perfect sense once you've seen the town's gorgeous surroundings. The combination of the steep bluffs, the curve of the beaches, and the ocean is pretty darn spectacular. If you come into the town along Laguna Canyon Road from the 405 freeway, you'll go through a stunning coastal canyon, large stretches of which are happily undeveloped. This canyon is a testament to the residents' priorities; in 1990 the community took on an extra tax in order to purchase the land and save it from impending development. The area is now part of the Laguna Coast Wilderness Park.

Arty, crunchy, hippie—the adjectives you'll hear applied to Laguna vary, but it's an undeniably welcoming town. One of southern California's largest gay communities gathers here, a tolerant standout in conservative Orange County. The Hare Krishnas run a restaurant, the environmentalists rally—there seems to be room for everyone.

Laguna has plenty of outdoor diversions: At Main Beach, studded with a 1920s lifeguard tower, you can join a game of pickup basketball or volleyball, scramble over the tidepools at the north end of the beach, or watch the ubiquitous guitar-strumming beachniks. The water is quite clean and since the weather's so good, you'll see people swimming even in November. This is also a great area for scuba diving; just a few miles up the coast is an underwater dive park, part of Crystal Cove State Park (*see* Outdoor Activities, *below*).

## VISITOR INFORMATION

You can call the **Laguna Beach Visitor Information Center** (252 Broadway, tel. 949/497–9229 or 800/877–1115, www.lagunabeachinfo.org) for recorded information on lodging, restaurants, and activities, or stop by for maps and brochures. They're generally open Monday through Saturday, but stay open daily in July and August.

*Laguna's welcome mat is legendary. On the corner of Forest and Park avenues hangs a 1930s gate that reads "This gate hangs well and hinders none, refresh and rest, then travel on." Nearby is a statue of the town's greeter, who used to wave to visitors.*

## WHERE TO SLEEP

Laguna is the most popular stopover south of Newport, but it's priced way out of the budget traveler's reach. The **Crescent Bay Inn** (1435 N. Coast Hwy., at Crescent Bay Dr., tel. 949/ 494–2508) isn't the classiest place in town, but the rooms ($55–$69 weekdays, $65–$99 weekends) are perfectly adequate, and some even have kitchens and partial views of the ocean. Hit up the ultrafriendly sorts staffing the front desk at the **Sea Cliff Motel** (1661 S. Coast Hwy., at Bluebird Canyon Rd., tel. 949/494–9717 or 800/500–2164) for one of their clean and comfortable rooms. Basic rooms are in the $55–$75 range, but superior rooms can cost much more.

## FOOD

Laguna's hotels and galleries may be prohibitively expensive, but finding a cheap, well-prepared meal is easy. In the center of town are more than 30 restaurants, ranging from greasy spoon to china-and-crystal. **Royal Thai Cuisine** (1750 S. Coast Hwy., at Pearl St., tel. 949/494–8424) has delicious, authentic dishes for less than $10, and the inexpensive **Wahoo's Fish Tacos** (1133 S. Coast Hwy., at Oak St., tel. 949/497–0033), a popular local hangout, serves the best—repeat, the *best*—fish tacos on the coast. Another local favorite is stylish **Café Zinc** (350 Ocean Ave., at Forest Ave., tel. 949/494–6302), which does brisk business at lunch (pizzettas, $6) and brunch (huevos rancheros, $6.25). The outdoor tables are wonderful for lingering. If you're craving a sugar-and-caffeine fix, drop into the local, oceanfront branch of **Diedrich's** coffee house (180 N. Coast Hwy., at Broadway, tel. 949/497–7660) for an intense espresso or luscious coffee shake.

## WORTH SEEING

**LAGUNA ART MUSEUM •** The offbeat, intriguing exhibits here often highlight local artists. For instance, recent shows included a group of Impressionist-style paintings done in Laguna and a collection of miniature and small-scale art, where many pieces were under three inches. A free docent tour is given daily at 2. *307 Cliff Dr., at PCH., tel. 949/494–6531. Admission $5. Open Tues.–Sun. 11–5.*

## FESTIVALS

Laguna's many festivals give it a worldwide reputation in the arts community. The **Pageant of the Masters** (tel. 949/494–1145; for tickets call 800/487–3378), held in July and August, is by far the town's most impressive event. Each evening in Irvine Bowl Park on Laguna Canyon Road, actors re-create some of the world's most famous artworks as "living pictures." Participants must hold a perfectly still pose while on stage; though you may not realize it at first, every figure in these life-size tableaus is alive—from the man in the bathtub in Jacquet-Louis David's *Death of Marat* to the Cubist women in

Picasso's *Les Demoiselles d'Avignon*. Hundreds of locals pitch in to create these tableaus, and the results are astonishing. Even when they take apart a setup and show you how it's done, it fools the eye. The Irvine Bowl is an outdoor amphitheater, so bring a sweater and perhaps a seat cushion. Tickets for the pageant start at $10 but can go up to $50; get them as far in advance as possible. It may sound like a slightly bizarre show, but it's impressive—hence its rising popularity and the hopeful, loitering couples trying to buy extra tickets. Paired with the Pageant of the Masters is the **Festival of the Arts,** held on the grounds in front of the Bowl. Over a hundred painters, sculptors, and jewelers set up booths to display and sell their work. You can get in free if you have a ticket to that night's Pageant performance; if not, admission is $5. The **Sawdust Festival** (tel. 949/494–3030), held in July and August as well, is a raucous arts fair in a eucalyptus grove across Laguna Canyon Road from the Irvine Bowl. Unlike the Festival of the Arts, this art show is not juried, so there's a relaxed, feel-good vibe. You can stroll around the displays with a drink in hand, checking out the handmade arts and crafts and demonstrations, listening to the bands, maybe even catching a belly dancing act. The festival grounds also host a series of winter holiday weekends in late November and December. Tickets are $6. Parking for all events is limited, and it's recommended that you park in one of the marked lots along Laguna Canyon Road. A $1 shuttle runs between the lots and the festival grounds.

## AFTER DARK

The **Boom Boom Room** (1401 S. Coast Hwy., tel. 949/494–7588), located within the Coast Inn, is a hot spot for the gay and lesbian community. This nightclub/bar is definitely laid-back—you can step right off the beach and onto the dance floor.

Launched by Bette Davis, the **Laguna Playhouse** (606 Laguna Canyon Rd., tel. 949/497–2787 or 800/946–5556) mounts a variety of performances, from Eugene O'Neill to Neil Simon. At press time there were plans afoot to expand onto an adjacent lot.

## OUTDOOR ACTIVITIES

Some of the best scuba diving in the county is here; join an organized expedition originating in Newport (*see* Outdoor Activities *in* Newport Beach, *above*), or rent equipment at one of the many local dive shops, including **Laguna Sea Sports** (925 N. Coast Hwy., at Wave St., tel. 949/494–6965). A complete rental will cost you $45 a day. In particular, **Moss Point** (off PCH at Moss St., south of Main Beach) is an excellent and rarely crowded dive spot. Only a few short miles north of Laguna Beach, **Crystal Cove State Park** (8471 N. PCH, tel. 949/494–3539) has a 1,000-acre **underwater park** for scuba divers and snorkelers. Much of the trail was wiped out by El Niño, but splendid scenery still remains. The above-ground portion of the park is a popular place for hiking and mountain biking. Rangers offer free guided tours most weekends.

# SAN JUAN CAPISTRANO

Just 6 mi south of Laguna, San Juan Capistrano is a serene inland town—a welcome respite from the frenzied commercialism so common in other coastal towns. Aside from visiting surfers who sometimes meet on the shores of Capistrano Beach at dawn, most people see San Juan only from the freeway. Don't make that mistake: The town's clean beaches and historic Mission District deserve a day's visit.

## VISITOR INFORMATION

The ultrapleasant folks at the **San Juan Capistrano Chamber of Commerce** (31781 Camino Capistrano, tel. 949/493–4700, www.sanjuanchamber.com) will be happy to set you up with info on local sights, upcoming events, and the like.

## WHERE TO SLEEP

The **Mission Inn** (26891 Ortega Hwy., right off the I-5, tel. 949/234–0249) is close enough to the mission (architecturally and geographically) to be mistaken for part of it, and it's only two blocks from the train station. Rooms are clean, the service is friendly, and guests have use of a pool, Jacuzzi, and a VCR (videos are $2). You're encouraged to pick fruit from the orange trees on the premises. Double rooms start at $55 during the week, $65 on weekends.

If camping's more your speed, you'll have a couple of options. The **Doheny State Beach** campground (25300 Harbor Dr., Dana Point, near intersection of I–5 and Pacific Coast Hwy. at entrance to Dana Point Harbor, tel. 949/496–6171) overlooks the ocean from its perch on Dana Point, nestled among sand dunes and trees. They've got 122 sites, most of which are RV or tent spaces; these fetch $17–$18. One of the 33 beachfront spots will cost you $22–$23. Facilities include fishing areas, swimming, a general store, a picnic area, and food service. Drinking water, fire grates, firewood ($5), flush toilets, and showers are also available. This campground is popular with backpackers and families, so reserve online or by phone through ReserveAmerica (tel. 800/444–7275; www.reserveamerica.com). The **Ronald W. Caspers Wilderness Park** campground (33401 Ortega Hwy., tel. 949/728–3420) is best suited for car campers and RVs. (It allows tents, but the ground is uneven and strewn with rocks.) Hordes of retired folks flock here, so excessive noise isn't tolerated. All campers must obtain a free wilderness-use permit, available on the premises. Camping costs around $12 per night per site. Numerous hiking trails and scenic walks surround the campground, but the beach is a disappointing 10 mi away. Because of the presence of mountain lions (however unlikely you are to see them), those under 18 are required to be with a legal guardian to hike.

## FOOD

Those who are camping or pinching pennies should head to the **Marbella Plaza Farmers Market** (31109 Rancho Viejo Rd., north of Ortega Hwy., tel. 949/248–0838), which has the usual staples, plus artfully arranged produce, a full deli and bakery (sandwiches $6), and several indoor tables. Near the mission lies a string of unremarkable taco shops and chain restaurants, but the delicious Mexican entrées at sprawling **El Adobe** (31891 Camino Capistrano, south of Ortega Hwy., tel. 949/493–1163) are worth the extra outlay; meals here will cost $9–$18. Portions of the romantic, dark, honeycombed interior were once the town's *juzgados* (jails). **Sarducci's Capistrano Depot** (26701 Verdugo, next to the Amtrak station, tel. 949/493–9593) serves a little bit of everything, from rosemary chicken ($13.95) to pasta piccata ($11.25). Enjoy it on the restaurant's outdoor seating area.

*In Laguna's seemingly time-warped Candy Baron (231 Forest Ave., tel. 949/497–7508) you can drool over barrels and barrels of candy, with old-fashioned goodies like candy cigarettes, gumdrops, and more than a dozen kinds of saltwater taffy.*

## WORTH SEEING

**MISSION SAN JUAN CAPISTRANO** • Founded in 1776 by Father Junípero Serra, this was once the major Roman Catholic outpost between Los Angeles and San Diego. Although an 1812 earthquake left the great stone church in ruins, many of the mission's adobe outbuildings have been restored. One of them, the **Serra Chapel,** is believed to be the oldest building in California in continuous use. In the week surrounding St. Joseph's Day (Mar. 19), the mission hosts the *Fiesta de las Golindrinas* (Festival of the Swallows), celebrating the springtime return of the swallows from Argentina; unfortunately, the birds have been temporarily driven off by restoration projects, meaning you're more likely to see pigeons than swallows. Nevertheless, the site has a genuine air of history, the likes of which are not often found in these parts. Nearby are several adobe buildings dating back to the Mexican era. *Camino Capistrano and Ortega Hwy., tel. 949/248–2049. Admission $5. Open daily 8:30–5.*

**SAN JUAN CAPISTRANO REGIONAL LIBRARY** • This striking public library was built in 1983 by postmodern architect Michael Graves. It has a peaceful and shady courtyard with private spots for reading. *31495 El Camino Real, tel. 949/493–1752. Open Mon.–Wed. 10–8, Thurs. 10–6, Sat. 10–5, Sun. noon–5.*

# SAN CLEMENTE

San Clemente, the southernmost city in Orange County, is only 15 mi south of Laguna Beach on I-5, but in lifestyle and spirit it's a world apart. San Clemente looks like the California that Hollywood portrays: Blondes in bikinis, surf dudes streaking nude across the pier, and surfboards resting against the lifeguard stand as the sun sets. Well . . .except for the reactors of the San Onofre Nuclear Power Plant looming in the distance. The town is probably best remembered as the site of **Casa Pacifica,** Nixon's "Western White House." The massive 25-acre estate is visible from San Clemente State Beach; just look up to the cliffs for a large Spanish-style mansion (one of several) perennially surrounded by flowers. Because of its proximity to **Camp Pendleton,** one of the largest military bases in the state, San Clemente is a popular weekend beach retreat for military personnel. The town's main street is **Avenida del Mar,** which winds through picturesque hills of stucco-and-tile houses, eventually reaching the **Municipal Pier.** South El Camino Real is main street for the motel business, so if Motel San Clemente is booked, don't despair.

## VISITOR INFORMATION

Call the **San Clemente Chamber of Commerce** (1100 N. El Camino Real, at El Portal, tel. 949/492–1131, www.scchamber.com) for maps, brochures, and news on upcoming events.

## WHERE TO SLEEP

The spotless and incredibly comfy **Motel San Clemente** (1819 S. El Camino Real, near exit off I–5, tel. 949/492–1960) lies inland from the coast, but many rooms still have ocean views. Rooms start at $50, slightly more on weekends. There's a $5 charge per extra person.

The seasonal **San Clemente Beach AYH-Hostel** (233 Av. Granada, off El Camino Real, tel. 949/492–2848) is a friendly spot where you're likely to be greeted by a makeshift barbecue and gregarious international hostelers. The hostel provides a spotless, safe 40-bed haven only 2½ blocks from a tranquil beach. It's outfitted with a kitchen and laundry, and there's even an Amtrak stop on the beach nearby, the San Clemente Auxiliary (*see* Coming and Going *in* Orange County Coast, *above*), where you can catch a bus to Disneyland or Laguna Beach. Members pay $10 a night, nonmembers $14. It generally opens May 1 and closes in November. There's an 11 PM curfew and lockout 11 AM–4:30 PM; you'll need to check out by 11 AM.

The **San Clemente State Beach** campground (3030 Av. del Presidente, tel. 949/492–3156) sits atop bluffs overlooking the beach. The 157 developed sites are open to both tent and RV campers, and additional undeveloped sites are available. During peak season (Mar.–Nov.) fees are $17, $23 with hookups; on the weekends you'll pay an extra buck. Facilities include picnic areas, barbecues, hiking trails, and fishing. There are also fire grates, showers, and drinking water. Bring your own food, since there are no stores, although the county beach immediately to the north has a snack shack. Reservations can be made by phone or online through ReserveAmerica (tel. 800/444–7275; www.reserveamerica.com). To get here from the I–5 south, take the Av. Calafia exit and follow signs.

## FOOD

Come to **Fisherman's Restaurant** (San Clemente Pier, tel. 949/498–6390) for the stunning view but not the pricey mediocre food (dinners average around $20). Across the street, the **Tropicana Grill** (610 Av. Victoria, off El Camino Real, tel. 949/498–8767) has standard restaurant fare (burgers, Caesar salads, pasta) for less than $10; you'll also hear live jazz and local rock bands most weekend evenings. Also in the vicinity is **Cassano's Pizza** (626 Av. Victoria, off El Camino Real, tel. 949/361–0522), where a tempting slice of pepperoni is only $1.60. Vegetarian dishes—including the delectable tofu burger with avocado ($4) and delicious fruit-and-yogurt drinks ($2.75)—can be found at the inviting counter of **Captain Culver's Counter Culture** (149 Av. del Mar, at Ola Vista, tel. 949/498–8098).

# INDEX

# NOTES

# NOTES

# NOTES

# Looking for a different kind of vacation?

**Fodor's** makes it easy with a full line of specialty guidebooks to suit a variety of interests—from adventure to romance to language help.

**Fodor's.** For the world of ways you travel.

# IT'S YOUR TURN TO TALK BACK!

## FILL OUT THIS QUICK SURVEY AND RECEIVE A FREE COPY OF FODOR'S *HOW TO PACK.*\*

**Which Fodor's upCLOSE guide did you buy?**

_____

**What was the duration of your trip?**

_____

**How much did you spend per day, not including airfare?**

❑ $100        ❑ $300
❑ $150        ❑ Other_____
❑ $200

**Why did you choose Fodor's upCLOSE?**

❑ Budget focus
❑ Fodor's reputation
❑ Opinionated writing & comprehensive content
❑ Other_____

**Would you use Fodor's upCLOSE again?**

❑ Yes        ❑ No

**Which guides have you used in the past two years?**

❑ Frommer's $-A-Day   ❑ Let's Go
❑ Rough Guides       ❑ Rick Steves'
❑ Lonely Planet      ❑ None
❑ Other_____

**Did you like Fodor's upCLOSE better?**

❑ Yes     ❑ No

**Please rank the following features (1 = needs improvement / 2 = adequate / 3 = excellent).**

| | | | |
|---|---|---|---|
| Accommodations listings | 1 | 2 | 3 |
| Dining listings | 1 | 2 | 3 |
| Major sights | 1 | 2 | 3 |
| Off-the-beaten-path sights | 1 | 2 | 3 |
| Shopping listings | 1 | 2 | 3 |
| Nightlife listings | 1 | 2 | 3 |
| Public transportation | 1 | 2 | 3 |

**Please feel free to elaborate.** _____

_____

_____

_____

**Which of the following destinations would you like to see Fodor's upCLOSE cover?**

❑ Alaska         ❑ Pacific Northwest
❑ Australia      ❑ South America
❑ Austria        ❑ Southeast Asia
❑ Eastern Europe   ❑ Switzerland
❑ Greece        ❑ Turkey
❑ Israel         ❑ More European cities
❑ New Zealand    ❑ More U.S. cities
❑ Other_____

**You are**  ❑ Male  ❑ Female

**Your age is**
❑ 18-24  ❑ 45-54
❑ 25-34  ❑ 55-64
❑ 35-44  ❑ 65+

**You are** ❑ Single  ❑ Married

**Your occupation is**
❑ Student (undergraduate)
❑ Student (graduate)
❑ Professional
❑ Executive/managerial/administrative
❑ Military
❑ Retired
❑ Other_____

**Which choice best describes your household income?**
❑ Under $10,000
❑ $10,000-$19,999
❑ $20,000-$29,999
❑ $30,000-$49,999
❑ $50,000-$74,999
❑ $75,000+

**Your name and address are**

_____

_____

_____

**Your E-mail address is**

_____

**Would you like to receive informational E-mails from Fodor's?**
❑ Yes  ❑ No

Please return this survey to Fodor's Travel Publications, Attn: Fodor's upCLOSE Survey, 1540 Broadway, New York, NY 10036, for a free copy of Fodor's *How to Pack* (while supplies last). You can also fill out this survey on the Web at www.fodors.com/upclose/upclosesurvey.html.

The information herein will be treated in confidence. Names and addresses will not be released to mailing-list houses or other organizations.

* While supplies last